WHEN MONTEZUMA MET CORTÉS

When

MONTEZUMA

Met CORTÉS

*The True Story of the Meeting
that Changed History*

MATTHEW RESTALL

ecco
An Imprint of HarperCollins*Publishers*

HarperCollins books may be purchased for educational, business, or sales promotional use. For information, please e-mail the Special Markets Department at SPsales@harpercollins.com.

FIRST EDITION

Designed by Michelle Crowe

Library of Congress Cataloging-in-Publication Data has been applied for.

ISBN 978-0-06-242726-7

18 19 20 21 22   LSC   10 9 8 7 6 5 4 3 2 1

To
all the
Catalinas

Contents

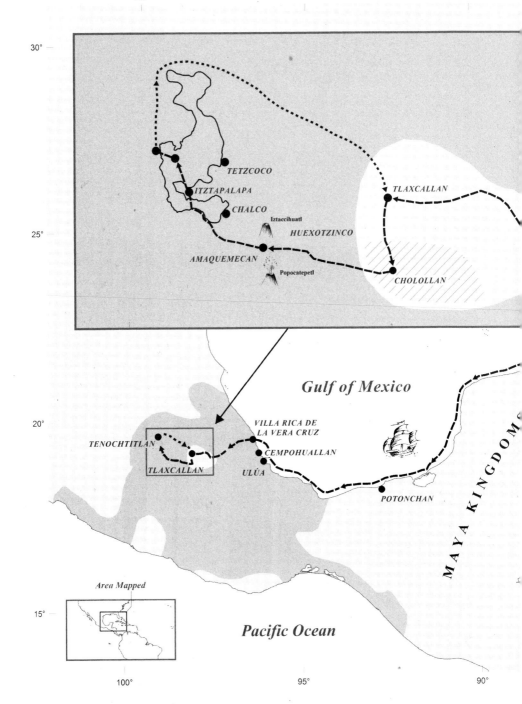

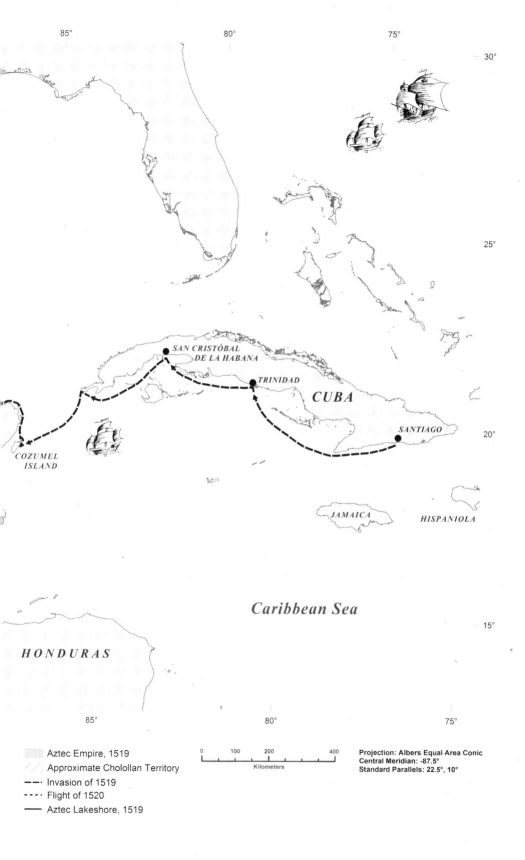

85° 80° 75° 30°

25°

SAN CRISTÓBAL
DE LA HABANA

TRINIDAD

CUBA

SANTIAGO 20°

COZUMEL
ISLAND

JAMAICA HISPANIOLA

Caribbean Sea

15°

HONDURAS

85° 80° 75°

Aztec Empire, 1519
Approximate Cholollan Territory
—·— Invasion of 1519
···· Flight of 1520
—— Aztec Lakeshore, 1519

0 100 200 400
Kilometers

Projection: Albers Equal Area Conic
Central Meridian: -87.5°
Standard Parallels: 22.5°, 10°

MEETINGS. This engraving ran as a banner across the top of the first page of the first chapter of John Ogilby's great *America: Being an Accurate Description of the New World*, first published in 1670 in London. The image lacked a title ("Meetings" is my invention), nor were those portrayed identified by name; for this is a generic representation of Native American and European leaders, armies, cultures, and of the supposedly peaceful meeting of civilization with barbarism.

Preface

---------------⚐---------------

WHAT MAKES THE "CONQUEST OF MEXICO" SO GREAT A SUBJECT? There is no shortage of answers to that question. For half a millennium, the story of the invasion of the Aztec Empire by Spanish conquistadors has consistently inspired and fascinated writers and readers, playwrights and audiences, painters and filmmakers. For many, the story's greatness has religious, political, or cultural foundations. For others, the tale is worth telling again and again because it is simply a ripping good yarn.

In contrast, and somewhat perversely, I have written this book because I believe the "Conquest of Mexico" is *not* great; at least, not in the sense that it has overwhelmingly been seen for the past five centuries. I have therefore tried to make this book more than just another telling of the same story. The story is told, to be sure, but the book is more concerned with how and why so many have seen it as "one of the greatest Subjects"—and how wrong they have been. That is a bold conceit, but it has a purpose. Whether you know nothing at all about Aztecs and conquistadors, or you are an expert on them, this is intended as a book for you. Because in the end I hope to persuade everyone who turns these pages that adjectives other than *greatest*—monumental but misunderstood, dramatic yet distorted, tragic not triumphal—are better applied to this history. And because I'm challenging the superlative nature of "the Conquest" (and the conquistador captain most famously associated with it), I imply that such adjectives might also be applied to other histories, if not to "all History." After all, the Spanish-Aztec meeting is a central chapter in the larger story of the European invasion of the Americas, leading to the transformation of global history and the making of today's world.

Before beginning, some explanations, scene-settings, and a time-line of key events may be useful.

I use the terms *Aztec, Mexica* (pronounced "mesh-EE-ka"), and *Nahuas* ("NA-wahs") to refer to specific groups of people within the Aztec Empire. Some scholars refer to the empire as the Triple Alliance, in order to emphasize the roles played in the empire's creation and maintenance by its three dominant cities: Tenochtitlan (the city of the Mexica, and the empire's great island-capital), Tetzcoco (an equally splendid lakeside city), and Tlacopan (smaller but also significant); I use the phrase too (sometimes as "the Triple Alliance of the Aztec Empire"). Further explanation of ethnic terminology is included in the Appendix, along with a diagram aimed at helping those more visually oriented (I am one of you).

With respect to the names of the book's central protagonists, I follow sixteenth-century usage and call Hernando Cortés just that, although "Fernando" is more accurate. He was never called Hernán, which is a modern rendering ("Cortez" is forgivable as an English version that goes back to the mid-sixteenth century). Although I follow conventional Spanish spellings for Spanish personal names and toponyms (for example, Velázquez), I do not put Spanish accents on Nahua ones (for example Tenochtitlán and Cuauhtémoc have accents in Spanish, but not in English; besides, their pronunciation in Nahuatl is uninflected).

As for the emperor of the Aztecs, it was tempting to render his name as accurately as possible, as Moteuctzomatzin (pronounced, roughly, "moh-teh-ook-tsoh-mah-tseen"). But for the ease of the reader, I chose "Montezuma." It is a convenient, familiar shorthand (like "Aztec") that originated in Spanish, English, and other languages in the late sixteenth century (perhaps even earlier). An early variant was "Moctezuma," the conventional form in modern Spanish, perfectly acceptable in English too.

A third person whose name requires some explanation is Malintzin. The original Nahua name of this interpreter to the Cortés-led invasion force, or company, is unknown, but Spaniards renamed her Marina. The importance of her role gave her a status that justified her soon being given the honorific *-tzin* in Nahuatl. In Spanish, she received the equivalent, the *doña* prefix. As a result, she was variously called doña Marina, Malintzin (as Nahuas tended to turn an *r* to an *l*), and Malinche (a Hispanization of Malintzin).

Cortés, Montezuma, and Malintzin are three of the sixteen Spanish and Nahua protagonists in the Spanish-Aztec War whose short biographies I have included in the Appendix. You may find it helpful to refer to those biographies when Aztecs like Cacama and Cuauhtemoc, and conquistadors like Ordaz and Olid, appear and then reappear in the chapters to follow. I have also created a kind of family tree, which I have called a Dynastic Vine (in the Appendix), that shows how kinship and marriage tied together the branches of the Aztec royal family in Tenochtitlan and Tetzcoco—and then tied them to Spanish conquistadors.

Timeline

———✦———

1428
* Foundation in the Valley of Mexico of the Triple Alliance of the Aztec Empire (centered on Tenochtitlan, Tetzcoco, and Tlacopan)

1440–69
* The first Montezuma (Moteuctzoma Ilhuicamina) rules as *huey tlahtoani* of Tenochtitlan (i.e., as Aztec emperor)

1468
* Birth of the second Montezuma (Moteuctzoma Xocoyotl); Axayacatl, Montezuma's father, rules as *huey tlahtoani* until 1481; he and two of his brothers head a generational cohort that will rule until the younger Montezuma takes the throne in 1502

1481–86
* Tizoc, Montezuma's uncle, rules as *huey tlahtoani*

1482–92
* War of Isabella, queen of Castile, against the Moorish kingdom of Granada, ending with Boabdil's surrender to her and Fernando, king of Aragon

1486
* Ahuitzotl, uncle and predecessor to Montezuma, elected *huey tlahtoani*

1492–93
* First voyage, under Columbus (Cristóbal Colón), to reach the Caribbean and return to Europe

1493–96
* Second Columbus voyage resulting in first Spanish colony in the Indies, on the island of Hispaniola (today's Haiti and Dominican Republic)

1502

* September 15, Montezuma elected *huey tlahtoani*

1503–09

* Series of Aztec conquest campaigns in Oaxaca and other southern regions

1504

* Cortés, age nineteen, arrives in Hispaniola; Queen Isabella dies (her four-year-old son, Carlos, will ascend to the thrones of Castile and Aragon when King Fernando dies in 1516)

1511

* The Spanish viceroy in the Indies, Columbus's son Diego Colón, appoints Diego Velázquez to invade and govern Cuba

1515

* Nezahualpilli, the *tlahtoani* (king) of Tetzcoco, dies and is succeeded by Cacama (with his brother Ixtlilxochitl in revolt)

1517

* February 8–April 20, Francisco Hernández de Córdoba leads Spanish expedition from Cuba, explores and battles Maya forces along Yucatec coast

1518

* May 3–November 15, Juan de Grijalva leads Spanish expedition from Cuba, explores and interacts with indigenous groups on Yucatec and Gulf coasts; October 23, Cortés appointed head of a third expedition, tasked with finding Grijalva and continuing to explore

1519

* February 10, expedition company under Hernando Cortés leaves Cuba, follows coastal route taken by Córdoba and Grijalva; Malintzin joins the company in Tabasco
* April 21, expedition lands on the Gulf coast, at San Juan de Ulúa, within the tribute-paying zone of the Aztec Empire
* May, Vera Cruz (the first of three towns of that name, moved to another site in 1521) founded by the company, which appoints Cortés as leading captain

* June 3–August 16, expedition camps in Cempohuallan; the nineteen-year-old Spanish king becomes the Holy Roman Emperor Carlos V

* July 26, Cortés and other leading captains send a ship to Spain

* August 16, Spanish-indigenous force begins march inland

* September 2, Spanish-Tlaxcalteca hostilities begin

* September 23, having been offered a peace treaty, the Spaniards enter Tlaxcallan

* October 10–11, Spanish-Tlaxcalteca expedition marches from Tlaxcallan to Cholollan

* October 14–18, massacre in Cholollan

* October c. 25, Spanish-Tlaxcalteca expedition leaves for Tenochtitlan

* November 8, the Meeting of Cortés and Montezuma

* November 14, Cortés later claims to have taken Montezuma captive on this date (disputed in this book)

1520

* April 20 (or by May 1), large Spanish company under Pánfilo de Narváez lands at San Juan de Ulúa

* May c. 16, Alvarado leads massacre of Aztec nobles during the Festival of Toxcatl in Tenochtitlan

* May c. 27–28, Cortés loyalists under Sandoval reach Narváez's camp at Cempohuallan and successfully attack it

* June 24, enlarged Spanish force returns to Tenochtitlan

* June 28, 29, or 30, Montezuma killed, along with the other triple *tlatoque* rulers (kings of the Triple Alliance of the Aztec Empire)

* June 30 or July 1, in what is later called the Noche Triste (Tragic Night), the Spanish-Tlaxcalteca force flees Tenochtitlan; close to a thousand Spaniards and well over a thousand Tlaxcalteca are killed

* July 9 or 10, series of skirmishes, battles, and Aztec attacks culminate in the Battle of Otumba (near Otompan)

* July 11 or 12, the fleeing survivors reach Tlaxcallan

* August 1, Spaniards massacre the men and enslave the women and children of Tepeyacac (Tepeaca)

* September c. 15, coronation of Montezuma's brother, Cuitlahua, as tenth *huey tlahtoani* of Tenochtitlan

* Mid-October to mid-December, smallpox epidemic kills many (some claim a third or half; disputed here) in Tenochtitlan (including Cuitlahua on December 4)

* December 25–31, Spaniards march back to Valley of Mexico, met by Ixtlilxochitl on the 28th, enter the valley on the 29th and Tetzcoco on the 31st

1521

* Late January or early February, Cuauhtemoc (a nephew of predecessors Montezuma and Cuitlahua) elected eleventh *huey tlahtoani* of Tenochtitlan

* February, Spanish-Tlaxcalteca-Tetzcoca (allied) attack on Xaltocan, then Tlacopan and its tributaries; Tetzcoco firmly established as base for campaign against Tenochtitlan

* April 5–13, allied attacks on Yauhtepec and Cuauhnahuac, which is sacked

* April 16–18, allied force defeated in attack on Xochimilco

* April 28, thirteen brigantines built by Tlaxcalteca laborers launched onto the lake at Tetzcoco

* May: 10th, implementation of siege of Tenochtitlan begins; 22nd, three Tlaxcalteca-Tetzcoca-Spanish forces, with conquistadors led by Alvarado, Olid, and Sandoval, leave Tetzcoco to take up positions surrounding the island-city; 26th, potable water to the city cut off; 31st, Sandoval and Olid join forces at Coyohuacan

* June 30, in a Spanish-Tlaxcalteca defeat on the causeway, sixty-eight Spaniards are captured and executed at the Great Temple

* July, ships land at Vera Cruz with hundreds more men, horses, and munitions

* July 20–25, battle for great plaza of Tenochtitlan

* August 1, Spanish-Tlaxcalteca-Tetzcoca forces enter great plaza of Tlatelolco, where Aztec defenders make their last stand

* August 13, Aztec survivors surrender and Cuauhtemoc is captured

* August 13–c. 17, invaders massacre, rape, and enslave the survivors, sacking the city

1522

* October 15, Carlos V names Cortés governor and captain-general of New Spain
* November: 1st, Catalina Suárez, Cortés's first Spanish wife, dies of unknown causes in Coyohuacan; 8th, his so-called Second Letter is published in Seville

1523

* Cortés and Francisco de Garay, Jamaica's governor, agree that Garay may claim Pánuco (region northeast of central Mexico); December: Garay dies in Coyohuacan; Pedro de Alvarado leads conquest company to Guatemala

1524

* Spaniards begin to settle in central Tenochtitlan; January, Cristóbal de Olid leads conquest company to Honduras, but stops in Cuba en route; June, the first two Franciscan friars arrive in Mexico; Olid renounces Cortés's authority; October, Cortés leaves Mexico for Honduras

1525

* February: as in 1520, the captive triple *tlatoque* are murdered; this time the kings, including Cuauhtemoc, are hanged on Cortés's orders in the capital of the Maya kingdom of Acalan-Tixchel; don Juan Velázquez Tlacotzin (who had been Montezuma's *cihuacoatl*, or viceroy, and had similarly governed Tenochtitlan since 1521) appointed governor of the city; dies later in the year and succeeded by don Andrés de Tapia Motelchiuhtzin

1526

* June 25, Cortés returns to Mexico, but July 2, royal official Luis Ponce de León removes Cortés from the governorship and initiates his *residencia* (administrative inquiry; it will drag on until 1545)

1527

* Royal official Estrada bans Cortés from Tenochtitlan

1528

* April, Cortés leaves Mexico for Spain; December, fray Juan de Zumárraga arrives as Mexico's first bishop

1529

* Cortés receives title of Marqués del Valle, marries the daughter of the Count of Aguilar; Nuño Beltrán de Guzmán appointed president of the first Audiencia (court of administration and justice) of New Spain

1530–31

* Don Andrés de Tapia Motelchiuhtzin, *tlahtoani* and governor of Tenochtitlan (indigenous Mexico City) is killed in a conquest campaign against Chichimecs, succeeded by don Pablo Tlacatecuhtli Xochiquentzin (a cousin of Montezuma), in turn succeeded by don Diego de Alvarado Huanitzin (a nephew of Montezuma), who rules until 1541; Ixtlilxochitl dies and is succeeded as *tlahtoani* of Tetzcoco by three of his brothers, each in succession

1530–40

* Cortés lives in Mexico, in Cuernavaca, managing his estates run on slave labor and sending a series of expeditions to Baja California and into the Pacific Ocean

1539

* First book published in the Americas, a catechism in Nahuatl, printed in Mexico City; don Carlos Ometochtzin, brother of the *tlatoque* of Tetzcoco, burned alive at the stake in Mexico City

1540

* Cortés returns to Spain; accompanies Carlos V's failed campaign to Algiers in 1541; dies near Seville in 1547

1794

* Cortés's remains (brought back from Spain in 1629) reinterred in a new mausoleum in the Hospital de Jesús in Mexico City; mausoleum destroyed in 1823; bones hidden in hospital chapel, where they remain

Illustrations

———✧———

EPILOGUE

Conquest as Crucible. *Reproduced courtesy of the Museo Soumaya.*

IN THE GALLERY

Introduced in:

CHAPTER 1

The Urtext. *Courtesy of the John Carter Brown Library at Brown University.*
Civilization, Barbarism, and Nature. *Courtesy of the John Carter Brown Library at Brown University.*
The Valley. *Courtesy of the Sutro Library, California State Library, San Francisco.*

CHAPTER 2

Shock and Awe. *Reproduced by permission of the Jay I. Kislak Foundation.*
The Meeting. *Reproduced by permission of the Jay I. Kislak Foundation.*
Stoned. *Reproduced by permission of the Jay I. Kislak Foundation.*
The Conquest. *Reproduced by permission of the Jay I. Kislak Foundation.*
Spanish Ingratitude. *Courtesy of the John Carter Brown Library at Brown University.*
Triumphal Entries. *Courtesy of the John Carter Brown Library at Brown University.*

CHAPTER 3

His Heart Was in the Right Place. *Courtesy of Scholastic Inc.*
Sacrificing Humans. *Courtesy of the John Carter Brown Library at Brown University.*
Idol Worship. *Courtesy of the John Carter Brown Library at Brown University.*
Divine Images. *Courtesy of the John Carter Brown Library at Brown University, and the Bibliothèque national de France.*
Ruffled Feathers. *Courtesy of the John Carter Brown Library at Brown University.*
A Noble Savage. *Courtesy of the John Carter Brown Library at Brown University.*

CHAPTER 4

The Zookeeper. *Original in the Biblioteca Medicea Laurenziana.*
Picturing the War. *Courtesy of the John Carter Brown Library at Brown University.*
Carved in Stone. *Drawing by Patrick Hajovsky, reproduced with permission.*

A CONQUEROR CAPTURES A KING. The engraved title page to Bernal Díaz's *Historia Verdadera de la Conquista de la Nueva España* [True History of the Conquest of New Spain], first published in Madrid in 1632. Edited by a Mercedarian, the edition gave prominence to the role played by a friar from that order in baptizing indigenous Mexicans (right of the title). Cortés is on the title's left; he rests his hand on a cartouche depicting him, backed by his fellow conquistadors, capturing Montezuma and his crown.

Invention

> I say and affirm that what is contained in this book is absolutely true.
> —Bernal Díaz, preface to the 1632 edition of his
> *True History of the Conquest of New Spain*

> In [my Poem] I have neither wholly follow'd the Truth of the History, nor altogether left it: but have taken all the liberty of a Poet, to add, alter, or diminish, as I thought might best conduce to the beautifying of my Work. It being not the business of a Poet to represent Historical truth, but probability.   —John Dryden, *The Indian Emperour*, 1667

> I often think it odd that it should be so dull, for a great deal of it must be invention.   —Jane Austen, 1799, on "history"[1]

H ow do we know what happened when the Spaniards invaded the Aztec Empire? The most widely read account of "one of the greatest Subjects in all History" is the gripping narrative of the invasion by Bernal Díaz del Castillo. Díaz has been frequently praised as a foot soldier with extraordinary literary talent. A member of the 1519 expedition into Mexico, this "captain conquistador" was trumpeted in the preface to his book as the original "eye witness" to the events he recalled. Díaz billed his book as the *True History of the Conquest*; Carlos Fuentes, the famous Mexican novelist, canonized it as the true foundation of Latin American fiction.[2]

The title page to the first edition of the *True History,* published in 1632, featured a full portrait of the conquistador who had led that invasion, Hernando Cortés. In the engraving, Cortés presents to the reader a dramatic scene, simply rendered, on a shield. In effect, the legendary conqueror opens a window onto the story, with a single moment selected to symbolize the narrative—an icon, if you like, that gives access to the narrative.

In that moment, we see a conquistador—clearly Cortés—approaching a king sitting on a throne. Although bearded, with features similar to those of Cortés, and wearing a simple European-style crown, the king is dressed in a feathered skirt. Just as the crown was an iconic and universal representation of kingship to Europeans of the day, so did a feathered skirt represent "the Indian" of the Americas. The king was thus clearly Montezuma, the emperor of the Aztecs, whose island-capital was depicted in another circular shield, or cartouche, at the bottom of the title page.

As Cortés approaches Montezuma, he reaches out with both hands: with his left, he appears to be grabbing the emperor's crown; with his right, he has a set of manacles, which he is slipping onto Montezuma's wrist. The seated emperor appears passive, offering no resistance. Yet this is hardly a peaceful meeting. Cortés's aggressive pose, the trio of armed soldiers crowded in behind him, and his symbolic seizure of crown and emperor suggest an encounter with violent intent, diplomacy gone wrong, an unnegotiated seizure of king and kingship.[3]

Does this small engraving, therefore, offer us a visual shortcut to the crux of the story? Can the epic history of the Conquest of Mexico—indeed, the larger world-changing phenomenon of the European discovery, invasion, and settlement of the Americas—be distilled to an emblematic, bold capture of an indigenous king? Perhaps it can; perhaps the history of the world, from the fifteenth to twentieth centuries, can be reduced to an engraving of imperial man, invading and taking.

But perhaps such an image is only the very start of the story. Perhaps it is merely a hint, in fact, on the title page of an 863-page book; and a misleading hint, to boot. For as we enter that book, read Díaz's lines closely, read between them, and compare them to other written and visual sources on this "greatest Subject," that simple image of seizure pixelates and crumbles. The late historian Hugh Thomas's comment that "on occasion Bernal Díaz's memory is at fault" turns out to be classic British understatement. Mexican historian Juan Miralles's catalog of the many inconsistencies and outright errors that pepper the *True History* turned into a book-length study, *Y Bernal Mintió* [*And Bernal Lied*]. For Díaz was neither a captain nor an eyewitness to much that he described, often relying instead on the earlier accounts (Cortés's included) that he claimed to be correcting. Pondering the "flashbacks, digressions, repetitions, ellipses, and incendiary passages" of the *True History*, Christian Duverger became convinced that Díaz witnessed little of what he claimed to see, and wrote not a word of it; the French scholar went so far as to argue that the book was actually written by none other than Cortés, during his retirement in the Spanish city of Valladolid in the 1540s.[4]

In the *New York Times* and *Chicago Sunday Tribune*, reviewers of a modern edition of Díaz's *True History* called his words "the most reliable narrative that exists" and "the most complete and trustworthy of the chronicles of the Conquest." But what if it is the opposite of that—utterly unreliable, incomplete, and untrustworthy? Where does that leave us? If we must take literally Fuentes's verdict on Díaz's book as foundational to the Latin American novel, and see it as a work of historical fiction, then how do we find the "Historical truth" to which Dryden alluded—let alone some "probability" regarding the great events of the sixteenth century? As an historian recently wryly remarked, "Historians explain why things turned out the way they did. Since we already know the outcome, this might seem a simple matter of looking back and connecting the dots. But there is a problem: too many dots."[5]

I suggest that we begin again, that we go back and trace the dots once more. "Every good mystery takes place on three planes," a celebrated mystery novelist has said, "what *really* happened; what *appears* to have happened; and how the sleuth figures out which is which." Five centuries after Spaniards launched themselves against the indigenous peoples of Mesoamerica and then wrote thousands of pages describing what they saw and did, we live in an intellectual world in which the phrase *testigo ocular* (eye witness) is viewed with skepticism and suspicion, as indeed it should be. But that does not mean that we must throw the baby out with the bathwater and dismiss sources such as Díaz as lies, as fiction, as invention. We can return again to Díaz, to the writings of Cortés himself, to the dozens of accounts and chronicles written by Spaniards in the sixteenth century and beyond, to accounts written by Aztecs and other Mesoamericans and their mixed-race descendants, to engravings and paintings and codices, and to the thousands of pages of legal documentation still held in the archives of Seville and Mexico City. We can sort through the probabilities and possible historical truths, sift through the lies, fictions, and inventions, until new understandings and perspectives start to come into focus.[6]

In seeking to begin again, to approach from new angles the oft-told story of Mexico's Conquest, I take my cue from Juan de Courbes (1592–1641), the French engraver who worked in Madrid in the 1620s and '30s and created the cartouche that is our initial window onto Mexico in 1519 (facing this Prologue's title page). The essence of the miniature scene engraved by Courbes is an encounter between two famous men. The accuracy of the scene, either as a literal depiction or a symbolic one, is not important for now (but we shall certainly return to it later). What matters is that Cortés, through Courbes's invention, offers us his encounter with Montezuma as a starting point.

That encounter was not just a meeting, but also one of the greatest meetings of human history—the moment when two empires, two great civilizations, were brought irreversibly together. "If that mythical moment—the birth of modern history—can be said to exist, it occurred on November 8th, 1519." So suggested one historian; another has proposed that the morning when Cortés first met Montezuma at the entrance to the imperial capital city of Tenochtitlan was "the real discovery of America." In this book, I call it the Meeting, with a capital *M*.[7]

The Meeting is the outermost layer of the story. We shall begin, in the first chapter, with Cortés's own version of the Meeting. Intriguingly, he never claims to have taken Montezuma's crown or manacled him on November 8; the alleged arrest came later. Instead, he depicted the Meeting as an unambiguous surrender by the Aztec emperor. That depiction has remained the dominant narrative, underpinning the way in which Cortés, Montezuma, and the entire story of the Conquest of Mexico have been seen for five centuries. As Cortés's account of the Meeting is peeled back, the layers beneath are revealed: how that encounter was remembered, interpreted, and invented; and beneath that, the entire exposed artifice of the legendary Cortés, the enigmatic Montezuma, and the messy, chaotic, brutal war of invasion that ever since has been seen through distorting lenses as "the Conquest of Mexico." And as the names we use for things matter a great deal, with the "Conquest of Mexico" a highly partisan label coined to evoke a triumphalist narrative (which it has done well for five centuries), we shall from this point on refer only to the Spanish-Aztec War (1519–21) and to the larger conflict of which it was a crucial part, the Spanish-Mesoamerican War (1517–50). (Those dates, as well as the terms *Aztec* and *Mesoamerican,* shall become clearer as we proceed; also see the Appendix, "Language and Label, Cast and Dynasty.")

I wish I could claim a Road-to-Damascus moment when I realized why and how I had to write a book on the most-studied subject in the history of Latin America, a foolhardy task that surely demands an explanation up front. But the truth is that I have experienced a series of such moments stretched between two quincentennials—that of Columbus's 1492 landing in the Americas and that of the first Spanish contacts with native Mesoamericans in 1517. Some of those moments took place in the archives (for example, reading documents written or dictated by the conquistadors themselves, preserved for centuries in Spain's extraordinary imperial archives in Seville); or in libraries (like the British Library in London, or the John Carter Brown Library in Providence, Rhode Island, with its unparalleled collection of rare books and manuscripts); or in conversation with the brilliant scholars of the Conquest period in Mexico, the United States, and elsewhere (either in person, or through reading and rereading the studies that made this book possible, and which are scattered through its endnotes); or in the classroom (where students in Pennsylvania, London,

Bogotá, and many points in between have kept me on my toes and forced me to second-guess every assumption and conclusion); or in Mexico City (walking where the streets and canals of Tenochtitlan once ran, realizing that Montezuma had often strolled through his zoo, for example, right beneath my feet); or simply at home (where I benefit from the extraordinary mind of a generous spouse).

As a result, I researched and wrote, lectured and wrote more; and yet the questions kept coming, often the same questions, and with the explosion of the Internet came increasing numbers of questions by email—from a high school student in New Zealand, from a retired naval officer in Argentina, from a postman in Barcelona, from a doctoral candidate in Canada, from a convict in a California prison, and so on. Gradually, it dawned on me that the wrong questions were being asked, or they were being asked in the wrong way—not by students or email correspondents, but by scholars and writers, by me.[8]

The challenge must be, therefore, to resist asking—let alone answering—why "Montezuma and the Mexican people were so quickly conquered by the Spanish?" (as a recent book phrased it). Instead, let us first entertain the notion that they were *not* "quickly conquered." Then let us ask why that question has been phrased in that way. Let us *not* ask, "How could a small army of hundreds of Spanish soldiers crush millions of Mexica and their powerful military theocracy?"—because it leads inevitably to the next sentence in that quotation: "This has been one of history's great mysteries." Instead, let us revisit and challenge common answers; for example, that the Aztecs were "weakened psychologically" because they believed Cortés or the Spanish king had "a prior claim to the Mexican throne," or "their ritualized style of combat unfitted them to confront Europeans who fought to win rather than to take sacrificial captives; but, in a contest of hundred against thousands, it was their horses that gave the invaders the decisive advantage."[9]

The quotations above come from four authors, deliberately unnamed in the paragraph because my purpose is not to criticize them personally (they have all written books I admire greatly), but to show

how such phrases reflect the larger perspective made up of thousands of books and articles, plays and films, going back hundreds of years. That perspective has always centered on a profoundly leading question, or—as I hope to persuade you—a profoundly misleading question. We will encounter it many times in the coming chapters. But for now, consider one more example, chosen because these are the beautifully phrased opening lines of an award-winning article by a superb scholar:

> The Conquest of Mexico matters to us because it poses a painful question: How was it that a motley bunch of Spanish adventurers, never numbering more than four hundred or so, was able to defeat an Amerindian power on its home ground in the space of two years? What was it about Spaniards, or about Indians, that made so awesomely implausible a victory possible?[10]

The outcome of the war—not just Tenochtitlan in smoldering ruins by August 1521, but Spanish colonial rule for three centuries and its deep, complex legacy in modern Mexico—must and will be explained. But we can reach that place of new understandings by fully questioning the above assumptions, and many more. For example, is there evidence that Montezuma ever surrendered, or that any Mesoamerican saw the Spanish invasion as legitimate? Has the emphasis on the Aztecs as devotees of so-called human sacrifice distorted our view of their civilization? Is a twenty-eight-month invasion really a "quick" war? Why are conquistadors typically numbered in the hundreds when in reality thousands of Spaniards fought the Aztecs? Is there really an advantage to being on "home ground" or having a dozen horses in battles of thousands of men? Do we prejudice our discussion and privilege traditional answers by styling the invaders as "adventurers," the invaded as "Indians," and their war as the "Conquest of Mexico"? Does viewing the Conquest as a compelling conundrum—as one of history's great mysteries—tend to lead us unavoidably back to the "mythistory" of the traditional narrative (as I label it)?

I think it does. And I have thus resisted the temptation to structure the chapters that follow as a simple narrative. That narrative is a
trap, drawing writer and reader alike into the familiar old Cortesian
chronology, turning the war into "the Conquest of Mexico," with its
predictable denouement. It is also monolithic, pushing counternar-
ratives to the margin as sidebars. Never fear, the story will be told,
but it will be told multiple times, with narrative pieces removed from
the story, examined in detail, and then reinserted.

But note that this book is not a synthesis of previous accounts,
another telling of the tale albeit from a different angle. Rather, it is
a reevaluation of previous accounts stretching from the 1520s to the
present; an examination not just of the events of the Conquest story
but of their half-millennium afterlife; an argument for seeing the
traditional narrative of the "Conquest of Mexico" as one of human
history's great lies, whose exposure requires us to better grasp both
what really happened at the time and why the traditional narrative
has prospered.

The book unfolds with eight thematically paired chapters. The
first pair (Part I) anatomizes the Meeting and the story of the
Spanish-Aztec War, exploring how and why their history evolved
into a traditional narrative that dramatically distorts the events of
the early sixteenth century. The next pair of chapters (Part II) describes how Aztec civilization and Montezuma have been seen over
the centuries. The West's long-standing view of the Aztecs is con-
trasted with suggestions as to how we might understand differently
their culture, their response to the invaders, their emperor, and his
perspective on the Meeting.

The Cortés legend is probed in the third and fourth pairs of
chapters, punctured not in order to demonize him, but to shrink the
inflated conquistador and make way for other protagonists. Those
other actors, both Spanish and Nahua, afford us revealing, alternative perspectives on the invasion through to Montezuma's death
(Part III) and then through the 1520s and beyond (Part IV). These
chapters suggest how we might select different dots and connect
them in new ways, seeing the Spanish-Aztec War through the ex-

periences of people marginalized in the traditional narrative—Taíno slaves from Cuba, for example, or women of all ethnicities. We can also place at the center of the story the violence and mass enslavement that characterized the conflict, which were sufficiently horrific to suggest that even "invasion" and "war" (let alone "conquest") are inadequate descriptors of a watershed moment in world history, for too long glorified as "the greatest adventure story of modern times."[11]

Thus new portraits of Cortés and Montezuma emerge, turning upside down the legends and stereotypes of the traditional narrative; beneath the layer of the famous men of imagination lie the layers revealing whom those men really were. But, even more important, there too at the heart of the story we see the perspectives and roles of all the other men and women who lived and died in Mexico during these tumultuous years. The Meeting of November 8, 1519, is thus the outside layer of a story driven by a great cast of characters—with the most famous members of that cast playing very different roles to those traditionally assigned to them. As the layers are peeled back and the book unfolds, we see in a new light the Meeting; Cortés and Montezuma; the "Conquest of Mexico"; the Spaniards and Aztecs of the era; the posthumous persistence of the mythistorical traditional narrative; the history of great encounters; and ultimately the very nature of history itself—and its invention.

PART I

Lies are sufficient to breed opinion,
and opinion brings on substance.

—Francis Bacon's essay on "Vain-Glory," 1612

Myth is birthed by ideology,
and only by attacking ideology
can myth be dispelled.

—Octavio Paz[1]

IMAGINING TENOCHTITLAN. The caption reads, in German: "Great Venice has five gates / at each of the gates there is a bridge / which reaches the land / and on these same five bridges / there are many drawbridges with towers on them / so that the city is impregnable." This woodcut (on both the fifth and seventh pages of the *Newe Zeitung*, printed in Augsburg in 1521 or 1522) is the earliest surviving European illustration of Tenochtitlan. Depicting the Aztec capital as a medieval city, it is almost completely inaccurate.

———✦———

CHAPTER I

Mysterious Kindness

Do not believe more than what you see with your eyes.
—Montezuma to Cortés, according to Cortés, 1519

The empire [of the Aztecs] received him with mysterious kindness.
—Maurice Rowdon, 1974

The career of Hernando Cortez is one of the most wild and adventurous recorded in the annals of fact or fiction, and yet all the prominent events in his wondrous history are well authenticated. All *truth* carries with itself an important moral.   —John Abbott, 1856

Facts are history, whether interpreted or not.
—Barbara Tuchman, 1964

History is a muse you glimpse bathing between leaves.
—Felipe Fernández-Armesto, 2014[1]

I MAGINE SEEING TENOCHTITLAN FOR THE FIRST TIME.
Imagine how they must have felt, those few hundred Spaniards and their African slaves, the first people from outside the Americas to see the great Aztec metropolis. The setting was spectacular, the scene breathtaking. The imperial capital was a massive island-city floating on a lake, surrounded by volcanic mountains. It was possibly the most stunningly beautiful combination of the natural and built environments in human history. Who among us would not want to see such a sight? Those first visitors must have been overwhelmed with disbelief, wonder, and fear. We certainly would be.

Those at least were the three emotional reactions that ran through surviving written accounts of Tenochtitlan before the Spanish-Aztec

War devastated it. Diego de Ordaz, a conquistador who would survive the war only to drown in the Atlantic, was the first person from the Old World to see this "other new world of great settlements and towers and a sea, and in the middle of it a city, very grandly built." Claimed Ordaz, "he had been amazed by what he had seen" and "in truth it appeared to have caused him fear and astonishment." Bernal Díaz wrote that the conquistadors were not sure "whether what appeared before us was real." The place "seemed a thing of enchantment," said Juan Cano, who would later marry a daughter of Montezuma; "one could hardly believe it was true or that one was not dreaming it." Cortés himself told the king of Spain that it was "so wondrous as not to be believed." The "great city of Temixtitan"—as Spaniards first called it—was so full of "grandeur, of strange and marvelous things" that "we here who saw them with our own eyes could not understand them with our minds."[2]

An Aztec description of the Spaniards' first arrival in the valley captured something of the nervous fascination that gripped the conquistadors:

> *Mocuecueptivi, ommocuecueptivi, onteixnamictivi, . . .* : They kept turning about as they went, facing people, looking this way and that, looking sideways, gazing everywhere between the houses, examining things, looking up at the roofs. Also the dogs, their dogs, came ahead, sniffing at things and constantly panting.[3]

Most of the Spaniards would have been familiar with Seville, the effective capital of the fledgling Spanish Empire. But although Seville was one of the largest cities in Europe in the 1510s, it only contained about thirty-five thousand people; Tenochtitlan was a staggering twice that size. Including the population of the towns that ringed the valley's network of lakes—such as those seen by Ordaz from the mountain pass above the valley—the Aztec metropolitan area was ten times as populous as Seville. As one Franciscan friar imagined later in the century, "the Indian people were so numerous that most of their towns and roads had the appearance of anthills, a thing of admiration to those who saw it but which must have instilled a terrible fear in the few Spaniards that Cortés brought with him."[4]

In view of what we now know of Tenochtitlan, Cortés's assertion that the city was "as big as Seville and Cordoba"—even if we read that as meaning the two Spanish cities combined—is rather weak. There may have been as many canoes plying Tenochtitlan's canals and waters as there were people in Spain's largest city. His estimate that the "main tower is higher than the tower of the cathedral in Seville" does not come close to conveying the shape and scale of the pyramid and twin temples that towered over the city's main plaza. And his statement that the city's other main plaza was "twice as big as the city of Salamanca's plaza" likewise barely hints at the well-kempt order and symmetry of a city that made medieval European towns seem like cramped warrens of squalor.

But the comparisons to European cities were inevitable, as numerous in Cortés's descriptions as in those by other Europeans, and consistently favorable to Tenochtitlan. Cortés imagined how perfect such a city would be, were it saved just for Spaniards. Its location on an island in a lake was noteworthy not just for making the place "very beautiful," he told the king, but because it could allow the conquistadors to create a segregated urban environment—with Spaniards living "separate from the natives, because a stretch of water comes between us."[5]

News of the discovery of a city whose scale and engineering were unprecedented in the European experience spread rapidly on the other side of the Atlantic Ocean. Eyewitness observations mixed with rumors; inadequate comparisons to European cities merged with imaginative speculation. A newsletter printed in the German city of Augsburg, in late 1521 or early 1522, described how the "Christians" who two years earlier had discovered the Aztec metropolis called it "Great Venice." The anonymous author of the newsletter was intrigued by the five causeways linking Tenochtitlan to the lakeshore, which an engraver attempted to depict in what is the earliest surviving illustration of the Aztec city (facing this chapter's title page). The newsletter announced that "Great Venice" was "enormously rich in gold, and in cotton, wax, and honey," that it and the cities around the lake were all "well built" with "roofs made of pure silver, and out of lime and sand." The urban inhabitants were "strong people," who "fatten and eat dogs, which are the only animals in the land," and "they eat much honey, and also human flesh."[6]

Literate Germans were not the only Europeans to be fed the delicious detail that the inhabitants of this newly discovered and wondrous metropolis were cannibals. In the autumn of 1525, the senators of the real Venice sat and listened with fascination to the description of a city that was, like their own, built on an island and laced with canals. The description was read to them by Gasparo Contarini, who had just finished serving as ambassador to Carlos V, the Spanish king, Holy Roman Emperor, and ruler of an empire whose expansion seemed disturbingly boundless.

"That city is marvelous," the ambassador told the senators, "for its size, its location, and its ingeniousness, placed in the middle of a lake of saltwater whose circumference is almost two hundred miles." The city was also adjacent to "a freshwater lake," and all these waters "rise and fall twice a day, as they do here in Venice." But unlike Venice, this far-off city was connected to the shore by several causeways, and "its inhabitants are idolaters" who "sacrifice people to their idols," and "they eat people, but not all; they only eat enemies captured in battle."[7]

By 1525, the Venetian senators had access to a far more detailed account of the city, written by none other than Cortés himself, who was already famous across Europe as the conqueror of that distant pagan empire and its capital. The previous year, a Venetian printer had sold off the first Italian edition of two letters written to the Spanish king by Cortés. Those letters had been written in Mexico in 1520, in the middle of the Spanish-Aztec War, and in 1522, after the war had destroyed much of Tenochtitlan. The letters were published soon after reaching Spain.

The first (known to us today as the Second Letter) was typeset in Seville on November 8, 1522—three years to the day after

Cortés first set foot in Tenochtitlan. Its frontispiece (in the Gallery) featured an extended title that acted as a blurb, promising that the book would tell of a newly found "very rich and very great province named Culua, in which there are very large cities and marvelous buildings, and great commerce and wealth; among these there is one more marvelous and rich than all of them, named Timixtitan."[8]

Cortés's account sold out quickly, inspiring its publisher, Jacobo Cromberger, to print the Third Letter as soon as he could the following year. By the time of the Venetian edition of 1525, there were multiple Spanish editions, as well as editions in Latin, Dutch, and French, presenting various combinations of the Second, Third, and Fourth letters. The Cortés version of events in Mexico was so successful that in 1527 the Crown prevented further printings (lest the conquistador's fame threaten the authority of the king). But the ban did little to squelch the success of the books, which have remained in print in many languages for the last five centuries. One of history's recurring ironies is that those who have destroyed something often dominate our perception of it, and this is true of Cortés and his "Timixtitan."

Although Cortés devoted pages to describing the city, Cromberger surely knew as well as did the printer of the Augsburg newsletter that words were not enough. Fortunately, Cromberger was also given a hand-drawn map (one that seems to have been sent from Mexico attached to Cortés's original letter). From that map an engraving was carved. Both the original map and the engraving that accompanied the 1522 Seville edition are lost. But copies from the Latin edition of 1524 have survived, as have some of the Italian versions accompanying the Venetian edition (one opens Chapter 4).[9]

The result has for centuries been an object of mystery and fascination. It is, in its own way, as wondrous as was the city itself, which— by the time Europeans admired "this impressive metropolis set like a jewel in the center of an azure lake" (in the words of art historian Barbara Mundy)—lay half ruined. The map was a sort of hybrid cultural creation. It combined elements from three sources available to the engraver. One was medieval European buildings similar to those that dominate the Augsburg engraving. Another was Islamic architecture, as represented in images such as those of the 1493 *Nuremberg Chronicle;* the mosques and minarets of Constantinople and Jerusalem may have served as models for the "mosques" that Cortés wrote were ubiquitous to Aztec cities. A third element provided the engraver with cartographic conventions and urban features not included in Cortés's Second Letter, and which could only have come from an Aztec source (probably the lost original Aztec-made map). For example, the map's schema of a square plaza set within a circular city set within a circular lake reproduced "the idealized geometries" of the Aztec conception of a city.[10]

It is not just the style of the map that is hybridized, but its very details, positioning Tenochtitlan in two moments in time—two universes—all in a single frame. The map thus takes us right to the Meeting and the months that followed it, when Tenochtitlan was the Aztec imperial capital but with a Spanish presence; when the "Temple where they sacrifice" (*Templum ubi sacrificant*) still stood but with a small cross raised upon it. At the top of the map, on the eastern horizon, an oversize Hapsburg banner flutters. The message to King Carlos was clear: here is a city and empire of marvels and riches; its rotten religious core (the central plaza of "sacrifice") justifies all means to conquer and convert its people; that enterprise has begun (the cross on the pyramid) and will soon be completed (the banner will be carried from the edge to the center).

More than a mere promise of victory, the map's very existence was a claim of possession; maps in the Europe of the day were tightly controlled and guarded objects of intelligence. Cortés told the Spanish king that during the months when Montezuma was under his control, the emperor had given him "a cloth upon which was drawn the whole [Gulf] coast," a map that was surely one of the sources of the coastal sketch included by the Nuremberg printers. Both maps were intended as evidence of the Aztec ruler's submission. The Nuremberg Map is thus a cartographic manifestation of the Spanish-invented surrender of Montezuma.[11]

But Montezuma did not surrender; and as the original maps made their way across the Atlantic Ocean, Tenochtitlan was not in the hands of Spaniards. Montezuma was dead, but the city had always been his, as reflected in one of the map's details: Of its seventeen inscriptions or labels (all in Latin on the Nuremberg version), only one person's name is mentioned. That person is identified three times as *D. Muteezuma:* Dominus, or Lord, Montezuma, the Aztec emperor. Without him, the city was incomplete; without him, the story of how Cortés and his fellow Spaniards entered Tenochtitlan was incomplete. Although he was not often seen or heard in public, the emperor was everywhere in the city—his image inscribed on monuments, his power evoked by palaces, his name cited by officials, his fame invoked in the monthly festivals that ran ceaselessly. In those first moments of encounter—before the distorting clutter of later events and the varied ways in which they were remembered by Spaniards and Nahuas alike—it was clear to everyone that the city, the country, and story belonged to Montezuma. Indeed, on the title page to the first published edition of Cortés's Second Letter, while the conquistador captain is mentioned once, the Aztec emperor is named twice: "Of this city and province, a very great lord is king, named Muteeçuma"; the letter "tells at length of the vast dominion of the said Muteeçuma, and of its rituals and ceremonies."[12]

Ritual and ceremony, presided over by Montezuma, were in store for those first Spaniards who saw and entered Tenochtitlan—despite their fear of ambush as they apprehensively approached the city, checking the rooftops and alleys, looking this way and that. Because Cortés's Second Letter is the foundational account, or urtext, of the Meeting, let us first approach that momentous November 8th of 1519 via his telling of it.

The mainland journey of the Spanish invaders had begun some six months earlier, on the coast of the Gulf of Mexico. According to Cortés, it was his own skill, combined with God's blessing, that explained how the expedition had made it this far inland, surviving a series of confused diplomatic and hostile encounters, including a number of open battles. In fact—as we shall see later in detail—the Spaniards owed their survival to the local Mesoamericans (the umbrella term we use to describe the many ethnic groups within and adjacent to the Aztec Empire). For rather than systematically wiping out the invaders, the city-states of the region had variously opposed them, tested them, or allied with them—all with a view to encouraging them, one way or another, to continue their journey toward the capital.

We pick up that journey on November 1, one week before the Meeting. On that day, the surviving three hundred Spaniards, accompanied by at least ten times that many indigenous warriors and porters, set out from the city of Cholollan (Cholula) to make the climb over the mountain pass into the Valley of Mexico. Cholollan was about fifty miles as the crow flies from Tenochtitlan, but much farther on foot, mostly because two volcanoes, Iztaccihuatl and an active Popocatepetl, stood in the way.

There were several routes available to the Spaniards, although Cortés seems to have been aware of only two. One was the route that Montezuma's envoys suggested. It was the easier of the two, running north around both volcanoes. But Cortés suspected that the Aztecs "wished to persevere in making a trap for us." So he chose the route that had been found by "ten of my companions." Cortés does not name Diego de Ordaz here, but it was Ordaz whom the conquistador captain had sent up earlier to inspect the volcanoes, and who had "brought down much snow and icicles for us to see"—despite the fact that an eruption was in progress.[13]

The expedition spent that first night (November 1) in "some hamlets" subject to Huexotzinco (Huejotzingo). There the locals "live very poorly" because they were allied with Tlaxcallan (Tlaxcala)—the city-state that was the chief enemy of the Aztecs in central Mexico—and "Muteeçuma has them surrounded by his territory." The next day (the 2nd), the Spaniards and their allies climbed the pass between the volcanoes. Disappointingly, Cortés failed to dramatize the moment, saving for later in the Second Letter his expressions of wonder over the view of the valley. No other conquistadors claimed to have seen the city and lake from the pass on the 2nd, either, so perhaps that chilly morning was overcast. Whatever the case, Cortés's emphasis is on the uneventful descent into the upper edges of the valley, where the invaders found buildings in which they could lodge. Now they were in the Aztec heartland, and the contrast was notable; there was "plenty to eat for all, and in all the rooms very large fires and much firewood."

In the afternoon, an embassy from the emperor arrived, led by a lord "whom they told me was a brother of Muteeçuma's." According to Cortés, the envoy's goal was to bribe the Spaniards into returning to the coast, by giving Cortés "some three hundred gold pesos" and begging him to turn back because "the land was scarce of food and the road to get there was very bad"; furthermore, the island-city could only be reached by canoe. On the other hand, the Aztec prince "then said that I had only to say what I wanted and Muteeçuma, their lord, would command it to be given to me." The embassy left, but Cortés claimed that the hospitality showed to the visitors revealed that "they planned to attack us that night"—a plot he said he foiled by increasing the guard.

Cortés's description of this meeting with the unnamed prince, and the night that followed, is marked by three themes that run through his account of this first week in November (and indeed, much of his story of the two-year war). First, Cortés was convinced that Montezuma was repeatedly trying to persuade the Spaniards, one way and another, to turn around. Second, he believed he periodically received submissive statements by indigenous lords, who thereby tacitly recognized the legitimacy of his presence in Mexico. Third, he suspected that spies were everywhere and ambushes were being planned at every turn.

Interlocked and often contradictory, the three themes reflected the Second Letter's purpose, which was to justify the invasion and its violence. For by projecting surrender and submission onto Nahua attitudes, Cortés classified them as vassals of the Spanish Crown, which in turn made any hostility a form of rebellion—with cru-

cial legal implications in the Spanish world. The three themes also
reflected the inadequacy of communication between Cortés and
Montezuma's envoys, as well as the Spanish failure to understand
Montezuma's strategy. We know that during the autumn of 1519,
Cortés relied on a pair of interpreters—Gerónimo de Aguilar, a
Spaniard who spoke Spanish and Yucatec Mayan, and Malintzin
(aka doña Marina or Malinche), a Nahua woman who spoke a dialect
of Yucatec Mayan and Nahuatl, the Aztec tongue. We shall return
in later chapters to the important topics of the role of interpreters,
of Malintzin herself, and of Montezuma's mysterious strategy. But
for now, note that Cortés mentions Malintzin and Aguilar just once
in his Second Letter—crediting them with helping him uncover an
alleged Aztec plot in Cholollan in October. He otherwise gives the
utterly false impression that he is communicating clearly and directly
with the untrustworthy local lords.[14]

ON NOVEMBER 3, the expedition made the slow descent to Amaquemecan (Amecameca), an Aztec city of several thousand inhabitants. Here they were again generously lodged and fed "in some very
good houses," so much so that they stayed two nights. According to
Cortés, there were again bribes ("some forty female slaves and three
thousand *castellanos* [and] all the food we needed"), and obsequious
promises of loyalty by high-ranking lords telling the captain that
Montezuma had ordered them "to provide me with all the necessary
things."[15]

Cortés's fear of ambush also remained constant. On November
5, the expedition reached Lake Chalco, which connected to the waters surrounding Tenochtitlan, although their view of the capital was
obscured by the spur of land upon which the town of Ixtlapalapan
stood. They seem to have spent one night in Chalco (although Cortés
omits that night in his account), and then one night in Ayotzinco
(Ayotzingo), about five miles along the lakeshore. The region was
heavily populated—the city of Chalco alone probably had some ten
thousand inhabitants—and so there were Nahuas everywhere, no
doubt hoping to catch a glimpse of the strange foreigners. But Cor-

tés saw only spies and warriors with ill intent; he was convinced that
"there they wished to test their forces against ours, only it seemed they
wished to do it very safely by catching us at night unawares." Thus all
during the night of November 6, Cortés had guards assault any locals
who came close enough to catch, by foot or in canoes, so that "by the
breaking of dawn some fifteen or twenty of them had been taken and
killed by us."[16]

On the morning of the 7th, Cacama (more properly, Cacamatzin),
Montezuma's nephew and *tlahtoani*, or king, of Tetzcoco—Cortés
only identifies him as "a great young lord of about twenty-five"—
arrived on a litter with a large entourage. In Cortés's telling, Cacama's message was as contradictory as that of the lords with whom he
had spoken over the preceding days. On the one hand, Cacama offered to guide Cortés to meet Montezuma in Tenochtitlan, assuring
the Spaniard that "we would see and learn from him the willingness
he had to serve Your Highness"—that is, Montezuma's willingness
to serve the Spanish king. On the other hand, Cacama and the Aztec lords with him "greatly insisted and persisted" in warning Cortés
not to continue in his journey, for in doing so the Spaniards "would
endure much effort and need." As always, Cortés implied that
the Aztecs were simply untrustworthy—that they recognized the
Spaniards as a legitimate presence, yet continued to threaten them.
Cortés's narrative thus seems nonsensical, an illogical jumble of justifications. In fact, it was logical only as a precursor to his telling of
the fantastic encounter with Montezuma, now only a day away.[17]

During the course of November 7, the expedition moved along
the lakeshore past the town of Mixquic and onto the causeway that
crossed the lake—marking where Lake Chalco flowed under the
causeway's bridges into Lake Xochimilco. In the middle of the causeway was a small island, covered by the town of Cuitlahuac. This city,
wrote Cortés, "although small, was the most beautiful we had seen
up to then, both in regard to the well-built houses and towers and in
the good nature of the foundation, for it is entirely assembled on the
water." After being "fed very well," the Spaniards continued on the
causeway, reaching the spur or peninsula of land that led to the cap-

ital city. Near the peninsula's tip was Ixtlapalapan, a large city of some fifteen thousand people, which sprawled from the shore into Lake Tetzcoco. Cortés once again details the largesse with which the local lords "made me very welcome," including "some three or four thousand *castellanos* and some female slaves and clothing." He is also as effusive about Ixtlapalapan as he is later about the capital itself, insisting that the houses of the city's rulers "are as good as the best in Spain," praising the "workmanship both in their masonry and woodwork," and detailing the elaborately landscaped gardens.[18]

Ixtlapalapan faced Tenochtitlan, and thus, at last, offered the invaders a close view of the great city. Cortés again saved his descriptions of the capital for later, but this is the moment when other conquistadors—most notably Bernal Díaz—commented on the view in their accounts. In an often-quoted passage, Díaz marveled at the entire panorama, from Tenochtitlan to Ixtlapalapan, noting that the curiosity and amazement went in both directions; for the Spaniards were "seeing things that had never been heard of or seen before, not even dreamed about," while the Aztecs came in massive crowds to see the invaders, "which was not to be wondered at, for they had never before seen horses or men like us."[19]

Curious Aztecs were out en masse on November 8, as Cortés and his Spanish-Tlaxcalteca force made their way out of Ixtlapalapan and onto the causeway that led to Tenochtitlan. The road was wide enough, wrote Cortés, "that eight horsemen could ride right down it side by side." The causeway passed through three towns, each with thousands of inhabitants and featuring "very good buildings, both houses and towers" (referring to pyramids), all "built on the shore, with many of their houses on the water." The invaders stopped at a fortified gate, built where the causeway met another one running from the western lakeshore. Here began the extended ritual of welcome that was the Meeting.[20]

The ritualized encounter started with the arrival of "about a thousand men, leading citizens of that city," each of whom "placed his hand on the ground and kissed it." That ceremony took "almost an hour." Beyond the gate was a bridge, and "past this bridge, that lord Muteeçuma came out to receive us with some two hundred lords, all barefoot and dressed in a different livery" but very richly so. "Muteeçuma came down the middle of the street with two lords, one on his right hand and the other on his left." Both of these Cortés had already met over the previous twenty-four hours: one was Cacama, Tetzcoco's ruler and Montezuma's nephew; the other was the emperor's brother, Cuitlahua (more properly, Cuitlahuatzin, and not to be confused with the town of Cuitlahuac), the ruler of Ixtlapalapan. They held Montezuma's arms, and "were all three dressed identically."

Cortés then succinctly described the awkward first moment of thwarted personal contact: "When we met I dismounted and went to embrace him alone, but those two lords who were with him stopped me with their hands so that I should not touch him." The three Aztec kings then "performed the ceremony of kissing the ground." After that, they each greeted Cortés, as did every one of the two hundred lords. When it was Montezuma's turn, Cortés took the opportunity to give the emperor "a necklace of pearls and glass diamonds"; Cortés "placed it around his neck." Montezuma quickly reciprocated: after they "had walked up the street ahead, a servant of his" brought two necklaces featuring gold shrimp, which Montezuma placed over Cortés's neck. Continuing up the street, they reached "a very large and beautiful house." The emperor took his guest "by the hand" and led him to "a very rich throne" in a large room facing a courtyard. Montezuma left but soon returned with gifts—"jewels of gold and silver and featherwork and up to five or six thousand pieces of cotton clothing"—and sat on another throne beside Cortés.

The emperor then delivered an astonishing address, written down a year later by Cortés as if it were reported speech. The verb that Cortés used to introduce the speech is significant. He avoids *decir* or *hablar;* that is, Montezuma does not simply talk, speak, or address his visitor. Instead, Cortés styles the speech as a formal, reasoned, legally valid discourse. The introductory phrase is rendered as *ppuso eñsta manera* in the 1522 and 1523 editions, and as *prepuso en esta manera* in the 1528 manuscript; in modern Spanish, *propuso en esta manera*. Thus Montezuma "suggested" or "proposed" or "reasoned in this manner," or "he made the following proposition." The speech is cast as an offer, one supported by a rationale.[21]

As a voluntary capitulation, supported by a kind of legal logic, Montezuma's speech correlated perfectly with the Crown's requirement that invasion companies attempt to secure surrender from indigenous rulers prior to waging war on them. There was even an official text, called the Requirement (*requerimiento*), which was routinely recited or read to indigenous defenders before battle. Bartolomé de Las Casas (the Dominican friar to whom we shall return frequently) famously remarked that he did not know "whether to laugh or cry at the absurdity" of this ritual. The Requirement offered two options: peaceful submission to king and church; or slaughter and servitude, "death and damages" that would thereby legally be "your fault" (indigenous rulers were told). In this fantasy of imperial ritual, indigenous lords would fully grasp their choices, and willingly surrender in terms that were as legally logical and binding to the Spanish mind as was the Requirement.[22]

That never happened. But Spaniards came to imagine that it did, in Tenochtitlan in 1519. For the Requirement was only absurd if taken literally as a speech aimed at indigenous audiences (the pretense that incensed Las Casas); likewise, Montezuma's voluntary articulation of the legal tenets of the Requirement is equally absurd if taken literally. But (as anthropologist Paja Faudree recently argued), the Requirement's audience was not indigenous, it was "other European powers, critics within Spain, and, crucially, the Crown itself." Thus Montezuma's speech, like the Requirement, was a Spanish legal ritual performed for a Spanish (primarily royal) audience, designed to officially transform the political Spanish-Aztec relationship—in Spanish eyes.[23]

Montezuma's speech, as composed by Cortés (and his fellow surviving captains), is worth reading in its entirety:

"For a long time we have known from our scriptures that we have from our ancestors that I, and all those who dwell in this land, are not natives of it, but foreigners who came to it from very foreign parts; and likewise we hold that our ancestors brought to these parts a lord, whose vassals they all were, and who returned to his homeland. And then he came again after a long time, so long that all those who had remained were married to local, native women and had many offspring and built villages where they lived. And when he wished to take them with him, they did not want to go nor even receive him as lord; and so he departed. And we have always held that those who descended from him would come and subjugate this land and us as their vassals; and thus because of the place from which you say you come, which is where the sun rises, and the things you say of that great lord or king who sent you here, we believe and hold as certain that he is our natural lord, especially as you tell us that he has known of us for a long time. Therefore you may be certain that we shall obey you and hold you as our lord in place of that great lord of whom you speak; and in this there shall be no mistake or deceit whatsoever. And you may well command as you will in all the land—that is, all that I pos-sess in my domain—for you shall in fact be obeyed; and all that we own is for you to dispose of as you wish. And thus you are in your own homeland and your own house; take your ease and rest from the labors of the journey and the wars you have had. For I know full well of all that has happened to you from Puntunchan to here, and I know well that those of Cempoal and Tascaltecal have told you much evil of me. Do not believe more than what you see with your eyes, especially from those who are my enemies; and some of those were my vassals and have rebelled against me upon your arrival and said those things to gain favor with you; and I also know that they have told you that I have houses with walls of gold, and that the floor mats in my rooms and other things in my household are likewise of gold, and that I was, and made myself, God; and many other things. The houses that you see are of stone and lime and clay." Then he lifted his clothes and showed me his body, saying to me: "See me, that I am of flesh and bone like you and like everyone, that I am mortal and tangible"—gripping his arms and body with his hands—"see how they have lied to you! It is true that I have some things of gold left to me by my grand-parents; all that I might have, you shall have, every time that you want it. I am going to other houses where I live; here you shall be provided with all the things that you and your people need, and you shall receive no hurt, for you are in your own house and homeland."[24]

Cortés then stated that he replied to the part of the speech "that seemed to me most agreeable, especially in making him believe that Your Majesty was he whom they were expecting." And with that, Montezuma left and the Meeting was over. Its coda, in Cortés's telling, is oddly anticlimactic (at least, until the reader turns the page). Provided with plenty of "chickens and bread and fruit and other necessary things," Cortés and his compatriots "spent six days very well provided with all that was needed." The question of who was the host and who the guest remained hanging (and will remain so for us, for now).

If only the story ended there, with the Spanish invaders enjoying a week of Aztec hospitality—before returning to the coast with fantastic tales to tell their compatriots in Cuba and Spain. But, of course, it did not, and therein lies the significance of the Meeting: the moment when Cortés met Montezuma would prove to be one of our past's great milestone encounters, one that forever altered human history.

Why was the Meeting such a milestone? The answer lies in part with the universal relationship between history and meetings. There is an enormous literature on historical theory that could profitably be discussed here; for the past century and more, historians have relished debating history and discussing historians. But let us step around such debates and consider this: History is encounter. The past comprises all the encounters—both simple and complex, peaceful and conflictual—that have brought people together. History, as a discipline, is thus the sum of all the *narratives* of those encounters. But that sum of narratives is untidy—replete with omissions, fabrications, and contradictions. Human memory is wildly unreliable, "wired to be warped." As a result, a traditional narrative (as I call it throughout this book) tends to be privileged over others, an appealing tale to mask the unappetizing mess that is reality. The English historian E. H. Carr asserted a half-century ago that history cannot exist without interpreters; for Carr, history was "a continuous process of interaction between the historian and his facts," so that "without their historian the facts are dead and meaningless." What I am suggesting here is that history—being all the encounters of the past—only exists for us through that "continuous process of interaction" between alleged and apparent facts and all their historians.[25]

But by historians, I do not mean just the professors and writers of modern times; I mean all the witnesses and writers whose narrations and interpretations have allowed past encounters to survive. With respect to the Meeting and the events surrounding it, accounts by "historians" therefore include every narrative ranging from Cortés's own version to this very book, any comments made in legal documents, all interpretations embedded in plays and poems, and all visual representations from the earliest colonial codices to the statues of Cortés, Malintzin, and their son that provoked controversy in Mexico City near the end of the twentieth century (more on that in a later chapter).

It may seem obvious that "the more you shift your point of view, the more is revealed" (in the words of Felipe Fernández-Armesto), and indeed that observation has been made for as long as histories have been written. And yet Fernández-Armesto, one of our era's most original historians of the Americas, is right to repeat it. Traditional narratives achieve biblical tenacity; Cortés's triumph and Montezuma's surrender persist as Conquest gospel. As Carr warned a half-century ago, it is "very hard to eradicate" not just the "fetish" that history is facts and nothing but them, but also the idea that a particular history is a particular set of well-established facts, amounting to a "true history" (to poke at Díaz again). The traditional narrative of the Spanish conquests in the Americas has been particularly tenacious because "persuasion is at the heart" of its canon of chronicles—from Cortés into modern times—a literature that its leading scholar, Rolena Adorno, has called a "polemics of possession." Historians of those conquests have thus had to work hard in recent decades to develop new viewpoints—revisiting well-worn texts, digging deeper in well-scoured archives, and analyzing sources written in Mesoamerican languages, all in an attempt to create what we like to call a New Conquest History.[26]

Yet the traditional narrative is like the Aztec defense of Tenochtitlan during the siege of 1521: by day, the attackers would take a section of the city, fighting house by house, block by block; at night, the Aztecs would take most of it back. Likewise, despite recent assaults by historians on numerous aspects of the traditional narrative, it holds its ground, even gaining some, as readers, listeners, and viewers remain as drawn as they have been for centuries to the narcotic effect of its simplified coherence and inevitable climax.[27]

The tragic mess that was the destruction of old Tenochtitlan resulted not from the tidy sequence of triumphal moments that marks the traditional narrative, but from the complexity that was the Spanish-Aztec War and the combined mess of its many histories and images. The messiness of narrative and interpretation that lies between us and any given past encounter has profound implications for our understanding of the story unfolding here, for it suggests that the traditional narrative of the Cortés-Montezuma Meeting is an unfaithful, distorted, or even dramatically fictitious rendering of the event. The real encounter that day must have been seen, understood, interpreted, remembered, and recorded in diverse ways, creating a picture far less simple than the one painted by Cortés. The promotion of Spanish mastery and control, of legitimacy and superiority, of a monopoly on truth and on knowing what really happened, must necessarily have marginalized or silenced alternative memories, perceptions, and realities. In short, the depiction of the Meeting as Montezuma's surrender is likely to have been a lie.

This brings us to a more specific reason why the Meeting is such a milestone: the traditional narrative of the "Conquest of Mexico," as well as the traditional portraits of Cortés and Montezuma, effectively stems from that account of the Meeting. If we rethink the Meeting, we can rethink its protagonists and the invasion war. Indeed, we might thereby rethink the entire history of conquest and early colonization in the Americas. And while the dominoes of traditional narratives are falling, we can go even further.

Consider this: the Spanish conquests are not only viewed as if "inscribed in the genes of the conquistadors," but that "retrospective illusion" is usually extended to include the genes "of modern Europe." Put another way, Spain's conquests funded its creation of "the first modern global configuration," and as primacy passed from nation to nation, the superior destiny of the West was confirmed. There has been a deep-rooted assumption, for centuries on both sides of the Atlantic, that the sixteenth-century rise of Spain and the modern triumph of the West are not just linked by a causal chain, but that each confirms the other, each echoes the other, each tells the same primal tale. The traditional "Conquest of Mexico" narrative resonates because it is a universal one, in which civilization, faith, reason, reality, and a progressive future are victorious over barbarism, idolatry, superstition, irrationality, and a retrogressive past.[28]

That narrative may be more broadly familiar than any in human history. For it underpins the multimedia fables that have been embraced by hundreds of millions of people worldwide in the decades straddling the turn of this century—the books, movies, and games of *The Lord of the Rings*, Harry Potter, and *Star Wars* are just three examples. At the heart of those fictional universes are conflicts between civilization and barbarism, good and evil, configured in highly racialized terms (even if the racial Others are imaginary anthropomorphic species) and complete with reassuring triumphal endings. No wonder the "Conquest of Mexico," in traditional narrative form, seems surprisingly familiar to modern audiences.[29]

Thus while Cortés and Montezuma continue to crop up again and again in the chapters that follow, this is not just a book about them. It is about something much larger—the pernicious prevalence and insidious ubiquity of traditional narratives that justify invasion, conquest, and inequality. And it is also about something "smaller"—the many men and women whose lives and stories from the age of the conquest wars were left on the margins, forgotten, or never told. They are included not for inclusion's sake, but because they are the tools that permit us to dismantle the traditional narrative and see the "Conquest of Mexico"—and, perhaps, hopefully, much more—from numerous new angles.

SURRENDER IN MEXICO. Scenes 3 ("Cortes and Montezuma at Mexican Temple") and 15 ("American Army Entering the City of Mexico") in the *Frieze of American History,* in the Rotunda of the U.S. Capitol, designed by Constantino Brumidi in 1859. The composition of these two events as moments of manifest destiny, as meetings of peaceful triumph and surrender, reflects the nineteenth-century U.S. appropriation of the traditional narrative of the Meeting. Each surrender—Montezuma's in 1519 and Santa Anna's in 1847—is used to legitimize the other, setting both incontrovertibly into the edifice of "American" history.

———✦———

CHAPTER 2

No Small Amazement

[Then] appear'd *Montezuma* himself, who put a Chain of Gold, imboss'd with Pearls, about *Cortez* his Neck, and immediately conducted him to the City, where having entred, and being come to the Palace, *Montezuma* plac'd *Cortez* on a Golden Throne, and surrendred up his Right to his Catholick Majesty of *Spain*, in the presence of all his Peers, to their no small amazement.   —Ogilby's *America*, 1670

Cortés entered triumphant, and to the Empire
Of Spain was added that hemisphere
                          —Final lines of Juan de Escoiquiz's epic
                          México Conquistada: Poema Heroyca, 1798[1]

WITH A TILT OF THE HEAD, AND A GESTURE OF THE HAND, Montezuma capitulates to Cortés on Capitol Hill.

It is a milestone moment, but you might miss the Aztec emperor's surrender—even if you are able to visit the U.S. Capitol Building in Washington, D.C., stand in its spectacular Rotunda, and admire the *Frieze of American History* at the base of the dome. For the frieze is fifty-eight feet from the floor, and the meeting of Cortés and Montezuma is but one of nineteen scenes.

The surrender is a subtle one: Montezuma's pose is one of proud welcome, not abject defeat. Yet the context and ramifications of the encounter seem clear. The forward motion of the scene is with the advancing, armed conquistadors; the Aztecs are adorned with feathers, not weapons, and one of three Aztec princesses is on her knees. Furthermore, the scene is a link in a chain of events that mark "American" history, from Columbus's first landing in the hemisphere through to the discovery of gold in California (the artist, an Italian named Constantino Brumidi, drew the original designs in 1859). This, the third of Brumidi's scenes, is echoed in the fifteenth scene, a depiction of U.S. troops taking possession of Mexico City in 1847. The parallel is inescapable: General Scott is Cortés, and General Santa Anna is Montezuma; the two acts of surrender in Mexico City echo, illuminate, and legitimize each other, representing resonant moments in the march of progress that is "American" history.

The *Frieze of American History* in the Capitol Rotunda illustrates the simple fact that three and a half centuries after the Meeting took place, it was still being remembered, represented, and reinscribed as a surrender. The clash of civilizations, the conquest wars, the protracted process of colonization are all eclipsed and elided into a single symbolic moment. For Cortés (and the West), that moment is providentially triumphal; for Montezuma (and Native America), it is one of voluntary capitulation, an acceptance of fate. Brumidi left space (accidentally) for later artists to update America's history, so that today the final scene depicts the Wright brothers and the "Birth of Aviation." Because the frieze is circular, Wilbur Wright is adjacent to Columbus, separated only by an allegorical female "America" (the Wright-Columbus comparison was frequently made in the twentieth century, typically updated since 1969 to pair the Genoese navigator with Neil Armstrong). The twenty-first century's millions of visitors to the Capitol can gaze up to see Columbus and the Wrights virtually side by side, just as they can see the mirrored pairs, across the Rotunda from each other, of Cortés and Scott, Montezuma and Santa Anna. The impression of the monumental weight of great events, of a predestined sequence of past moments, of facts carved in stone, is irresistible.[2]

Yet the frieze is not carved in stone. It is a mural, painted in grisaille, a fresco of whites and browns designed to look like stone. Likewise, the frieze depicts a series of encounters that actually took place, but those encounters are styled and juxtaposed to eliminate their ambiguities and complexities, all in the service of a greater message. Thus the frieze's use of content, like its technique of composition, is an artful trick. We can let ourselves be fooled, and accept

Montezuma's surrender to Cortés as a fact carved in stone. Or we can open our eyes to the spectacular trickery of a lie that has lived for five hundred years, surviving like a virus as it moves from page to page, image to image.

Brumidi did not include Montezuma's surrender to Cortés in his frieze simply because it happened (it did not) or because he believed it happened (he surely did, as did his peers). It was included because Montezuma's surrender was seen as a momentous example of barbarism accepting the progressive march of civilization, a strong link in that chain of "American" history, reflecting how the United States sought to build itself and promote its legitimate place in the world.

This may seem like a wild leap—from sixteenth-century Tenochtitlan to nineteenth-century (and twenty-first-century) Washington, D.C.—but Brumidi was not alone in making such a leap. During his lifetime, the Spanish Conquest of Mexico was very much on the minds of U.S. Americans and Mexicans, as the two carved out identities as independent nations, going to war with each other in the process; U.S. soldiers carried copies of William Prescott's new bestseller, *The Conquest of Mexico*, on their march from Veracruz to Mexico City, writing home that they were walking in the footsteps of the great Cortés.[3]

The perspective from the Mexican-American War is only the tip of an iceberg of preoccupation with the "Conquest of Mexico" that has not ceased, on both sides of the Atlantic, for five centuries. Our challenge is to grasp how and why a small lie became so massive, how a grossly distorted interpretation of a major event in world history has persisted as its traditional narrative—its mythistory—for half a millennium, staring at us still—from history books, from television screens, from the walls of the Capitol Rotunda.

Sir Hugh Cholmley was an English officer and gentleman who spent much of his adult working life in Tangier. The English acquired the Moroccan port city from the Portuguese in 1661, and the following year Sir Hugh took up a post in the colony, where he served for two decades. At some point he acquired a set of paintings, which he sent to be hung in his ancestral home in Yorkshire. There they remained for three centuries, noticed on occasion by guests, such as the Victorian visitor who described "a most curious and valuable series of eight ancient Spanish pictures, supposed to have come into possession of Sir Hugh Cholmley, of Tangier, from a captured Dutch vessel."[4]

We will probably never know for sure who created these paintings, where, and why, but art historians have reasonably argued that they were made in Mexico during the three decades after 1660, commissioned by a viceroy or even by King Carlos II himself. For the eight paintings told one of the young king's favorite stories, that of the glorious "Conquest of Mexico." Either way, destined for Spain, they never arrived. If the Cholmley family lore of "a captured Dutch vessel" is true, it is likely that the Dutch took the paintings from a Spanish ship carrying them across the Atlantic, and the Dutch ship in turn fell into English hands; during Sir Hugh's Tangier years there were two Anglo-Dutch wars.[5]

Meanwhile, Carlos II had commissioned his court historian, Antonio de Solís, to write a new telling of Spain's "Conquest of Mexico." The resulting book was published in Madrid in 1684. It was an immediate hit. Cholmley's eight looted paintings reflect Solís's telling of the Conquest story so closely that some scholars (myself included) have suggested the paintings were composed between 1684 and Cholmley's death in 1689 to illustrate Solís's *Historia*. I now suspect that the paintings were already hanging in Sir Hugh's house in Yorkshire when the *Historia* went to the printers, and that the parallels between the two stem from the fact that they both rely heavily on the traditional narrative of the Conquest established decades earlier (especially the 1632 first edition of the account by Díaz, who is depicted and named in two of the paintings).[6]

We shall turn momentarily to Cholmley's paintings, as they offer an engaging way to illustrate the traditional narrative. But first, it is worth clarifying the core elements and events of that narrative. Although Solís's version is a good example, his *Historia* is merely a link in the chain stretching from Cortés's own accounts through to the present, made manifest in recent times in every imaginable medium from serious history books to television shows.[7]

Imagine the traditional narrative as a drama in three acts. For across the centuries, it has been told as a tripartite tale of discovery, loss, and recovery—following a structure that is fundamental to human storytelling (not coincidentally, as we shall see shortly). The first act sets the scene and introduces the cast—most notably the hero (Cortés), the villain (Velázquez), and the tragic hero (Montezuma). This is primarily a Spanish story, beginning with the arrival of its Spanish hero. It is also a tale of underdog triumph, of the extraordinary bravery of a small conquistador company, but the heroism of the group always stems from Cortés's lead. The narrative follows the hero and his companions into Mexico, culminating in the cliffhanger moment of the Meeting. Following Cortés's lead, established in his Second Letter, this first act is full of signs that it will climax not only in discovery, but in the winning of a prize—confirmed, in the act's closing scene, with Montezuma's surrender to Cortés.[8]

The second act begins by consolidating that win, but the logic of the drama requires immediate challenges to it, and sure enough it soon falls apart. Despite heroic efforts to hold on to what Cortés has won for his king, the barbarism of the Aztecs and the treachery of Velázquez bring catastrophe to the conquistadors. Hundreds of Spaniards die in the battles fending off Aztec warriors as the conquistadors fight their way out of Tenochtitlan. But hope remains: the villain is neutralized, as the army Velázquez had sent to arrest Cortés had instead joined him; and the stoic survivors find refuge with their allies, the Tlaxcalteca. The second act closes with Cortés's promise to his king to reconquer what has been temporarily lost.

The third act comprises the events covered by Cortés's Third Letter, in which the final year of the war against the Aztecs is presented as a predestined yet masterful act of recovery by Cortés—in His Majesty's name. A year of turning towns subject to the Aztec Empire into allies allows the Spaniards to lay siege to Tenochtitlan, culminating in its destruction and the capture of Montezuma's successor, Cuauhtemoc. The empire is declared conquered—and re-deemed as New Spain.[9]

LET US NOW FILL in some of the details of this traditional narrative by looking closely at some of Cholmley's paintings. (All eight can be seen in the flesh—in oil and canvas—by visitors to the Library of Congress, where the paintings hang as part of the Kislak Collection; acquired by the Kislak Foundation in 1999, they are now usually called the Kislak Paintings; four are included in this book's Gallery.)[10]

The Kislak canvases are continuous narratives; most of them image multiple events within a single frame, as if the story were divided into eight chapters. The paintings reflect well several of the traditional narrative's key elements. For example, Cortés is the hero of the story. Aside from his name in the title of half the paintings in the series, he is also tagged in the key with a "1" in the six paintings where he appears. Three other captains are also introduced to let us know that this is a tale of glorious battles fought by a small company of brave conquistadors. Gonzalo de Sandoval, Cristóbal de Olid, and Pedro de Alvarado appear five or six times in the painting series (as often as Cortés), identified with numbers on their helmets. In the first painting, for example (not reproduced here), the three appear—in the tradition of battle paintings of the Baroque period—on horseback, wielding swords. The captains, along with the anonymous throng of conquistadors presented in the paintings, are in full armor and carrying banners of the seventeenth century. The traditional narrative is full of anachronisms of this kind, turning the conquistadors from armed colonists into an army of soldiers.[11]

Let us turn specifically to Kislak Painting #2, which graphically evokes further aspects of the traditional narrative of the war. In late April 1519, Cortés's fleet anchored in the same natural harbor found by a previous expedition (that of Juan de Grijalva), on what is now the central Veracruz coast. The next three months featured a series of events that are weaved into the traditional narrative, all essential to the cloth of Cortés's legend as a general of genius. Those events (as traditionally told) were as follows: The coast was part of the kingdom of the Totonacs, who were tribute-paying subjects of the Aztecs. Cortés was able to turn Totonac suspicion of the foreigners into an alliance against the Aztecs, setting a precedent that would allow him systematically to dismantle the empire by a combination of diplomacy and warfare over the next two years. At the same time he initiated diplomatic relations with the Aztecs themselves, through a series of meetings and gift exchanges with ambassadors from Tenochtitlan, artfully fomenting discord and alarm in the empire—from its margins to its center.

Meanwhile, seeing how wealthy the empire was, Cortés determined not to return to Cuba to report to Velázquez, but to press on and conquer the Aztecs in the Spanish king's name. With a trio of brilliant moves he dispatched a ship to Spain laden with Aztec treasures (Montezuma's gifts) and letters to the king; he then sank the rest of his fleet so none of the men could betray him to Velázquez; and he manipulated his company of some 450 men into founding a town on the coast, named Villa Rica de la Vera Cruz. They elected a town council; the council or *cabildo* officers, acting according to Cortés's secret plan, used their new authority as Crown officials to declare the Velázquez expedition fulfilled and terminated, and to appoint Cortés as their captain-general to lead them to conquer and settle for the king.

This impression of Cortés's masterful ability to maintain control of the situation in the face of all obstacles is powerfully reflected in the dominant scenario of this Kislak Painting #2—at Cortés's command, the conquistadors have put on a theatrical display of military shock and awe. The canvas is bristling with lances, cannon, galloping horse legs, and ship masts. The eight ships are mostly heavy galleons (in reality, not yet invented at the time of the war), their gun ports open. Onshore, six cannon are being fired simultaneously, while six horsemen gallop in formation with lances raised. To the far right, half-naked indigenous warriors fall to the ground in fear and wonder; the heavy dress and weaponry of the conquistadors contrasts in all the paintings with the light feathered costumes of the indigenous warriors, whose faces mostly show alarm or amazement.

To the far left, a large Aztec embassy presents lavish gifts to Cortés, who is seated at a white-clothed table (a reframing has cut off all but Cortés's hands and a knee). In the traditional narrative, these gifts were bribes from Montezuma, who was already hoping to persuade Cortés to go home; cleverly, the conquistador converts them into bribes with a different purpose. He is seated with other Spanish captains and with Malintzin. This was his Nahua interpreter (whose name is explained in the Preface, and whose life is further discussed in Chapter 8). Mayas had earlier "given" her to Cortés, as the expedition worked its way from Yucatan along the Gulf coast toward Vera Cruz; she thus spoke Nahuatl (the tongue of the Aztecs) and Yucatec Maya. Before that, the Spaniards had rescued Gerónimo de Aguilar on Cozumel. Because he had been shipwrecked on the Yucatec coast seven years earlier, he too had learned Maya. Together, Aguilar and Malintzin formed an invaluable translation chain, credited in the traditional narrative to a combination of good fortune (or God's intervention) and Cortés's astuteness.[12]

Kislak Painting #2 thus promotes a core theme of Conquest mythistory: Spanish superiority and the indigenous perception, even acceptance, of that superiority as something supernatural, possibly divine and providential. Such a vision of the story, an encounter of civilization and barbarism with its inevitable outcome, is clearly a setup for the Meeting. That is no doubt why the artist leapt straight to that moment for Painting #3. As a result, the battles outside Tlaxcallan and the massacre in Cholol[l]an (today's Tlaxcala and Cholula) are not depicted in the painting series; this was a tidy way to avoid events that were problematic and usually presented in the traditional narrative in contrived, contradictory ways (detailed in later chapters). Instead, Tlaxcalteca warriors appear in Painting #3 as a background presence, allies hidden behind advancing conquistadors. (If there is any echo in this painting of what had happened in Chololan, it is in the passivity of Montezuma's entourage, portrayed as dignitaries and servants, not a force of warriors; readers of Díaz, Solís, and their ilk would have learned that the massacre intimidated the Aztecs and their emperor into subjection.)[13]

Cortés's pose in Painting #3 is intended to illustrate an oft-repeated detail of the Meeting, that the Spanish captain attempted to embrace Montezuma, but was stopped from doing so by his brother or other noblemen (here it is the emperor himself whose hand seems to gently dissuade Cortés from coming closer). That moment of physical awkwardness likely did take place, and therein lies its function: as a tiny element of verisimilitude, it helps persuade the viewer of the truth of the entire scene and its larger meaning—Montezuma's surrender, Cortés's triumph.

Montezuma's appearance, his features and clothing, are pure European fantasy and imagination—combining visual stereotypes of the "Orient" and of the American "Indian"—but the artist invented a recognizable figure who is also at the center of Painting #4 (also in our Gallery). The busy composition of the fourth painting features dozens of feathered Aztec warriors in the foreground, beneath a wall; on top of the wall is a crowd of Spaniards, with Montezuma in their midst. His gesture is the same as in the previous painting, only this time he is gesturing to his people to stop the fighting that has overtaken Tenochtitlan.[14]

Note that in the leap from Kislak Painting #3 to #4, the action has jumped again, across the 235 days in which the Spaniards (according to the traditional narrative) lived in the royal palaces in Tenochtitlan, effectively controlling the empire through the emperor—whom Cortés, in another brilliant move, had taken prisoner while also developing a close friendship with him and convincing him to make a notarized statement of surrender to the Spanish king. Spanish-Aztec détente had collapsed when Pedro de Alvarado attacked Aztec celebrants during a monthly religious festival, while Cortés was on the coast confronting the expedition sent by Velázquez. Cortés returned to war in Tenochtitlan. As Painting #4 picks up the story, the unruly, barbarous Aztecs have abandoned their once-revered leader and are hell-bent on expelling the invaders. The caption reads: "Finding themselves surrounded in the Mexican palaces, the Spaniards make Montezuma appear on a rooftop and from there calm them [the Aztec mob], but an Indian threw a stone and others shot arrows, which killed him."

The four canvases that constitute the second half of the Kislak Painting series follow the traditional narrative's emphasis on loss and recovery, catastrophe and redemption. Paintings #5 and #6 (not included in the Gallery) depict two moments in July 1520 when the Spaniards bravely and miraculously escaped destruction at Aztec hands. The defeat during the Noche Triste (as Spaniards came to call it; the Tragic Night) is composed as a heroic battle scene, with Olid, Sandoval, and Alvarado on horseback in the foreground, glancing back at the tangle of Aztec and Tlaxcalteca warriors. Cortés is a smaller figure, but dead center, well lit, also on horseback, and brandishing his sword. Again identified in the key as "1," in both the fifth and sixth paintings, he is undeniably still the principal hero of the epic. Cortés's stoicism and heroism are further emphasized in Painting #6's depiction of the Battle of Otumba. There he rallied the survivors of the nocturnal escape from Tenochtitlan for a heroic last stand. In this painting, Cortés is in the foreground stabbing an Aztec warrior in the chest, while the other Spanish captains turn the tide of battle in the background.

Sacrifice and survival set the scene for triumph in the final pair of paintings. Kislak Painting #7 is again a continuous narrative, with the full title of "Conquest of Mexico by Cortés, No. 7" (in the Gallery). The painting is a highly fanciful reconstruction of the siege that the Spaniards and their indigenous allies laid to Tenochtitlan in the spring and summer of 1521. The geographical setting is distorted, the architecture absurdly European. Months of horrific urban conflict are compressed into a single glorious tableau in which there are more conquistadors sweeping across causeways into the city than there are indigenous allies fighting Aztec defenders. In the traditional narrative, this is overwhelmingly a Spanish victory, achieved through perseverance and the ingenious use of brigantines built especially to enforce the siege of the island-city. Reflecting that spin, the painting places a brigantine prominently in the foreground, its technological superiority echoing that of the galleons in Painting #2. The Tlaxcalteca, Tetzcoca, and other allies (who in reality outnumbered the Spaniards some 200:1) are restricted to a small group in the distant right corner, led by Spaniards on horseback and not even engaged in the battle.[15]

One might expect this canvas to be the finale, but there is a coda to the story: in the traditional narrative, Montezuma's surrender is repeatedly confirmed by his restatement of it, by his loyal efforts to calm the mob (costing him his life, as shown in Kislak Painting #4), and by his successor's surrender. Painting #8 thus shows Cuauhtemoc, looking almost identical to Montezuma, standing in a canoe that has been boarded by three conquistadors, allowing them to capture him. As if justifying the subsequent torture of Cuauhtemoc, in the effort to find the missing royal treasure (an incident not shown here), the painting includes piles of gold bars in Aztec canoes. As the caption explains: "Guatemoc [sic], the last king of Mexico, fleeing with his men in canoes that carry gold, silver, and other jewels." His capture "concluded the siege of Mexico in the name of His Majesty."

Whether we view the three-act drama of the traditional narrative through the Kislak Paintings, or whether we suspend our disbelief and surrender to the historical-novel pleasures of Cortés or Díaz or Solís or Prescott or Madariaga or Thomas, the pivot of the story is always the Meeting. It is thus impossible to see the story differently—to turn the mythistorical traditional narrative of the glorious "Conquest of Mexico" into reality's grim and messy Spanish-Aztec War—without asking these questions: How has the Meeting been seen and explained over the past five centuries; and why?

In the premodern world, without jets and smartphones, the movement of information was—from our perspective—extremely slow. News from the Americas (from "the Indies") took weeks or months to reach Europe, longer when ships were wrecked or lost, when documents were damaged by fire or water, or when witnesses died. Yet, despite all this, word traveled; stories spread, letters were copied and delivered, pamphlets set and printed.

Thus it was that Cortés was able to establish his account of the Meeting with Montezuma, and the events surrounding it, remarkably quickly. And yet, his was not the first account to spread across Europe. In March 1521, while Spaniards and their indigenous allies fought bloody battles besieging Tenochtitlan, Peter Martyr (Pietro Martire) d'Anghiera received copies of two letters that Spanish settlers had sent from Cuba. The missives included descriptions of the Aztecs, their emperor, and their capital city. Peter Martyr made copies of the letters, as others must have done too. Since the 1490s, Indies news had traveled this way, and pamphlets describing Spanish expeditions along the coasts of Yucatan and Mexico, including that of Cortés, had been printed in Nuremberg and other northern European cities as early as March 1520. Soon after Peter Martyr read them in Spain, such descriptions had reached as far as Germany, been translated, set with wood-carved illustrations, and printed.[16]

We have already seen an image (at the start of Chapter 1), and read an excerpt, from one example: the newsletter titled *Late News of the Land that the Spaniards Discovered in the Year 1521 Named Yucatan*. It was probably made possible by the communication system of the Fugger banking family, based in Augsburg but highly active in Spain, especially in its commercial capital of Seville. Printed in Augsburg in late 1521 or early 1522, this newsletter was the first printed account of the Meeting that we know of today. The passage is worth quoting in full:

> The Captain of the Spaniards made peace with the king Madozoma, lord of the Great Venice, and asked him to allow him and his people to see the city, and the king promised, and then went back to the city and called his advisors about him and told them that he had promised the Christian that he could come into the city, but his men answered that they would not permit such a thing, as the Christian would capture the city if he were allowed

to enter it, so they imprisoned the king so that he could not allow the Christians to enter the city, and then the king told his people to kill him, as he could not keep his word, and to make his son king, and the people did as their king commanded and made his son king.[17]

This account of the Meeting has been almost completely ignored by historians for the last five centuries. Indeed, it is easy to dismiss. It is too short to be a compelling narrative, it is remote (anonymous and in German, as opposed to eyewitness Spanish accounts), and peculiar (the narrative twist of "Madozoma" ordering his own assassination is unique, not found in other Conquest accounts, perhaps borrowed from a medieval folktale).

Yet this briefest of accounts is important for a couple of reasons. On the one hand, as the first printed description of the Spanish arrival in Tenochtitlan, it is not influenced by Cortés's published version of events. It omits any mention of surrender; the riddle of why Montezuma allowed the Spaniards to enter the city is solved with the statement that he and Cortés "made peace." On the other hand, it offers variations on the theme of Montezuma's capture and death, squeezing narrative detail into the paragraph in an attempt to make sense of the story. As such, it is typical of the dozens of versions of the Meeting that were written down in the decades and centuries that followed. No two accounts were identical—all shuffled the details around differently, omitting some, adding or inventing others—yet all sought to give the Meeting, and the events around it, a ring of truth, to tell a story that was wondrous and yet logical and credible, to add "corroborative detail intended to give artistic verisimilitude to an otherwise bald and inconvincing narrative."[18]

The crucial detail of Montezuma's surrender, missing from that earliest German account, was very quickly insinuated into the story—a shift that can be seen happening over the course of 1522, when news from the New World was brand-new. In another German newsletter printed in Augsburg, for example, surrender, not peace, was offered as the solution to the riddle of the Meeting. In

this pamphlet, the emperor "Mantetunia" makes a laudable decision
to capitulate. The account makes no mention of his death or of the
war at all; his response to the Spaniards is presented as right and
admirable, logically obviating the need for warfare:

> When Mantetunia heard that these people had come from the
> most powerful lord of the whole world, he received them honor-
> ably and submitted obediently to your Imperial Majesty, and told
> them that this was due to the prophecies handed down to them
> from their ancestors that one day a lord of the whole world would
> find them, and come to them with the people who lived in their
> land in ancient times and from whom they are descended.[19]

Significantly, this newsletter was printed at the very end of 1522,
almost two months after Cortés's Second Letter was published—
in Spain, but by a German printer. That same month, an Italian
printer and bookseller named Andrea Calvo published in Milan a
tiny book that consisted of an excerpt from Cortés's Second Letter, very loosely translated by Calvo himself. The excerpt focused
almost entirely on the description of Tenochtitlan ("Temistan") and
Montezuma ("Moralchie," oddly enough), culminating in Cortés's
astonishing claim that the subjects of this "great King . . . do all
that I command in the royal name of Your Highness." Calvo then
completed his booklet with a paragraph attempting to explain such
an unlikelihood, composed by him but in Cortés's voice (also worth
quoting in full):

> The principal reason that this great King and all the others of
> this New Spain have so peacefully accepted Your Majesty as lord
> is because they say they are not native to this country but that a
> King from the east once came to conquer the said country and
> left his people to guard it and departed. Then, after a certain time
> he returned and found that all his people had taken wives of the
> country and thus no longer wished to obey him. He therefore had
> to leave, but threatened to return with an army so great that they

would be forced to do what they would not do voluntarily. Since those times, their ancestors and they themselves have lived in fear of the coming of the said King; and now, seeing that a Captain of Your Majesty was conducting himself in a similar way [*simili deportamenti*], they actually believed him to be their Lord and thanked God that he had not sent forces to destroy them but to treat them with love, and with this they all voluntarily offered to be subjects of Your Majesty.[20]

The difference between the account from early 1522 and the two from December of that year is striking. Cortés's version of the Meeting as a surrender had quickly taken root. Five centuries later, it remains well rooted and still flourishing.

Calvo imaginatively attempted to make plausible Cortés's improbable explanation of the Surrender (let us now give it a capital *S*), by drawing upon the doctrine of the Second Coming of Christ, thus turning Cortés's arrival into a Second Coming for indigenous Mexicans. In trying to make sense of the Surrender, Calvo was at the start of a literary and historical tradition that has preoccupied writers of all kinds on both sides of the Atlantic for half a millennium. To navigate the hundreds of texts and images that make up that tradition, I have identified three themes that run through it, and dubbed them the Prophecy, the Coward, and the Ambush.

There is evidence that in the first few decades after the war, some people viewed the Meeting not through the lens of Cortés's lie, but as a brief moment in a bloody invasion; in other words, they remembered the war as just that, a war. Hints of this view survive in accounts from Tlatelolco, the part of the island-capital where the final battle of the siege was fought, and also in remarks made by fray Bartolomé de Las Casas—one of the few Spaniards in a position both to denounce the Surrender as immoral fiction and to write so much that many of their words have survived (we shall be hearing later from both the Tlatelolca and the good Dominican friar). None-theless, in the second half of the sixteenth century, the Cortesian account of the Meeting was strengthened by the success of the 1552 bestselling biography of Cortés by Francisco López de Gómara, and also by the writings of influential Franciscan friars in Mexico (especially Mendieta, Motolinía, and Sahagún). Meanwhile, indigenous views evolved from war memories to complex understandings of the Spanish arrival seen through the prism of Christianity. Perspectives on the Meeting thus seldom questioned it as the Surrender, instead seeking to explain it using some variant on the themes of the Prophecy, the Coward, and the Ambush.[21]

The theme of the Prophecy was central to Cortés's account and it remains the predominant theme to this day. The canon of early accounts by conquistadors and royal chroniclers—Cortés, Gómara, Díaz, Herrera, Solís, each one copying the previous ones—depicted the Surrender as an intertwined trio of moments: Montezuma's first speech of welcome and surrender on the day of the Meeting; his imprisonment by Cortés; and the emperor's second surrender speech, made tearfully before the Aztec nobility and notarized by the Spaniards. We shall return later to the (alleged) seizure of the emperor and his second Surrender; for now, suffice to note that in the traditional narrative the seizure is a soft arrest, to which Montezuma effectively acquiesces, as explained by his two statements of surrender. Those speeches, in turn, are explained by this crucial claim: Montezuma believed that the arrival of the Spaniards had long been prophesied and anticipated. Some variants were extensive, with Montezuma giving lengthy speeches (as in the Cortés version that we read earlier) and Cortés giving long replies; others were stripped down to the essential elements of Montezuma expecting the Spaniards, welcoming them to the city, and offering his allegiance to the Spanish king in fulfillment of the prophecy.[22]

During the sixteenth century, the Prophecy explanation was embraced and developed the most by a pair of intertwined groups—the Franciscans who came to convert the Nahuas to Christianity and then to educate their elite and tend to their new parishioners; and those Christianized and educated Nahuas themselves. Fascinating Conquest histories emerged from this cultural melting pot. The best known is fray Bernardino de Sahagún's collaboration with "as many as eight or ten" educated Nahuas from Tlatelolco; the result was the final book in a twelve-volume study of Nahua culture and history known to us as the Florentine Codex. Although the first draft was written in Tlatelolco in 1555, the earliest surviving manuscript version is from 1580. It can rightly be called a Tlatelolca-Franciscan account. It is thus an example of what I call quasi-indigenous sources (a scholar of Peru has called the Andean equivalent "nativelike"); to call the Florentine Codex a native or indigenous source is to mis-leadingly eclipse its Franciscan content and complex coauthorship. The Florentine Codex's version of the story heavily emphasizes the Prophecy not only as the reason why Montezuma surrendered his empire, but indeed as an underlying explanation for the Conquest.[23]

A version of the Prophecy explanation is also included in the *Historia* by the Dominican friar Diego Durán, who drew upon Nahua sources from Tenochtitlan in the 1570s. It appears as well in the account that don Fernando de Alva Ixtlilxochitl wrote to promote the role in the war played by his great-great-grandfather, Ixtlilxochitl, the *tlahtoani* of Tetzcoco. Ixtlilxochitl insisted that prophecies and omens did not bother Montezuma, but that his subjects generally "held as very true the prophecies of their ancestors who predicted that this land would be possessed by the children of the sun" (a phrase he picked up from Gómara); and that the arguments in Montezuma's court over how to welcome Cortés were irrelevant, because "the outcome was predetermined."[24]

Back in Milan in 1522, Calvo had drawn upon the Second Coming as an explanatory model, and once Franciscans and other priests began to preach in Mexico, generations of Nahuas made the same connection. Indeed, it is hard to escape the conclusion that Franciscans and Nahuas deliberately drew upon millennarian models to rewrite the distant and recent Mexican past—a process that both Christianized Nahua history and Nahuatlized Christianity. A wonderful example of that cultural interplay, one that reveals how Nahuas sought to use the Prophecy theme to understand the Conquest story, is *The Three Kings,* a drama written in Nahuatl around the end of the sixteenth century.

This Epiphany play centers on the reactions of Herod, as *tlah-toani* of Jerusalem, to the three Magi as they approach the city to announce the birth of Christ. The story's details blatantly evoke the Meeting, as it came to be constructed by this time: an ancient prophecy predicts the coming of a new king; the strangers come from the east and follow a star that evokes the comet and other omens that supposedly unnerved Montezuma. Herod welcomes the Magi with speeches that echo Montezuma's speech to Cortés: "Ascend to your home, your *altepetl* [city]. Enter. You are to eat, since it is at your home that you have arrived." Herod then undergoes a transformation, just as Montezuma does in the Conquest's traditional narrative. He threatens and insults his priests, becoming both enraged by the threat to his right to rule ("Am I not the king?" [*Cuix amo nitla-tohuani*]) and unnerved ("I am about to faint!"). The story's origin is biblical (in Matthew, chapter 2, Herod turns troubled and angry). In other words, Nahuas in the late sixteenth century did not see the story of Herod and the Magi through their memory of the Meeting and Montezuma; on the contrary, the Meeting and Montezuma were imagined and reinvented through the lens of biblical tales like this one. The play, like quasi-indigenous accounts such as the Florentine Codex, tell us little about what actually happened in 1519 but offer great insight into how later indigenous generations used Christianity to rewrite and understand the past.

Although Herod did not suffer Montezuma's sudden demise, *The Three Kings* shifts in order to retain echoes of the Spanish-Aztec War: at the moment in the Conquest story when Montezuma disappears, Herod goes from representing him to representing the Aztecs who resisted the invaders. There is violence, the Magi leave the city (as the Spaniards did on the Noche Triste). But, in the end, this is the Epiphany story, and the essential parallel is between the birth of Christ and his coming to Mexico; the Magi, who seem at first to be stand-ins for the first Spaniards, turn out to be Nahua lords embracing the new and true faith. The motives and reactions of Herod, like those of Montezuma, are ultimately eclipsed by the prophesied, providential sweep of Christianity's arrival.[25]

During the sixteenth century, the Prophecy theme became embellished with a few details that subsequent writers picked up to add dramatic flavor. For example, Francisco de Aguilar, a veteran conquistador remembering the war some forty years later, was one of the first to add that the Aztecs believed "bearded and armed men" were prophesied. That "fact" has reappeared ever since; a pithy example is in the verses that Lewis Foulk Thomas placed in Montezuma's mouth in his 1857 play, *Cortez, the Conqueror:*

> O! then, alas! The ancient prophecies.
> That did foretell the downfall of our race,
> By bearded white men from the Eastern seas,
> Are near fulfilment.[26]

Another detail that was added to the prophecy story—and which blossomed to become its central feature in the twentieth century—was the idea that Montezuma believed Cortés to be a manifestation of Quetzalcoatl, an Aztec deity supposedly destined to return and rule. Cortés made no mention in his account of the Meeting, or in any of his writings, of Quetzalcoatl; nor does he claim to have been taken for a returning god. But there was a rich and complex mythology surrounding Quetzalcoatl throughout Mesoamerica, and as it evolved under the influence of Christianity it became attached to the prophecy theme underpinning the Surrender. We shall return to Quetzalcoatl in the next chapter, so suffice to note here that most scholars would agree that Quetzalcoatl's return is "a postconquest elaboration of an indigenous tradition" (in the words of Quetzalcoatl expert Davíd Carrasco); the evidence suggests that such an elaboration took place after Montezuma's death and the war's end.[27]

Nonetheless, the story became central to the mythistory of the Meeting. In Juan de Escoiquiz's "heroic poem" of 1798, Montezuma declares to Cortés that "I am persuaded / that the great King who has sent you / is descended directly from the feared / Quezalcoal [*sic*], architect of the extensive / Mexican Empire," and that "the infallible prophecy of Quezalcoal . . . was fulfilled when you came to this kingdom." The "Conquest of Mexico" became a highly popular theme in the nineteenth century. In one typical rendering of the Meeting as Surrender, explained by the prophecy theme, "some tears fell from Montezuma" as he accepted that "the predictions of our ancestors" had been fulfilled and that he thus had to "offer all my kingdom" in "obedience" to Cortés's king. The prophecy, tailor-made for the Spaniards, anticipated men coming from the east, "differing in habit and customs from us, who were to be lords of this country." "Signs in the heavens" confirmed that the Spaniards were "the people we looked for." After all, Montezuma and his predecessors had "ruled these nations only as viceroys of Quetzalcoatl, our god and lawful sovereign."[28]

The fact that Montezuma did not mention Quetzalcoatl in his speech, as recorded by Cortés, has not deterred modern writers from inserting it. As one recent version of the traditional narrative put it: "Obviously Montezuma was recounting the story of Quetzalcoatl." On the other hand, others have seen the entire prophecy story as a metaphor for Mexico's destiny, with Montezuma's belief less important than the faith and acceptance of all his people. In one of the theatrical dialogues by Mexican poet and playwright Salvador Novo, Cortés's indigenous interpreter, Malintzin (here Malinche), explains the Conquest to the nineteenth-century French empress of Mexico, Carlota. Belief in Quetzalcoatl underpinned Mexico's surrender, but the symbolic capitulation to Cortés was Malinche's, not Montezuma's. Says Malinche, her people

> awaited, going back many generations, the return of Quetzal-
> coatl. CARLOTA.—And they believed he arrived, with Cortés.
> MALINCHE.—He arrived as him. For me, at least.[29]

In other words, Malinche is Mexico, and Cortés-Quetzalcoatl is her god, to whom she had no choice but to surrender.

The notion of belief in the prophecy myth being more expansive—
not just Montezuma believing Cortés to be Quetzalcoatl, but the
Aztecs taking the Spaniards to be gods—goes back to the mid-
sixteenth century. Francisco de Aguilar mentioned it, as did Francisco Cervantes de Salazar, who wrote in his *Chronicle of New Spain*
that as the Aztec commoners watched the Spaniards enter Tenochtitlan, some said, "These who come from where the sun is born must
be gods." The old men and those familiar with local lore and prophecy, said, "These must be those who have come to command and rule
over us and our lands." In Herrera's telling of 1601, they "sighed,
saying, those must be the ones sent to rule us and our lands, for
they are so few yet so strong to have defeated so many men"; the
Surrender is presented as so inevitable that it is accepted by Aztec
elders before it even happens, before Montezuma has yet to deliver
his speech.[30]

In the eighteenth century, the Scotsman William Robertson's
bestselling account included Aztecs in the streets thinking the conquistadors were "divinities," while Montezuma welcomes Cortés
with a speech centered on the prophesied return of relatives, people
descended from the same ancestors, with legitimate right to "assume
the government." This was another detail of the prophecy theme incorporated early on into the traditional narrative; in the words of
the friar Gregorio García, the Aztecs were "of the same lineage as
don Hernando Cortés, as Moteçuma told him." No wonder, as one
recent retelling of the traditional narrative puts it, "Montezuma was
happy to regard Cortés and the Spaniards as descendants of Quetzalcoatl."[31]

Conquest history has very often been interpreted through contemporary filters (think of Brumidi's frieze), and that is true of one
final way the Prophecy theme of the Surrender has been seen: the
arrival, welcome, and speech of surrender as a moment of peace, of
calm before the storm of war. This was how it was viewed, rather
poignantly, by Mexican writer Francisco Monterde in 1945. The
Meeting as providential and peaceful must have resonated in a
Mexico that had witnessed generations of violence (following the

outbreak of the revolution in 1910), while the world was likewise
torn apart by war. The Surrender promised a peace that would be
destroyed, thereby setting the stage for the tragedy and triumph of
the Conquest. This was not unlike the late-sixteenth-century indigenous perspective on the Meeting, which must have seemed pregnant with a tantalizing promise of peace to the survivors of decades
of violence and of lethal epidemics. And indeed Monterde borrowed
liberally from the Tlatelolca-Franciscan phrases in the Florentine
Codex. Says Montezuma, "It was prophesied that you would come
to your city, that you would return to her, and it has come to pass.
Be welcome; rest yourself. Our lord has arrived in his land." Cortés
replies, "Be reassured, sir; we all love you."[32]

UNIVERSAL LOVE FOR MONTEZUMA has not, however, been central
to how the Meeting has been depicted. On the contrary, the second
theme in such depictions has been that of the Coward, with Montezuma's surrender explained by his own weakness of character and
failing as a ruler. His cowardice likewise explains how he ends up
a prisoner of the Spaniards, unable to prevent the subsequent Aztec
revolt, resistance, and yearlong war that follows his death. Thus at
the Meeting, Montezuma "surrendred up his Right to his Catholick
Majesty of *Spain*, in the presence of all his Peers, to their no small
amazement"—according to Ogilby's 1670 version of this variation.
Those "Peers" were "much discontented" with Montezuma, "because
he had without the least resistance or consideration settled a handful
of Strangers to domineer over his whole Dominions, by which his
weakness and pusillanimity, he was now a Prisoner, like a common
Malefactor, which had formerly govern'd so mighty Territories." In
this account, there is no speech of surrender, nor any mention of
prophesy, nor an attempt to reconcile the "pusilanimous" emperor
with the valiant one described elsewhere in Ogilby's compendium;
Montezuma simply loses his nerve and turns over his throne.[33]

We shall turn in detail to Montezuma, and the ways in which
he has been imagined and misunderstood over the centuries since
his death, in the next two chapters. But it is worth briefly mention-

ing now how Montezuma the Coward came to be invented and kept alive, especially because his nurturing in the twentieth century helped to perpetuate the mythistory of the Meeting as the Surrender.

The canon of early Spanish accounts, and the traditional narrative they birthed, used a pair of arguments regarding Montezuma's role in the Surrender. One was a simple, circular logic, based on a complete acceptance of the truth of the Surrender: because Montezuma gave up his empire without a fight, he must have been cowardly and weakened by superstition, by the power of prophecy; and thus because he was weak and cowardly, he gave up his empire. The other argument used Montezuma's ignoble personality as a foil for Cortés's heroic one: Sepúlveda was one of the first to summarize this dyad in print, comparing the "noble, valiant Cortés" with a "timorous, cowardly" Montezuma. Such a pairing has proved irresistible to Cortés biographers and Conquest storytellers, from Gómara ("cowardly little man") to Prescott to the present. The main goal of that negative depiction of the emperor, however, has been to glorify Cortés and highlight his fortitude and potency as the anti-Montezuma; Montezuma as Coward helped explain the Surrender, but it was a by-product of the traditional narrative's explanation of the "Conquest of Mexico" as the product of Cortés's heroism and skill, combined with the guidance and intervention of God. Thus Montezuma the Coward was important to explaining the Meeting, but less central to explaining the entire Conquest story.[34]

It is hardly surprising to find Spanish accounts belittling Montezuma. But it may be surprising, and is therefore more interesting, to discover that in the sixteenth century there developed among Nahua accounts a version of Montezuma the Coward. There is no single Nahua account or perspective on the Spanish-Aztec War, or even one that can accurately be termed "the Aztec account." But there were various manuscripts written by Nahuas in the century after the war that told its story from the viewpoint of that author and his hometown—allowing us to speak of Conquest accounts from Tlatelolco (such as the Tlateloca-Franciscan Florentine Codex), Tetzcoco (the account by the mixed-race Nahua nobleman Fernando de Alva

Ixtlilxochitl), Tlaxcallan, and so on. In those various accounts and within their micropatriotic perspectives, Montezuma does not fare very well.

Alva Ixtlilxochitl does not insult Montezuma, but he does note that the day the emperor was killed, "the Mexica insulted him, calling him a coward and an enemy of his homeland." This is not necessarily a Tetzcoca perspective, as Ixtlilxochitl seems to draw heavily here on Gómara, but it does evoke the highly critical Tlatelolca view in the Florentine Codex, in which Montezuma "was greatly afraid" at the approach of the invaders in 1519; "he seemed to faint away; he grew concerned and disturbed . . . he was afraid and shocked." Earlier Tlatelolco accounts certainly blame the Tenochca—that is, the Mexica on the Tenochtitlan side of the island, which fell first to the invaders during the siege of 1521—but they do not scapegoat Montezuma the way that later accounts do. For example, a Tlatelolca account written in Nahuatl around 1545 ignores Montezuma altogether, claiming that Cuauhtemoc had actually been made king (*tlahtoani*) of the Tlatelolco part of the city before the war:

> The Spaniards arrived four years after Cuauhtemoctzin was seated
> as ruler of Tlatelolco, when war was waged there. When the war
> was over, there was no *tlahtoani* in Tenochtitlan. Only a dwarf
> named Mexicatl Cozooloitic, whose calves were as round as balls,
> as his name suggests, and some of his friends, were in charge.

The manuscript's focus is the fate of Cuauhtemoc, who was hanged by Cortés four years after the war, with the blame assigned squarely on the upstart Tenochca dwarf, Mexicatl. One could argue that Mexicatl's traitorous behavior acts as a metaphor for Montezuma's surrender, but I think far more likely it is a larger metaphor for Tenochca unreliability and illegitimacy.[35]

Similarly partisan and micropatriotic were accounts written by Tlaxcalteca. The mixed-race Tlaxcalteca Diego Muñoz Camargo, for example, wrote a *Historia de Tlaxcala* in 1592 in which the Tlaxcalteca converted to Christianity before all other Nahuas, making their conversion possible by defeating the Aztecs. In this Tlaxcallan-centric narrative, the Meeting became the Surrender because the Tlaxcalteca had succeeded in terrifying Montezuma with the "great victory and capture of Cholula" by "our Spaniards and the people of Tlaxcala." Thus a few days after the "victory" in Chollollan, "the captain Cortés was very well received by the great Lord and King *Moctheuzomatzin* and all the Mexican Lords." The Aztec ruler is "great," and yet weak in the face of the moral power of the Spaniards and Christianized Tlaxcalteca.[36]

Whether promoting a Nahua city-state or Cortés's genius, the use of Montezuma the Coward to explain the Meeting has made for some feeble arguments. The Italian traveler-writer Gemelli, for example, like Ogilby, Montanus, and many others before him, attempting to explain how the fearsome Aztec emperor was so easily "terrify'd" by the approach of the Spaniards, weakly resorted to the emperor's own sudden weakness. In Gemelli's 1699 account, Montezuma decided that as "there was no putting a stop to this Evil," he might as well make "a virtue of Necessity" and welcome the conquistadors into Tenochtitlan. In such versions of the story, Montezuma goes instantly from being a bold ruler to being a passive actor in the tragedy. He is almost infantilized—or feminized, in line with the perceptions of female roles and behavior at the time. For example, he is easily tricked into becoming a prisoner, and when Cortés asks him "to swear Fealty to the King of *Castile*," he does it, "with the Tears standing in his Eyes" (possibly a sign of weakness, or emotion inappropriate to a ruler; but perhaps, on the contrary, reflecting a medieval Iberian notion of lordly tears as a mark of commitment to a significant act, a subtlety presumably lost on Gemelli).[37]

Montezuma's cowardice, and hence arrest or imprisonment, is not only as much of an invention as the Surrender (as we shall see in a later chapter); it actually adds to the nonsensicality of the Surrender (logically, each renders the other redundant). Yet, faced with its repetition in the traditional narrative, poets and playwrights and authors of all kinds have attempted to twist the arrest into an explanation of the Meeting as Surrender. For this, the third theme—that of the Ambush—we turn to the brilliant Spanish poet Gabriel Lasso de la Vega.

IN HIS EPIC POEM *Mexicana* (the 1594 extended edition of his *Valiant Cortés*), Lasso depicted the opening moments of the Meeting by borrowing details from the Cortés-Gómara traditional narrative, including the giving of necklaces and the thwarted embrace of the emperor ("to nobody is such licence given"). But his emphasis is on the grandeur of the imperial entourage, the pomp and circumstance of the Meeting; an epic moment fit for epic verse. As the canto's subtitle announces, this is about Cortés's "reception with great acclaim by King Moteçuma and his Court." Montezuma is "unbeaten and exalted" and "great and powerful." At this first meeting, there is no surrender. Montezuma lavishes luxurious gifts and palatial accommodations on his guests, leaving Cortés in his new lodgings without returning to deliver a speech of capitulation. Instead, Lasso ends the canto with the sidebar story of "nine Spanish soldiers" killed on the coast. The tale's twist is the next canto, titled "Cortés Imprisons King Moteçuma." In a ruthless but valiant move, the captain turns the tables on the emperor. Montezuma's speech is an indignant one, but he has been outwitted and successfully ambushed.[38]

Lasso had spotted one of the massive contradictions built into the traditional narrative: If Montezuma had surrendered, why did Cortés need to seize him and put him in irons? Gómara had spun the seizure as a masterful act of daring—"no Greek nor Roman nor anyone since there have been kings has done anything equal to Hernando Cortés in seizing Montezuma, so powerful a king, in his own house, in a place so fortified, among a multitude of people having no more than 450 Spanish comrades, and allies." Authors since then have copied or echoed Gómara, or buried the contradiction of the imprisonment beneath an emphasis on the Surrender, sandwiching it between the emperor's two speeches of capitulation—the engraving on the frontispiece to Díaz's *True History* captures that approach, with Cortés reaching out to manacle a Montezuma whose passive, seated pose suggests the seizure is merely a symbolic confirmation of his surrender. Lasso's solution—the Meeting as Ambush—would appeal in particular to Protestant writers less sympathetic to the conquistadors. In early modern English accounts, for example, Montezuma's surrender is taken for granted as a known fact, with the subsequent placing of the emperor in fetters presented as a gratuitous act of hostility, an example of dishonorable Spanish ingratitude. In one version of an illustration of the ambush used in various eighteenth-century books (and included in our Gallery), the caption sarcastically read "Spanish Gratitude."[39]

Ever since Lasso's *Valiant Cortés*, the pomp and circumstance of the Meeting has proved irresistible to dozens of poets and playwrights. Like Lasso, Lewis Foulk Thomas did not wish to mar the moment with a surrender speech that might have undermined the majesty of the imperial host and the logic of the narrative. The American's play, while a lesser-known and indeed lesser work in every way, similarly emphasized how the emperor sought to welcome the invader

> In manner worthy of thy high estate,
> As our accredited and honor'd guest,
> And our own dignity as royal host.

Yet, as with Lasso's poem, the Meeting is pregnant with Montezuma's undoing. In Thomas's drama, the Aztec ruler's passivity is determined by his belief that the Spanish arrival "was long foretold us by our Gods," while the Spaniards see the peaceful and elaborate welcome of the Meeting as a perfect cover for their conquest plans. Realizing that Montezuma assumes the Spanish presence is temporary, Cortés and Alvarado murmur to each other: let him "eject us—if he can."[40]

One might imagine that Protestant American writers like Thomas and John Abbott—whose 1856 *Cortez* biography was part of his *Makers of History* series—would embrace the Ambush theme unambiguously as typical of Spanish treachery (or "gratitude"). Certainly they were the heirs to a negative view of Spanish colonialism that swirled around the Protestant world for centuries (and was dubbed, at the turn of the twentieth century, the Black Legend); Abbott saw a morality tale in Velázquez's violent conquest of Cuba, which his own country had recently invaded: "God has not smiled upon regions thus infamously won. May the United States take warning that all her possessions may be honorably acquired." Yet Abbott had imbibed Prescott and the canon of Spanish sources. Thus while he skips Montezuma's surrender speech, he still has Montezuma confessing to Cortés "his apprehension that the Spaniards were the conquerors indicated by tradition and prophesy as decreed to overthrow the Mexican power." The Meeting initiates a "kind reception" and "extraordinary hospitality" by Montezuma, turned by Spanish "sagacity, courage, and cruelty" into a "marvelous" triumph, in which they brought "both monarch and people into almost entire submission to their sway." Such an unappetizing stew of the Prophecy and Ambush ingredients, spiced with a touch of the Black Legend, was typical of how the Meeting as Surrender was served up in the century to follow.[41]

There is one great question simmering under all these themes, as they flowed through the centuries in their efforts to make sense of the mythistory of the Meeting as Surrender: Why cling to Cortés's lie and that mythistory? Before picking up the clues scattered in this chapter and systematically answering that question, let us linger for a moment on a twist to the Ambush theme. That twist flips the theme on its head, and makes Montezuma the trickster.

For example, in the Conquest account by a minor English writer named W. H. Dilworth (it was first published in 1759), the speech given by the emperor at the Meeting is an original mix of elements from Dilworth's imagination and from Solís and other Spanish chroniclers. There are hints that Montezuma may be on the verge of surrender: he returns the "profound reverence" offered by Cortés, and admits that "we believe that the great prince you obey is descended from Quezalcoal [sic]." But Dilworth's Montezuma is far from naïve, ignorant, or passive. He tells Cortés that he has realized that the Spaniards are not gods, but "made like other men"; that their horses are "large deer, tamed and trained"; and their guns are "barrels of metal" using "compressed air striving for a vent." Furthermore, he concedes that these descendants of "Quezalcoal" have not come to rule, but "to model our laws and reform our government"—as if the Spaniards were not invaders, but political consultants.[42]

Cortés responds with a speech asserting that Spaniards are "more intelligent than your vassals, because born in a climate of more powerful influence," and yet he claims only to be an ambassador for his monarch, who, he reassures Montezuma, "desires to be your friend and confederate." The Aztec emperor accepts this "confederacy and friendship," later signing a "treaty of commerce and alliance," and then "a voluntary acknowledgment of that vassalage which he owed to the King of Spain as successor to Quezalcoal." There is a crucial catch, however. For in Dilworth's version, Montezuma's "whole aim in this transaction, was to forward the departure of his guests, without any intention to fulfil the terms of his submission for the future." In short, the emperor has been playing an elaborate diplomatic game, in which his surrender is bait dangled repeatedly before an arrogant invader.[43]

There are other versions and variants on this notion of Montezuma's Surrender as feigned, as a bait to ensnare the invaders. An early example appears in a document authored by the leaders of two Nahua towns—probably late in the sixteenth century, but fraudulently claiming to be written in 1519 and signed by Cortés in 1526. In this version, the Spaniards and their indigenous allies are in Tenochtitlan because "the malicious plan of the great Montezuma consisted of having us there as guests, showing us false affection" in order to spring an ambush. Similarly, a recent retelling of the traditional narrative has Montezuma acting on divine orders "to encourage the Spaniards to relax their guard" and Cortés stunned by "his good fortune," for the emperor "had, in effect, handed over the keys to his kingdom." None go far enough—if the Surrender is a trick, does that not undermine the traditional view of a cunning Cortés and a stumbling Montezuma? But flipping the Ambush theme thereby flips the assumption of who is in control, itself an intriguing clue as to what really happened at the Meeting.[44]

The entry of Cortés and his fellow conquistadors into the city was a joyful triumph. The Spaniards, wounded and weary from weeks of combat against wily native warriors, were dizzy with relief. Both the country outside and the streets inside the city were "filled on both sides with innumerable Indians" yelling the "shouts and gestures" of "their major fiestas," the same loud welcome used for "applauding and blessing new allies." This enthusiastic popular reception led to a lavish feast, with the invaders lodged in "some very beautiful houses and palaces," where they heard speeches that acknowledged the sovereignty of the king of Spain with "courtesy and affection."[45]

As much as this sounds like a typically imaginative depiction of the Spanish entry into Tenochtitlan on the day of the Meeting, it is in fact drawn from later Spanish descriptions of the entry into Tlaxcallan two months *before* the company reached Tenochtitlan. The "new allies" were the Tlaxcalteca, and this meeting was not, of course, *the* Meeting. But sidestepping into this alternative triumphal entry helps us to answer the question, Why did the mythistory of the Meeting as Surrender quickly grow deep roots and continue to flourish for half a millennium?

This, the Tlaxcalteca episode, introduces the theme of the Spanish and European culture of triumphal entry as the first of a series of answers to that question (for those counting, I propose eight answers).

In the traditional narrative of the Spanish Conquest, the war and peace with Tlaxcallan is presented as anticipating the subsequent war with the Aztecs—but with a twist. Because pre-Conquest Tlaxcallan was later styled, by Spaniards and Tlaxcalteca alike, as a *república* ruled by "Senators" (*los Senadores*), Cortés's triumphant entry evoked triumphant entries into Rome. In typical images of the moment (the Gallery includes one), the Tlaxcalteca wear togas and their buildings look more Italian than Mesoamerican. Cortés's march into the city of Tlaxcallan anticipated his entry into Tenochtitlan; "the Senators" came out to welcome the Spaniards, as Montezuma and his nobles would do. But the Tlaxcallan entry marked the start of a permanent peace and acceptance of Christianity; the entry into Tenochtitlan would lead to a long war. The Tlaxcalteca, as future allies ruled by senators, were the good "Indians," in contrast with the bloodthirsty and recalcitrant Aztecs. (Bernardo de Vargas Machuca, a virulently prejudiced conquistador, saw the "respectful, courteous, and brave" Tlaxcalteca as the exception that proved the rule.)[46]

The triumphal entry into Tlaxcallan was thus a salve for the pain of what happened after the entry into Tenochtitlan. By being the one entrance into a city with permanently positive results, it helped to legitimize, by association, the march into the Aztec capital. Its significance—and its gradual development over the centuries into a grander, more enthusiastic and unambiguous moment than it surely was—was also its connection to the larger Spanish culture of urbanism and triumphal entries. Spanish civilization was profoundly urban, and entries of procession or triumph into cities were deeply resonant and symbolic moments. Drawing upon centuries of medieval tradition, itself threading back in time to ancient Rome, Spaniards expected a ritual surrender by a defeated lord at the city gates, followed by a triumphal entry into that city, celebrated by the populace. That tradition was reinforced in 1492, when the Spanish monarchs, Ferdinand and Isabella, accepted the surrender of Boabdil outside the gates of Granada; Boabdil had been the last ruler of the last remaining Islamic kingdom in the Iberian Peninsula, so Granada's capture had strong political and religious significance for Spaniards. I can find no evidence that any of the conquistadors at the Meeting were also at Granada in 1492, but many of their fathers and other relatives surely were—including Cortés's own father, Martín.

Cortés would go on to make a number of entries into Tenochtitlan (or into the city of Mexico, as Spaniards came to call it). Each of those was used to reinforce the notion of that first arrival as a triumphal entry, each one serving to reiterate the Meeting as the Surrender. Just as later Spanish accounts exaggerated the entry into Tlaxcallan of 1519, so did they imagine Cortés's entry into Mexico-

Tenochtitlan in 1526 as another great triumph; he "returned to Mexico, where he was received by the inhabitants with the same demonstrations of joy that they used to show one of their emperors." When Juan de Escoiquiz ended his thousand pages of "heroic poetry" on the war of conquest with the lines "Cortés entered triumphant, and to the Empire / of Spain was added that hemisphere," he was referring specifically to the fall of Tenochtitlan on August 13, 1521; but the larger referent was to the initial triumphant entry.[47]

August 13 happened to be the feast day of St. Hippolyte, whose celebration rapidly evolved in sixteenth-century Mexico into a ritual annual reenactment of the Meeting. "In memory of that event and happy victory," as Diego Valadés put it in 1579, a festival and "solemn prayers" were celebrated each year. The anchor of the celebration was a procession out of the central plaza to the "magnificent temple" of St. Hippolyte, built on the city's edge where the Noche Triste had claimed the greatest Spanish casualties. Both religious and civil authorities processed out and back to their respective buildings on the plaza—the archbishop to the cathedral, the viceroy and the president of the Audiencia to their respective palaces of government— thereby ritually reentering and reclaiming the city as a Spanish seat of power. The annual procession specifically referenced moments of defeat in 1520 and then triumph in 1521. But the march into the city was also a ritualized reenactment of that first Spanish entry of November 8, 1519, not as the ambiguous arrival that it actually was, but as the providential triumph that it was later claimed to be.[48]

This first answer to the big question—why has Cortés's lie survived as truth for so long?—is thus the European cultural tradition of the triumphal entry. That cultural tradition leads us to the second answer: the dire circumstances of the moment when that lie was first put to paper. The genesis of the invention of the Meeting as Surrender was October 30, 1520, when Cortés sat down with paper and ink to describe to Carlos, the young king of Spain, the events of the previous fourteen months. But rather than simply draw upon his memory of the war's events, Cortés drew upon a cultural reference point that all Spaniards shared—that of the triumphal entry into a city—and reimagined the Meeting both as a triumphal entry and as the milestone moment in the story.

For the context in which Cortés composed his Second Letter to the king was utterly bleak. His campaign was a disaster. Most of the Spaniards who had accompanied him from Cuba were dead. Without the arrival of reinforcements (sent embarrassingly by his nemesis, Governor Velázquez), Spanish numbers would have been so low as to oblige a hasty retreat to the Caribbean. The great island-city was not only lost, it had never been captured. Its seizure was a sham. Months of restricted lodging in the center of Tenochtitlan had given way not to Spanish control of the capital, but to the violent eviction of the invaders from the valley. The survivors were now more dependent than ever on their Tlaxcalteca allies. Cortés and the other captains faced mortal enemies to the west, in Tenochtitlan, and to the east, in Cuba; they had no choice but to invent a tale of victory, in the hope that the defeat of their Aztec enemies might disarm their Spanish ones.

The Second Letter is Cortés's composition, and thus its contents— whether seen as eyewitness reporting or political artifice—are always credited to him. But surely we must resist the temptation to credit the Meeting story entirely to him; to do so would be too facile, too slavish to the legend of his alleged genius. Seeing the Meeting as a Surrender—with the war in 1520 as a rebellion, and the task ahead as a recovery of a prize already won once—was patently appealing, comforting, morale-boosting. It turned a messy war full of atrocity and chaos into a simpler, nobler narrative. It must have begun circulating among the surviving Spaniards in Mexico before Cortés wrote it down. By October 1520, the Spaniards must have collectively begun to remember the Meeting rather fondly. Tenochtitlan, as a *lieu de mémoire*—a place evoking meaningful memories—was a highly complex such locus for the conquistadors, and it would become even more so for those who survived the second half of the war. In view of what the Spaniards subsequently experienced in Tenochtitlan, culminating in the slaughter of most of the conquistadors during their Noche Triste, the survivors surely saw through rose-tinted lenses the weeks in November 1519 when they were welcomed and feasted by Montezuma.

The dire circumstances under which the Surrender was invented lead us in turn to the next answer to the question, because the need in October 1520 to justify the war in progress birthed the need in the decades and centuries that followed to justify the war's outcome. Much of what happened in the war came under scrutiny in its wake; in the 1530s and '40s, Cortés's political stock fell and his actions during the war were put under the microscopes of scores of private lawsuits and a massive royal investigation. But one looks in vain in the thousands of pages of legal documentation—preserved in the imperial archives in Seville—for statements denouncing Montezuma's Surrender as fiction. That is a place none of the conquistadors, giving testimony before lawyers and Crown officials, were willing to go. Nor were such officials interested in asking outright if the Surrender was a lie. It was simply there, in the background, as something believed, accepted, but seldom directly confirmed or discussed.[49]

I have searched sixteenth-century documents and books for years, looking for insight into how the Meeting was talked about in Mexico in the generation or two after the war. Most references are one-liners. But a couple of more detailed and defensive mentions are worth quoting. One was a letter sent to Carlos V in 1553 by Ruy González, a veteran of the Spanish-Aztec War. The aged conquistador was incensed by Las Casas's *Very Brief Account of the Destruction of the Indies*, which had been published in Seville the year before and was now circulating in Mexico City, where González lived as an *encomendero* (recipient of indigenous tribute and labor) and former city councilman. How dare the bishop "call us conquistadors tyrants and thieves and unworthy of the name of Christians," say "we came here unlicensed [illegally]," and "cast doubt on [the legitimacy of] Your Majesty's rule"![50]

González asserted four reasons to prove "the just title of Your Majesty to this new world" and "to shut up the backbiters [*murmuradores*]." One was that the conquistadors had come under license from king and pope; another was that "these people" (indigenous Mexicans) were "idolatrous" cannibals and "filthy sodomites" (a common accusation and justification for conquest to which we shall return later). The remaining two proofs were roundabout ways of using the Surrender as justification. Montezuma "was not a legitimate lord," because he had usurped the throne from his elder brother, "unmade the contract [*compaña*] of his ancestors" (the Triple Alliance with Tetzcoco and Tlacopan), and tyrannized and enslaved his subjects. Thus, as a result, "the lords of the land were on our side," willingly joining Cortés and the Spaniards, who "made them free of all captivity and servitude." González thus dismissed Montezuma as illegitimate, thereby dismissing his surrender; instead, the Surrender was applied to "all those natives, admitted into the service of Your Majesty of their own free will; they asked for it and we ratified it."[51]

One can imagine González and his fellow veterans sitting round the dinner table cursing Las Casas and other "backbiters," discussing the Surrender and its importance in these terms. Similar conversations are reflected in a 1589 book written by Juan Suárez de Peralta. Born in Mexico City in 1537, Peralta was a nephew of Cortés's first wife (murdered, Peralta's aunt later alleged, by Cortés). Peralta insisted that the speech of surrender recorded in Cortés's Second Letter, and repeated in Gómara's biography, was true:

> [Montezuma] said those words, as recounted by old Indians, from whom I heard them, as did certain conquistadors, especially my brother-in-law Alonso de Villanueva Tordesillas, who was secretary to the government of the Marqués del Valle [Cortés], and to whom one can give much credit, seeing as he was so prominent and honored and very noble, a native of Villanueva de la Serena.[52]

One gets the strong impression that Peralta heard the story only from his brother-in-law—whose truthfulness, in accordance with the early modern Spanish legal system, was based on his socio-racial status more than plausibility or corroborating evidence. As for the brother-in-law's source—"old Indians"—Peralta told us nothing of them or those from whom they may have heard the story. The surrender speech Peralta reproduced was a somewhat fantastical version of the Cortés-Gómara account, complete with ancient prophecies and the Aztecs believing the conquistadors to be gods.

Las Casas was the one man willing to question the Surrender story in public—because he was willing to question the legitimacy of the invasion, the very rationale behind the story. The friar told several stories of conversations he had with Cortés in Mexico City. In one, Las Casas said he reproached the conquistador for attacking Montezuma without cause and taking him prisoner—and then taking his kingdom. Cortés replied, *"Qui non intrat per ostium fur est et latro.* [He who does not enter by the front door is a thief and a brigand.]" This seems to have been Cortés's style—to joke about the war, and to do it at the friar's expense by vaguely comparing himself to Christ (the Latin phrase is from John, chapter 10).[53]

Las Casas's indignance over the conquistador's immorality and arrogance was similarly characteristic. Thief, brigand, and liar were precisely the accusations levied at Cortés by Las Casas, who had no qualms confronting him in person or denouncing his deeds and deceptions in print. And, in 1547, while Cortés's bones were still settling into their coffin, Las Casas prepared to confront in Spain the apologist forces for the Conquest. A series of debates were held, over several years, in the university town of Salamanca and in Valladolid, where they culminated in the convening of a special council or junta of 1550–51 (when Las Casas took five days to read out loud in Latin his 550-page *Argumentum apologiae*). Conquistador veterans were there, like Bernal Díaz (or so he claimed), and other minor figures like Gómara (hard at work on his hagiography of Cortés, soon to be published as *La Conquista de México*); both men could scarcely have imagined the influence their books would have on perpetuating the mythistory of the Conquest for centuries to come. Also at the debates were Historians Royal like former conquistador-administrator Gonzalo Fernández de Oviedo (whom Las Casas once called "the greatest enemy that the Indians ever had"), and Juan Ginés de Sepúlveda, the "intellectual figurehead of the conquistador cause."[54]

The result of the years of argumentation was a moral victory for Las Casas, as reflected in laws curbing conquistador practices and a book that has yet to go out of print (1552's *The Very Brief Account of the Destruction of the Indies*). The achievement of Las Casas was the permanent establishment of the principle that conquests—both in general and in each specific act of invasion and territorial claim—required justification. But in practice that did not mean that Spain's colonies ended up being run by bishops and friars, as Las Casas wanted; it meant that conquistadors had to justify their actions by following certain legal procedures to avoid losing out to rivals or to Crown officials, or being denied the lucrative and prestigious right to rule the provinces they had won. The many New World readings of the Requirement—along with related ritual performances of Spanish authority, like Montezuma's invented surrender speech—had, despite their apparent absurdity, done their job. Conquistadors continued to be granted licenses to "pacify" and "populate" (thereby enjoying the title of *adelantado,* literally "the advance man," the licensed invader). But if they survived the wars they started, and the internecine violence among conquistadors and Crown officials of the early sixteenth-century Americas, they increasingly ran the risk of being bedeviled by decades of lawsuits and legal wrangling back in Spain, while another governed what the *adelantado* had fought so hard to conquer.

Consequently, the concept of justification was the battleground upon which all sides of the debate on conquest and colonization fought. In this sense, Sepúlveda had won the argument. For the debate was no longer about the humanity of indigenous peoples, but about how to define "just war" against them—how to remove "doubt" regarding the king's "lordship" over "this new world" (in Ruy González's words). As one conquest led to another, like stepping-stones of violence taking the invaders and all their deadly baggage across the hemisphere, the controversial cases piled up. From the 1520s into the '40s, accusations against Cortés of the use of excessive violence continued to circulate; but in the face of new cases of conquistador atrocities—in Michoacán, in Guatemala, in southeast Yucatan, in Peru—the Mexican stories seemed less and less shocking. Above all, tales of the treatment meted out to indigenous kings and rulers comprised a litany of torture and murder. Yes, Cuauhtemoc had suffered the same fate, tortured in 1521, hanged in 1525, and Montezuma himself was probably murdered (as we shall see). But no other conquistadors could come close to claiming a surrender story like that of the Meeting. Preserving and perpetuating the Meeting as Surrender thus became increasingly important not just to the Mexican case, but to the entire enterprise of Spanish conquest and colonization in the Americas. It was the paramount parable of justification.[55]

THUS WAS THE TRADITIONAL narrative propagated in the Spanish world. By the time of the Salamanca debates, a set of key versions of specific conquest events—above all, the Meeting as Surrender—was already in print, most notably in accounts by Cortés and by Oviedo. Gómara's was soon to follow, consolidated in the next century by Herrera, Díaz, Solís, and on into the eighteenth century. But a further answer (the fourth of our eight) is needed to explain why the same narrative is repeated in accounts in English, French, Dutch, and eventually a dozen other languages, perpetuated in paintings, poems, plays, and operas, through the nineteenth and twentieth centuries. That answer is, to borrow a term from modern psychology, confirmation bias.

An eighteenth-century Frenchman, the Abbé Prévost, seemed to hit the nail on the head when he noted that Spanish accounts of Montezuma's speech, full of "skill and ingenuity," were based on sources that "were mostly highly suspect." Yet, mused the historian-abbot, "they seem otherwise, because they draw on a sort of authenticity through their resemblance to accounts by all historians, all of whom must have drawn from a common source." Prévost was right; the similarity of all the sources available to him in the 1750s was due to the fact that they stemmed ultimately from a single root—the surrender speech invented by Cortés. However, rather than go on to question the veracity of the speech, the abbot—of brilliant mind but ultimately a man of his times—concluded the opposite. He then simply repeated the version created by Solís, whose account was in Prévost's day the best-known descendant of Cortés's version.[56]

In other words, the story of Montezuma's surrender was repeated so often that it acquired the timbre of truth, the way that statements uttered over and over or made in print again and again tend to do. Century after century, chroniclers and historians simply repeated the same story, each new account a new branch stemming from the same tree trunk. Gómara and Díaz in the sixteenth century, Solís in the seventeenth, Robertson and Prescott in the eighteenth and nineteenth—none were able or willing to act like modern historians and strive to create an objective, balanced (some might say, cynical) reconstruction of the past. Nor should we expect that of them. Instead, they leaned on their own briefs and biases—Gómara in Cortés's employ, Solís in the king's, Robertson influenced by the anti-Catholic, anti-Spanish Black Legend—to forge minor variations on the theme of the Meeting as a Surrender.

Even more recent generations of historians, subjecting the Meeting and the Conquest to scholarly scrutiny and international debate, as the pile of books rose higher and higher, have not escaped the shadow of that tree—with its hundreds of branches all stemming from Cortés's letter. Some have certainly rejected Cortés's account as an outright invention, with Montezuma's surrender speeches as "fabrications." But the overwhelming majority of modern accounts—in print, online, on film—are mere variations on the same endlessly repeated theme of the Meeting as Surrender.[57]

As the Elizabethan essayist Francis Bacon famously noted, opinion "brings on substance"; once formed, "it draws all things else to support and agree with it." The weight of "received opinion" is as great as that which simply seems "agreeable." Or, to draw on a more recent commentator (and an historian of colonial Mexico), James Lockhart once remarked that scholars were subject to what he sardonically called "the law of the preservation of the energy of historians." Consequently, historians tend to turn first to "the easiest (most synthetic) sources." In this case, those sources are the canon of conquistador and chronicler accounts that underpin the traditional narrative, further rendered "fact" by confirmation bias.[58]

Related to confirmation bias is another subliminal factor (and another answer to the question posed a few pages back). This factor is the structure of the traditional "Conquest of Mexico" narrative, a subliminal factor because we are drawn to it as something familiar and predictable (and thus something that just makes sense), without being consciously aware of the deep roots of the attraction. To be more specific: not only is the Conquest story a ripping-good yarn, but its core elements have allowed it to harness the power and logic of the Classical narrative. It is typically called such because it is traceable back to Aristotle. But today's literary theorists have also reduced it to a five-stage model, labeled A/B/-A/-B/A.[59]

Applied to our story: A is the initial state of equilibrium (a New World granted to the Spanish Crown by the pope, with Cortés as one of the agents of God and crown, tasked simply with claiming it); B is the disruption of that equilibrium (the Spaniards meet with resistance); -A is the acknowledgment of that disruption (the Spaniards realize that they have invaded a powerful, centralized state to which they assign blame for all disruptions); -B is the attempt to repair that disruption (they attempt to forge alliances in order to reach Montezuma and Tenochtitlan); the final A is the restoration of equilibrium (Montezuma's surrender). The rest of the story is a repeat of the B/-A/-B/A stages, with the Spaniards facing a setback, building alliances, and restoring equilibrium through the defeat of the Aztecs and the recovery of Tenochtitlan.

This is arguably the only way Cortés could have structured the narrative, and the only way (or certainly the most likely way) that subsequent narrators and chroniclers could have seen it. For this is *the* traditional narrative structure in the West, deeply embedded in the medieval European mind, perpetuated through the early modern centuries, and given renewed strength in the nineteenth and twentieth centuries with the explosion of different media for telling stories—from the novel to the full-length motion picture. The traditional Conquest of Mexico narrative is tailor-made for modern storytelling, complete with hero, villain, and tragic hero, as well as an ambiguous romantic theme that can be twisted to suit contemporary purposes (the Cortés-Malintzin relationship that has blossomed in the last two centuries). Whether we view it as a three-act drama or a five-stage narrative, its win-loss-recovery structure is echoed in a myriad range of dramas stretching from Shakespearean tragedy to Hollywood's romantic comedies.

Meanwhile (returning to the sixteenth century for the sixth answer), a similar narrative was becoming rooted, traditional, and repeatedly confirmed among the indigenous nobility in Mexico—but for different reasons than those underpinning its Spanish and European equivalent. The colonial system brought to Mexico from Spain a new political culture of reward and privilege. Claims to a deeply rooted and unswerving loyalty to church and crown, God and king, were essential to how indigenous rulers, dynasties, and towns petitioned for rewards (such as exemption from paying tribute, rights to traditional titles, and control over landed estates). As a result, a surrender mythistory spread across Mesoamerica. For centuries, all across the former Aztec Empire and south into the Maya regions of Yucatan and Guatemala, ruling families and former city-states and towns claimed that they had immediately and peacefully embraced Christianity and the sovereignty of the Spanish Crown. Some genuinely had, but many downplayed or omitted their past resistance to invasion.[60]

That larger surrender mythistory gave structural support and cultural affirmation to the more specific mythistory of Montezuma's Surrender to Cortés. Who was most motivated to embrace and perpetuate the Surrender? Montezuma's own relatives and descendants. Despite suffering heavy losses in the war, the Aztec royal family survived as a ruling dynasty (albeit at the local level), successfully maneuvering and negotiating their status for generations (there is copious legal documentation on family members' efforts to sustain property and position from the early sixteenth into the twentieth centuries). There are numerous examples of the consistent claim by

Aztec dynasty members that Montezuma voluntarily conceded sovereignty. Perhaps the best-known such examples are by his daughter, Tecuichpochtzin (doña Isabel Moctezuma Tecuichpo), and her sixth (and final) husband, the conquistador Juan Cano, who promoted the notion of Montezuma as a Christian martyr—welcoming Cortés from the very start, eager to convert, dying "in Your Majesty's Service." The argument was clear. In Cano's words: "it befits your royal conscience to show favor to [the Aztec imperial] lineage, especially to doña Isabel, because she is the successor to Moctezuma, who gave obedience and vassalage to Your Majesty." We shall return to doña Isabel in a later chapter, so let us turn here to an example written by another Aztec noble, don Pablo Nazareo, a nephew by marriage of Montezuma's.[61]

Nazareo was a boy during the Spanish-Aztec War, educated after it by Franciscan friars in the college in Tlatelolco (part of the island-capital slowly turning into Mexico City). Trilingual in Nahuatl, Spanish, and Latin (of which he became a teacher), Nazareo wrote a series of letters in Latin to the Spanish king, petitioning for privileges on behalf of himself, his wife, and the father-in-law whom he cared for in his old age. That old man was don Juan Axayacatl (or Axayaca), Montezuma's brother; Nazareo's wife was a niece of Montezuma's, baptized doña María Axayaca Oceloxochitzin. Nazareo repeated in various ways in his letters to the king that Montezuma and his brother had not only surrendered to Cortés, but that don Juan's loyalty throughout the war made the Spanish Conquest possible. For example:

> Our forebears, the lord Moteucçoma and our father the lord Juan Axayaca, Moteucçoma's brother, were easily the first of anyone who rose up in favor of the Spaniards who were the first to travel in these parts of the Indies, and with humble souls yielded to Your Royal Crown with the greatest reverence, giving, via the Captain [Cortés], to Your Sacred Catholic Caesarean Majesty infinite goods, a great quantity of gifts, and infinite kinds of weaponry made of pure gold, as a sign, or rather as proof, that they recog-

nized the true rule of the vicar of God, almighty and living, one shepherd and one flock.[62]

It would hardly be an understatement to say that, for don Pablo Nazareo, his uncle's Surrender had cosmic significance. This simple pair of facts—Montezuma's Surrender was a fiction, but his relatives and descendants bent over backward for generations to insist it was an essential truth—tells us a great deal about the role that mythistorical moment played in Mexican history, as it unfolded after 1519. One can hardly blame Nahuas like Nazareo and doña Isabel Moctezuma for deploying the myth of Montezuma's surrender as a legal and political strategy. After all, they were Christians and surely preferred to believe that the emperor had died one too. For them, the Surrender was no lie; it was the sacred moment that made sense of their new world.

Montezuma is the next answer to the question—not the man himself, but his five-century afterlife. In the first century after his death, the emperor's reputation was destroyed and upended, all in the service of justifying and explaining Spanish invasion and conquest. We have already been introduced to Montezuma the Coward, and we shall turn to the details of his character assassination in the next chapter, so suffice to note here that Spanish and Nahua sources alike depicted Montezuma as "superstitious, depressed, weak, cowardly," a one-dimensional ruler "incapable of overcoming the fate imposed" upon him. Considering that Cortés and his promoters invented Montezuma's Surrender, it is ironic that blaming the emperor for Aztec defeat became an appealing alternative to traditional Spanish explanations for their triumph in the Conquest. When such explanations—God's will, Cortés's genius, European superiority—faded in popularity in the modern era, more attention became focused on Montezuma's alleged failure.[63]

Another layer of irony was added as quasi-indigenous accounts of the war gradually emerged—most important, Sahagún's *Historia General* (the so-called Florentine Codex), whose Nahuatl text slowly became available to the world in translation. The account in the Florentine Codex of the Conquest is, as we saw, a late-sixteenth-century Tlatelolca-Franciscan narrative, but it was misleadingly read for most of the twentieth century as an authentic Aztec or even "Indian" view of the Conquest. It even featured a version of Montezuma's surrender in Nahuatl, lending the speech a linguistic veneer of authenticity and giving new life to this core aspect of the traditional narrative. Writers unsympathetic to the Aztecs used the Florentine Codex to bruise Montezuma's reputation more than ever (mostly in the Anglophone world, for a century starting in the 1880s); but even those sympathetic to Montezuma tended to perpetuate the mythistory of the Surrender, by arguing that it was not a result of the emperor's weakness, but of his deep-rooted belief in Aztec prophetic traditions (the Prophecy theme, in more sophisticated form).[64]

This putatively pro-Montezuma trend began in Mexico and has had sporadic success there at a popular level, while working its way into academia worldwide. However, a full revisionist rehabilitation of Montezuma has yet to happen, and cannot happen without the busting of the mythistory of the Meeting as Montezuma's Surrender. Montezuma may never avenge the posthumous bruising of his character and reputation, for the simple reason that Cuauhtemoc has increasingly served as a better candidate for the role of Aztec hero—especially in Mexico. For example, Mexican textbooks in the final decades of the twentieth century still depicted Montezuma according to the traditional narrative—as intimidated by the approach of the Spaniards and subservient to Cortés once he reached Tenochtitlan—with Cuauhtemoc's resistance to the siege given passing attention. In this century's textbooks, however, Montezuma's Surrender, while still accepted as fact, is downplayed and Cuauhtemoc is given a heroic treatment; he is, Mexican students are told, a *fundador de tu patria*, a "founding father of your country."[65]

For the eighth and final answer, we return to another national hero, General Scott—via Napoleon.

As France's Emperor Napoleon Bonaparte prepared for his 1808 invasion of Spain, he commissioned the Italian composer Gaspare Spontini to write an opera. The subject: the Conquest of Mexico. The parallel was clear: Napoleon was the heroic Cortés of the story, and Spain his Mexico. Titled *Fernand Cortez,* the opera even featured a fictional Cortés brother, named Alvaro, who was captured by the Aztecs and rescued just before he was to be ritually sacrificed; when the opera debuted in Paris, in November 1809, Napoleon's brother was already installed as Joseph I, the new king of Spain, and France's massive army dominated the peninsula.

Spontini navigated around the incongruity of a Spanish Montezuma surrendering to a French Cortés by keeping the Aztec emperor—and his capture—offstage. The production's bombastic music and seventeen live horses supposedly entertained Parisian audiences (Hector Berlioz found it inspirational, making it of some import in modern music history). But critics found it hard to swallow other ironies of the parallel between the invasions (for example, earlier in 1809 thousands of Spanish troops had been slaughtered outside Cortés's hometown of Medellín; his childhood home was also a casualty) or its absurdities (such as devilish Aztec priests as substitutes for evil Spanish Inquisitors). The production was canceled before the year was out.

As Spontini's opera flopped, so too, gradually, did Napoleon's war. His triumph proved to be as fleeting and illusory as Montezuma's surrender. Spanish resistance turned into guerrilla warfare, the atrocities mounted, the British invaded, hostilities dragged on for five years until the French finally retreated from the peninsula in 1814. But the composer and his librettists (Étienne de Jouy and Joseph-Alphonse Esménard) were undeterred; they revised the opera, promoting Montezuma from an offstage reference to a character second only in billing to "Cortez" himself. In the 1817 revival, the "King of the Mexicans" was an ineffective sovereign willing to die with his empire—but then easily convinced to accept Cortés's "friendship" and bless his romantic union with a fictional niece of Montezuma's. As the final curtain fell, the choir sang "*O jour de gloire et espérance* [Oh day of glory and hope]!"

Unlike the original propaganda piece, this version was a hit. From its debut in 1817 it remained in the repertoire of the Paris Opera through 1830, performed 218 times. Audiences were less interested in the grim realities of war—be it Napoleon's in Spain or Cortés's in Mexico—than they were in the comforting romanticism of the traditional Cortesian narrative, with its pivotal moment of mythistory: Montezuma's surrender to civilization's providential march of hope and glory. Above all, the gendering of the Conquest as a romance caught the spirit of the age. Malintzin (or an Aztec princess of invented name) emerged from a marginal or occasional character to a central one, both in histories and dramas on Cortés and the Conquest and in her own literature. In the great run of "Conquest of Mexico" operas—composed in five European nations, stretching from Antonio Vivaldi's *Motezuma* of 1733 to Ignacio Ovejero's *Hernán Cortés* of 1848—the story grew increasingly romanticized and a Malintzin-type character increasingly important. The lithographs of Nicolas-Eustache Maurin—a Parisian contemporary of Spontini's who produced a popular series of prints inspired by his *Cortez* opera and by Giovanni Pacini's *Amazilia* (debuted in 1825 in Naples)—are an early example of the Malintzin industry in art and literature that the romantic era would spawn.[66]

If the revised version of Spontini's opera was a hit, Prescott's history of the Conquest of Mexico was even bigger; only in his case, contemporary historical events worked in his favor. At first a modest success, the book exploded when President Polk ordered U.S. forces to invade Mexico. The Mexican-American War may be largely forgotten in the United States; the irony of anti-immigration policies designed to keep Mexicans out of lands that were once theirs seems lost on the promoters and supporters of such policies. But in Mexico, the War of the U.S. Invasion is far from a distant memory. The Mexicans and Mexican-Americans interviewed for a recent study on present-day attitudes toward the Spanish Conquest tended to "emphasize a relationship between the violence of the Spanish conquest, the loss of half their land in 1848, and the violence on the U.S. border today."[67]

Nor was 1848 the last time that Mexico was invaded. Napoleon Bonaparte's nephew, ruling France as Emperor Napoleon III, joined a Spanish and British debt-collecting expedition into Mexico in 1861, soon turning it into a conquest campaign. Napoleon eventually placed an Austrian archduke on the Mexican throne as Emperor Maximilian I, but for three years, until he was executed in 1867, Maximilian ruled a country that never ceased to resist its latest conquerors. The Mexican defeat of French forces at Puebla on May 5, 1862, is today commemorated by Mexican-Americans (as the Cinco de Mayo holiday) to celebrate their "Mexicanness" in the country whose conquest of Mexico launched an empire that now tries to keep Mexicans out, and whose marines still sing of victory in the halls of Montezuma (a song to which we shall return). The refrains of triumph and tragedy, linking empires and nations, past and present, always seem to echo back to that November day in 1519 in Tenochtitlan.

The story of the "Conquest of Mexico" is thus a *lieu de mémoire*, a place of memory and meaning that has broad geographical and deep temporal range. The ways in which we can approach the topic are almost limitless. But whether our guides are doña Isabel Moctezuma and don Pablo Nazareo, Brumidi and General Scott, or Napoleon and Spontini, it always becomes clear that the "Conquest of Mexico" narrative is never just—or even never really—about the Spanish-Aztec War. Far from simply a set of historical events, the Conquest is a living locus that has been repeatedly refashioned over the centuries "to serve official, regional, and personal ends," appropriated and reinvented "by individuals, communities, and the state" to redefine present experience.[68]

At the heart of that oft-appropriated narrative is an imagined moment—Montezuma's surrender to Cortés—that has persisted and proliferated in print and paint not because it happened, but because so many people for so many different reasons believed it happened or needed it to be so. For (and as) an invented event, the Meeting as Surrender tells us a great deal about the last five centuries of human history.

PART II

Tlein ticmotenehuilia aquin tlatohuani . . .
Cuix amo nitlatohuani Cuix amo nitlatocati
Cuix ye onipoliuh Cuix ye Onimic
Cuix ye onitlan Cuix acmo nicmati

"What are you talking about? Who is the king (*tlahtoani*)? . . .
Am I not the king? Am I not the lord?
Am I already defeated? Have I already died?
Have I already been finished off? Am I no longer of sound mind?"

—Herod, in a seventeenth-century Nahuatl drama of
The Three Kings[1]

KINGS OF THE BEAST. Portraits of the eighth, ninth, and tenth Aztec kings, from the 1704 English edition of Gemelli's 1699 *A Voyage Round the World*. While in Mexico City, Gemelli had access to various manuscripts, such as those in the library of the great Mexican intellectual don Carlos Sigüenza y Góngora. Because of the chain of copying going back to Aztec times, these portraits are early modern European in style but include elements adapted from Mesoamerican artistic traditions. Access to colonial copies of indigenous codices did not stop Gemelli from emphasizing the satanical nature of Aztec kingship and religion.

CHAPTER 3

————⚘————

Social Grace and Monstrous Ritual

Every impulse of his natural Ferocity gave Way to Fear and Weakness.
—Townsend's 1724 translation of Solís's
History of the Conquest of Mexico

One cannot help feeling that Montezuma was a monster and [his] sacrifice of the captives a ritual murder . . . [yet] on learning that the god
wanted to come to Mexico city, he was overwhelmed with awe.
—Maurice Collis, 1954

I wish to be united in friendship with your King, and at his request, I will
happily abolish the eating at my table of human flesh, abhorred by him.
—Montezuma's surrender speech to Cortés
in Escoiquiz's *México Conquistada*, 1798

Surely, never were refinement and the extreme of barbarism brought so
closely into contact with each other.   —William Prescott, 1843

Europeans, from the first Spanish conquerors who saw Mexica society in
action to those of us who wistfully strive to, have been baffled by that un-
nerving discrepancy between the high decorum and fastidious social and
aesthetic sensibility of the Mexica world, and the massive carnality of the
killings and dismemberings: between social grace and monstrous ritual.
—Inga Clendinnen, 1991[1]

THE NAMES OF THE TEN AZTEC KINGS CONTAIN A NUMERICAL
code. By assigning a number to each letter used in their names,
the monarchs can be reduced to a set of numbers. Thus the first king,
Acamapichtli, becomes 56; the two Montezumas are each assigned
84; and Cuauhtemoc, the last emperor, is 77. Add the ten numbers

up and they "together make 666, the number of the Beast." In other
words, the Aztec monarchy was, in its totality, a manifestation of
Satan—"the Beast describ'd by St. John."[2]

This numerological wisdom was explained to Giovanni Gemelli
when he visited Mexico City in the late 1690s. When the Neapoli-
tan lawyer-turned-adventurer (and, some said, Vatican spy) returned
to Italy from his five-year voyage around the world, he published
a detailed account of all he saw and learned. His six-volume book
enjoyed multiple editions in Italian, French, and English during
the eighteenth century. Gemelli's story was later dismissed as overly
fantastical (he argued, for example, that both the Egyptians and
Native Americans were descended from refugees "from that Island
Atlantis") and even as fictional (his journey helped inspire a bestselling imaginary travelogue, Jules Verne's *Around the World in Eighty
Days*). But Gemelli did not imagine his journey, nor did he invent
the people he met and the things they told him. He even had access to the incredible library and didactic company of don Carlos
Sigüenza y Góngora, the celebrated Mexican polymath who was elderly but still alive when Gemelli visited. In other words, Gemelli's
views were not outlandish at the time; they were mainstream, and
his book's success helped to keep them that way.[3]

Thus when generations of Europeans read that some people
thought the ancient Aztec monarchy was diabolist—and that the
proof was in the numbers—they were the recipients of a belief that
had been circulating in Spain, Mexico, and elsewhere, in some
form or another, for centuries. When Gemelli wrote that Aztec
emperors like Montezuma regularly performed "abominable Sacrifices," personally "ripping open the Breast" of a victim and "taking
out the Heart immediately, which was thrown into the Face of the
Idol, while it was still leaping," he was summarizing commonplace
knowledge. And when Gemelli noted that New Spain's "Indians
are naturally very Fearful; but excessive Cruel," that "they are very
great Thieves, Cheats, and Impostors," and that they lack a "Sense
of Honour (for they make nothing of robbing one another of it; besides the Incest they commit with their Mothers and Sisters)," he

was merely repeating—and helping to perpetuate—pejorative notions about the otherness of America's "Indians" that went back to Columbus's time.[4]

Those notions were part of the swirl of prejudicial perception and misinformation regarding Native American culture and history in the early modern Atlantic world. At the center of that swirl were, and still are, the Aztecs. Although seldom seen today as satanical, Aztec civilization continues to be viewed primarily through the lens of human sacrifice. Even at the level of a humorous book for children (such as the bestselling *Horrible Histories* volume whose cover is included in the Gallery), the Aztecs can be "angry" because that is an alliterative association that resonates with readers of all kinds. In such a context Montezuma has existed for five centuries, suffering a long afterlife of negative judgment. To give Montezuma a little revenge—and to solve the mysteries of the Meeting—we must first explore how and why the Aztecs became "angry," how Montezuma became posthumously mistreated, and how the Aztecs might be seen through different lenses.[5]

For many centuries before 1492, Europeans had believed that in remote regions of the world there lived strange and alien people, some marvelous, some monstrous. Books like Pliny the Elder's *Natural History* and Sir John Mandeville's *Travels*, with their mixing of the realistic and the fantastic, were written in the first and fourteenth centuries respectively but still wildly popular at the turn of the sixteenth. Europeans came to the Americas expecting to find bizarre humans and outlandish cultural practices. Often they believed they found them.

Stories circulated in Europe in the 1490s that Columbus had found islands where the people were all cannibals (who ate human flesh daily), that they had discovered one island of giants and another exclusively inhabited by women warriors. Traditional tall tales persisted for centuries, as new ones developed. European expectations were not dampened by decades of living among indigenous peoples, because each new discovery encouraged the circulation of wild stories, with letters and reports from the New World often mixing accurate observations with fantastical claims. When Diego Velázquez issued Cortés orders for his voyage to Mexico, Velázquez had been living in the Caribbean for twenty-five years (since crossing on Columbus's second voyage) without seeing monstrous humans; yet he still instructed Cortés to ascertain the truth of reports "that there are people with broad and massive ears, and others who have faces like dogs," and to find out "where the Amazon women are."[6]

Yet while the quest for the curious and monstrous would continue across the Americas for decades, a grimmer image of "the Indian" was already being invented. As early as the 1490s, Columbus and his collaborators and successors constructed an abiding myth of cannibalism in the Caribbean (whose very name derives from the word). They were motivated by beliefs—backed up by royal law, beginning in 1503 (but based on earlier codes)—that cannibals could rightfully be enslaved. Spaniards called these alleged man-eaters *caribes* ("the term that they used to make free people into slaves," as Las Casas put it), and expected (some hoped) to find them on the American mainland too. Accounts by Juan Díaz and Peter Martyr d'Anghiera, published in 1520 and 1521 and based on what Spaniards claimed to see on the 1518 Grijalva expedition along the Yucatec and Mexican coastline, generated engraved imaginings of indigenous orgies of idolatry, sacrificial slaughter, and cannibalism that were reproduced for many generations. It was as if Dante's *Inferno* were transformed into a kind of earthly "Indian" inferno.[7]

The European imagination of satanic horror in the Americas was enormously stimulated by the Spanish discovery of a fully developed religious world in Mexico—complete with temples and statues, priests and rituals, all bewilderingly incomprehensible unless simply classified and condemned as the work of the devil. Aztec religion soon became conceived by Europeans on both sides of the Atlantic as centered on three interrelated elements: public executions, characterized from the sixteenth century up to the present as "human sacrifice"; habitual cannibalism; and the worship of monstrous, satanic "idols." Attached to these were a set of negative stereotypes, sometimes aimed at the Aztecs in particular, sometimes smearing Mesoamericans in general: a propensity for sodomy, licentiousness, a weakness for alcohol, dishonesty, and credulity.

For example, an account of "Some Aspects of New Spain" by an "anonymous conquistador" (first printed in 1566 in Italian as a *Relatione*) claimed that in some regions the people "worship the member of the body that is between a man's legs" and were such drunkards that they took wine enemas when they were too drunk to swallow; and Aztec men urinated sitting down, while the women did it standing up. The focus of the account, however, was on the trifecta of savagery. The Aztecs were "so solicitous in sacrificing men, and offering their hearts and blood" to their "idols" because those idols, possessed by the devil, had convinced the credulous natives that they only ate human hearts. Allegations of cannibalism were inevitably made, both against the ancient Mexicans—who "used to have great wars and great differences among themselves, and all those captured in war were eaten or enslaved"—and even their sixteenth-century descendants, who "are the cruelest people to be found in warfare, for they spare neither brother, relative, nor friend, taking their lives even if they are beautiful women, killing them all and eating them." The *Relatione* concluded:

> All the people of this province of New Spain, and including those of other neighboring provinces, eat human flesh, and they value it more than all the other foods in the world, so much so that they often go to war and risk their lives just to kill someone and eat them; and, as I have said, most of them are sodomites and drink excessively.[8]

It may be tempting today to dismiss such stereotypes as silly, or to view them in the larger context of the unadorned bigotry of the age in which modern racism was born. Yet whatever the stereotype, it was always connected to the twin topics of human sacrifice and cannibalism, and the use of these allegations to justify centuries of conquest and colonization.

Take this example: In 1554, two Spaniards strolled through Mexico City, chatting in Latin. Their dialogue was fictional, but it tidily reflected the popular perception of the Aztecs that had rapidly taken hold in the colony (as in Europe). Walking through the plaza that had been, since long before the Spanish invasion, the ceremonial center of the city, one Spaniard pointed out where "men and women were offered up and sacrificed as victims to idols . . . as if in a butcher shop." This horror, "incredible as it may seem," occurred "almost monthly," taking the lives of "numberless thousands." The other Spaniard responded,

> O Indians, most blessed by the arrival of the Spaniards, who were transformed from their former great misery to their present happiness, and from their previous slavery to true liberty![9]

The more grisly and diabolist the image of Aztec religion, the more profound the redemption of the indigenous Mexican people— and the more justified their conquest and subjugation. Just as accusations of cannibalism had been used to justify enslaving indigenous peoples in the Caribbean, so did the conquest and colonization of mainland "Indians" such as the Aztecs become justified and legalized through accusations of "idolatry," sodomy, and cannibalism.

"Because of the care and devotion the natives of these parts devote to the nurturing and veneration of their idols and of the devil," declared Cortés in the orders read out to the invasion force gathered in Tlaxcallan in December 1520, prior to the assault against Tenochtitlan, "your primary motive and goal is to separate and uproot all the natives of these parts from those idolatries." This was not a reflection of Cortés's mythical piety (more on that in a later chapter), but another small yet significant link in the manufactured legal chain of conquest justification. The cluster of edicts issued by Emperor Carlos V in October 1522, when he appointed

Cortés "governor and captain general of New Spain," included a grant of prerogatives to the conquistadors in Mexico. Almost a quarter of the document was devoted to an astounding royal confirmation that allegations of sacrificial cannibalism now legally justified Spaniards not only waging a war of invasion, but depriving survivors of their freedom. It is worth quoting at length. Carlos reasoned that, as he had

> received reports that many chiefs and lords and others of the land hold many local people as slaves, which they capture and retain through the wars that they wage against each other; and many of those slaves they keep to eat and to kill and to sacrifice before their idols; and that this gives us license to recover [*rescatar*] those Indian slaves; and it will serve us and be to the advantage of the settlers and benefit those Indian slaves if I hereby give license and authority . . . to the settlers . . . to recover those Indian slaves and take them as their own slaves.[10]

Spanish theologians and other officials debated these issues for much of the sixteenth century. But even though those on one side—most famously, Las Casas—seemed to win the argument when "Indians" were legally deemed *not* to be "natural slaves," the conquest and colonial subjugation of millions of Native Americans had long ago become a fact, and its ideological rationale deeply established. Men like the Dominican Francisco de Vitoria and the royal chronicler Juan Ginés de Sepúlveda wrote at length in Latin and Spanish to prove why and how "just war" had been waged against Native Americans. But their arguments were surely grasped by Spaniards and other Europeans in simple terms: the conquest had spared the innocent from being "sacrificed" and eaten; Christianization sealed the deal. Sepúlveda himself could put it in terms simple enough: "For this cause alone—not keeping the law of nature or being idol-worshippers—the Indians can be conquered and punished."[11]

In his epic poem about Spanish conquests, first published in 1610, Gaspar de Villagrá wrote that

not more than one hundred years ago,
every year in the City of Mexico,
were offered up in tribute, in horrific inferno,
more than one hundred thousand souls.

But in the contrastingly bright present, the poet-conquistador proclaimed, that dark past had been forgotten by the contentedly Christian "Indians," just as "the trees and plants [are] forgetful in the happy spring of the hardships of the winter past."[12]

As the vanguard of Christianization in central Mexico, the Franciscans were at the forefront of detailing and circulating such a perspective, but over the centuries it was developed and spread by writers of all kinds, not only ecclesiastics and not only Spaniards. In presenting religious rituals in pre-invasion Mexico not as somber or pious ceremonies, but as satanic orgies of cruelty and bloodletting, the emphasis was often on the horrors of scale. The gods of the Aztecs, whose "idols" were worshipped with obsessive violence, numbered more than two thousand (the number claimed by fray Diego Valadés and other Franciscans). Valadés asserted that fifteen or twenty thousand men were routinely sacrificed, and that after one war with Tlaxcallan, the Aztecs sacrificed seventy-six thousand prisoners—"certainly a lamentable and mournful spectacle." The Franciscan don Juan de Zumárraga asserted that twenty thousand were sacrificed a year, an oft-quoted figure that morphed over the decades into twenty thousand children; the figure happened to match the exact number of "idols" or religious statues that Zumárraga claimed he had destroyed within a year or two of becoming Mexico's first bishop. By the late sixteenth century, it was widely "known" that the emperor Ahuitzotl's coronation ceremony in 1486 featured the nonstop sacrifice of 80,400 victims.[13]

It was not only readers of Spanish, Italian, and Latin who learned these "facts" about the Aztec past. English and Dutch readers learned from the twin compendium on *America*, first printed in 1670 (Ogilby's version) and 1671 (Montanus's), that the "business of the Satanical Religion" of the Aztecs was to sacrifice "to their Devil-god

Vitzilopuchtli" thousands of people a year, "whose flesh likewise afterwards they did eat in a solemn Banquet." Rather than sharing in this religion, however, the peoples subject to the Aztecs increasingly grew to "abhor" their "particular Religion," with its "cruel slaughters and butcheries of Men." This, the English and Dutch authors concluded, echoing earlier Spanish arguments, "was the chief reason why they so easily receiv'd the *Roman* Religion."[14]

The images that accompanied such books offered lurid illustrations of Aztec butchery. Some became well known and influential, copied again and again; a good example is "Human Sacrifices of the Indians of Mexico," used for centuries to accompany numerous accounts and histories in many languages. Variations on this visual theme often included an Aztec priest holding aloft a human heart, freshly torn from a sacrificial victim (as examples in the Gallery illustrate). These images tell us far more about the Europeans and Christianized indigenous Mexicans who made them than they tell us about the Aztecs, a crucial point since "much of what the world thinks it knows about Aztec human sacrifice derives from visual images" like these.[15]

The dawn of a more objective, open-minded view of the Aztec past came in fits and starts. A Greco-Roman view of the Aztec pantheon was commonly expressed from the sixteenth century on, casually mentioned by the likes of Cortés and Las Casas, explored in detail by certain Franciscans (most notably Valadés and Juan de Torquemada, another chronicler of Mexico's early church), and often seen in drawings of long-destroyed "idols." Although Franciscan writers still emphasized the gory satanism of Aztec religion, classical analogies encouraged the development of more positive comparisons; and in 1680, when Sigüenza y Góngora was asked to design the triumphal arches for the entry into Mexico City of the new viceroy, he chose to place images of the eleven Aztec emperors and the god Huitzilopochtli where traditionally classical figures would have gone. The images were based on drawings by native artists from the previous century, with each Aztec figure associated with one of the heroic virtues of a model ruler.[16]

The undercurrent to Sigüenza y Góngora's choices was one of Mexican patriotism—specifically the view that it was the Aztec past that made Mexico a unique and bright star in the sweeping constellation of Spanish imperial territories. Such ideas surfaced with increasing force in Mexico from the late eighteenth century into the present one. When construction in Mexico City's central plaza in 1790 uncovered two gigantic monoliths—a statue of the earth goddess Coatlicue and the now-famous Calendar Stone—Mexicans were fascinated by a civilization that colonialism had denigrated and buried. Perhaps the Aztecs had not been "irrational or simpleminded," mused astronomer Antonio de León y Gama. In a book about the stones he declared "the Indians of this America possessed great knowledge in the arts and sciences." Soon afterward, a Dominican friar, Servando Teresa de Mier, delivered a sermon before the viceroy and archbishop extolling the virtues of Aztec civilization; that civilization, built on the preceding achievements of the Toltecs, was the basis of Mexican greatness, not the Spanish colonial regime. In response, the regime arrested, excommunicated, and exiled Teresa de Mier.[17]

These events hardly amounted to serious efforts to rehabilitate the Aztecs, however. Shortly after its discovery, the Coatlicue statue was reburied—under one of the corridors of a university building in the city. If the Aztec past could not be buried, it would be defaced; a few decades earlier the viceroy ordered the destruction of the stone carved portrait of Montezuma that had survived on a rock face in Chapultepec since its creation in 1519. And Teresa de Mier's revolutionary sermon did not exactly seek to evaluate the Aztecs on their own terms; he gave credit, rather, to St. Thomas, who he claimed visited the Toltecs a millennium earlier, civilized them, and lived on in Aztec memory as the deified holy ruler Quetzalcoatl.[18]

The Franciscan filter of prejudice and judgment, it turned out, was not so easily destroyed; it had grown so virulently over the centuries that few seemed aware of its roots (and many, especially Protestant writers, would have denied them). This was even more the case outside Mexico. Across Europe and the Americas, generations of students in the late eighteenth and nineteenth centuries learned about the Aztecs through the books of German educator Joachim Campe. Despite being "For the Use of Children and Young Persons" (as the subtitle of his *Cortes: or, the Discovery of Mexico* declared), Campe's books on the early Americas depicted Aztec religion as a nightmarish sequence of "barbaric superstitions" and ritualized atrocities.

The books were structured as tales told by a father to a group of children, in the style of children's literature of the time. Thus in *The Discovery of America* a fictional father described an Aztec heart sacrifice to his young audience, sparing no details as he told of the heartless bodies thrown down the pyramid steps to the waiting populace, who took pieces of the corpses "home, and ate them with their friends." The father asked, "Is it not true, my children, that this is horrible? Well, prepare to hear something that is even more so." And he goes on to detail the flaying of living victims by Aztec priests. Campe sought to use education in order to instill moral lessons about civilization and colonialism two centuries later; in contrast, two centuries further on, in *Angry Aztecs,* Terry Deary used humor to inspire interest in history. But both are manifestations of a long tradition of perpetuating specific Aztec stereotypes among all readers, even the youngest.[19]

ANOTHER ASPECT OF AZTEC practice that has been a perennial fascination is the numbers game played by Franciscans in the sixteenth century. Ever since, writers have used their assertions to debate how many tens of thousands of people were sacrificed annually. Mused Englishman John Ranking in 1827, was it twenty (as Zumárraga claimed), fifty (Gómara's claim), or fifty to a hundred (Las Casas)? And were the thirty thousand sacrificed at Montezuma's coronation a typical number for a coronation? Ranking has been ridiculed for claiming that Mongols on elephants invaded the Americas in the thirteenth century, but his fixation on quantifying annual Aztec "atrocities," rather than questioning the supposed evidence for them, puts him well in the mainstream of his day. He even rightly noted that the estimate of Tenochtitlan's population by some Spaniards as only sixty thousand was reasonable—without asking if the claim that as many people were executed each year in the same city was unreasonable.[20]

The same numbers game, with the same myopia, was still being played a century later. Sherburne Cook, a pioneer scholar of demographic history, examined the logistics of large-scale human sacrifice in a 1946 essay—cited for decades as authoritative. Unconcerned with the Spanish origins of stories of such ceremonies, Cook took a putatively scientific approach, measuring sacrificial slabs and calculating cutting times to conclude that by removing a heart every fifteen seconds, a team of Aztec priests could indeed have sacrificed 88,320 people in four days.[21]

As modern academic disciplines came slowly into being, defenders of Aztec culture (or those seeking to study it objectively) were regularly drowned out by those determined to keep the Aztecs in a category far below that of Western civilization. Although William Prescott's *History of the Conquest of Mexico*—which was a smash hit for generations beginning in the 1840s—was restrained in its revisionism, being based overwhelmingly on the traditional conquistador canon of Cortés, Gómara, and Díaz, it nonetheless argued that the Aztecs had built a real civilization. For that, Prescott was roundly denounced. Lewis H. Morgan, for example, called the book "a cunningly wrought fable." A lawyer and politician (eventually a New York state senator), Morgan was also a founding father of modern anthropology, whose "influential" *Ancient Society* firmly placed the Aztecs in the middle category of barbaric (between savage and civilized). There was no state, he insisted, "nor any civilization in America when it was discovered," and there was "but one race of Indians, the Red Race." For Prescott, the Aztecs presented a paradox, for cannibal consumption was an elite "banquet" that was "prepared with art" and unfolded "with all the decorum of civilized life." Here was Prescott's "refinement and the extreme of barbarism" sitting uncomfortably beside each other. But for Morgan, there was no paradox: "Montezuma's dinner" was no more than the simple "daily meal" of barbarian "Indians."[22]

There was considerable irony in Morgan's insistence that to claim the Aztecs and other "Indians" were civilized was to "caricature the Indians and deceive ourselves." For he was hardly alone in applying moral indignation to the caricaturing of "Indians" as uncivilized by virtue of their devotion to human sacrifice and cannibalism. The centuries-old theme was seized upon by writers such as John Abbott, a New England minister and author of moralistic biographies; in his *Makers of History: Hernando Cortez*, first published in 1856 but in print well into the twentieth century, the Mayas encountered by Cortés were howling savages whose "horrible entertainment" was "midnight orgies" of cannibalism, while the Aztecs routinely ate "the flesh of the wretched victims" of their abominable human sacrifices.[23]

The proliferation of such characterizations of the Aztecs over the past hundred years has been extraordinarily extensive. Perhaps it is not surprising to find it in books aimed at broad audiences; be they plays, novels, or history textbooks, such works tend to depend for their success upon dramatic narratives, vivid imagery, and even lurid sensationalism. Nor is it surprising to see Aztec caricatures work their way into the new media of the modern age, from comics and graphic novels to television documentaries and video games. What is perhaps surprising is how profoundly such views have been perpetuated in scholarly publications: judging the Aztecs for "the horrible sacrifices that they made to their gods" has been, and remains, a deep-rooted, mainstream perspective, even in international academic circles. The following string of quotes is intended not to single out individual scholars and writers, but—on the contrary—to offer a glimpse into the long, strong march of this judgment ("horrible sacrifices" is from 1928).[24]

Aztec Mexico was organized "so as to be able to sustain, and thereby mollify, the unseen powers with as many human hearts as it was possible to give them" (1955). The two cornerstones of rule by the Aztec nobility were "human sacrifice and a methodical exaction of tribute" (1966). Aztec nobles developed a "rule of terror" in which "death was lurking everywhere," and by Montezuma's reign "the sacrificial engine was forging ahead at frantic speed"; tens of thousands of infants every year were "wrenched" from the breasts of "sobbing mothers," and "the epitome of dehumanization was achieved when the lords could with good appetite sit down and eat the flesh of the plebeian" (1967). Aztec priests were butchers, literally, as they "can legitimately be described as ritual slaughterers in a state-sponsored system geared to the production and redistribution of substantial amounts of animal protein in the form of human flesh" (1977). Early in their history the Aztecs developed "an evil reputation for savagery among their more civilized neighbors," their warriors being Mexico's "most bloodthirsty" (1984). The "one activity for which the Aztecs were notorious" was "the large-scale killing of humans in ritual sacrifices" (1991). "Lines of despondent captives must have been a familiar sight" in Tenochtitlan, as "human sacrifice was central to Aztec religion" (2008)—"potentially the fate of all, the linchpin that held the indigenous system together," the "bloody keystone of religious beliefs"; "violence, and the threat of its use, was endemic in Indo-Mexico," so that at Montezuma's coronation, the parade of prisoners progressed up the pyramid steps to the sacrificial altar, "blood, the food of the gods, dripped down and pooled on the steps as the celebratory orgy of death and political elevation continued" (2015).[25]

No WONDER THAT "no topic has caused more controversy and confusion about Aztec life than human sacrifice," as leading Aztec scholar Davíd Carrasco has deftly put it. Carrasco is among those who have sought to offer a less prejudicial and more objective view of Aztec civilization. Such efforts might be summed up as taking three lines of argument.[26]

The first I have implied earlier in this chapter: the supposed evidence for characterizing Aztec life as built around rituals of slaughter and cannibalism is another example of confirmation bias. Like the story of the Meeting as the Surrender, the original lie or exaggeration became truth by its repetition as fact, buoyed by the bias of Aztec stereotypes. Conquistadors and Franciscans, theologians and chroniclers, all seeking to justify some aspect or another of the Spanish invasions, conquests, colonization, and campaigns of conversion, repeated the same denunciations of the Aztecs so many times that they became fact. After several generations, the distortions and lies were widely believed; there was nobody to argue against them. Even the indigenous elite, based on their contributions to Sahagún's great *Historia* (the Florentine Codex), seemed to believe them (after all, they were now Christians too). When Bernal Díaz's account of the invasion was finally published in 1632, with its lurid descriptions of such rituals based on alleged eyewitness observation, the lies seemed truer still. Their repetition in the bestselling histories by Solís, Robertson, and Prescott carried them across the centuries and to readers worldwide. When, in the modern era, Sahagún's *Historia* was discovered and began to be published, its inclusion of the same distortions, highly detailed and in Nahuatl, helped give sixteenth-century prejudice a whole new veneer of authenticity.

A second way to view the Aztecs more objectively is to adopt a comparative perspective—a persuasive line of argument, to my mind. For is there not a glaring irony to denunciations of Aztec violence written during "the century of genocide," the era when 187 million people perished in political violence, "more killing than at any other time in history"? We do not even need to turn to the violent twentieth century to compare Aztec and Western civilizations; European practices of the fifteenth and sixteenth centuries will do the job just as well (including the atrocities of the Spanish-Aztec War, to which we shall return in later chapters). Thus modern judgments, based on sixteenth-century Spanish sources, reflect two layers of irony, hypocrisy, and ethnocentrism. These comparisons are obvious, and have thus for long been periodically made; in 1955, for example, the French anthropologist Jacques Soustelle noted:

> At the height of their career the Romans shed more blood in their circuses and for their amusement than ever the Aztecs did before their idols. The Spaniards, so sincerely moved by the cruelty of the native priests, nevertheless massacred, burnt, mutilated, and

tortured with a perfectly clear conscience. We, who shudder at the tale of the bloody rites of ancient Mexico, have seen with our own eyes and in our own days civilized nations proceed systematically to the extermination of millions of human beings and to the perfection of weapons capable of annihilating in one second a hundred times more victims than the Aztecs ever sacrificed.[27]

But such damning comparisons have, for centuries, tended to be dismissed, using various dubious argumentative techniques. One is the use of categories, embedded deeply in how we talk about the Aztecs: we wage religious wars and execute prisoners; the Aztecs practiced "human sacrifice" before "idols." As Montaigne famously remarked in his essay "On Cannibals," "everyone calls barbarian what is not his own usage." In the same centuries that Aztec prisoners were executed at the Great Temple of Tenochtitlan, Christians burned other Christians alive at the stake; in both cases, men and women were ritually killed in public for political and religious reasons. That commonality must have been starkly clear to the Aztecs themselves, when in 1539 the Christianized indigenous ruler of Tetzcoco, don Carlos Ometochtzin, was condemned of clandestine "idolatry" by Zumárraga (former witch-hunter in Spain and Mexico's first bishop), then burned alive at the stake in the plaza where the Great Temple had stood. But of course nobody then, or since, called Ometochtzin's killing a "human sacrifice." For by deploying different categories, that commonality is buried, allowing us to emphasize the many differences that also existed in practice and meaning; from there it is a short step to the slippery slope of dismissal.[28]

Take examples from two very different studies of the Aztecs. The North American anthropologist Marvin Harris absorbed uncritically the negative depictions of the Aztec past by sixteenth-century Spaniards like Díaz, Durán, and Sahagún, calling the empire a "cannibal kingdom." He dealt with the Spanish-Aztec comparison of cultures of violence by dismissing it on the opening page of his discussion (in a widely read 1977 book): the conquistadors were not surprised to discover that "the Aztecs methodically sacrificed human beings," because they themselves "broke people's bones on the rack, pulled people's arms and legs off in tugs of war between horses, and disposed of women accused of witchcraft by burning them at the stake." Yet, according to Harris, they were unprepared for "what they found in Mexico" not just because Aztec practices were different, but also because they were categorically worse. "Nowhere else in the world had there developed a state-sponsored religion whose art, architecture, and ritual were so thoroughly dominated by violence, decay, death, and disease."[29]

The echo of sixteenth-century Spanish rhetoric is not surprising. When Spanish critics of conquistador practices denounced "the unheard-of cruelties and tortures inflicted" upon indigenous people (the judge Alonso de Zorita), "the devastations and cruelties, the slaughters and destructions" by Spanish invaders (Las Casas), Conquest apologists simply flipped the comparison; "it is my opinion and that of many," wrote the conquistador-author Vargas Machuca, "that to paint cruelty in its full colors, there is no need to do more than portray an Indian." The rhetorical trick is simple and transparent, yet it has been successfully repeated for centuries.[30]

Far more sympathetic to the Aztecs was Inga Clendinnen, whose beautifully written exploration of Aztec culture based on Sahagún's *Historia* is one of the last century's most sophisticated and widely read studies on the topic. She too noted that in Europe, for many centuries, large crowds watched the "judicious tortures and exemplary maimings" of public executions. But, then, by a quick sleight of hand, she dismissed the relevance of such comparisons, on the grounds that public executions "were relatively infrequent, certainly peripheral to daily life," with the victims "seen as culpable to some degree"; by contrast, "Mexica victims were purely victims." Clendinnen's goal was to show that Aztec executions were not more horrific than Western ones, just couched in a different cultural context. Yet the dismissal of the comparative context, and the devotion of many pages to "sacrificial" rituals, meant that her influential study struggled to escape the revulsion for Aztec religion that suffused her book's source, Sahagún's *Historia*.[31]

The story of Aztec public executions may be one "which chills" (as Clendinnen asserts). But is there any story of state-sponsored violence and public executions that does not chill? Even the most sensationalist Franciscan or Dominican account of Aztec killings is no harder to read than the records of Inquisition tortures, than accounts of protracted public executions in colonial Spanish America, or even than Las Casas's *Destruction of the Indies*. Regardless of how one seeks to mute or dismiss the comparison, the fact remains that Western traditions of ritualized public killing for political and religious purposes have been as extensive and deadly, if not more so, than Aztec practices. As Carrasco puts it: "Even though the Aztec image in Western thought ranks them as the biggest sacrificers in the world, there is no substantial archaeological or documentary proof that they ritually killed more people than other civilizations."[32]

THIS TAKES US BACK to issues of evidence and the context of Aztec civilization, and thereby to yet another way of seeing through negative Aztec stereotypes. The two lines of argument above do not claim that the Aztecs did not publicly execute prisoners at all. Carrasco again: "That the Aztecs practiced ritual human sacrifice is beyond doubt, but it is also clear that Spanish chroniclers exaggerated the numbers and purposes of these sacrifices as a strategy to justify their own conquests and prodigious violence against" indigenous peoples. Maya archaeologist Elizabeth Graham goes further, rightly arguing that neither Aztecs nor Mayas had a term that translates as "sacrifice," that Spaniards introduced the concept to Mesoamerica, and that executions took place "as part of warfare" and not "on the basis of gods' needs." Warfare in Mesoamerica mixed "goals of economic gain with cosmic justification," just as it does today (consider the complex economic and ideological justifications behind our own century's long wars waged by the West in the Middle East).[33]

So how can we go through or around the distorting filters of Spanish accounts to see Aztec rituals of execution more clearly—to see human sacrifice (a loaded phrase that arguably should only be applied to the Aztecs with quotation marks) as wartime killing, without judgmental hyperbole?

One illuminating and fascinating new source of evidence is the Great Temple itself. No records survived of its destruction in the 1520s, and it remained buried for centuries; yet the Great Temple was precisely where almost all the executions, most notably the alleged mass sacrifices, took place. However, in 1978 Mexican archaeologists began to excavate the foundations of the Great Temple—that is, the pyramid upon which the twin temples stood, and its surrounding structures. Directed for four decades by Eduardo Matos Moctezuma, the project has gradually revealed that the Great Temple was rebuilt seven times, helping to preserve more than 126 caches of ritual offerings buried by generations of Aztec priests. The objects in these caches are a kind of unintended time capsule, and we shall return to look at them in detail in the next chapter. For now, what of the bones of the hundreds of thousands of alleged victims of Aztec brutality? Or, if we believe that the empire was "a cannibal kingdom" and those victims were all taken off to be eaten in Aztec homes, what of the human skulls "too numerous to count" that Díaz later claimed he had seen in the square facing the Great Temple?[34]

The archaeologists did indeed uncover two large carved stones, which more or less match conquistador descriptions as those upon which prisoners were executed. They also found ritual knives, most of flint, finely carved and decorated, deposited over many years. In addition, the floors of some buildings, and remnants of some altars and statues, contained traces of human blood. Human remains were also found, those of 126 people; forty-two were children. The children all suffered from disease, and their throats had been cut. Forty-seven adult heads were found, spread through various offerings from different time periods.

But none of those adults had been decapitated. Of Díaz's skulls, perforated to fit onto skull racks, only three were found prior to 2015 (three skulls from almost four decades of excavations). More than ten times that many decorated facial skull masks were found under the Great Temple floors. Even when archaeologists found the larger of the two skull racks, the *huey tzompantli,* in 2015, it revealed scores—but not hundreds, let alone thousands—of human skulls, with those outnumbered by two-dimensional carved stone skulls. Furthermore, the ritual knives do not appear to have been used; they were symbolic offerings. Archaeologists have found more human remains at Teotihuacan than in Tenochtitlan (Teotihuacan is the spectacular site north of Tenochtitlan whose heyday was a millennium before that of the Aztecs). Of the eighty thousand prisoners supposedly sacrificed over four days in 1486, "no evidence approaching one-hundredth of that number has been found in the excavations"; put another way, compared to Zumárraga's imaginary 2 million children executed during the century before Spaniards invaded, the Great Temple yielded evidence of 0.0021 percent that many.[35]

Thus when Prescott declared that the unequaled scale of Aztec human sacrifice was incredible ("The amount of victims immolated on its accursed altars would stagger the faith of the least scrupulous believer"), he had no idea that his rhetoric was literally accurate: it is not to be believed because it is a monstrous lie. If we allow the centuries-old monolithic image of the Aztecs as bloodthirsty cannibals, devotees of monstrous ritual, to pixelate and crumble, a very different picture becomes visible behind it.[36]

Just as a clearer picture of early modern Spanish culture might balance Zumárraga with Cervantes, Cortés with Las Casas, traditions of Inquisition torture with achievements in poetry and oil painting, so would a clearer picture of Aztec civilization include an appreciation of Aztec poetry and *xochicuicatl,* or "flower-song"; the extraordinary beauty of Aztec featherwork; the sophistication of Aztec aesthetic sensibilities; the system of education for both girls and boys; the literary and legal culture that supported historians, judges, ministers, and clerks; the orderly accomplishment of cities like Tenochtitlan and Tetzcoco—masterpieces of urban engineering, architectural harmony, and organizational ingenuity. One of the conquistador legacies is that we tend to see Aztec cities through the distorting lens of their obsession with human sacrifice and cannibalism. But Tenochtitlan was not a dark locus of doom and death; it was a place of festivals and families.

The Aztecs were heirs to the larger civilizational tradition of Mesoamerica. In their achievements in sculpture and painting, in the language arts, and in urban design, they are no less an impressive manifestation of that tradition than the Mayas, Mixtecs, and other Mesoamerican cultures. In the island-capital and in towns across the steadily expanding empire, kings and merchants, warriors and slaves, shamans and corn farmers, featherworkers and birdkeepers, priests and scribes interacted peacefully within "a highly stratified, intensely ritualized, wealthy urban society." The Spanish invasion may have prevented the Aztecs from "attaining new levels of material, social, and intellectual greatness." But the levels attained by 1520 were extraordinary and will inspire marvel and study for centuries to come.[37]

By way of further developing a clearer, less prejudicial picture of Aztec civilization, let us linger for a moment on a pair of Aztec deities. One of them, Huitzilopochtli, helps us to see how the Western view of the Aztecs became distorted, and the other, Quetzalcoatl, leads us back to Montezuma and the Meeting.

Huitzilopochtli has variously been called the war god, the patron god, and the principal god of the Aztecs (pronounced "wheat-seal-opotch-tlee," the conquistadors instantly changed the name to Huichilobos, Ochilobos, and Orchilobos). Over the centuries since the fall of the Aztec Empire, the deity "came to epitomize Aztec religion and, to a broader extent, Aztec culture." Frequently depicted in text and engraving as the grim and gruesome deity to whom human hearts were offered, Huitzilopochtli became *the* Aztec icon in the Western mind; to this day popular notions of the Aztecs, even in the minds of those who cannot name Huitzilopochtli or describe any Aztec deity, are essentially based on that deity's imagery and mythology. Where did such a god originate?[38]

In short, Europeans invented him. The seed of the invention seems to have been planted by Cortés in his Second Letter to the king. There he remarked that Aztec idols in temples were larger than a man and made of dough from seeds mixed with human blood. Peter Martyr, who was the Spanish Crown's Chronicler of the Indies when Cortés's Second Letter was published in Spain, repeated the description, inventing the detail that the blood was from children. The conquistador Andrés de Tapia, whose eyewitness but fanciful account of the war of invasion was written in the 1540s, added that the blood was that "of virgin boys and girls." Not a single piece of evidence has ever emerged to support the idea that human blood, let alone children's blood, was mixed into this dough (we shall explain the dough's nature and purpose shortly), yet it was repeated as fact in dozens of books for centuries; by the turn of the seventeenth century the story had evolved into another invention—that the bread the Aztecs gave to Cortés and the other Spaniards in Tenochtitlan had secretly been mixed with human blood.[39]

Tapia also described stone statues of deities with necklaces and decorations of serpents, golden human hearts, and skulls; as these would seem to be descriptions of two statues uncovered beneath Mexico City in 1790 and 1933 (Coatlicue and another deity, Yolotlicue), it has been suggested that Tapia muddled up his "idols" in his later recollections. This was not the only possible muddling up of Aztec statues, mixed with conquistador imagination; the temple tour described by Cortés (and Bernal Díaz) was not actually that of the Great Temple at the heart of Tenochtitlan, but took place in the neighborhood of Tlatelolco.[40]

Tapia's account was not published, but it was read by Gómara, who merged all these ingredients to create an imaginative description of Huitzilopochtli as a grim, fearsome, bejewelled stone idol in the Great Temple. Gómara's semifictional, hybrid Huitzilopochtli was copied over and over by chroniclers and churchmen (Franciscans like Mendieta and Torquemada in particular relished the detail of sacrificed children's blood). Even Las Casas, with his deep skepticism of the conquistadors, swallowed it wholesale. Bernal Díaz, despite insisting his account was to rectify Gómara's errors, himself copied the Gómara version.[41]

Meanwhile, a slightly different Spanish description of the "idol" developed in Mexico. Probably originating among the indigenous elite in the late sixteenth century, in oral tradition or a long-lost codex, the earliest surviving record of this description is in fray Diego Durán's *History of the Indies of New Spain*. From there it was copied by a Jesuit, Juan de Tovar; Durán and Tovar included drawings of the god in their books (and Tovar's is included in our Gallery). Both books also remained unpublished for centuries, but another Jesuit, José de Acosta, copied Tovar's description into his *Moral and Natural History of the Indies*. First published in 1590, Acosta's book soon became an international hit, quickly published in six other European languages.[42]

Acosta's description of Huitzilopochtli was for centuries worked into various bestselling histories of the Americas, from Theodore de Bry's *Americae* series to Solís's *Historia*. Some combined the Acosta version with the Gómara version, with emphasis usually placed on the more satanic elements. For example, Ogilby's influential book, along with its Dutch twin, regaled readers with lurid images of Aztec sacrifices, flesh-eating, and idols—including a vast goat-monster of a Huitzilopochtli, complete with a ghoulish face on his torso. Thus whatever authentic, indigenous elements may have worked their way into the Durán-Tovar descriptions, or even the first conquistador accounts, they were distorted or lost amid the Europeanized ones. "In the centuries following the Conquest," art historian Elizabeth Boone concluded in a landmark study, Huitzilopochtli "comes to be a new pagan god or a diabolical idol."[43]

All of which raises the question: What did Huitzilopochtli really look like? No stone statues of the god have survived (so much for Tapia's description), but there are descriptions and drawings in early colonial codices. Their imagery is similar to that found on stone sculptures made before the Spanish invasion; examples are in the Codex Telleriano-Remensis (in our Gallery) and on the backrest to a stone throne called the Teocalli. In these and comparable examples, the artist has not simply drawn or carved the "idols" that Europeans imagined Aztecs worshipped. Such images are neither the god himself, nor a priest dressed up to represent the god, but to some extent both of those things. The decorative elements—heron and quetzal feathers, a hummingbird-head helmet, paint stripes on face and body, a smoking shield, and so on—evoke the characteristics of the deity; they call up his sacrality, his divine and sacred power.[44]

Only one of these sacred elements is unique to Huitzilopochtli, the hummingbird (*huitzilin* in Nahuatl); all the others can be found as sacred elements of other Aztec deities. Furthermore, some of the descriptions and drawings of Huitzilopochtli that have survived from the sixteenth century do not actually refer to the god himself, but rather to priests or rulers representing the deity. For example, the Aztec king Chimalpopoca (who ruled 1417–27) is portrayed in the Codex Xolotl as dressed in the accoutrements of the god—from striped face and headdress of heron and quetzal feathers to hummingbird device. This wasn't so much an impersonation of the god as it was a borrowing of his sacred power, a projection of authority through association with the deity—one whose mythology closely associated him with the genesis of the Aztec state (Huitzilopochtli was said to have guided the ancestors of the Aztecs from their mythical home of Aztlan to the island where they built Tenochtitlan). A similar association is achieved in the Teocalli carving, in which Montezuma mirrors and is paired with the deity, while both "talk" war; the symbols for fire and water, representing warfare, stream from their mouths.[45]

One final aspect of Aztec representations of Huitzilopochtli is worth explanation: the dough mentioned earlier, which Spaniards imagined was made with the blood of sacrificed children. In fact, the *tzoalli* dough was formed of ground amaranth seeds and cactus syrup. It was used to make an image of Huitzilopochtli for the festival of Panquetzaliztli, held in the month of that name. The image was adorned with the symbols of the deity (the feathers, the hummingbird device, the stripes, and so on), carried through the streets of the city, set up at the Great Temple, and at the climax of the festival it was broken up and eaten.[46]

The *tzoalli* image is depicted and described in colonial sources such as Sahagún's *Historia* (Florentine Codex), more or less in ways that seem to reflect accurately how it was used. But at the same time, the transformation of the Aztec deity into the demon-god of European imagination can be seen emerging in Franciscan and other Spanish sources. Indeed, the transition can even be seen occurring within Sahagún's *Historia:* the drawing of the dough statue of Huitzilopochtli in Book I is similar to the sideways rendering in various codices; but in Book XII, composed years later, the traditional accoutrements and side view were replaced by a frontal view of a leg-splayed pagan god, a stark precursor to the devil-idol to be found on the pages of European books for centuries to come. The iconography and meaning of Aztec images of Huitzilopochtli have been explored and debated at great length by scholars, and it would be easy to devote many more pages to them. But the point should already be clear: Huitzilopochtli, as represented by the Aztecs themselves, was a far cry from the pagan devil-monster of post-invasion renderings.[47]

ALTHOUGH THE SACRIFICIAL PRACTICES associated with Huitzilopochtli are still the primary popular images of Aztec culture, the deity himself became eclipsed in the last century or so by another: Quetzalcoatl, the Feathered Serpent (or Plumed Serpent), "for most people the quintessential Aztec god." The story of how the modern manifestation of Quetzalcoatl evolved is very different, and more complex, than the parallel post-invasion history of Huitzilopochtli. But the end result is the same: so much was invented by Europeans, mostly for specific political, religious, and cultural purposes, that the surviving aspects and meanings of the original Aztec deity are diluted, eclipsed, difficult to discern.[48]

What does seem clear is that there was memory or folk history in ancient Mexico of a legendary ruler of Tula (the city-state that dominated central Mexico before the Aztecs but after the decline of Teotihuacan), named Topiltzin Quetzalcoatl. Topiltzin is really a title (in Nahuatl, *to* means "our," *pilli* means "nobleman," and *tzin* is a part of speech that conveys reverence; making "Our Noble Lord," or, very colloquially, "Sir"). The title was probably held by a series of rulers, so Topiltzin Quetzalcoatl was various historical men who became merged into a single legendary figure, with various folktales attached to him. For our purposes, one such group of tales is important: Topiltzin Quetzalcoatl was forced to leave Tula, due to political conflict or religious differences, and in some variants he did not die but disappeared, perhaps across the Caribbean Sea. That final detail was probably added after the Spanish invasion, as was a further twist in the tale: the legendary man, or man-god, was destined one day to return.[49]

One of Quetzalcoatl's many manifestations was that of a man-god, because at some point he merged or was muddled up with a deity named Quetzalcoatl—himself a complex nexus of gods, including a deity of rain and fertility, and a wind god named Ehecatl. A god named Quetzalcoatl was thus part of the pantheon of the Aztecs, associated in particular with the town of Cholollan (Cholula, a pilgrimage site for more than a millennium, with the world's largest pyramid; it was devoted to Quetzalcoatl). Meanwhile, during the first decades after the Spanish invasion, two unrelated concepts began to circulate in Mexico and Europe: one was the idea, put into Montezuma's mouth by Cortés when he wrote his account of the Meeting, that the Aztecs believed the descendants of ancient lords of the land would one day return to claim their kingdom; the other was the idea, first written down by Durán, that St. Thomas reached Mexico and preached there in ancient times.[50]

By the late sixteenth century, the first of these had merged with the tale of Quetzalcoatl's return. It is significant that the linking of the two stories had not been made by the conquistadors; Cortés never once mentions Quetzalcoatl in his writings of the 1520s and '30s, and Gómara's mention of Quetzalcoatl follows Tapia, who only refers to him as a man-god founder of Cholollan who wore a white robe covered in red crosses and who banned human sacrifice. Despite this incipient Christianization of the god by the 1540s, it was not until Sahagún compiled his *Historia* a few decades later that the legends of the returning lords and of Quetzalcoatl's return were merged into one ("They say he lives, and will return and reign . . . and when don Fernando Cortés came, they thought he was him").[51]

The idea that Montezuma thought Cortés was Huitzilopochtli had circulated earlier—Viceroy Mendoza recounted that rumor in a letter to his brother in Spain in 1540—but by the second half of the century the Franciscans and their Christianized indigenous collaborators on the *Historia* project had settled on Quetzalcoatl as a far better candidate. The appeal to the early colonial-period indigenous elite of a man-god Quetzalcoatl destined to return was obvious: such a figure made Christianity more local, tying it to native Mexican culture past and present, and helped recast "the Conquest" as predestined and providential, rather than an inexplicable tragedy.[52]

Then, in the seventeenth century, the notion that St. Thomas had visited Mexico also became attached to the evolving legends and understandings of whom Quetzalcoatl had been. The first full development of the idea was an essay by Sigüenza y Góngora, unpublished but widely circulated into the next century, when the St. Thomas–Quetzalcoatl myth reached fruition in the hands of writers and churchmen like Lorenzo Boturini, Francisco Javier Clavigero, and the controversial Teresa de Mier. This saintly Quetzalcoatl was a benign ruler who abolished human sacrifice and cannibalism, preached monotheism, prophesied the Spanish conquest, and promised to return. The patriotic significance of the reinvented Quetzalcoatl was profound, and was the basis for his resurgence in twentieth-century Mexico; in the era of *indigenismo* (a postrevolutionary political and cultural movement that sought to rehabilitate the nation's indigenous heritage), Quetzalcoatl was the subject of a "literary renaissance," manifested in poetry, theater, and painting.[53]

A side effect of the long life of this modern Quetzalcoatl was the perpetuation of the Sahaguntine connection between the legendary Quetzalcoatl, the alleged Aztec myth of the returning lords, and Montezuma's supposed speech of surrender. The more Christianized that Quetzalcoatl became, the more benign and blessed he became in the Mexican cultural pantheon, the deeper the roots of that invented connection grew. The effect, in the end, was *not* to rehabilitate the Aztecs (who remained barbaric and bloodthirsty), but on the contrary, to emphasize their salvation through the surrender to Cortés and Christianity, thereby perpetuating the mythistory of the Meeting.

The combined effect of Spanish, European, and modern Mexican reinventions of Quetzalcoatl as Jesus-like and Huitzilopochtli as satanic was to reinvent Aztec religion and culture as anticipating and justifying the Spanish invasion. One showed how Satan's grip on the Aztecs had placed human sacrifice and cannibalism at the heart of their culture, requiring their rescue from barbarism and damnation; the other showed how God had predestined the Aztecs to be saved, laying the foundation through St. Thomas–Quetzalcoatl, bringing it to fruition through Cortés. The final key piece to this elaborate, imaginary puzzle was Montezuma's identification of Cortés with Quetzalcoatl, inspiring his otherwise incomprehensible surrender, thereby opening Tenochtitlan's gates to providence, turning an otherwise indefensible invasion into a morally justifiable fulfillment of divine will.

Montezuma was a general in the armies of the Inca emperor of Peru.

Never mind that the Aztec and Inca empires were thousands of miles apart and never knew of each other's existence. Such details did not trouble London's theatergoers a century and a half after Montezuma's death. For it was as a general, serving the Inca emperor, that Montezuma appeared in *The Indian-Queen,* a play written by John Dryden and his brother-in-law Sir Robert Howard, first performed in London in 1664. The brief, five-scene tragedy was later turned into a semi-opera, with music by Henry Purcell. In that form it has been performed from 1695 until today (Purcell's satisfyingly Baroque melodies offsetting the absurdities of the poets' plot).[54]

The play's central, heroic character is an entertainingly imaginary Montezuma. As a young Peruvian general, he defeats the Mexicans in battle; but then, when the Mexicans turn the tide and triumph over Inca Peru, Montezuma switches sides. His primary goal, it turns out, is to marry Orazia, the Inca's daughter—in the face of her father's opposition, of competition from rival suitor Acacis (son of the Mexican queen), and of that same queen's desire to have Montezuma for herself.

The play is thus a royal love story about legitimacy, with romance as a metaphor for kingship: Who has the right to rule and who has the right to love or marry whom? Such a universal theme might have been given a European setting. But by placing the drama in the generically exotic otherness of the ancient Americas, Howard and Dryden were also able to deploy crowd-pleasing themes of incest and human sacrifice—long established in European minds as attributes of "Indian" life. The essentializing of Native American cultures, place, and historical characters—Peruvians and Mexicans mixed up and their kingdoms made adjacent; Mexico's "Usurping Indian Queen" is named Zempoalla; her general (and secret lover) is Traxcalla—was made possible by the 150-year-long European reduction of historical figures like Montezuma to stereotypes and symbols.

Dryden soon returned to these themes, this time without his brother-in-law, to write *The Indian Emperour*. In defiance of today's wisdom regarding sequels, this longer play was better and more successful; first performed on London's Drury Lane in 1665, it was a popular hit at the time, and has gone down in literary history as a seminal work of rhymed heroic tragedy.[55]

Dryden attempted to fix the second play more securely in historical reality than *The Indian-Queen* had been. The Incas are absent, for example, and Montezuma rules Mexico, which is invaded by Spaniards led by Cortés ("Cortez"). The sequel takes place twenty years later, with Montezuma the sole character to have survived (although children of the Indian queen, Zempoalla, play roles). In an explanation of the link between the two plays, handed out to audiences, Dryden stated that the sequel was about the conquest of Montezuma's "flourishing Empire," and that he had "neither wholly followed the story nor varied from it."[56]

Dryden's poet's liberty included making Pizarro one of Cortez's "commanders" in Mexico, as well as giving all his Aztec characters decidedly non–Native American names, such as Odmar and Alibech. His theme is, once again, the legitimacy of rulership and love (one cannot, it seems, have both: Montezuma chooses love, and dies; Cortez chooses rule, and wins Mexico). Yet while the plot and characters varied from "the Truth of the History" more than Dryden would have had his audiences believe, the play captured important aspects of the early modern (and even modern) perception of "the Spanish Conquest" and its protagonists—most notably that of Montezuma.

In *The Indian Emperour* the title character is the conflicted, and contradictory, ruler that we know today, the character that he has been for most of the past five centuries. He is the doomed yet "great and glorious Prince" that Dryden declares him from the very start, often firm in his resolve to protect his empire, and steadfast under torture. His captain-goes-down-with-ship sense of pride and honor would have resonated well with an early modern audience: when Cortez, magnanimous to a fault, proffers a compromise to the defeated emperor ("Despair not, Sir, who knows but Conquering *Spain* / May part of what you lost restore again?"), Montezuma responds:

"No, Spaniard, know, he who to Empire born,
Lives to be less, deserves the Victors scorn:
Kings and their Crowns have but one Destiny:
Power is their life, when that expires they dye."
Taking up his sword, the proud Aztec continues:
"————Name Life no more;
'Tis now a Torture worse than all I bore:
I'le not be brib'd to suffer Life, but dye
In spight of your mistaken Clemency.
I was your Slave, and I was us'd like one;
The Shame continues when the Pain is gone:
But I'm a King while this is in my Hand,——[*His sword*].
He wants no Subjects who can Death Command:

You should have ty'd him up, t'have Conquer'd me,
But he's still mine, and thus he sets me free [*Stabs himself*]."[57]

Thus does Montezuma become a martyr. He insists that his martyrdom is to his throne, and thus to the empire itself (the notion of
royal martyrdom was no doubt an echo, for Dryden and his audiences, of the execution of England's King Charles I in 1649). Yet
he opts not to work with Cortés to govern his people, nor to lead
those of his subjects who go into a happy exile (where they will enjoy
"Love and Freedom"), because he chooses a principle over his surviving subjects.

That principle is a romantic one; his self-sacrifice is really to love.
His final two words—"Farewel *Almeria*"—are a reminder of the
love quincunx that has driven the plot: Montezuma loves Almeria (daughter of the deceased "Indian Queen"), who loves Cortés,
who loves Cydaria (Montezuma's daughter), but she is betrothed to
Orbellan (son of the "Indian Queen"). Dryden's Montezuma is certainly the tragic hero of the tale, but he is also the emperor who, in
the end, one way or another, simply gave up.[58]

Montezuma's role was central in the "highly unstable edifice of
synecdoche, analogy, and allusion" by which Spaniards reconstructed
Aztec history and religion, and reinvented its gods, in order to make
just and moral "the Conquest." And although Protestant Europeans and Americans would come to condemn the Spanish conquests,
their view of the Aztecs and the tragic, doomed Montezuma was
taken from that Spanish reconstruction. Thus in England as much as
in Spain and Mexico, Montezuma's peaceful and willing surrender
to Cortés—his role as the emperor who simply gave up—was not
just important, it was the most important thing he did, the defining
element in his biography.[59]

Yet therein lies the rub. Montezuma did not surrender to Cortés. It is neither plausible that he did, nor easily reconciled with the
images and evidence of him as a ruler that survived from the early
sixteenth century; indeed, the emperor who voluntarily gave up his
empire is particularly difficult to reconcile with the king of the can-

nibals. Over the last five centuries, Montezuma has thus evolved
into a particular kind of contradiction, one oft repeated but never
resolved. Sahagún's claim that Montezuma participated unflinch-
ingly in sacrificial rituals himself, but that when he heard descriptions of the Spaniards he "trembled with fear and almost fainted,"
is echoed over and over by modern writers. The Mexican writer of
children's books Heriberto Frías wrote in 1925 of "the sadly famous
Moctezuma Xocoyotzin, doubly cursed as a great general of rapa-
cious, conquering armies and as the Supreme Pontiff of wily, stul-
tifying priesthood." English diplomat and historian Maurice Collis
confessed in 1954 that "one cannot help feeling that Montezuma
was a monster and the sacrifice of [his] captives a ritual murder." Yet
this monster, quickly believing that Cortés was a returning Quetzalcoatl, "was overwhelmed with awe" at the prospect of the god's
approach. Here was the sadly famous emperor portrayed as a lily-
livered serial killer.[60]

Because understandings and images of Montezuma grew so
emblematic and stereotypical in the decades and centuries after his
death, he no longer needed to be anchored to historical reality. As a
generic "Indian" prince, he could be drawn or described as any artist,
playwright, or historian wished—as Dryden entertainingly proved,
and as was reflected in the engraved portraits of the early modern
centuries (examples of which are in the Gallery). As a result, of
course, the early modern and modern Montezuma became increasingly removed from the Montezuma that died in 1520.

To MAKE BETTER SENSE of these many Montezumas, of the emperor's
multifaceted afterlife, let us linger on his posthumous personalities.
These should be seen not as distinct textual or visual portraits, but
as threads that run in confused and contradictory ways through the
vast quilt of Montezuma imagery. Montezuma the Monster has
already been introduced, and is primarily a personification of the
Aztec stereotypes already discussed. This emperor was the cannibal
king, the dark lord who "fed now and then of man's flesh, sacrificed"
but preferred to have children "slain and dressed for his table." This

Montezuma did not merely preside over the culture and kingdom defined by idolatry, human sacrifice, and cannibalism, but led it by example, removing hearts himself, literally getting his hands dirty. Yet the vast majority of such portraits, from Sahagún to Collis, Gómara to Ranking, mixed such characteristics with others, thereby contributing to the contradictions.[61]

Another personality, mixed in uneasily with the Monster, was that of Montezuma the Magnificent. The deepest origins of this Montezuma lay in the years of the emperor's reign (1502–20), in how his kingship was projected onto his subjects, and in the memory of that image among survivors of the invasion war. This personality comes closest to the real Montezuma, the man who mastered the difficult job of ruling an empire. However, that historical Montezuma was muted after the invasion by the duplicitous, capitulating Montezuma of Cortés's Letters, and the weak and cowardly Montezuma of Gómara's telling. It is only later in the century that the Magnificent begins to reemerge, and he does so in surprising (and, predictably, contradictory) ways and places.

For example, the Spanish poet Gabriel Lasso de la Vega was devoted to promoting the Cortés legend, most notably in a pair of long epic poems. But for Lasso, Montezuma was not the anti-Cortés of so many Spanish accounts; rather, he was a great ruler of an awe-inspiring kingdom, an epic figure, powerful and indomitable, as befits the poet's verse. Lasso's position was that the greater the "Indian" emperor, the greater the triumph of the man who beat him, and indeed, that argument is made clear in a brief essay appended to Lasso's *Mexicana* of 1594.

Written by one Gerónimo Ramirez, the essay insists that "the Indians of New Spain were not bellicose, but neither were they cowardly, simpleminded, ignorant, without ingenuity or skill or way of living." Far from being "weak-hearted and feminized (as some have said)," they were "very skillful at arms" and "fought valiantly." To deny "the spirit and fortitude of the Indians" is "to diminish the merit that Cortés won in conquering them." As for "the astonishing name and power of Moteçuma, King of Mexico," no other ruler in the Americas approached "the grandeur of his kingdom, neither in the number of vassals nor in the abundance of riches." Only the ferocious resistance of the Tlaxcalteca could be said to "diminish the power of this supreme [*superbissimo*] king."[62]

The Montezuma the Magnificent of the seventeenth and eighteenth centuries was usually tempered to various degrees of disconnection with the Monster. In the *America* of Montanus and Ogilby he is virtually a model monarch; his domain is vast, due to "his Valor and good success in the Wars," but he is at the same time "a wise and good Prince, just, affable, and tender of his Subjects good." His only flaw is his fanatical devotion to his "Satanical Religion."[63]

A particularly vivid modern manifestation of Montezuma the Magnificent is in the 1964 book of that name by Mexican lawyer and historian Ignacio Romerovargas Iturbide (although only published in Mexico, and long out of print even there, the book resonates across Mexican websites in the present century). Romerovargas sought to make of Montezuma a model statesman who might inspire modern imitators. He was a "great reformer and educator" who was "the only ruler of his time in the world who required the compulsory education of every member of society." He allocated state lands to those who had served the community well. He built a great hospital and orphanage. His palace of dwarfs, albinos, and deformed people was a state home for humane care, not a place of "morbid curiosity, as it was interpreted by the Spaniards, who spoke so much of charity but understood it poorly and never practiced it." He opened up his storehouses in times of drought or crop failure. His legal system was not equaled in Europe until after the French Revolution. He protected trade and maintained peace throughout the empire. With his "deeply artistic temperament," he turned Tenochtitlan into a massive urban artwork, an engineering and architectural masterpiece. He was powerful and feared, but also "loved by his people to the point of being almost adored," and seemed sometimes cruel only due to his extreme devotion to justice.[64]

How can this compelling if imaginative emperor be reconciled with the cruel coward of Spanish depiction? Romerovargas himself

poses the question, and answers it by arguing rightly that the Spaniards were invested in a negative characterization of the Aztecs, a
view that tainted their portrait of the ruler; he rejects, therefore, the
Monster. But he cannot resist the myth of the returning Quetzalcoatl, leading him to resort to Montezuma the Fearful (my label for
another posthumous personality). Following so many before him,
Romerovargas gives the emperor a dramatic personality change in
the face of the Spanish invasion. Believing a "far off king" had sent
the invaders, this "sublime figure" and "national hero" let them in,
but once "taken by surprise and imprisoned" he could not withstand
"the physical and moral tortures" of his captivity, and was "tor-
mented and reduced to impotence." Romerovargas is keen to promote the martyrdom of the fallen emperor, but the contrast with
his pre-invasion magnificence makes him a rather pathetic martyr.[65]

This tempering of the Magnificent with the Fearful, like the
other contradictory personality threads, went back into the early
modern centuries. By the time Sepúlveda called Montezuma "timorous and cowardly" in 1543, the story of the emperor's capitulation
was well established as fact, with a derogatory view of his alleged
faintheartedness hot on its heels.[66] Montezuma the Fearful was an
easy target, a convenient scapegoat. In the *Historia* by Sahagún and
the one by Durán, Aztec defeat in the war was blamed squarely on
Montezuma, specifically on his fearfulness—his superstitious, depressed, weak, cowardly demeanor. This tidy way of explaining the
conquest through a reimagined Montezuma was surely the prevail-
ing view as much among Nahuas as among Franciscans (as reflected
in Sahagún's *Historia*). Montezuma was the antithesis of an exemplary *tlahtoani*: a warrior-king who failed to lead his armies; a Great
Speaker who had little to say. Durán took the interpretation a step
further, inventing a mirrored pair of personalities for the first and
second Montezumas—the one (ruled 1440–69) explaining the Aztec Empire's expansion, the other (ruled 1502–20) its collapse.[67]

The Sahagún-Durán historical fiction stuck—as historical fact.
Gemelli, writing a century later, translated "Montezuma" as "Wise
Lord," for he was "Grave, and Majestick, a Man of few Words, and

discreet, which made him much honour'd, and fear'd." Yet faced with ominous portents and predictions of "some great Calamity" by his astrologers, this same emperor was quickly reduced to "Repentance," passively awaiting "his Ruin, to be wrought by the Children of the Sun, coming from the East." In a variant on this theme (in a 1778 heroic poem by Joseph María Vaca de Guzmán), in which "the terrible Montezuma" was not loved by his people at all, but was "the most arrogant King" (almost a Magnificent Monster), the emperor nonetheless sank quickly into "a mortal lethargy" when "the great Cortés" appeared on the horizon. Likewise, Ranking depicted a warlike and bloodthirsty Montezuma who set up *a stone of excessive size* to accommodate the increase in human sacrifices, beginning with 12,210 victims at his coronation; yet this same man was overcome with emotion when offered the crown, his acceptance thrice "interrupted by tears," and at Cortés's approach seventeen years later "was terribly perplexed by his [own] superstition and fears." The emperor of Gemelli, Vaca de Guzmán, Ranking, and Romerovargas, and myriad interpretations in between, whether feared or loved (or both) by his subjects, always crumbles in the face of prophesied doom.[68]

The irony of the renewed popularity in the twentieth century of the Quetzalcoatl myth was that writers sympathetic to the Aztecs ended up perpetuating Cortés's lie about the surrender. Thus the traditional narrative of Cortés's triumph and Montezuma's failure became enhanced, not undermined, by an indigenist attention to the Aztec cultural context. Montezuma the Fearful increasingly appeared in print in the twentieth century. French historian Jean Descola—whose history of the invasion, written in the 1950s, was titled *Hernán Cortés; or The Return of the White God*—offered a slightly updated version of the traditional narrative, in which the genius and awesome destiny of Cortés (based, as so often, on a reading of Cortés himself and Gómara) was reinforced by the ancient prophecies, terrifying omens, and providentialism of the Quetzalcoatl myth. Similarly, the Mexican Jesuit priest and scholar Esteban Palomera, who studied the sixteenth-century Franciscan Diego Valadés from the 1940s to 1980s but was also a devotee of Maya history, concluded that the legend of Quetzalcoatl, "pregnant with fatalistic omens, influenced the religious soul of the [ancient] Mexicans, especially the superstitious spirit of Montezuma." Valadés, whose 1579 book was Palomera's subject, makes no mention of the Quetzalcoatl-Montezuma myth; Palomera was simply articulating the conventional wisdom of his own era.[69]

By the twenty-first century, judgments passed on Montezuma the Fearful had piled high, with Internet commentary added to books of all kinds and languages. As the Prophecy interpretations of the Meeting showed (in the previous chapter), the defeat of the empire has again and again been blamed on Montezuma's "superstition," "delusion," his naïve "fatalism"; he was "blinded," "paralyzed with foreboding, confused and indecisive;" he was simply "frightened."[70]

Over the centuries since Montezuma's death, as these three personalities developed and collided with each other to create a complex mythology about the emperor, how was he drawn and painted? What did the Monster, the Magnificent, and the Fearful actually look like? Early colonial visual representations of the emperor tended to follow those that had survived the Spanish invasion, in which artists attempted not to create a faithful likeness of the man but to depict his status and power, his essence as emperor. In some of these images (and in some in our Gallery), there is perhaps the echo of Montezuma the Magnificent. And in later illustrations, especially in the nineteenth and twentieth centuries, depictions of the Meeting or of Cortés's seizure of the emperor portray him as crestfallen, head drooping in defeat. Nonetheless, there is an overarching motif to the five centuries of Montezuma portraiture, one present in almost every image: feathers. The final personality is thus Montezuma the Feathered.[71]

The use of feathers as an iconic shorthand to convey native peoples of the Americas is strikingly ubiquitous. It began immediately: Columbus returned from his first voyage to the Americas in March 1493, and the following year a mural in one of the Borgia palaces in Italy already featured American "Indians," naked save for feathered headdresses. Clearly, and not surprisingly, Europeans already had at their disposal an icon of dress (or lack thereof) to represent the alien or the Other; feathered dress had for long been associated with Turks and other "Oriental" peoples. So, just as they expected to find in the Americas freakish people, barbaric customs, monstrous idols, and tales of the expectedly unexpected, so did they assume that these "Indians" would wear feathers, and often nothing else. With the discovery that many native societies in the Americas did indeed value bird feathers and had developed dazzling featherwork cultures—from the Aztecs to the Tupí of Brazil—the stereotype deepened. By the seventeenth century, the feather was exclusively *the* "Indian" image, the early modern equivalent to the icon for a smartphone app.[72]

The role of the feather was thus simple and it was used everywhere—on maps, engravings, paintings, and sculptures. An elaborate but fairly typical example is the frontispiece to Ogilby's *America* (included in the Gallery); the word was included as the book's title, but it was rendered redundant by the presence of feathers on all the "Indians." At the same time, feathers were also used to convey differences among "Indians," as perceived by Europeans; an "Indian" wearing only a feathered headdress was more barbaric or of lower status than one with feathered skirts or anklets, and a complete garb of feathers conveyed a ruler.

De Bry included a vaguely identified Montezuma as a generic feathered "Indian" ruler in the frontispiece image to his *Peregrinationes in Americam* of 1601, and—inevitably—Montezuma emerged during that century as the most feathered of them all. The first European-style portrait of Montezuma to be printed was by a Frenchman, André Thevet, in 1584. He gave his subject classical garb and an ambivalent stare, an ambiguity of dress and gaze that reflected the contradictions that had already become embedded in descriptions of the emperor, both in Thevet's own writings (where he is "philosophical, virtuous, misguided and even diabolical," as a recent study observed) and in the larger literature. Thevet's portrait held hints of the Monstrous, the Magnificent, and the Fearful—but also the Feathered, for in addition to feathers on his head and spear, the emperor is pointing to an elaborate feathered shield, as if to draw attention to its symbolism and his kingship.[73]

Thevet's portrait was borrowed widely for centuries, sometimes unaltered, sometimes changed to reflect different combinations of the contradictory textual depictions that such images often illustrated. In the Ogilby and Montanus version, Montezuma wears nothing but feathers, the classical toga gone, his outfit that of a warrior prince. There is little of the Fearful here, and one can imagine that English readers of Ogilby recognized something of the tragic, savage, but "Glorious Prince"—the kingly Noble Savage—that Dryden had put onstage just a few years earlier.

Another variant was the full-length and colorful painting by a Mexican artist, sent to Cosimo de' Medici in the 1690s (it still hangs in Florence, in the Medici Treasury). The painting was copied in engraved form and appeared that way in various books, including Italian editions of Solís's *History of the Conquest of Mexico* (such as the one in our Gallery). This image gives the impression of a noble, barbaric lord (hints of the Magnificent), but despite the spear he is somewhat effeminized (evoking the Fearful). Above all, he is Montezuma the Feathered, an allegory vacated of meaning so that he can represent anything or nothing. Like the disembodied feathered headdress that is the image for the "Moctezuma" station in the Mexico City subway, he is an icon, not an individual. He is the prince with a personality so contradictory that it crumbles and disappears, leaving instead the icon of Indianness, the image of a generic heathen prince—one who might, for example, be an Aztec general leading an Inca army.[74]

———

"When I was young and runnin' wild, I talked with Montezuma," began a ditty sung by British sailors in the nineteenth and early twentieth centuries (and perhaps for a century or two before that). "Now Montezuma said, says he to me, Friend Jim, I wish you'd go to sea. / And smite each person you might see, who happens to be my enemy. / And so said Montezuma, said Montezuma to me."[75] Reducing Montezuma to a generic ancient king, a single stereotype, made him a fitting topic for popular song. Just as Henry VIII's pop-song characteristic was his six wives, Montezuma's was his impotence or tragic demise as ruler.

The conquistadors liked to claim both that Montezuma willingly gave them his empire and also that they had destroyed it with remarkable rapidity—early in the 1520s Cortés wrote regularly of how he had already "conquered and settled" all of New Spain. But the destruction of the Aztecs and their emperor was actually a slow process, not just in terms of Spanish colonization (which, contra Cortés, took decades, even centuries), but in terms of the steady, widespread construction of negative and stereotypical perceptions and depictions of Aztec civilization and the personality of the ruler who welcomed the invaders that November day in 1519. Most important, the understanding of the Meeting as the Surrender by Montezuma both underpinned and was reinforced by those perceptions.[76]

The organizers of a 2009 British Museum exhibition, *Moctezuma: Aztec Ruler*, noted that "today Moctezuma is an ambivalent and little-celebrated figure," although "his name still carries a ring of familiarity." Their reference was to Mexico, but the statement surely applies more broadly too. The British sailor song suggests that the emperor needed assistance in avenging the wrong done to him by his enemies, and it is perhaps the ultimate sign of how bruised his reputation is that most people today associate Montezuma's name with a phrase that did not even originate in Mexico or Spain, but with the intestinal distress of British administrators in India and other regions of their empire. As "Montezuma's Revenge" is also the name of a video game and a roller coaster, even the original meaning of that phrase is presumably lost to many. In the interests of permitting the emperor that vengeance, therefore—and also by way of bringing us closer to a new understanding of the Meeting—we now turn to look at Montezuma with fresh eyes.[77]

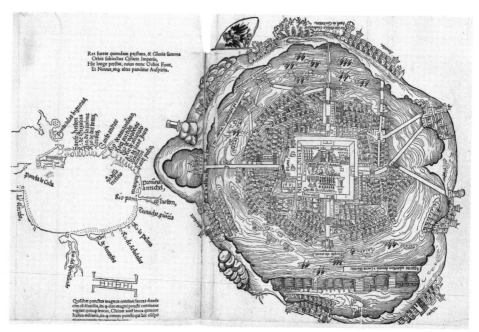

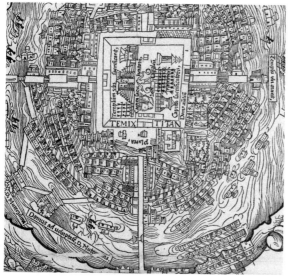

DOWNTOWN. The map of Tenochtitlan printed with the 1524 Latin edition of Cortés's Second Letter, published in Nuremberg. The labels were in Italian in the 1525 Venice edition. A few hand-colored versions also survived. The map is hybrid in style and content, a Europeanized version of a lost Aztec original. The smaller circular space on the left is the Gulf of Mexico, likewise a European rendering of a cloth original acquired from Montezuma. The larger detail has been rotated to place north at the top. The closer detail is in its original orientation, and depicts Montezuma's zoo.

———— ⚜ ————

CHAPTER 4

The Empire in His Hands

They unanimously gave him their votes, saying he was mature, virtuous, very generous, of invincible spirit, and adorned with all the virtues that could be found in a good ruler; his advice and decisions were always right, especially in matters of war, in which he had ordered and undertaken things that showed his invincible spirit.

—fray Diego Durán's account of Montezuma's election to emperor in 1502, in his *History of the Indies of New Spain*, 1581

Moteczuma found himself on the greatest throne that he or his ancestors had ever held. The whole empire was in his hands. And so, considering the great power he had, he did not believe that he could be conquered by any ruler, even the greatest in the world.

—don Fernando de Alva Ixtlilxochitl, *Thirteenth Relation*, 1614

His story is, perhaps the greatest, which was ever represented in a Poem of this nature.   —John Dryden, referring to Montezuma, in the dedication to *The Indian Emperour*, 1665[1]

I T IS ONE OF THE MOST BEAUTIFUL MAPS IN THE HISTORY OF CAR-tography. It is also one of the most significant and enigmatic—the sole surviving cartographic depiction of a unique and spectacular city on the eve of its destruction. And yet nobody knows who created the map.

Sometimes wrongly (and ludicrously) attributed to Cortés, the earliest version of the map seems to have been a long-lost print of 1522, made in Seville to accompany the first edition of the conquistador's Second Letter to the king (as we learned in Chapter 1). A Spanish engraver probably created it by combining a sketch sent from Mexico with details found in the Letter. The original Mexican cartographer would thus have been indigenous, most likely an Aztec who knew Tenochtitlan well. But the engraver in Seville had never seen the Aztec capital, or any buildings in Mexico, and his embellishments thus created a strange hybrid metropolis—as can be seen in the earliest surviving versions.[2]

The map seized the imagination of printers, writers, and readers, and it has not let go for five centuries. Known today as the Nuremberg Map, it was copied and adapted over the years, taking on a life of its own. It accompanied accounts of explorations and conquests published in French and Dutch and Italian, printed in Germany, England, Spain, and Mexico. Details were dropped and added, islands in the lakes were moved, the scale and orientation were shifted. In some versions, there was only one, circular lake. In others, the causeways were bridges and the dikes were strings of fortified towers. In one branch of variants, there were as many as eight islands on the lake, all with city buildings on them, all connected by causeways. Over time, buildings tended to look more and more European, with the center of Tenochtitlan gradually losing the detail of the original version.[3]

Yet despite this complex and fascinating story of cartographic evolution, certain key details survived in the rendering of the city. One detail in particular is, I suggest, of crucial importance to understanding Montezuma. In fact, I believe it is the key to his worldview, to grasping who he was, and why he responded the way he did to the arrival of the Spaniards. That detail was a part of the city destroyed in 1521, but remembered for centuries: Montezuma's zoo.

On the Nuremberg Map, located within the central plaza of "Temixtitan" are the usual architectural elements that appealed to the European imagination: the pyramid and "Temple where they sacrifice" (*Templum ubi sacrificant*); skull racks, with silhouetted heads still sporting hair, both labeled "Sacrificial heads" (*Capita sacrificatorum*); and a headless, vaguely androgynous statue, called a "Stone Idol" (*Idol Lapideum*). But on the edge of the stylized city in the Nuremberg Map appears another label: "Montezuma's Garden," and next to it, "Montezuma's Pleasure Palace." Adjacent to the central plaza is "Montezuma's Palace," and nearby a structure labeled "House of the Animals" (*Domus animalium;* in the Italian version, *Casa de li animali*). The map thus gives the impression of a city and its ruler that were not solely concerned with violence and death, but with pleasure and life. Is it possible that—amid the imaginative fantasy of a map evolved far from geographical and architectural reality—this depiction of the city captured something revealingly essential about the world that Montezuma controlled?[4]

The answer is a resounding yes. I believe that Montezuma's complex of palaces, gardens, and zoos is the key that unlocks a new way of looking at the emperor, his empire, and his response to the arrival of conquistadors. The key has been in front of us all along—in the Nuremberg Map, for example—but we simply have not seen its significance or appreciated how it makes sense of the Meeting. For this reason, the zoo is worth dwelling on for a moment.

The Aztec emperor's palaces, gardens, and zoos were so extensive, well ordered, intensely maintained, aesthetically impressive, and—to foreign eyes—exotic and strange, that they drew immediate interest in Europe. The very earliest letters and pamphlets that spread word of the Aztecs in European cities in the 1520s emphasized such wonders. For example, a newsletter that seems to have been written in November 1522, and printed in German in Augsburg, probably by year's end, contextualized the zoo of "Mantetunia" (Montezuma) thus:

> This Mantetunia has many large and beautiful palaces, the doors of which are as much as seventy or ninety feet wide, with such a maze of corridors that those who loiter there cannot easily find their way out and sometimes get lost. The land has an abundance of gold, pearls, and precious stones, and the palace contains an enormous treasure. There are many beautiful gardens and parks such as have never been seen before, and many strange trees and

fruits unknown to us, and a very beautiful and rare zoological garden in which there are many strange fowl and animals of this country such as tigers, lions, leopards, bears, wild boars, and lizards, as well as wild and wondrously shaped human beings from among their own people, which they watch, and they are of both sexes. All these are kept separated.[5]

The newsletter would have drawn upon letters arriving with every ship that came from the New World, such as one written in Cuba by the royal judge Alonso de Zuazo in November 1521. Zuazo had not yet seen Mexico for himself, but he saw the booty that Cortés sent back to Spain in 1520 and he clearly spoke with some of the conquistadors who were in Tenochtitlan before its fall—among them Diego de Ordaz and Alonso de Ávila. His summary of the zoo thus reflected the details that were circulating in these earliest days:

Monteuzuma [sic] had for show a house in which he had a great diversity of serpents and wild animals, which included tigers, bears, lions, wild boar, vipers, rattlesnakes, toads, frogs and many other various snakes and birds, right down to worms; and each one of these things was in its place and in cages as needed, with people assigned to give them food and all that was necessary to take care of them. He also had other people that were monstrous, such as dwarves and hunchbacks, some with one arm and others that were missing a leg, and other monstrous races [naciones] that are born as such.[6]

Zuazo also included the usual stereotypes about the Aztecs (they were all godless, cannibal sodomites who sacrificed live victims daily) and some tall tales (one province was inhabited by giants, proof of which was a massive bone that Ordaz had taken back to Spain, and another region was ruled by the "Lady of Silver"). But the details regarding the zoo more or less match those in other early reports, from the earliest (Cortés's Second Letter and Andrés de

Tapia's account) to the late-sixteenth-century accounts that blended the threads of prior accounts with indigenous community memory and with Franciscan and Dominican versions. So, did Montezuma's zoo really exist or was it a myth (to use the terms of a long-standing debate in Mexico)?[7]

Conquest history is certainly full of tall tales and long-lasting legends. This book, after all, is built upon my argument that a linchpin of that history—Montezuma's surrender—is the tallest tale of all. But the repeated reports and mentions of the imperial Aztec zoo do not smack of such invention, nor do they smell of political or religious spin. Both colonial and modern accounts certainly contain exaggeration, invention, and plenty of imagination—especially, as we shall see shortly, on the link between the zoo and the ubiquitous theme of human sacrifice. But I see no reason to question the zoo's existence. Indeed, in addition to early colonial accounts of it, there are two other relevant sources of evidence: the lists of war booty and loot, gifts, and tribute items that Cortés and other conquistadors sent back to Spain between 1519 and 1524; and the thousands of objects discovered by archaeologists buried underneath the ceremonial center of Tenochtitlan.[8]

The sum of all that evidence opens up a window onto Aztec life and Montezuma's court that is illuminating and compelling, offering an important series of steps toward a new understanding of the Meeting. I suggest we look through that window in a trio of distinct ways. The first way is to emphasize organization and categorization: how the zoos were laid out as part of the larger royal collections of flora, fauna, and other objects—what we might call the zoo-collection complex. Another perspective is to analyze acquisition, maintenance, and observation: how the zoo-collection complex was built, and the relationships between the collections and Montezuma himself, his courtiers, and those who worked in the zoos. The third way of looking at the zoo-collection complex is to think about representation and meaning: how did all the animals, birds, plants, people, and objects reflect the Aztec cosmology or view of their empire and the universe. As far as that may seem to take us from the day that

Cortés first met Montezuma, it actually sharpens our vision of that event in surprising ways.

VARIATIONS IN COLONIAL ACCOUNTS of the zoo make it hard to tell what kinds of categories the Aztecs themselves used. The Nuremberg Map suggests that the zoo-collection complex had two levels of organization: discrete palaces or compounds (simply called "houses" on the map and in Spanish accounts), within which were separate cages, rooms, or walled zones for different kinds of creatures (as mentioned by Zuazo and shown in the map). Colonial writers often made an attempt to describe the zoo-collection complex categorically, but then either allowed their imagination to get the better of them or ended the topic by lumping categories together. (Gómara, for example, divided live birds into two chapters, one of birds kept for their feathers, the other of hunting birds—but threw into the latter chapter wild cats, other animals, and deformed humans.) Ogilby, drawing upon a century and a half of such descriptions, labeled the zoo-collection complex Montezuma's "Strange Garden-houses" and identified three categories:

> The King hath in *Tenustitan* three great Structures, whose Magnificence, for Cost and rare Architecture, can hardly be parallell'd. The first is the Residence for all deform'd People: The second, an *Aviary* for all manner of Birds and Fowl, being a spacious open place, Roof'd with Nets, and surrounded with Marble Galleries. The third, being a Den for Wild Beasts, was divided into several Rooms, wherein were kept Lions, Tygers, Wolves, Foxes, and all manner of Four-footed Animals.[9]

In my own research journey through these "Strange Garden-houses" I identified seven categories of living things, and seven of nonliving objects. That classification is loosely reflected in the pages to follow, but the zoos and collections were varied and complex enough to support any number of categorizations and emphases.

We might begin with plants, organized by the Aztecs into various subcategories located in multiple gardens and palaces. As Na-huas later told Sahagún, *moxuchimiltia* ("flower gardens were laid out"), and many flowers were tended for their "delightful Variety and Fragrancy" (according to Solís). But more important, Solís and others claimed, were the herbal and medicinal gardens, whose prop-erties were studied by Montezuma's physicians and applied freely to the sick—a sort of Aztec national health-care system, which satis-fied the emperor's vain sense of obligation to take "such Care of the Health of his Vassals."[10]

Then there were reptiles. Without the glass that is customary in modern reptile houses, the Aztecs apparently used "large pots" and "jugs" or "great pitchers." There were "poisonous snakes that had in the tails something that sounded like bells," and—Díaz claimed—when "the serpents hissed, with the lions and tigers roaring, and the wolves and foxes howling, it was awful to hear and seemed like hell itself." Solís concluded that the reptile house was an "improbable" invention "of the Indians," made up "to represent the savage Dispo-sition of a Tyrant"—although he nonetheless included details on the kinds of snakes it contained, "even Crocodiles."[11]

Birds comprised a pair of categories. The Aztecs were dedicated ornithologists; they called aviaries *totocalli* ("birdhouse" in Nahuatl). Ogilby imagined a single aviary, roofed and netted with "Marble Galleries." Gómara, as we saw, stated that the Aztecs kept colorfully feathered and hunting birds separate. Solís decided some birds were kept "for their Feathers, or Singing," with "Sea-Fowl" maintained in separate saltwater or freshwater "Pools." And the Nuremberg Map shows five or six separate bird areas. So it is likely that the aviary of feathered birds was itself divided up into a series of cages and ponds, with a wide variety of birds kept for their song and for observation, but above all for their feathers—carefully harvested, considered "of great Value," and used "in their Cloaths, in Pictures, and in all their Ornaments." In addition to geese, brown herons, and white peli-cans, there were "cranes and crows, many parrots and macaws, and a different sort of large bird they say are wild pheasants." Cortés later admitted that during the siege of Tenochtitlan, he deliberately destroyed these aviaries. Having set fire to the palaces where Montezuma had hosted the invaders some eighteen months earlier, he then turned to

> others next to them which, though somewhat smaller, were very much prettier and more refined; Mutezuma had kept in them every species [*linajes*] of bird found in these parts. And although it greatly grieved me, I decided to burn them, for it grieved the enemy very much more; and they showed much grief, as did the others, their allies from the lakeside cities.[12]

Birds of prey were kept apart from other feathered creatures for obvious reasons. They included "lanners, sparrow hawks, kites, vultures, goshawks, nine or ten kinds of falcons, and many assorted eagles, among which there were fifty larger than our own golden eagles" (the artists of the Florentine Codex conveyed a similar list, sampled in our Gallery). According to fray Toribio de Benavente (who took the Nahua name Motolinía), writing not long after the zoo was destroyed, Montezuma's eagles could "really be called royal because they are extremely large"; kept in vast cages, they ate entire turkeys and were treated respectfully as if they were "lions or some other wild beast." Solís remarked that one of his sources claimed "one of these Eagles would devour a Sheep at a Meal"—which he thought an exaggeration. Sheep did not exist in Aztec Mexico, which is perhaps why the illustrator of an Italian edition of Solís's book changed the sheep to a dismayed, feathered Aztec carried off in an eagle's talons (perhaps, one might imagine, a careless zookeeper).[13]

Another category was that of those animals described above by Zuazo; in Solís's words, "Lions, Tygers, Bears, and all others of the savage Kind which New-Spain produc'd." According to Díaz, there were "tigers and two kinds of lions, one of which was a kind of wolf which here they call a jackal, and foxes and other small carnivorous animals." "In short," wrote Gómara, "there was no kind of four-footed beast that was not represented."[14]

As colonial sources tend to simply repeat the same list of wild animals, let us step sideways here into the archaeological evidence from the Great Temple project. Among the 126 (and growing) caches of objects collected and ritually buried by the Aztecs, direct zoo-related evidence has recently been found (inspiring a Mexican newspaper to run a 2014 story titled "Montezuma's Zoo Is Not a Myth"). One cache contained more than nine thousand animal bones, most of them from Mexican gray wolves. Some wolf bones had also been placed in other caches. Thus far, more than twenty individual wolves have been identified, some with entire skeletons. Not only do animal bones outnumber human bones found beneath the Great Temple precinct, but wolf remains alone rival human ones in quantity. Now an endangered subspecies of gray wolves, the Mexican wolf was native to northern Mexico in Aztec times; some, perhaps many, of the depictions of coyotes in sixteenth-century codices are now thought to be representations of this wolf, the smallest gray wolf subspecies.[15]

At least one of the wolves uncovered by archaeologists suffered from arthritis and dysplasia, and could not have survived to the age that it did unless being cared for in captivity. That fact, combined with the location of most wolf bones within or adjacent to the zoo complex, as well as references in colonial sources to the inclusion of wolves in the "Wild Beasts" section, strongly suggests that at least some of these wolves had lived in the zoos of Montezuma and his predecessors.

The remaining categories of living things in the zoo comprised human beings. One was that of deformed humans—"monstrous men and women, some crippled, others dwarfed or hunchbacked" (in Tapia's words). Motolinía claimed that the court was "served" by "dwarfs and little humpbacks" that were "intentionally made so in childhood by breaking and disjointing their bones." According to Solís, fathers were inspired to maim their children in this way because the palace of "Buffoons" and "Monsters" contained apartments where these "Errors of Nature" were given instruction and meals. Modern Mexican historians took that interpretation a step further, arguing that it was the uncharitable Spaniards who assumed Montezuma kept a palace of the deformed out of "morbid curiosity."

In fact, his motivation was "humanitarian" (one such historian asserted); the palace's purpose was "so the state could directly care for them."[16]

Women—the final category of living things—lived in the palace, or compound of houses, designated for the emperor. This is not to suggest that women in Aztec society were viewed or treated like animals, or even that Montezuma saw them as zoo creatures. Women enjoyed considerable status in Aztec culture, albeit one restricted to gender-specific roles (as was the case worldwide). But the conquistadors and Spanish chroniclers described the residential palaces of Montezuma's wives and concubines as if the women were a category of royal possession. Colonial accounts claimed that Montezuma took for himself the noblemen's daughters who most appealed to him, although this was surely more a matter of strategic alliance and political control than one of the emperor's taste; the royal practice of polygyny was so fundamental to the maintenance and structure of the empire that Aztec scholar Ross Hassig recently wrote an entire book about it (women, he argues, were "the dark matter of Aztec history"). I suggest that the identities of such women, combined with their maintenance in a discrete compound, make it useful and appropriate to consider them part of the zoo-collection complex. For our purposes, it is crucial to understand that the zoo, as conceived by the Aztecs, included human beings; people too could be collected.[17]

The Nuremberg Map labeled buildings on the edge of the city as *Domus ad uoluptase D. Muteezuma* ("The Pleasure-House of Lord Montezuma"). Claims by conquistadors that the palace contained astonishing numbers of women soon settled into the figure of a thousand, repeated for centuries with the same assurance as the invented numbers of sacrificed humans. Herrera's phrasing of it in 1601, copying from Gómara, was fairly typical: in this palace, "few men slept; but there were a thousand women; although others say there were three thousand, and that is more probable, taking into account the ladies, servant women, and slave women." Herrera also mentioned the detail, repeated by many others, of Montezuma's fecundity; in Ogilby's words, "he was likewise much given to Women, but it was only to such as were counted his Wives; of which he is said to have had no less than a hundred and fifty with Child by him at one time."[18]

HOWEVER WE CATEGORIZE the living things in Montezuma's zoo complex, it clearly contained hundreds of species of flora and fauna, and thousands of people (some as part of the collection complex, many more as workers), offering us tantalizing glimpses into life at court and in the imperial city. Those glimpses are sharpened a little more by the nonliving or material objects also collected by Montezuma—the details of which can be gleaned from colonial accounts, conquistadors' lists of loot and booty, and archaeological evidence.

Cloth and clothing is one example. Cortés claimed that Montezuma wore four outfits a day, "all new, and he never wore them again." Whether that was an exaggeration or not, the emperor certainly seems to have maintained a wardrobe that amounted to an important part of the royal collections—as evidenced by the spectacular apparel included in the first two big shipments of gifts and loot sent to Spain by Cortés.[19]

The first shipment, sent from Vera Cruz in July 1519, comprised some 180 objects, many presented to Cortés and the other captains on board one of the ships anchored offshore. This haul of treasure was entrusted to Francisco de Montejo and Alonso Hernández de Puertocarrero, who ignored Cortés's wishes and stopped in Cuba to show off the loot, before sailing on to Spain. The shipment was inventoried in Seville on November 5, so it is quite possible that on the very day of the Meeting in Tenochtitlan, high-ranking Spaniards in Seville were feasting their eyes on a sample of the kinds of clothes, featherworks, and jewelry that were in massive quantities in Montezuma's collections. (The loot, accompanied by a group of Totonac men from the Gulf coast, then toured several Spanish cities before traveling north to Brussels.)[20]

The second shipment was assembled after Tenochtitlan was captured, and sent from there in May 1522; it was actually a trio of shipments, two intended for the king, one to be distributed accord-ing to detailed instructions among thirteen churches and twenty-three church and state officials. Almost none of it reached Spain—it was captured by Jean Florin, a French corsair, to Cortés's "great chagrin"—but various inventories survived. One of them lists this war booty as comprising 116 items, almost all featherworks. Many of these must have been taken from Aztec warriors or from Monte-zuma's collections in the city. Feathers and featherworks thus make up another important category of nonliving things in the royal col-lections. They were highly valued and, by all accounts, spectacular. The feather headdresses that were part of the shipment that reached Seville in November 1519 left Oviedo breathless; "there was just so much to take in."[21]

Featherworks overlap with clothing (as many were used as such), and with another collection category, armor and weaponry. Aztec shields were often adorned with featherwork, examples of which were included in both the 1519 and 1522 treasure shipments. Con-sidering the brutal war that Spaniards waged in order to plunder Montezuma's collections, it is not surprising that Montezuma's ar-mory caught the Spanish imagination. Generations of descriptions, from Cortés on, were used by Solís to compose his long one of the manufacture, maintenance, and display of various weapons in a two-building armory. The artistry and splendor of these weapons reflected not only the "Opulency" but also the "Genius" of Monte-zuma the "Martial Prince."[22]

Aztec emperors also collected what we would classify as objects of art, and indeed hundreds, perhaps thousands, of these objects have ended up in the art musems of the modern world. Two cat-egories of such objects are works of sculpture produced by "cutters of stone, workers in green stone mosaic, carvers of wood" in the workshops within the zoo-collection complex; and metalworked jewelry and figurines. Cortés, Tapia, and Gómara all mentioned small "carved pieces" worked from precious metals, and figurines "so realistic in gold and silver that no smith in the world could have done better." The emperor's "gold and silver-smiths, and coppersmiths" were described by Sahagún, and much later Gemelli noted that he had read and heard in Mexico City that Montezuma had kept "all sorts of Birds, and Beasts, and Sea-Fish in his Salt Fish-ponds, and River-Fish in fresh Water. If any kind could not be had, he kept them in Gold, and for Grandeur." In other words, the living zoo was paralleled by a nonliving one of representations of the empire's creatures.[23]

Montezuma was also a collector of books. His library must have held many hundreds of the painted scrolls and screenfolds that were almost all destroyed in the war and during the subsequent centuries of Spanish colonial rule; their heirs were the early colonial codices. Artists called *tlacuilloque* (plural of *tlacuillo*), of whom "there was never a shortage, for the office passed from father to son and was highly esteemed," painted with a pictographic writing system. As Tovar later explained to a fellow Jesuit, Aztec artists "had figures and hieroglyphs with which they painted" and could thus "draw whatever they wished." Díaz called them "very skillful [*sublimados*] painters." When the Spaniards arrived on the Gulf coast in 1519, a group of *tlacuilloque* quickly painted them and their possessions in scrolls destined for Tenochtitlan (as depicted in one of the frames in our Gallery's "Picturing the War").

The library there also included Aztec histories, structured as annals. These year-by-year sequences of events give an impression of objectivity, of lists of simple facts, although early Aztec history was primarily origin and migration mythology, while later Aztec history was highly partisan and political, charting the glorious rise of the empire. Montezuma's library ("a great house for all his books") also included tribute lists detailing the items each subject city and province of the empire owed to the emperor; again, some of these were created or re-created in the early colonial period, giving us some sense of what the lost library looked like.[24]

Two of the most important tribute lists, known to us as the Codex Mendoza and the Matrícula de Tributos, detailed the feathers, precious stones and metals, jaguar skins, and sacks of cacao delivered by each province—and also shells, mostly unworked

Spondylus shells from Cihuatlan, on the empire's Pacific coast. The inclusion of shells on tribute lists and in caches of offerings around the Great Temple is evidence that they formed a part of the royal collection, both unworked and as carved artworks. In one group of eleven caches of offerings, buried during the construction of an expansion of the Great Temple in the 1470s, shells and other items from the sea (such as coral and bones of fish or marine animals) were layered to represent the cosmological layers of the under-world. The connection of these objects to water also linked them to Tlaloc, the deity of rain and fertility to whom the Great Temple was partially dedicated (Tlaloc effigies were also in this same group of caches). The conquistadors and chroniclers ignored or dismissed shells and related objects (they were of little value to Spaniards). But they were of great symbolic value to the Aztecs, reflecting the belief that Montezuma ruled over sea as well as land, and that his zoo should therefore include objects and creatures that came from those waters.[25]

I COULD CONTINUE CLASSIFYING, listing, and detailing for many pages the innumerable things collected by Montezuma, but the point is made: he was a collector. More than that, he was a collector imperial and extraordinaire, one of the great collectors of human history; collecting was at the very heart of his identity as emperor. So how did he do it? How was the zoo-collection complex built and maintained, and what was its relationship to the people of the city surrounding it?

"It is true that I have silver, gold, feathers, weapons, and other objects and riches in the treasure of my parents and grandparents," Montezuma told Cortés, "kept from a long time ago until the pres-ent, as is the custom among kings." This statement is most likely apocryphal (it comes from Gómara, and he and Cortés tended to put words into the Aztec emperor's mouth, words designed to appeal to their own emperor, Carlos). But the implication that the royal col-lection had roots going back into the fifteenth century and earlier is surely accurate, supported by the layers of buried objects discovered around the Great Temple. Montezuma neither created his zoo-collection from scratch nor invented the concept. He both inherited it from his ancestors and also competed with the king (*tlahtoani*) of Tetzcoco across the lake; Nezahualcoyotl, who ruled an important city-state but was subordinate to Montezuma, maintained his own zoo-collection complex (according to his descendants).[26]

Like any collection, then, the royal Aztec one must have started small and gradually grown; like the empire itself—of which it was a product and reflection—the collection contained a growth dynamic, inherited by Montezuma along with the animals and objects. Art historian Amara Solari has identified seven mechanisms of procurement, loosely copied here (using groups of seven is our invention; the Aztecs would have preferred fours or eights). Foremost among these mechanisms were the spoils of war (including religious statues or objects taken from the temples of defeated towns), and the wide variety of animals, birds, pelts, feathers, clothing, precious stones, and other objects brought to Tenochtitlan four times a year as tribute payments from subject towns. Tribute's purpose was to show the magnificence and authority of the Aztec nation, claimed Durán, so subject peoples were awed by "the grandeur" of the Aztecs, by "the ease with which they did what they wanted." Tribute proved to the people that the Aztecs were the lords of creation, and Montezuma was like "the sun, warming you with his heat and fire, the most excellent Lord of Created Things."[27]

Merchants and ambassadors also brought in items through two ways: diplomatic exchange and commercial trade. The empire's long-distance traders, called *pochteca*, were a large and prestigious group in Aztec society. They plied an extensive network of trade routes that had evolved centuries before the Spanish invasion and which survived for centuries after it. The *pochteca* traded for themselves, and for the emperor and his court, thus supplying both the massive markets in the capital and the royal zoo-collection. Merchants also acted as, or accompanied, ambassadors, as Sahagún detailed in his *Historia* (with a whole book of the Florentine Codex devoted to the *pochteca*). The famous shipboard exchange of 1519, mentioned earlier, was an example of a long-standing tradition of diplomatic gift giving in Mexico.[28]

Other mechanisms of acquisition featured a more direct involvement by Montezuma. Specialized craft manufacturing was maintained in the city, some of it apparently within the palace complex itself, and a portion of the production went straight into the emperor's collections. Smaller collections within the empire were also subject to royal requisition; for example, Durán tells a story of the requisition by the first Montezuma of all the plants from a garden in Cuetlaxtla, on the Gulf coast, replanted in the royal Aztec nursery at Huaxtepec, gardens that Díaz called "the best that I have ever seen in all my life." Finally, the whimsy of the emperor played a role, for he collected whatever "caught his fancy." The phrase is by Motolinía, who claimed that,

> a trustworthy Spaniard, when in the presence of Moteuczoma, saw a sparrow hawk that was flying in the air catch his fancy. To show off his greatness in the presence of the Spaniard, Moteuczoma gave orders that the hawk be brought to him; and so great was the zeal and the numbers of those who went after it that the wild hawk was caught and delivered to him.

Or he hunted birds himself; Nahua informants told Sahagún that one of the ways that Aztec emperors "amused themselves" was to "hunt birds with a bird-net [*tlatlapechmatlauia*]."[29]

Once acquired, all the many categories of living and nonliving things were placed in their corresponding locations in the zoo-collection complex; some would remain there, others would become interred as sacred offerings (from the beautifully crafted ceremonial knives to the skeletons of wolves uncovered centuries later). Colonial accounts and archaeological evidence support the Nuremberg Map's impression that the zoo-collection complex was arranged adjacent to and surrounding the city's ceremonial center (with only the botanical gardens located off the island on the lakeshore). Parts of the collection were probably housed within Montezuma's palace complex, with the animal zoos immediately to the east, and the aviaries, armory, and library adjacent to the west. According to Tapia and Gómara, "gold plates and bars, jewels, and carved pieces," as well as "gold and silver and green stones" were kept in rooms that Montezuma accessed through the aviaries.[30]

On the one hand, therefore, the zoo-collection was a network of elite spaces, belonging exclusively to Montezuma and his family, located in a city heart that was dedicated to religious ceremony, political rule, and royal life. Montezuma was, according to Cortés, particularly keen on bird-watching; some aviaries and zoo patios supposedly had galleries or "Apartments capable of receiving [the emperor] and his whole Court," where, for example, they could observe the birds of prey and enjoy "the Diversion of Hawking."[31]

On the other hand, it took hundreds, if not thousands, of specialists and workers to build and maintain theses spaces, create the crafted artifacts, and take care of the animals. The aviaries and animal cages were extensive and sufficiently well designed ("big cages made of very thick timbers very well cut and put together") to inspire specific comment in the colonial sources, where note was also made of the staff. The Nahuatl term for zookeepers was *tequanpixque,* and according to Sahagún's informants they were numerous. Cortés claimed the aviaries alone "gave Employment to above Three Hundred Men, skilful in the Knowledge of their Diseases."[32]

THIS BRINGS US TO our final way of looking at the zoo-collection complex: How did all the animals, birds, plants, people, and objects reflect the Aztec cosmology or view of their empire and the universe? What did the zoo mean?

The conquistadors and other Spaniards had a trio of relatively simple answers to that question. Primarily, the zoo-collection complex in its totality meant wealth; it confirmed that the empire of the Aztecs could make its invaders and colonists prosperous. That perspective was reflected in how the collection was described by Spaniards, with an emphasis on precious metals (which, unlike stone figurines or feathered shields, had an immediate and fungible value in Europe), and often as part of a description of markets and market goods. Put together, the great markets and the massive zoo-collection complex were evidence not just of the richness of the land, but of well-oiled mechanisms for concentrating that wealth in a capital city—an ideal basis for a colony.[33]

Another Spanish explanation was that the zoo, in particular the wild animals and reptiles, was just further evidence of Aztec satanic barbarity—because the zoo could be tied to the Aztec stereotype of human sacrifice and cannibalism. Early colonial assertions that the animals were fed human flesh were few, but Díaz echoed Gómara's comment on the hellish noise of the zoo, adding details on the diet of "bodies of sacrificed Indians." Like so many "facts" about the Aztecs, this detail was passed on across the centuries, so that by the nineteenth it had evolved into a portrait of the zoo whose wonder was offset by the terrible truth that "the snakes and beasts" were fed with "the flesh of men sacrificed," and that the hissing, howling, and yelling of the animals made the zoo seem like "a dungeon of hell and dwelling place of the devil"—which "it was indeed," as another building attached to the zoo complex was an ornate "chapel" in which, at night, "the devil appeared unto" Montezuma. The detail of the devil has disappeared from discussion of the Aztecs, but the man-eating zoo animals linger on.[34]

A third Spanish explanation for the zoo-collection complex was that its splendor and organization were a reflection of Montezuma's grandeur. In other words, it was "the custom among kings" (as Gómara noted); or (as Solís put it), the zoo was "a Custom established from all Antiquity, by the Number of Wild Beasts any Prince had in his Possession, to make an estimate of the Grandeur of the Possessor." This explanation comes very close to what I think the zoo-collection was really about. But the history of this perspective also contains a twist, one that is fascinating, ironic, and worth a brief digression. For while medieval European kings kept menageries of hunting animals and birds of prey, and maintained armories and treasuries, it was not in fact their custom to develop massive zoos and collections—that is, until *after* Montezuma's zoo-collection was discovered and plundered, and objects from it and descriptions of it circulated around Europe.[35]

Medieval European princes and bishops had maintained treasuries of holy relics, which "served as signs of accrued sacral authority" (similar to the function of royal Aztec collections). But starting in the second quarter of the sixteenth century, such collecting practices shifted to include material objects, more secular than sacred, that represented the outside world. This new culture of collection was part of a larger European cultural development; it spread through all ranks of society where it was affordable, and the idea and popularity of *Kunstkammern* and *Wunderkammern* (cabinets of curiosities and wonder) would lead eventually to galleries and museums. Explanations include religious changes (the Protestant Reformation and the questioning of the sacred status of relics) and the rise of European overseas empires.[36]

But an additional factor, usually overlooked, is crucially and ironically important: the cultural impact of those shiploads of objects—diplomatic gifts, war booty, and loot from Montezuma's palaces—sent to Spain and to other parts of the Hapsburg domain (including the Spanish Netherlands, parts of Italy, and Austria). The shift in royal collecting practices in sixteenth-century Europe was thereby influenced by the discovery of royal Aztec collections and their partial appropriation by Carlos V. Beginning in the 1520s, the Hapsburg collections developed to reflect the empire that the royal family was acquiring—just as Montezuma's collection had reflected *his* empire—and even featured some of the exact same objects.

There was even a further twist: among the chests of objects sent throughout the 1520s (and Cortés alone dispatched at least seven shipments between 1522 and 1529), items taken from Montezuma's collections and elsewhere in Mexico were mixed in with objects commissioned by Spaniards and created by indigenous craftsmen. For example, Cortés claimed that during his months in Tenochtitlan with Montezuma, he "drew" various "things" (such as jewelry, crucifixes, bowls) that the emperor then "had made in gold," and which were intended for Carlos as part of the Royal Fifth (the 20 percent tax owed to the king on everything of value acquired during a conquest campaign). Even before the Cortés expedition reached Mexico, thousands of Spanish objects had entered the Aztec Empire as a result of gift exchanges and trading by Grijalva and others. Some must have gone into Montezuma's collection, in turn inspiring the objects that went back to Spaniards; Gómara and Las Casas claimed that the gifts given to Cortés by Montezuma's ambassadors in 1519 had originally been prepared for Grijalva. In other words, from the earliest moments of contact, the material cultures of the Spaniards and Aztecs had begun to influence each other—one dimension of which was the seeding of early modern European collection culture by the concept and objects of Montezuma's zoo-collection complex.[37]

The link between Montezuma's zoo and the development of zoos in Europe was less immediate and more tenuous. This was partly because the zoo and its living occupants were deliberately destroyed in 1521, and partly because its remnants could not easily be shipped to Europe (unlike nonliving looted objects from the collection); the conquistadors tried to ship zoo animals, but "many died" (as Cortés admitted). Descriptions of the zoo became shorter and less frequent over the centuries, while it was included less and less frequently in maps of Tenochtitlan. Although there were exceptions (such as the Ramusio Map), the general trend over the early modern centuries was for the zoo to be vaguely depicted but not labeled (as in a 1564 French version), then to be folded into the gardens (as in a 1580 Italian one or a 1634 print made in Frankfurt), and then eclipsed altogether (as in a 1754 image that was subsequently reproduced often). Chorographs, or slightly elevated views, of Tenochtitlan included in early modern books tended to identify "the Pleasure House and Garden," but not the zoo. Even in the late twentieth century, when Aztec studies exploded as a field, the zoo and aviaries were not given archaeological attention (their potential for illuminating the Aztec past is far less than that of the Great Temple, hardly justifying the destruction of early colonial churches and other buildings). The only book written about Montezuma's zoo is a children's book.[38]

Montezuma's zoo was thus an astonishing novelty to foreign observers of the sixteenth century because they had no frame of reference with which to understand its purpose and meaning. There was nothing like it in Europe, and there would not be for centuries. As Romerovargas Iturbide observed, by "ordering the creation of zoological parks three centuries before Darwin," Montezuma seemed to modern observers far ahead of his time. In fact, as with the development of nonliving collections, the Aztec zoo complex was so ahead of the development of modern zoos as to suggest it may have acted as a foundational precedent. Descriptions of it surely influenced the development of royal menageries in the early modern Europe—the most famous of which was incorporated into Louis XIV's palace and garden complex at Versailles. Of course, the Aztec genesis of the modern zoo was soon forgotten; the concept became seen as a European invention. Those courtly menageries evolved in the eighteenth century into a handful of public, urban zoos, the earliest of which was in Vienna (from 1752). Zoos then opened across European capitals in the early nineteenth century (starting in Paris in 1793), spreading to North America with the founding in 1859 of the Philadelphia Zoo (which labels itself "America's First Zoo," with nary a nod to Montezuma). The concept eventually returned to Mexico City with the opening of the zoo in Chapultepec in 1924.[39]

In 1527, Cortés sent his father a tiger. The cat, probably an ocelot, came with a letter, which began:

> Sir: here in my house, there has grown up since it was very little a tiger [*un tigre*], and it has turned out to be the most handsome animal that has ever been seen, for in addition to being very pretty it is very tame and walks freely about the house and eats at the table whatever it is given; and it therefore seems to me that it could go on the ship very safely and will escape the fate of so many that have thus died. I implore Your Mercy to give it to His Majesty, for in truth it is booty to be gifted.[40]

What are we to make of this nugget of historical detail? Is it no more than a curiosity? Historians have certainly made nothing of it, although the letter survives in the Spanish archives, and has even been published.

I suggest that the tale of Cortés's tiger is in fact very meaningful, that its significance lies in its connection to empire. But while the more obvious connection, that of European colonialist plundering, is interesting, I think the link back to Aztec animal collecting is more important. Cortés kept a tiger because Montezuma had kept tigers; he wanted it to be given to Emperor Carlos because the Aztec emperor had acquired such animals as symbols of his power and majesty. That ocean-bound ocelot thus takes us to the very *meaning* of Montezuma's zoo-collection. For the zoo was a stunning statement about empire.

The incorporation of local and foreign objects, of things living and crafted from across the empire and beyond, underpinned the Aztec understanding of the world, their empire, and the man who ruled it. The zoo-collection complex allowed Montezuma to develop and maintain "an image of himself, and the Aztec rulers who preceded him, as semi-divine" (in Solari's words). Natural objects represented and reflected the geographical and ecological scope of the empire, crafted objects its political scope. Aztec methods of collection, organization, and categorization—as well as their completist impulse (Alva Ixtlilxochitl and other chroniclers emphasized how "there was not lacking" in the zoos a single species)—revealed an ambitious desire to know about and control the world.[41]

Thus through his zoo-collection complex, Montezuma could attain universal knowledge, the ultimate acquisition. That made him unique among his subjects, so much so as to connect him directly to the gods; for only the creator deities and the emperor who ruled their creations could have universal knowledge. It was therefore imperative that Montezuma collect the Spanish newcomers in order to *know* them. Their arrival on the edges of his empire made his universal knowledge incomplete. By acquiring them—not surrendering to them or slaughtering them—he was able to study and understand them, thereby restoring the wholeness and universality of his imperial knowledge.

Montezuma's zoo-collection complex legitimized "his placement at the apex of the Aztec social hierarchy and at the center of the known world." The emperor's physical presence in the heart of Tenochtitlan was highly symbolic. The physical epicenter of the known world, the world Montezuma knew and ruled, was the Great Temple. It represented the world vertically: the massive pyramid embodied the earth, the twin temples at its top embodied the heavens; the base, and the layers of sacred offerings below it, embodied the underworld. But the Great Temple was also the center of the world in horizontal terms: imagine its pyramid as the entry point of a stone landing in a pond (or, to use the metaphor from Aztec mythology, the spot where an eagle with a serpent in its mouth landed on a cactus); the first ripple in the pond is Tenochtitlan's center, with its ceremonial precinct, its temples and palaces and zoos; the next ripple is the island-city itself; the next is the Basin of Mexico, then the empire of the Aztecs, then the rest of Mesoamerica, bounded by seas.[42]

Montezuma was able to look down upon his city, his world center, from a sacred place—literally. A short distance to the west of the island-capital, across a causeway and on a gentle hill overlooking the lake, was Chapultepec (where today's zoo is). Montezuma had inherited a palace complex at Chapultepec, one with elaborate gardens, its own zoo and aviary, and bathing pools, all centered on a spring, which for almost a century had provided Tenochtitlan with fresh water via a twin-channel aqueduct. Montezuma not only liked to spend time at Chapultepec, but he seems to have expanded the entire complex considerably, including a restoration of the aqueduct in 1507. Then in 1519—when conquistadors had already set foot in his empire—he made his presence on the hillside permanent. There he had a portrait of himself carved into the rock, more than six feet tall, with a view of Tenochtitlan and the imperial heartland. By facing the rising sun and standing beside the source of fresh water, the stone Montezuma was "conceptually related" to the Great Temple, with its twin patron deities of the sun and rain. By fixing himself into the rock near his predecessors, at least four of whom (including his namesake, the first Montezuma) were also portrayed on the hillside, Montezuma laid claim to a permanent dynastic legitimacy.[43]

Astonishingly, although severely damaged, the portrait survives. It is important for that reason alone, and because "it is, perhaps, the last Aztec monument." But it is also important for what it tells us about the emperor, his self-image and the image he projected onto his people. His name glyph alone—a deceptively simple-looking cluster of pictorial elements—conveys a highly complex set of metaphors. The glyph conveyed both the name of Montezuma and his status as supreme ruler, as central to the world as the sun itself. In the Chapultepec carving, as in most surviving stone carvings of the name glyph, a speech scroll is included—evoking both his imperial office of *tlahtoani* (recall that the term literally meant "speaker"), and his fame, carried across the empire as his name was spoken. At Chapultepec, as in Tenochtitlan, the emperor conveyed to his subjects his status as an individual man of prowess, as an elite representative of his lineage, and as the epitome of kingship—and all this after the Spanish invaders had already set foot in his empire.[44]

Montezuma was the first Aztec king to turn his name glyph into "an icon of divine kingship," and the glyph thus literally symbolized his efforts to elevate his status and office to new levels of cosmic significance. That ambitious political promotionalism in turn reflected his record as ruler; when the Chapultepec portrait was carved, he was seventeen years into his reign, aged fifty-two, a man who was allegedly just months away from surrendering his city and empire to a small force of foreigners. Yet the historical sources on Montezuma's reign, while they are sparse and distorted by the cultural filters of the colonial period, overwhelmingly support the impression given by that stone portrait, making the later image of Montezuma the capitulating coward even more paradoxical and unbelievable.[45]

Montezuma was directly descended from Acamapichtli, the dynastic founder, who became *tlahtoani* in the 1360s. According to some early colonial sources, that title became elevated to *huey tlah-*

toani ("great speaker"), beginning with the fourth ruler, Itzcoatl (historians often treat the two titles as "king" and "emperor," as I have done here). The *huey tlahtoani* was chosen from among the relatives of the last ruler by a council of Aztec noblemen and members of the royal family, including the rulers of Tlacopan and Tetzcoco (the junior partners in the empire's Triple Alliance). In practice, the succession tended to go to brothers before sons, as each generational cohort held onto power for as long as possible: for example, Montezuma's father and two uncles had ruled before him, and when he was killed, it was his brother Cuitlahua who succeeded him. In other words, the throne did not automatically pass to the eldest son, as it did in European monarchies; a prince had to prove himself before being chosen, and (according to Durán), Montezuma, already thirty-five, was selected "for his great valor and excellent deeds."[46]

Accounts of Montezuma's accession and coronation were, of course, all written in the Spanish colonial period, so we cannot be sure which details were invented or distorted. That said, Montezuma was apparently unanimously selected to succeed his uncle in 1502. It is possible that he took the name *Moteuctzoma*, "Angry Lord," at his succession. But more likely he renamed his great-grandfather Ilhuicamina as Moteuctzoma, thereby further cementing his legitimacy. A small investiture ceremony took place immediately, with the four-day public coronation festival not held until the following summer, after the war season. That gave Montezuma a chance to lead a campaign and return with prisoners of war, to be executed with due ceremony during the coronation. A stone was carved on all six sides to commemorate the event; displayed in the plaza, the stone connected that day to the day the earth was created, signaling Montezuma's sacred title to rule the world.[47]

Of particular significance to the events at the end of his reign, Montezuma also invited the rulers of eight city-states not yet paying him tribute to attend the coronation (some, like Cholollan, he later conquered; others, like Tlaxcallan, were still independent in 1519). Supposedly this was unprecedented; in any case, they all attended, were showered with gifts, shown lavish hospitality, given hallucinogenic mushrooms during the execution of prisoners, and danced in disguise at the height of the festivities in the city center. If the anecdote is at all true, it suggests that the new emperor understood well how power could more effectively be exercised through diplomacy combined with the implied threat of violence, rather than simply through brute force. (The conquistadors who were shown similar hospitality in the city in 1519 and 1520 would surely have heard the story, if not from their hosts then from the Tlaxcalteca officials who accompanied them. Not surprisingly, and as we shall see in the next chapter, Spaniards reacted rather differently to Montezuma's message.)[48]

Of the two uncles of Montezuma who had ruled as emperor before him, the first was Tizoc. Tizoc's reign of only six years was cut short by an allegedly unnatural death (in 1486); according to colonial sources, his disinterest in military campaigns and imperial expansion led to his regicide by poisoning. Whether this story is accurate or not, it shows that the Aztec understanding of kingship in the sixteenth century included the notion that a *tlahtoani* might prove to be weak and lacking in martial spirit; furthermore, such a ruler could be removed from office. Yet, despite the Tizoc precedent, and despite the derogatory interpretation of Montezuma's response to the Spanish invasion, no colonial sources depict Montezuma as Tizoc-like before 1519. On the contrary, not only do colonial sources almost uniformly emphasize Montezuma's personal bravery in military campaigns, but some even exaggerated his hawkish stature (claiming, for example, that under him the Aztecs campaigned as far away as Nicaragua).[49]

During his seventeen years as *huey tlahtoani*, Montezuma faced his share of natural disasters and man-made threats to his empire. There were famines three years, earthquakes in three others, and one brutal snow-filled winter. Roughly a third of his military campaigns were against towns or provinces rebelling against Aztec tribute demands. Yet the fact remains that not only did he survive in office, but the empire persisted and continued to expand. Early colonial documents like the Codex Mendoza and the related Matrícula de

Tributos list impressive numbers of city-states defeated and brought into the empire. Tlaxcallan remained autonomous, but Montezuma shrank its territory, cutting its access to the coast, surrounding it with Aztec client states, "tightening the noose." Meanwhile, the dominance of Tenochtitlan within the Triple Alliance increased, as Tetzcoco became more markedly a junior partner, a distinct second, with Tlacopan a distant third (with implications for the course of the war in 1520–21, as we shall see).[50]

Montezuma thus proved himself worthy of the association with his warlike namesake great-grandfather. His record of imperial expansion substantiated his image on public monuments and in public rituals. The elaborate claim to a supreme and mystified rulership, promoted by his name glyph, was not a hollow one. His devotion to acquiring living things, objects, and knowledge did not hinder his ability to acquire territory and tribute, but in fact helped it. He was not a bookish zookeeper, timid and retiring, but a fearless master collector, a bold zoological imperialist. In other words, this emperor was clothed.[51]

We know little of what Montezuma was thinking and doing in Tenochtitlan in the six months leading up to the Meeting. But his state of mind and his intentions were understandably the subject of intense speculation among the conquistadors as they marched closer to the emperor's capital city. After the war, such speculations became tainted by the triumph of the Meeting-as-Surrender narrative and by the scapegoating of Montezuma. His inscrutable behavior during the course of 1519 thus became interpreted (and even invented) much later as further evidence of his mental collapse. By the late sixteenth century, the Montezuma of these months had become firmly established as vacillating, paralyzed, panic-stricken, and fatally weakened by his superstitious belief that a series of omens foretold the end of his empire—and that Cortés-as-Quetzalcoatl was the agent of that doom.[52]

Yet despite that later reinterpretation of Montezuma's behavior to fit the story of the Surrender, one can still see in conquistador accounts some echoes of Spanish confusion regarding his strategy. For example, Aguilar took the standard line that because the Spaniards had fought the Tlaxcalteca until they agreed to an alliance, Montezuma "grew fearful and dismayed to think that the captain [Cortés] was on the way to his great city." The series of gift-bearing embassies that Montezuma sent to meet the advancing conquistador company was thus interpreted as attempts to bribe the Spaniards into turning around (illustrated in the Gallery's "Picturing the War"). This nonsensical interpretation of Montezuma's gifts by Aguilar, Cortés, and others has been repeated into the present day, even though the opposite conclusion—that the emperor sought peacefully to lure the foreigners into his city—is far more logical. Aguilar himself seemed to realize that such an interpretation did not quite add up, noting too—without being able to explain it—that "Montezuma appeared to have stationed a great army along the way, although we only heard report of it and never saw it."[53]

Tapia likewise claimed that such an army was shadowing them, adding that it surely could have "quickly crushed" the invaders and "put an end to the war." Tapia added, seeming to refer both to the pre-invasion Tlaxcalteca and to the Spanish-Tlaxcalteca invasion:

> I asked Montezuma and some of his captains why, having these enemies surrounded, they did not finish them off in a day; and they answered: "Well, we could easily do so. But then we would have nowhere to train our young men, except far from here; and we also always wish to have people at hand to sacrifice to our gods."[54]

Even if we take this conversation between Tapia and Montezuma with a grain of salt, it suggests that at the time of the war, the Spaniards were aware that the emperor was *not* seized by fear and inaction, but in fact was in control and had a strategy. The conversation also suggests that Montezuma's strategy was not clear to the Spaniards as they approached the city, provoking concern and speculation; and that it nonetheless seemed likely that the company was able to march into Tenochtitlan solely because Montezuma had permitted it.

Indeed, Montezuma's mastery of the situation becomes much clearer once we stop trying to cram the vast square peg of evidence on his strategy into the tiny round hole of the Meeting-as-Surrender. Ross Hassig has persuasively argued that Montezuma chose not to attack the Spaniards in 1519 because he wished to learn more about them before committing to outright war, and because he needed to be sure of his control over subject city-states in the eastern region of the empire, which had been destabilized by the invasion. Furthermore, the labor demands of harvest restricted the war season to December through April; thus the force of warriors shadowing the invaders in the autumn of 1519, if it existed at all, was most likely a modest one, not yet the "great army" of Aguilar's comment.[55]

I agree with Hassig's analysis, which I think makes even more sense when viewed in the context of Montezuma's collection mentality. Like a cat toying with a mouse, for months the emperor was watching the conquistadors, testing them, playing with them, studying them. Even before he could examine them in person, he was gathering accounts and images of them. He was fascinated by these *Caxtillan tlaca*, these *Caxtilteca* ("people from Castile"). His goal was neither to destroy nor drive the newcomers away, but to confuse, weaken, and draw them in—so they could be collected. Montezuma was not afraid of the Spaniards; he was hunting them.[56]

In the short run, the strategy worked. The emperor peacefully acquired these strange new people, and housed them in buildings that were adjacent to the royal zoo-collection complex, effectively incorporating them into his collections. But the Caxtilteca could not be contained for long as novelties, as new subjects of study, in the zoo-collection complex; they were too numerous, too dangerous, too savage (let alone accompanied by a contingent of Tlaxcalteca warriors). So what was Montezuma's long-term plan?

We shall never know for sure, although the various accounts of the ensuing months in Tenochtitlan—the 235 days from the Meeting to Montezuma's death—suggest several possibilities. We shall come to those in a subsequent chapter, but for now let us consider just one possibility, and propose a tantalizing theory rooted in the seasonal cycles of the life, death, and celebration in the city.

Aztec life—like daily life for sixteenth-century Spaniards and indeed for us today—was marked by a sequence of months, each with its particular activities and holidays, repeated annually. There were eighteen months, each of twenty days, in the Aztec calendar. This 360-day cycle was called the *xihuitl* ("year" in Nahuatl), leaving five days, called the *nemontemi*, to round out the solar year. Each month had its own public festival. For example, the festival and month of Ochpaniztli ("Sweeping of the road" or "Sweeping the way") was dedicated to a goddess of sexuality and fertility; celebrants wore outfits and wielded implements associated with the goddess, most notably a broom, a symbol of cleaning and cleansing.

The Meeting and the initial Spanish entry into Tenochtitlan took place near the end of Quecholli ("Macaw" or "Precious Feather," the hunting god's month). The month that followed, the first full month the conquistadors witnessed in the life of the city, was Panquetza-liztli ("Raising of flags" or banners). Its festival was a major event each year, dedicated to Huitzilopochtli. It was also the last of the year's four tribute months, when the subject towns and provinces of the empire delivered food, luxury goods, and other tribute items to the capital city. The other tribute months were Ochpaniztli (in the autumn) and Etzalqualiztli (in early summer), but the first tribute month of each year was Tlacaxipehualiztli ("Flaying of men"), whose festival is, I propose, of great significance to our story.[57]

It is tempting to imagine that Montezuma and his court were conscious of the fact that, as the Caxtilteca settled into their quarters in the city, the month dedicated to hunting was drawing to a close. The festival of Quecholli featured various ritual deer hunts, bringing venison into the city and including the execution of a warrior dressed like a deer. Yet here were men who had been drawn into the city through an elaborate kind of hunt, and who brought with them huge deer that could be ridden (the Aztecs and other Nahuas called horses "people-bearing deer," *in mamaça in temamani*). Likewise, it was surely not lost on the city's rulers and warriors that, when the warfare season began that December, they already had foreign warriors in their city—armed guests who quickly began to wear out their welcome. Indeed, as the months passed and Tlacaxipehualiztli approached (it fell around March in our calendar), it must have occurred to the Aztecs that their Spanish guests might have a special role to play in the festival, one that may well have been in the minds of Montezuma and his more hawkish courtiers since the previous Quecholli. For Tlacaxipehualiztli marked the high point of war season, celebrating Aztec martial prowess by turning Tenochtitlan into a ritual, theatrical battlefield—complete with real enemy warriors and a guaranteed Aztec victory.[58]

Each year, for forty days spanning Tlacaxipehualiztli and the month before it, warriors captured in imperial campaigns were brought into the city. There they gave a series of ritual, public performances—including dancing with the Aztec warriors who had captured them—and eventually, with their hair shorn, bodies painted in red stripes, and given new names, they were executed. This was not the indiscriminate slaughter of war prisoners that sometimes happened on European battlefields (Agincourt comes to mind), but a ritualized reenactment of victory intended to show respect for the defeated—and to spiritually transform them into divine offerings.

At one point (at the month's end, in some accounts), a captive and his captor drank pulque together in the plaza (pulque, made by fermenting agave sap, is still drunk in Mexico today), before giving a gladiatorial performance. The captive won his freedom if he defeated his captor and then three other warriors in succession, but he alone was tied by his ankle or waist to a stone platform, given a club decorated with feathers to fend off clubs embedded with razor-sharp obsidian blades. In the battles of Tlacaxipehualiztli, the Aztecs always won.

Executions took the form of the swift removal of the heart, after which the bodies were taken to local temples around the city and skinned (the "flaying" or *xipehua* of Tlacaxipehualiztli). Those who had captured the executed warriors then wore their skins, going door-to-door to show off their achievement, engaging in mock battles with other warriors (with turkeys as prizes), dancing in the central plaza, receiving gifts and public praise from Montezuma in front of his palace.

The skin-wearing ritual turned captor and captive into one, both dubbed *xipe* ("flayed one"; the festival's god was Xipe Totec, "Our Flayed Lord"). The captor acquired his captive's life essence or energy in this celebration of individual warrior courage and prowess. When the flayed skin rotted and was then removed at the festival's end, timed with the appearance of spring flowers, the captor ritually bathed, emerging—like a fresh ear of corn from its dried-out husk—as a renewed and celebrated warrior of status.[59]

There is no direct evidence that Montezuma or other ruling Aztec nobles planned or hoped to turn their Spanish guests into involuntary participants in the "flaying of men" festival. But it seems inconceivable that it did not occur to them as a possible—even serendipitous, appropriate, and divinely arranged—solution to the Spanish problem. If there had been such hopes, the deterioration of diplomatic relations near the end of the 235 days following the Meeting would have dashed them, but only in terms of the timing of the attack, capture, and execution. For in the end, it was in June, during Etzalqualiztli, when Aztec warriors killed hundreds of Spaniards in the city, some half of the invading force, executing scores of them at the top of the Great Temple pyramid.

By then Montezuma—speaker, emperor, collector—was dead. He did not live to see the rest of his collections plundered, his zoos burned to the ground, his city buried like a vast sacred offering. Like his jaguars, wolves, and ocelots, Montezuma's Spaniards could not be tamed. They had imprisoned their zookeeper, humiliated and discarded him, leaving posterity to do him the greatest violence of all—the assassination of his character, transforming the great collector into a cowardly captive.

PART III

What? Are they really planning
To keep the people away
From plundering the Indies?

—Satan, referring to Saints Francis and Dominic,
in Carvajal's *Complaint of the Indians in the Court of Death*, 1557

Great Hercules *of old, did mighty things*
And overcame at last his sufferings.
But Ferdinando *second unto none,*
By nobler Acts has Hercules *out-done.*
Cortez *a greater Traveller then He*
Though not so strong, has compass'd Land and Sea.
Made the Antipodes *obey his* Nod;
And what is more, acknowledg one true God.

—English edition of Thevet's
"Life of Ferdinand Cortez," 1676

He came dancing across the water
Cortez, Cortez
What a killer

—Neil Young, "Cortez the Killer," 1975[1]

HOW CONQUISTADORS DISCOVER. The frontispiece to a 1697 French edition of Las Casas's *Very Brief Account of the Destruction of the Indies*, retitled *La Découverte des Indes Occidentales par Les Espagnols* ("The Discovery of the West Indies by the Spaniards"). The "discovery" is symbolized by Spaniards carrying off the wealth of the land, using forced indigenous labor: in the distant background, women are grabbed and men beaten on the ground; in the foreground, a proprietorial Cortés meets a passive Montezuma—an example of how, even in a context critical of conquistador practices, the Meeting was presented as surrender and submission.

CHAPTER 5

The Greatest Enterprises

Oh ingenious man, excelling all others in spirit, and born only for the greatest enterprises!   —A character admiring Cortés's palace in
Francisco Cervantes de Salazar's *Dialogues,* 1554

He was soon disgusted with an academic life, which did not suit his ardent and restless genius.   —William Robertson, 1777

As an Italian poet said, with good reason, in a sonnet of his: *Qui esparge il seme et qui recogle il fructo.* Which means, some sow the seeds and others collect the fruit.   —Gonzalo Fernández de Oviedo, 1535,
referring to Velázquez and Cortés[1]

A T THE MOMENT OF HIS BIRTH, HERNANDO CORTÉS WAS CHO-sen by God for greatness. That, at least, was the conclusion drawn by Gerónimo de Mendieta.

As the Franciscan friar sat in a convent in Mexico City in the 1590s, composing his history of the spiritual conquest of the Aztecs, he was struck by the apparent coincidence in 1485 of three events. For surely they were not, he realized, coincidental at all. In that year, a German woman in Saxony gave birth to Martin Luther, destined "to place beneath the banner of the Devil so many of the faithful." At the same time, on the other side of the Atlantic Ocean, at the dedication ceremony for the new main temple in Tenochtitlan, 80,400 people were sacrificed by Aztec priests. But God had a remedy to "the clamor of so many souls and the spilling of so much human blood, to the injury of their Creator." The divine response was the birth of Cortés, who would bring into the fold of the Church "an infinite multitude of people who for countless years had lived under Satan's power."[2]

In fact, neither Luther nor Cortés was born in 1485. The German entered the world in 1483, and Cortés was probably born in 1484. Nor was the new temple to the Aztec god of war, Huitzilopochtli, dedicated in 1485; that ceremony seems to have taken place in 1487. Furthermore, the figure of 80,400 human sacrifices comes from Franciscans such as Mendieta himself and (as we saw earlier) is now generally believed to be a wild exaggeration. But the point here is not to correct Mendieta; on the contrary, the dubious factual basis for his claim only serves to bring into focus the mythological smoke and mirrors that surround the entire first half of Cortés's life.

Mendieta was not the first—nor the last—to imagine the providential noncoincidence of Cortés's birth and early life. The idea was probably already circulating in the Spanish world when the poet Gabriel Lasso de la Vega put it in print. Sponsored by the Cortés family, Lasso had published in 1588 in Madrid a great epic poem titled *Valiant Cortés;* an expanded second edition of 1594 included the lines that native Mexicans had forever been blind,

Without being given any news of Christ the King,
until this man came to the world,
which was in the same year as Luther,
horrible and ferocious monster against the Church.

Whether Lasso invented it or not, by the end of the century the notion of Cortés as God's antidote to Luther had become part of the fabric of the conquistador's legend. In his own epic poem in praise of Cortesian conquests, Antonio de Saavedra fine-tuned the imaginary providential coincidence, noting, "When Luther was born in Germany / Cortés was born the same day in Spain." Not long after, Torquemada solved the dating problem by moving Cortés's birth year to 1483. Similar contrivances, including the claim that both men were born not only the same year but on the very same day, continued to appear in chronicles and poems through to the eighteenth century.[3]

The casting of Cortés as destined for greatness from the moment of birth has forever distorted accounts of his early years—indeed, of his entire life and the Conquest story. Biographies composed as part of accounts of the "Conquest of Mexico," from the sixteenth century into the twentieth, are overwhelmingly hagiographic in nature. All imagine the pre-1519 years as a preparation for greatness, with Cortés as a young man pregnant with an incipient and energetic genius, eager to burst forth upon the world.

The tone was set primarily by Gómara. His *Conquest of Mexico*, started during the old conquistador's final years, under the patronage of Cortés's son (don Martín), was a foundational hagiography of the Cortés legend. Did direct access to Cortés give Gómara important original material, revealing anecdotes, and unique insight into the man? For centuries, readers of Gómara have assumed that his book has such qualities, encouraged by his "clear and unaffected prose" and the inclusion of a few critical judgments (of Cortés's treatment of the last Aztec emperor, Cuauhtemoc, for example). In fact, Gómara made it perfectly clear that his book's purpose was not an objective and accurate depiction but rather the glorification of its subject. Las Casas insisted that Gómara was Cortés's crony (*criado*) and personal historian, and "he only wrote what Cortés himself told him to write" (although more likely he wrote what don Martín wanted him to write).[4]

In Gómara's book we find the three key characteristics of almost all subsequent accounts of Cortés's early life. The first is providential destiny (later to be fully developed at the hands of Franciscan writers). Take, for example, the trio of close calls with death that Gómara had the young Cortés survive. First, he was saved from fatal childhood illness by the piety of his wet nurse. Then, as a carousing teenager, he was rescued from the violent anger of a jealous husband by the intervention of the mother of the woman he was caught visiting. Finally, he was saved from shipwreck on his initial crossing of the Atlantic Ocean when on Good Friday a dove appeared—"a good omen" and "a miracle," "sent by God"; the bird guided the lost vessel and its despairing passengers to Hispaniola, reaching the Caribbean island on Easter Sunday.

The details of these three moments were sparse, but Gómara set a pattern to be followed throughout his book, one that loosely echoed the similarly little-known early life of Christ: as a man, Cortés was flawed, but he was blessed, to be spared by God through various means for higher purposes.[5]

The second characteristic of traditional Cortesian biography, prominent in Gómara's foundational account, is the construction of the young Cortés as a frustrated genius, impatiently awaiting the heroic stage upon which he was destined to perform. He abandoned the study of law in Salamanca after only two years, "fed up with, or regretting, studying," which "weighed upon and angered his parents," and as a teenager in Spain "he was boisterous, haughty, mischievous, and liked weapons." But, in Gómara's telling, this was because the scale of Cortés's abilities and ambition was too great for his homeland. For "he was very clever and capable in all things" (in the 1578 English version: "of a good witte and abilitie"), and he was "determined to get on and go away." He chose the Indies over Italy because he supposedly knew the new governor on Hispaniola, Nicolás de Ovando, and there was "much gold" there. In the early English version, Cortés "was a very unhappy ladde, high minded, and a lover of chivalrie, for which cause he determined with himselfe to wander abroad to seeke adventures." "His Nature was boiling, hasty, various, addicted to Arms," as a French version put it; "so that his Genius seemed rather destined to exploit high and Martial affairs, then to decide a controversie in Law either by Tongue or Pen."[6]

As accounts of the Mexican conquest and of Cortés's life multiplied over the centuries, so did these biographical themes become reduplicated and reiterated. Cervantes de Salazar began a chapter of his 1560s *Chronicle of New Spain* with the statement that "It was Hernando Cortés whom God, along with those of his company, chose as his instrument for so great a matter." He borrowed Gómara's smattering of early anecdotes, adding some twists; thus Cortés quit Salamanca after two years because—rather than despite the fact that—he was "very talented," for he only needed two years to master grammar.[7]

Similar variants perpetuated the themes through the seventeenth century—most notably in the chronicles by Díaz and Solís—and into the eighteenth, when Robertson worked them into his top-selling *History of America* (unchallenged until Prescott's volumes of the 1840s). Robertson emphasized Cortés's innate and impatient military abilities. Thus the young Spaniard dropped out of university because student life was ill-suited to "his ardent and restless genius." And despite his immersion in "active sports and martial exercises" he became "so impetuous, so overbearing, and so dissipated" that his father dispatched him "abroad as an adventurer in arms."[8]

Robertson, following the Spanish chroniclers of the preceding centuries, upon whom he based his book, offered no details of the Hispaniola years. He simply told readers that when life as a colonist on Hispaniola was unable to "satisfy his ambition," Cortés joined Diego Velázquez in his expedition to Cuba. Robertson then glossed over "some violent contests with Velázquez, occasioned by trivial events, unworthy of remembrance," to focus on a portrait of a turbulent youth mellowing and maturing into a prudent and graceful man of "winning aspect" and "extraordinary address in martial exercises." No details of Cortés's life on Cuba are offered either, only the verdict that on that island he mastered, "with what is peculiar to superior genius, the art of gaining the confidence and governing the minds of men."[9]

This brings us to the third characteristic of biographies of Cortés's early life: the treatment of time. Cortés arrived in the Caribbean when he was nineteen or twenty years old; he left Cuba when he was thirty-four; he died at sixty-three. His years before the expedition to Mexico thus made up more than half of his life, and a good portion of his adult life. Yet less than 2 percent of Gómara's book was devoted to the pre-Mexico years. Over the centuries, instead of digging up more (or more reliable) information about the early Cortés, historians offered even less. Some (like Francisco Cervantes de Salazar, writing in the 1560s) created abbreviated versions of the

Gómara stories; others (like the poets Lasso de la Vega and Saave-dra) jumped straight to the departure from Cuba, thereby more or less following Cortés's own account in his Letters to the king. The more that Cortés became the archetypal conquistador, the legendary conqueror of the Aztecs, the more his pre-Mexican life (and the real Cortés) disappeared.

Robertson, for example, dispensed with Cortés's seven years on Hispaniola in these two lines: the young Spaniard arrived in 1504 and "was employed by the governor in several honorable and lucrative stations. These, however, did not satisfy his ambition," so in 1511 he left for Cuba. The eight years on Cuba were given a few pages. But the two years of the Spanish-Aztec War were given 128 pages. A more extreme example is Thevet's short biography, in which the Caribbean years are literally sailed right through: Cortés, "aged nineteen years, *Anno 1504,* was bound for the *Indies,* and embarqued in the Ship, of *Alonso Zuintero* an inhabitant of *Palos de Moguer,* who took along with him four more laden with Merchandise, and Sailing towards the *West,* he found out the Kingdom of *Mexico*"—which he immediately proceeded to subdue.[10]

Thevet's complete elision of fifteen years is perhaps forgivable, given that his biography is only a few pages long. Robertson's disproportionate allotment of space is likewise understandable—his narrative target was the Spanish-Aztec War. And although such writers perpetuated a distorted view of Cortés's life, they were simply part of the great chain of misperception, inheriting and passing on the myths, half-truths, and omissions. Yet the misleading impression given that Hispaniola and Cuba were mere brief stops on the way from Spain to Mexico surely raises this question: What on earth was Cortés doing for that long decade and a half in the Caribbean?[11]

Keats, it turned out, was wrong. It was not "stout Cortez" who "with eagle eyes star'd at the Pacific—and all his men / Look'd at each other with a wild surmise— / Silent, upon a peak in Darien," despite the claim by the English poet in his famous sonnet. It was Vasco Núñez de Balboa and an African slave who in 1513 were the first non–Native Americans to see that ocean. Keats seems to have been reading Robertson and conflated his accounts of Balboa first seeing the Pacific with Cortés first seeing Tenochtitlan. Or perhaps the poet merged the two moments on purpose. After all, "stout Cortez" was the emblematic conquistador, the archetype of a European amazed by what he had discovered; for Keats, he fit the bill.[12]

For us, however, it does matter that Cortés never set foot—let alone the first Old World foot—"on a peak in Darien." It matters that there was unceasing Spanish activity across the entire Caribbean basin, its islands and its surrounding mainland coasts, during the fifteen years that Cortés was there—activity in which the budding conquistador played a very minor role. Indeed, there is evidence of him participating in only one expedition of exploration or conquest, the invasion of Cuba.

Not that Cortés was inactive. He was assigned allotments of indigenous villagers on both Hispaniola and Cuba. Called *encomiendas,* these grants gave their holders the rights to the labor and tribute products of their subjects.[13] *Encomiendas* were not land grants, but their holders often claimed nearby lands, as was the case in these early Caribbean years; nor did *encomiendas* give license to enslave villagers, although they were often treated as slaves. Thus Cortés, like his fellow Spanish settlers, used his *encomiendas* to run a cattle ranch and sent "his" Taínos to look for precious metals (especially river gold). He was literate (as his later Letters to the king attest), and for some years worked as the official governmental notary in Azúa, a tiny Spanish settlement near Santo Domingo on Hispaniola. Later, on Cuba, he appears to have served for a time as Diego Velázquez's secretary (that is, as the governor's personal notary). He lived with a Taíno woman, whom he had baptized as Leonor Pizarro (as we shall see later, they had a daughter, whom he named Catalina, and whom he would recognize fondly in his will).

Cortés certainly participated in the Velázquez-led Spanish invasion of Cuba in 1511. It is not clear how much fighting he did. He may have done some, but there were some 330 Spaniards in the invasion company and they met little resistance (the greatest opposition came from the Taíno leader Hatuey, who had fled from Hispaniola; he was captured and burned). The claim by an anonymous writer in the 1550s that Cortés effectively orchestrated the Cuban conquest and that Velázquez did very little "due to his obesity" smacks of Gómara-style partisanship and is not supported by any archival evidence.[14]

All these activities mark Cortés as being an ordinary or typical Spanish settler in the early Caribbean. There are no signs of him being particularly "restless" or "ambitious." He failed to initiate a single expedition. He followed rather than led, and even then, he did not follow far. He participated in none of the campaigns that Spaniards undertook during these fifteen years to locate, raid, or attempt to conquer other islands or sections of the circum-Caribbean mainland. It was Alonso de Ojeda and Diego de Nicuesa, not Cortés, who explored and fought indigenous warriors along the coasts of Colombia and Central America (some said Cortés was supposed to be on that expedition but was prevented from going by a bad leg—or a bout of syphilis). It was Francisco Pizarro, not Cortés, who explored and fought alongside Balboa and Pedrarias de Ávila in places like Darién. It was Juan Ponce de León and Juan de Esquivel, not Cortés, who discovered Florida and conquered Puerto Rico and Jamaica, and Juan Díaz de Solís and Vicente Yáñez Pinzón who first found the Mexican coastline. Nor was it Cortés who discovered Yucatan and the Mexican mainland in 1517, or who led the second expedition there in 1518. Typical of the distorted impression given in centuries of accounts of these early explorations and conquests is the image chosen to illustrate *The American Traveller;* covering Spanish activities in the Caribbean from the 1490s to 1518, Cortés does not appear until the very last of the three hundred pages, yet it is his portrait that faces the title page.[15]

Some writers, faced with the incompatibility of the Cortés legend and his early record in the colonies, simply imagined his participation in some campaign or another; Velázquez chose him because "he had already helped conquer what is now Nicaragua" is an example of such inventions. Even Maurice Collis—whose 1954 *Cortés and Montezuma* overwhelmingly follows the trail of Cortesian hagiography left by Gómara, Solís, Robertson, et al.—spots the red flag that is Cortés's quiet life in the Caribbean. Insisting that Cortés "was a military genius and a great man of affairs," Collis mused why his friends on the islands seemed not to notice, or at least not think to write such observations down; he wondered if Cortés was "himself unaware" of his "latent powers," and asked why "was he content to remain for fifteen years in the little world of Cuba doing little more than amuse and enrich himself?" Collis's weak answer to his own question—"One can only surmise he was waiting his opportunity"—avoids the obvious conclusion: Cortés lived an ordinary life on Hispaniola and Cuba because he was an ordinary man of ordinary abilities.[16]

There is a purpose to deflating the myth of Cortés's Caribbean years. For in inflating the Cortesian legend, the traditional narrative has hidden or downplayed the earlier careers of other Spaniards. Men like Juan Ochoa de Elejalde, a Basque veteran of the conquest wars on Hispaniola, Puerto Rico, and Cuba, who fought as a captain throughout the Spanish-Aztec War, going on to participate in the bloody campaign in Tehuantepec; he held Nahua villages in *encomienda* and owned indigenous and African slaves. Or men like the Alvarado brothers. Not just the infamous Pedro, but Gómez, Gonzalo, Jorge, and Juan, who all arrived between 1510 and 1517 to fight in the islands, going on to play leadership roles in Mexico, Guatemala, and elsewhere—winning reputations as men of violence, if not cruelty. Or the men who had originally crossed the Atlantic on one of Columbus's voyages. An example of one who sailed with the first Columbus crossing (1492) is the pilot Diego Bermúdez, who participated in later expeditions to Florida and various Caribbean islands before dying in the Spanish-Aztec War (Bermuda is named after his brother, also a ship's pilot). An example of one who joined the final Columbus crossing (1502) is Sancho de Sopuerta, who fought

Taínos on Hispaniola and Cuba, sailed with Grijalva, and barely survived the wounds he received both on the Noche Triste and during the siege of Tenochtitlan (according to his own florid claims); he lived in the city with his Nahua wife in the 1520s.[17]

Such men are crucial to understanding the Spanish-Aztec War. As veterans of campaigns against indigenous communities they brought with them experiences and expectations that partly shaped the war. Higher-ranking veterans, men with resources to invest in the company, brought with them their status as captains, horsemen, or comrades with ties of loyalty to other veterans. They did not expect to take orders, but to act within cohorts and factions to promote their interests and safeguard their investment. Furthermore, all veterans of Caribbean campaigns, regardless of rank and status, had become accustomed to two ways of interacting with, subduing, and profiting by indigenous people: violence, often extreme, often deployed against unarmed families; and slave-raiding, ideally on a large scale.

The *quebrantamiento,* the great "breaking" of the Taíno population of the first decade of the century as a result of violence, enslavement, and overwork in placer gold mining, led to a decade of slave-raiding across the Caribbean—from Florida to the northern coasts of South America. The islands in between were decimated. Tens of thousands were enslaved; the slaughter and disruption to family life and food production caused the indigenous population to drop within a generation by hundreds of thousands (or by millions, as some have claimed—from Las Casas to some modern scholars). Then a smallpox epidemic hit the region in 1518, prompting a dramatic increase in the issuing of slave-raiding licenses. Faced with increasingly poor "harvests" of "Indians," Spaniards in the Caribbean jumped at the opportunity to reap the benefits of an untapped newly discovered mainland; under these circumstances, the decisions of hundreds of men to join the Cortés company in 1518, betray Velázquez in 1519 and 1520, or join the war in 1520 and 1521 should come as no surprise.[18]

These three themes—the ubiquity of conquistador factionalism;

the development of habitual violence against indigenous communities; and the centrality of the enslavement of indigenous people—will be explored in various ways in this and successive chapters. As we work our way first through the events of 1519 and 1520, and then through the 1520s and beyond, these themes will help us to grasp the war's gruesome reality. They will also help us to see through the traditional narrative's mythistory of Cortesian control—the compelling fiction of the general as a master conductor, bending to his will a massive orchestra of diverse players, leading them all to the Conquest's final triumphal chords. The evidence plays a more somber tune.

To that end, let us turn now to Diego Velázquez and his relationship with Cortés, the relationship that spiraled into the great factional feud at the heart of the company, outliving that company, the Conquest war, and its principal protagonists.

One night in Cuba, Cortés and Velázquez slept in the same bed together. Or so Gómara claimed. In his telling of the tale, the two men had fallen out over a Spanish woman—Catalina Suárez, whom Cortés had seduced and then shown reluctance to marry (more on her unhappy fate later). Velázquez had locked up Cortés as a result. But he escaped and found the governor at a ranch where he was camped out. "Diego Velázquez was afraid, seeing him armed and at such an hour; he begged him to dine with him, and to rest without suspicion." Cortés responded that he only wished to know what accusations the governor had made against him; he insisted the governor remained "his friend and servant." Then, wrote Gómara, "they held hands as friends, and after much conversation they lay down together in the same bed, where Diego de Orellana found them in the morning, when he came to tell the governor how Cortés had escaped."[19]

The incident has a certain irresistible, cinematographic charm. It also captures a few of the key elements of the legendary Cortés personality, in their formative stage—he is seductive and persuasive, adventurous and victorious. This is just what Gómara intended with the anecdote; he ends the chapter with the comment that "through such dangers and detours runs the road that the very best men take to reach their good fortune." Chroniclers and historians have been following his cue ever since. For example, in his 1942 biography of Cortés, Salvador Madariaga used this incident to show how the conquistador's "winning way" would shape his life: "he was gifted with that most precious yet most rare of combinations: presence of will with presence of wit."[20]

Velázquez's role in the story is just as important, for it feeds into the larger part played by Cuba's governor in the traditional narrative of Cortés and the Conquest. The basic outline of their relationship is this: In 1518 Velázquez selected Cortés to lead an expedition of exploration into what turned out to be Mexico; the governor changed his mind before Cortés left Cuba, but Cortés left anyway, denying Velázquez's authority over the expedition throughout the war against the Aztec Empire; as a result, Cortés claimed full credit for the "Conquest of Mexico," being confirmed as governor-general of the new kingdom in 1522, despite a concerted legal campaign by Velázquez. The anecdote above thus anticipated a complex conflict, one in which an angry Velázquez is outwitted by a triumphant Cortés, seduced into—literally—sleeping with the enemy.[21]

As with so much of Conquest history, Cortés and Gómara together established the narrative regarding Diego de Velázquez. According to Gómara, Velázquez was "greedy [*codicioso*]" and "extremely womanly [*mugeril*]" (meaning he was swayed and influenced by women to the extent of being himself feminized); he was also quick-tempered and vengeful, constantly "very angry with Cortés," or "furious and indignant." By contrast, throughout his dealings with the Cuban governor, Cortés was portrayed by Gómara as calm, confident, and capable; justified in his positions and destined to triumph. Velázquez was, in other words, a foil for Cortés, the anti-Cortés, the villain of the piece. He is the man who—before Montezuma appears on the scene to take on the role—exhibits the opposite characteristics to Cortés in order to highlight the great man's qualities.[22]

There is, of course, another side to this story. Bartolomé de Las Casas was living in Cuba during these years, and personally knew both Velázquez and Cortés (whom he knew later in Mexico too). Las Casas recorded his version in his *Historia de las Indias,* not published until 1875 (by which time Gómara's book had sold out dozens of editions in multiple languages for centuries). But we can freely compare the two, and the friar's indignation over Gómara's apocryphal anecdote is far more convincing. According to him, Cortés was the governor's disloyal secretary, caught stealing documents in order to file complaints against his patron. Furious, Velázquez had arrested Cortés, threatened to hang him, but after a few days had cooled off and released him ("but he did not want to go back to receiving him in service as his secretary"). Gómara's version was "all a big lie, and any sensible person could easily judge." After all, "Velázquez was governor of the whole island," but Cortés was just

an ordinary man [*hombre particular*], not to mention his crony and secretary, whom he had held captive and wished to hang, which he could have done, justly or unjustly. So how can Gómara say that he did not wish to speak to him for many days and that he had come armed to ask him what complaints he had with him and that he came to be his friend and that they held hands and that they slept that night in the same bed!

Furthermore, continued Las Casas, "I saw Cortés during those days, or very shortly afterwards, very bowed [*bajo*] and humble, like the very lowliest crony [*mas chico criado*] that Diego Velázquez might wish to favor." Cortés was lucky to have been spared, then, and he knew it, for the governor demanded respect at all times, "and nobody sat down in his presence unless they were very much a gentleman [*muy caballero*]." If he had sensed

from Cortés even a pin prick of pride or presumption, he would have hanged him, or at least exiled him from the land, where he would have cowered without raising his head for the rest of his life. Thus did Gómara attribute to Cortés, his master, what in those days one would not even, while awake, imagine could possibly happen, let alone dream it while sleeping.

As for Velázquez, his image as an obese, bad-tempered buffoon is restricted only to later pro-Cortés propaganda. Even Las Casas, who was famously unforgiving of conquistador brutality, had this to say about the Cuban governor:

> He was very much a gentleman in his bodily appearance, and consequently amiable; he did become fat, but still lost little of his gentility; he was prudent, and when people thought he was being slow [*grueso:* thick], he was deceiving them . . . when he was in conversation he was very affable and gracious [*humano*], but when it was necessary or if he was angry, those before him trembled, and he always wished to be treated with complete respect.[23]

Velázquez was a member of the first generation of Spaniards to come to the Americas. A Castilian nobleman from Cuéllar, he later became known as Diego Velázquez de Cuéllar, in part to distinguish him from the famous seventeenth-century painter Diego Velázquez (not a relation). He was possibly a young veteran of Ferdinand and Isabella's war against the Muslim kingdom of Granada in the 1480s, and thus a witness to the ritual surrender to the Catholic monarchs at the city gates—his presence there, if true, would prove to be ironic in view of the fact that he missed the Meeting, whose reconstruction as a surrender drew upon the 1492 triumph at Granada as one of its models.

In 1493, Velázquez joined Columbus on his second Atlantic crossing, faring better than did Columbus himself in the years that followed. Successfully navigating the politics of the early Caribbean, Velázquez attached himself to Columbus's brother, Bartolomé, and then to fray Nicolás de Ovando, Hispaniola's governor. He showed himself as willing as any conquistador to treat the indigenous people of the islands with merciless violence. The massacre of the so-called queen of the Taíno, Anacaona, and her followers on Hispaniola, was mostly his doing. He captained the Spanish conquest of Cuba with unflinching brutality. The burning of Hatuey was also his doing (Cortés was a witness). By 1516, when three Jeronymite friars took over as commissioners in Hispaniola—in charge of all the Spanish colonies, but highly ineffectual—Velázquez was arguably the most powerful man in the Indies. In 1517, two events made his position even stronger. First, the young King Carlos reached Spain to assume the throne, and in the ensuing shake-up at court, Juan Rodríguez de Fonseca, the bishop of Burgos, who had been Ferdinand's principal councilor for Indies affairs, returned to favor; he was Velázquez's uncle-in-law. Second, an expedition that Velázquez sent to explore the coasts of a large island adjacent to Cuba returned with tantalizing evidence of a wealthy, well-settled new land.[24]

That "island," of course, was the peninsula of Yucatan, whose coastline led to Mexico. Francisco Hernández de Córdoba led the expedition, designed to explore but mostly to plunder and enslave "Indians" on the "island" (as we have seen, the so-called discoverers were also enslavers). He and two partners provided three ships. Although they "discovered Yucatan," they met with fierce resistance from the local Mayas. For once, Gómara's one-line summary of the expedition seems apposite: although Hernández de Córdoba "brought nothing back from the expedition but wounds"—from which he soon died in Cuba—"he did bring back word that the land was rich in gold and silver, and the people were clothed." Cortés had neither the connections nor funds, neither the initiative nor reputation, to be part of the Hernández de Córdoba expedition.[25]

Indeed, not only did Cortés not participate in the 1517 expedition, but Velázquez passed him over when choosing leadership for both that and the subsequent expedition to Yucatan. Why? Might it have been because he was ordinary, without a track record of leadership, a mediocrity, and—above all—untrustworthy? Velázquez also had family members to choose from, such as his twenty-eight-year-old nephew, Juan de Grijalva, commissioned to lead the 1518 expedition. Grijalva had also proved his mettle, not only in the 1511 conquest of Cuba but also on a slaving expedition to Trinidad in 1517 (while Hernández de Córdoba was receiving fatal wounds on the coasts of Yucatan). Meanwhile, Cortés had been enjoying the comfort and safety of life in Cuba, and was not even asked to join the 1518 company.

Other Castilian hidalgos (lesser nobles) did accompany Grijalva: Pedro de Alvarado, Alonso de Ávila, and Francisco de Montejo all went as captains; they were the principal investors in the expedition, after the governor and his nephew. These men would go on to help lead the invasion of Mexico as captains, and in the 1520s and '30s bring conquest violence to the kingdoms of the Mayas. But by 1518 they had also participated in more expeditions than had the relatively inactive Cortés; Montejo, for example, had explored and fought in Panama with Pedrarias de Ávila. Other men on the 1518 expedition would go on to participate in the wars in Mexico: fray Juan Díaz, chaplain to Grijalva and author of an eyewitness account of the expedition, was one; the notary Diego de Godoy was another; so too was Bernal Díaz; yet another was Bernardino Vásquez de Tapia, who would play a leading role as a captain in the Spanish-Aztec War, surviving to live as a founding settler and councilman in Mexico City into the 1550s.[26]

Cortés was conspicuously absent from an expedition about which he was later rudely dismissive, accusing Grijalva of having sailed back to Cuba "without having done anything at all." Gómara claimed that Grijalva was so pathetic that "he wept" when some of the men opposed returning to Cuba. The later claim that Velázquez was frustrated by Grijalva's failure to found a colony, that the governor regretted "having sent an idiot [bobo] as a captain," does not ring true. On the contrary, Grijalva did exactly as instructed. He was not supposed to settle or conquer. Velázquez intended to do that, once the king had granted him the title of adelantado of the newly discovered lands; and in the wake of the Hernández de Córdoba expedition, the governor had sent envoys with his petitions to Hispaniola and Spain.[27]

Looking past the distorting filter of the pro-Cortés comments of later years, it is clear that the Grijalva expedition was significant for its personnel, its discoveries, the knowledge it garnered, and the groundwork it laid. The four ships charted more of the coastline of Yucatan—still thought to be an island—than had Hernández de Córdoba, and the Gulf coast of Mexico was also explored. Totonacs, as well as Yucatec and Chontal Mayas, were engaged in attempted communications, exchanges of material goods, and in battle. Although the Spaniards did not know this in 1518, they had made first contact with the Mexican mainland, with Nahuatl-speakers, and with the Aztec Empire.

At the point on the coast that the Spaniards named Ulúa, local subjects of the Aztecs tried to tell the visitors about the "Culhúa"—a name used widely across the empire and beyond for the Aztecs. Spaniards misunderstood (hence the place's name), but they grasped that a large and wealthy kingdom was nearby, and that some or all of these "islands" might constitute a mainland. As fray Juan Díaz reported, here were people who "lived in stone houses, and had laws and regulations, and public places assigned for the administration of justice." They had fine clothing, gold, abundant food, and were "skillful [*ingeniosa*]" in various ways. Even Gómara, who was ruder still about Grijalva than Cortés was, listed more than 350 hand-crafted items acquired through trade and theft on the expedition. Far from doing nothing at all, Grijalva had discovered a civilization and possibly an empire, charted the way to them from Cuba, established friendly relations with a people who lived at one of the entry points to that empire (the Totonacs), and even set a precedent for communicating with local people (Grijalva used various interpreters, including a pair of bilingual speakers, anticipating the double-interpreter system for which Cortés would later claim credit). In turn, Montezuma now knew of these foreigners, their ships, weapons, and proclivities. The scene was set, the encounter of empires was now inevitable. And Cortés had nothing to do with it.[28]

In the political maneuverings that consumed the small Spanish community on Cuba after news of the Grijalva expedition reached the island (before Grijalva himself had even returned), Velázquez worked to persuade various men to lead a third expedition. Baltasar Bermúdez supposedly balked at the cost, which the governor sought to place mostly on the expedition's leaders (Velázquez, sniped Gómara, "had little stomach for spending, being greedy"). Two Velázquez relatives, Antonio and Bernardino, were considered too, as was Vasco Porcallo. The conventional narrative of this moment was that while these were "all Persons of great Courage and undoubted Qualifications" (in the words of a 1741 English account), Velázquez "wanted a Man who should be entirely at his Devotion." In other words, the governor struggled to find a man who was capable both of leading an expedition and of bringing it back to report to him; that is, up to the task, but not so ambitious that he would betray Velázquez and carve out a province for himself. In the words of Solís, he sought "a man with much heart, but of little spirit."[29]

As with almost every detail of Cortés's life before Mexico, this moment in the story is tainted by hindsight. Because all the historians from Gómara to Solís to Madariaga went on to write of Cortés as a man with heart *and* spirit, the logic of the narrative requires Velázquez to have sought a lesser man. By having Velázquez anticipate betrayal, Cortés's triumph seems ordained. By having Velázquez seek mediocrity, Cortés's success seems justified.

All of which masks three intertwined realities. First, the material goods and detailed information from the mainland put the governor in an impossible situation; any Spaniard who could win a license to invade and settle, or even just explore and raid, was now going to do just that, as soon as possible. The situation was fine-grained sand in Velázquez's hands.

Second, these expeditions were dangerous and expensive, so men able and willing to provide and supply ships were inevitably going to be leading members of the expedition company, regardless of how closely they were related to, or trusted by, Velázquez. Third, most of the men of some standing and wealth who had accompanied Hernández de Córdoba or Grijalva, or both, were going to likewise play leading roles—such as the Alvarado brothers, Montejo, Alonso de Ávila, and Francisco Maldonado. This was also true of lesser-ranked men whose experience on the earlier expeditions made their inclusion likely—such as Juan Álvarez, pilot and ship's master (*maestro*); Juan de Camacho, who was also a pilot; Martín Vásquez (who became one of Montezuma's so-called guards and later brought his Taíno wife from Cuba to Mexico), Alonso de Ojeda (who lost an eye on the Grijalva expedition but lived another half century), Juan Ruiz, Domingo Martín, and many others.[30] Add to these factors the ties of kinship, of hometowns in Spain, and the partnerships and dependencies of business activities in the islands, and the cohorts of personnel on each of the ships become inevitable—or, at least, far more of an organic process than the traditional narrative of gubernatorial selection implies.

In view of all this, Cortés emerged as the expedition's leader by virtue of his very lack of qualification; he was the ultimate compromise candidate. Where Velázquez erred—and he seems to have realized his mistake almost immediately—was in underestimating Cortés's duplicity. Cortés was, above all, a survivor, and in the lethally dangerous world of the sixteenth-century Spanish Indies, that made him highly untrustworthy.

Assuming this revised portrait of Velázquez and Cortés is accurate, how can we reconcile our new perspective with the events that followed? In the traditional narrative, Cortés sails to triumph and glory in Mexico, while the Cuban governor spends the next five years fulminating and plotting against his former secretary, until 1524, when his fury and frustration send him to his grave. How might we view that story differently? I suggest we shift our viewpoint in three ways, by looking at events through the lenses of (first) the Cortés-Velázquez feud, (second) the role played by cohort and faction, and (third) the nature of the Spanish political system.

The Cortés-Velázquez feud has tended to be seen through the distorting lens of the Cortesian legend, as a conflict that served to create a villainous Velázquez as foil to Cortés the emergent hero—with the governor consumed by "illiberal jealousy," by fear and envy of "Cortés's superior personality."[31] But it serves us better to see the enmity between the two men as an increasingly bitter and brutal feud that was often violent—verging on provoking civil war—and maintained by factions of family and supporters for years.

We need momentarily to jump ahead of the story here, in order to detail how the feud not only exploded in 1519 but lasted through the 1520s, influencing that decade's events. The conflict was pursued unceasingly through gossip and letters and lawsuits, in which Velázquez's faction had the early advantage of access to Bishop Fonseca and the court, while Cortés's faction later made use of the platform of the rapidly developing Cortesian legend. But the conflict was also a violent war that cost lives, often resulting from Cortés's poor judgment and spiteful defense of his perceived domain.

The first months that the company spent on the Gulf coast of Mexico were largely consumed by factional maneuvers and negotiations (to which we shall turn shortly). The initial reports sent to Spain from Mexico stemmed entirely from the Cortés-Velázquez feud. On July 1, another ship reached Vera Cruz from Cuba, sent by Velázquez with news that he had been granted that *adelantado* license to settle the mainland (and thus be governor of whatever he conquered). It took the rest of the month for the company to develop a response; on the 26th, Alonso Puertocarrero and Francisco de Montejo sailed for Spain with letters to the king and other officials (they also carried that first massive shipment of gold, jewelry, and other luxury goods, mentioned in the previous chapter). But the political machinations and double-dealing was just getting under way. Although the letters were fiercely anti-Velázquez, Montejo hedged his bets by making an unscheduled stop in Cuba, where he showed his friends the treasure from Montezuma that was to be delivered to the king of Spain. Word quickly reached Velázquez, who sent a ship to intercept them. Montejo and Puertocarrero surely knew he would, for they slipped into the Atlantic by an unusual route.

Meanwhile, in Vera Cruz the factional jostling had become violent. With the letters and treasure on their way to the king, the

Cortesian faction moved against a cohort of particularly staunch *Velazquistas;* two of them, Juan Escudero and Diego Cermeño, were hanged. In Cuba, the governor dispatched an envoy (Gonzalo de Guzmán) to Spain to persuade the king that Cortés was a traitor and should be arrested, and he began to assemble a large invasion force to go to Mexico and do just that. Led by Pánfilo de Narváez, it was more than double the size of Cortés's original company. Crown officials on Hispaniola, learning of these preparations, sent Lucas Vásquez de Ayllón to stop them; instead, Vásquez joined Narváez.

Montejo and Puertocarrero reached Seville at the beginning of November (just as the conquistadors who had stayed behind were descending into the Valley of Mexico, days before the Meeting). Unfortunately, Velázquez's chaplain, Benito Martín, was in the city (he had brought over Velázquez's successful *adelantado* petition). The chaplain persuaded customs officials to embargo the ships and Montezuma's treasure, forcing Montejo and Puertocarrero to pursue an audience with the king—without the treasure. Joined by Cortés's father, Martín, they chased the king to Barcelona, only to find he had already left for Burgos; not until March, seven months after leaving Vera Cruz, did they catch up to Carlos in Tordesillas, to find both Bishop Fonseca and Velázquez's agent Guzmán already making their cases. At the same time, across the Atlantic, Narváez's massive company of eleven hundred men left Cuba for Mexico.

The stakes were now very high, with the fate of thousands of Spaniards in the balance. However, the two sides were not divided by principles or ideas, nor were any of the men particularly loyal—if at all—to Cortés and Velázquez; their loyalty was to their own cohorts, and their perception of which path led to wealth and status (and this was even true of King Carlos). Therefore, as spring came on, Velázquez found his efforts to get Cortés declared a traitor, arrested, or killed stymied. For Carlos was rightly fascinated by reports of Montezuma's treasure, and had it sent to him from Seville. Although Fonseca allegedly hid some of it from the king, it was enough for judgment to be deferred. In effect, Carlos was willing to give Cortés and his faction a chance, as long as they could produce more of the same. That attitude was more or less that of the men who sailed with Narváez; contrary to the traditional narrative's claim of more Cortesian brilliance, it took little more than tales of Tenochtitlan, from men who had just been living there for half a year, to convince the Narváez company to join the Cortés company.

Velázquez's purpose had hardly been to send reinforcements to aid Cortés; yet that, effectively, is what happened. By quadrupling (at least) the conquistador force within Tenochtitlan, Velázquez made it possible for some Spaniards to survive the Noche Triste. That irony, combined with the fall of Tenochtitlan over a year after that, might seem to have been the final straw for the Velázquez faction. But neither Velázquez nor Fonseca nor their allies were ready to give up. Within months of Tenochtitlan's fall, a royal envoy (Cristóbal de Tapia) reached Mexico from Hispaniola, empowered to take over the government of the new territory (and arrest Cortés if he resisted). The captains who had fought in the siege of 1521 were not going to let that happen, and Tapia was met on the coast and paid off.

Still undeterred, Velázquez assembled yet another expedition of invasion in Cuba, this one led by the governor of Jamaica, Francisco de Garay, and by Grijalva. It did not land until 1523, by which time envoys from Spain had brought documents confirming Cortés as governor-general of Mexico and undermining the legality of Garay's new colony (intended to comprise Pánuco, northeast of the Aztec Empire). Like Narváez and Tapia before him, Garay was more interested in lucrative negotiations than civil war, as was the Cortés faction in Tenochtitlan—where the Jamaican governor was given a cordial reception. But when Garay fell ill and died, after a Christmas Day dinner in Cortés's house, there were rumors of foul play—"a murmur as if *Cortez* had poyson'd him, to rid himself of a Partner in his Government," as Ogilby later put it, "for it had been generally observ'd, that his Ambition suffer'd no Equal."[32]

Still the great factional feud persisted. Cortés's Letters to the King (the Third in 1522 and Fourth in 1524) had grown increasingly long and marked by paranoid rants against his enemies—not just Velázquez and Narváez, but Tapia and Garay, and even old Diego

Colón and Fonseca himself. The tone of Cortés's accusations, combined with mounting counteraccusations that Cortés had abused his position in multiple ways, played into Fonseca's hands (a handful of Noche Triste survivors returned to Cuba in 1520 and testified that Cortés ordered slaughter and enslavement of "Indians," encouraged cannibalism among indigenous allies, and stole gold that should be shared with other conquistadors and the Crown). At the supposed peak of Cortés's success, the moment of his appointment as governor-general, the king also appointed four royal officials to assist him (in effect, to police him). Both Fonseca and Velázquez died in 1524, but that same year the four royal officials arrived and began immediately to undermine what authority Cortés had in Mexico.[33]

Meanwhile, Velázquez had left Cortés another parting gift. Cristóbal de Olid, one of the few captains who had survived the entire Spanish-Aztec War and remained loyal to Cortés's cohort, set off in January 1524 to conquer Honduras for Cortés. But he stopped in Cuba en route, where Velázquez turned him; Olid took violent possession of Honduras for himself, denying Cortés's authority. Cortés ranted to the king that he was "thinking of sending for the aforementioned Diego Velázquez and arresting him" in order to "cut out the root of all the evils that [stem from] this man, so that the other branches wither." Alarmed, Crown officials dispatched a judge (Ponce de León) to Mexico to conduct a full-scale inquiry into Cortés's actions. Meanwhile, as Olid had seized the man Cortés had sent to arrest him, Cortés decided to travel to Honduras himself—a lengthy, pointless expedition with enormous cost in resources and human lives. In his absence, Spaniards in Tenochtitlan formed into two violent factions; Cortés's cousin Rodrigo de Paz, who headed the pro-Cortés faction, was arrested and tortured to death by the other faction. A counterattack brought the Cortesian group back to power before his return from Honduras in 1526, but a few days later Ponce de León reached the city and immediately suspended Cortés as governor. The ghost of Velázquez had won another round. After eighteen difficult months, Cortés left for Spain. He would never again rule New Spain in any capacity. As the great historian of Spain

Sir John Elliott memorably put it, "Fonseca's hand stretched beyond the grave."[34]

And yet the feud was still not dead. Family and cohort members who were or had been tied in some way to Cortés or Velázquez continued to fight in the law courts for decades. Letters written by Cortés's parents throughout the 1520s have survived, and they show an intense preoccupation with waging a political and legal battle against the faction of Velázquez, Narváez, Garay, and their allies. Those letters are a mere drop in the bucket; the legal records of investigations and lawsuits stemming from the feud run to thousands of pages (and those are just the documents that have survived).

In sum, this was far from a simple, short-lived battle between two men, in which one emerged the absolute victor; it was a relentless political war of attrition between two factions.[35]

WITHIN THOSE TWO LARGE FACTIONS were numerous smaller ones, the cohorts that made up all conquest companies and groups of early settlers in the Spanish Indies. Individual action was seldom possible in the conquistador world. The indigenous perception that the conquistadors "had no lord, they all looked like brothers in their clothing, way of talking and chatting, eating and dressing" was a reading not of egalitarianism, but of informal group clubbishness. Hierarchy was social, not military (there was no formal army in the Indies). The men of conquistador companies survived and prospered—or perished—due to cohort loyalties, and even when cohort members betrayed each other, as they often did, there was usually another cohort or faction involved. Half a dozen examples should suffice (as cohort details are infused through these chapters).[36]

How do we know who made up specific cohorts and factions among the conquistadors of the Spanish-Aztec War? In some cases, surnames or hometowns offer evidence. As it was common to travel to the Indies with close relatives, cohorts centered on groups of brothers or other family members. The roster of the over two thousand men who fought in the war is full of brothers, sons, nephews, and cousins. In addition to family members, there were numerous hometown comrades with ties of blood and marriage that are invisible to us but which held cohorts together. The five Alvarado brothers have already been mentioned; other examples include the three Monjaraz brothers, the four men from the Andalucian village of Alanís (who all used Alanís as a surname and were probably kinsmen), and the five Alvarez brothers with their cousin Francisco de Terrazas (one of the brothers died in the conquest of Puerto Rico, but the other four fought in Mexico with their cousin, who was a captain).

There are also other clues. Near the end of his account of the war, Bernal Díaz wrote brief biographies of dozens of the conquistadors—some a paragraph, some a single sentence—which the historian John Fritz Schwaller cross-listed with the clusters of signatures on the recently discovered First Letter, sent to the king from Vera Cruz in 1519. The correlations confirm cohorts such as those centered on the Monjaraz and Alvarez brothers, and suggest other members (for example, the Alvarez brothers may have been close to the two Carvajal brothers, and to the Alaminos men). They also reveal other cohorts, such as one centered on three of the men who owned horses: Vásquez de Tapia, Francisco Donal, and Cristóbal Ortiz. Three of the captains who formed the core of another cohort were Rodrigo de Castañeda, Francisco de Granada, and Ojeda *el tuerto* ("one-eyed," because of the Maya arrow that took out an eye on the Grijalva expedition). The Basques also made up a loose cohort, centered on four men from Vizcaya (Biscay), Pedro Vizcaíno (a crossbowman who settled in Chiapas after the war), Cristóbal Rodríguez, and the brothers Martín and Juan Ramos de Lares; the most prominent Basque in the company (from the Guipuzcoa region) was Ochoa de Elejalde.[37]

Another cohort comprised veterans whom Díaz and others referred to as the *viejos;* these "Old Men" were Andrés de Paredes, Santos Hernández, and Lorenzo Suárez. They had fought together in the Conquest of Cuba. Although Paredes died in the Mexican war, four other men of that name joined the company (and perhaps Old Man Paredes's cohort). Suárez *"el viejo"* achieved notoriety for murdering his Spanish wife (more on him later). Hernández (dubbed the *Buen Viejo,* according to Díaz) might have had the dubious distinction of fighting in more conquest companies than any other Spaniard of his generation: beginning in 1502, he participated in campaigns throughout the Caribbean, then survived the Spanish-Aztec War, fought in invasions from Pánuco to Guatemala, dying around 1558 in his seventies or eighties.

Men who survived the war are more likely to appear in the archival record, especially those who lived into the 1530s, and even more so those who testified in the massive *residencia* investigation into Cortés. What men said about whom adds further clues as to the ties and loyalties of cohort and faction. The swirl of such relationships that surrounded Cortés himself was highly complex, yet Cortés, like other men of the company, was part of a cohort of relatives and hometown comrades: Puertocarrero was a native of Medellín, and a distant cousin to Cortés on his father's side; Diego Pizarro, related to Cortés on his mother's side, was a loyal captain until his death in the second half of the war; also killed late in the war was the young Alonso de Monroy, who served as one of Cortés's pages and may have been a relation.

Perhaps the best-known member of this cohort was Gonzalo de Sandoval, who shared Cortés's hometown of Medellín, and consequently sought out Cortés when he arrived in Cuba in 1517 (aged about twenty). He remained so consistently loyal and invaluable to Cortés that his 1961 biography was titled *The Constant Captain,* reflecting his reputation in the traditional narrative. He fell ill on the 1528 voyage back to Spain with Cortés and Andrés de Tapia, dying at a roadside inn before reaching Seville (Díaz invented a touching deathbed scene featuring the three conquistadors, but in fact Cortés traveled on, leaving Sandoval to be robbed by the innkeeper and to die alone).[38]

Andrés de Tapia illustrates how complex cohort loyalties could be. He was related to Velázquez by marriage, and probably came to the Indies to join him in Cuba as a household (and cohort) member. But he had also known the Cortés family in Medellín, and once he joined the Cortesian company, he remained an unswerving loyalist—tied, perhaps, as much by self-interest and a friendship with Sandoval as anything else. Tapia was one of several men who formed a loose Velázquez cohort in Mexico, and who managed to survive the vicissitudes of factional politics during and after the war. Olid was another on-and-off *Velazquista,* having been a teenager in the governor's household in Cuba; he saw that his best interests lay with the Cortés faction throughout the war, when he acted as one of the dominant captains, not switching sides again until 1524. Francisco de Montejo was also in the governor's cohort, but succeeded better than the decapitated Olid in playing both sides until acquiring his own governorship (even if it took decades and the blood of thousands to achieve).[39]

At the heart of the *Velazquista* cohort were the men whom Cortés loyalists seized during the months of factional quarreling at Vera Cruz (in the traditional narrative, they are "arrested" by Cortés): Juan Velázquez de León, a kinsman of the governor from his hometown of Cuéllar, and a stutterer with a reputation as a fighting man; Gonzalo de Umbria; Diego de Ordaz; Juan Díaz, the friar; a pageboy of the governor's named Escobar; and Pedro Escudero, who in his role as a constable in Cuba had imprisoned Cortés in 1515 under the governor's orders. Cortés clearly begrudged him that, for while a kangaroo court sentenced two men to be hanged and Umbria to lose a foot, only Escudero was executed. A couple of sailors were flogged, but the others were all released after a few days, probably as a result of negotiations between Cortés loyalists and Ordaz—who thereafter served as a cooperative captain throughout the war.[40]

THE FEUD BETWEEN the Cortesian faction and the Velázquez-Fonseca faction was in a way a manifestation of the larger system, a complex version of the Crown-conquistador relationship. Put another way, the Cortés-Velázquez feud was one corner of a triangle, the primacy of cohort loyalty was a second, and the third corner was the complex system of patronage and reward that formed the skeleton of the Spanish royal state; many officials, settlers, and conquistadors—not just a famous handful—were the flesh on those bones. The sinews of the state—which was a loose collection of kingdoms, dominated by Castile, with Spain still in its genesis—were the ties of kinship, hometown, and the contractual agreements that underpinned business ventures and conquest companies. Navigating this system was not easy; indeed, its very challenges were intrinsic to its maintenance of hierarchy, to ensuring the perpetuation of the elite—and above all, in every sense, the monarchy.

Elliott, who has long grasped this system, once commented that Cortés "played the game according to the rules, but these had been laid down by the Spanish Crown." Thus he ended up "a disappointed and disillusioned man" because he "had overlooked the most important fact of all: that those who devise the rules are likely, in the last round, to win the match."[41]

I agree that the Crown was bound to win in the long run, in Mexico as in Peru and elsewhere in the Americas; after all, the system was the Crown's. But we lose sight of the significance of that fact if we imagine that Cortés might have won the match, that he resented not winning, and that his disillusionment (if it was real) had basis to it. Cortés played the game reasonably well (he was good with words) but not exceptionally well (he was too quick to betray, deceive, and lie). His abilities as a conquest company leader were limited (there are other explanations for the events in Mexico, as we have already begun to see), and he was deluded in hoping to retain the governorship of Mexico, or even to be appointed viceroy. Yet he enjoyed considerable power and excessive wealth in the last two decades of his life, as he surely knew. He also seemed to believe sincerely in the king's divine right to be the fountainhead of the system (as most Spaniards did), in the evident truth that God and the pope had tasked the Spanish monarchs to bring the New World into the fold of Christian civilization. In other words, if we believe the Cortesian legend, his disappointment seems logical; however, if we see him more realistically as a mediocre captain with a talent for survival and deceit, he did better than might be expected. If we remember that this was the Crown's game, that Cortés bought utterly into the game but that he was just one among many players, it becomes easier to see past the distortions and oversimplifications of the Cortesian narrative.

Cortés's final petition to the king—written from Valladolid in 1544—is illustrative. Began the sixty-year-old *marqués*,

> Your Sacred, Catholic, Caesarean Majesty: I thought that the labors of my youth would earn me some rest in my old age, and yet I have spent forty years not sleeping, eating badly, or if not badly not well either, always with weapons ready, placing myself in danger, spending my life and property all in the service of God, bringing sheep to their pens in the remotest corners of our hemisphere . . .

He continued in this vein for pages, lamenting how he achieved so much "without help from anyone," and despite the obstacles of "the copycats and the covetous bursting like leeches with so much of my blood." "Defending myself from Your Majesty's treasurer has been harder than winning the land of the enemy," leaving him impoverished, strapped with debt, virtually a vagrant, "having to work, without rest in old age, until death." Not that any of this was "the fault of Your Majesty," who was "magnanimous and powerful" and had generously so honored Cortés in the past. (The king's prime minister scribbled at the foot of the petition: "Not to be answered.")[42]

Read with modern eyes, the letter might be seen as a pleading protest from a disappointed, shunned courtier; Prescott found it "touching," a poignant reminder that "it was possible to deserve too greatly." Or it might be judged as pathetic and sycophantic, alternating between pomposity and self-pity. In fact, it is all of those things, but they are all beside the point. For if read with an eye to the patronage system, the document is an example of the old conquistador using conventional petitionary language right up to the end, employing the same rhetorical techniques of his peers—playing the Crown's game, in other words, in ways that were predictable, unoriginal, unexceptional, and (as was often the case) ineffective.[43]

And therein lies the crucial point to which this chapter has been leading. We can better understand the Spanish-Aztec War if we accept that Cortés was not the master of the game, but just a player within it (sometimes winning, sometimes losing). Consequently, he was not "the model of calculation, rationality, and control he is so often taken to be." The word *control* has been applied to his actions for centuries, not only by his hagiographers but also by those seeking objectivity yet drawn nonetheless by the rhetorical rhythm of his Letters to the king into believing his false claims of masterful manipulation. This myth of Cortesian control has pernicious side effects: it gives shelf life to Cortés's own boast that "the oeuvre that God did through me was so great and marvelous"; it permits the idea that Cortés had a unique vision, that he had the power to implement that vision; it implies that scores of Spanish and indigenous captains and leaders of all kinds had no agency; finally, it ignores the role played by chaos in the war, thereby helping to deny the war's very existence as such, turning it into a "carefully calculated military and political exercise," one man's brilliant achievement.[44]

In reality, decisions were made by numerous individuals—like Xicotencatl of Tlaxcallan, Ixtlilxochitl of Tetzcoco, Pedro de Alvarado, Vásquez de Tapia, and Ordaz—and even more so by councils of noblemen and by groups of captains, by factions and cohorts. Moreover, those decisions were often quick reactions more than considered implementations of strategy, being offset by the chaos and unpredictability of war, and by the need to respond to initiatives by other groups—be they Spanish or indigenous, local or distant. Above all, Nahua leaders played far more decisive roles than the traditional narrative has allowed, and they came closer to being in control—even in localized moments—than Cortés did.

As for vision, neither Cortés nor the other captains held a unique one, but rather shared the broad Spanish expectation that war with indigenous peoples was inevitable, and that it would lead to their mass enslavement, sexual exploitation, forced conversion, and subordination as pacified residents of *encomienda* towns and villages; the invaders would become wealthy, city-dwelling holders of *encomiendas* and various Crown-sanctioned posts and privileges. For the minority who survived the invasion, that expectation would more or less be realized.

In the tiny coastal town of Antigua de la Veracruz (population: nine hundred), Cortés stands with his arm around "Malinche," staring out into the Gulf of Mexico. The scene is a mural painted on the wall of the Hotel Malinche, a modest inn that is dependent on the occasional *Ruta de Cortés* (Route of Cortés) tourists. For this was the spot where the Cortés expedition made its first landfall, on April 22, 1519. Here the mythmaking began, as the two histories of the expedition—the traditional narrative and the messy, murky truth—diverged.[45]

Without knowing what was on the muralist's mind, we can imagine which elements of the traditional narrative she may have found inspiring. Perhaps she sought a more romantic version of Orozco's depiction of Cortés and Malinche (painted in a stairwell of a convent-turned-college in Mexico City), softening the possessive position of the conquistador's arm in Orozco's version to suggest a gentler message: Veracruz is for lovers. Or perhaps the lovers' gaze is wistful, anticipating a future in which the Spaniard sails to Spain without his Nahua interpreter—but with their young son, never to see his mother again. Or perhaps they are to be imagined staring not where ships will sail once more, but where they recently sailed and anchored—before being destroyed on Cortés's orders; a contemplation, then, of what was missing, and what that meant.

That mythical act—a burning of the boats, dramatic but invented—was the last of a trio of legendary Cortesian achievements that followed the April 22 landing of the company on the Mexican coast, and, in the traditional narrative, made his successful march to Tenochtitlan possible. The first was the diplomatic manipulation of local rulers and Aztec ambassadors, allowing Cortés to secure supplies and allies for the march inland. The second was the founding of a town, whose new officials then appointed Cortés as their leader, breaking the connection to Velázquez—a legal maneuver usually credited to Cortés. The third, the boat burning, completed a trio that formed a compelling and consistently Cortés-centric story, placing him not only at the heroic center of events but in control of them.

And yet this trio of triumphs is historical fiction, a mixture of inventions, elisions, and distortions. Cortés was not in control, neither at Veracruz nor in the months that followed.

These are the essential facts. When the expedition made landfall that April 22, they had already spent two and a half months on the move. (The eleven ships simply traced the route along the Yucatec coast charted by the 1517 and 1518 expeditions, engaging Maya communities with periodic violence; a ship was lost, some Spaniards killed, dozens more wounded; a shipwreck survivor, Gerónimo de Aguilar, was rescued on Cozumel, and a number of indigenous slaves were acquired, including the Nahua girl who became Malintzin.) From their April landfall until the expedition's march inland, four months passed. During that time, some Spaniards died from their wounds, at least one was hanged as a result of conflict within the conquistador company, a few sailed to Spain, and some seventy more arrived from Cuba. There was considerable factional disagreement. Various exploratory expeditions were made, on land and by sea, along what is now the coastal zone of Veracruz. Three towns were founded (but not built), two with the hopeful name of La Villa Rica de la Vera Cruz (Rich Town of the True Cross, since April 22 was Good Friday). The Totonac town of Cempohuallan (Cempoala) was renamed Seville; its new name did not stick. The Spaniards interacted extensively both with local groups—Nahuas and Totonacs—and with Aztec embassies, starting almost immediately.

The first embassy sent by Montezuma reached the company on Easter Sunday, less than two days after the landfall. The speedy arrival of that embassy is a clue to exposing the Cortesian lie of his manipulation of local politics. The Aztec leadership had been tracking the expedition as it made its way from Maya country into the territories of the empire (Montezuma had probably known of the

Spaniards since 1517, and perhaps since 1513). The diplomatic encounter of Easter Sunday was not initiated by Cortés nor by any other Spaniard; it was determined by the Aztecs, who brought gifts from Montezuma, provided food and water, and gathered detailed information on the Caxtilteca expedition.[46]

According to some accounts, an invitation to visit Tenochtitlan was extended, and refused. This seems plausible. From the Easter Sunday meeting through to the Meeting in Tenochtitlan, Montezuma's policy was consistently that of the collector—deploying ambassadors and gifts, learning all he could, using loyal subjects and enemy towns alike to test the newcomers as they were lured slowly to his capital. Had the Spanish company been united and resolute, under firm command, and armed with knowledge of the region, they might have accepted that initial invitation. But—contra the claim by Cortés and his biographers—the company was none of those things.

Deeply divided, under ambiguous and weak leadership, unsure of their purpose, ignorant of their surroundings, the company was at the mercy of indigenous initiatives. Montezuma's was not the only one. Another embassy also visited the Caxtilteca at their mosquito-infested camp on the beach at Ulúa (renamed Vera Cruz), this one from the Totonac-speaking city-state, centered on Cempohuallan, which was a modest city located up the coast and a little inland. In late June, the company abandoned the failed first Vera Cruz and decamped to Cempohuallan, at the invitation of the Totonacs. There a complex political game was played out by three protagonists: the Totonac leadership, the Spanish captains, and Aztec officials.

In the traditional narrative, Cortés is the game master, exploiting Totonac resentment of their Aztec overlords to forge a military alliance, to make the Totonacs vassals of the Spanish Crown, and to begin to convert them to Christianity. At the same time, Cortés continues to reassure Montezuma of his friendship, seizing Aztec tribute-collectors in front of the Totonacs, but then secreting them to Spanish ships and later releasing them. But such claims to elaborate Cortesian double-dealing were designed to mask the fact that the Spaniards could not possibly follow Aztec-Totonac political pos-turing and negotiating. The Spanish captains knew nothing of the historical relationship between Mesoamerican groups, and the Aztec Empire was a vague entity of unknown distance, power, and wealth. The language and culture gaps were immense, with four languages being translated. Although Malintzin was learning Spanish, and there were Nahuatl interpreters among the Totonacs, the company's initial communication system comprised the captains speaking to Aguilar in Spanish, him translating into Yucatec Mayan to Malintzin, she translating into Nahuatl, and in places like Cempohuallan another interpreter translating into local tongues like Totonac.

While the Spaniards were operating in the dark, the Totonac leadership and Aztec officials were part of the same world, able to talk around the dangerous but ignorant foreigners and negotiate an outcome that was of potential benefit to both. The Totonacs established a loose alliance with the invaders that did not represent anything close to the capitulation claimed by Cortés. They succeeded in preventing the guests in Cempohuallan from overstaying their welcome, encouraging them to move up the coast to the small town of Quiahuiztlan, where Vera Cruz was again founded; in August, a small contingent of Spaniards stayed there while the majority marched inland toward Tenochtitlan—accompanied by Totonac warriors, who could report back to Cempohuallan and fight on whatever side seemed to be winning. The Aztecs, for their part, were able to prevent a full-scale regional revolt without having to dispatch an army, while also succeeding in drawing the invaders toward Montezuma. To where did the Spanish-Totonac force march in August, and why? As we shall see shortly, the answer reveals indigenous actors, not Spaniards, continuing to play the leading roles.

Meanwhile, as the Spaniards struggled to understand indigenous motives and regional politics, they were also fighting among themselves. Throughout these four months, there was constant squabbling, fractious negotiating, and periodic violence as the company's many factions ("conquistadors-in-waiting") shuffled and jostled for position. The disputes centered on pretty much everything—where they should go, who should lead, how best to acquire food and gold,

how the spoils should be divided, how they could ensure royal reward when all was said and done. But one issue in particular tended
to split the men into two sides. Should they return to Cuba or continue exploring the mainland? Returning meant honoring the orders
given by Velázquez, and thus remaining loyal to him and, by extension, the king; staying meant violating the governor of Cuba's mandate, necessitating an alternative strategy to ensure that disloyalty to
the governor would not be construed as disloyalty to the king. The
line dividing the two sides was not clearly drawn, with men switching back and forth as smaller factions shifted and the company's
prospects rose and fell.[47]

The messy reality of conquistador bickering and indecision, as
weeks turned to months, while the company had barely left the Gulf
coast, is disguised in the traditional narrative behind a spectacular
Cortés-Gómara lie: that Cortés convinced the company to found a
town and elect a town council (a *cabildo*); that body then declared the
Velázquez-mandated expedition over, and, in the name of the king,
launched a new expedition and appointed Cortés as their captain-
general (an invented theatrical moment that illustrators seldom resisted; an example is in the Gallery). The truth was so obvious that
Bernal Díaz blurted it out: the plan was hatched by the dominant
group of captains. Díaz was eager to place himself at the center of the
group, which was surely unlikely. But in doing so he plausibly identified many of the captains who hatched the plan—Puertocarrero,
Olid, Ávila, Escalante, Lugo, and the five Alvarado brothers.

At least half a dozen documents were composed, signed, and
sent to Spain over the next six months, revealing a clear agenda and
commitment on the part of a core faction of captains. The first, a
petition written on Ulúa island on June 20 (and only recently discovered hiding in plain sight in the imperial archives in Seville),
identified Puertocarrero, Montejo, Olid, Pedro de Alvarado, Alonso
de Martín, and Alonso de Grado as the six councilors of the (as
yet, imaginary) new town; Francisco Alvarez Chico acted as agent
for the town, and Pedro's brother Gonzalo was the first to sign—
followed by almost the entire company (318 signatures survive on

the document, damage to which has erased probably a hundred or more). Another document, written a fortnight later and charging Puertocarrero and Montejo to represent the company's interests in Spain, was signed by Ávila, Olid, Grado, Vásquez de Tapia, Sandoval, and Diego de Godoy. Puertocarrero, Montejo, Ávila, and Grado put their names to a third letter, composed a week later and offering a narrative of the expedition thus far (in which Velázquez appeared as motivated by greed and personal profit, in contrast to Cortés's and the company's desire to serve the Crown).[48]

These captains formed the loose leadership of the company that would march inland at summer's end. The language of the documents they sent to Spain—statements to which almost all the company hitched their prospects—was very clear. In the first, for example, the king and his mother, Queen Juana, were asked

> not to benefit Diego Velázquez with any responsibility or profit of any kind from this region, nor grant it to him, both because of the harm and prejudice that all of us here would receive and because it is obvious that [we have] settled, and chosen a judge in Your Majesty's name, and offered this land to your royal crown—land where Diego Velázquez would work and strive hard to damage in any way possible those people involved in it; and if he were to come to this region, nobody would escape being hurt and thrown out as people who did not want to do what he wanted, but rather to serve your Highnesses as your vassals should . . .

The other documents written that summer were equally and consistently blunt in their factional partisanship and their open declaration of loyalty to the king—in the form of a collective commitment to a company that should be, and they hoped would be, licensed to Cortés, not Velázquez. These records were exactly what they purported to be (and not artifices, ghostwritten by Cortés). As his father, don Martín, wrote to the king's Council of the Indies a year later, "some four hundred men . . . having founded a town . . . elected and named for among themselves *alcaldes* and *regidores* and other council officers and named Hernando Cortés as governor and chief magistrate of the land." Don Martín's letter was highly partisan, but that statement captured a simple truth.[49]

As for Cortés's own ambiguous involvement in the plan, Díaz managed to convey it well (despite his usual contradictions of tone and narrative). He seemed to recognize that the captains needed Cortés to be captain-general (as Velázquez had appointed him thus, thereby minimizing the rebellious potential of their plan), while Cortés was in turn unlikely to oppose his reappointment by the captains: "Cortés agreed to it, although he pretended to need much pleading; as the saying goes: 'You beg me to do what I already want to do.'"[50]

Las Casas also spotted the implausible lie in the traditional narrative, suggesting, like Díaz, the obvious truth (despite the fact that he was keen to demonize Cortés as an illegitimate leader). Referring to the rebellion against Velázquez from its inception in Cuba, the friar asked:

> How could these ship captains be excused from being participants in this rebellion of Cortés's? Alonso Hernández Puertocarrero, Francisco de Montejo, Alonso de Ávila, Pedro de Alvarado, Juan Vázquez, and Diego de Ordáz had been named by Velázquez as captains of the other ships, and it is unlikely that they were ignorant of Cortés's dealings. . . . It hardly seems credible that these captains could claim ignorance of the deceit.[51]

In other words, the majority of the captains and the men in their cohorts saw that the Velázquez commission limited their ability to conquer, profit, and claim reward. There is no reason, or evidence, for assigning credit entirely or even mostly to Cortés. As Ogilby put it,

> finding themselves to have fall'n upon an Adventure that was certainly rich and good, and having got such looting and interest in the Countrey already, by their Success and Victories, and chiefly

by their Confederacy with so many of the Natives and People
of the Countrey, revolted to them, did almost at first, by a general consent, renounce their Commission, and dependency upon
Velasquez, and profess'd to act immediately from and for the King
of *Spain.*[52]

THE THIRD AND FINAL moment of mythical Cortesian control, according to the traditional narrative, occurred in the days between
Puertocarrero and Montejo sailing for Spain and the departure of
the Cortés-led company inland toward Tenochtitlan. According to
Cortés himself, "I came up with a way to pretend that the ships were
not seaworthy, and ran them aground, so that everyone lost hope
of leaving." He feared that some of the men would "rise up against
me," being unnerved by how well populated the land was and "how
few we Spaniards were," and because so many were "dependents and
friends of Diego Velázquez." The idea that Cortés could simultaneously fool hundreds of Spaniards while having a fleet of ten ships
grounded defies credulity. For perfectly good reasons explained in a
moment, a group of captains surely decided to ground and dismantle
the vessels, and Cortés simply took credit for it, as he did so much
else.[53]

Yet it might have remained a harmless fib, had not the biographers and chroniclers blown up the moment so dramatically that by
the 1840s Prescott could exclaim: "The destruction of his fleet by
Cortés is, perhaps, the most remarkable passage in the life of this remarkable man." Dozens of parallels to heroic feats of ancient Greeks
or Romans have been made, with Cortés's boldness growing greater
as the centuries passed. Gómara's mention of a speech by Cortés
taunting those "unwilling to wage war in that rich country," restyled
by Díaz as Cortés comparing the moment to "the heroic deeds of
the Romans," evolved over the centuries into a stirring speech to
match the Rubicon-crossing milestone. "Julius Caesar on the Ru-
bicon cast his die. Tiny streamlet was the Roman's glory. You vanquished an ocean," sings a "heroic, irresistible" Cortés to his soldiers
in the opera *Montezuma.* In the fulsome prose of the great Galician

intellectual José Filgueira Valverde, "the captain's words lit up a fire of triumph and greed on the ashes of the broken timbers"; the assembled conquistadors "all felt themselves to be the clay of history, shaped by the supremely strong hands of a Hero." As one historian remarked: "No other episode in the total career of Hernando Cortés has received so much attention or has been the object of so much rhapsodic writing."[54]

The fact that there is an entire body of literature on this molehill-turned-mountain of a topic, from epic poems to scholarly articles, should surely inspire us to question the entire traditional narrative and its literature. Indeed, the only reason to give it our attention now is the chasm between what most likely really happened and what has been generated by Cortesian mythistory. Bridging that chasm allows us to fit this artificially enlarged piece of the puzzle into our emerging new picture of the 1519 invasion.

Let us first be clear on what Cortés did not do. He did not set fire to his fleet. That detail was added in the late sixteenth century, as many before me have observed. But it survives because it echoes the torching of boats on the Tigris by the Roman emperor Julian, because "boat burning" alliterates nicely (throw in "bold" and "brave" too), and because it evokes an irresistible visual (used to effect in *Captain from Castile*, in which the ships light up the night as they float flaming in the bay). Nor did he scuttle or sink his ships, then justify the action with a stirring speech to rally angry sailors, despite the repetition of such a story by centuries of chroniclers; there was no reason to go to that much trouble, and scuttling would have made it harder to remove items of value from the ships.[55]

In fact, this was *not* a decision brilliantly made by Cortés alone to destroy his *entire* fleet, in order that the surviving four hundred men of the company had no choice but to follow him to victory. Instead, as with the other decisions made at Vera Cruz, he acted with some of the other captains, who realized that, as the remaining ships had been at sea for six months (without access to a full array of supplies for maintenance and repair), their wooden hulls were beginning to rot. Left at anchor, they would slowly sink and the valuable hardware on board be lost. By grounding or beaching the ships—a far simpler task than scuttling or burning them in the bay—the sails, rigging, cables and cordage, tackle, nails, and other metal fittings could be removed and saved. This was done, and the equipment left in Vera Cruz with the sixty to one hundred fifty men who remained there under Juan de Escalante as captain. Saving such valuable equipment was not visionary; it was simple common sense. Puertocarrero and Montejo, questioned the following spring in La Coruña (Spain), testified that it was ship captains and pilots who determined that their ships were rotting—and they proposed the beaching. Even Tapia, who otherwise follows Gómara's contrived tale of Cortésian cleverness, admitted that several captains reported that "their ships were unseaworthy"; Díaz, despite wrongly claiming that boats only were saved, with all ships destroyed, insisted that it was done "with our full knowledge, and not [in secret] as is said by the historian Gómara."[56]

Were there complaints about the ship grounding? Naturally. The men of the company argued about everything. The developing Cortés-Velázquez feud exacerbated the squabbling. Many of the captains and men were absent when the decision was made and executed. And those captains who owned the ships feared they would not be fully compensated (three of them later sued Cortés, claiming he owed them the value of the equipment removed from the ships). But the men left in Vera Cruz were in no way stranded; the ship in best condition remained at anchor. Furthermore, as we have already seen, there was a steady traffic of ships from Cuba and Hispaniola to the Veracruz coast and back, as well as traffic with Spain, through the entire period of the invasion and war. Nor could any of the captains, Cortés included, have possibly known that much of the ship's salvaged hardware would end up being used in the small ships or brigantines that would be built for the lakeside siege of Tenochtitlan.

The Rubicon-crossing, no-turning-back, to-Tenochtitlan-or-bust turning point—complete with a rousing speech by a crafty, seductive, Caesarian Cortés—is dramatic and resonant. But it is pure fiction, as much an invention as the burning of boats.

Returning to Cortés's original statement on the boats, we can now see how it contains that combination of truth, half-truth, and lie that is the essence of all his Letters to the King (and, by extension, the entire traditional narrative of the war): he did "run the ships aground," but the decision was not his alone; the decision was not artfully "contrived," although it was controversial; and the ships being "unfit for sea service" was not a "pretense" but an evaluation of their imminent state.

Such was the Cortés-Gómara spin on the entire mess of the four months on the Veracruz coast: a mix of memory, accurate reporting, half-truths, and outright fiction. To credit Cortés with a masterful manipulation of all the Spanish and indigenous protagonists over these four months turns him into a superhuman puppet-master, reducing all others to gullible, craven, passive fools. A recent example is the narration to the "Cortés" episode of the History Channel's *Conquerors* series, in which "one of the most daring acts in the history of conquest" (not just the "Conquest of Mexico," but conquest in world history) is Cortés's ship-burning: "Now, the only option for his soldiers is victory or death, and victory depends on the leadership, diplomacy, audacity, and cunning of one man: conquistador Hernán Cortés."[57]

The traditional narrative thus makes Cortés so Machiavellian, it has even been suggested that he literally followed Machiavelli's (as yet unpublished) playbook. Over and over, a circular argument has been repeated by the peddlers of the traditional narrative: Cortés triumphed at Vera Cruz because he was so gifted, heroic, even godlike, and proof that he was those things was the fact of his triumph on the coast—and then inland. Like the fiction of Montezuma's surrender, it would be "a splendidly implausible notion, save that so many have believed it."[58]

Death of Montezuma.

P. 210.

A LAMENTABLE END. The Victorian newspaper editor William Dalton wrote adventure novels and history books on the side, entertaining generations of children with tales of derring-do. This illustration of the *Death of Montezuma* is from *Cortes and Pizarro: The Stories of the Conquests of Mexico and Peru, with a Sketch of the Early Adventures of the Spaniards in the New World. Re-Told for Youth,* first published in 1862. Reflecting the dominant narrative of the emperor's death, as established by the conquistadors and repeated for centuries, the Spanish invaders do not cause the tragedy, but lament it; having tried to protect Montezuma from his own people, they are concerned, even devastated, by his fatal wounding.

CHAPTER 6

Principal Plunderers

Motzume also surrendred himself, and left all his people to *Cortez* his kindness, but after he had thus submitted, *Ferdinand* hearing there was a secret Rebellion in the Countrey, put him in chains, which so inraged these *Barbarians*, that they furiously ran to the place where *Motzume* was imprisoned (whether it was to deliver him from the indignity he suffer'd, or else were vexed at his compliance with *Cortez*) and threw great stones at their King, wherewith (notwithstanding all the *Spaniards* endeavours to drive them away) they miserably killed him and dash'd out his brains.
—1676 English version of Thevet's *The Life of Ferdinand Cortez, A Spaniard*

Did King Montezuma really learn our language so quickly that he could understand the stipulations of this principal plunderer [*primer salteador*], the ones in which he was asked to surrender his kingdom or cede his entire royal estate? Is it not true that such contracts are only valid where the contractual parties understand each other?
—Bartolomé de Las Casas, 1561

A mysterious convergence united them from the outset: they wanted to understand each other, to decipher each other.
—Enrique Krauze, 2010, on Cortés and Montezuma[1]

WHO MURDERED MONTEZUMA? AS WORD OF HIS DEATH spread across Tenochtitlan, the question must have been on the lips of Spaniards and Aztecs alike—and then, in the succeeding weeks and years, the lips of other Mesoamericans and Europeans. Indeed, to this day, the smoke and mirrors that surround the traditional narrative of the "Conquest of Mexico" have kept the question alive and its answer unsure. The Aztec emperor suffered a violent death in June 1520; that much is clear. But how did he die and by whose hand?

There has been no shortage of theories and dramatizations, with the emperor's demise inspiring many a scene, and even entire works, of theater, opera, and film. Writers and composers, drawn for centuries to the dramatic thrust of the traditional narrative, have always been particularly taken by its inconsistencies—and a popular one has been the emperor's death, with its mysteries (whodunit?) and ambiguities (was it noble or ignominious?).[2]

To explore the moment, we must jump into the exact midpoint of the twenty-eight-month war of invasion. Full-scale, open Spanish-Aztec warfare had finally broken out a few weeks earlier—after fourteen months of cold war coexistence—and the slaughter would not now cease for another fourteen months. By the last week of June (1520), the Spaniards were besieged within Axayacatl's palace complex (which Cortés then called "the fortress"), along one side of Tenochtitlan's great plaza. The conquistadors—some fifteen hundred of them—were more numerous than at any point in the war so far, and they had with them thousands of Tlaxcalteca warriors (how many is uncertain), as well as an unknown number of African and Taíno slaves and servants. But Aztec warriors and the city's population had surrounded them and were seemingly hell-bent on their destruction—a goal that the Aztecs would, to a significant extent, achieve within a matter of days.

To see what happened next, through the fog of competing claims and verdicts, I have grouped accounts of Montezuma's death into five versions of the story. The first is the one most commonly given in the traditional narrative, found, not surprisingly, in Cortés's Second Letter. Considering that he described the June battle in detail—giving a day-by-day, almost blow-by-blow, account—Cortés's summary of the emperor's end was perfunctory:

Mutezuma, who was still a prisoner, together with one of his sons and many other lords who had been captured from the beginning, asked to be taken out onto the rooftops of the fortress so that he might speak to the captains of those people and have them end the war. I had him taken out, and when he reached a parapet which went out beyond the fortress, wishing to speak to the people who were fighting out there, his own people gave him a stone's blow to the head, so great that he died three days later.[3]

There is no accusation of murder in these lines. The cause of death is clearly Aztec projectiles, but the implication is that it was accidental, with the verdict thus manslaughter (you may remember Kislak Painting #4, in the Gallery). This ambivalent version, in which nobody is really to blame (save, perhaps, the unruly Aztec mob and even Montezuma himself), was copied by Gómara and Oviedo, and then repeated for centuries. One example suffices: in a seventeenth-century English account, the emperor attempts to order "his Subjects to retreat" from a window of his palace, but "thinking to be more easily heard or seen, [he] went to a higher Window, where looking out, he was unfortunately hit with a Stone, of which he died three days after."[4]

Version two took the same elements, but assigned intent and blame more clearly: Aztec "Rebels" were the deliberate killers. This explanation first appears in the second half of the sixteenth century, stemming from the same quasi-indigenous sources (like the long-lost so-called *Crónica X*) that turned Montezuma into a scapegoat for Aztec (and specifically Mexica) defeat. In this version, predominant by the seventeenth century, the Mexica insulted the cowardly, captive emperor as they tried to kill him. In Solís's telling, for example, Cortés and Montezuma agreed that the emperor would persuade the "Rebels" to lay down their arms and the Spaniards would then leave the city. But the rebels threw stones and insults, calling Montezuma "the opprobrious Names of pusillanimous, effeminate Coward, an abject, a vile Prisoner, and Slave to his Enemies." Despite efforts by two conquistadors to shield him, he was fatally hit by two arrows and a stone to the head.[5]

The more the Aztecs were guilty, the more the Spaniards were not only blameless but also distraught. In Escoiquiz's epic poem, for example, the Spaniards tried to stop the "lamentable stone," then to salve the emperor's wound and save his life, and, finally, to save his soul with conversion. Their noble efforts were in vain. Montezuma's soul "fell hopelessly into the abyss," through the fault not of the conquistadors but of the rebellious Aztec mob and the emperor himself, stubbornly superstitious to the end.[6]

Robertson likewise was typical in making it clear who was to blame. In his 1777 telling, the Aztecs, accustomed to revering Montezuma "as a god," listened to his speech, "their heads all bowed." But disapproving of his words, they soon let the arrows fly "so violently" that before the Spaniards could protect the emperor, "two arrows wounded the unhappy monarch, and the blow of a stone on his temple struck him to the ground." The Spaniards carried him "to his apartments; and Cortes hastened thither to console him under his misfortune. But the unhappy monarch now perceived how low he was sunk," angrily "scorned to survive this last humiliation, and to protract an ignominious life," tearing off his bandages, refusing "any nourishment" so that "he soon ended his wretched days, rejecting with disdain all the solicitations of the Spaniards to embrace the Christian faith."[7]

The suggestion that Montezuma contributed to his own death in some way, either through his foolhardy attempts to address a hostile, armed populace, or by refusing food and medical attention, is fully developed in the third variant of the story: death by suicide. We have already seen a metaphorical dramatization of that variant in Dryden's *The Indian Emperour*, in which Montezuma stabs himself to death, preferring martyrdom to reigning as Cortés's puppet. But it certainly goes back into the sixteenth century. Cervantes de Salazar, for example, wrote that the emperor willed himself to die, "wishing neither to eat nor be cured" of his wound. In this imaginative rendering of the death scene, Montezuma exclaimed to Cortés that the stones thrown at him "broke my heart into pieces," to which Cortés responded that indeed "you do not have a mortal wound; you are dying from despair and discontent." This was the variant picked up by Herrera and by Díaz—the latter's similarly imaginative account helping give this third variant life up to the present.[8]

The fourth variant also retains Aztec-hurled stones as the proximate cause of death, but adds a new assassin: Cuauhtemoc. This accusation has its own thread in text and image going back centuries. For example, in one seventeenth-century depiction of the emperor's "stoning by his own people" (Kislak Painting #4), Cuauhtemoc is not identified by name, but he could be the Aztec who seems to be leading the attack—yelling back at Montezuma, sporting a prominent head feather, the sole Aztec holding a steel sword. Montezuma, arms out, brought into focus by the white-robed friar, Olmedo, is Christlike, betrayed by his own, a martyr in the making. Indeed, the similarities between this moment and the Ecce Homo scene in the Passion of Christ—when Pilate displays the captive and condemned Christ to a hostile mob, an increasingly popular scene in the fifteenth and sixteenth centuries—gives pause to wonder how much of the story of Montezuma's stoning was a later invention.[9]

The depiction of Montezuma as a Christian martyr may be a subtle and minor thread in his posthumous fabric, but it has been persistent. A vivid example comes in *Montezuma*, a 1960s operatic telling of the story. When the Aztec mob insult Montezuma and Malintzin as traitors, egged on by Cuauhtemoc, Montezuma uses the prophecy myth to justify his surrender. But Cuauhtemoc sings mockingly, "He pleads for the pale-face ladrone, his master," and the Aztec chorus chant, "Kill him!" Although Montezuma does not actually convert in this operatic version, Cuauhtemoc rallies the mob to hurl the fatal stones and shoot arrows by singing, "He's a Christian! Kill him!" With Montezuma dead on the spot, the opera draws to a close with the Aztecs singing, "Long live Cuauhtemoc the King!"[10]

The fifth and final variant on the story is the only one that absolves the Aztecs and firmly points a finger either specifically at Cortés or at the other Spanish captains. Sometimes called "the Indian version," this variant in fact goes back to the sixteenth century and is not solely or simply an indigenous or even quasi-indigenous version.

In the quasi-indigenous Codex Ramírez, Montezuma and the other royal captives are all stabbed to death by Spaniards, a version that the friars Acosta and Durán followed. In an odd detail mentioned by the Jesuit Tovar, "there were those who said that in order for the wound not to be seen, they put a sword into his nether regions [*parte baja*]," which Ixtlilxochitl repeats (and Francis MacNutt translates as "his fundament"). No matter how delicately one puts it, there was clearly a story circulating many decades after the event in which conquistadors shoved a sword up Montezuma's rear end (no doubt, as Belgian scholar Michel Graulich points out, seen as fitting for the emperor of habitual sodomites)—a distasteful symbol of how profoundly Montezuma's reputation has been shafted for centuries. In other accounts, Spaniards beat the captive emperor to death, or "dash'd out his brains"; and in one quasi-indigenous version, Montezuma and Cacama (*tlahtoani* of Tetzcoco) were strangled "when the Spaniards fled the city at night." The image of Montezuma on the balcony in the Codex Moctezuma is often taken to show him being strangled or stabbed by a Spaniard.[11]

This fifth variant, a square verdict of Spanish homicide, was very much a minor one until the nineteenth century, when it gradually became predominant in Mexico. By 1892, Alfredo Chavero could claim that "it is not certain that Montezuma died from the stone: it is well proven that Cortés ordered him killed." When, more than a half-century later, Mexican historian Ignacio Romerovargas Iturbide remarked that Montezuma "was assassinated by the Spaniards," he was expressing the common view in the land that had been Montezuma's.[12]

There is one final twist to the tale: What happened to the emperor's body? Spanish accounts devoted little attention to the topic, following the tone set by Cortés (he remarked that "Indian prisoners" took away the corpse "and I don't know what they did with it"). But quasi-indigenous accounts offered revealing details. According to the Florentine Codex, the body was carried to Copulco and cremated there. Copulco was where the priests of the New Fire Ceremony lived; as the ceremony was held every fifty-two years, and Montezuma was fifty-two when he died, this might have been seen as a way to ritually inspire an Aztec rebirth or recovery in the midst of a difficult war (it also calls into question Montezuma's birth date; was it adjusted posthumously to give him a fifty-two-year life?). In the Codex Tudela, the priests ate Montezuma's ashes, a mark of reverence and also a ritual of rebirth and renewal. And in the account from the Annals of Cuauhtitlan, the body was processed through towns at the four cardinal directions prior to cremation. Presumably these variants were less local memories of the event and more early colonial ideas on how the burial of a *huey tlahtoani* would or should have been conducted. Either way, they consistently convey one key point: the burial was one of ritualized respect and reverence, not the irreverent disposal of a corpse by its murderers.[13]

There was another possible twist to how Christianized Nahuas, decades later, understood that burial. Mexican art historian Diana Magaloni has pointed out that the illustration in the Florentine Codex of two Mexica men lifting Montezuma's body out of the lake (where Spaniards had thrown it) echoed imagery of the Descent from the Cross (it is included in "Burned" in the Gallery). The theme, showing Christ being cradled as he was taken down from the cross, was popular in European religious art throughout the late medieval and early modern centuries, and would have been seen in sixteenth-century Mexican churches. The same illustration then shows the emperor's body being cremated in the same pose. (By contrast, another frame shows the body of the murdered ruler of Tlatelolco, Itzquauhtzin, taken by canoe and cremated in a more traditional Nahua bundled pose.) Did the same Mexica who scapegoated Montezuma for the war's defeat also emphasize the Christlike reverence with which he was buried? This speculative but persuasive idea suggests a deep-rooted memory of an emperor who was never scorned—let alone murdered—by his own people.[14]

Amid the competing claims and contradictory accusations over Montezuma's death, everybody who testified or offered opinions—Spanish and quasi-indigenous—consistently adopted the same set of four positions: they did not kill him; they lamented his death; they were quick to point fingers at who did it; yet they were also willing to blame him for the outcome of the war, to judge him as a weak leader, effectively making Montezuma himself the guilty party. For now, the mystery of his murder shall remain unsolved (until the chapter's end); for that solution only makes sense if we first clarify why the mystery and its many contradictory accounts existed in the first place. After all, there is little doubt that the Spaniards burned alive the Taíno ruler, Hatuey, on Hispaniola; that they garroted the Inca ruler, Atahuallpa, in Peru; and that they tortured to death the Muisca ruler, Sagipa, in Colombia.[15] What happened in Mexico that made for a more ambiguous outcome?

To answer that, we must pick up the story of the invasion where we left it—on the Gulf coast in August 1519—and then approach the Spanish-Aztec War, through to Montezuma's death ten months later, with a perspective very different from that of the traditional narrative.

Quauhpopocatl was an Aztec nobleman, a Mexica from Tenochtitlan. His name was more properly Quauhpopocatzin, with the *-tzin* suffix to reflect his high rank. He himself was distantly related to the royal family, and his wife was the great-granddaughter of Huitzilihuitl, the second Aztec king (ruled 1391–1415). Quauhpopocatl was sufficiently valued and trusted by Montezuma that in the summer of 1519—as the invading foreigners marched and sailed up and down the Gulf coast, fighting local townspeople and each other—the emperor sent him to the coast to meet them.

Under Montezuma's orders, Quauhpopocatl welcomed the invaders at Vera Cruz, then

> brought, guided, and protected the Marqués [Cortés] and the Christians [the Spaniards] along all roads on which they came, until they entered this city of Mexico, using various means and much astuteness so that the townspeople along those roads, who

were disturbed by the arrival of the Christians, would not kill them.

This, at least, was according to Quauhpopocatl's son. A boy during the war, the son witnessed both the 235 days of the Spanish sojourn in Tenochtitlan and the Noche Triste battle that killed his father. The boy survived the siege of the city and saw his elder brother— who had succeeded as *tlahtoani* of Coyohuacan (Coyoacan)—leave on the Cortés-led expedition to Honduras, along with four hundred of the town's warriors, never to return. In 1526, now in his teens and with the hybrid Christian-Nahua name of don Juan de Guzmán Itztlolinqui, he himself assumed the governorship of Coyohuacan. He would rule it until his death in 1569. Reinforcing that astonishing continuity of local rulership, don Juan, already Mexica royalty, married into the Tetzcoco side of the Aztec royal dynasty—his wife was doña Mencia de la Cruz, one of the granddaughters of Nezahualpilli (ruled 1473–1515)—just as his royal ancestors had been doing for generations.

Don Juan de Guzmán Itztlolinqui was one of three rulers of Nahua towns in the former Aztec heartland who rode beside Viceroy Mendoza in the Mixton War of 1540–41 (a campaign northward against "rebel" Chichimecas that was yet another violent episode in the protracted Spanish invasion). In 1551, the king granted Itztlolinqui his own coat of arms—making him Spanish, as well as Nahua, nobility. Five years later he was one of thirteen royal or noble Nahua lords who wrote to Carlos V "humbly begging" him "to appoint the bishop of Chiapas, fray Bartolomé de Las Casas, to take on the position of our Protector"—an official judicial post in Spanish American provinces—"against the many grievances and abuses that we receive from the Spaniards, for them being amongst us and we being amongst them."[16]

Clearly Itztlolinqui was a successful Aztec politician in New Spain's earliest decades; that characterization is slightly anachronistic ("Aztec" was an imperial entity that ended in 1521, and "New Spain" existed mostly in name only when Itztlolinqui became ruler of his hometown), but it conveys his ability to navigate the hybrid Aztec-Spanish imperial system that was Mexico in his lifetime. He had learned to write Spanish and Latin from the first Franciscans in Mexico, and had a fine grasp of the new legal system. He was educated, informed, and connected.

This context helps us to read the forty-page brief Itztlolinqui filed in Tenochtitlan/Mexico City in 1536. Addressed to the king, it outlined the sacrifices and services of don Juan's father, Quauhpopocatl (such as that quoted previously), as just reason for the king ordering local Spaniards to stop treating the people of Coyohuacan "like slaves." Showing a mastery both of Nahua oratorical tradition and the Spanish petitionary language of the era, Itztlolinqui argued that despite being loyal Christians, his subjects were "hit, kicked, beaten with sticks, thrown in jail, put in stocks and chains like the worst prisoners in the world." Their tribute burden was so onerous that people were fleeing into the hills, where they had no access to the sacraments of Christianity.[17]

Thus Itztlolinqui's very brief narrative of the moment in the war to which we now turn (the march of August–November 1519, from Vera Cruz to Tenochtitlan) was in service of a particular political agenda. Itztlolinqui was not alone in his goal or his chosen tactic; towns and noble families across Mesoamerica (from the Nahuas to the Mayas) claimed after the war that they welcomed and aided the Christian invaders from the very beginning (as discussed in Chapter 2). Because the evidence shows it was untrue in many cases, it is tempting to ignore Itztlolinqui's claim. Indeed, historians have done just that.

I suggest, however, that we can learn something from Itztlolinqui—for several reasons. First, the Spanish conquistador and chronicler accounts that underpin the traditional narrative are no less partisan or agenda-driven; they have the benefits of repetition and availability, but not that of objectivity (or, as we shall see, believability). Second, there is no doubt that the Aztecs were tracking the Spanish ships along the coast, and that multiple Aztec embassies traveled to meet, observe, and accompany the company from the moment they landed. Such contacts are mentioned in dozens of Spanish and indigenous accounts, along with the detailed evidence (written and material) of Montezuma's gifts. The names assigned to Aztec ambassadors, however, are inconsistent and incomplete, so there is no reason why Quauhpopocatl could not have been among them—performing or contributing to the task given to him by Montezuma. Multiple sources state that Cacama (the *tlahtoani* of Tetzcoco) traveled east to meet the Spaniards, a story entirely compatible with Itztlolinqui's. The Tetzcoca chronicler Alva Ixtlilxochitl claimed that it was actually his namesake (and one of Cacama's brothers) who made the trip—and made it as far as Vera Cruz.[18]

Third, Itztlolinqui brought witnesses to corroborate his story. They had their own obvious reasons to support their *tlahtoani,* but the details they offer are worth our attention. Pedro Tlilantzin, for example, testified that he himself went halfway from Tenochtitlan to Vera Cruz, joining Quauhpopocatl en route to the capital; that "he knows they were put safely in this city of Mexico without any danger or risk, because he saw it." Pedro Atenpenecatl added that he too made that journey, with his own father, going as far as Amaquemecan (Amecameca), "which is half way between Vera Cruz and this city," and thus he saw how Quauhpopocatl "brought the Christians by good roads and protected them until putting them safely in this city." Andrés Mecateca said he was with Quauhpopocatl in Coyohuacan (in the service of the *tlahtoani*) when Montezuma's messenger arrived calling him to Tenochtitlan; they were told to bring food to the Spaniards and guide them to the city; this they did, catching up with them at Amaquemecan. Martín Hueytecotzin was also with Quauhpopocatl when he was called to see Montezuma, but he added the detail that they brought from Coyohuacan "many flowers" which "they threw on the floor before" the emperor. Finally, don Diego Cuitecotle said he was "present at the conversation" between Montezuma and Quauhpopocatl, who then ordered Cuitecotle to take a canoe back to Coyohuacan to fetch "his blankets," join him at the lake, and go welcome the Christians; Cuitecotle thought it was at Chalco where they met Cortés, who in recognition of Quauhpopocatl's status gave him "a necklace of pearls."[19]

Obviously this is not a story that can be swallowed whole, any more than any such recollections can, be they by Castilians or Coyohuacan Nahuas. We do not know if the details of flowers and blankets lend credibility or are mere imagination; if Quauhpopocatl led his men as far as Vera Cruz or only to nearby Chalco. Nonetheless, I think that Itztlolinqui's story offers us a glimpse of what really happened (and did not). Montezuma and the Aztecs responded to the arrival of the Spaniards in an intelligent and pragmatic manner. They were neither terrified nor overwhelmed with superstitious foreboding. They neither took the Spaniards to be gods, nor viewed them as a racial Other; even the perception of the newcomers in quasi-ethnic terms—with hitherto-unknown language, customs, and material culture—was muted by the predominance in the Nahua world of *altepetl* identity. The *altepetl* of the Spaniards (who more often called themselves Castilians) was Caxtillan, making them Caxtilteca, with Cortés as their *tlahtoani* (as *capitán* was taken to mean). From the start, the Aztec leadership sought contact, communication, and information; they wanted to understand Caxtilteca intentions, strengths and weaknesses, their capacity to hurt or help the Aztec Empire. Quauhpopocatl thus represents one of scores, if not hundreds, of Aztecs who brought word back to Tenochtitlan, as the invaders were queried, tested, and lured with one set of gifts after another into the capital.[20]

The traditional narrative tells a different story—indeed, there are three other versions of the march to Tenochtitlan, each as well established and misleading as the other. The Cortesian version predictably placed Cortés in almost total control, winning one indigenous ally after another, gaining first the Totonacs and then the Tlaxcalteca. Initial Tlaxcalteca hostility and the outbreak of a deadly eighteen-day war were downplayed as a Spanish victory, a precursor to the winning of another ally.

Predominant for centuries, the Cortesian version was given a boost by the increasing popularity of the Tlatelolca-Franciscan version in the Florentine Codex (as it began to be published and translated, starting in the late nineteenth century). This variant imagines the dithering, unnerved Montezuma described earlier, as part of a trifecta of invented notions about the emperor: a set of eight omens that presage the invasion and Aztec defeat; Montezuma's reaction; and the Surrender at the Meeting. Although this detracts a tad from Cortés's control (Montezuma's weakness makes it easier for Cortés to prevail), the two versions are clearly compatible.

The third version is the Tlaxcalteca one, in which the eighteen-day war is downplayed or erased, in order to emphasize the role of Tlaxcallan as the first and most important convert to the Spanish and Christian cause. In this version, Tlaxcalteca leaders and war-riors save the Spanish company from an ambush in Cholollan, from total annihilation during the Noche Triste, and from permanent re-treat in the summer of 1520; the fall of Tenochtitlan and the spread of the true faith to New Spain are made possible by the Tlaxcalteca.

We cannot embrace Tlaxcalteca partisanship any more than we can accept Cortesian mythistory, but it—like the Itztlolinqui story— contains a crucial kernel of truth. For if we weigh the likelihood of Cortesian control against that of indigenous control, the latter is far heavier. Cortés was doubly removed from the total control of which he later boasted; first, by the captains who decided for themselves where and when to fight or not, and second, by the fact that the company was forced to react at every turn to initiatives taken by the Aztec and Tlaxcaltec leadership. As one historian has noted, "The relentless march on Mexico impresses, until one asks just what Cortés intended once he had got there."[21]

THE FIRST MAJOR TEST of the Caxtilteca engineered by the Aztecs was a trap set for them by the Totonacs of Cempohuallan—who led the company straight into Tlaxcalteca territory. Tired and hungry after two weeks' travel, the company was led right to the eastern defensive wall of the Tlaxcalteca. The Totonac ambassador-guides went ahead to procure a friendly welcome; instead, they delivered the invaders to the Tlaxcalteca, who began a series of ambushes and major assaults. The Totonacs were hedging their bets, hoping to achieve greater autonomy by sending the invaders west to battle one or both of the regional powers (the Aztecs and the Tlaxcalteca). But they surely calculated that the Aztecs were most likely to prevail, and thus they did what the Aztecs wanted—for the empire benefited from the death of every Tlaxcalteca warrior and every Spanish conquistador, from the weakening of both sides.

The eighteen-day war was punishing to both sides. The Tlaxcalteca warriors attacked the Spanish camp at dawn, and kept up the assault all day. At night, the Spanish captains rode out to nearby hamlets and villages, burning the houses and killing everyone they found. The next day, the pattern was repeated. After several days, the Tlaxcalteca sent an embassy of fifty men to discuss a treaty; according to Cortés's account, one of them revealed under questioning (in other words, torture) that while the elder *tlahtoani*, Xicotencatl, genuinely wished for peace, his son (of the same name) intended to trick the Spaniards into letting down their guard. Cortés then ordered a hand to be severed from all fifty emissaries (or so he claimed); thus continued the Tlaxcalteca attacks and the conquistador raids on unarmed villages.

The Tlaxcalteca warriors were well trained and organized professionals, "skilled beyond any the Spaniards had yet encountered in Mesoamerica"—indeed, in the Americas. The conquistadors fought mostly on the defensive, and while their weapons (especially steel swords) allowed them to kill many more of the enemy than the Tlaxcalteca could, their numbers steadily fell; by the second week, they had lost half the horses (the rest all wounded) and a fifth of the Spaniards had died or taken wounds that would prove fatal. The company was outnumbered by its porters—some two hundred Totonacs, several hundred Taíno slaves, and scores of African and other indigenous slaves and servants. They were vital for transporting artillery, food, and other supplies; but with supplies dwindling, they became a liability. Totonac porters surely began to slip away back to the coast, but the Taínos—who had already begun to die from cold and hunger on the march into Tlaxcalteca territory—suffered greatly. The strategy of the captains (we should not blame Cortés if we are also to deny him credit), if it can even be called such, was a disaster. If the Tlaxcalteca had persisted, the invaders would have been killed to a man.

But they did not. Under the rules and customs of Mesoamerican warfare, the Caxtilteca should have retreated and sued for a peace in which they paid tribute to Tlaxcallan. But lacking that option, the Spaniards perpetuated a war of attrition whose cost was proving too high for the local leadership. A hint of that cost is given by Cortés's own chilling descriptions of nocturnal attacks on Tlaxcalteca villages, where, he later crowed to the king, "I killed many people." On one dawn raid, he reached "another large town, which, according to an inspection I had made, contained more than twenty thousand houses. And because I took them by surprise, they rushed out unarmed, the women and children running naked through the streets, and I began to do them some harm."[22]

There is no doubt that the Tlaxcalteca decision *not* to destroy the invasion force was the right one. In the long run, such a massacre would only have led to brutal Spanish reprisals from the much larger force that Velázquez was already assembling in Cuba—although Xicotencatl and the other Tlaxcalteca rulers could not possibly have known that. Still, in the short run, many Tlaxcalteca lives were saved. And if the Caxtilteca-Tlaxcalteca war was beneficial to the Aztecs—their doing, at least in part—then the subsequent peace was far less so. During the days of negotiations between the Spanish captains and the Tlaxcalteca, Aztec envoys urged the captains not to trust the enemy (again, it seems clear that there were Aztecs with the company every day of the journey). But a new supply of gifts and reassurances from Montezuma could not match the promise of immediate relief in nearby Tlaxcallan. On September 23, the invaders limped into the city and the Tlaxcalteca leadership took control.

The badly bruised company spent seventeen days in Tlaxcallan (roughly a day of recovery for each grim day of warfare). Almost every Spaniard had suffered wounds of some kind, and while most recovered, some died, reducing total Spanish numbers to fewer than 250 (half the force that had left Cuba). The survivors must have been traumatized and terrified. Their relief at being able to experience the hospitality, rather than the hostility, of the Tlaxcalteca must have been tempered by the knowledge that the invaders were at the mercy of their hosts, dependent upon them for food and supplies, for information about the Aztecs, and for allied warriors to protect them from whatever came next.

Viewed from the perspective of the traditional narrative, it is a mystery why the Spaniards did not stay longer in Tlaxcallan. Viewed from the same perspective, it is also difficult to explain the shocking incident that followed: the brutal slaughter of thousands of residents of a neighboring Nahua city. As with so many moments in the traditional narrative, the mystery and inexplicability are rooted in the great narrative of the conquistadors and chroniclers, and its mythistory of Cortesian control. The massacre in Cholollan (today's Cholula) is less mysterious if we step back from that traditional narrative, take into account the reduced circumstances and state of mind of the conquistadors, and accept that it was the Tlaxcalteca leadership, not Cortés and his captains, who were in control.

THE BARE FACTS of the Cholollan massacre are as follows. On October 10, the surviving Spaniards and some six thousand Tlaxcalteca warriors made the daylong march to Cholollan. They camped for the night outside the town, where Chololtec nobles delivered welcome speeches and food. The next day, the Spaniards entered the town (with Cempohualtec and Tlaxcalteca porters; the allied warriors were asked to remain outside). There they were housed and fed for two days, but for the three days after that they were brought only firewood and water (according to Spanish reports). Cortés also claimed (echoed by other Spanish accounts) that there were barricades in the city, pits with stakes sharpened to kill falling horses, piles of stones on the rooftops (ready to be thrown), and rumors of a massive Aztec army hidden nearby. Decades later, a final detail of supposed evidence of a planned Chololtec ambush was added to Spanish accounts: a local woman revealed the ambush plot to the interpreter Malintzin, who informed Cortés.

Around the 16th or 17th, a large number of Chololtec porters assembled in the central plaza of the city, either at Cortés's behest or in preparation for the departure of the Spaniards; there seem also to have been hundreds of other locals there too, including women and small children, possibly to watch the Caxtilteca marching off. Suddenly, the conquistadors began to wade into the crowd with their swords, butchering the townspeople. Armed Spaniards blocked all four exits from the plaza, killing those who tried to flee. Meanwhile, the Tlaxcalteca army that was camped outside stormed into the city. For the next several days (one conquistador said it lasted four), the Spaniards and Tlaxcalteca slaughtered, plundered, and burned. Thousands of Chololteca were killed. Not a single Spaniard died.

Cortés later claimed that he had marched to Cholollan for supplies. But Cholollan was neither on the way to Tenochtitlan, nor any closer to it than Tlaxcallan itself (it was a detour to the south). The fact is, neither Cortés nor his fellow captains were in control: the Tlaxcalteca led the Spaniards to Cholollan for their own political purposes, telling the Spanish captains that it was on the way and rich in supplies. The alleged Chololtec ambush was probably a Tlaxcalteca ruse devised to manipulate the captains—or, as Alva Ixtlilxochitl later wrote, "an invention of the Tlaxcalteca and some of the Spaniards." The Spaniards did not know that another city, closer to Tlaxcallan, was also well supplied: Huexotzinco. And therein lies the rub.

Part of the mythistory of Tlaxcallan as the city of "good Indians," the antidote to the Aztec "bad Indians," was the supposed difference in their governmental system—a virtual republic run by senators. In fact, Tlaxcallan was organized socially and politically just like any Nahua *altepetl* (town or city-state), with local variations similar to those of the Aztecs. Tlaxcallan itself was a complex *altepetl*, made up of four constituent *altepeme* (plural of *altepetl*), each with its own *tlahtoani* (one of whom, Xicotencatl, was most senior); Tenochtitlan was also a complex *altepetl*, comprising Tenochtitlan itself (with its own four subordinate neighborhoods) and the sibling *altepetl* of Tlatelolco at the north end of the island (whose *tlahtoani* had been demoted to the level of a governor by the *huey tlahtoani* of Tenochtitlan).

There was another similarity between Tlaxcallan and the Aztecs, one central to the events of 1519. The Aztec Empire was a Triple Alliance of unequal partners, with Tenochtitlan dominant over Tetzcoco, both of whom were more powerful than Tlacopan (as we shall see in the next chapter, this uneasy partnership played a crucial role in the war's outcome). Tlaxcallan was also the dominant partner in its own regional triple alliance (let us call it the Tlaxcallan Triple Alliance); its junior partners were Huexotzinco and Cholol-lan. Huexotzinco's warriors had fought the Spaniards alongside their Tlaxcaltec allies in September's eighteen-day war, and in October they too marched to Cholollan; they would go on to fight the Aztecs, and later insist in eloquent petitions to the king of Spain that from the very beginning they had embraced the Spaniards and the Christian religion. And what of Cholollan? A year or two earlier, it had abandoned the Tlaxcallan Triple Alliance and become a loyal tributary of the Aztec Empire.[23]

The march to Cholollan and the sacking of the city thus constituted a well-executed Tlaxcalteca plan to test the new alliance with the Caxtilteca invaders, to punish the Chololteca for switching sides, and to restore in Cholollan a leadership loyal to the Tlaxcallan Triple Alliance. The political tide had turned not only in favor of Tlaxcallan as a regional power—better equipped than ever to resist Aztec encroachment—but also in favor of Xicotencatl. One of his fellow kings, a *tlahtoani* named Maxixcatl, had been jostling to replace the elderly Xicotencatl as senior ruler, but he was related to the Chololteca ruler who had switched to the Aztec side and been killed in October's massacre.

After two weeks in Cholollan, the company moved on to a subject town of Huexotzinco's, and from there began the march between the volcanoes and into the Valley of Mexico. The surviving Spaniards made up roughly 5 percent of the expedition: in addition to the surviving Taíno slaves, African slaves and servants, and remnant Totonac warriors and porters, the vast majority of the force were warriors and other support personnel from the Tlaxcallan Triple Alliance. There were women too—Spanish, Taíno, Totonac, and

Tlaxcalteca (to whom we shall return in a later chapter). All in all, something close to ten thousand people descended into the Aztec heartland.

For a moment, let us put aside Tlaxcaltec confidence in their newfound situation, as justified as it may have been, and let us reject the traditional narrative's mythistory of Cortesian control (the captains were being pushed by the Tlaxcalteca and pulled by the Aztecs, with any semblance of control on their part mere delusion); forget the sibling myth of Montezuma the Fearful (some of his noblemen may have been apprehensive, but the emperor was keen to see the Caxtilteca for himself). Instead, let us accept that all the protagonists in this unfolding drama were familiar with war, and all must have felt the visceral, anticipatory fear—or thrill—of the violence that they knew was coming.[24]

But the violence did not come; not yet, at least. It would remain contained for months, like the wild beasts in Montezuma's zoo, threatening periodically to break out, their roars sounding to the conquistadors "like hell itself." Perhaps the Spaniards sensed—assumed—that, when the killing did eventually come, it would indeed be as if all hell had broken loose.[25]

Meanwhile, the months of marching and fighting, the memories of slaughter and reminders of one's own mortality, gave way to a surreal ease and tranquility. Montezuma welcomed Cortés and the other Caxtilteca captains, extending to the invaders a level of hospitality that was incredible, inexplicable. The Meeting initiated a long interlude in the Spanish-Aztec War of some 235 days (more or less, if we end it on the uncertain date of Montezuma's death). Certainly there was violence during this time, even within Tenochtitlan itself. But relatively speaking the interlude was a period of "phoney war" or *drôle de guerre* ("strange war")—phrases coined to describe the period of roughly the same number of days at the start of World War II, when no major military operations were launched in Western Europe. Similarly, only toward the end of the 235 days of our story's phoney war did Spaniards or Aztecs engage in major attempts to destroy or subdue the other.[26]

During these months, Montezuma and Cortés seem to have spent considerable time in each other's company, most of it in the relative seclusion of the royal palaces in the center of Tenochtitlan. One is reminded of the months that Julius Caesar and Cleopatra spent together in Alexandria, thereby influencing the course of Egyptian and Roman history. That interlude produced a notorious romance; did the phoney war in Tenochtitlan nurture a political romance?

All this makes the 235-day interlude sound paradoxically both mysterious and uneventful, and indeed Conquest accounts have tended to focus on the year before the Meeting and the year after Montezuma's death, skipping over or shrinking the time in between (typical of the temporal distortions of the traditional narrative). An extreme example is by Vásquez de Tapia, who was in Tenochtitlan for most of this period, summing it up thus: "The next day, we entered Mexico and we were there for eight months, more or less." But such a summary was deceptively simple, as reflected in Vásquez de Tapia's next sentence: "During that time important things [grandes cosas] happened that, in order not to be longwinded, I shall leave out."[27]

Important things, indeed; for the Meeting had planted a seed. Or rather, the lie of the Meeting had planted a seed that, just as one lie begets another, germinated into a sprawling tree of inventions and embellishments. The captains had reached Tenochtitlan hoping to do what conquistadors had done before and would continue to do in the Americas: seize the ruler; and by threats, selective acts of violence, and the performance of possession, make a conquest claim. (In his Second Letter, Cortés claimed he had told the king about Montezuma in a prior report, "and I assured Your Highness that I would take him, either captive or dead or subject to Your Majesty's Royal Crown.")[28]

Such an outcome was not, in reality, possible. It was the Spaniards, not the Aztec ruler, who had been detained; Montezuma had collected the Caxtilteca, not surrendered to them. But the audience for the legalistic performance of possession was not indigenous; it was Spanish, ranging from the rank-and-file conquistadors camped out in the city to the royal officials in Spain who would eventually read reports of these events. And so—surely soon after the Meeting—the captains began to nurture the seed that would produce that tree of lies, of which we can identify three main branches.

The first such branch was that of the arrest or capture of the emperor (an act introduced at the very start of this book). Conquistador sources are vague and contradictory as to when exactly the arrest took place, how Montezuma responded, and where he subsequently was detained. This is because the very notion, like the Surrender at the Meeting, is pure nonsense—implausible in the extreme, unsupported by any of the evidence of life in Tenochtitlan during these months. If Montezuma was ever physically detained, whether in irons or under guard, it was after war broke out in the city center in May; in other words, it happened within weeks, if not days, of his death. But Cortés and others later moved the "arrest" forward in time; they admitted that Montezuma still ran his empire, but by inventing his capture, they could claim that Cortés controlled Montezuma and thus controlled the empire. The story only hangs together if one accepts cartoonish stereotypes of Montezuma as naïve and acquiescent, and Cortés as brilliantly and boldly Machiavellian (as illustrated literally in a recent "graphic biography" of Cortés; see the Gallery). This period, then, was less of a phoney war, closer to a political romance, and more of a phoney surrender and captivity (let us call these 235 days the Phoney Captivity).[29]

The second branch of the metaphorical Phoney Captivity tree was the claim in Cortés's Second Letter that Montezuma's speech of surrender at the Meeting was restated by him several times—that, in effect, he kept on surrendering, month after month. Montezuma's second great Surrender speech became a famous scene, because Cortés made of it an irresistibly theatrical one, in which a tearful emperor not only swore allegiance to the king of Spain, but persuaded the Aztec nobility to likewise "promise to do and comply with all that was demanded of them in the name of Your Majesty" (Cortés told the king) and to henceforth pay to the Spanish monarch "all the tributes and services which formerly they made and owed to Mutezuma." As if laying to rest any doubts regarding the veracity of so spectacularly implausible an event, Cortés added that "all of this took place before a public notary, who set it down in an appropriate document."[30]

The scene was repeated, painted, and engraved (our Gallery includes an example), and embellished scores of times, included in almost every account for the last five centuries. As usual, Gómara set the unquestioning tone. In a 1578 English edition, for example, the emperor ordered all "his Noble men" to submit to "the king of Castile," because he is "the king whiche wee have looked for so many yeares." As for the conquistadors, added Montezuma, "wee are their kinsmen," and he then broke down "with the sobbes, sighes, and teares, that fell from hys eyes. All his subiectes there present fell into a crie, weeping and mourning." Elizabethan readers of Gómara might have taken Aztec tears to be a mark of submission, but just as likely they read the scene as one of emotional expression appropriate to the import of the moment—as Spaniards did. For in the European (and possibly Aztec) culture of these centuries, weeping was associated with prayer and petition, with both the request and receipt of favors, from both divine and earthly lords.[31]

In Cortés's account, this scene took place in early December; then again, some unspecified number of weeks later, he supposedly had another discussion with the emperor and Aztec notables on matters of religion. While admitting that he could not impose a destruction of religious "idols" or the conversion of the Aztec rulership, he nonetheless claimed that the emperor conceded that "I would know better than them the things they should hold to and believe, and I should explain to them and make them understand, and they would do what I told them was best." (Francis Brooks, the Australian friar-historian who years ago brilliantly dissected the Phoney Captivity, called this "perhaps the most extraordinary sentence in the whole letter.")[32]

A few pages (perhaps a month) later, Cortés reported again on the many conversations he had had with Montezuma, emphasizing how much he had learned about the "mines" and "the secrets of Mutezuma's lands." This knowledge was shared "with such free will and contentment on the part of Mutezuma and all the natives of these lands that it seemed as if *ab initio* they had known Your Sacred Majesty to be their king and natural lord." In addition to such statements, Cortés's Second Letter is peppered with implications of Montezuma's amiable subordination and Aztec subservience. These were repeated and expanded by subsequent writers, with imaginative new scenes invented from the onset. Cervantes de Salazar, for example, turned the Phoney Captivity into a lengthy political romance, culminating in a poignant final conversation between Cortés and a dying Montezuma, in which they both shed tears and declared their mutual affection. The emperor (now ex-emperor and vassal of King Carlos) yet again articulated his subordination and acknowledgment of Spanish sovereignty, making one last "formal expression of Spanish imperial theory" (Brooks again).[33]

That fictional deathbed scene leads us to the third metaphorical tree branch: Montezuma's keen interest in the Spaniards, and his seemingly calm and amiable demeanor (he had, after all, succeeded in neutralizing the invaders and turning them into collected specimens) was imagined by them as love—love for the conquistadors in general, for Cortés in particular, and for his new status as a vassal of the king. (Some even claimed later that Montezuma wished to convert to Christianity, but Cortés said he needed further instruction.)

This "mysterious convergence" tying the two men together was laid on thickly by Gómara and his successors (to reflect Cortesian control and magnetism, in contrast to Montezuma's innate inferiority and passivity). But other writers seized upon the notion of Montezuma's Stockholm syndrome with an enthusiasm equal to the Spanish chroniclers. In the eighteenth century, for example, Dilworth stated that Montezuma grew "particularly fond of" Cortés, and on one occasion embraced him "with great affection." The emperor was "perfectly well satisfied" with his state of virtual captivity within the city center, becoming "every day more and more attached" to his captor.

When Cortés returned to Tenochtitlan with Narváez, Montezuma came "as far as the outward court to meet Cortes"—an echo of the Meeting of a few months earlier—"whom he caressed in a transport of joy, which could not possibly be the effect of dissimulation." Similarly, Campe told young readers that while the Aztec emperor hoped the Spaniards would soon go home, and was thus overjoyed when Cortés told him ships were being built, he was also exuberantly fond of the captain; upon hearing of the ships, "Montezuma could not conceal the extravagance of his joy upon this expected answer; he fell upon the general's neck, overwhelmed him with caresses."[34]

In one French account, the flow of affection was reversed and the theme used to make a wry joke about Spaniards: "From that time [Cortés] attempted to become their Master, and at the first he endeavoured to gain them by all possible kindness, and to win the hearts of the Mexicans [Aztecs] by his courteous and sweet comportment, and indeed he was so affable and loving, that they thought him not to be a *Spaniard*."[35] But by and large, Montezuma's demeanor during the Phoney Captivity became elemental to the evolution of his personality; Sigüenza y Góngora, quoting Torquemada, emphasized that "while among the Castilians, this king was so affable, so loving, that hardly a day passed when he did not do favors for someone." Or, in the words of the twentieth-century Galician intellectual Filgueira Valverde:

> There were almost happy days when the Aztec lord and the Spanish captain lived familiarly together, showing each other favors and proofs of friendship, the hours enlivened by the vagaries of game-playing, by bouts of hunting, by fine singing, and by the pleasant humor of the captive king, always generous toward both guards and servants.[36]

As another historian recently remarked, in response to Díaz's story of the conquistadors and Montezuma laughing at Pedro de Alvarado cheating at the Aztec game of *totoloque:* Montezuma had been turned into "a king from out of a chivalric romance."[37]

Filgueira Valverde was simply a link in a chain of repetition going back centuries, whereby conquistador recollections of their extraordinary sojourn as guests of Montezuma—the food, the women, the excursions to palaces and markets and zoos, the hunting and game-playing—were repackaged as details from the emperor's joyful captivity. Evidence of Montezuma learning about Spanish technology was recast as Cortés patronizing or deceiving the adoring emperor; thus Cortés showing Montezuma how to use a crossbow was part of their games together, and the four forty-foot brigantines that the Spaniards built for Montezuma, which he then used on hunting trips, grew into a ruse whereby "the conquistadors gained priceless information about the lake."[38]

No doubt both Aztecs and Spaniards saw the brigantines as useful to them, as a reflection on their status as hosts and captors, and were unaware or in denial regarding how the other side saw the boats—and the entire situation. This double-sided perception helped to create confusing accounts of some of Vásquez de Tapia's mysterious "important events" of the Phoney Captivity—events already confused by the traditional narrative's inversion of who was in control and who captive.

Examples are the incidents involving Cohualpopocatzin (or Qualpopoca) and Cacama (more properly, Cacamatzin). Qualpopoca was the *tlahtoani* of a town in the empire's eastern region, where Spaniards were still maintaining a semblance of a settlement (Vera Cruz). Early in the 235 days of the Phoney Captivity this lord and some of his noblemen were arrested, brought to Tenochtitlan, and publicly executed (by "dogging"—mauled by Spanish mastiffs—and then burned alive). Cortés claimed this was punishment for killing Spaniards near the coast, thus supporting the lie of his control over the empire. But the details of what Qualpopoca did, and why, were contradictory and unpersuasive in accounts by Cortés and other Spaniards. For, in fact, the machinations of Aztec imperial politics were also at work, beyond the grasp of the conquistadors (and therefore us). The execution that the Spaniards witnessed was surely seen by the Aztecs as a variant on what those same Spaniards were denouncing as "human sacrifice," probably presented to the populace as part of that month's festival (and, for Montezuma and his noblemen, a fascinating display of a Caxtilteca variant on ritual killing).[39]

Cacama was the *tlahtoani* of Tetzcoco; he had met the Spaniards near the borders of his domain and escorted them to Tenochtitlan in early November. He was Montezuma's nephew and the second-ranked king in the empire's Triple Alliance. According to Cortés and the traditional narrative, Cacama objected to his uncle's surrender to Cortés, and began to plot an attack on the Spaniards with the third king in the Alliance, that of Tlacopan. Quauhpopocatl of Coyohuacan may also have been implicated, along with the ruler of Ixtlapalapan. Cortés then claimed to cleverly conspire with Montezuma to have them all arrested and brought to Tenochtitlan to swear allegiance to none other than Cortés—who claimed he then replaced Cacama with his brother Coanacoch. (This absurd claim has been the basis for centuries of even greater ones, such as "Here *Cortes* made Kings, and comaunded with as great authoritie as though he had obtayned already the whole Empire of *Mexico*.")[40]

While the presence of the Spaniards in the city may have been a factor in the incident, its larger non-Cortesian context was the power-jostling among the three kings that underpinned the Alliance; never an equal partnership, the balance of authority was constantly tested, further complicated by the fact that intermarriage had turned the royal families into one sprawling dynasty (see the Dynastic Vine in the Appendix). There was also another twist: after forty-three years as Tetzcoco's *tlahtoani*, the great Nezahualpilli had died four years before the Spanish invasion, leaving many sons and a succession dispute that was complicated by the Spanish-Aztec War. Six of the those sons would end up as *tlahtoani* of Tetzcoco—Cacama the first, then Coanacoch, followed by Ixtlilxochitl, whose role in the last half of the war would prove crucial. In short, while the Spaniards may ultimately have benefited from the Aztec Empire's intra-dynastic and inter-*altepetl* politics, in the early months of

1520 they were a long way from understanding its complexities, let alone controlling them.

If MONTEZUMA's SURRENDER was an invention, and his captivity phoney, why did the Spaniards not denounce the lie later on—when, for example, some gave testimony in the Cortés *residencia* investigation that was critical of him? As MacNutt remarked, only "unanimity of testimony served to remove from the sphere of fable" history's "most supremely audacious act . . . so stupefying in his conception and so incredible in its execution." In fact, there are many reasons to question that testimony and restore the Phoney Captivity to "fable."[41]

To begin with, consider that most of the conquistadors who sailed from Cuba in 1519 were dead by the end of 1520, or alive but had never set foot in Montezuma's Tenochtitlan. And most of the men who fought in the battle in Tenochtitlan that marked the end of the Phoney Captivity had come with Narváez, so that even the survivors of that battle had entered a city that was already up in arms. In short, fewer than 10 percent of the thousands of Spaniards who participated in the war were both in Tenochtitlan during the Phoney Captivity and survived beyond 1521 to talk about it.

Furthermore, an even smaller percentage were able to see the Meeting, and only a handful could have heard any speeches or the subsequent conversations that took place between the Spanish captains and Montezuma and his nobles. For most the conquistadors in the city, their information and understanding of what was going on came from the captains and the discussions within cohorts. With their immediate needs met—an abundance of servants, including indigenous "wives" and sex slaves, plenty of food, a stockpiling of precious metals and other valuables, no apparent threat of sudden attack—there was little reason to question the official story.

Indeed, any Spaniard later questioning the Surrender and calling the captivity phoney would have run the risk of crossing the line of treason and committing lèse majesté (*lesa majestad*). As Brooks noted, even Las Casas did not deny "the natural right of Spain to rule." In time, "the myth of Montezuma's submission was so established that it was unquestioningly accepted, even by people who had been present" (to quote Thomas, despite his verdict of this being "certainly possible" but not probable). By the 1570s, Durán could show a genuine curiosity in the truth, because it hardly mattered; he found it "difficult to believe" sources showing Montezuma seized right after the Meeting, and thereafter kept "in irons, wrapped in a mantle, carried on the shoulders of his caciques," because "I have yet to meet a Spaniard who will concede this point to me." But such skepticism was too little too late; the lie was already too well established.[42]

In addition, dozens of conquistadors staked a personal, political investment in Montezuma's alleged captivity by later claiming to have been his guard. Martín Vásquez was one, later known for hosting card games at his Mexico City house, where he lived with his Taíno wife. Another was Pedro Solís, a horseman in Sandoval's cohort who claimed to have been head guard, as did Juan Velázquez. Francisco Flores later stated that he witnessed one of Montezuma's surrender statements, and probably did guard duty; as did crossbowman Pedro López, one of the Noche Triste survivors who ate Martín de Gamboa's horse after it was fatally wounded during the escape. Díaz claimed Cortés had López flogged when he complained about guard duty and referred to Montezuma as "a dog." Díaz also wrote that another guard, named Trujillo, could not stop staring at the emperor; Montezuma gave him a gold nugget and asked him to stop, but when Trujillo still could not help himself, he was removed from the guard.[43]

In reality, the "guard" was a rotation of conquistadors who served as part of the emperor's entourage, as indeed it must have looked to city residents who saw him going about his business. In other words, contingents of Caxtilteca became part of the imperial guard, protecting not detaining the *huey tlahtoani*. This enhanced the ruler's prestige, while also giving him opportunities to study and learn more from the Caxtilteca; in return, he patronized them with attention and trinkets (jewelry and other items that conquistadors later bragged about). The prestige for a conquistador of having been "a guard of Montezuma's" only increased in the years and decades after the war, as the legends of city (its wealth!) and captivity (his generosity!) blossomed. None had reason to admit—or even to choose to remember—that the captivity was a sham.

Despite all these reasons to misremember the past, however, surviving conquistadors did in fact reveal the reality of the Phoney Captivity in numerous ways. To start with, throughout the entire 235 days, neither Cortés nor any other Spaniard in Tenochtitlan wrote a letter or report to the king, or to anyone outside the city, detailing their supposed control of city and empire. Yet they claimed to have ink and paper—to notarize Montezuma's surrender. The Aztecs had writing materials anyway. Moreover, scores of other documents have survived from the turbulent, violent years bracketing the Phoney Captivity.[44]

When, after the escape from the city, the survivors began to insist the dead emperor had surrendered and been seized, they nonetheless offered abundant details of life in a city where Montezuma had clearly continued to rule freely—details that are highly revealing for what they do and do not contain. The sum of all such descriptions, from Cortés's own to those of Tapia and Aguilar to the testimonies given in lawsuits and investigations, give a powerful impression of a fully functioning city and ruling regime. Earlier historians conceded that Montezuma "was to all outward appearances free," and recent ones have observed that, even in the canonical accounts by Cortés, Gómara, and Díaz, "Moctezuma is remarkably free"; he is "a man at liberty, at the center of an enormous household operating according to its familiar routines." The putative prisoner, under "the guard" of up to half a dozen conquistadors at all times, nonetheless traveled at will to other palaces, to temples to make offerings, and to hunting grounds, moving around and outside the city with an entourage of "always at least three thousand men" (Cortés's own admission). He "received ambassadors from distant lands" and envoys delivering tribute, "speaking publicly and privately" as he wished, "always with many lords and high-ranking people in his company."[45]

Similarly, the markets continued as usual, as did religious festi-

vals and rituals. All were mentioned by the conquistadors, anticipating the changes that *would* come—wealth appropriated by them,
their religion imposed—while tacitly or explicitly acknowledging
that no such changes had begun. Cortés claimed he made attempts
to destroy and replace Aztec "idols," but even he and Gómara admitted that "the moment was not fitting, nor did he have the force
necessary to carry out his intent."[46]

It is almost as if the Caxtilteca were ignored, even invisible. And
while they must have stood out, they were a minuscule presence,
confined much of the time to the massive Axayacatl palace complex.
Recall that this was a city of some sixty thousand inhabitants—not
the two hundred thousand or more that is often erroneously claimed,
but with hundreds of thousands of additional residents in the myriad towns on the lakeshores. Many of those visited Tenochtitlan by
day in order to work, deliver goods, and trade, swelling the city and
helping to make it the noisy, smelly, bustling imperial capital that
conquistadors remembered and described. As the Spaniards numbered no more than 250, they made up less than a quarter of 1 percent of the island-city's daytime population.[47]

Yet, at the same time, for all the unwitting revelations of a city
functioning freely and normally—not under new management—the
descriptions by conquistadors lack a personal engagement with the
Aztec population. We can sense the Spaniards' avaricious amazement at the splendor of the imperial court and capital, and the paradox of the fear that tinged their boasts, but they remain curiously
disconnected from individual Aztecs other than Montezuma and his
close entourage. The real city of festivals and families is not visible
or available to the conquistadors, a sign of their isolation as collected
guests, as unwitting zoo specimens, of an emperor remote and inac-
cessible to ordinary Aztecs.

When Cortés left the city in May to confront the Narváez company sent by Velázquez, Montezuma did not send a contingent of
warriors (only observers); he was, after all, still *huey tlahtoani*, and it
was his decision where and when Aztec warriors fought. Cortés left
with several of the leading captains and most of the men, leaving

Carta de relació ēbiada a su. S. majestad del ēpa-
dor nɼo señoɼ: poɼ el capitā general dela nueua spaña: llamado fernādo coɼ-
tes. Enla ql haze relació dlas tierras y prouicias sin cuēto q hā descubierto
nueuamēte enel yucatā del año de.xix.a esta pte: y ha sometido ala corona
real de su. S. H. En especial haze relació de vna grādissima prouicia muy
rica llamada Culua: ēla ql ay muy grādes ciudades y de marauillosos edi-
ficios: y de grādes tratos y riqzas. Entre las qles ay vna mas marauillosa
y rica q todas llamada Timixtitā: q esta poɼ marauillosa arte edificada so-
bɼe vna grāde laguna. dela ql ciudad y prouicia es rey vn grādissimo señoɼ
llamado Muteeçuma: dōde le acaecierō al capitā y alos españoles espāto-
sas cosas de oyɼ. Cuenta largamēte del grādissimo señoɼio del dicho Muteeçuma y de sus ritos y cerimonias. y de como se sirue.

THE URTEXT. *(top, previous page)* The title page to the first publication of Cortés's 1520 report to the king, the so-called Second Letter, printed in Seville in 1522 by Jacobo Cromberger, and recently dubbed "the urtext on the conquest of Mexico."

CIVILIZATION, BARBARISM, AND NATURE. *(bottom, previous page)* Undaunted Spaniards and fearful Aztecs before the twin erupting volcanoes of Popocatepetl and Iztaccihuatl. The version in *America* (English 1670, Dutch 1671) of this imaginative illustration popular in the early modern centuries.

THE VALLEY. A nineteenth-century rendering of the Valley of Mexico in 1519 shows the route that the Spanish-Tlaxcalteca forces took in November 5–8 from Chalco (bottom right) through Ayotzinco, Cuitlahuac, and Ixtlapalapan, to the Meeting at Tenochtitlan's edge (marked here as "Camp of Cortez").

SHOCK AND AWE. Kislak *Conquest of Mexico* Painting #2, oil on canvas, late-seventeeth-century Mexico. Labeled "The Arrival of Cortés at Veracruz and the Reception by Moctezuma's Ambassadors," and later "Veracruz No. 2."

THE MEETING. Kislak *Conquest of Mexico* Painting #3, oil on canvas, late-seventeenth-century Mexico. Labeled "The Meeting of Cortés and Moctezuma," and later "Volcano of Mexico. No. 3."

STONED. Kislak *Conquest of Mexico* Painting #4, oil on canvas, late-seventeenth-century Mexico. Labeled "Moctezuma Stoned by His People."

THE CONQUEST. Kislak *Conquest of Mexico* Painting #7, oil on canvas, late-seventeenth-century Mexico. Labeled "The Conquest of Tenochtitlan," and later "CONQUEST OF MEXICO BY CORTÉS. No. 7."

Spanish Gratitude.
Cortes orders Motezuma to be Fetter'd.

T.II   Fol. 202.

Entra Hernan Cortés triunfante
en Tlascala.

J. Rodriz.^{te} lo del.   J. Garrido lo sc.

SPANISH INGRATITUDE. *(left)* "Spanish Gratitude. Cortes orders Motezuma to be Fetter'd"
is a 1741 English example of a widely used early modern illustration. An imperious, bearded
Cortés points a baton of office at a feather-dressed Montezuma, whose wrists are being chained
by another Spaniard. The caption is sarcastic, as the "fettering" shows Spanish ingratitude for
Montezuma's surrender.

TRIUMPHAL ENTRIES. *(right)* "Hernan Cortés enters Tlaxcala in triumph." From a 1798 Madrid
edition of Solís's *Historia de la Conquista de México*. Every reinvention of every Cortesian city
entry reinscribed the Meeting as a triumph.

HIS HEART WAS IN THE RIGHT PLACE. *(top)* As reflected on the cover of this volume in the multimillion-selling *Horrible Histories* series, human sacrifice is at the heart of its tongue-in-cheek take on Aztec civilization and its conquest.

SACRIFICING HUMANS. *(bottom left)* "The Human Sacrifices of the Indians of Mexico," showing executions taking place atop a highly stylized and imaginary Great Temple in Tenochtitlan, first appeared in 1601 and then in numerous publications through to the present century. Its bizarre architecture, horned devils, and sinister sacrificial setting made Mesoamerican culture utterly menacing.

IDOL WORSHIP. *(bottom right)* "Uitzilipuztli: Principal Idol of the Mexicans," from the Abbé Prévost's *Histoire Générale des Voyages Possible of 1754*, is a version of an image of Huitzilopochtli and the heart sacrifice that appeared in various European books from the late sixteenth to nineteenth centuries.

DIVINE IMAGES. In the Codex Telleriano-Remensis *(top)*, Huitzilopochtli represents the fifteenth month in the Aztec calendar, Panquetzaliztli. The Codex Tovar, completed around 1585 by the Jesuit Juan de Tovar, and here depicting Huitzilopochtli *(middle)* and Montezuma *(bottom)*, drew upon indigenous sources to create a hybrid perspective on the Aztec past (similar to that of books created in the same decades by Sahagún, Durán, and other friars).

RUFFLED FEATHERS. *(top images)* The frontispiece *(left)* to Ogilby's *America* (1670), depicting native Americans of all kinds as feathered, with "America" embodied as a topless woman wearing the emblematic feathered skirt and headdress; and Montezuma *(right)* ("The Last King of the Mexicans") as a generic, feathered Native American warrior prince.

A NOBLE SAVAGE. *(left)* Montezuma— in an Italian edition of Solís's *History*, based on the portrait sent to Florence in the 1690s—as young and virile, yet unthreatening as generic, feathered, and Orientalized.

THE ZOOKEEPER. *(left)* One of the illustrations added to the manuscript of Sahagún's *Historia* (aka the Florentine Codex) conveyed the extent of Montezuma's zoo complex with sample images of birds and beasts, a building and a zookeeper.

PICTURING THE WAR. *(left)* Images of the Spanish-Aztec War, from a 1733 Italian edition of Solís's *History of the Conquest of Mexico:* an Aztec embassy submissively offers gifts; Spaniards show off cannon, while an Aztec artist draws the scene (to be shown to Montezuma); a horse head taken by Aztec warriors; and an eagle carrying off a careless Aztec zookeeper.

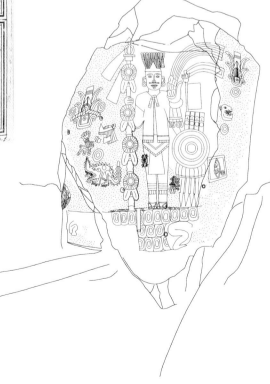

CARVED IN STONE. *(right)* Portrait of Montezuma at Chapultepec. Carved in 1519, damaged by order of the Spanish viceroy in the 1750s. A portrait of Montezuma's father, the emperor Axayacatl, and at least three predecessors were also deliberately destroyed in the Spanish colonial period. Montezuma's name glyph is to the viewer's left of the portrait (the head, headdress, and speech scroll).

CORTÉS OUTWITS. *(right)* "Cortes outwits and takes leave of Velasquez," an illustration from Dalton's *Stories of the Conquests of Mexico and Peru* for Victorian-era young adults, depicting Cortés giving an insouciant wave of his hat to a glowering Governor Velázquez. Cortés as heroic rebel (answering to the higher authorities of God and King) held obvious appeal to young readers.

CORTÉS RENOUNCES. *(bottom left)* "Cortés renounces the title of General given to him by Velázquez, and the Townspeople [*el Pueblo*] reappoint him by election," an Antonio Rodríguez engraving for the 1798 edition of Solís. The artifice of the formal, legal proceeding is underscored by the imaginary setting, complete with carpet and canopy. Following the traditional narrative, Cortés is the center of attention, both visually and via the caption's assertion of popular election.

Cortes outwits and takes leave of Velasquez.   P. 61.

CORTÉS ORDERS. *(bottom right)* "Cortés orders the ships to be sunk," another 1798 Rodríguez engraving, centers the legendary (and fictional) moment on Cortés's commanding gaze over his handiwork and the horizon he has determined not to cross until the conquest is achieved.

Fol. 7.   *T. II.*

Renuncia Cortés el título de General que le dio Velazq. y el Pueblo le vuelve à elegir.

T. II.   *Fol. 74.*

Manda Cortés dar al través con las naves

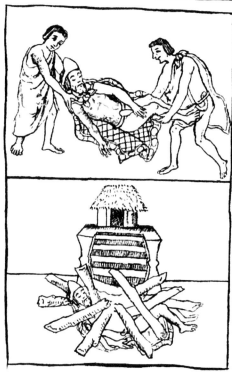

BURNED. The Cremations of Montezuma and Itzquauhtzin: This trio of illustrations from Sahagún's *Historia General* (Florentine Codex) show *(top left)* two Spaniards throwing their bodies into the lake, *(top right)* two Mexica lifting Montezuma's body out, for it to be cremated, and *(right)* the body of Itzquauhtzin moved and differently posed.

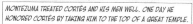

I CONTROL MONTEZUMA. *(above)* From Dan Abnett's *Hernán Cortés and the Fall of the Aztec Empire*, a graphic version for young readers that captures well many of the elements of the traditional narrative: a clever Cortés controlling a passive Montezuma, happily complicit in his own manipulation; and a hotheaded Pedro de Alvarado destined to wreck the peace.

MONTEZUMA SURRENDERS SOVEREIGNTY. *(right)* The emperor, seated on his throne, repeats his speech of surrender to Cortés, before a Spanish notary and the astonished Aztec nobility. Following the traditional narrative, the Aztecs weep. In the middle frame, Spanish and Aztec armies fight in the field (the 1520 Battle of Otumba), but in the lower one, Cuauhtemoc is captive—thus restoring the equilibrium of Montezuma's surrender. From a 1733 Italian edition of Solís's *History of the Conquest of Mexico*.

WHERE IS MARTÍN? This *Monument to Mestizaje* was originally erected in 1982 in Coyoacan, the former Aztec *altepetl* where Cortés made his headquarters right after Tenochtitlan's fall. Sustained protest forced the sculpture's relocation to an obscure park, where it is seldom seen (coincidentally not far from the location of the Meeting). The statue of Martín as a boy, standing in front of his parents (Cortés and Malintzin) was stolen and remains missing (see inset).

PORTRAIT OF THE CONQUEROR AS AN OLD MAN. Almost all portraits of Cortés are apocryphal or imaginary, but many

derive from an original, long-lost painting of the Marquis gazing piously upward, probably on his knees praying—as reflected in the engraving (left) used in all Lasso de la Vega's works praising the conquistador (1588, 1594, and 1601), and with gaze adjusted (right) in a 1778 Italian edition of Solís's *History*.

A CLEMENT CORTÉS. Nicolas-Eustache Maurin, "Clémence de Fernand-Cortès." One of a series of early-nineteenth-century lithographs created in Paris, depicting the "Conquest of Mexico," with fictional characters interspersed with historical ones.

ONCE AND FOR ALL. The events in Tenochtitlan of 1520–25 were recorded on this page of the Codex Aubin, a Nahuatl-language annals written by an educated Mexica man in the late sixteenth century.

FAMILY MATTERS. The second page of the Codex Cozcatzin, an early colonial manuscript from Tenochtitlan, shows Montezuma sitting on a high-backed throne *(tepotzoicpalli)*, beside the hill-cactus glyph for Tenochtitlan—at the top of which is the miter or Aztec crown of the *huey tlahtoani*. Facing the emperor is his daughter, doña Isabel Moctezuma Tecuichpo, dressed like her father, with the royal headdress glyph above her head to mark her status as principal royal heir (not her brother, don Pedro Moctezuma Tlacahuepantli, who sits behind her).

MARINA, ET AUTRES FEMMES DONNÉES A CORTEZ.

TO MAKE CORN BREAD. "Marina and other women given to Cortez" appeared in various eighteenth-century accounts of the Conquest, illustrating the moment when "the Cacique [ruler] of Tabasco gave to Cortés twenty Indian women, to make corn bread for his troops" (as the Abbé Prévost put it, in his 1754 *Histoire Générale des Voyages*, from which this image is taken). Behind this portrayal of civilization's contrast to barbarism is a grim contrast between "Indian" innocence and the services these girls were forced to perform for the conquistadors.

MEXICO CITY IDEALIZED. Detail from a map of the city painted around 1692 onto a *biombo*, the Japanese-style folding screen popular in elite Mexican homes of the seventeenth century (oil on canvas 213 x 550 cm). The arrow marks the walk we take in the Epilogue.

LONG LIVE TENOCHTITLAN! The location of the Meeting ("*El Encuentro*") was marked in the late twentieth century by this concrete plaque, attached to the outside wall of the Hospital de Jesús. Often damaged or defaced (this example reads, "Genocide! Long Live Tenochtitlan!"), it was recently replaced by a Meeting scene in colored tiles.

barely more than a hundred in Tenochtitlan. In his absence, the ambiguous arrangement of the Phoney Captivity slipped quickly into open warfare. In the traditional narrative, this is no coincidence: Cortés had consolidated the Surrender as a triumph of civilization over barbarism, but others then ruined it—the impetuous Alvarado, the villainous Velázquez and his agent Narváez, the pugnacious, superstitious Aztecs. But in fact, there were those on both sides who had been spoiling for a fight, for an end to Montezuma's collection experiment.

THREE THINGS HAPPENED IN MAY. We cannot be sure of their sequence, of their precise relationship of cause and effect, but they all seem well evidenced enough and all had an exacerbating (if not causative) effect on the others. One was the celebration of Toxcatl. The Spaniards had arrived during Quecholli, and stayed long enough to witness eight more Aztec months with their festivals: tribute was delivered on two of them, and ritual executions ("human sacrifices") took place during most, although if Montezuma or anyone in his government had planned to execute the Caxtilteca during Tlacaxipehualiztli (as I suggested earlier), such a ritual usage of the emperor's guests never occurred. But perhaps such a plan was intended for Toxcatl, the ninth festival since the Meeting; that at least was what Pedro de Alvarado later claimed he was told.[48]

May's second happening was war—open, punishing urban warfare between the Aztecs and the Caxtilteca. The latter had the advantage only for the opening hours of the conflict, when they waded through unarmed festival celebrants, slaughtering and dismembering with their swords. After that, being massively outnumbered, they holed up for weeks in Axayacatl's palace.

The third thing that happened was that Montezuma seems finally to have been seized, along with every high-ranking royal and noble member of his government. The emperor whom Cortés was not allowed to touch at the Meeting, who had surely remained untouched since then—free and in command of his government—was now shown the indignity of being shackled.

Let us turn to a perspective on these three happenings from Tlatelolco, written down in Nahuatl in the mid-sixteenth century. An annals, or a record of yearly events, from this sibling *altepetl* to Tenochtitlan included a twelve-page account of the invasion war. The first year is covered very briefly in half a page, and then Cortés, here called the Captain,

> left for the seashore; he left behind don Pedro Alvarado, Tona-
> tiuh. Then he asked Moteucçoma how they celebrated the festival
> of their god. He said to him, "How is it? Set up all the equipment
> for it and do it." When Tonatiuh gave the order, Moteucçoma
> was already being detained, along with Itzquauhtzin, the *tlaco-
> chcalcatl* of Tlatelolco. At this time they hanged the nobleman of
> Acolhuacan, Neçahualquentzin, at the wall near the water. The
> second who died was the ruler of Nauhtla, named Cohualpopo-
> catzin. They shot him with arrows; when they had shot him, he
> was burned while alive.

In this version, then, Qualpopoca's burning, Montezuma's arrest, and the rounding up of other Aztec lords all happen in May, as Toxcatl begins—its celebration encouraged by Alvarado, planning to attack. The Annals go on to describe the costumes and singing and dancing of the celebrants, culminating on the second day with a sudden three-hour onslaught (the drummers were targeted first; "they struck off their hands and lips"). Montezuma and Itzquauhtzin try to restrain the Spaniards. The violence seems to subside; twenty days pass; the Captain returns to the city "uncontested." But "the next day we pursued them, and there was clamor, with which the war began."

Tzinti yaoyotl, the war began. In the traditional narrative, at this point the story is halfway over. But in the Annals of Tlatelolco, ten of its twelve pages are devoted to the fighting and killing of the year that followed this moment. In sources in Nahuatl and in quasi-indigenous accounts, the temporal distortions are very different from those of the traditional narrative; memory and attention are devoted to the devastating disruption and mortality of the year after Montezuma's death, and even to the ensuing decades of pro-tracted warfare.

And what of Montezuma's fate? "In the year Two Flint Knife, Moteucçoma died; it was also when Itzquauhtzin, the *tlacochcalcatl* of Tlatelolco, died."[49]

When I was six years old, I saw Montezuma. I cannot remember the moment, but I know it happened because I have photographic evi-dence: a moldy old Kodak slide of me standing in the gardens of the Royal Palace at Aranjuez, squinting in the Spanish sunshine, with a row of statues in the background. The statues are unidentifi-able in the photograph, but I know now that the one closest to me was—according to the engraving on its stone plinth—"Montezuma. Emperor of Mexico. D. Yr. 1520" (*Montezuma. Emper[ad]or de Mexico. M[uert]o A[ñ]o 1520*). There is no hint as to how or why the emperor died in 1520, and I doubt my six-year-old curiosity extended that far.[50]

But now, in contrast, I am fascinated both by the question of Montezuma's mysterious demise and by the significance of the vari-ous claims and supposed solutions. So this is what I think happened that fateful final week of June 1520, and this is why the contrast between reality and the traditional narrative matters.

The fifth of the set of five verdicts on Montezuma's death that began this chapter pointed at the Spaniards. A young museum em-ployee in Mexico City (with the surname Moctezuma, as it hap-pens) recently told an interviewer an interesting variant on that verdict. In the story familiar to her, she said, "the Spaniards killed Montezuma, inserted a pole through him, and then held him up on his balcony, making him look as if he were alive. Then his people stoned him, thinking he had sided with the conquistadors." This seems to borrow from the legends surrounding the 1099 death of El Cid (posthumously propped by a pole on his horse to help rally demoralized troops). But it is also a solution that wants to have its cake and eat it too: although the Spaniards committed the murder, both Spaniards and Aztecs had homicidal intent and believed they succeeded. And therein, I think, lies some truth.[51]

I do not doubt Montezuma appeared on a rooftop, thereby placing him in danger as the battle raged below, projectiles flying in all directions. The general fact of it was recorded too often to be a complete invention, just as the Meeting itself was not made up (the fiction was its meaning as Surrender). We cannot be sure if he spoke, or attempted to do so, but if he did, his speech and the Aztec responses, as recorded in Spanish chronicles and subsequent histories, are mostly—if not entirely—imaginary. I suspect that he was attempting to speak to somebody below, and that he suffered an accidental blow from a stone in the attempt.

That wound, as deep or shallow as it may have been—or even just the rumor of such a wound—was a godsend to the captains who dispatched Montezuma and the other captive members of the regional royal family. For this was a mass murder of the entire Aztec kingship or *tlahtohcayotl*. The *tlahtoani* of each city-state that made up the empire's Triple Alliance, as well as the royal governor of Tlatelolco, were all executed: Cacama of Tetzcoco ("stabbed forty-five times," according to Alva Ixtlilxochitl); Tlacopan's *tlahtoani;* and Itzquauhtzin of Tlatelolco. These deaths are well evidenced, lacking the controversy or mystery surrounding Montezuma's death. Nor should this mass murder surprise us; in fact, it would be surprising if the rulers had *not* been killed. Conquistador fatalities were mounting as the days passed. The Spanish captains were becoming increasingly fearful and desperate. Montezuma no longer served any purpose. He may have been wounded, or he may have been capable of resuming a leadership. Either way, leaving him alive was a needless risk. At that moment, the overwhelming Spanish priority, all that mattered, was to slaughter the enemy and escape their city to safety. Executing the captive *tlahtohcayotl*—then throwing their perforated bodies out to the Aztec mob—might have improved their chances. Thus in the bloody chaos of battle did a handful of captains—there is no reason to assign blame or control specifically to Cortés—put the emperor and his fellow kings to the sword.[52]

Montezuma's murder by the Spaniards is thus logical and expected in the context of the mass execution of all the *tlahtoque*. His possible wound from a stone or arrow, or even the fact that he came close to receiving such a wound, gave the Spaniards the idea of blaming the Aztecs. This leads us to what is most important about the entire riddle of Montezuma's death: the persistence of the Spanish claim that they were not responsible. If the conquistadors were so willing to admit that the other rulers were executed, and indeed to admit to the killing of indigenous rulers on other occasions (from Atahuallpa and Sagipa to Montezuma's own successor, Cuauhtemoc, hanged by Cortés five years later in a Maya town), then why not admit to Montezuma's murder? Why did Cortés and other survivors from the company deny it, and why did subsequent tellers of the traditional narrative elaborate upon that denial? Indeed, why go as far as Díaz did, claiming "Cortés and all the captains and soldiers wept as though they had lost a father" (tears, once again, marking the moment)? That imaginatively implausible detail was repeated by Clavigero in the next century, and by Prescott in the next (believe it if you can, was MacNutt's sardonic aside). Those authors were not alone in indignantly defending the conquistadors and denouncing the "monstrous imputation" that Cortés was guilty; why?[53]

Because Montezuma's murder by Spaniards undermined the Surrender. Imagine Montezuma's life as a sequence of dominoes, stretching from the Meeting to his death. In the traditional narrative, those dominoes stood in a tidy row, connecting the Surrender at the Meeting to the conquistadors weeping over his death; in between lay the characterization of the 235 days as a consolidation of Spanish control over the empire and of the emperor's friendly subservience to Cortés. Nudge the domino at either end and the whole row goes down, destroying the Spanish justification for their invasion and all it entailed. And while writers in later centuries were not as invested in the maintenance of Spanish Conquest justification, they were still bound by the logic of the traditional narrative. Why would "Spaniards take the life of a king to whom they owed so many benefits" (as one put it)?[54]

According to the traditional narrative, because Montezuma surrendered, it was Aztecs, not Spaniards, who were motivated to kill him. In fact, because Montezuma did not surrender, but conquistadors claimed he did, it was *they* who were motivated to kill him—and to deny it. The traditional narrative transformed a murderous moment in a messy and chaotic war into a clean and clear twist in the plot, with "Cortés and all the captains and soldiers" emerging as victims themselves. The astonishing absurdity of that contrivance could not remain hidden, and for centuries it has bubbled under the traditional narrative. Our challenge now is not to pick a side or assign blame—and in particular it is not to demonize Cortés, as that only serves to give him the control he lacked and feed his legend (to which we now turn in the next chapter). Rather, it is to reorient the narrative to emphasize disorder and the role of multiple protagonists, thus to better understand the war and its outcome.

We are left, then, with a pair of contrasting images for this chapter's closing scene. In one, the conquistadors weep over Montezuma's body. In the other, they commit mass murder in cold blood, repeatedly stabbing the chained and unarmed Aztec leaders. The first sets up the traditional narrative of the war's second half, in which Cortés leads his men to safety and then builds a righteous alliance for the recapture of the imperial capital. The second guides us into a more realistic understanding of the bloodbath into which Mexico would be plunged in the year that followed.

PART IV

What fields have now not been watered
With blood crying up to God,
Spilled from our honest parents,
Our sons, our servants, our brothers,
Fighting theft and rape?
What daughter, sister, or wife
Have we been able to guard
From being used like a whore
By these vile and ruthless tyrants
Who corrupt all that they touch?

—Michael de Carvajal, "Complaint of the
Indians in the Court of Death," 1557

Warfare is almost as old as man himself,
and reaches into the most secret places of the human heart,
places where self dissolves rational purpose,
where pride reigns, where emotion is paramount,
where instinct is king.

—John Keegan, *A History of Warfare*, 1993[1]

CONQUERED MEXICO. In the frontispiece to Juan de Escoiquiz's epic poem, *México Conquistada: Poema Heroyca*, angels hold aloft a version of the "Fat Cortés" portrait widely reproduced in the eighteenth century; below, a maiden queen representing Spain sits on a throne, handing the word of God to another maiden, whose feathered headdress and subordinate position mark her as representing the Aztecs or "conquered Mexico." The providential theme of the engraving—with the Conquest justified by civilization's superiority over barbarism, and guided and planned by God, using Cortés as His agent—is central to the Conquest's traditional narrative, which Escoiquiz's poem helped perpetuate (it was published in 1798, a few years after Cortés's bones were reburied in a grand mausoleum commissioned by the viceroy).

———✦———

CHAPTER 7

The Epic Boxer

He was the epic boxer [*el púgil épico*], and he fought for his king; he was the mystical crusader [*el cruzado místico*], and he fought for his God; he was the quixotic gallant [*el galán quijote*], and he adored his lady.
—Mateo Solana on Cortés, 1938

Cortés certainly had his faults, like all men; he was perhaps not as politically adroit, nor as contemplative, as Solís describes him to us.
—Preface to the 1704 French edition of Solís's *History of the Conquest*

Rather than a man, Cortés is a myth, a myth whose aspects have always been disputed by concurrent schools of thought and ideological rivals, in such a way that allowed each one to think of "their" Cortés: demigod or demon, hero or traitor, slaver or protector of the Indians, modern or feudal, a greedy or great lord.   —Christian Duverger, 2005

The true aid, after God's, was what we gave them . . . because the Spaniards were few and so poorly supplied and were going through lands where they would not have known the way if we had not shown them; a thousand times we saved them from death.
—Rulers of the *altepetl* of Xochimilco, 1563[1]

HOW SHOULD THE ANNIVERSARY OF THE MEETING BE CELE-brated in the city where the historic encounter took place? The viceroy of New Spain had the perfect answer to that question.

Exactly 275 years after the Meeting, the Count of Revillagigedo had Cortés's bones dug up and reburied at the site where the Aztec emperor had welcomed the legendary conquistador. By entering the ground on that spot and that day, Cortés symbolically reentered Mexico in triumph.

The date was November 8, 1794. The bones were placed in a crystal urn, topped by a bronze bust, in a mausoleum in the church of the Hospital de Jesús. The building was the palace, still standing today, that Cortés had constructed for himself on the site of the Meeting. It was converted into a hospital and religious foundation just a few years later when a larger mansion was built for him. The kingdom's leading dignitaries all witnessed the reinterment ceremony (although not the viceroy, who was recalled to Spain just months before the event), and they heard a sermon by fray Servando Teresa de Mier. The young Mexican-born Dominican was a rising star in the capital. His sermon of November 8 has not survived, but he presumably waxed lyrically about Cortesian triumphs and the providential purpose of the Meeting, no doubt mentioning the great Calendar Stone and other Aztec monuments recently dug up and displayed in the city.

Fray Servando probably flirted with controversy but cannot have said anything too controversial, or he would have been arrested—as he was the following month, a week after a now-famous sermon that he delivered before the new viceroy on the feast day of the Virgin of Guadalupe. He was stripped of his doctoral degree and his right to preach and exiled from Mexico; the text of his sermon was burned. The earlier sermon on Cortés was probably destroyed at the same time. Even though Teresa de Mier was exiled for his comments on the Virgin of Guadalupe, St. Thomas, and (since 2002, St.) Juan Diego—not for his Cortés eulogy—the history of the conquistador's bones proved once again to be a magnet for controversy and conflict.

Although Cortés had died in Spain, and in December 1547 his body had been buried in Santiponce (outside Seville), his remains had been disinterred in 1567 and shipped to Mexico. That reburial was intended to be a grand and symbolic affair, but Cortés's three sons had meanwhile become ensnared in a half-baked plot to overthrow the viceregal government in Mexico City. By the time the bones reached Mexico, the illegitimate don Martín (Malintzin's son) had been brutally tortured and remained imprisoned, while the legitimate don Martín and his brother Luís had been exiled to

Spain. Cortés's remains were thus quietly interred in Tetzcoco. His triumphal reentry into Mexico-Tenochtitlan would have to wait.

As it turned out, the wait was only two more generations. When, in 1629, don Martín's grandson, don Pedro Cortés, died, the viceroy decided that alongside his body in the Franciscan monastery in Mexico City the bones of his great-grandfather would also be buried. The conquistador was, at last, now within Montezuma's capital. But, as always, there was a catch: don Pedro had died without an heir; Hernando's line was extinguished and buried with his own bones.

The surging popularity of Cortés in the decades surrounding his move to the new mausoleum in 1794—reflected in literature and art (as we shall see shortly)—would soon run into a new controversial chapter. Lucas Alamán was a prominent Mexican scientist, historian, and politician who in 1823 started his first term as a minister in the government of the newly independent Mexico. Despite his political career, he was a monarchist sympathizer and shuddered to think how anti-Spanish sentiment might inspire the destruction of Cortés's remains. That year, therefore, shortly before the mausoleum was smashed, he illicitly hid the urn behind a beam in the Hospital de Jesús, spreading the story that the tomb had been opened and the bones secretly shipped to Italy.

Alamán never publicly revealed what he had done, but in 1843 (ten years before his death) he filed a burial record with the Spanish Embassy, requesting it remain classified for a century. Sure enough, the location of Cortés's urn was thus a mystery for much of the nineteenth and twentieth centuries—dubbed recently by a Spanish newspaper as "one of the greatest historical mysteries of the Americas" and "the biggest enigma surrounding Hernán Cortés." Spanish officials honored Alamán's request (or simply forgot about the document) until 1946, when an official made the burial record public. The bones were found, removed, and declared to be those of the long-dead Marqués del Valle.

A furor erupted over what to do with them. Various suggestions were made as to how best to commemorate the infamy with which

Cortés was then viewed: grind the bones to dust, for example, or throw them into the Atlantic Ocean. Hoping to put the cat back into the bag, Mexican officials simply returned Cortés to his hiding place in a corner of the hospital. The strategy worked. His bones are still there, marked only by a simple plaque: "Hernán Cortés 1485–1547." The location is obscure, photography is restricted, and there are seldom visitors.[2]

Cortés's memory enjoyed an equally bumpy ride across the centuries in another medium of commemoration, that of the public statue. Not until 1890 was a statue erected in his Spanish hometown of Medellín. High on a plinth in militaristic pose, fully armored with his foot on an Aztec "idol," the conqueror still stares east over the little town and toward the Indies. The statue seems to celebrate both the local boy made good and Spanish arms in the spirit of the epic poems by the likes of Escoiquiz and Vaca de Guzmán; it is ironic that within a decade, most of what remained of the Spanish Empire would be taken by a younger nation that had appropriated Cortés's victory over Montezuma and commemorated it in public art—not in a small provincial town, but in the capital's Capitol.

In 2010, the Medellín statue was defaced with red paint. "Anonymous citizens" left a note denouncing it as "fascist" and "a cruel and arrogant glorification of genocide and an insult to the Mexican people." The vandals objected to Cortés standing on a decapitated Aztec head; in a statement of response, the mayor of Medellín corrected them, lamented their "lack of historical understanding," and defended the statue as a simple "homage to a son of this town." The protestors also noted that the red paint was significant because that very night the Spanish and Mexican national soccer teams played in Mexico City (the Spanish team plays in red and is nicknamed "La Roja").[3]

Meanwhile, in 1982, the Mexican government erected a statue in Coyoacan whose purpose was not to memorialize Cortés but to celebrate *mestizaje*—the mixing of the Spanish and Mesoamerican peoples—with a depiction of the conqueror with Malintzin and their son, Martín, as a naked boy (labeled "Where is Martín?" in our Gallery). A century earlier, Cortés's image had appeared in bronze in a very public part of Mexico City, the great Paseo de la Reforma, but in a decidedly negative context; the statue itself portrays Cuauhtemoc, with Cortés appearing only in bronze reliefs on its plinth, as the Aztec emperor's captor and torturer. By contrast, in the 1982 sculpture, Cortés is not the antihero but the founding father. It provoked uproar. There were denunciations, demonstrations, and defacings, and the statue of little Martín was stolen. The remaining installation was moved to an obscure corner of another park, where, like the plaque marking where Cortés's urn is hidden, it attracts little attention today. Martín has never been found.[4]

"There is so much to say about the prowess and invincible courage of Cortés that on this point alone a large book could be written." These words, penned by Motolinía, one of the first Franciscans in Mexico, were more farsighted than the friar could have imagined.[5]

When Motolinía penned that prophecy, Cortés was still alive and Gómara was busy laying the foundation (using Cortés's published Letters to the King as crucial building material) for a literary tradition that combined a narrative of the Spanish-Aztec War styled as a glorious, predestined Conquest of Mexico with a life of the conqueror as a hagiography—a hero-worshipping, legend-forming biography. Blooms of intense popularity have periodically sprung up, but the topic's popularity has remained deeply rooted for five centuries. Serious attempts to uproot the legend are few and far between; almost every book has sought to lionize or demonize, to celebrate the hero or denounce the antihero. Like his bones, the real Cortés has been either obscured by the trimmings of a celebratory mausoleum or hidden behind a beam. Like his vandalized statues, he is seen increasingly through presentist eyes, less and less understood as a historical figure. As one of his modern biographers noted, Cortés long ago ceased to be a man, surviving only as "a myth."[6]

For us to uproot the legend, we need to understand its nature, to see how Cortés became Caesar, Moses, and Hero, and also to see how "Cortez the Killer," the antihero, has served as the fourth side of the same frame containing the Cortés legend, completing the myth rather than shattering it.

THE MOTTO CHOSEN by Cortés for his coat of arms was *Judicium Domini apprehendit eos, et fortitudo ejus corroboravit bracchium meum* ("The judgment of the Lord overtook them, and his might strengthened my arm"). Taken from an account of the siege of Jerusalem by Titus Flavius Josephus, the line implied that Cortés had besieged and captured a second Jerusalem. The reference reflected Cortés's own embrace of the exalted notion that his actions in Mexico were divinely guided, that his role was that of a universal crusader. It also reflected the Spanish tendency, commonplace in the early modern centuries, to compare Spain's imperial achievements to those of the ancient Greeks and Romans.[7]

By the 1540s several specific comparisons had become commonplace in Spanish accounts of the war in Mexico, including that of Jerusalem and Tenochtitlan, and that of Cortés and Julius Caesar. Cortés himself made no such claim; the purpose of his Letters was, after all, to display his undying loyalty to a king who, as Holy Roman Emperor, was *the* Caesar of the day. But the clerics and intellectuals who formed the pro-Cortés, anti–Las Casas faction in Spain during the conquistador's final years pointed out three similarities: both men were remarkable generals; both were unique literary figures for recording detailed accounts of their greatest campaign (Cortés's Letters; Caesar's *Gallic Wars*); and both had administrative vision, guiding the Mexican and Roman worlds, respectively, into new eras.[8]

Gómara made much hay with the comparison to ancient Rome. In addition to printing his coat of arms, Gómara insisted that "never has such a display of wealth been discovered in the Indies, nor acquired so quickly" as that found by Cortés. Enthused his secretary-hagiographer:

not only were his many great feats in the wars the greatest—
without prejudice against a single Spaniard in the Indies—among
the many achieved in the regions of the New World, but he
wrote them down in imitation of Polybius, and of Salust when
he brought together the Roman histories of Marius and Scipio.[9]

Gómara used his giddy comparisons of Cortés to the great generals of ancient Greece and Rome—and to their historians—as buildings blocks for his construction of the exemplary conquistador. By
contrast, the other famous conquistador, Francisco Pizarro, was portrayed as illiterate and ignoble, and his assault on the Inca Empire as
little more than a plundering expedition by avaricious bandits. This
allowed Gómara to better promote Cortés as the noble, pious model
of a literate man-at-arms, and his invasion of Mexico as "a good and
just war." Gómara went a little too far—his criticism of the Conquest of Peru prompted his *History* to be quickly banned in Spain.
But by century's end there were ten Italian editions, nine in French
too, and two in English, making it "so widely read that it served, almost by default, as the official history of the Spanish New World."[10]
Comparisons were not restricted to Julius Caesar—in his ode to
Cortés of 1546, for example, Francisco Cervantes de Salazar also
compared Cortés to Alexander the Great and to St. Paul—but the
Cortés-Caesar leitmotif tended to predominate, and it lasted for centuries. In his 1610 account of the Spanish Conquest campaigns in
New Mexico, composed as an epic poem, Gaspar de Villagrá repeatedly invoked Cortés as the paradigmatic conquistador. When, in Villagrá's telling, Cortés's efforts to campaign in northwest Mexico were
opposed by Viceroy Mendoza (who had by now assumed rule of New
Spain), the conflict had classical echoes: "Greed for power, like love,
will permit no rival. Even as Caesar and Pompey clashed over their
rival ambitions for world power, so now Cortés met with opposition."
Similarly, the splendors and religious devotion of Mexico City were

all due to the noble efforts of that famous son who set forth to
discover this New World, whose illustrious and glorious deeds,

after the years have passed, will surely be seen as no less great and admirable than those of the great Caesar, Pompey, Arthur, Charlemagne, and other valiant men, whom time has raised up.[11]

The theme was prominent too in the histories by Díaz (who also compared *himself* to Julius Caesar) and by Solís—the latter prefaced with the assertion that "whoever will consider the Difficulties he overcame, and the Battles he fought and won against an incredible Superiority of Numbers, must own him little inferior to the most celebrated Heroes of Antiquity." Solís's book was a bestseller in multiple languages for well over a century. Meanwhile, Cortés was promoted inside and outside the Spanish world as a kind of model, modern Caesar. For example, in his *History of the Conquest of Mexico, By the Celebrated Hernan Cortes* (first published in 1759 but seeing dozens of editions through to the twentieth century), W. H. Dilworth sought to improve and entertain "the BRITISH YOUTH of both Sexes." The book claimed to contain "A faithful and entertaining Detail of all [Cortés's] Amazing Victories," with a story "abounding with strokes of GENERALSHIP, and the most refined Maxims of CIVIL POLICY."[12]

From Dilworth to Prescott to modern authors (entire books have been devoted to comparing Cortés to Caesar or to Alexander), the Spaniard has generally come off well in relation to ancient generals, whether the focus is on military logistics, governmental vision, or moral justification. For a 1938 Mexican biographer of the conqueror, Julius Caesar was more self-interested than Cortés; the Spaniard was not only glorified, but also sanctified, an "epic boxer" and "mystical crusader" who embodied his age more than his own personal ambitions.[13]

Other Latin American intellectuals suggested that Cortés "was a Caesar, but more like Caesar Borgia than Julius Caesar"—meaning Cesare Borgia, the duke made famous by Machiavelli in *The Prince*—and that Cortés's "political vision" was so similar to Machiavelli's that one imagines the conquistador reading *The Prince*. That scenario is impossible, as the now-classic political treatise was not published until 1532, as literary scholars acknowledge. But some have argued that Machiavelli's ideas were circulating before the book saw print, allowing Cortés to be "the practical Spaniard" to Machiavelli's "theoretical Italian."[14]

FOLLOWING THE LOGIC OF the Cortés legend, political disunity among Mesoamericans has traditionally been read as the conqueror's achievement, with the question being who most influenced his divide-and-rule strategy: Julius Caesar, Cesare Borgia and Machiavelli, or the Bible. The Christian element (Solana's "mystical crusader") inevitably gave Cortés the moral edge over any of his possible influences (the Bible aside). Thus, beginning with the earliest writings on the Conquest by Franciscans and other ecclesiastics, Cortés was promoted as a pious version of a classical general, better than the ancients because he carried the true faith with him.[15]

"I do not wish to deride the noble achievements of the Romans," wrote Diego Valadés in 1579, for they subdued and organized an impressive number of provinces. "Yet one must exalt with the highest praise and with new and illuminating phrases the unprecedented fortitude of Hernando Cortés, and the friars who came to these new worlds." Comparing the possessions of the Roman Empire with "the parts of the Indies that have come into our hands, ours are infinitely greater." But for Valadés, it was not just a question of scale. The Cortesian achievement was a religious one, and thus "the sign of how Cortés exercised his power for the good" was how he and the earliest friars destroyed temples, expelled priests, and prohibited "diabolic sacrifices." It was thus the nature, as well as the magnitude and speed, of the enterprise that made it "the most heroic."[16]

Valadés, the son of a Spanish conquistador and a Tlaxcalteca mother, was the first mestizo (mixed-race man) to enter the Order of Saint Francis. His perspective was thus as much colonial Tlaxcalteca as it was Franciscan. Valadés was one of the earliest to articulate the invented but long-lasting tradition that the Tlaxcalteca were the very first—at Cortés's urging—to receive baptism as new Christians in Mexico.[17]

Another mestizo son of a Spanish conquistador and Tlaxcalteca mother, Diego Muñoz Camargo, also contributed to this core element of the Cortés-as-Moses legend. His *History of Tlaxcala*, completed in 1592, recounted a meeting that supposedly took place between Cortés and the four rulers of Tlaxcallan in the middle of the Spanish-Aztec War (as anti-Aztec forces regrouped). At the meeting, Cortés delivered a virtual sermon, confessing that his true mission in Mexico was to bring the true faith. "We call ourselves *Christians*," he declared, being sons "of the only true God that there is." Explaining Christianity and its rituals, he urged the lords to destroy their "idols," receive baptism, and join him in a vengeful campaign of war against Tenochtitlan. The rulers then persuaded their subjects, who all gathered for a public mass baptism, at which Cortés and Pedro de Alvarado acted as godfathers.[18]

The incident was almost certainly fiction. It may have echoed real conversations between conquistador captains and city rulers in 1520, but the scene depicted by Muñoz was a mythistorical mix of his imagination and Tlaxcalteca folk history. Yet—like the mythistory of the Meeting in Tenochtitlan—it took root. For it placed both Tlaxcallan and Cortés in a positive light, promoting one as the voluntary starting point for Christian baptism, and the other as an effective agent for conversion. These Tlaxcalteca were the good Nahuas; they listened to religious reason and to their wise lords, in stark contrast to the Aztecs and their failed ruler. This Cortés was a peacemaker, a spiritual conquistador who deployed the word, not the sword, inspiring conversion without coercion.

The Franciscan promotion of Cortés as a New World Moses, both during and long after his lifetime, had three roots. First, the twelve founding fathers of Catholicism in Mexico were Franciscans, arriving in 1524 with Cortés's support. Second, many of the Twelve (as they came to be known), including their leader, fray Martín de Valencía, and the influential Motolinía (fray Toribio de Benavente), shared a millenarian vision of their mission; their goal was to convert indigenous Mexicans in order that Christ could return, a holy task made possible by Cortés. Third, the Cortés-Franciscan alliance became cemented by the political schism that divided Spanish Mexico in the 1530s. The Franciscans were forced to compete in Mexico with secular clergy and rival orders, especially the Dominicans, who aligned themselves with the first royal officials sent to govern New Spain. The Dominicans were critical of Cortés; the Franciscans penned narratives that praised him.[19]

One such Franciscan was fray Gerónimo de Mendieta. He spent roughly the last quarter of the sixteenth century composing his *Historia Eclesiástica Indiana* in the Franciscan convent in Tlatelolco, once part of the Aztec capital and in Mendieta's day a Nahua neighborhood of Mexico City. Although Mendieta's history of the evangelization in Mexico was denied publication permission (for its overly millenarian tone), it reflected the opinion of the day and influenced subsequent chronicles and accounts of the Spiritual Conquest. As we read earlier, Mendieta believed that Martin Luther and Hernando Cortés were born the same year, and that this was part of God's plan for the Spaniard. This providential numerology was reinforced by the bloody orgy of human sacrifice that Mendieta thought occurred in Tenochtitlan that same year. The remedy to "the clamor of so many souls" and "the spilling of so much human blood" was Cortés, dispatched to Mexico "like a new Moses to Egypt."[20]

"Without any doubt," wrote the friar, "God chose specifically to be his instrument this valiant captain, don Fernando Cortés, through whose agency the door was opened and a road made for the preachers of the Gospel in this new world." Mendieta's nineteenth-century editor printed in the margin: "Cortés chosen as a new Moses to free the Indian people." Proof of Cortés's role, divinely appointed since birth, was another meaningful synchronicity with Luther: in the same year that the German heretic "began to corrupt the Gospel," the Spanish captain began "to make it known faithfully and sincerely to people who had never before heard of it." No less a "confirmation of the divine election of Cortés to a task so noble in spirit" was the "marvelous determination that God put in his heart."[21]

Down through the centuries, authors writing in multiple languages wove these threads of Cortés's religious devotion and the evidence of God's intervention in the Conquest's glorious story. It was the stuff of epic poetry: for Mexican-born Spanish poet Antonio de Saavedra, Cortés was a brilliant and godly agent; for Italian poet Girolamo Vecchietti, he was *il pietoso Cortese*. He guided indigenous people to the light so effectively that "the reverence and prostration on their knees that is now shown to priests by the Indians of New Spain was taught to them by don Fernando Cortés, Marqués del Valle, of happy memory" (as García put it in 1607).[22]

In the hands of Protestant authors in later centuries, the Moses leitmotif shifted into something slightly different—"religious fanaticism," one American historian called it in 1856—but the core legendary element persisted. Upon assuming command of the expedition to Mexico, Cortés took up his "heavenly mission" with the zeal of "a frank, fearless, deluded enthusiast." His destiny was "to march the apostle of Christianity to overthrow the idols in the halls of Moctezuma, and there to rear the cross of Christ." In the less judgmental words of another turn-of-the-century historian, Cortés's "religious sincerity" was "above impeachment." Indeed, he was virtually a saint, "a man of unfeigned piety, of the stuff that martyrs are made of, nor did his conviction that he was leading a holy crusade to win lost souls to salvation ever waver." Later scholars were decreasingly adulatory, arguing that Cortés and his colleagues were, "so far as religion was concerned, simply products of their times." But many remained convinced that Cortés's character and goals were, above all else, religious, and that no other explorer or conquistador of the Americas could match Cortés "in the constancy or the depth of his zeal for the Holy Catholic Faith."[23]

MAXIME HEROICUM—"MOST HEROIC"—was how Valadés had summed up Cortés's enterprise of military and spiritual conquest. *Hero* was increasingly popular as a descriptor of Cortés from the late sixteenth century onward, typically tied to a set of adjectives that defined his heroic qualities: *great, invincible, valiant*. Although sometimes tied to religion (as Moses-Hero), the purpose of such praise was usually political and patriotic, to promote Cortés as an inspirational national hero. The Hero leitmotif ran thick through the familiar canon of conquest sources—from Gómara to Madariaga—as well as in a wide variety of other sources. Villagrá, for example, exclaimed to the king that Cortés was the hero who "conquered an entire world," inspiring the insight that "there is nothing in the world to compare with the presumptuousness of man"; Cortés, as the exemplary *homo heroicus,* was *the* man.

> He attempts things which it seems are reserved for God alone. You will note, worthy king, that the great Cortés, Marquis of the Valley, who, after braving the dangers of the mighty deep, burned his fleet, determined either to conquer or to perish; this very one in whom the spirit of adventure still burned with an unconquerable desire to discover not one more world but one hundred if possible . . .[24]

Cortés is found in archival documents of the early modern centuries as a heroic reference, but these tend to be repetitive, passing mentions, knee-jerk nods to his iconic status as patriotic hero. A more natural and vivid medium for Cortesian adulation and legend promotion was epic poetry. One of the best examples—both for its quality of verse and its wide circulation for centuries—is Gabriel Lasso de la Vega's *Valiant Cortés* (*Cortés valeroso*) of 1588, comprising more than nine thousand lines of epic verse praising "the great Cortés." A second edition of six years later was more than twice as long. Five years later, Saavedra rose to the challenge (he and Lasso were friends) and published a similar chronicle. *The* Indiano *Pilgrim* (*El Peregrino Indiano*) used more than sixteen thousand lines of epic poetry promoting the Cortés legend, likewise built around a version of the traditional "Conquest of Mexico" narrative.[25]

That put the ball back in Lasso de la Vega's court, and within two years he had published his *Elegies in Praise of Three Famous Men* (*Elogios en Loor de los Tres Famosos Varones*)—one of whom was Cortés, compared favorably to another, Jayme the Conquistador, King of Aragon.[26] Lasso's devotion to lionizing the legendary conquistador of Mexico was as much necessity as it was ideologically motivated; he was supported and sponsored by the Cortés family. One of them, don Gerónimo Cortés, was an amateur poet who contributed prefatory verses both to Lasso's *Valiant Cortés* and to Saavedra's *Pilgrim*. This example, included in the former of the two books, captures the tone both of don Gerónimo's efforts and the more elegant lines of the poets his family kept solvent:

> Once again there pours forth
> the sweet sound of the greatness,
> the labors, dangers, and bravery, with which
> my invincible grandfather won eternal fame.[27]

"Invincible" was a favored adjective, used both by Saavedra and don Gerónimo, and in the caption to the portrait of Cortés printed in all three of Lasso de la Vega's hagiographies (and included in our Gallery). "Valiant" was also popular—"valorous, great gentleman and Christian"; "illustrious and valiant gentleman"—as was "fame"; Cortés was often "the most famous and most adventurous Captain." Above all, Cortés was the "great hero."[28]

While Cortés never disappeared as a popular, patriotic topic, Cortesiana came in waves: that of the decades surrounding 1600; another in the reign of Carlos II (1661–1700), who commissioned and collected books and paintings on the "Conquest of Mexico" (Solís was his royal chronicler); and another in the late eighteenth century (culminating in the reburial of Cortés's bones and in Juan de Escoiquiz's *Heroic Poem*—introduced at the top of this chapter). This latter wave can be explained generally in terms of Bourbon Spain's more profitable, more robust empire, and specifically as a result of new Spanish publications of Cortés's Letters to the King (most notably by Mexican archbishop Lorenzana in 1770).[29]

A larger cultural context was also the increased popularity of the epic poem, with Cortés as a traditional, fashionable subject. For example, in *Hernandia*, Francisco Ruiz de León wove themes from ancient Greek and Roman literature into the traditional narrative of

Mexico's Conquest. The title may have been pithy, but the poem was a dense 383 pages of ottava rima, an Italian verse form associated primarily with heroic poetry. Although the poem's title suggested its topic was Cortés, in effect the conquistador was deployed as a figure from classical mythology, with the primary target being to praise Spain, the true faith, and heroism itself. By embodying that triad, Cortés was virtually deified, recognizable as a legendary icon, not as a credible, historical human being.[30]

In subsequent decades, more Spanish poets turned to the same theme and genre of verse. Two of them even used the same motif and title, *The Ships of Cortés Destroyed*. One of these poems, a sixty-stanza ode to "the great Hero," won the Royal Academy's annual poetry prize. This giddily patriotic celebration of Spanish glory, as embodied in "the new Cid, the Spanish Achilles," took Cortés's alleged destruction of his ships on the shores of the Gulf of Mexico as a symbolic moment that turned the Atlantic into a "theatre" and "fountain" of Spanish triumph. "The great Cortés" thus brought to Spain national glory and global respect. Escoiquiz's stirring verse in praise of "the valiant Hernando" ran to more than a thousand pages; *Mexico Conquered: Heroic Poem* included a prologue that proclaimed Spain's glowing record of moral rectitude, legitimacy, and generosity toward "Indians."[31]

That prologue noted how favorable Spain's colonial record was in contrast to the dire reputations of other European empires, and in refutation of the lies spread by Las Casas and his foreign disciples. Anti–Las Casas apologias for Spanish conquest and colonialism formed a tradition stretching from Sepúlveda and Vargas Machuca, through the Bourbon era of epic poetry, into the early twentieth century (when a Spanish historian coined the phrase "Black Legend"). Yet despite this defensive tradition, and the abiding popularity of Las Casas's *Very Brief Account of the Destruction of the Indies,* depictions of Cortés as Hero persisted in the Protestant world.[32]

For example, for Thomas Nicholas, the Elizabethan translator of Gómara's *Conquista,* the "delectable and worthy" exploits of Cortés were a model and precedent to be emulated. Any Englishman contemplating the ambition of discovery and conquest could learn from the Cortés case,

> how Glorie, Renowne, and perfite Felicitie, is not gotten but with greate paines, travaile, perill and danger of life: here shall they see the wisdome, curtesie, valour and pollicie of worthy Captaynes, yea and the faithfull hartes whiche they ought to beare unto their Princes service.[33]

Nicholas presented Cortés as an exemplar but not an exception among his people. Indeed, there is nothing in his introduction to his *Pleasant Historie of the Conquest of the Weast India, now called new Spayne* that anticipates later Black Legend stereotypes about Spaniards in the Americas (the first English edition of Las Casas's *Destruction of the Indies* was still five years away; the Spanish Armada of 1588 a decade in the future). Not only does he echo the praise for Cortés that he has found in Gómara's text, but Nicholas also suggests that something can be learned from the steely spirit of Spaniards as a whole. His portrait of the Spaniards is the opposite of later stereotypes; they are people so committed to king and country, so full of the "zeal of travayle," that they have built a "greate" and "marvellous" empire. Englishmen, Nicholas implies, should envy and seek to emulate such men.[34]

A century and a half later, another English translator of a bestselling Spanish book—Solís's *Conquest of Mexico*—articulated a similar admiration for Spain's achievements, arguing that the English should even be grateful to their rivals; for that "the Discovery and Conquest of that new World have enrich'd *England* with no small Share of the wealth of it; which makes it a Point of Gratitude in Behalf of my Country to publish the Actions of this Hero . . . so illustrious a Conqueror."[35]

The persistent perception of Cortés as a heroic figure in the Protestant West can in part be explained by the simple fact that a great story needs a great hero. By the late eighteenth century, the "Conquest of Mexico" came prepackaged as a narrative with Cortés as that hero (sometimes flawed, but always triumphant), Montezuma as the doomed and tragic half-hero, and Velázquez as the antihero. It is hardly surprising that the story was appealing to Spanish poets hoping a patriotic theme would bring them success. But it was equally attractive to the painters, poets, composers, and writers of the Romantic era. In particular, the Romantics—who emphasized individual emotional responses over the rationalism of the Enlightenment—found Malintzin a compelling character, ripe for reinvention. She became central to the story by being transformed into a sort of female version of Montezuma—a representative of the indigenous Mexican world who surrenders not through weakness or superstition, but because of the overwhelming emotions of romantic and sexual attraction. The effect was to transform Cortés, in turn, into a rugged leading man, sexually irresistible to women, a symbol of machismo, a modern hero, "the Romantic Caesar" (as Mexican intellectual José Vasconcelos dubbed him).[36]

Cortés the Romantic Hero would have been recognizable to Parisians, for example, who saw Spontini's opera *Fernand Cortez,* and likewise to Europeans who saw copies of Nicolas-Eustache Maurin's lithographs depicting scenes from the "Conquest of Mexico." In "Clémence de Fernand-Cortès" (included in the Gallery), the Spanish captain is the archetypal Romantic Hero—martial yet magnanimous, triumphant both on the battlefield and in love. Stated the caption: "placing himself proudly on the throne" of the defeated and manacled Moctezuma, Cortés informs his captive that "your empire is destroyed, I am the sole master here, and you shall suffer the fate that is reserved for you; resisting Cortés will cost you your life." But there is hope for Montezuma, in the form of Alaïda—a fictional, generic, pale-skinned Indian princess, far removed from the historical Malintzin but fitting her stereotype of the period. "Your heart is noble, Cortés," declares Alaïda, putting herself between the fallen emperor and his Spanish executioner: "It will also be generous, and this moment will determine if it is a magnanimous hero or a barbarous soldier to whom I have given my love."[37]

The question is left hanging, as it should be. For Cortés is both the magnanimous, macho, barbarous, soldier-hero who seduces an empire and founds a nation. From Gómara's day to Maurin's, and through the twentieth century, Cortés has retained "an uncontested place amongst the heroes of the nations." Hyperbolic evaluations of this heroism have grown, rather than faded, across these centuries. For some, Cortés was simply the ultimate "hero"; for others his "inner greatness" burned too bright to be contained. The "Conquest was a thing of superlatives and the men who took part in it were supermen," with Cortés *the* superman. Even when modern historians and writers attempted to evaluate Cortés in a balanced way, to see him as both hero and villain, in both "bright light and shadow" (as one Mexican biographer put it), he has remained a larger-than-life figure, a "truly extraordinary" and "riveting character." Apologetic hero worship has served only to give modern legs to the legend: "It may be impossible for us, nowadays, to approve of men like Cortes [*sic*] and the *conquistadores,* but we may at least admire their courage, resourcefulness, and strength."[38] Statues and monuments to Cortés have had a mixed history. But in text and image he has remained inextricably tied to the monumental events for which he is routinely given credit. Thus did Cortés himself become monumental.

––––––––––––

Cortés: smooth enough to seduce an entire empire into submission. The dashing, handsome, beautifully dressed—yet ruthless—ladies' man of Maurin's lithographs survived in the popular imagination long enough to be played by Cesar Romero in the 1947 Hollywood movie *Captain from Castile.* Romantic consummation is reserved for a subplot that does not include Romero's Cortés, as if his seductive appetite is far too vast for a mere love interest; in the final scene, it is a kingdom he rides off to woo and take. But by the time of the 2015 Spanish television drama *Carlos, Rey Emperador,* Cortés had become more of a promiscuous predator, a macho megalomaniac, a wife-killing brute.[39]

Those two images of Cortés are arguably two sides to the same coin, for the Antihero legend is often little more than the revision of his Romantic Caesar-Hero characteristics to emphasize brutality over boldness, cruelty over cunning, seizure over seduction. In specific, historical terms, three roots of negative perception created the Antiheroic Cortés: the Cortés-Velázquez feud, the Black Legend, and Mexican nationalism.

As explored in an earlier chapter, Cortés's complex and ultimately bitterly contentious relationship with Diego Velázquez underpinned and influenced most of his adult life. For his last two and a half decades, Cortés was ensnared in a massive legal and political battle, both directly with Velázquez and with his allies after the governor's death. Dozens of private lawsuits were filed against Cortés in the 1520s to '40s, while the sprawling *residencia* investigation into his conduct dragged on inconclusively. Portions of the *residencia* were terminated shortly before Cortés died, but they lacked clear verdicts (the murder inquiry never went as far as an arrest or trial, judgments of his governorship of New Spain became irrelevant as the years passed since his removal from the office, and in the meantime the Crown had repeatedly exacted funds from him as fines and loans). The Velázquez feud was thus at the center of a vast legal-political web whose numerous insinuations, accusations, and absence of ringing exonerations echoed down the centuries, where they could once more be alleged (making a wife-murder scene in a television show not only possible, but plausible to audiences).[40]

The second root to the modern Antiheroic Cortés is a similar set of sixteenth-century accusations revived centuries later. Las Casas was one of the most vocal critics of Cortés during the conquistador's lifetime and for years after it (they first met in the Caribbean shortly after Cortés arrived in 1504; for four decades they crossed paths in Cuba, Mexico, and Spain, and on occasion, the friar confronted the conquistador in person). But his scathing written denunciations were largely restricted to Spanish and Latin manuscripts not published until the late nineteenth and twentieth centuries. Modern apologists for Spain's empire wrongly imagined past centuries of Protestant writers using Las Casas to demonize Cortés; ironically, only after such apologists invented the Black Legend did the Dominican's criticisms become part of a modern Cortesian Black Legend. The Antihero may be "sterile, anachronistic, and ultimately false," but for a century it has been fueled by modern interpretations of past texts and events far beyond the discovery of works by Las Casas—fueled by a powerful movement that is Mexican nationalism.[41]

For Ignacio Romerovargas, the midcentury Mexican champion of "Moctezuma the Magnificent," Cortés was no more than a "bandit," and his "invasion . . . an act of barbarism contrary to just law and a violation of the laws of human civilization." In an era in which Las Casas is hailed as anticipating the modern human rights movement, and Montezuma and Cuauhtemoc are periodically subject to attempts at rehabilitating them as national heroes, some see Cortés as something of a precursor to today's monsters and megalomaniacs.[42]

Over the last two centuries, Mexicans have sought to come to terms with the Conquest and Spanish colonialism as part of the process of forging a national identity. This process has been a complex political and cultural one, and is still very much ongoing, articulated in sophisticated terms by generations of intellectual figures from Lucas Alamán to José Vasconcelos, from Eulalia Guzmán to Octavio Paz. Along the way, Cortés has been tossed back and forth, denounced and defended in numerous ways, but in the end persisting as a highly ambiguous figure. Even the great muralists of the Mexican Revolution gave him varying treatment, from Diego Rivera's deformed and syphilitic Cortés to the naked Cortés elevated by José Clemente Orozco into the Adam of a Mexican genesis. On the five hundredth anniversary of Cortés's birth, Paz commented on the paradox of Mexican feelings toward the conquistador as both violator and founder: "hatred of Cortés is not even hatred of Spain. It's hatred of ourselves." As another Mexican scholar noted, Cortés is "a very controversial character" because "to Mexicans he represents that ambivalence, the presence of the destructive European; but he's also the great European warrior, the conqueror." Likewise, even scholars in the English-speaking world whose sympathies lie with the Aztecs more than the conquistadors have let slip their grudging admiration for the "devious, masterful gentleman-adventurer."[43]

In other words, Cortés has evolved in modern times into a reluctantly but relentlessly admired Antihero. Like Satan in Milton's *Paradise Lost* or J. R. Ewing in the 1980s television drama *Dallas,* he is an Antihero so compelling, so central to the story, so necessary to the formation of the other characters, that he draws our primary attention; in the end, we love to hate him.

Cortés the Antihero, the modern monster, is of course no closer to being a credible historical figure than Cortés as Caesar, Moses, or national Hero. In Neil Young's song "Cortez the Killer," Cortés is simply the medium by which the idyllic society of the Aztecs is destroyed, as if he were a weapon, not a man ("What a killer"). By the song's time, Cortés had become associated with destruction for so long as to be a well-recognized symbol of loss; indeed the final verse reveals the Mexican subject matter to be merely metaphorical, with the paradise lost of Montezuma's world standing for the romantic paradise that Young lost with the end of a relationship.[44]

Young later claimed that the song was banned in Franco's Spain; when, after the generalissimo's death in 1975, the album upon which the song appeared was released in that country, the song's title was softened to "Cortez, Cortez." The Cortés legend had come far enough for a song about a different kind of conquest and loss to be a battleground between images of Cortés as the Romantic Caesar, the National Hero, and the lethal Antihero. In this, as in the vandalism of the Cortés statue in his hometown, the tragedy of the original war is hidden behind presentist squabbles tinged with unintentional comedy.

The comedy in Xochiquetzal Candelaria's 2011 poem "Cortés and Cannon" is darker, and its use of old threads of the Cortés legend more subtle. Here is the Black Legend Cortés who mutilates and murders, who seems deranged with attachment to his largest weapon of destruction, the cannon. But his pantomime of affection for "his field piece," the stroking and dancing and ordering "his men to lie on the ground in homage to the iron," amuses and endears him to the local Totonacs, who "laugh" and believe him "wild with love for the enormous, hollow thing he has hauled from the hull of his ship" (also see the epigraphs to Chapter 8). Candelaria comes close to an old stereotype of innocent, gullible indigenous people doomed to die at the hands of the blood-crazed conquistadors. But in the end the poem's hint of homoerotic humor, its evocation of the war's violence as completely lacking in glory or justification, and Candelaria's willingness to imagine a real Cortés, suggest with deft brevity a new way to look at this old Antihero.[45]

As long as the battleground is Cortés—not just his Hero or Anti-hero status, but Cortés in any historical or posthumous form—the conflict is unlikely to result in a better understanding of the war that made him (in)famous. How, therefore, can we view that war without Cortés getting in the way? If we eschew the Cortesian traditional narrative, who is left as our guide through the events of the 1520s? What optical strategies might we use to see around the five-hundred-year-old gorilla in the room?

To start with, we can cut the temporal cake in a different place. The traditional narrative makes the fall of Tenochtitlan in August 1521 the climax of the tale. Most accounts either end there or treat subsequent events (the death of Cuauhtemoc, Cortés's remaining years, New Spain's three centuries) as an epilogue. This phenomenon is rooted in part in the royal system of patronage, which gave conquistadors motive to make premature claims of success in discovery and conquest; such claims underpinned the rewards of being *adelantado* (official invader) and captain-general, and then provincial governor and more. Early success, however imaginary, also reclassified resistance as "the rebellion that took place in this recently conquered province," thereby legalizing the enslavement of local populations. Columbus made grandiose assertions of success as early as 1493, and Spanish conquistadors continued to do so into the seventeenth century (I have elsewhere called this "the myth of completion").[46]

Although the cutting of the narrative cake in 1521 has sixteenth-century roots and rationale, it actually became more prevalent in recent centuries; Prescott did it, for example, as do the most-read modern editions of Díaz's *True History* (although the original manuscript continues to 1568). At the same time, the canon of traditional narrative sources—and the histories based on them—tend to give detailed attention to what Cortés and his company were doing early in the invasion (1518–20); Gómara and Prescott are typical in devoting almost half their accounts to that period. The Hispanocentric story begins with Cortés leaving Cuba and climaxes with him capturing Tenochtitlan. (Perhaps I follow suit myself in dating the Spanish-Aztec War as 1519–21.)[47]

So, what alternative criteria might we use for determining where to cut? I suggest a closely related set of determinants: When did the conflict became an open war, with both sides deploying full force unsparing of noncombatants? When did that end? And when did indigenous (or quasi-indigenous) accounts mark the start and end of the war?

The starting point of open war was clearly May 1520, when the Aztecs began for the first time an unambiguous campaign to destroy the invaders, and the Aztecs in turn became the target of elimination. Open war in and against Tenochtitlan ended in August the following year, with the city's fall—and as the Aztecs thereby ceased to be a functioning political entity, the Spanish-Aztec War ended then. But warfare within the former Aztec Empire and outside its boundaries continued, against Nahuas, Tarascans, Mayas, and other Mesoamericans—from the regions northwest of central Mexico that Spaniards named New Galicia, to the Maya regions that they called Yucatan and Guatemala—through the 1540s. Throughout these three decades, most combatants were indigenous Mesoamericans, invaders and defenders. Indeed, thousands of ex-Aztec warriors—Mexica, Tetzcoca, Xochimilca, Quauhquecholteca, and others—as well as Tlaxcalteca forces, marched far north and south to fight and settle new imperial provinces. But the empire was increasingly a Spanish one, and this therefore can be dubbed the Spanish-Mesoamerican War of 1517–50.[48]

Quasi-indigenous accounts more or less support such cutting points. The origin, genre, and authorship of such sources are complex, making this an inexact science, but a rough pattern can be detected in accounts from the Aztec heartland (Tenochtitlan, Tlatelolco, Tetzcoco): minimal attention is given to the period before the outbreak of open war in May 1520; the majority of pages are devoted to the war from then through the summer of 1521; but considerable space is given to ongoing violence and invasion-related developments into the late 1520s (and sometimes beyond). This first narrative strategy therefore is to adopt a less Hispanocentric chronological focus, turning a 1519–21 story into a 1520s one.[49]

Another narrative strategy we can adopt is simply to remove Cortés from the center of the stage (as other conquistadors tried to do in their unpublished and largely unread reports to the crown). He was nominally the senior captain of the company waging war in Mexico, and then governor-general of the province of New Spain; we cannot remove him from those posts. But the events of the 1520s come into clearer focus if we place other Spanish captains, as well as indigenous leaders, at the center of the events they guided and influenced. There is a lesson to be learned from how the Toxcatl Massacre has tended to be blamed on Pedro de Alvarado; I suspect that if Cortés had been present in the city at that moment, a different spin would have been invented, a pro-Cortesian one such as the tale of the foiled ambush used to justify the Chololllan Massacre. The Toxcatl Massacre is not the exception that proves the rule of Cortesian control; it is a glimpse into the real world of conquistador decision making, in which men like Alvarado, Olid, Ordaz, Sandoval, and Vásquez de Tapia acted and reacted in semiautonomous cohorts of captains and their followers.[50]

A good example is that of the confrontation with Narváez and his company at the end of May 1520, usually credited as another "brilliant victory" by Cortés. It was nothing of the sort. Luck played

a role (receiving an arrow in the face at the start of hostilities motivated Narváez to come quickly to terms), as did the presence on the
Cortesian side of thousands of indigenous warriors. But above all,
it was Sandoval who successfully used the tactic that was supposedly Cortés's forte—the combination of diplomatic persuasion and
threatened violence—and he was aided by dozens of conversations
that took place between men of the two camps during the weeks of
May. In those conversations, the new arrivals all heard of the splendor of Tenochtitlan, the wealth of the Aztecs, the peaceful entry of
Cortés's company into the city, and the supposed surrender of Montezuma. The key persuaders were men like Bartolomé de Usagre. A
gunner with the Cortés company, his brother Diego was also a gunner and had crossed from Cuba with Narváez. Bartolomé walked
into the Narváez camp (with, according to Díaz, some gold nug-
gets) and soon talked Diego—and his cohort—into joining him. The
promise of spoils and slaves, made by kin and comrade, was far more
powerful than any captain. (Bartolomé died in the siege; Diego went
on to fight Mayas in Guatemala under the Alvarado brothers.)[51]

One further example is the simple and apparent fact of who
led which groups of conquistadors and warriors in the campaign
of January to August 1521. The traditional narrative relies on the
fiction that Cortés commanded everybody, masterminding the en-
circling and besieging of the Mexica, fighting everywhere or coming to last-minute rescues. In fact, Cortés seems to have done very
little, if anything, on his own. Rather, he remained in a captains'
cohort with Olid, Andrés de Tapia, and Pedro de Alvarado. Sandoval operated separately, working with captains like Pedro de Ircio,
Luís Marín, and Juan Rodríguez de Villafuerte—and coordinating
with Ixtlilxochitl. Sandoval's military and diplomatic successes in
the crucial region extending from Ixtlapalapan to Chalco, following failed efforts by Cortés's group, owe much to his ability to work
better with the Tlaxcalteca and Tetzcoca leadership. The logistical
challenge of getting the disassembled brigantines from Tlaxcallan to Tetzcoco—requiring cooperation from both sets of Nahua
leaders—was managed not by Cortés but by Sandoval and Rodrí-

guez de Villafuerte. It is surely telling that in the final assault, while Olid, Alvarado, Sandoval, and others fought along with Tlax-calteca, Tetzcoca, and other indigenous allies up the causeways into the city, Cortés remained in the relative safety of a brigantine on the lake—pretending to lead, like the fictional Duke of Plaza-Toro, from behind (or, as Alva Ixtlilxochitl put it, Cortés proved "what they say about all cruel men being cowards").[52]

The January–August campaign took as long as it did because cap-tains like Sandoval and Olid were not simply taking orders from Cortés, and were only loosely working together; it took as short as it did because ultimate control of the campaign lay in the hands of the leaders who knew the language, the terrain, and the enemy, and who commanded the loyalty of 99 percent of the fighting men. Indigenous initiatives were decisive throughout the war. Leaders in Tlaxcallan, Tetzcoco, Tenochtitlan, and elsewhere must therefore also be given credit as actors (not just re-actors)—from rulers such as Montezuma, Cacama, Ixtlilxochitl, and Xicotencatl, to lesser-known Nahuas whose roles we can only begin to discern, such as Quauhpopocatl and don Juan Axayacatl.

THIS LEADS US TO yet another narrative strategy that we might adopt to see around the obstacle of Cortesian legend: we can take spe-cific *altepetl*-based indigenous perspectives. There is no such thing as *the* indigenous or native or "Indian" viewpoint, but we can glean new insights by trying to see events the way the dynastic elite did in Tetzcoco, for example. Two crucial facts set the scene for this portion of our story and this angle on Mexico's tumultuous 1520s: Tetzcoco was the second-ranking power in the unequal Triple Al-liance that was the Aztec Empire; when its *tlahtoani*, or king, Neza-hualpilli, died in 1515, among his hundred-plus children were half a dozen sons with royal mothers from Tenochtitlan and thus with claims to the Tetzcoco throne.

Tetzcoco was the dominant *altepetl* or city-state on the eastern shore of the eponymous lake. Its heartland was the highly fertile and well-populated territory that stretched from the lake east to the mountains, but the city also exercised power and collected tribute from as far eastward as the Gulf coast. Thus by the end of the fifteenth century, there was "a veritable Tetzcoca empire." It could not extend westward, because there lay the great lake, with Tenochtitlan set bright and jewellike in its center. A century before the Spanish invasion, a Tetzcoca nobleman named Nezahualcoyotl had allied with the Mexica lords of the island-city to destroy the regional dominance of an *altepetl* on the far western lakeshore. Having humiliated that town (Azcapotzalco), the victors effectively turned their military alliance into a permanent power-sharing arrangement (Tlacopan, an *altepetl* just south of Azcapotzalco, took control of the western territories, completing the tripartite alliance). Nezahualcoyotl became *tlahtoani* of Tetzcoco, ruling half a century until his death in 1472 (the poet-prince is famous as a folk hero and cultural icon in Mexico today).[53]

Tetzcoco and Tlacopan were thus important imperial partners, acting as breadbaskets for Tenochtitlan (that is, providing corn and other foods) and as buffer zones between the imperial capital and outlying enemies (the Tlaxcalteca Triple Alliance to the east and the Tarascan Empire to the west). But Tenochtitlan was unambiguously the dominant partner. It took the first and largest cut of spoils and of subsequent tribute payments from all joint conquests. Only its ruler was the *huey tlahtoani* (the Great Speaker, the emperor). Nezahualpilli (ruled 1472–1515) sought wives as closely related as possible to Tenochtitlan's *huey tlahtoque*—Axayacatl (ruled 1469–81), Tizoc (ruled 1481–86), Ahuitzotl (ruled 1486–1502), and Montezuma (ruled 1502–20).

And therein lies the first twist in the tale. Sources differ greatly as to the identity, fate, and offspring of Nezahualpilli's wives, with some claiming he fathered up to 145 children. But the consensus is that the most important wives were Mexica royalty, producing six or seven sons with reasonable claims to the Tetzcoca throne in 1515. The chance timing of the resulting succession dispute and the arrival of the Spaniards meant that eight (and possibly nine or ten) of those sons would end up serving as *tlahtoani* over the next thirty years—

right through the "Conquest" period (see the Dynastic Vine in the Appendix).

The three sons with the strongest claims in 1515 were Cacama, whose uncle was Montezuma, and his half brothers Coanacoch and Ixtlilxochitl (who shared the same mother, by whom the *huey tlahtoani* Tizoc was their great-uncle). Not surprisingly, Cacama had the support of Montezuma and was declared his father's successor. Sources disagree as to how heavy-handed Montezuma needed to be in influencing or imposing his choice, but all agree that one brother, Ixtlilxochitl, refused to accept it. He fled Tetzcoco, gathered supporters, and established loose control over the northern portion of Tetzcoca territory. Neither brother apparently felt confident or strong enough to crush the other, and so a deal was made: Ixtlilxochitl would govern the north, Cacama the center and the city of Tetzcoco itself, with Coanacoch given an area in the south (presumably to discourage him from joining either of his two ruling brothers). This tripartite sharing of power among unequal partners had obvious parallel and precedent in the Aztec world. It also benefited Montezuma, who surely had a hand in it: a divided but peaceful and productive Tetzcoco helped the *huey tlahtoani* maintain Tenochtitlan's dominant position in the empire's ruling alliance.[54]

The arrangement might have lasted many years more, but the arrival of the conquistadors destabilized it. We know that Cacama met the Spaniards as they descended into the Valley of Mexico and led them to the Meeting. But what happened next is unclear. According to the traditional narrative, Cacama objected to Montezuma's surrender, and Cortés thus imprisoned him and placed another brother, Cuicuizcatl, on the Tetzcoca throne. The notion of Cortés as kingmaker within weeks of arriving in Tenochtitlan is one of the many absurdities stemming from the lie of his seizure of emperor and empire. Even Cortés effectively admitted that he had no control over Tetzcoco, stating that the Tetzcoca rejected Cuicuizcatl (who had to remain in Tenochtitlan) and instead chose Coanacoch (who had Cuicuizcatl killed when he fled home during the Noche Triste). In fact, Cacama probably remained as *tlahtoani* until he was murdered by the retreating Spaniards, along with Montezuma, in that June of 1520. In the meantime, during the months of the Phoney Captivity, there was clearly intense political jostling between Cacama, his brothers, and Montezuma. The Spanish captains, failing to grasp what was really happening, imagined causes and outcomes, and periodically lashed out; a story told by Alva Ixtlilxochitl (Ixtlilxochitl's great-great-grandson) rings true, whereby Cacama sent an escort with twenty conquistadors to Tetzcoco to fetch a gift of gold objects, and the paranoid Spaniards killed the leader of the escort (yet another brother of Cacama's).[55]

Whatever the truth of those months, by the summer of 1520, Cuitlahua was *huey tlahtoani* in Tenochtitlan and Coanacoch was *tlahtoani* in Tetzcoco. The empire's center was relatively secure and stable—for now. During the second half of that year, the war's initiative was again in the hands of the Tlaxcalteca (despite the traditional narrative's ubiquitous claim that Cortés was in charge and control); with the conquistadors at first diminished and battle-scarred, then increasingly fortified by recovery and resupply, the Tlaxcalteca were able to expand their territorial control at the expense of the easternmost Tetzcoca regions of the Aztec Empire. With the onset of the local war season in December, the Tlaxcalteca campaign began in earnest and with sufficient confidence to move into the Tetzcoca heartland. With the restoration of the Tlaxcalteca Triple Alliance, the invasion force of Caxtilteca and Tlaxcalteca was reinforced with warriors from Huexotzinco and Chololan (those left after the previous year's massacre). On December 29, the combined company descended the mountain pass into the Valley of Mexico.

On the last day of 1520, the city of Tetzcoco was occupied. There was no resistance. Alvarado and Olid climbed the great temple-pyramid, from which they could see that the city, spread out over a larger area than Tenochtitlan, was almost empty; its population, roughly as numerous as that of the imperial capital (some sixty thousand), was in flight, their canoes peppering the lake as they rowed with their king, Coanacoch, to the safety of Tenochtitlan. The Spaniards, Tlaxcalteca, and other invaders sacked the city; any men left behind were slaughtered, women raped and enslaved along with their children.[56]

With Coanacoch gone, and Tetzcoco triumphantly in Spanish-Tlaxcalteca hands, one of the absent king's many brothers, Tecocol, was installed as ruler—baptized as don Fernando Cortés Tecocoltzin. Or was he? By the end of January, Tecocol was dead, cause unknown. Hassig has argued that in the wake of the city's sacking, there was insufficient time or stability for such a decision, and that "his kingship was a convenient fiction." Alva Ixtlilxochitl downplayed Tecocol's supposed brief rule thus:

> Everyone agreed to make Tecocoltzin their lord, even though he was King Nezahualpilli's illegitimate son, because they did not dare nominate the legitimate ones until they saw how things would turn out.[57]

To make sense of this, we need to back up to the night of December 29, when the Caxtilteca-Tlaxcalteca force was camped out in the Tetzcoca town of Coatepec, having descended that day from the mountains. In the night, the captains received a visitor: Ixtlilxochitl. Cacama's rebellious brother had held on to his domain in northern Tetzcoca territory throughout the fourteen months since Spaniards had first entered the valley; he had stayed sufficiently clear of Tetzcoco and Tenochtitlan to survive, waiting to make his move. That night Ixtlilxochitl seized his opportunity not only to become *tlahtoani* of his father's entire territory, but to expand it at the expense of the Mexica—whose rulers had supported both his brothers, Cacama and then Coanacoch. With the help of the Tlaxcalteca and their foreign allies, he could shift the balance of power in the valley and turn *his* Tetzcoco into the imperial capital. If that meant surrendering tributary towns east of the mountains to the Tlaxcalteca Triple Alliance, it was a price worth paying to control the great valley.

Ixtlilxochitl's role in the events of 1521 has, I believe, been overly ignored or downplayed. This is not surprising. The traditional narrative slavishly submits to Cortés's claim that he, as kingmaker, appointed and controlled "Indian" lords like Ixtlilxochitl; the taking of Tetzcoco and its use as a base for the siege of Tenochtitlan has for five centuries been credited to Cortesian genius, without room to recognize indigenous initiative. Where credit has been given to the role played by "Indian allies," it is the Tlaxcalteca who traditionally win star billing—praised by Díaz and Prescott and most chroniclers and historians between and since. Tlaxcallan's own officials and mestizo historians maintained an extraordinarily successful campaign throughout the colonial period to promote the Tlaxcalteca as *the* Christian converts and crucial allies who made the "Conquest of Mexico" possible. As for the pair of accounts by Ixtlilxochitl's great-great-grandson, they are not well known outside scholarly circles, typically ignored or dismissed as overly biased.[58]

In fact, the accounts by Alva Ixtlilxochitl are no more biased or partisan than the pro-Cortés canon, and arguably the exaggerations are more easily peeled away to see a revealing and persuasive picture beneath. That picture suggests that it was the Tetzcoca, led by Ixtlilxochitl as *tlahtoani,* who played as crucial a role in the war in 1521 as did the Tlaxcalteca—and arguably a more crucial one. Sources differ as to how and when he became *tlahtoani;* perhaps in the autumn of 1520 (as I suspect), but certainly by the spring of 1521, he was recognized as such by the Spaniards and by his subjects in Tetzcoco, many of whom had slipped back home from Tenochtitlan, and would continue to do so as the balance of power in the valley shifted. Ixtlilxochitl would rule Tetzcoco until his death in 1531. (Coanacoch, meanwhile, remained in Tenochtitlan as the Mexica-recognized *tlahtoani* until being captured by Spaniards in 1521, along with Cuauhtemoc and the Mexica-recognized *tlahtoani* of Tlacopan; Cortés hanged all three in Maya country in 1525.)[59]

We might take with a pinch of salt the claim by Alva Ixtlilxochitl that his ancestor captured a great Mexica warrior in hand-to-hand combat outside Ixtlapalapan, ritually burning him alive to send a message to Coanacoch and Cuauhtemoc. But such combat was characteristic of Aztec warfare and helps us to see the conflict as an internecine Aztec war rather than part of "the Spanish Conquest." Furthermore, Alva Ixtlilxochitl's brief description of the Ixtlilxochitl-led campaign to cement Tetzcoco's rise to prime position in the valley rings true in terms of its details: having defeated Ixtlapalapan on the lake's southern shore, to prevent the Mexica using it as a base against Tetzcoco, Ixtlilxochitl then led northward sixty thousand Tetzcoca warriors, accompanied by twenty thousand Tlaxcalteca and three hundred Spaniards. The object was to neutralize the third *altepetl* in the Triple Alliance, Tlacopan. The allied force defeated the Mexica at Xaltocan, a small island-*altepetl* in the lake's northern waters, before sweeping through the lakeshore towns down to Tlacopan. "At dawn, they sacked the city and burned as many of the houses and temples as they could," wrote Alva Ixtlilxochitl, also "killing as many as they could" in the course of a week of battles with Mexica warriors in the Tlacopan region. The victorious army returned to Tetzcoco, where the Tlaxcalteca were granted "permission to leave, and they returned to their lands rich in plunder, which was what they always sought."[60]

This was warfare fought according to local tradition and precedent, both in its timing (during the war season) and its purpose (two *altepeme* joining forces to curb the regional power of two others and to acquire spoils). Spanish sources and the traditional narrative do not disagree with the facts of the campaign; they simply appropriate it as one conceived and directed entirely by Cortés. Likewise the supposed winning of support for the allied cause among towns on the eastern side of the valley; in reality, these were Tetzcoca subjects, following the lead of their own king. Spanish sources also follow the Cortés-Gómara lead in blaming unrest among the conquistadors in Tetzcoco on Nárvaez loyalists and *Velazquistas,* crediting Cortés with the bold restoration of discipline with the hanging of Antonio de Vallafaña; but the obvious fact that the Spaniards were pursuing a Tetzcoca-Tlaxcalteca agenda surely stirred up factional conflict, resolved by the dominant captains, not by Cortés alone. Finally, the reluctance of the Tetzcoca to maintain a war front against the Chalca cities (along Lake Chalco south of Ixtlapalapan) was presumably a source of unrest among the Spaniards; Sandoval had attempted to extend the alliance's control down there, using Spanish horsemen and Tlaxcalteca warriors, but it was in vain. Other captains also led assaults against the southern towns, doing enormous damage and forcing families not killed or enslaved to flee; Aztec canoe-based warriors repeatedly returned, though, turning the war into one of attrition.

In the traditional narrative, the first half of 1521 comprised a brilliant campaign by Cortés, as he gradually took control of the valley and put his siege of Tenochtitlan in place. Setbacks and incidents not well fitting to this narrative have been explained in terms of the unreliability of "Indian" allies, the bloody-mindedness of the Aztecs, and the vast logistical challenges. But viewed through the lens of the Tetzcoca agenda, the war's unfolding makes more sense. The Tetzcoca and their Tlaxcalteca allies sent companies of warriors where they—not the Spaniards—wanted. Their goal was not to establish permanent territorial control, but to force a town into accepting Tetzcoco or Tlaxcallan as the dominant regional capital to which tribute would henceforth be sent—thus explaining why the campaign comprised dozens of raids and minor campaigns, with the same towns "taken" by the conquistadors over and over. Spanish captains tried in vain to turn the assaults into a concerted attack on Tenochtitlan, failing when indigenous warriors went home with spoils and captives rather than staying in the field continually. Nobody in this war was a soldier in a standing army, but while the Caxtilteca were a long way from Castile and committed to their semilegitimate enterprise, the Nahua fighting men expected to stay home once the war season wound down in April.

The war should have ended in May, therefore, as a standoff. Had the Spaniards simply left at that point, the region would have settled down for the rest of 1521 into a postwar recuperation, with the Aztec Empire dismantled, and the new powers consolidating their tribute-paying regions: a Tlaxcalteca Triple Alliance, stronger than ever; a Tenochtitlan reduced in power and reach; a Tetzcoco unified under Ixtlilxochitl.

But rather than leave, the Spaniards grew in number—by May there were more than seven hundred, and even as men died, by August total numbers approached a thousand. These men greatly outnumbered the survivors of the original company, and they were keen to get their share of slaves and spoils. Their horses, harquebuses (the clumsy handgun of the day), and crossbows grew in number too. As did their willingness to kill: sackings and slave raids, disguised as the punishment of rebels, proliferated. When Xicotencatl (the son) expressed reluctance in May to keep fighting after the war season, a handful of Spanish captains conspired with some Tetzcoca nobles and a Tlaxcalteca rival (named Chichimecateuctli): Xicotencatl was seized and hanged. Chichimecateuctli was probably the architect of the conspiracy, but he found the captains quick to believe Xicotencatl was a traitor and to kill him for it. As for the Tetzcoca, their city had been turned into a massive war camp, complete with the newly constructed brigantines designed for the direct assault on Tenochtitlan. They must have understood that the only way to get their city back was for that final assault to take place, and successfully. There was no turning back for Tetzcoco.[61]

The siege of Tenochtitlan, then, might perfectly validly be seen as both a dramatic denouement to the Tetzcoco succession dispute begun in 1515, with Ixtlilxochitl the last-standing brother triumphantly reuniting the regions of his father's domain; and as a violent tipping of the balance of power within the old Triple Alliance, with Tetzcoco knocking Tenochtitlan down to second partner. The degree to which Tetzcoco's triumph was a Faustian bargain, with the Spaniards and the Tlaxcalteca playing major and minor devils, respectively, was not immediately apparent.

The war itself was of course a horrific disruption to family life in Tetzcoco. But its immediate aftermath, what the Spaniards claimed as their "conquest," was not a radical suspension of a tranquil and static prewar past, but an extension of a political history that had always combined volatility with adaptability. In this case, deeper adaptations were required, most notably religious conversion and the recasting of governmental structures. But the importance of the *altepetl* was recognized by the new Spanish authorities, who designated it as one of only four urban centers in the Valley of Mexico to be a *ciudad*, "city." And the Tetzcocan royal family continued to rule, according to traditional patterns of legitimacy. As had been Aztec practice throughout the valley for many generations, cohorts of brothers inherited the throne, then sons of the next cohort, with claims underpinned by blood ties to Mexica royalty in Tenochtitlan.[62]

Thus when Ixtlilxochitl died, he was succeeded by three of his brothers, don Jorge Yoyontzin (to 1533), don Pedro Tetlahuehuetzquititzin (to 1539), and don Antonio Pimentel Tlahuitoltzin (to 1545); the latter's nephew (and a son of Coanacoch), don Hernando Pimentel Nezahualcoyotzin, would then rule as *tlahtoani* and *gobernador* for two decades. Ixtlilxochitl's postwar rule thus ushered in a return of governmental stability, with the succession dispute and lethal warfare of 1515–21 a relatively short disruption to the otherwise calm dynastic century and a half from Nezahualcoyotl through his great-grandson Pimentel. The dynasty would lose control of the city's top political office after that, but would persist as landed aristocracy for centuries. Tetzcoco's decline as a regional power would likewise be very gradual, beginning at the end of the sixteenth century.[63]

THE TETZCOCA PERSPECTIVE on the war is thus crucial and eye-opening. But there is one final optical strategy we can take to see around that gorilla (the myth of Cortesian control): we can try to see the 1520s from the viewpoint of the Mexica (the inhabitants of Tenochtitlan-Tlatelolco). From that perspective, a world disrupted in 1520 by the prolonged presence of foreign guests in the capital, culminating in the shocking attack on unarmed Toxcatl festival celebrants in May, was then set right by the costly but stunning victories of June and July. Most of the newcomers had been killed, scores of them in the ritual executions that suitably honored captors and captives. In Ochpaniztli (which began early September), a new *huey tlahtoani*, Cuitlahua, assumed office, and tribute from across the empire was delivered in Tenochtitlan as scheduled.

But equilibrium had not quite been restored. Tribute no longer came in from the east, as towns that had been under Tetzcoca control now suffered sweeping Tlaxcalteca-Caxtilteca attacks, or they switched allegiances to the expanding Tlaxcalteca Triple Alliance. Auspiciously, perhaps, at the onset of the month of Tititl (the Festival of Shrunken Things), Tetzcoco itself broke away from its Triple Alliance with Tenochtitlan and Tlacopan. A shrunken empire was hardly an empire at all. In Etzalqualiztli (the Bean-Eating Festival), it was more than beans that were in short supply; the island-city was becoming encircled by its enemies, cut off from the world it had so recently commanded. By the end of Miccailhuitontli (the Small Festival of the Dead), the dead were piled high in the streets; as Huey Miccailhuitl (the Great Festival of the Dead) began, the metropolis was sacked, the dead burned in great funeral pyres, the survivors made slaves or refugees.

From the perspective of the Spaniards and the traditional narrative, August 1521 completed the bloody birthing of New Spain, of three centuries of colonial rule. As a 1697 French version of Las Casas's *Destruction of the Indies* put it, "*Mexique*" was the name of "a great Empire, of which Montezume was the last King; Fernand Cortez entered it in the year 1519, seized that Prince, and conquered the whole country." Solís, having devoted hundreds of pages to the war, wrapped up the story in a single final paragraph: after "the Conquest of the Capital City," the lords and "Tributary Princes" of the fallen empire came "to do Homage to the Conqueror"; thus "in a short time was erected that noble Monarchy, which merits the name of *New Spain*."[64]

For the conquistadors, the business now was to continue to pacify (*pacificar*) and settle (*poblar*). All local people were to be enslaved or allotted as sources of labor and tribute to *encomenderos* (conquistadors granted such "Indians" in trust, or *encomienda*). Ongoing hostilities with "Indians" were classified as the suppression of "rebels." Cooperative "Indian allies" (*indios amigos*)—those who had fought for what the Spanish perceived as their cause, and who now accepted Christianity and the labor and tribute demands of the new settlers—were granted the privilege of local self-rule. Top billing in this category were the Tlaxcalteca. As conquest apologist Vargas Machuca later put it, "don Hernando Cortés entered and kept Mexico with their help. . . . After which, all the remaining provinces of New Spain were conquered in the briefest of times by the Marquis del Valle."[65]

Solís's closing line is dated in its enthusiasm for the war—"A Wonderful Conquest, and a most Illustrious Conqueror, among those which many Ages rarely produce, and of which there are but few Examples in History!"—but its finality continues to be reflected in today's accounts. A (literally) graphic example is a recent version for young readers, which neatly captures the spirit of the traditional narrative in cartoon images and captions. At Cuauhtemoc's surrender, "Cortés was delighted"; he had "won the war." But "sadly the great city of Tenochtitlan was in ruins" and "the glorious Aztec civilization has been destroyed." However, "Cortés built Mexico City on the site of Tenochtitlan." The penultimate frame depicts a ruined, empty city; the final frame, a courtyard with Spanish buildings.[66]

The three elements of that impression—the finality of the Conquest at war's end in August 1521, the sharp break between a city obliterated and a brand-new one built on the same site, and Cortés in charge of it all—are fundamental to the traditional narrative, and are fundamentally wrong. From other perspectives—the advantages of hindsight, the weight of historical evidence, the memories of indigenous communities—the 1520s look very different. From the specific viewpoint of the surviving Mexica in Tenochtitlan, their world did not simply contract with the end of empire; it also expanded. Examples of expanding horizons included the introduction into Tenochtitlan in 1519 of Taínos, Africans, and Spaniards; the experience, the following year, of epidemic diseases brought by those foreigners (most notably a smallpox epidemic that struck around October, killing thousands, including Cuitlahua); and the acquisition of new material objects (for example, in the fighting at Xochimilco in the spring of 1521, Spaniards noticed that Mexica had attached Spanish swords to wooden lances, giving them deadly steel points). What's more, at the war's end in the valley in 1521, the Mexica and other Nahuas did not cease to fight; on the contrary, they went out as warriors and colonists, far to the north and south into Maya kingdoms in Yucatan and Guatemala. Others traveled as far as Spain, a few as representatives of Aztec nobility, many as slaves (a pair of ships crossed the Atlantic in 1528 with two of Montezuma's sons, three Tlaxcalteca princes, a son of the Mexica ruler of Tenochtitlan, and more than thirty Nahua servants and slaves).[67]

Nor was it only Spanish religion, culture, and language to which the Mexica were increasingly exposed; young noblemen soon became fluent in Latin, taught (and some eventually teaching) at the college opened in the Tlatelolco district of Tenochtitlan (the New World's first European-style institution of higher learning). For Spaniards, the Tlatelolco college was a New Spain institution. But its pupils were all Nahuas, and for them it was an institution in the life of postwar Tenochtitlan.

Tenochtitlan's death turns out to be a myth, created by the chronological cutting of the cake at August 13, 1521. The emphasis by historians on Cortés dividing up urban lots among the conquistadors in 1522, or Alonso Gracía Bravo measuring the central grid or *traza* in 1524, or the "seventh great plague" (as Motolonía called it) of forced construction work for the indigenous builders of Spanish palaces, have all acted as nails in that mythical coffin. For while Tenochtitlan was largely in ruins that August—a hellscape of rubble, corpses, and half-starved survivors—it was neither dead nor abandoned. A reduced Aztec population, scarred from battle and smallpox, remained in the capital. In the early days and weeks, those not "too sick to leave" no doubt stumbled out along the causeways, "so thin and yellow and dirty and stinking that it was pitiful to see them" (as Díaz put it). But that was to find food and escape the sacking of the city—the raping and slave-taking and torturing for information on hidden treasures that followed every urban assault since the Chololan Massacre. Within months, if not weeks, the Mexica reclaimed their neighborhoods and homes, gardens, and *chinampas*—despite a gallows supposedly set up in the main plaza to hang returnees.[68]

Before the siege, Cortés had imagined the city as ideal for a segregated and secure settlement, with Spaniards on the island and "Indians" across the water in lakeshore towns. But the reality of the early 1520s was the opposite. In 1521, the conquistadors settled on the shores, most of them in Coyohuacan, to the south of Tenochtitlan; ironically, the Spaniards had to ride up the same causeway they had traveled in November 1519 in order to reach the city they had so massively damaged and did not yet occupy. Even when they did start to move into new buildings, starting in 1524, they did so only within the *traza*, the gridded central zone reserved for Spanish administrative buildings and houses—the very concept of which, in addition to the location, was Aztec. Churches were built on the foundations of temples. Palaces were built on palaces. Plazas, streets, and canals remained in place. Aztec space persisted underneath or within Spanish-Aztec space.[69]

Most of the city still comprised the five Aztec neighborhoods that had originally been separate *altepeme*. Each *altepetl* survived, its name intact but with a prefixed saint's name: Santiago Tlatelolco in the north; and surrounding the *traza*, the four that comprised San Juan Tenochtitlan—Santa María Cuepopan, San Sebastián Atzacoalco, San Pablo Teopan, and San Juan Moyotlan. But perhaps even more notable than continuities of space and polity, people and neighborhoods, was the astonishing perpetuation of Aztec royal rule.

Going back at least to the first Montezuma, the Aztec emperor had appointed a high official to act as a viceroy or first minister, with the title of *cihuacoatl*. Montezuma's own brother, Tlacaelel, had served as his *cihuacoatl*; and Tlacaelel's grandson, Tlacotzin, served as *cihuacoatl* to the second Montezuma. Not only did Tlacotzin survive the war, but he survived within a besieged Tenochtitlan, acting (according to Cortés) as a negotiator between the Mexica and the allied forces in the closing weeks of the war. After the war, he retained his title of *cihuacoatl* and—with Cuauhtemoc as a captive *tlahtoani*—effectively ascended to the throne, now named don Juan Velázquez Tlacotzin. Indigenous annals and codices include him in the succession of rulers, following Cuauhtemoc. In the Codex Aubin he appears as ruler beside the entry for 1523 (reproduced in our Gallery); above his head is a pictograph of a woman-headed snake (*cihuatl* means "woman"; *coatl* means "snake"). The traditional responsibilities of the *cihuacoatl* seem to have included the infrastructure and functioning of Tenochtitlan itself, and sure enough Tlacotzin took on that role in the early 1520s. For example, he reopened the great city market and renamed it after himself; it just happened to be located adjacent to his own (rebuilt) residence.[70]

Although Tlacotzin was effectively already ruler of indigenous Tenochtitlan, he was appointed *gobernador* by the parallel Spanish administration upon Cuauhtemoc's execution in 1525. However, he died soon after Cuauhtemoc, as he too was on the Honduras expedition. Cortés then appointed don Andrés de Tapia Motelchiuhtzin, who was also with him on the expedition; Motelchiuhtzin was "only a Mexica eagle-noble" (as Nahua chronicler Chimalpahin later put it), not Aztec royalty. He governed the city during the late 1520s, when Spanish rule was in its infancy, its effectiveness undermined by virtual civil war among the conquistadors, and between them and the first waves of royal officials and early settlers. In 1530, Motelchiuhtzin was killed in action, as one of the leaders of an expedition against Chichimecs to the north. On the same campaign was a distant cousin of Montezuma's, don Pablo Tlacatecuhtli Xochiquentzin, who then assumed the governorship of Tenochtitlan.[71]

This took the governorship closer to its direct line from the Aztec emperors, and it moved even closer still with the appointment of don Diego de Alvarado Huanitzin; as a grandson of Axayacatl and nephew of Montezuma, Huanitzin was recognized by the Mexica as *huey tlahtoani*. In quasi-indigenous sources like the Codex Aubin, Huanitzin is depicted wearing the *xiuhhuitzolli*—headdress of high office that was effectively the Aztec crown—and seated on the high-backed reed throne of the emperors. Huanitzin's image was not just a veneer of continuity or a sign of Aztec nostalgia: he was chosen, according to Aztec tradition, from a pool of royal eligibles, including two surviving sons of Montezuma; his appointment was sanctioned by Viceroy Mendoza, with whom he worked closely and who clearly relied heavily upon him.[72]

After Huanitzin, the rulership of the Mexica city would remain within the lineage of the old Aztec imperial dynasty for generations, passing to grandsons of the emperors Tizoc and Ahuitzotl, to a son and to a nephew of Huanitzin's, and by the 1620s to one of his great-grandsons—a man therefore directly descended from Acamapichtli, who had become king back in 1376. Continuity of dynastic rule thus long outlasted Cortés's coming and going; he had left Mexico for good by Huaniztin's death in 1541. The story of Tenochtitlan had ceased to be Cortés's. But then, in reality, had it ever been?

Cortés stood on the beach, waving his sword, yelling at Martín de Castro. Write this down, he told Castro, the senior notary among the men and horses gathered on the sand. Write, he "loudly declared," that I am "the very illustrious lord don Fernando Cortés, Marquis of the Valley of Oaxaca, Captain General of New Spain and the South Sea for His Majesty the King"; that "I have discovered this land, that I have come with my ships and fleet to conquer and settle it!" Shouting that he was thereby "taking control and possession of this newly discovered land," the Marquis

> "gave the port and bay the name of the Port and Bay of Santa Cruz, and he walked back and forth" across the beach "from one part to another and with his sword struck certain trees which were there, and ordered the men who were standing there to accept him as Governor of these lands for His Majesty."[73]

It is tempting to see something pathetically quixotic in this scene. For it has no place in the traditional narrative of Cortesian triumph. The ceremony of possession occurred not during the invasion of Mexico, but in May 1535, on a beach at the tip of the peninsula known today as Baja California. For all the talk of discovery and conquest, there was no civilization on the horizon, no embassy to engage, not even a few unsuspecting locals to enslave or ensnare. A small map was sketched, ending up in the archives in Seville, along with Martín de Castro's record of the moment. The map shows only the tip of the peninsula, its short coastlines going nowhere—just like Cortés's expedition.[74]

For all his titles, his ships and horses, his shouting and striking trees with his sword, Cortés might as well have been don Quixote tilting at windmills. A week later, he had the expedition's public crier read out loud on the same beach a royal edict, issued years earlier, in 1529, giving Cortés license to "discover, conquer, and settle any islands in the South Sea of New Spain" (that is, off Mexico's Pacific coast), and the notary made a record of that reading. It was as if Cortés were repeating the legal rituals from the beach at Veracruz of sixteen years earlier, only this time he really was in control of his company. But there was another difference: no city-states were nearby. There was no conquest to come. He was not even in charge of the lands for whose conquest he was given credit.[75]

A few days later, he wrote to Cristóbal de Oñate (conqueror of New Galicia—the region northwest of central Mexico—and its governor for most of the next decade) to inform him that he had found "pearls and fishing grounds," but that he was not yet writing to the governor of New Spain (Nuño Beltrán de Guzmán) or the archbishop (fray Juan de Zumárraga) until he had discovered "the secrets" of these new lands. In fact, there were no secrets. A paltry Spanish colony set up at Baja's tip in 1535 was abandoned within a year; a permanent one would not be established for another sixty years, and it would remain poor and tiny for centuries.[76]

Hollow titles, pointless paperwork, fruitless expeditions, and virtual exile from the kingdom he supposedly won but was now ruled by others. Such were the final decades of Cortés's life (1529–47), dubbed by his biographers the period of "Self-Conquest" or that of "The Powerless Marquis." And it is certainly tempting to knock the wind out of the sails of Cortesian mythology by mocking moments like the one on the Baja beach. But that misses the point, which is not to turn him from hero to antihero, legend to loser, but to dismantle his exceptionalism. For Cortés waving his sword and dictating documents on that beach was not actually a figure of fun; he was a typical conquistador, doing what Spaniards of the era did all over the Americas and beyond. Like other Europeans, they claimed lands wherever they explored, proclaiming possession and claiming legal title before going on to conquer, settle, and rule. Most expeditions failed; most claims led to nothing; the mortality rate of conquistadors and would-be conquistadors was extremely high. Remove the Spanish-Aztec War from Cortés's biography and his unexceptional and typically unsuccessful participation in that pattern comes into focus.[77]

Purveyors of the traditional narrative of the Conquest and Cortés's life have always struggled to make sense of his movements and priorities in the final quarter century of his life. How to explain the conundrum of a supposed visionary leader failing to focus on his prize, constantly distracted by other regions, squandering thousands of lives on travesties like the pointless and costly expedition to Honduras? The facile solution had been to follow Cortés himself, who never failed to point fingers at old enemies and ungrateful friends. A more complex, but better evidenced, solution lies in accepting that Cortesian control is a myth, that his capture of the Aztec Empire was as much an illusion as the surrender of Montezuma, that he inevitably and hopelessly struggled to maintain even a semblance of control over both the Spaniards in New Spain and the vast, destabilized network of indigenous states and communities. Furthermore, the conundrum disappears if we also accept that if Cortés had a vision, it was not for New Spain, but for his own glorious future, one in which he—not Velázquez—was to initiate expeditions, discover new lands under indisputable license from the king, and find a passage to Asia and the Spice Islands.

This was the old Iberian dream, circulating long before Cortés's generation was born, the one Columbus had clung to all his life and that had inspired scores of voyages for decades. Thus all the captains who set off to explore regions of Mesoamerica in 1521—Juan del Valle to Tehuantepec, Pedro de Alvarado to Oaxaca, Olid to Michoacán, and Pedro Alvarez Chico to Guerrero—were instructed to look for a way to sail from the Caribbean to the Pacific (or South Sea). Until such a passage were found, and in order to help find it, a shipyard was needed on the Pacific; to that end indigenous slaves and porters were put to work carrying cables, rigging, and anchors all the way from Veracruz across central Mexico to Zacatula (today's Petacalco, on Guerrero's Pacific coast). In his Third Letter to the king, of May 1522, Cortés reported that four ships were already under construction.[78]

As it happened, during the very weeks when Montezuma had been welcoming Cortés in Tenochtitlan, Ferdinand Magellan (Fernão de Magalhães) and Sebastián Elcano were leading an expedition through the straits that would be given the Portuguese captain's name. On November 28, 1519, they reached the Pacific, sailing on to the Spice Islands or Moluccas (today called Maluku, part of Indonesia) and the Philippines (where Magellan was killed). Elcano's return to Spain in the autumn of 1522 prompted the king to order Cortés to freeze his explorations while another expedition (under Jofre García de Loaysa) was launched from Spain to try to improve on the Magellan-Elcano route. That expedition finally set off in 1525, and by the summer of 1526 was presumed lost; Cortés was ordered to search the Pacific for survivors. In fact, while Loaysa himself and most of his crew had indeed perished, survivors had made it to the Moluccas and one ship even found the new Spanish shipyard in Tehuantepec.[79]

Seeing an opportunity to save the day, Cortés organized an expensive trans-Pacific expedition under the command of one of his cousins, Alvaro de Saavedra Cerón. Hoping to be responsible for placing Asia's islands "under the imperial scepter," Cortés wrote that he was "convinced that in our time we shall see His Majesty become king of the world." He wrote a letter for his cousin to deliver to the Chinese emperor, informing him that God had given "preference" to the Spanish king above all other Christian princes, and "in His bounty has wished that he should be emperor of the world." (He also sent "ten letters in Latin, the [addressees'] names blank," "as it is the most general language in the universe," and "there may be Jews who can read it.") Saavedra's fleet set sail in July 1527; the years passed, with no word. Meanwhile, in 1528, crown officials led by Guzmán had wrested from Cortés what little control he had of the Spanish administration in Mexico; Cortés's shipyards were seized, and he was recalled to Spain.[80]

What had happened, meanwhile, to the Saavedra expedition? In the end, it did make it to the Moluccas. But there the ships were lost and most of the men died; a few survivors eventually reached Spain, seven years after leaving Mexico.

Having returned to Spain, laden with the spoils of war, Cortés pursued the Spanish king. Eventually, on July 6, 1529, in Barcelona, Carlos V signed four *cédulas* granting privileges to Cortés. In the first two, he is still recognized as governor and captain-general of New Spain, and at the same time elevated to marquis of the Valley of Oaxaca. Along with the marquisate came the granting and confirmation of his tenure of considerable lands and *encomiendas* in central Mexico and Oaxaca. He was now, by royal decree and in reality, an extremely wealthy and powerful nobleman.

The moment lasted only minutes. For that morning the king went on to sign two more decrees. At first glance, they appear simply to further burnish the privileges of the new marquis. One made him captain-general of the coasts and provinces of the South Sea (meaning the Pacific Ocean). The other granted him further lands in Mexico for hunting. But in both, the title of governor of New Spain was absent. It had been revoked. His right to rule was gone, and would never be recovered. His marquisate was a consolation prize. The title of captain-general, without the governorship, amounted to an order to sail off and find new lands for the king, or perish doing so, but to leave Mexico to others.[81]

Cortés's extensive properties and access to labor in Mexico and Oaxaca made him a wealthy man. But the 1529 document granting him the right to be captain-general of the South Sea—in effect, to rule the Pacific—would lead him nowhere but to an empty beach in Baja. His kingdom of imaginary islands grew further and further beyond reach. Harried by the Guzmán administration (he sued the

governor for impounding ships of his), his Pacific possibilities were
limited by Crown-backed claims in northern Mexico and beyond
by Guzmán himself and by an old enemy, Pánfilo de Narváez. Furthermore, unaware that the king had sold all rights to the Moluccas
to the Portuguese crown, Cortés built and outfitted two new ships.
Led by another Cortés cousin, Diego Hurtado de Mendoza, the expedition left Acapulco in 1532. One ship sailed north and made
landfall in what is now Nayarit, where all members of the crew were
slaughtered. The other ship disappeared without a trace.

Increasingly obsessive, Cortés sent out another pair of ships, under Hernando de Grijalva. Some islands south of Baja were found,
but Guzmán's men seized one of the ships. Cortés's own expedition
to Baja then followed, despite the fact that the Crown had now
authorized Alvarado to take the lead in Pacific explorations. Thus
when, in 1536, word reached Mexico that the Pizarro expedition
in Peru had appealed for reinforcements, Cortés prepared a pair
of vessels, placing Grijalva in command and ordering him to sail
to the Moluccas, instead of Peru. Grijalva almost made it, reaching the Gilbert Islands, where his crew murdered him and abandoned ship. Still Cortés kept building ships and preparing Pacific
expeditions. A fleet of three sailed north in 1539, returning with
nothing but descriptions of the California coast. When Cortés left
for Spain shortly after this, a fleet of five was being prepared in
Acapulco; Cortés never returned to Mexico and the expedition was
abandoned.[82]

One historian recently found in all this "the beginnings of a European modernity in which an insatiable quest for profit and a projection into space and the future were combined."[83] That may be true, in
terms of the larger context of sixteenth-century European exploration and expansion. But Cortés's role in that larger development was
dismal. His derivative and self-centered sense of purpose led to little
that was original or creative. He achieved nothing of note in his fifteen years in the Caribbean, but at least the relative modesty of those
years did relatively little damage; by contrast, during a similar number of years, his Pacific endeavors likewise achieved very little—yet

he exploited indigenous labor, drained resources from communities still suffering or recovering from warfare and epidemic disease, and sent hundreds of men to die at sea. There was no profit, no return, no result other than waste, misery, and failure. The success of the Aztec war—the "Conquest of Mexico"—did not transform Cortés from a mediocrity into a brilliant man of vision. But it gave the illusion of him being such a man, and having always been one.

That illusion was certainly believed by Cortés himself; he birthed and nurtured it in his Letters to the King, and in the 1540s it blossomed through conversations with his son, don Martín, and with his biographer, Gómara. It was also evident in a few incidents of these final years in Spain. The failures of his Mexican and Pacific expeditions of the late 1520s and '30s were topped by the failure of a Mediterranean campaign in 1541. It was not, of course, led by Cortés, nor was its outcome his fault. But his own hubris matched that of Emperor Carlos V and his troops. The campaign began with a Spanish assault on the Ottoman stronghold of Algiers and ran into trouble almost immediately, with the invasion fleet damaged and scattered by violent weather, and the land attack driven back and saved from complete disaster only by making a two-day march back to the coast. Cortés allegedly tried to compare the retreat to his position in Mexico after the Spanish expulsion from Tenochtitlan, urging Carlos to turn back and seize Tunis just as he had rallied and seized the Aztec capital. Fortunately for Cortés, his plea fell on deaf ears, or else the old conquistador might have met an ironic—and arguably appropriate—death at the hands of non-Christian defenders of a besieged overseas city.[84]

Throughout his half-millennium afterlife, whether Cortés has been seen as Moses or Caesar, as Hero or Antihero, two core Cortesian characteristics have persisted: exceptional and masterful. Spanish composer of epic poetry Vaca de Guzmán colorfully put it thus:

If you want to see the valiant spirit,
that has given so much glory to your nation,
prepared for risks and prudent,

resolute in endeavors and bold,
a General of the Spanish people,
whose valor the world has respected,
in the great Cortés you will see it all, . . . [85]

Remove the twin assumptions of his exceptionalism and his mastery of events, however, and two mutually dependent and explanatory things collapse: the heroic legend of Cortés, and the traditional "Conquest of Mexico" narrative. To paraphrase Paz, to dispel a myth, one must attack the ideology that spawned it. If Cortés is no longer exceptional, nor the man in control, an opening is created—a whole world of openings—into which other people and other explanations can be discovered.

And then there is the war itself. Divorcing Cortés's biography from the "Conquest of Mexico," and then banishing that phrase, with its connotation of a campaign that was a remarkable yet inevitable triumph, allows us to see the Spanish-Aztec War for what it was: a horrific conflict that raged for more than two years, marked by civilian massacres and atrocities of all kinds, with mortality rates around two-thirds among Spanish invaders and Mesoamerican communities alike (as we shall discuss in detail in the next chapter). Indeed, seen through the lens of war's unpredictable chaos, the image of Cortés as exceptional and masterful becomes absurd, divorced from reality, a portrait of a fictional commander of an imagined campaign. But viewed within the context of the war as it really was, Cortés's exceptionalism recedes to one small but revealing fact: he survived. A tiny percentage of the Spaniards who sailed to Mexico in 1519 experienced the entire Spanish-Aztec War, survived additional expeditions and campaigns, and died a natural death in Spain (Duverger, making the point rhetorically, asserts that "he was the only one of all the conquistadors to die in his bed.") A recent study of recipients of the Carnegie Medal for heroism found "almost no examples of heroes whose first impulse was for self-preservation." In the end, perhaps Cortés's greatest accomplishment was self-preservation.[86]

GIFTS OF WOMEN. "Cortes receives Donna Marina w[i]th other female Slaves as a present from the Cacique of Tabasco" was included in *A World Displayed,* first published in London in the 1760s. Its visual details reflect the symbolic imagery of the traditional narrative, long established by this time, including Cortés's imperious pose, his armored men arrayed like early modern cavalry, and the "Indians" wearing only feathers, with a feathered headdress indicating the local ruler ("cacique"). But there are heavy hints here of a darker theme, not shocking to sixteenth-century Spaniards or eighteenth-century readers of English, but suggesting to us a different perspective on the war of invasion: the trafficking in teenage girls as sex slaves.

———✦———

CHAPTER 8

Without Mercy or Purpose

In this year the prostitutes who were supposed to be daughters of Moteucçoma died. The Christians said, "Let women be brought, your daughters."

—Codex Aubin

We receive many grievances and abuses from the Spaniards, for them being amongst us and we being amongst them.

—Thirteen royal and noble lords of the Valley
of Mexico, in Tlacopan, to the king, 1556

War makes ordinary people do horrible things. Frightened soldiers in foreign lands murder the locals without mercy or purpose. One wishes that this happened rarely. In truth, it happens all the time.

—Adam Gopnik, 2015

Before Cortés lops off a messenger's
hands and has another trampled,
before the branding and burning,
there is wonderment
and, for a moment, endearment
as Cortés dances, off beat, around
the long neck of his field piece.
Stroking it, he whispers into its mouth,
then cocks his ear to the darkness.

—Xochiquetzal Candelaria, "Cortés and Cannon"[1]

As Cortés stood over the warm but lifeless body of his wife, he must have known he would be accused of murder.

In an episode of the Spanish television drama *Carlos, Rey Emperador*, Catalina Suárez catches her husband kissing and groping

Malintzin in an upstairs hallway of his new Mexican palace. The resulting argument continues into their bedroom, where Cortés demands her respect. "I am your husband, I am governor of New Spain!" he yells. "I have a whole world at my feet, here I am a god— a *god*!"

"You're a demon!" Catalina shouts back at him. "An insane demon!" As she reaches for paper, threatening to write a denunciation to the king, he grabs her by the throat. The action cuts to the rowdy dinner party downstairs, where Malintzin sits looking worried, and then cuts back up to the bedroom—where Catalina lies dead in Cortés's arms.[2]

For television audiences in the Spanish-speaking world, the depiction of Cortés as a megalomaniac and murderer—and specifically as an uxoricide—offered not a shock but a confirmation of the popular belief, going back at least into the nineteenth century (certainly in Mexico), in the conquistador's guilt. As we read earlier, Cortés's antihero legend, while primarily a modern phenomenon, bubbled under his heroic legend even in his own lifetime. Thrust into the invasion's lead role by his fellow conquistadors, he had claimed it with such duplicity, avarice, and self-righteousness that he spent the rest of his life fighting lawsuits, official investigations, and accusations of all kinds—including the murder of rivals and royal officials. It was thus inevitable that Catalina Suárez's death, sudden and witnessed by him alone, would raise suspicions. Indeed, in 1529, the question of his guilt in the matter, prompted by a lawsuit filed by doña Catalina's mother, became an official part of the Crown's massive *residencia* inquiry (the timing surely not coincidental). It has remained a mystery ever since, a small corner within the sprawling edifice of Cortesian legend.[3]

So was Cortés guilty? Or does it not matter?

The royal inquiry into doña Catalina's death resulted in an implied acquittal. That is, the initial gathering of testimony produced insufficient evidence to justify a criminal investigation. Some witnesses, like Gerónimo de Aguilar, insisted his guilt was clear and common knowledge. A few of Catalina's maids said that right after her death they saw bruises on her neck, and a broken necklace on the floor. On the other hand, others testified to her chronic illness, her frequent fainting and periodic pain; her nephew and a couple of other men said she died of a disease of the womb (*"mal de madre"*).[4]

Modern verdicts have also gone both ways. Abbott's opinion was still, in the nineteenth century, the majority one: that the accusation derived from the fact that her death "was so evidently a relief to Cortez, and so manifestly in accordance with his wishes," but despite his "many and great faults," such a crime was "quite foreign to his character. The verdict of history in reference to this charge has been very cordially *Not proven*." More recent historians have been less generous:

> Certainly a man who did not flinch at torture, who believed women existed for men's convenience, who had been drinking— and who probably had threatened his wife before—might have ended by strangling a spouse who harped on his bad behavior.[5]

This takes us closer to what concerns us here. For I suggest that Cortés's innocence or guilt is unimportant. With Montezuma's murder, the questions of who did it, whether or why they lied, and where fingers were pointed, all have significance. But in doña Catalina's case, what matters is where the details, the context, and the implications of the alleged murder lead us.

―――

The incident took place in Cortés's new palace, still under construction, in Coyohuacan (Coyoacan)—the *altepetl*, just outside Tenochtitlan, where Spaniards based themselves for three years while the capital city was being rebuilt. Doña Catalina died in October 1522, three months after arriving from Cuba. She was not alone in traveling to Mexico after hearing word of Tenochtitlan's fall. For example, her maids accompanied her, as did her family members, and their inconclusive testimony would help perpetuate the mystery of her death.

Many Spaniards would eventually testify in the inquiry, and the detailed account by one has caught the attention of modern historians, and for good reason. During the All Saints Day dinner, on the fateful evening, doña Catalina was overheard chatting with Francisco de Solís (a captain in the war, a leader in the Ávila cohort, and a Cortesian loyalist). "You, Solís," said doña Catalina, "you don't want to employ my Indians in things other than what I've ordered, yet you don't let them do what I want." "But, señora, it is not I who employs them," responded Solís, "the privilege [*merced*] is yours to employ and command them." Remarked Catalina: "I promise you that before many days pass, I shall do something with what's mine and won't have to answer to anyone." At this, Cortés exclaimed, "With what's yours [*con lo vuestro*], señora, I don't want anything [*yo no quiero nada*]!"[6]

At this rebuff, doña Catalina stormed up to her room. The double entendre of Cortés's remark seems clear, and one can imagine the conquistadors enjoying a good laugh. According to the above witness, the other slave-owning women (*las otras dueñas*) also laughed. The dialogue may be apocryphal (after all, other witnesses described Catalina leaving because she felt unwell, and several told of her falling ill earlier that day while walking in the orchards owned by the black conquistador Juan Garrido). But even if it is, it illuminates an environment in which ownership of "Indians" was a regular dinnertime topic, in which multiple hierarchies of race and gender were in play, and in which men (and perhaps women, but only Spanish women) joked about sex and slaves.

Those slaves were, for Spaniards, the spoils of war, be they Taínos from Cuba or Nahuas in Mexico, and there was a nameless, numberless quantity of them in the Coyohuacan house that night, along with African and other Mesoamerican slaves and servants also long lost to us. But there were other indigenous people present too, adding layers of context to the dinnertime conversation. For example, before doña Catalina had arrived from Cuba, another woman had also made the journey, a Taíno woman with whom Cortés had lived in Cuba prior to marrying doña Catalina. He had named her Leonor

Pizarro (his maternal grandmother's name), and she was—so far— the mother of his only child, a daughter to whom he had given his mother's name: Catalina Pizarro.

It was suggested that Cortés's affection for Leonor had motivated his reluctance to marry doña Catalina (seducing her was one thing, marrying her another, and only agreed to after heavy-handed intervention by Velázquez—although he was baby Catalina's godfather). It was also claimed that doña Catalina came to Mexico only after learning that her husband had already sent for Leonor (doña Catalina's arrival was a surprise, claimed Díaz). It is not clear if Leonor brought her daughter too, nor do we know how long Leonor lived in Mexico. It seems quite possible that she was the same Leonor Pizarro who was briefly one of doña Catalina's maids, and who later married the conquistador Juan de Salcedo. But the half-Taíno Catalina Pizarro outlived her father, who remembered her with rare and revealing affection in his will (in the same document he disinherited his son Luis for planning to marry a niece of comrade-turned-enemy Vásquez de Tapia). Cortés admitted he had drawn income from the properties given to Catalina as a dowry, and ordered that she be reimbursed. In the end, the dowry was taken by doña Juana de Zúñiga—Cortés's second wife and now widow—who blocked Catalina's marriage to Francisco de Garay's son and sent her to a convent in Spain. Cortés's affection for half-Taíno Catalina was thus sufficient to anger both his Spanish wives.[7]

The Spanish and Taíno women in the Coyohuacan house were, not surprisingly, outnumbered by Nahua women. There were untold servants and slaves, many used as sex slaves by the conquistadors. Ana Rodríguez, one of doña Catalina's maids, claimed that "don Fernando courted ladies and women who were in these parts"—and that made his wife "jealous." Vásquez de Tapia later claimed that between arriving from Cuba and leaving for Honduras, Cortés "had slept with at least forty Mexican women." Another conquistador said the Coyohuacan house was full "of the daughters of the lords of this land." Partisanship and exaggerations aside, Ana Rodríguez was surely right in referring to a scene that was widespread during and after the war, that Cortés participated in, and that doña Catalina found distasteful (and, no doubt, distastefully familiar). And because several of the Nahua women were not slaves but of high status, yet nonetheless forced or obliged to participate in this scene, and consequently impregnated, we know details.[8]

One was Montezuma's senior daughter, Tecuichpochtzin, who had been baptized doña Isabel Moctezuma Tecuichpo—the "Isabel" a nod to her royal status (reflected in the Gallery's "Family Matters"). During the war, while still a girl, she had been betrothed to her father's two successors, Cuitlahua and Cuauhtemoc. She survived the siege, and in the 1520s went on to marry a series of conquistadors. The first two, Alonso de Grado and Pedro Gallego, soon died, but her marriage to Juan Cano produced five children and lasted until her death in 1551. Tecuichpo held Tlacopan in *encomienda*, maintained noble status, and achieved lasting fame. When Gemelli visited Mexico City in the 1690s—the viceroy at the time was the Count of Montezuma, a descendant of the famous emperor, although mostly descended from Spanish aristocrats—he commented on families claiming descent from Aztec royalty, particularly from the children of "*Tecuhich potzin*." Most were descendants of her and Cano.[9]

But one of doña Isabel's children was Cortés's, apparently fathered in the Coyohuacan house after she had already married Gallego (claimed Vásquez de Tapia). One can only speculate as to the circumstances of the conception of the child, but it was within a month or so of doña Catalina's death, as the child was born in 1523; baptized Leonor Cortés Moctezuma, she eventually married a Spaniard.[10]

It was also known "very publicly" that Cortés had "slept with two or three of Montezuma's daughters"; that he "kept" one, baptized doña Ana, as a "girlfriend" (*amiga*) during the months of the Phoney Captivity; and that in the same months he also impregnated a sister or cousin of hers. A few conquistadors claimed this was doña Francisca, a sister of Cacama and his many brothers, and that as the Spaniards prepared to fight their way out of Tenochtitlan (on the eve of what would become the Noche Triste), Aztec noblewomen were assaulted—and Cortés took "a final opportunity to rape the sister of the king of Tetzcoco" (in the words of a modern historian). Reading through the various accusations, it seems likely that during the first half of 1520, Cortés and other captains kept as concubines, or eventually raped, at least two of Montezuma's daughters (renamed Ana and Inés) and at least two of Cacama's sisters or daughters (renamed Ana and Francisca). All were killed right before or during the Noche Triste save for one of the Tetzcoca "princesses," a doña Ana. She survived to later marry two conquistador veterans of the war—Pero Gutiérrez, then Juan de Cuéllar, supposedly arranged by Ixtlilxochitl (her uncle or brother). Doña Ana may well have been in the Coyohuacan house in 1522.[11]

ANOTHER OF THE NAHUA WOMEN in the Coyohuacan house was also already well known in the tiny conquistador community. Before arriving in Mexico, doña Catalina would surely have heard of the "Indian" slave girl with a knack for language, whose role as interpreter had earned her freedom and the honorific *doña* Marina (in Nahuatl, Malintzin). But did doña Catalina know, before she arrived, that Malintzin was pregnant, and that her own husband was the father? We do not know, nor do we know if Malintzin was still living in Cortés's house, nor exactly when she gave birth. But she was certainly living in Coyohuacan, and present in the Cortés residence much of the time, and the son that she bore Cortés—whom he named Martín, after his father—may even have been born shortly before doña Catalina's death.[12]

In the extensive testimony given in Cortés's *residencia* inquiry that relates to his sexual behavior, it is noteworthy that Malintzin receives almost no mention. Spaniards were more concerned with the question of doña Catalina's death, with Cortés's relationships with Montezuma's daughters, and with his alleged carnal knowledge of women who were related to each other ("with cousins and with sisters," or with a crude attempt to seduce a woman whose "daughter he had publicly slept with in Cuba"). When Malintzin is mentioned, it is mostly as part of a similar accusation: for example, that in his house "he was sleeping with Marina, who was a local woman [*de la tierra*], by whom he had some children, and with a niece of hers"; or that "he lay carnally with two of Montezuma's daughters and with Marina, the interpreter, and with a daughter of hers," and that "two or three Indians were hanged from a tree inside the house" in Coyohuacan, on Cortés's orders, because "they had slept with Marina."[13]

What are we to make of this? The rumors that Cortés slept with relatives of Malintzin are surely untrue (she was herself a teenager during the war). Those accusations thus reflect the fact that to Spaniards at the time, it was a certain kind of incest that was objectionable, not the use and abuse of indigenous women, which was widespread and endemic to the war and its aftermath. As for the tale of the hanged "Indians," if true it reflects the theme that emerged from the details surrounding doña Catalina's death: that in the 1520s, "Indians" were Spanish possessions, to be commanded or killed, given away or sold, kept or impregnated, as their "owners" wished. We would be wrong to imagine the tale as a sign of Cortés's romantic jealousy over Malintzin. In his will—the same final testament that revealed his affection for his daughter Catalina and her Taíno mother, Leonor ("probably Cortés's first love," one historian speculated; perhaps his only one?)—there is no mention at all of Malintzin.[14]

And yet, several centuries later, the dark reality of sex and slavery in the 1520s had become this imagined dialogue:

Cortez.   My sweet interpreter, most eloquent,
            Thy tongue interprets 'twixt these tribes and me:
            Let they meek eyes interpret love for me.
Marina.   Can Cortez speak of love to his poor slave?
Cortez.   Ay, by my soul! For I do feel it here.
            O! my dear captive, thou hast captured me!
            No more art thou my slave, for I am thine.
Marina.   I am thine own.
Cortez.   My love, my life, my joy!
Marina.   O! My beloved lord![15]

By the time this poet—the American Lewis Foulk Thomas—had placed a red-hot romance at the heart of his 1857 play, *Cortez, the Conqueror,* the supposed love affair between Cortés and Malintzin had become common fodder for the page and stage. Malintzin had been ignored for centuries (note that in the cited comments from 1529, conquistadors already felt the need to identify "Marina" as "a local woman" or as "the interpreter"). But, starting in the early nineteenth century, several Malintzins were gradually invented.

The first imaginary Malintzin took form when three cultural threads intertwined: the spread throughout the West of the artistic and literary movement of Romanticism; the fascination with Cortés as a suitable subject for epic poetry or prose, renewed (as we saw earlier) in the late eighteenth century; and the genesis of a legendary "doña Marina" who embodied the nineteenth-century stereotype of the ideal woman. She was thus "of noble birth, beauty, and quick genius," with "an affectionate heart and generous temper." Her services as interpreter were "invaluable" and saved Spanish lives. And, most significant of all, "she was the first Mexican who embraced Christianity." This "extraordinary woman" was "exceedingly beautiful" and had "winning manners, and a warm and loving heart." She quickly became fluent in Spanish and "deemed herself the honored wife of Cortez"—oblivious to the sinful bigamy committed by the conquistador in entering "this unhallowed union."[16]

This "Marina" was above all sanctified by the qualities of love and loyalty: "'I am more happy,' said she one day, 'in being the wife of my lord and master Cortez, and of having a son by him, than if I had been sovereign of all of New Spain.'" That was how an Anglo-American pastor put it at the dawn of the twentieth century, but a Mexican playwright generations later imagined these breathless words of hers: "I dreamt his dreams of gold, his childish and tireless dreams of wealth and power. But I caressed the living gold of his hair. Mine was the treasure of his breathing, living body."[17]

Few authors who borrowed Malintzin as a literary character made claims to historical accuracy. Yet the vast majority imagined her as a figure of—or metaphor for—tragic romance or romantic tragedy. And that Malintzin has persisted as a virtual industry of creativity, due to the sheer volume of attention given to her—from late-nineteenth-century figures of lasting significance (like Eligio Ancona and Ireneo Paz) to twentieth-century writers of particular importance to Mexican culture (like Salvador Novo and Rodolfo Usigli) to others who have achieved an international impact (like Laura Esquivel and Carlos Fuentes).

Thus, arguably, regardless of how complex or sophisticated the intention of poets, novelists, screenwriters, and historians has been, the net effect is to turn the Spanish-Aztec War into a tragic romance. And as such, it is never too far from the Maurin lithograph in which a fictionalized Aztec lord gives his Malintzin-like sister to Cortés, with the caption "Cortés accepted the invaluable gift of the cacique chief, and that was the first day of a passion that cast some sweetness onto the bloody triumphs of the conqueror of Mexico."[18]

The second of the three invented Malintzins emerged in Mexico as something of a reaction to the romantic, sanctified, white-washing version. This was the "lustful, conniving traitor" who made early appearances in nineteenth-century plays and novels, achieving deep cultural roots in the early twentieth century, when Mexican Spanish adopted the neologism *malinchista* to refer to a turncoat or traitor. The third Malintzin evolved in turn in reaction to that deeply negative one, developing when late-twentieth-century feminists argued that she was repeatedly victimized (both in her lifetime, and in her image in modern Mexico); that emphasis was later modified to argue that she was a victim with agency—a survivor.[19]

Malintzin the victim/survivor is in some ways no closer to the historical Malintzin than any of her other invented manifestations; as a "transfigured symbol of fragmented identity and multiculturalism" she is more of an expression of modern (or postmodern) anxieties than a recognizable figure from the Aztec world. And yet in other ways this Malintzin better helps us to get around the distortions and distractions of the Malintzins and Marinas and Malinches invented over the past two centuries.[20]

For whether Malintzin is seen as the saintly doña Marina or the devilish la Malinche, her legend leads back to a legendary Cortés. For better or worse, "as moth falls into the torchlight, / She fell to his brilliant alluring" (as a second-rate poet put it in 1885). Or as Abbott put it (in 1856), she was so "devotedly attached" to him because his great "energy, magnanimity, fearlessness, and glowing temperament" served "to rouse a woman's love." The issue here is therefore not just Cortés as legend, but the irresistibility (for male historians) of Cortés as a legendary womanizer.[21]

Gómara and Solís relished that reputation; Díaz listed all Cortés's children and their various mothers (as did Hugh Thomas, under "Cortés's ladies"). For Abbott, Cortés was an "ardent lover" as a teenager; he "cruelly trifled" with the affections of doña Catalina; he is overwhelmingly alluring to the lovestruck Malintzin. "In his relations with women," mused one historian, Cortés "reveals a primitive, polygamous temperament." For others, the conquistador's need to sow his seed was similarly a primal mandate, determined by the desire to populate the New World and plant in it "a new type of human being." His "progression of carnal love . . . has all the magnitude of a biblical verse in which Jehovah blesses the fecundity, often incestuous, of the patriarchs, for that perpetuates the species."[22]

There was, in other words, cosmic significance to "this conquistador's amorous leaps [lances amorosos] at kingdoms and ladies." Over the centuries, Cortés the womanizer evolved into a tripartite symbol: one of male dominance and machismo, swashbuckling and seductive, sword-wielding yet heart-winning; the emblematic founding father, both the first example and the symbol of the male fertility required to germinate a new race in a New World; and, in the gendered vision of the Spanish conquest and of the encounter of European and "Indian" civilizations, the masculine Christian conqueror of the feminized heathen.[23]

The problems with all this are many, but a couple are important to us here. Most obviously, the notion of Cortesian exceptionalism once again rears its ugly head. Yet Cortés was by no means unique among the conquistadors in having multiple sexual relationships of varying kinds with indigenous women—as we shall see shortly.

Furthermore, his Coyohuacan palace full of women was arguably a function of his inheritance of the mantle of imperial office. With the *huey tlahtoani* captive and his palace in Tenochtitlan destroyed, the surviving royalty and nobility initially gravitated toward what appeared to be the new center of imperial power. This meant not only filling the palace with women, just as Montezuma was believed to maintain thousands of concubines, but maintaining as many as possible of the very same women—Montezuma's own daughters, Cuauhtemoc's own wives, the royal women of the Aztec dynasty of Tenochtitlan and Tetzcoco.

Vásquez de Tapia, either unwittingly or knowingly, hit the nail on the head when he remarked that Cortés "in some ways lived more as a heathen than as a good Christian, especially in having an infinite number of women within his house." In other words, Cortés's famous womanizing was less about him as an individual, and far more about him as just another conquistador (Spanish men in this war almost all behaved this way) and, somewhat paradoxically, about the position he held; for as inheritor of the mantle of ruler, he had to take on the role of a *tlahtoani* impersonator.[24]

But whether Cortés's "ladies" are seen as mere evidence of his machismo or as conquest metaphors, a crucial issue has tended to be marginalized, ignored, or sugarcoated—with respect to both women and Mexico: that of consent. Here, then, is the rub. Did Cortés kill doña Catalina? I suspect he angrily assaulted her, causing her sufficient physical distress for her illness to end her life; a modern verdict might be manslaughter, although it would surely stick in the craw of judge and jury. But pondering the possibility of foul play distracts us from the more compelling and revealing themes exposed by the moment: the roles and experiences of women, Spanish and indigenous, in the war and its aftermath; the ubiquitous evidence and echo of violence; and the disturbing intersection between those two themes.[25]

Was Malintzin another of his victims, drawn to his flame like a moth; was she a slave struggling to survive, or a sly manipulator of men? By focusing on one Nahua woman, however unusual or extraordinary her personal story may seem to be, we run the risk of forgetting what aspects of her experience were shared by thousands of others. What do glimpses into the lives of Malintzin (or doña Catalina or Leonor Pizarro or Tecuichpo) tell us about the other women—Spanish, Taíno, Nahua; probably Totonac and African too; wives, concubines, slaves—in the Coyohuacan house and in the houses of other conquistadors? What had they endured, and would they endure, as a result of the war men had waged and the new political arrangements they fought to forge? What kind of place had Mexico become that we can contemplate whether Cortés was a wife killer—and then dismiss the question as beside the point?

Consider, then, the engravings that accompanied accounts of the moment when Malintzin first met Cortés—another meeting within this story, and one that, like the Meeting, has been romanticized as surrender. Specifically, consider the engravings common in the eighteenth century (one example began this chapter, another is in our Gallery), before the many Malintzins had been created. In the version printed in 1754 with the Abbé Prévost's *Histoire Générale des Voyages,* for example, there is a tiny anticipation of Romanticism in the accompanying text: the granting of "twenty Indian women" to make bread, opined the abbot, was just "the excuse for them to be received; for it is certain that Cortés took an inclination toward one of these women, whom he had baptized under the name Marina and made his mistress. She was, according to Díaz, of a rare beauty and elevated bearing."[26]

Yet the image itself captures something very different: a group of teenage girls, completely naked, innocent, being sized up by armed men, among whom they are to be divided up as slaves; and there could be no doubt—either in 1519, or in 1754, or today—that they were to serve as sex slaves. This is where the death of doña Catalina leads us: to her Taíno and Nahua rivals, to the many Malintzins, to "Indians" that a Spaniard can call his or hers, to the other nineteen girls "given" to conquistadors along with Malintzin, to the thousands of indigenous teenagers forced into sexual slavery, to the tens of thousands of indigenous families torn apart by war and disease and the oft-ignored scourge of mass enslavement.

In the spring of 1548, just a few months after Cortés's death, the Spanish king and Holy Roman Emperor, Carlos V, issued an extraordinary edict. Over two pages of dictation to his secretary, Juan de Sámano, the king came close to a denunciation of conquistador atrocities that would have made Las Casas proud. (Indeed, the friar surely had much to do with the edict; he sailed to Spain the previous summer, and earlier in 1548 pleaded with the king to order his officials to enforce the 1542 laws restricting indigenous slavery.)[27]

Addressing the royal government in New Spain, Carlos began by raising the specter of the twenty-year investigation into Cortés—the *residencia* inquiry that had petered out a few years earlier. "Among the various charges made against him," stated the king, were five specific allegations of the mass enslavement of "Indians" during the conquest war. As "nobody can in good conscience and title hold such Indians as slaves," noted the king, he therefore ordered all of Cortés's surviving slaves "to be freed, and the same goes for their children and the descendants of all the women taken as slaves."

The edict effectively condemned Cortés posthumously, not only for enslaving indigenous people but also for his role in the five massacres that accompanied the seizures. First, according to Carlos's reading of the *residencia* files, Olid "seized peacefully" the entire population of the town of Quecholac and brought them to Cortés, who was nearby in Tepeyacac (Tepeaca; this would have been in September 1520, a few days after the attack on Tepeaca itself.) Cortés separated "the Indian men, some four hundred of them who were of fighting age, and had all of them killed; those who were left, some three thousand women and children, he had branded as slaves."

This pattern was allegedly then repeated. When Sandoval escorted porters carrying wood for the brigantines from Tlaxcallan to Tetzcoco, he passed through the town of Calpulalpan, where "the people had peacefully submitted." No matter: "many of them were killed, and many seized, women as well, and taken to Tetzcoco," where "they were branded as slaves and sold." The edict went on to third and fourth examples. When Cortés went to war against the provinces of Cuauhnahuac (Cuernavaca) and Huaxtepec, despite their peaceful submission the local men were again slaughtered, "and more than five hundred souls were branded as slaves." Finally, "when the said don Hernando went to war against the city of Chulula [Cho-lollan]" (here the king jumped back to 1519), the people peacefully gave him the supplies he needed. But when "four thousand Indians, more or less," were gathered in the plaza to serve as porters, Cortés "without any cause ordered the Spaniards to kill them, and thus had many killed and the others enslaved."

What are we to make of this document? It has been published several times, beginning as early as 1596, and yet given passing attention, if that, by historians. Should we dismiss it as too little, too late? Perhaps. Calling these atrocities, three decades later, "bad deeds for which there was no reason for them to have been done" was arguably a meaningless and mild condemnation. Or should we consider the edict merely a confirmation of events already known (and—in the case of Tepeaca, Quecholac, and Cholollan—already mentioned in this book, as in many before it)? Again, perhaps; for there is certainly plenty of corroborating evidence that the massacres and mass enslavements took place.

In fact, the edict of 1548 was conservative in estimating numbers of indigenous victims. When the elimination of Quecholac's population came up in Cortés's *residencia* inquiry, he himself admitted that he ordered five hundred men executed. His justification was that it served as a warning to others not to attack Spaniards traveling between Vera Cruz and Tenochtitlan—a rationale repeated by pro-Cortés witnesses. Vásquez de Tapia, however, estimated the slaughter at two thousand men, with some four thousand women and children enslaved. Nor does the edict mention what appeared to have happened days earlier to the people of Tepeaca itself: some four hundred Tepeacan warriors were killed in an open battle with a Spanish-Tlaxcalteca force outside the town, followed by a brutal sacking of the town. Hundreds were lanced or spiked, torn apart by

Spanish mastiffs (*aperreados,* or "dogged"), butchered in their own homes, or—one conquistador, Diego de Ávila, claimed—thrown alive from rooftops to waiting Tlaxcalteca warriors. Ávila and a couple of other conquistadors claimed that the Tlaxcalteca ate the Tepeacans (although Cortés justified the slaughter to the king on the grounds that the Tepeacans "are all cannibals"). Across the region, dozens of towns and villages (some said forty) were sacked, thousands executed, and the survivors—including tens of thousands of women and children—branded as slaves. They received the G (for *Guerra,* "war") on their faces. There were complaints that the captains monopolized the best-looking women, leaving only "old and wrecked ones" to the other Spaniards.[28]

We shall return shortly to some of these details that hint at scales of violence, rape, and slavery—and at issues of responsibility and culpability. But for now, let us follow the indigenous survivors, those who witnessed their family members being slaughtered, and were then branded, sold, and marched off to live as the property of Spaniards. Is it possible to find any of them still alive, at the time of that 1548 edict? As it happens, it is.

IN THE WAKE OF CORTÉS'S DEATH, there were dozens of lawsuits and legal proceedings related to his lengthy will and extensive estate (contrary to the persistent myth that he "died in deep poverty and all alone"). Among that documentation, scattered across archives in Spain and Mexico, is a hefty inventory of Cortés's property in and around Cuauhnahuac (running to some seventy pages in modern print, although including only part of the Cuauhnahuac holdings and none of the properties in Mexico City, Coyohuacan, the Toluca valley, the great marquisate in Oaxaca, and so on). Along with the buildings, lands, and equipment related to wheat, silk, and sugar operations were listed 287 slaves, 94 of them "blacks," mostly born in Africa. As a reminder of the violent nature of forced labor, iron equipment for the disciplining of slaves was also listed: braces, collars, chains, and "a cage [*prisión*] for slaves, with four iron chains."[29]

The other 193 slaves were "Indians." Those "Indians" were not listed as mere numbers; their names, ages, and towns of origin were included. "Juan Ucelote [Oçelote]," for example, was "an Indian man, native of Ecatepeque, fifty years of age, and he seemed as much." There is sufficient detail in the lists of slaves to even offer us a hint of human life, as if in reading each entry we are catching the glimpse of a ghost. "Isabel Siguaquesuchil [Cihuatlexochitl], an Indian woman, native of Tlaxcala [Tlaxcallan], forty-three years of age." "Juan Xitl, an Indian man, a native of Guaxaca [Oaxaca], forty-one years old, said to be an oven-worker." "Cecilia, an Indian slave woman, condemned to twenty years, native of Tepexi, forty years of age." And this poignant, thought-provoking entry: "Cristóbal, an Indian native of this New Spain, who says he doesn't know where he is from, because he was small when he came into the power of the Spaniards; he is [now] thirty-five years of age, a little more or less."[30]

This Cristóbal would have been about six years old at the height of the Spanish-Aztec War. Conquistadors thus enslaved him as a child. The slaves on Cortés's Cuauhnahuac estate were, on average, eleven years old in 1520. The slaves at Tlaltenango and adjacent sugar operations—some 165 in total—were between six and thirty-one at the war's peak, but averaged eighteen; the vast majority (93 percent) were under twenty-two, averaging seventeen years old. In other words, during the war and the subsequent campaigns of the 1520s across Mesoamerica, it was indigenous children and teenagers who were enslaved in massive numbers.

These survivors on the marquis's estates—outliving Cortés himself—represented the tip of an iceberg of child slavery. Their places of origin are highly varied (86 towns for the 193 slaves), reflecting the levels of displacement and shattering of families and communities. They also map many of the campaigns, and especially the massacres and mass enslavements, of the war: Tepeaca and Cholollan; Zacatepec, Izúcar, and Huaxtepec; Oaxaca and Guatemala. And towns that allied with the invaders in the war are equally well represented—especially Tlaxcallan and Tetzcoco (at 11 percent and 7 percent, the best-represented towns in the list)—a reminder that the myths of immediate welcome and surrender hid more complex tales of resistance, for which children paid a lifelong price.

The phenomenon has been grossly downplayed in the Cortesian legend: he "extended toleration rather than approval to the institution of slavery," later having "grave doubts of the equity or wisdom of enslaving the Indians"; he had enslaved "natives in the past but [then] appeared to find it abhorrent." A hideous truth was thus hidden. As Andrés Reséndez, a leading historian of "Indian enslavement," recently observed, "not only was Cortés the richest man in Mexico, he was also the largest owner of Indian slaves. And wherever Cortés led, others followed."[31]

Reséndez is right, but let us tweak the point to emphasize our concern here: Cortés was the biggest enslaver of "Indians" *because* he was the richest settler in Mexico. And others were not taking their cue from him; *all* conquistadors were taking slaves. Not just in Quecholac and Tepeaca, but in town after town across the Americas, for generations before and after Cortés's years in the Indies, adult "Indians" and their elderly were slaughtered, their women and children enslaved. Why?

Imagine the explanation as a matryoshka or Russian nesting doll. The outermost doll is that of the larger history of slavery in the early modern world—a subject in which there is little space for a moral high ground. Cortés's thousands of indigenous slaves (Vázquez de Tapia claimed it was over twenty thousand) may have been an exceptionally large number for one Spaniard, but they were a tiny percentage of the more than half a million enslaved across the Caribbean, Mesoamerica, Central America, and beyond, just in the early sixteenth century alone. And an even smaller percentage of those enslaved elsewhere in the Atlantic orbit. Holocaustic levels of slaughter and enslavement of non-European peoples marked the early modern genesis of our modern world. Cortés's era was just the beginning. Over the successive centuries, between 10 and 20 million Africans and indigenous Americans would be forced into slavery. Tens of millions more would be displaced and forced into servitude, would die from epidemic diseases, would suffer the tearing apart of families and the brutal exploitation of colonialism and imperial expansion. Such experiences were the political, economic, and moral platforms upon which our world was constructed.[32]

Nor was slavery limited to Europeans and Africans; there were indigenous slaves in the Americas before 1492. Arguably, conquistadors simply practiced a more devastating version of the slavery that had been practiced for centuries in the hemisphere. "More devastating" is the key phrase, however; sixteenth-century Spaniards magnified and transformed indigenous traditions of slavery, imposing a scale of dislocation that was unprecedented. At the same time, they used the prior existence of slaves in indigenous communities as an excuse, a justification for their own slaving (Europeans of all nations used a similar justification to enslave Africans). More than a simple justification, this was a legal loophole that was abused on a massive scale: Spaniards branded so-called *esclavos de rescate* ("ransomed slaves") with an *R* on the face, their status thereafter no longer requiring explanation, regardless of how spurious its origin.

This leads us to the second matryoshka doll, or reason why Mesoamericans were enslaved. Because Spaniards were accustomed to enslaving North and West Africans, as well as Muslims taken in the war against Granada of 1480–92, they did not hesitate to enslave indigenous peoples in the Caribbean—beginning with Columbus's first voyage, sponsored by the Castilian crown, in 1492–93. And because it was far cheaper and easier to "harvest" islands for slave labor than it was to buy and ship Africans across the Atlantic, the Caribbean was virtually depopulated by Spanish expeditions of exploration, conquest, and enslavement—motivating companies to search farther afield, including (as mentioned earlier) the Mesoamerican mainland. Although the more critical accounts of Spanish conquests in the Americas have tended to assign to Spaniards gold-lust as their darkest motivation, the evidence is extensive that the conquistadors came from the Caribbean to Mexico fully intending, above all, to carry on raiding for slaves—and they did exactly that on numerous occasions during and after the Spanish-Aztec War. As Díaz admitted, defensively:

If the Mexican Indians and natives of the villages rose up against and killed Spaniards, and after being summoned three times to come in peace still did not wish to come in, but made war, we were given license to make them slaves, and to burn a brand on their faces, in a *G* like this.[33]

So why does our vision of the Americas in the early sixteenth century tend *not* to feature enslaved indigenous peoples in the foreground? Why, more specifically, in the traditional narrative of the "Conquest of Mexico" are there few mentions of indigenous slaves? This is partly because of the eventual decline in indigenous slavery and its eclipse by African slavery throughout the hemisphere. (Black African slaves were brought to the Americas beginning with the earliest voyages of Columbus; a small but unknown number of black slaves and freedmen fought in the Spanish-Aztec War, the best known of whom was Juan Garrido.)[34]

But it is also because the prudence and legality of enslaving "Indians" was debated from the very start, regulated for much of the time, and periodically banned outright. Thus Spaniards tended not to mention it, or to do so in passing, because it was done with such routine regularity as to barely be worth mentioning, while—paradoxically—it was also understood to be illicit and illegal if not justified on vague moral grounds (idolatry, cannibalism, sodomy, and the old sawhorse of human sacrifice) or legal ones (rebellion). So while Crown policy more or less outlawed the enslaving of "Indians" throughout the sixteenth century and beyond, it always permitted loopholes. Rather than admitting small numbers of special cases, those loopholes actually fostered and encouraged the perpetuation of mass slaving practices, especially in zones of conflict or European expansion. That included pretty much every corner of the Americas at some time or another (and sometimes for generations), meaning no region escaped from being a "borderland of bondage." In the 1520s, it was Mexico's turn, and Mesoamerica's for decades to follow.[35]

In theory—and, again, in terms of Crown policy—it was preferable to leave indigenous men and women to be converted to Christianity and to labor in their homelands to produce food and tribute goods. Moving them was counterproductive, because it was "contrary to their nature, and because they are of feeble complexion," stated a royal edict banning the shipping of "Indians" to Spain. When they died in Europe—as did the majority of the hundreds transported on dozens of ships, from Columbus in the 1490s to Cortés in 1540— the blame was placed on "the change of climate, country, and food." But that edict was not issued until 1543.[36]

Furthermore, such edicts did not mean enslaved "Indians" across the Spanish world could suddenly take control of their lives; it meant that they had a right to file suit in the law courts, which a minority were able to do, and a minority of those achieved freedom. Legal cases of indigenous men and women, almost all enslaved as children during the war, fighting for freedom in Spain and New Spain (and elsewhere) in the 1540s and '50s (and beyond) are a gold mine for historians. From amid the faceless, nameless thousands, such cases bring to life individuals like Francisco Manuel (his full name). He was a small boy in 1527 when his hometown on the Pacific coast (near today's Manzanillo) was attacked by Alvaro de Saavedra Céron (as part of Cortés's plan to secure the region for a port). As was the pattern in the Spanish-Aztec War, and for many years following, the town was sacked, adult men killed, women and children enslaved— including Francisco Manuel, who a year later was on a ship to Spain, destined to spend his youth working as a servant/slave in Seville (not until 1552 did he escape to Madrid and file suit to be legally declared free).[37]

Yet such cases, as fascinating as they are, can be misleading; most Francisco Manuels never made that journey to Madrid, and thus never made it into the historical record. Meanwhile, in 1551 in Mexico City, the viceroy appointed a lawyer, Bartolomé Melgarejo, to free the kingdom's "Indian" slaves and return them to their hometowns. Melgarejo's plaintive, pathetic letters to the king are a sobering read. He proudly added up the number of slaves freed, as the years passed, yet after a decade the total barely topped three thousand—out of some one hundred thousand in central Mexico, and hundreds of thousands more across the viceroyalty. He also freely admitted that officials in Mexico forced him to respect the old loopholes, with face brands (*G* or *R*) trumping the legal process, and the tens of thousands enslaved in the wars to the north and west deemed "just" because the invaded peoples were classified as rebels. Finally, Melgarejo claimed that year after year the local treasurer refused to pay his salary; because "I cannot work as a lawyer for those who own slaves" and nobody employs "me due to the great communal enmity in which they hold me," "my odious job" has thus left "me in a worse condition than the Indian slaves I've freed."[38]

Meanwhile, new conquest campaigns meant new opportunities for harvesting indigenous communities for slaves, and the human spoils of those campaigns tended to stimulate the slave markets throughout the Spanish colonies. Thus the link between indigenous enslavement in the Caribbean and in Mexico was twofold: the history of enslavement in the Caribbean provided conquistadors with models and motives, while indigenous slaves were transported between the islands and the mainland—in both directions.

During the course of the war, Spaniards brought hundreds— possibly thousands—of Taíno slaves and servants into Mexico from the Caribbean (mostly from Cuba, although many were surely born and enslaved elsewhere before being taken to Cuba). There were numerous complaints from the Spaniards left in Cuba. Manuel de Rojas, for example, claimed that due to "the great quantity of Indians that Spaniards took on the fleets that went [to Mexico], this island was very depopulated and greatly damaged." Things went from bad to worse: "excessive allotments [*repartimientos*]" of "Indians" were then made to Spaniards on the island, "many of whom went to New Spain, taking with them many of the servants [*naborías*] and Indians who were given to them in *encomiendas* and others whom they then sold and bartered away."[39]

There is no evidence that these Taíno slaves and servants fought or were even used as arrow fodder. Instead, the men were porters, they built defensive works, and they put up and broke down camps; the women were sex slaves, and they carried and cooked. Many died from maltreatment. As Rojas alleged, they were also sold. Diego de Ávila claimed that Cortés approved "the Spaniards bartering Carib Indians—the Indians they brought with them on the campaign—for chickens and other things," and "I saw the Spaniards who were with Cortés publicly bartering many of those Indians." The statement was made in 1521, in Cuba, in a transparently *Velazquista* legal brief, but I suspect Ávila simply laid at Cortés's door a practice that was sanctioned by all captains and reflected the way that Taíno slaves were generally treated.[40]

This draining of indigenous Cubans did not stop Velázquez and other Spanish settlers on the island from continuing to exploit the surviving population. Despite a royal ban on any Spaniard other than Velázquez himself claiming more than one hundred "Indians" as "servants" [*personas de servicio*], a 1522 survey showed that the twenty most prominent settlers divided up three thousand Taínos among them that year, averaging 166 each; given that this included Mexican conquistadors such as Narváez, Vasco Porcallo de Figueroa, and the notorious slaver Juan Bono de Quexo, some of these "servants" were surely shipped to households or slave markets in Mexico.[41]

As Mesoamerica became part of the Spanish Indies in the 1520s through 1540s—the viceroyalty of New Spain would eventually encompass Mexico, Central America, and the Caribbean and circum-Caribbean—it also became a core part of the regional Spanish network of slave markets. Slaves taken in Mesoamerica were mostly moved to mining, plantation, or household enterprises elsewhere in Mesoamerica, but some were taken to the islands. Spaniards made little effort to hide the fact that they were enslaving "Indians" in one province to be sold in another; indeed, that was the nature of the business. Andrés de Tapia got rich doing this after the Spanish-Aztec War; he was so successful that decades later, when he was an old man, he was able to persuade Viceroy Mendoza to ask Prince Philip to appoint his son to a lucrative church position because "tribute" from the family *encomiendas* was insufficient—because "in the past they took so many of the natives of the province to the islands and to other regions."[42]

The third matryoshka doll is more specific to Mexico, and to the Spanish-Aztec War. The point can be summarized in one intriguing phrase: Montezuma's missing treasure. In their earliest reports back to Spain, Cortés and his allies planted a seed that would turn into a virulent weed. They exaggerated the extent of the gold, silver, and "treasure" that they had acquired—both during the months of plotting on the Gulf coast in 1519, and when persuading the Narváez company to join them in 1520. The consequences of their hyperbole were legion. Most of the decades-long *residencia* inquiry, along with scores of other lawsuits and investigations, was devoted to finding Montezuma's missing treasure. Cuauhtemoc and other Mexica were tortured to reveal the secret (the feet of the captive *huey tlahtoani* were doused in hot oil, which was then ignited). Spaniards tortured and murdered other Spaniards (a notorious example being the slow death of Rodrigo de Paz, one of Cortés's cousins). And—most germane here—the thousand or so Spaniards who joined the siege and survived the war acquired inflated expectations that fueled disappointment and anger. The solution was to turn on the local population. With shares upon victory in 1521 at fifty pesos or less for a conquistador of modest status, the potential profit from enslaving unarmed indigenous villagers was too tempting to turn down.[43]

The fourth matryoshka doll of explanation is the smallest, but it takes us back to the heart of the matter. Indigenous enslavement during and after the Spanish-Aztec War was endemic because it was mostly women and children who were being seized and branded. There were several reasons for this, in turn—explanations that apply to indigenous enslavement in the Indies as a whole (not just in Mexico). There was a market in Europe for indigenous American women and children as domestic or household slaves (women fetched the highest prices, then girls, then boys, with men the lowest); as Spanish settlements spread and grew in the Americas, so did that same market. In addition, women and children were more easily overpowered, restrained, and branded on the face than full-grown men. Children were also easier to trick into going with slavers—who then passed them off as paid servants, not forced slaves; or they worked as servants, ostensibly free, only to find themselves later sold as pieces of property. Such was the experience of hundreds of Nahua children and teenagers taken to Spain alone between the 1520s and 1540; thousands of Mesoamerican children became enslaved adults in lands far from home through this layered system of deception.[44]

But, above all, there was also a particular market in the Spanish Indies of the early sixteenth century for indigenous women and girls to play the roles of wives, concubines, and sex slaves. Such slaves were elemental to the trifecta of conquistador expectations and practices. Spaniards assumed that the "pacification" of "Indians" was likely to entail violence; that subdued indigenous populations would be exploited through slavery and the *encomienda* system (which provided unpaid goods and labor); and that indigenous women would meet the needs—sexual, reproductive, domestic—of conquistadors and settlers. As one historian rather bluntly put it, "sex was a driving force in the exploration of the Americas."[45]

The Spanish world in the Americas was for decades overwhelmingly male; in theory, growing numbers of Spanish women would replace indigenous women in such roles, but in practice they tended to displace them in terms of rank, not roles and services. The patterns were set in the islands; Cortés was typical in having a Taíno family in Cuba before having sexual relationships with Nahua women in Mexico. Diego González, for example, survived the entire Spanish-Aztec War, but his Cuban Taíno wife was less fortunate; she died from complications giving birth to their son. González remarried in Mexico, perhaps to a Nahua woman. Another example was Martín Vásquez, a horseman in the Mexican war; he had previously fought in Panama, under Pedrarias de Ávila, and in the conquest of Cuba—where he married a Taíno woman. They had four children, and by 1525 his wife was in his Mexico City household with him. (He held various *encomiendas* and owned numerous indigenous slaves, whom he used for gold panning; at one point he sold a crew of fifty indigenous slaves to his business partner.)

Lorenzo Suárez, a member of the cohort of *viejos*, left behind a Taíno woman and their child in Cuba when he joined the expedition to Mexico; the child meant something to him, for in 1527 he sent Alonso Botel to go look for him in Cuba and bring him to him in Mexico. Suárez had meanwhile married a Spanish woman, but he killed her with a stone used for grinding maize (he was one of several conquistador wife-killers, according to Díaz); the act earned him the nickname of "Grinding Stone," and as punishment he lost his *encomiendas,* although they were given to the son whose mother he murdered. In penance, he seems eventually to have taken orders as a friar, and as such denounced some Nahuas to the Inquisition for "idolatry."[46]

There are many other examples of conquistadors whose interactions with indigenous women in Mexico moved along, or existed simultaneously, at different points on the spectrum between rape and marriage. Sancho de Sopuerta fought in the conquest campaigns on Hispaniola and Cuba, then with Grijalva, coming to Mexico with Cortés. He settled in Tenochtitlan in 1524, marrying and having at least three children with Ana Gutiérrez, who seems to have been indigenous. Francisco de Granada was a veteran of the conquest wars in Mexico and Guatemala, famous for having taken an Aztec arrow in the face on the Noche Triste (Santos Hernández achieved similar renown for removing it in the heat of battle). Granada participated in the Tepeaca massacre and other such events, and owned many indigenous slaves. There is no record of a spouse, but Granada fathered an unknown number of children by one or more Nahua women. Juan Sedeño fought in the Mexican wars, after which he settled in Vera Cruz with an indigenous wife, renamed Isabel Sedeño; he had been given the nearby town of Xilopetec in *encomienda,* but its population complained so vigorously of his abusive treatment that it was appropriated by the Crown in 1531.[47]

Another conquistador, Francisco Gutiérrez, arrived in the Indies in 1517, joining the war in Mexico in 1520, right after the Tepeaca massacre. It is not clear if his first wife was Spanish or indigenous, but after the war she died and Gutiérrez married a Nahua woman, settling in Tenochtitlan; she bore him most of the ten children he had fathered by the 1550s. Similarly, Juan Galingo, a crossbowman

who joined the second half of the war in Mexico, married a Nahua woman when his Spanish wife died. Some men followed the
opposite pattern: for example, Bartolomé "Coyote" Sánchez, a veteran of the Spanish-Aztec War who received the town of Coyote-
pec in *encomienda*, married a Nahua woman in the 1520s; then in
the 1540s, after her death, he married a Spaniard. Likewise Juan
Pérez de Arteaga, who was called Pérez Malinche because he served
as Malintzin's guard during the war (and learned fluent Nahuatl),
married a Nahua who was renamed Angelina Pérez; they had six
children. Much later, after her death, he married the daughter of
another conquistador.[48]

We only know about any of these relationships because there was
marriage, formal concubinage (in the case of indigenous royalty or
nobility), or children. These examples must be taken, then, as the
seemingly consensual tip of an iceberg of nonconsensual ones. For
every Spaniard who we know left a Taíno wife in Cuba, hundreds
left behind in the islands concubines, mistresses, and victims of rape.
Likewise, for every Nahua woman who appears in the records, often
nameless, as the wife or mother of a conquistador's child, there must
have been many hundreds who were temporarily connected in some
sense—including involuntarily—with a Spaniard.

Evidence of sexual slavery and forced promiscuity takes the form
of passing comments in Spanish sources—all small but adding up
to an undeniable but oft-overlooked and dark reality. For example,
Cervantes de Salazar claimed that Cortés, while in Cuba, was too
sick to leave the island because "his friends said that he had syphilis
[*las bubas*], because he was always a womanizer [*amigo de mujeres*],
and Indian women infect those who go with them much more than
Spanish women do"—the final line revealing Spanish attitudes as
salt in the wound of their treatment of Taíno women. Other hints
come from remarks in archival sources: "the natives are very jealous,
and nothing causes them greater pain than when one goes with their
women." The comment's context is advice by Cortés to a cousin on
his voyage to Asia, but Cortés knew nothing of Asians (as was clear
from the rest of his letter), and he clearly had "Indians" in mind.[49]

Díaz makes passing mention of the acquisition of local women dozens of times: the phrase "good Indian women" or "pretty Indian girls"—*buenas indias* or *hermosas y buenas indias*—peppers his long account. The references range from a comment that one Spanish sailor impregnated various indigenous women during the war, to half a dozen descriptions of Spanish quarrels over *buenas indias;* most comments, however, simply note that "we took some women and girls." The frequent mention of how these captive women looked reveals why they were hunted: on one Sandoval-led sortie, the Chalca and Tlaxcalteca did most of the fighting, because "our soldiers . . . were chiefly occupied in hunting for a pretty Indian girl [*una buena india*] or getting some loot"; they return with "some fine pieces of Indian women" (*pieza*—"piece" or "catch"—was a hunting and slaving term, referring to an acquisition of high or full value); "here we grabbed some very good *indias* and loot"; on one occasion, they surprised a family "in their house and took three Indian men and two girls, pretty for *indias,* and an old woman"; one small group of conquistadors attacked a hamlet and "we seized thirty chickens and a local kind of melon . . . and three women; and so we had a great Easter"; battle spoils frequently included "many *indias* and children"; at times they took so many girls, Díaz described the haul as a *montón* ("a pile").[50]

After the sacking and enslaving at Tepeaca and Tetzcoco, there were complaints that the night before the formal dividing up and branding of captives, the Spanish captains stole for themselves "the best Indian women" and "the good pieces"; on other occasions, "in the night the captains took from the pile the good and pretty *indias* that had been put aside for branding." After that, Díaz claimed, the conquistadors hid "the good *indias*" they had grabbed in camp or among the Tlaxcalteca, claiming they were servants, so the captains would not take them for themselves—to keep or to brand and sell. Some of these girls, admitted Díaz, remained with their conquistador captors for several months—long enough for it to be known throughout the company "who treated well the Indian women and servants he had, and who treated his badly." The women who had been most abused, come auction time, tended "to suddenly disappear and never be seen again."[51]

Further hints can be found in quasi-indigenous sources. The line from the Codex Aubin, quoted at the beginning of this chapter, referring to the death during the Noche Triste of "the prostitutes who were supposed to be daughters of Montezuma," evokes community memory of how Spanish demands for sex slaves turned Aztec girls into concubines and perverted the purpose of diplomatic marriage alliances. Above all, the line reminds Nahua readers that the ultimate victims were *mochpochuan*, "your daughters."[52]

Two other quasi-indigenous sources contain variants on the same passage, describing the raping and looting that swept Tenochtitlan as it fell to its besiegers. The Mexica memory of Spanish conquistador lust for two things is in one Nahuatl account wrapped into a single hunt:

> On every street the Spaniards took things from people by force. They were looking for gold; they cared nothing for jade, precious feathers, or turquoise. With the women they looked everywhere, in their vaginas, up their skirts; with the men, they looked everywhere too, under their loincloths and in their mouths; and they picked out and took the beautiful women, with yellow bodies.

In the Spanish version of the same text, the passage is reduced to its essence: "they took nothing but gold and the pretty young women." But in another Nahuatl source, gold goes unmentioned, leaving an emphasis on the assault: "the Christians searched all over the women; they pulled down their skirts and went all over their bodies, in their mouths, in their vaginas, in their hair."[53]

Spanish commentary on indigenous reactions is rare, but Cortés's complaint that indigenous men "are very jealous" echoes in other accounts. For example, Díaz described an incident on the Honduras expedition in which the leaders of a town that had been attacked, seeing "their women taken," sent envoys with "small bits of gold jewelry" to "beg Cortés" to return the captives. He agreed, if they would deliver food; when they did as asked, and Cortés decided to keep three of the women anyway, "all the Indians of that town" attacked the camp "with darts, and stones, and arrows," injuring a dozen Spaniards "as well as Cortés himself, in the face"—a detail added by Díaz, one suspects, because it seemed just deserts.[54]

On other occasions, of course, indigenous leaders used women, even family members, to cement agreements and protect their towns. Díaz's casual description of the granting in 1519 by the so-called Fat Cacique of his niece and seven other "*indias,* all of them daughters of caciques," conveys the normalcy of this distribution of teenage girls from the viewpoint of the conquistadors (and, presumably, of the local noblemen too). Hints as to the Spanish reaction confirm our suspicions: they are interested in "the golden collar and gold ear-rings" that each girl wore, and when "they were baptized, the niece of the Fat Cacique was named doña Catalina, and she was very ugly; she was led by the hand and given to Cortés who received her and put on a brave face [*con buen senblante*]." No doubt this was laughed over many times (the ugly one given to Cortés and given his wife's name); men at war make jokes about sex and local women. One wonders if the poor girl—at whose expense the joke was ultimately made—was ever told why the foreign men smirked around her.[55]

For what is missing in all the documents and chronicles—what we must fill in with our imaginations, as best we can—is the terror of the experience for these teenage girls. At the fall of Tenochtitlan, "some women escaped" from being seized and made sex slaves by "putting mud on their faces and dressing in rags." But to imagine the larger picture, we need more than a snapshot image from the sacking of the Aztec capital, and more too than the example of Malintzin as a teenage slave whose experience was typical in some ways but surely not in others; instead, we must think of the other nineteen girls passed into the Spanish camp along with her, and of the Fat Cacique's niece and the other seven girls "given" to the same conquistadors; and the thousands of others "given" or taken, the "piles" of captured girls—consigned to a fate of sexual slavery, dragged across the country as the war developed, passed among the unintelligible invaders to satisfy their bodily needs as the violence mounted.

The paucity of information on such girls and women, combined with the sheer volume of victims, makes it all the more crucial for us to remember those individuals we can, and to try to imagine what this war and its aftermath was for them—even if all we know is that in 1549, María Xocoto was a forty-one-year-old slave in the Cuauhnahuac sugar mills, that she apparently looked her age, that she was a native of Cuauhnahuac, and that she was probably forced into sexual servitude when she was twelve, as Spanish-indigenous forces swept her hometown, killing or enslaving her family.[56]

"So great was the haste to make slaves in different parts" of New Spain, claimed Motolinía, "that they were brought into the city of Mexico in great flocks, like sheep, so they could be easily branded." The thirty-ninth charge made against Cortés in his *residencia* inquiry stated that (in Cuauhnahuac and Huaxtepec) he "and the people who came with him killed many Indians, and then branded more than five hundred souls as slaves." Statements of slaughter and enslavement like these, and many others quoted in this chapter, give the impression of a steady stream of numbers—of hundreds and thousands whose total tally is unclear. Any exploration of a history of warfare runs into questions of demographic scale, and that is particularly true in the Mexican case, where the impact of mass enslavement and civilian massacres must be considered alongside battle casualties and the impact of epidemic disease—let alone questions of pre-Columbian population levels, of conquistador numbers, and of numbers of indigenous allies during the war. Indeed, one of the mythistorical themes of the traditional narrative of the "Conquest of Mexico" has been that of numbers of people.[57]

The conquistadors and other Spaniards tended to downplay their own numbers, laying the foundation for the canard that an empire of millions was conquered by a "handful" of conquistadors: the conquest was achieved by "an isolated handful of Spaniards against a powerful and warlike race"; "unbelievable success came to Cortés with a handful of men and a few horses"; "with a mere handful of adventurous men" he "performed the greatest feat" in history, "toppled the most warlike of all American empires," and "subjugated a highly cultured people whose numbers ran into the millions." Thus by the same token, indigenous numbers were exaggerated, as Cortés and others boasted about the wealth of the land they had discovered and the scale of their triumph over it. That exaggeration has resurfaced in multiple ways over the centuries—from the numbers of victims of Aztec sacrificial ceremonies to the numbers of Tlaxcalteca warriors allied with the Spaniards; from the population of Tenochtitlan to the mortality rate from smallpox during the war.[58]

There is no doubt that some 450 Spaniards sailed from Cuba, reaching Cozumel in February 1519; fewer than three hundred, perhaps as few as 250, walked into Tenochtitlan in November that year. Does that make the achievement of the surviving "handful," and Cortés's supposed military genius, even more impressive? Not quite. In August 1521, at the war's conclusion and the city's surrender, there were at least 980 surviving Spaniards in the Valley of Mexico, and well over a thousand across Mexico. So how did the conquistador presence fluctuate and how do the real numbers help change our view of the war?

The first fact is that many more Spaniards entered the war than those original 450. In the thirty months between Cortés's departure from Cuba and the war's end, I estimate that at least 2,600 Spaniards crossed to the Mexican mainland, and I suspect the actual number was at least three thousand. At their most numerous moment, there were fifteen hundred. Cortés and Narváez then led them into the Tenochtitlan trap that became the Noche Triste, and a month later a thousand of them were dead. Over the next year, total numbers crept back up, getting close to fifteen hundred again, although never quite reaching it due to battle losses. So by the time Tenochtitlan was captured, almost two-thirds of all those who came to Mexico had died.

If we account for the small number who left for the islands or Spain during the war (Ordaz was one), the conquistador mortality rate was below 65 percent; but if more Spaniards arrived than my estimated twenty-six hundred, the rate was closer to 70 percent.[59]

Most Spaniards died as a result of wound-related infections or injuries from the arrows, small blades, and obsidian-studded clubs used by Mesoamerican warriors. But hundreds were taken alive and ritually executed in Tenochtitlan during the Noche Triste battle, and at least seventy-five suffered the same fate in June 1521, when Aztec defenders resoundingly won an engagement during the siege. A small minority died at the hands of other Spaniards. The point here is not that a few thousand conquistadors, instead of a few hundred, defeated a great empire, but that Tlaxcalteca, Aztec, and other Mesoamerican warriors inflicted such heavy casualties on the invaders that two-thirds of them died in the war. This was not an astounding victory of a handful led by a brilliant general; it was a punishing, costly war in which Spanish defeat was regularly averted by new arrivals—not to mention the tens of thousands of indigenous "allies." If Cortés really was in charge, then for every man whom he led to victory, he led two to their death.

A cluster of small but significant points stem from this reality check on conquistador numbers—points all to do with the capacity of the invaders to retain their toehold in Mexico and inflict violence upon the local population. For example, the enormous force of eleven hundred who came with Narváez in April 1520 were the exception to a pattern of steady flow; that is, men came in groups as small as half a dozen, but with regularity throughout the war, providing reinforcements at a useful and relatively undisruptive rate. They also brought with them additional horses, crossbows and harquebuses, powder and shot, and other supplies. Weaponry was not the smoking-gun explanation for Spanish victory (one "Cortés" television documentary, drawing upon the modern military variant on the traditional narrative, declares Cortés's "secret weapons" to be steel swords and crossbows, cannon and harquebuses, mastiffs and horses—which "the natives" thought were "dragons"). In fact, those weapons did not offer great offensive advantages, but permitted small, tight, strong defensive positions. Spanish weapons were useful for breaking the offensive lines of waves of indigenous warriors, but this was no formula for conquest, which small Spanish companies did not and could not have achieved. Rather, it was a formula for survival, until Spanish and indigenous reinforcements arrived; the story, in other words, of the Spanish-Aztec War.[60]

These factors all helped to determine the mindset of the conquistadors, to which we shall turn in a moment. But first, what of the indigenous side of the numbers question? For much of the last century it was believed that the indigenous population of Mexico before the Spanish-Aztec War was as much as 25 million, with more than a million living in the Valley of Mexico (a hundred to two hundred thousand of them in Tenochtitlan). As the region's indigenous population was perhaps as low as a million by 1600, the demographic impact of Spanish conquest and colonization was thus a population loss of 96 percent—an unprecedented demographic disaster. The major culprit has usually been identified as smallpox (the *Variola major* variant of *orthopoxvirus*), with the initial epidemic sweeping through central Mexico at the end of 1520, killing up to half the residents of many towns and cities—including Tenochtitlan—in just two months.[61]

These numbers have repeatedly been challenged, in a spirited debate that has simmered among scholars for decades, with lower figures now accepted by many scholars (but seldom appearing in books and documentaries aimed at larger audiences). We saw earlier that the island-city of Tenochtitlan could not have held as many as a hundred thousand residents; more likely there were some 60,000, with hundreds of thousands in the other cities around the lake, and more like 5 to 10 million in the Aztec Empire and Mexico as a whole. Likewise, we cannot be so sure that Mexican towns were cut in half in a matter of months, just because Motolinía asserted it as fact decades later. Sweeping verdicts on the causes of Aztec defeat—"the miraculous triumphs" of the conquistadors were "in large part the triumphs of the virus of smallpox"—no longer hold up.[62]

But that does not mean we can discount or dismiss the demographic impact of the diseases the Spaniards brought with them. For there remains strong evidence that epidemics of smallpox and other diseases devastated Mesoamericans during the war, and a 90 percent population decline (from 10 million to 1 million) in eighty years is still highly shocking. What it does mean is that we must look carefully at the smallpox evidence to see exactly how it affected the course of the war, in particular in conjunction with other factors. Specifically, the war's outcome can in large part be explained by the intersection of the smallpox factor with internecine conflict among the Aztec leadership and the role played by the Spaniards' indigenous allies—who were also impacted by epidemic disease. As Hassig noted, epidemic mortality within both the Aztec and the allied leadership added to the disruption of normal patterns of warfare. I would add that this did not facilitate Aztec defeat per se; rather, it made the war more protracted and less clearly guided. Aztec (then Mexica) leadership was interrupted, allied indigenous leadership was fractured, and high mortality rates opened up possibilities for upstarts and parvenus, further destabilizing the indigenous political landscape. In sum, if total indigenous numbers were not as high as once thought, with fewer Mexica both at the start of the war and as defenders of Tenochtitlan during the siege, and smallpox and other diseases killed fewer people than once thought, then outright slaughter, starvation, and enslavement accounted for more casualties at all stages of the war than has been recognized.[63]

At the same time, the impact of so-called indigenous allies is also thereby magnified. Herein lies an argument made many times (it was even made, in muted form, by Prescott), but it needs to be restated, with a crucial additional emphasis. Conquistadors massively downplayed the extent to which "the Conquest" was not theirs, but rather a war fought by indigenous warriors allied with them against the Aztecs and—eventually—just the Mexica. They did this for the obvious reason that their letters of report and testimonies were intended as evidence of their success and their sacrifice. But Spaniards also considered it ignoble for a Spaniard to use indigenous warriors to fight another Spaniard, and so accounts tended to ignore the presence of indigenous warriors during internecine conflicts. For example, the Cortés-Narváez standoff, depicted in the traditional narrative as yet another moment of Cortesian triumph against the odds, in fact pitted Narváez's thousand Spaniards against ten thousand indigenous warriors brought by Sandoval. Even more shocking was the claim that "Pedro de Alvarado captained fifty thousand Indians, when he went against Francisco de Garay, and he killed three hundred Christians in one night."[64]

Those numbers are probably exaggerated, but the point remains: there were indigenous warriors and porters involved in the war far more extensively than Spanish sources and modern histories tend to recognize. The recognition that Tlaxcalteca forces played crucial roles has never gone far enough; the deep roots of that perspective in Tlaxcala's successful self-promotion since the sixteenth century has only served to downplay or deny the roles played by other city-states. Above all, the failure to acknowledge the role played by the Tetzcoca in forging an agreement with the Tlaxcalteca Triple Alliance has meant a distortion of the war and a downplaying of total alliance numbers. Ironically, Gómara's figure of two hundred thousand men besieging Tenochtitlan may in fact have been close to the truth. I suspect there were at least that many. Thus in 1521 warriors from dozens of cities and regions outnumbered 200:1 the Spaniards with whom they were loosely allied; they outnumbered Mexica defenders four or five to one. No wonder the Tlaxcalteca/Tetzcoca-led alliance—not the Spaniards—defeated the Mexica.

The combination of these developments helps to explain why the Spanish-Aztec War became so violent. Prior to the arrival of the conquistadors, two factors acted to restrain warfare, to prevent or minimize any kind of total warfare being waged in central Mexico. One was the balance of power, operating on two levels: Tenochtitlan was dominant within the Triple Alliance, but the inclusion of Tetzcoco and Tlacopan served to offset that domination and discourage its abuse (with dynastic intermarriage helping too); the Aztec Triple Alliance was then itself kept somewhat in check by the Tlaxcalteca Triple Alliance. The events of 1519–20 shifted that larger balance in favor of the Tlaxcalteca—for the first time in their history. The events of 1521 destroyed the balance *within* the Aztec Empire, giving Tetzcoco dominance over its two former partners. At the same time, the Tlaxcalteca-Tetzcoca rapprochement magnified the effect of those two shifts.

The addition of Spaniards, their weapons, and the diseases brought by them and their Taíno and African dependents made the shift explosive and chaotic. Furthermore, the Spanish tendency to engage in a kind of total war (ideologically justified, aimed at unconditional surrender, with civilians as legitimate targets) destroyed the second factor of pre-Columbian restraint. Contrary to the Aztecs' reputation for bloodthirstiness, they shared with other Mesoamericans a culture of warfare that was bound by a war season, by rules of conduct, and by an emphasis on individual combat and ritualized killing. (The Aztecs and the Tlaxcalteca Triple Alliance even seem to have engaged in so-called Flower Wars, in which the unpredictable chaos of open battle was replaced by hand-to-hand combat and negotiated casualties.) Unlike the Iberian Peninsula, the Mexican countryside was not studded with castles and fortified towns; by and large, both urban and rural populations did not need to live in fear of sudden attack, slaughter, and enslavement—not until 1519, that is. Places like Cholollan and Tepeaca were thus highly vulnerable to the kinds of massacres inflicted upon them by the conquistadors. But—and this is important to emphasize—indigenous warriors also participated in those massacres, as they did in the violence of the siege of Tenochtitlan. In other words, the lesson of conquistador practices was that the rules no longer applied; the Spaniards let the genie of total warfare out of the bottle.[65]

Ruy González participated in the attack on Tepeaca. He missed the slaughter at Cholollan and the Toxcatl massacre—having crossed from Cuba with Narváez in 1520—but he survived the Noche Triste (allegedly saving the lives of many compatriots) and the Battle of Otompan (Otumba) in order to wield his sword at Tepeaca. There "he faced many dangers and hardships, fighting many times with the Indians" (in the words of the commendation that accompanied his coat of arms). He went on to survive his wounds from the siege of Tenochtitlan, and to settle in the city as a prominent veteran conquistador. He fought again in Conquest campaigns into Michoacán and New Galicia. In 1525 he was given a house plot in Tenochtitlan, and he spent the next three decades acquiring and losing property, entering into business deals, profiting from indigenous tribute payments through *encomienda* grants, and negotiating the shifting sands of Spanish politics in early Mexico. He died a moderately wealthy city councilman in 1559, by all accounts as close as a conquistador came to being an "ordinary man."[66]

In his old age, did memories of massacres like Tepeaca trouble Ruy González? We cannot really know the answer to that question. But we do know that he was so incensed by Las Casas's *Very Brief Account* of 1552 that mere months after its publication he wrote a letter to the king, attacking the friar and defending Spain's wars of conquest (quoted in Chapter 2). One passage touches so closely on our concern here—the mentality of the ordinary men who fought in the war—that it is worth quoting at length:

> The war and conquest of these kingdoms does not appear so twisted and senseless as certain unlettered people affirm and maintain. For these [indigenous] people were barbarous, idolatrous sacrificers, killers of innocent people, eaters of human flesh, most repulsive and nefarious sodomites. And if someone wished to tell me that such-and-such sins deserve war and loss of a kingdom—and furthermore that in war there are outrages, great mistakes, and notable excesses and sins—that I do believe. But let those who committed them pay for them, not everyone; punish them, and let us not lose that which we have earned so well and with such hard work in the service of God and of Your Majesty. And the truth is that once war begins, even though it may be very

just and among very Christian people, I don't believe that there can be any fewer excesses, as occurs in the wars in France and Rome and elsewhere.[67]

It may be tempting to view this simply as a conventional conquistador usage of racism (or its sixteenth-century manifestation) to justify and excuse war crimes (by others); Vargas Machuca wrote two books at the turn of the seventeenth century making just that argument. Or we could zoom back our lens and see it as an example of the universal claim by soldiers that collateral damage is unavoidable. And it is, of course, both of those things. But if we leave it at that, we come close to settling for an explanation that smacks of the Black Legend, as if it is enough just to pass judgment on the conquistadors—to condemn them as perpetrators, leaving indigenous people to be victims. As Tzvetan Todorov put it, "what if we do not want to have to choose between a civilization of sacrifice and a civilization of massacre?"[68]

Instead, we might see in Ruy González's defensive phrases a kind of confession, a sliver of an opening into the mindset that made the Spanish-Aztec War such a bloodbath. In two ways, he goes further than he needs to. First, in describing the people among whom he has lived most of his life—"these people [*esta gente*]"—he hammers away at their savagery with one negative stereotype after another, stripping away their humanity until they seem worse than animals, as if sparing their lives would itself be a sin. Second, the mild term for "excesses" used in the last line, *desordenes*, might have sufficed as a dismissive confession; many a conquistador referred to the slaughter of "Indians" with a single word, slipping it past king, royal councilor, modern historian, student. But, again, González lays it on thick, effectively admitting that he participated in a war that was characterized by atrocities. The term *atrocidad* was not in his sixteenth-century vocabulary, but his string of descriptors amount to a damning revelation of atrocity: *eçesivo, grandes ynadvertençias, notables desordenes, pecados*. In short, he is telling us this: we invaded the homelands of these people and committed atrocities against them; we were able to do it, justifying it to ourselves and others, by dehumanizing them, classifying them as evil subhuman creatures; but on some level, we knew this was wrong.

González challenges us to see the good and bad within each conquistador; he may make it difficult, but it is crucially important if we are to better understand why the "Conquest" was a war so lethal and brutal. There are easier alternative explanations, easily found in the literature. But they fail to satisfy. Condemning all conquistadors as bad is as facile as claiming all indigenous people are good; turning one entire ethnoracial group into perpetrators and another into victims is itself a kind of racism that no amount of moral indignation can redeem. More tempting is the sorting of conquistadors into two categories. After all, one wants to believe that in the very crucible of cruelty, there were men who chose not to torture, rape, or kill; that conquistadors who took holy orders did so in order to live lives of compassion, not corruption; that a butcher like Pedro de Alvarado was a bad apple.

This latter explanation, which effectively scapegoats Alvarado as an apologia for the rest or majority of the conquest company, is the one most commonly found in traditional narrative accounts. Even Las Casas, with his litany of "tyrants" and their atrocities in his *Destruction of the Indies,* seems to condemn all conquistadors by not naming the accused. But in fact he does the opposite; by failing to denounce the larger enterprise of conquest and colonization, he implies that the "tyrant" captains are the bad apples ruining what would otherwise be a fine orchard. A variant explanation for conquistador cruelty—a rather Lascasian one, smacking too of the Black Legend—is the view that most conquistadors were bad apples, thereby highlighting the nobility of the exception. Sandoval, that "constant captain," has tended to be favored for such a role, as have Aguilar and Ordaz. In the 1826 anonymous Conquest novel, *Xicoténcatl,* the "sincere and selfless" Ordaz serves to underscore how all his colleagues are immoral brutes; the Nahuas, or "Americans," are the mirror opposite, all decent and honorable, with a duplicitous Tlaxcalteca traitor in the role of the one bad apple.[69]

A third variant on the question of how to explain conquistador behavior comes closer to our goal. This one sees the moral balance shifting within the conquistadors as a result of the war experience. As the great Mexican intellectual and historian José Luis Martínez once said of Cortés: "after the Noche Triste he was infuriated by [Aztec] Mexico; little by little he became tougher and he ended up being cruel—a very tough and cruel man." There is surely some truth to this, and it surely applies to hundreds of *indianos*—Spaniards who fought and settled in the Indies. But the danger in the argument lies in slipping toward the old Franciscan position—more justification than explanation—best articulated by Mendieta.[70]

"Some, in their writings," wrote the old friar, had judged Cortés to be a "tyrant" (a reference to the famous Dominican). Rather than deny the captain's "excesses," the Franciscan excused them on two related grounds. First, he had no other option, as he was surrounded by "such a multitude of enemies, some visible and others hidden," with "so few *compañeros*" (and those "so greedy for gold"). Second, he had the greater good to consider. Thus:

> Although he himself pronounced the death sentence in cases that did not seem to justify it—saying, "hang this Indian, burn that one, torture so-and-so!"—in two words they provided him with the information regarding who was going to kill Spaniards, who conspired, who mutinied, who plotted, and other such things; and although many times he felt they [such measures] were not quite justified, he had to pander to the [conquistador] company and [indigenous] allies, so that they did not become enemies and abandon him.[71]

This rationale—the twisted logic of the civilizing mission requires cold calculations of violence—is chillingly compelling. But it contains a flaw, one ubiquitous in the traditional narrative: it assumes total Cortesian control, maintained at times by lesser-of-two-evils choices. I suggest that the truth was the opposite: Neither Cortés nor any other Spanish captain or indigenous leader controlled the company, campaign, or the overall arena of the war. As a result, many men made cold calculations of violence all the time, for multiple reasons. At the same time, some moments of violence were so extreme and explosive as to seem incalculable, inexplicable. Take Robertson's description of the massacre in Cholollan, written in the 1770s with only the obvious Spanish sources at hand, but perhaps informed a tad by his grasp of how such moments in human history unfold:

> The streets were filled with bloodshed and death. The temples, which afforded a retreat to the priests and some of the leading men, were set on fire, and they perished in the flames. This scene of horror continued for two days; during which, the wretched Indians suffered all that the destructive rage of the Spaniards, or the implacable revenge of their Indian allies, could inflict.[72]

As much as Protestant writers like Robertson, Prescott, and MacNutt relished the quick slip into barbarism of armed Catholics, one cannot help but read their use of terms like *carnage, merciless slaughter,* and *unchecked ferocity* as echoes of other massacres—the human record of which has piled up exponentially in the centuries since Cholollan. In the century before Robertson's, the Dutch jurist Hugo Grotius had written books imploring European rulers to respect international laws of war, having observed "throughout the Christian world" the speed with which men resorted to war "for no reasons at all, and when arms were taken up no reverence left for human or divine law, exactly as if a single edict had released a madness driving men to all kinds of crime." If writers from Robertson to MacNutt saw in the "Conquest of Mexico" a premonition of the kinds of butchery that Grotius witnessed in the Thirty Years' War, what would they have made of the human record of atrocity in the twentieth century?[73]

For example, on March 16, 1968, a company of about a hundred U.S. soldiers shot 404 unarmed Vietnamese villagers in My Lai. The bodies of the My Lai victims were thrown in a ditch in the village. They included 182 women and 173 children, of which 56 were infants. A mile away, in the village of My Khe, the soldiers of another company from the same battalion executed 97 Vietnamese villagers. The story hit the press in the United States a year and a half later, galvanizing the antiwar movement. The company's lieutenant was court-martialed and convicted of mass murder, and charges were filed against officers for covering up the massacre. But nobody else was convicted and nobody served prison time, including the lieutenant, who was freed from house arrest by President Richard Nixon and at the time of writing was living in Georgia.

The massacres at Cholollan and My Lai happened centuries apart and under circumstances so different that a deep comparison is unlikely to be revealing. But some superficial similarities are suggestive. In both cases, the lack of closure or accountability, the lack of a satisfying explanation, has allowed community scar tissue to permanently form. Despite the passing of centuries, "the aftermath of the massacre remains on most Cholultecas' minds." An elderly Tlaxcalteca who married into a Cholulteca family as a young woman recently bemoaned that "Cortés manipulated" the people of Tlaxcallan to come to Cholollan "and kill our brothers"; "I'm from there and everyone calls us traitors." "We forgive, but we do not forget" is a common comment by survivors; the phrase was said recently to a reporter by Pham Thanh Cong, a My Lai villager who was eleven at the time of the massacre and hid under the corpses of his mother and three sisters. The soldiers entered My Lai believing that it harbored enemy Vietcong soldiers; the conquistadors entered Cholollan believing an enemy army was hiding nearby and was plotting with the townspeople. But did it not become clear that such information was faulty, as unarmed families huddled apprehensively in the village center and the town plaza, and as American soldiers fired their guns and Spanish conquistadors swung their steel swords? We are left with the uncomfortable suspicion that, in the heat of the moment, that is all there was: the heat of the moment. As a Vietnamese veteran remarked of the massacre, noting that there were others, committed by Americans and by Vietnamese soldiers on both sides: "In war such things happen."[74]

As unsatisfying as those explanations may be—and interviews with soldiers who were at My Lai offered similarly predictable and routine reflections on the fog of war: we were afraid, we were avenging our fallen comrades, we were just following orders—they nonetheless help us to better understand what happened in Cholollan and throughout the Spanish-Aztec War. For whereas the Vietnam War has become infamous as a senseless, bloody conflict, the Spanish-Aztec War retains in the popular imagination a shimmer of glorious adventure. But it was no such thing. By thinking of the massacres at Cholollan and Tepeaca as manifestations of a certain kind of war, we can better see the whole story as a war that is replete with such moments—traumatized combatants, numb to the horror they are experiencing and perpetrating, civilian populations brutalized beyond all imagining, one sickening outbreak of violence leading to another.

How, then, did conquistadors who were "ordinary men" end up participating in—even creating—such moments? It is tempting to turn to the five Alvarado brothers as case studies, but their reputation for savoring violence and cruelty—especially Gonzalo and Pedro—leads us back to a "bad apple" argument. So let us take two lesser-known examples.[75]

Juan Bono de Quexo was a Basque with a long career as a conquistador in the Indies. Arriving as a pilot on Columbus's final transatlantic voyage in 1502, he went on to participate in expeditions to Florida, Puerto Rico, and Cuba; he had *encomiendas* of indigenous people on both those two islands, and on Puerto Rico owned mines and large numbers of Taíno slaves. A consummate plotter and backstabber, he joined the anti-Velázquez rebellion at Vera Cruz in 1519, but then stole back to Cuba only to return to Mexico with the pro-Velázquez company under Narváez. He survived the Noche Triste to participate in massacres such as that at Tepeaca (after which he accused the Tlaxcalteca warriors of mass cannibalism). He continued to plot against Cortés in the 1520s, eventually settling back in Cuba. One gets the distinct impression that he was a singularly unpleasant man, but within the spectrum—like Ruy González—of conquistador ordinariness.[76]

The same might be said of Jacinto "Cindo" del Portillo. He reached the Indies in 1514 and likely participated in both the Hernández de Córdoba and Grijalva expeditions. He survived the Spanish-Aztec War, going on to join various campaigns in the 1520s, by which he acquired as many as five hundred indigenous slaves. He seems to have used them in gold-mining or panning operations, and to have abused them so harshly that they rose up against him. Badly wounded in the resulting conflict, he swore to give up his worldly possessions if God saved him; when he recovered, he joined the Franciscans, freed his indigenous slaves, and signed his *encomiendas* over to the Crown. For decades, fray Cindo was one of the door-keepers of the Franciscan convent in Mexico City. But he still participated in expeditions of conquest and forced conversion—into Zacatecas around 1560, for example—and advocated not for the abolition of *encomiendas,* but for their income to be used to build churches (as he told the king in a 1561 letter). One wonders whether souls were saved—Portillo's included—by his transformation from veteran conquistador to friar (and whether such thoughts crossed his own mind while he died slowly from a poisonous spider bite in Nombre de Dios).[77]

Men like González, Bono, and Portillo crossed to the mainland alongside—or to join—groups of men to whom they were connected by kinship, hometowns, and other ties, in the hope of being in the percentage (it turned out to be only one-third) who survived the war to reap rewards of plunder and settlement. Allegiances among men were deep-rooted, complex, and personal; they killed for each other. (Contra the traditional narrative: larger allegiances, to captains like Cortés, were fleeting, strategic, and almost incidental.)

For the first two years of the war, men came to fight and survive. During the siege, they came to be part of the victory. Veterans of violence against indigenous peoples in the islands joined survivors of the first half of the war against the Aztecs; almost all had experienced the slaughter of "Indians" in their own homes. In Mexico, they witnessed the death—slowly by infection, or quickly in ritual executions—of most of their comrades. They had become hardened to mass killing, and the steady trickle of supplies from the islands gave them the means to do immense harm to the "Indians." Their small numbers and the limitations of their weaponry, especially cannon and harquebuses, meant that battles against large numbers of indigenous warriors were frustrating and exhausting. But against unarmed captives and civilians, such limitations evaporated; in the plaza of Cholollan or the fields outside Tepeaca, swords and knives could be deployed as riskless and efficient tools of mass butchery.

Each massacre was an act of revenge for Spaniards already killed. It did not matter that retaliation for Mayas killing the first Spaniards of the company was inflicted upon Totonacs or Nahuas. Or that revenge for the killing of scores of Spaniards by Tlaxcalteca was carried out against Chololteca, with Tlaxcalteca warriors as comrades. Or that the Tepeaca massacres were revenge for the Noche Triste, a defeat inflicted far away by the Mexica, who had themselves conquered the people of Tepeaca in warfare. It did not matter because in the frenzy of battle, revenge was revenge, and—after all—to the Spaniards, they were all "Indians."

In that simple fact—the Spanish reduction of all indigenous peoples to a single category—lies a crucial piece of the puzzle of violence in this war. A scholar of the Holocaust has written that "war, and especially race war, leads to brutalization, which leads to atrocity." The Spanish conquests in the Americas have tended *not* to be seen as "race wars," because modern concepts of race did not yet exist; Spaniards were ethnocentric, not racist, seeing themselves as Christians and Castilians or Basques, and others by similar terms and in categories of ethnicity, region, religion, or types of barbarism. And yet the Spaniards under our microscope were men like González, Bono, and Portillo; men whose experience in the Indies had led them to view "Indians" in a category that looks a lot like not only a racial one, but a racist one. They anticipated warfare against indigenous towns and villages, in which local men would be killed near or in their homes, and their women and children enslaved. All this could and would be done because "Indians" were in a separate human, or subhuman, category.[78]

Here, then, were the puzzle pieces. First, conquistador culture was a violent one, and Spaniards were quick to treat each other with brutality. But they tortured and murdered each other according to certain rules, giving their violence a judicial veneer (examples from the Mexico of the 1520s are the torturing to death of Rodrigo de Paz, and the torture and mutilation of García de Llerena). Second, those rules did not, however, apply to "Indians." By virtue of the same loopholes that permitted "Indians" to be invaded, conquered, enslaved, and otherwise subjugated—their "idolatry," cannibalism, propensity for "human sacrifice," and frequent rebelliousness—they also fell outside the protection of the rules of violent conduct. If men like Paz and Llerena could be judicially tortured, indigenous people could be indiscriminately slaughtered and enslaved. Third, the incipient racism that had developed toward "Indians" by Spanish *indianos* permitted revenge for conquistador deaths to take the form of massacres—even if the frenzy of such atrocities went against the logic of the fourth factor, which was the need to finance the war through the acquisition and sale of slaves.[79]

In wartime atrocities—from the Thirty Years' War to World War II to the Vietnam War—violence was committed by men who became "numbed to the taking of human life, embittered over their own casualties, and frustrated by the tenacity of an insidious and seemingly inhuman enemy." As different as the contexts are to those more recent conflicts, those factors undoubtedly apply to the conquistadors and their mounting record of brutality in the Spanish-Aztec War—and in Mesoamerica from 1519 through to the 1540s.[80]

THERE IS A FINAL STEP TO TAKE. What we must contemplate are battles comprising hours of casual slaughter, massacres of civilian populations, each side driven by what they have witnessed to commit their own atrocities, internecine violence, mass mutilations of prisoners, entire towns butchered or enslaved, families torn apart, women raped or forced into long-term sexual slavery, an apocalypse of violence striking the center and then devastating one region after another in waves lasting decades. The sum of all this so resoundingly makes the case that the "Conquest of Mexico" should be seen as a war—not a conquest war, not a short war, and certainly not a surprisingly short war, but fully and categorically a war—that it in fact does more than that. It suggests that we might do better to understand it as a genocidal war.

Genocide is, of course, a loaded and controversial term. There has been resistance to the application of the term to the extermination of indigenous peoples in North America—despite exhaustive recent studies that make powerful arguments for its relevance. As a term coined and officially defined by the United Nations in the 1940s, it is also anachronistic to the sixteenth century. A genocide requires, by definition, state policy of the kind not found in the Spanish world of five centuries ago (where the state was a far cry from modern). And even though twentieth-century atrocities "were too often tolerated, condoned, or tacitly (sometimes even explicitly) encouraged by elements of the command structure, they did not represent official government policy." Indeed, in the case of the Indies in the sixteenth century, individuals or conquest companies acting with extreme violence sought subjugation rather than total elimination; their "policy" was to gain slaves and *encomienda* tributaries, even if the violence used to attain those goals was consequently irrational and patently counterproductive.[81]

What I am suggesting, therefore, in rhetorical rather than categorical terms, is that the Spanish wars of invasion were genocidal not in intent, but in effect. Within what was in effect the genocidal Spanish-Aztec War, there occurred micro-genocidal moments. In town after town—Cholollan, Tepeaca, Quecholac, Cuauhnahuac, and even Tenochtitlan itself—the slaughter of combatants was followed or accompanied by the massacre of civilians and the enslavement and often deportation of survivors, most notably young women and children. The impact of such attacks on these communities was catastrophic and permanent (genocidal in effect) and tinged with a hint of deliberate destruction (genocidal in intent).

For rightly perceiving that there were millions of indigenous Meso-americans, Spanish captains were willing to obliterate certain communities knowing that there were hundreds of others. The survival of those communities—the cultural and demographic persistence of Nahuas and other indigenous peoples through these wars and up to the present—has helped to mask the fact of those micro-genocidal moments.

Even if we accept that Spanish institutional or governmental policy was not genocidal in intent, and indeed often comprised laws designed to protect and encourage the proliferation of indigenous communities, the fact remains that an invasion war could only be genocidal in effect with official acquiescence. Underlying the sixteenth-century Spanish debate regarding the nature of New World "Indians" lay an assumption that they had no rights until the Crown determined that they did, and that the limits to those rights and the loopholes in the laws permitted Spaniards to behave accordingly. A Spaniard who killed another Spaniard faced judicial retribution (or at least personal retribution that was state-sanctioned); but a Spaniard could kill or enslave an "Indian" with impunity if that victim met two simple criteria—being "Indian" and offering resistance.

The significance of the genocidal element in the Mexico of the 1520s is twofold. First, it marked the moment of genesis for the region's transition to New Spain and, in time, the Mexican republic, with profound implications for Mexican national identity (as Mexicans are well aware). But, second, Mexico is not unique in this respect; on the contrary, violence and warfare that was genocidal in effect (and, in some cases, in intent) marked the genesis of colonies that led to nation-states throughout the Western Hemisphere.

Scholars of the U.S. Wars of Independence, or the American Revolution, have pointed out that Americans have sought to portray the war as more of a revolutionary movement than a war, one based on high ideals rather than dangerous and wrongheaded ideas, a transition less violent than other revolutions. Americans made this comparative spin during the French Revolution of the 1790s, and during the Russian and Chinese revolutions of the twentieth century. It remains deeply ingrained in the popular understanding of 1776 and its aftermath. The Spanish-Aztec War has enjoyed a similar whitewashing—not labeled a war, but instead called an *entrada*, a *pacificación*, the "Conquest of Mexico."

Both cases, of course, were myths, lies, designed to render noble and just wars that featured atrocities, massacres, murders, rapes, enslavements, and all manner of brutalities inflicted upon civilian populations—in short, wars.

CONQUEST AS CRUCIBLE. Humberto Limón, *Crisol de razas* (1975). Oil on cloth, 90x70cm. The painting (titled "Crucible of Races") echoes the tradition of Mexican calendar art, originating in the nineteenth century, specifically the romance between the personifications of the two great volcanoes that overlook the valley (seen here on the horizon); it also draws upon a parallel mythical tradition, with roots going back to the seventeenth century, in which the "Conquest of Mexico" is seen through the metaphor of a romance, either specifically between Cortés and Malinche, or more generically between an heroic conquistador and a passionate "Indian princess." The fixing of this scene in November 1519 is suggested by Limón's depiction of a procession along the causeway leaving Tenochtitlan, presumably Montezuma coming out to meet Cortés. Thus that Meeting, with its thwarted embrace and its doomed political romance, is substituted for a metaphorical meeting that is seeped in sexual possession—with the conquistador the active protagonist, the indigenous one made female, passive, her unconscious pose ambiguously representing rescue or kidnap. The image reflects well the layered centuries of perceptions and interpretations that shroud the Spanish-Aztec War, making its many meetings a complex and unresolved phenomenon.

Halls of the Montezumas

Alvarado.   So, let's improve the time; then pledge me all—
              May we, thus met to-night, thus meet again,
              All joyously, *"to revel in the halls
              of the Montezumas!"*
Sandoval.   Fill bumpers, all!
All.   Halls of the Montezumas!

—*Cortez, the Conqueror*, 1857

We should not believe the historian who writes based on what others have told him. To see the reason for this, take a hundred people who have been to a sermon and you will see that each one will recount it to you in a different way. And take a thousand who have been to a battle and you will not find four in agreement about what happened.

—Pedro de Navarra, 1567

In many cases a real historic event is transformed into a myth, and the myth itself is reenacted through ritual.

—Eduardo Matos Moctezuma, 1987

These men, seen in their distant perspective, seem to us to move in an aura of romance, and even the most cut-and-dried chronicle of their deeds reads more like a troubadour's tale than the sober pages of history.

—MacNutt, *Fernando Cortes*, 1909

There's always a story that comes after the end of a story. How could there not be? Life doesn't come in tidy packages, all neatly wrapped up with a pretty bow on top.   —Sue Grafton, 2011[1]

THE KING HAD HEARD THE STORY MANY TIMES BEFORE. ONE OF his childhood playmates was Martín Cortés, Malintzin's son, who was sent to court as a page at the age of six, and remained in Prince Philip's entourage until going to war, at nineteen, in the disastrous Algiers campaign of 1541 (where he saw his father again). So Philip knew Martín for the first fourteen years of his life. He must have been told many times who the older boy was and of what glorious conquest he was the progeny. He also heard from his tutor and his governor (the latter related, by chance, to Cortés's second wife) the details of Spain's progression of conquests in the Indies—as a break from learning Latin and Greek and memorizing *The Song of El Cid*. In the early 1540s, the teenage Philip became regent of Spain, where he met Cortés and Las Casas—who gave him a manuscript copy of the *Destruction of the Indies*—and many others with strong opinions on Indies affairs. So he knew the story of the "Conquest of Mexico" well.[2]

Yet, in 1562, Alonso de Zorita felt the need to explain it again. As the royal judge (*oidor*) wrote to Philip (now king) from Mexico:

> When the captain don Hernando Cortés and the Spaniards came to this land, once Montezuma knew of them, he sent people to visit the port and to bring them food and other things as a sign of peace and friendship, and they did this at his orders along the whole road until the Spaniards arrived at this city, where he came out to receive them with all his people in peace. And as a sign of this he gave the captain a thick chain of gold and put it round his neck and received him and the Spaniards as brothers, and he put them up in his palace and he treated them amicably until they seized him, in order to take his gold, jewels, and precious stones and all his valuables, which were many, without he or his people giving them any occasion or reason to do so. And if later the Spaniards were thrown out, it was because they had imprisoned Montezuma and because of the killing and destruction, by don Pedro de Alvarado and the Spaniards who were with him, of the sons of the lords and principal men of those kingdoms and other people who were on the patio of the house where Montezuma was held captive, trying to comfort him in his prison.[3]

Zorita had presented the king with an interpretation of History as Encounter. Not only, suggested the judge, did New Spain originate in the encounter between Cortés and Montezuma, but its subsequent problems stemmed from how that encounter had gone wrong—with "peace and friendship" transformed into "killing and destruction" for no "occasion or reason." Furthermore, Zorita also understood how the encounters that compose the historical past are remembered and retold in ways that reflect multiple agendas and misunderstandings—as well as the distortions and agendas of subsequent encounters. The result is the blurring of lines between fact and fiction, truth and invention. Those blurred lines are not just *an* issue that historians must tackle; they *are* History.

Zorita's task, then, was a Sisyphean one, and he knew it. Perhaps this book is one too. For it has been as much about the invented history of the "Conquest of Mexico" as it has been about the reality (or *a* truth, as I have presented it) of the Spanish-Aztec War. Why? In part because I have had to describe the myth in detail, to expose history as mythistory, in order to bust it. But I am equally interested in the traditional narrative for its own sake, for what its half-millennium shelf life—from its Cortesian birth to its evolution through poetry and opera to its popular persistence today—tells us about how we retain and use the past.

The Meeting did not only take place on November 8, 1519. Both for the people who were there (the Castilians and Basques, Nahuas and Totonacs, Taínos and Africans) and for us today, the Meeting merely *began* on that day. It was—is—an encounter that has lived for five hundred years, fed by those who have appropriated it, given it meaning, rewritten or redrawn it for someone else to remake it as their own. That is true of the entire story of the Spanish invasions, remade and studied for centuries until its history has become a mountain of contradictory and competing claims. No wonder the traditional narrative has survived; it offers a tidy solution to all that clutter. But that also means that it is impossible to study the Spanish-Aztec War without studying its traditional "Conquest of Mexico" narrative. The events themselves and their traditional narrative long ago became inextricably intertwined.

Or perhaps the two are not completely inextricable. For example, consider these sentences, taken deliberately from a relatively obscure but middle-of-the-pack representation of the traditional narrative (a history of the Conquest, structured as a Cortés biography, by a Spaniard published in Edinburgh in 1829). Cortés's

> whole life is gilded by deeds so singular and splendid, as to invest the narration of them with the interesting character of chivalrous romance. The destruction of his fleet at Vera Cruz to compel his followers to conquer or die—his fearless entry into Mexico—the still bolder seizure of Montezuma, in the midst of the capital—his defeat of Narvaez—his exploit at the battle of Otompan—and his magnanimity in the siege of Mexico, present a series of events as striking as they are unparalleled.[4]

Here the threading of a heroic, omnipresent, omnipotent Cortés into the story is so visible as to make it possible to pull that thread out. As we pull on that thread, the traditional narrative unravels, allowing us to see that Cortés's life is indeed a "chivalrous romance"—as it has been imagined and invented, not as supported by the historical evidence. The reason why his "Conquest of Mexico has more of the atmosphere of romance than of sober history" (as a modern historian enthused) is not the content of "the Conquest" but how historians have packaged it. Without Cortés in control of events, those events no longer become his, or cease to have happened completely: he alone neither destroyed his fleet, seized Montezuma, nor defeated Narváez; ships were scuttled for practical reasons, the entry into Mexico was fearful and blind, there was no magnanimity displayed before, during, or after the siege of Tenochtitlan.[5]

Pulling the thread may be easier said than done. If the gorilla in History's room is Invention, then Cortés is the gorilla of the "Conquest of Mexico" (his name appears on most of the preceding pages—of a book arguing against Cortés-centrism). Yet done it must be. For the European invasion wars in the Americas rank not only among the great watersheds in global history, but "also among the most frequently misrepresented." More than just a pivotal moment in our past, the importance of the Meeting is magnified by being falsely depicted and grossly misunderstood for half a millennium—and, I have suggested here—because of the links between the justification of the Spanish Conquest and the glorification of the Rise of the West.[6]

With that last sentence (or even paragraph) we might have lost the good Spanish judge. So let us pick up Zorita's challenge, and in the spirit of his efforts to influence the Spanish king—but with the benefits of hindsight, access to multiple archives, and the efforts of hundreds of historians—write a brief, Cortés-free account of what happened "when the Spaniards came to this land."

The Meeting took place twenty-seven years and twenty-seven days after Columbus first set foot on American soil. During that time period, Spanish settlers sailed the Caribbean Sea and its edges in Florida, Central America, and the northern coasts of South America. They explored and founded small colonies. They introduced cattle, found gold, and built churches. But above all they massively disrupted indigenous life—killing, displacing, and enslaving hundreds of thousands of local peoples. Such was both the experience and expectation of the Spaniards who joined expeditions to the Yucatec coast and Mexican mainland in the late 1510s, when epidemic disease and over-enslaving had created a labor crisis in the Spanish Caribbean. Those expeditions were organized in Cuba by Diego Velázquez, who had been in the Indies (as the Spaniards called the Americas) since 1493.[7]

Expeditions mandated to explore, trade, and—if the appropriate procedures were followed—enslave, but not to conquer and settle, sailed from Cuba in 1517, 1518, and 1519. These were companies of armed settlers, not formal armies, divided into men on foot of various professions and "captains" who had invested in the company in various ways (paying for ships or supplies, bringing horses or men dependent upon them). The 1519 company comprised about 450 Spanish men and more than a thousand Taíno slaves and servants (mostly Cuban), as well as small numbers of African slaves and servants, some non-Taíno women, a dozen horses, and some mastiffs. That 450 would constitute less than 15 percent of the total number of conquistadors who would come to fight in the 1519–21 war. Most would die in the war. Upon reaching the region of the Gulf coast that was under the control of the Aztec Empire (around today's Veracruz), the leading captains of the company began a four-month quarrel over whether to return to Cuba or to betray Velázquez and reconstitute themselves as a new company answerable only to the Spanish king (soon to become Carlos V).

They chose the latter option, setting off in August 1519 on an inland march that would take the survivors into the valley and island-capital at the heart of the Aztec Empire—and would begin the two-year Spanish-Aztec War. The Spanish perspective on that war, what I have been calling its traditional narrative, has been presented in many ways in the preceding chapters. So let us summarize it one last time, using Bernal Díaz (as the book's dubious alpha and omega). Near the end of his manuscript, Díaz included a 213th chapter that was omitted from the 1632 edition, not published until the nineteenth century, and omitted too from almost all modern editions. He titled it "Why so many Indian men and women were branded as slaves in New Spain, and my statement about this."[8]

Díaz began the chapter by stating that "certain friars" had often asked him that question, and that he always explained that the king authorized slave-taking in New Spain—and that it was the fault of Velázquez for sending Narváez "to take the country" for him. These two somewhat contradictory explanations reveal both the war for what it was, and the defensive choreography of justification that conquistadors felt obliged to perform.

As Díaz went on to explain, Montezuma had surrendered his empire to the Spaniards and willingly become their prisoner. Thus at

the moment when Narváez's company landed on the coast, roughly
a year after the original company from Cuba had arrived there, the
land was already under legal Spanish control. Therefore when hostilities with the Aztecs broke out, their aggression constituted "a
rebellion"—and rebels could, under Spanish law, be enslaved. The
fault lay with Narváez because the arrival of his company obliged the
Spaniards in Tenochtitlan to split their small company in two, one
to meet the newcomers, the other to remain in the capital; the latter
group, numbering only eighty under Alvarado, panicked during an
Aztec festival, attacked the celebrants, and provoked the ire of the
local population. The "rebellion" rolled on, resulting in the Aztecs
"killing, sacrificing, and eating over 862 Spaniards." The survivors
prevailed only because "God favored us," the Tlaxcalteca "received
us like good and loyal friends," and reinforcements came steadily
from Cuba, Jamaica, and the other islands.

It was at this time that the Crown and royal officials "granted
us permission" to "enslave and brand on the face with this *G* the
Mexican Indians and those natives of the towns that had risen up
and killed Spaniards." That license was given because of the revolt,
and because evidence was provided of indigenous markets in which
slaves were "bound with collars and ropes much worse than those
the Portuguese use on the blacks from Guinea." Such slaves were
"redeemed," meaning they were branded on the face with an *R* and
sold to Spaniards.

Armed with reinforcements, local allies, and the righteous justification of royal law, the Spaniards regained the city and empire that
had been taken from them by Aztec rebels. In the process, many
"Indians" were branded. But Spaniards—incompetent, corrupt, traitorous ones—had prompted that rebellion, and thus inevitably the
recovery of the lost empire brought some abuses. As Díaz admitted,

certainly great frauds were committed over the branding of Indians, because as men, not all of us are very good—rather, there are
some of evil disposition [*de mala conçiençia*]; and because at that
time there came from Castile and from the islands many Span-

iards who were poor and so greatly covetous and avaricious and
ravenous to acquire wealth and slaves that they took measures
necessary to brand the free.

Díaz was not, of course, Las Casas. So he followed this seemingly Lascasian admission by first blaming the Spanish officials who
took over the incipient government in Mexico while many conquistadors (Díaz included) were on the Honduras expedition of the mid-
1520s (they "branded many free Indians who were not slaves," just
for profit); then he blamed bad "caciques" or local indigenous rulers
for selling their own people; and finally he told an unlikely tale of
how he and a priest named Benito López "broke the branding iron"
in Coatzacoalcos to stop slave laws being abused.

Crowed Díaz, "We took pride in having done so good a deed!" In
such boasts was the entire enterprise of enslavement, slaughter, and
colonization wrapped up in the artifice of righteousness and legality.
The Spanish-Aztec War and its aftermath, as a "good deed," became
"the Conquest of Mexico."[9]

What, meanwhile, of the other side of the story? There is, as
has become clear in the preceding chapters, no single vision of the
vanquished. But just as the Spanish perspective on the invasion can
be more clearly seen when we view it as a chaotic but collective enterprise, we can likewise access indigenous experiences by granting
agency to *altepeme*, that is, seeing how the leadership of the *altepetl*
of Tlaxcallan, and that of Tetzcoco and other city-states and towns,
exploited the disruption of the Caxtilteca invasion to expand their
own regional power at the expense of their enemies and their rival
partners.

The point is not simply the well-worn one that the Tlaxcalteca
role—downplayed by Spaniards, trumpeted by writers from colonial
Tlaxcala, highlighted by modern historians—was crucial. Nor is it
the equally tired point that early alliances revealed Aztec weakness
and spelled inevitable defeat. In the war's earlier stages, resistance to
the invaders was widespread, even among indigenous groups who
later switched sides. Numerous ethnic groups participated as war-

riors or support personnel in the invasion, including oft-ignored Taínos brought from the Caribbean. Above all, when the Aztec Empire's Triple Alliance collapsed in the war's second half, the role played by Tetzcoco proved to be more significant than that of Tlaxcallan. Meanwhile, the violence of the invasion destabilized Mexico and then all of Mesoamerica, largely because of the combined impact of two factors: epidemic disease, and a rapid slide into a kind of total warfare that was arguably genocidal in effect (albeit not in intent), genocidal as a result of the combined impact of battle mortality, massacres of civilians, enslaving of survivors, destruction of family units, and sexual predation.

The experience of atrocities by both Spanish conquistadors and indigenous warriors fueled further violence, generating a culture of conquest that resulted in the perpetuation of such patterns of warfare across Mesoamerica through the 1540s. Unprecedented levels of violence and mortality prompted competition for regional dominance; waves of violence across the empire and beyond spread that competition, into which the Spaniards—reinforced from the Caribbean and Spain in a steady stream during and after the war—were able to insert a new hegemony. But that hegemony was established in collaboration with the surviving indigenous nobility, whose role as "allies" was thus crucial not only during the war but in its aftermath. Local Mesoamerican rulers should neither be judged for choosing to act as "allies" nor criticized for misreading the long-term impact of the Spanish presence. More than 90 percent of combatants in the war were indigenous; they fought to defend their homes and to use the war's upheaval to carve out political space and regional autonomy. Men like Xicotencatl and Ixtlilxochitl made sound decisions based on the information at hand and the apparent best interests of their own positions and the security of their subjects.

Montezuma did likewise. He knew of the foreigners for years before their arrival. He had the company tracked along the coast in 1519, and when they landed in his territory in April, a large embassy immediately met the Spaniards with an elaborate and generous welcome. In the months that followed, he both tested them (he surely had a hand in them being guided into a Tlaxcalteca ambush) and lured them into his capital city. Once the Spanish-Tlaxcalteca force entered the Valley of Mexico, they were met by Cacama (Montezuma's nephew and the king or *tlahtoani* of Tetzcoco, the second-ranked city-state in the empire's Triple Alliance) and led into Tenochtitlan, although not by the causeway traditionally used by Aztec emperors upon their return from victorious campaigns; that was the route from Chapultepec to the east. Instead, the foreigners were guided in from the south to be welcomed by Montezuma and the full entourage of Aztec royalty and nobility.[10]

Montezuma's bait-and-switch strategy, designed to weaken the invaders while luring them into the center, worked brilliantly. The Spaniards were so confused that their frustration and bewilderment is clearly seen in their letters and testimonies, despite the self-promotional intent and tone of such accounts. They even seem to have convinced themselves that Montezuma was deeply shaken by their presence—while they slowly traveled, losing men, suffering battlewounds and other hardships, toward the emperor's net. They did not realize that Montezuma was not afraid of them; he was hunting them.

The conquistadors could not have known, of course, that the emperor was a collector. Even after they were successfully hunted, lured, trapped, and placed in a suitable structure in the center of the city, adjacent to the many other buildings and enclosures of the royal zoo, they could not have understood what had happened. Montezuma would hardly have attempted to explain to the Spaniards that their role was to be observed and studied, celebrated as a novel reflection of Aztec imperial power; then, if they proved too wild, they were to be transferred to the collections that existed beneath the sacred precinct—ritually executed, perhaps at the ceremony of the Flayed Man, and interred along with other foreign objects and the bones of exotic creatures.

That Montezuma's latest acquisitions proved to be his last, creatures so savage that they turned on their zookeeper, does not undermine the logic and efficacy—from the Aztec perspective—of his strategy. It worked: the conquistadors were collected, at first as additions to the zoo; later, most were indeed transferred to the sacred collection. That events subsequently turned against Montezuma, and then his empire and his people, was due to factors beyond his control: the sweep of Old World epidemic diseases; the lack of a common Mesoamerican or "Indian" sense of identity, combined with the inevitable shift of "alliances" within and between imperial states that had been built and wrecked and rebuilt on such arrangements for thousands of years; and the steady influx of Spaniards from the Caribbean and then from Spain itself.

Let us return, then, to the core moment in the Meeting: Montezuma's speech. Within the context of the emperor's strategy of collection, that speech takes on a different meaning. Clearly, he did deliver a speech. Just as clearly, it was not one of surrender; yet there is evidence that Montezuma's words contained historical and cultural references that in some way gave status to the guests, possibly at the expense of the hosts. In the sixteenth-century Nahua play *The Three Kings*, when Herod receives the Magi, he welcomes them in language appropriate to his status as *tlahtoani* of Jerusalem: "Ascend to your home, your *altepetl*. Enter. You are to eat, since it is at your home that you have arrived." These were exactly the kinds of phrases Montezuma used at the Meeting.[11]

To better grasp the purpose of such phrases, we must jump two decades forward, to 1541. In that year, a Spanish official named Jerónimo López wrote from Mexico City to the king, "every day there are more Indians who speak Latin as elegant as Cicero's." Noting that one could pass Nahua noblemen conversing in Latin on the streets of the city, he enthused "it is admirable to see what letters and colloquies they write in Latin, and what they say." Spaniards naturally credited Franciscans for their skill at turning "Indians" into literate Christians. Certainly friars played the central role in the conversion campaign that followed the war, and the college of Santa Cruz de Tlatelolco, the first school opened in the Americas, produced a generation or two of Latinized Nahua nobles (we met some, like don Pablo Nazareo, earlier). The first academic library in all the Americas, founded in 1536, survives in part today in San Francisco, California, where the breathless scholar can turn pages of books once turned by Aztec noblemen. But the college in Tlatelolco was a rapid success not just because of the efforts of a small group of dedicated friars, but because those Franciscans were able to build upon the existence and persistence of an indigenous intellectual tradition of higher learning, pictographic and phonetic writing, elegant and formal speech, and courtly address.[12]

Of particular relevance here is one key feature of the Nahuatl language. Whereas European languages (such as sixteenth-century Spanish) had ways in which vocabulary choices and use of grammar could make speech more polite, Nahuatl had a way of changing almost every word into a more formal, polite version of itself. By adding particular prefixes or suffixes to nouns, pronouns, prepositions, and many adverbs—and by changing the verb roots—regular speech could be turned into reverential speech. In the words of a Spaniard who studied Nahuatl in Mexico just a century after the Conquest war, the effect was "to elevate the Mexican language [Nahuatl] greatly and in this it outdoes even the languages of Europe." Speaking with reverential forms was thus a subtle, high art. Their use was sometimes determined by the status of the speakers (all Aztecs would have addressed Montezuma reverentially), but as a general rule it was the occasion that determined their use.[13]

One would never use reverential forms to refer to oneself; not even Montezuma would do that, and indeed his high status made it even more important that he speak modestly, even derogatively, about himself. But conventions of politeness and reverential address would have determined the way in which the emperor spoke to a visitor of status; thus the more reverentially Montezuma spoke to the Caxtilteca captains, the better it reflected on the emperor himself. In other words, the literal message of an address such as Montezuma's would be that the speaker was lower and lesser in every way than the recipient of the speech, but the status of the speaker and his use of reverential Nahuatl conveyed the real message—which was the opposite, that he was in fact of higher status and greater importance. This inversion was deeply built into the language, so that, for example, the terms for "noble" and "child" were virtually identical, allowing a nobleman to call himself someone's child, in the politest of language, thereby simultaneously conveying his nobility.

The impossibility of adequately translating such language is obvious. The speaker was often obliged to say the opposite of what was really meant. True meaning was embedded in the use of reverential language. Stripped of these nuances in translation, and distorted through the filter of multiple interpreters (the Aguilar-Malintzin system), not only was it unlikely that a speech such as Montezuma's would be accurately understood, but it was probable that its meaning would be turned upside down. In that case, Montezuma's speech was not his surrender; it was his acceptance of a Spanish surrender.

Walk with me through the streets of Tenochtitlan, simultaneously through the city on the day of the Meeting, across the Mexico City of the midcolonial period, and into today's downtown. Our stroll will cover a singular piece of ground, as we visit four locations on what was, for thousands of years, a small island on a spectacular lake. But it requires going back in time while remaining in the present—something we do all the time, whenever we watch historical dramas, read historical novels, or travel to places where the layers of the human past are still visible in the present.

We enter Tenochtitlan from the south, as the invaders did on November 8, 1519 (our entry point and walk through the city are marked with an arrow on the 1692 map that is "Mexico City Idealized" in the Gallery). What was the edge of the city in 1519 had become, by the seventeenth century, a small plaza several blocks in from the lake. The precise spot where Cortés attempted to embrace Montezuma has been hotly debated, but there are really only two candidates, and they are a short block apart. The first, near a diagonal canal in the *biombo* map, is today still a small plaza, but now also a bustling city intersection, below which is a subway station, and the remains of a small Aztec temple—underground but visible through an opening in the plaza. All around is the color and movement, smell and din, of modern Mexico City. The Aztec past is there, but buried, literally, belowground.[14]

The other Meeting site is just a stone's throw away, and in fact the short block between the two locations probably accommodated the two hundred or so Spaniards who stood there on November 8. To mark the spot, Cortés built a chapel, attached to a hospital for Spanish settlers. Known for centuries as the Hospital de Jesús (introduced earlier), the original structure still exists and still functions as a medical center—the oldest hospital in continuous use in the Americas. Sigüenza y Góngora called his book on the Hospital de Jesús—published in 1663 when it was called the Hospital de la Immaculada Concepción de Nuestra Señora—the *Piedad Heroyca de Don Fernando Cortés*. "Cortés's Heroic Piety": as if all the medical good works done by generations of hospital staff reflected back on the conquistador as the institution's founder, just as the saving of Mexican souls was to the credit of the captain who led the Conquest company, both enterprises representing a healing of some kind.[15]

But that was three and a half centuries ago. Today, "no street, no statue, no city, just a few places that mark his journey (the Sea of Cortés in California, the Pass of Cortés between the volcanoes, the Palace of Cortés in Cuernavaca) dare to mention the cursed name" (as Krauze has put it). The Hospital de Jesús is now a tribute to Cortés and his "Conquest of Mexico" only in a surreptitious, almost apologetic way. The ancient hospital is wrapped in a mid-twentieth century extension, its historical core invisible from the main street. Cortés's bones are hidden in the chapel, in an unmarked location separate from the unobtrusive brass plaque on an inside wall. A copy of the small bust made for the 1794 mausoleum is set up between the two sixteenth-century interior courtyards, near a modern mural of the Meeting; but they are seldom visited in the dark and secluded space, transparent to the hospital staff going about their daily business. Finally, there is the three-quarter-length oil-painted portrait of Cortés, often reproduced (and introduced earlier). It hangs in a beautiful, colonial-era room with period furnishings and other Cortesian portraits. But the room is a private, locked office.[16]

The room's seclusion is of course what makes it worth visiting. It has been preserved for its own sake, not as a tourist attraction, and it therefore acts as a portal to the sixteenth century—one that contrasts strikingly to the time portal of the submerged Aztec temple a block away. But the room evokes the past in another, more surprising way. For among those who gained access to this room in ages past were the senior officers of the foreign army that occupied the city in 1847. One of them, General William Jenkins Worth, was so struck by the Cortés portrait that he had a copy made and delivered as a gift to the First Lady of the United States. So the story goes; I suspect that Worth stole a colonial-period original. But whether it was a respectful copy, or war loot, the painting hung in the White House for the remaining months of the Polk administration, and in 1849 Sarah Childress Polk took it with her to the Polks' Nashville mansion. There it was displayed prominently in the front hall, a reminder that the acquisition of half of Mexican territory, resulting from her late husband's "Mexican war," was (in her words) "among the most important events in the history of this country" (on the day she hung the painting, she heard of Worth's death from the cholera epidemic that a month later killed her husband too). After Sarah Childress Polk died in 1891, the painting remained part of the Polk estate, and it can be seen today in the President Polk Home and Museum in Columbia, Tennessee.[17]

On the exterior, fortresslike wall of that secluded room in the Hospital de Jesús, out in the busy street, there was until recently a concrete plaque to commemorate the location of the Meeting. Its crumbling surface, with its message periodically rewritten by vandals, is long gone (but captured as the closing image in our Gallery). The applicability of the term *genocide* to the Spanish-Aztec War is debatable (as suggested earlier)—but debatable in both senses of the word: questionable, yet also worth debating for as long as the war remains disguised behind the old narratives of the "Conquest of Mexico." For as we are attempting here to view specific spots in

Tenochtitlan/Mexico City at multiple moments in time, let us imagine what the early conquistador-settlers might have made of that recent graffito—"Genocide / Long Live Tenochtitlan!"—on the walls of the hospital chapel. I suspect that of all the historical details just mentioned—the half-millennium persistence of the hospital, the periodic disputes over Cortés's bones, the U.S. invasion and military occupation of Mexico City, the Worth copy of the Cortés portrait still hanging in Tennessee—the detail that would have been *least* surprising to the conquistadors would have been that plaque and its graffiti. Explanations would have been required (*genocide* would not exist in any language for centuries; the city was still Tenochtitlan, or "Temixtitan," to Spaniards as well as Nahuas into the 1530s, and Tenochtitlan to Nahuas for centuries). But an act of protest or rebellion would not have surprised them; they would have assumed that it was carried out by the descendants of the people against whom they had waged a brutal war of slaughter and enslavement.[18]

IF THE DUAL SPOT of the Meeting is a provocative reminder of how the "Conquest of Mexico" is both distant history and an unresolved problem of the present, the same is true of the *zócalo,* as the city's massive central plaza became known. It was, and is, a few blocks' walk to that plaza from the plaque marking the Meeting (on our map, we enter the plaza from its top, right corner). Those exact same blocks were walked by the conquistadors—and the Taínos and Totonacs and Nahuas and Africans who came with them, led by their Aztec hosts—that November morning in 1519. As they entered the Aztec plaza, to their left stood the palace of Axayacatl (where the Caxtilteca would spend the next five months), and to their right, Montezuma's palace. On that site, Cortés would build his own palace, but it was soon appropriated by the Crown and became the palace of viceregal government. Rebuilt many times (it was largely destroyed in the riot of 1692, within months of the painting of the map that is guiding our walk; would that act of rebellion by the descendants of Tenochtitlan's defenders have surprised the conquistadors?), it is now the Mexican republic's Palacio Nacional.[19]

That corner of the *zócalo* is also one of the ways whereby U.S. troops entered the city's center on September 14, 1847—as conscious then as they had been throughout their march from Veracruz that they were walking in the footsteps of the conquistadors. Here, at last, were "the halls of the Montezumas."

In George Wilkins Kendall's classic account of the war between Mexico and the United States, published within a few years of the conflict and influential for many decades after it, his description of General Winfield Scott's "Entrance into the City of Mexico" was accompanied by a Carl Nebel lithograph of the *zócalo*. This now-famous image was a virtual copy of an earlier lithograph by Nebel, only with the stunning addition of U.S. troops filling much of the plaza. Kendall did not explicitly draw the parallel to the last time a foreign invasion force entered the city's central plaza, but he hardly needed to do so. Likewise, the tenor of his depiction of responses by the city's residents to the surrender and U.S. occupation echoed Spanish accounts of the Aztec uprising following Montezuma's supposed surrender (and, again, would not have surprised the conquistadors of the 1520s). Kendall was indignant that despite Mexican capitulation and the raising of "the American flag" on the presidential palace, the "dastardly inhabitants," particularly the city's "lowest scum" and its thousands of "idle yet able-bodied vagrants," engaged in "treacherous" and "cowardly" hostilities. Regardless of the legitimacy of the original invasion—indeed, eclipsing the very question— the flight of Santa Anna and the surrender speech of Montezuma validated and legalized the Spanish presence in the city in 1519 and the U.S. presence there in 1847. The Halls of Montezuma had been taken. Subsequent local resistance was illegitimate revolt.[20]

The connection between the two invasions was made explicit in Lewis Foulk Thomas's play *Cortez, the Conqueror*. This "Tragedy, in Five Acts" (which was "also prepared as a Dramatic Equestrian Spectacle"), published in 1857, was dedicated to John A. Quitman, the Mississippi general and congressman who showed "high chivalry" in "the late war between our country and Mexico." The play was inscribed to the general, wrote Thomas, because its plot was "founded on events of old occurrence on the same fields where you so lately and so largely contributed to render the name of our country and your own, illustrious." A scene in the play's middle featured four conquistadors eating and drinking one night in a house in "Cho-hula." Raising their glasses to the impending march to victory, their dialogue (quoted at the top of this Epilogue) ended with the "Halls of the Montezumas!" toast. In a note, the playwright admitted that the phrase was "an anachronism," and that "the words were uttered on a memorable occasion, by the hero of San Jacinto," General Sam Houston, "who, in a spirit of prophesy, foretold and pointed the path of our countrymen to 'the Halls of the Montezumas.'"[21]

The phrase persisted through to the twentieth century, during the decades that Prescott's *Conquest of Mexico* was read by generation after generation of English-speakers, while U.S. expansionism took troops to territories that had been or still were Spanish colonies—from the Philippines to the Caribbean to Central America; and back to Mexico, with the occupation of Veracruz by the U.S. Navy and Marines in 1914. A few years later, the new battle hymn of the Marine Corps was written with the opening lines "From the Halls of Montezuma, / To the shores of Tripoli, / We fight our country's battles, / On the land and on the sea." Since then, the phrase's specific reference has become lost in a more general association (used, for example, as the title of a 1951 movie about the Corps fighting on a Japanese island in World War II, and the name of a 1990 video game featuring the "battle history" of the Marines).[22]

Arguably, it is not important whether the phrase accurately evokes the invasion wars of 1519–21 or 1546–49. Like "Genocidio / Viva Tenochtitlan!" the phrase acts as an icon, calling up images and ideas relevant to the present. Such words are not intended to be a key to unlock the truths of the past, and that places them firmly within the long tradition of writing, singing, engraving, and otherwise appropriating and representing the "Conquest of Mexico." The Mexican-American War is both "the forgotten war" and one of the United States' most controversial, because its justification remains elusive. As long as Mexico and the United States exist as nation-

states, that war will not go away; just as the Spanish "Conquest of
Mexico" will not go away as long as the descendants of Spaniards
and Aztecs and other Mesoamericans live together in the lands once
ruled by Montezuma.[23]

Thus to stand in the *zócalo* of Tenochtitlan/Mexico City and to
contemplate the layers of history that are both invisible and visible (from the exposed foundations of the Aztec Great Temple, to the
sequence of imperial, viceregal, and national palaces, to the massive
open space where people have paraded and protested, danced and
died) is to surround oneself with ghosts. The great plaza is a place
of cosmic resonance, a magnet for centuries of festivals and fights,
of celebrations and conflicts. There are specters here; Mesoamerican
and Aztec, Spanish and African, Mexican and American.

Now stand at the foot of the Great Temple and mentally walk
due west out to Montezuma's zoo. This requires imagination, as the
Great Temple is an archaeological site, and the skull racks and other
Aztec structures through which one would walk have long been
razed or buried beneath the cathedral (what's more, there are no
signs pointing the way to the zoo). But by walking around the front
of the cathedral, one can exit the *zócalo* from a street at its lower
middle (marked in the 1692 map by a stone fountain, long since
removed). Walk straight ahead along a street that in Aztec times
led to the zoo, in colonial times was called Calle San Francisco, and
today is a pedestrianized shopping street. At that street's end is one
of those Mexico City corners about which a book could be written.
But our focus is, first, just one of the buildings that we can see today
from that corner. In the 1692 map, we are at the edge of the small
park nestled beside the Aztec-Spanish aqueduct and the convent of
Santa Isabel. Both aqueduct and convent are long gone, but on the
convent's site now sits the Palacio de Bellas Artes.

In this beautiful theater—built between 1904 and 1934, and featuring an Art Deco interior and murals by the pantheon of Orozco,
Rivera, Siqueiros, and Tamayo—Antonio Vivaldi's opera *Motezuma*
was recently performed. The performance was noteworthy for several
reasons. To start with, this was the first time the opera had ever been

sung in the land of the Montezumas. Although the libretto of the
opera had survived since Vivaldi's day (it was published in 1733), the
music was lost for centuries. The score was only discovered in 2002 in
a library in Berlin (after the library's contents, looted in World War II
and deposited in Kiev, were returned to Germany). Following a legal
dispute over the library's rights to charge for performances, the score
was made public in 2005; the Bellas Artes debut was in 2007.

For the Mexican performance, the libretto and its newly redis-
covered score were altered to fit the time and place. Some phrases
in Nahuatl were added, and some pre-Columbian instruments were
included. The Mexican violinist Samuel Máynez Champion, in con-
sultation with the venerable Mexican historians Alfredo López Austin and Miguel León-Portilla, made plot adjustments, muting the
original opera's happy ending with a reminder to audiences of Montezuma's tragic death. Máynez felt that the original libretto, based
on Solís's *Historia de la Conquista* and with "an invented and very
trivial romance" plot, was "hog-wash, absurd, and tragicomic farce."
In fact, Tenochtitlan in 1520 was no more than an exotic backdrop
to the use by Vivaldi and Giusti (the librettist) of a romantic-comedy
plot that was conventional to opera (as it is in Hollywood movies).
That plot—absurd indeed—focused on a pair of fictional lovers, a
brother of Cortés's named Ramiro, and a daughter of Montezuma's
named Teutile. Montezuma opposes the romance, but his wife in-
tervenes, permitting a final matching of the lovers—despite their
mismatched identities and the Conquest context.[24]

The opera was written in Venice in an effort to improve Vivaldi's
financial state. It did not much help; he died eight years later a pauper
in Vienna. But in retrospect the composer's choice of topic and his
invention of a love story to "cast some sweetness onto the bloody triumphs of the conqueror of Mexico"—to borrow a line from the caption to one of Maurin's lithographs of a century later—anticipated
the flurry of attention to Cortés and Montezuma during the era of
Romanticism. Vivaldi's opera was not just a link in the long chain of
(often absurd) dramatizations of the Spanish-Aztec encounter, from
The Indian Emperour to *Captain from Castile*; it was a link in the

greater chain of the appropriation, distortion, and invention of the Meeting and the events surrounding it.

The twenty-first-century revival of *Motezuma*, which has now been staged in cities across Europe and the Americas, and the Mexican reaction to its plot, reminds us that the "Conquest of Mexico" has never ceased to be a topic of entertainment, debate, celebration, and conflict. Furthermore, this has been because its story and its appropriation is so often about something else—about reviving a career (Vivaldi in 1733) or saving a library (the legal dispute of 2002–05) or indulging in a fantasy that European colonial expansion was about romance, or at least a fitting setting for romance, with happy endings that might act as metaphors for civilization's joyful triumph over barbarism.

THERE IS STILL ONE final stop on our time travel of a walk in this extraordinary city—as if Vivaldi's *Motezuma* being sung, with Nahuatl phrases added, in the Art Deco theater where the Aztec-Spanish aqueduct once poured fresh water into Tenochtitlan was not mind-boggling enough. Step out of the Palacio de Bellas Artes and walk across lanes of traffic to the immediate southwest; in the 1692 map, one steps out of the convent of Santa Isabel and across the street into the complex of buildings and gardens that was the convent of San Francisco (hence the old name of the street).

In the 1520s, when the new Tenochtitlan, eventually to be called the city of Mexico, emerged phoenixlike from the old capital's rubble, Spaniards and Nahuas claimed or returned to city blocks between streets and canals to build homes. One group of new settlers were the Franciscan friars, preaching poverty but armed with sufficient wealth and power to claim a large section of the city upon which to construct their church and convent. Equivalent to four city blocks, with access to fresh water, the canals, and the lake, the massive plot was the site of much of Montezuma's old zoo complex.[25]

Where the emperor's gardeners and zookeepers had tended plants and birds, the indigenous slaves of the friars maintained an orchard and gardens, chicken coops and fishponds. Where Montezuma had studied the natural world, Franciscans pondered how to obliterate all memory of Montezuma's world. Gradually, the ghosts of the zoo beneath the convent faded. And then the convent itself shrank and faded—walls and buildings razed, plots sold or stolen, a city street carved through its heart in the nineteenth century, and in the next century a skyscraper raised in one corner. The Torre Latinoamericana, once the tallest building in Latin America, still offers a panoramic view of the city to visitors—for whom Montezuma, his zoo, his empire, and the reasons for their passing are buried as deep into Tenochtitlan's bedrock as the skyscraper's foundations.

Acknowledgments

———— ♠ ————

MOST BOOKS ARE MADE POSSIBLE BY A HOST OF HELPING HANDS, and this one is no exception. Numerous authors and students, scholars and librarians, colleagues and friends, audience members with challenging questions and email correspondents with interesting observations—you have all made crucial contributions. My apologies go to those of you who did not make it, simply through oversight on my part, onto this page or into the notes.

This book's sources are translated from Nahuatl, Spanish, French, Italian, German, and Latin. All translations are by me, unless otherwise stated; however, as I do not claim full fluency in all those tongues, I have benefited from the assistance of various colleagues, who are thanked individually in the relevant notes. Their help is illustrative of how myriad moments of generosity allow a project like this to reach completion.

Three decades ago, when I was an undergraduate at Oxford University, I took a seminar offered by a brilliant young scholar on the Conquest of Mexico. I was introduced to Cortés's Letters to the King in a way that planted the seed of my future career and—it now turns out—this book. That scholar was Felipe Fernández-Armesto. This is a lesser book than Felipe would have written on the topic, but it is nonetheless infused with his influence. I will always be grateful to him.

During the years that this book developed, while reading the work of many scores of scholars, I found myself turning repeatedly to a relatively small group who have all produced multiple books and articles over decades. They deserve specific mention for influencing my thinking through at least half a dozen, and in some cases over a dozen, publications each (not all included in the Bibliography): Rolena Adorno, Elizabeth Hill Boone, Davíd Carrasco, Inga Clendinnen, J. H. Elliott, Felipe Fernández-Armesto again, Ross Hassig, James Lockhart, José Luis Martínez, Eduardo Matos Moctezuma, Barbara Mundy, Susan Schroeder, and Hugh Thomas.

Many friends and colleagues were exceedingly generous with their time and thought, reading various drafts, sections, and earlier versions of the book. I am deeply grateful to all of them. They include Felipe yet again, Susan Evans, Miguel Martínez, John Fritz Schwaller, Stuart Schwartz, Peter Villella, and Louis Warren; in particular, Richard Conway, Kris Lane, Denise Oswald, Robin Restall, Amara Solari, and Linda Williams gave many hours of their time and many pages of feedback, providing invaluable encouragement and insightful comments that influenced and improved the book in manifold ways. The project was also fueled through countless conversations and correspondences with Daniel Brunstetter, María Castañeda de la Paz, James Collins, Garrett Fagan (conversations and classroom discussions over many years with Garrett were particularly encouraging and influential), Martha Few, Michael Francis, Jorge Gamboa, Enrique Gomáriz, Amy Greenberg, Ken Hirth, Ronnie Hsia, Mark Koschny, Enrique Krauze, Andrew Laird, Domingo Ledesma, Mark Lentz, Russ Lohse, Andrea Martínez, Iris Montero, Ian Mursell, Linda Newson, David Orique, David Orr, Michel Oudijk, Emma Restall, Kathryn Sampeck, Stuart Schwartz, Tatiana Seijas, Emily Solari, Ian Spradlin, Mark Thurner, Peter Villella, David Webster, Caroline Williams, and many others whom I have shamefully forgotten to list; and also with some of the doctoral students with whom I have worked at Penn State—and who have blessed me in so many ways—Samantha Billing, Jana Byars, Laurent Cases, Scott Cave, Mark Christensen, Spencer Delbridge, Scott Doebler, Jake Frederick, Kate Godfrey, Gerardo Gutiérrez, María Inclán, Emily Kate, Rebekah Martin, Megan McDonie, Ed Osowski, Robert Schwaller, Michael Tuttle, and Christopher Valesey.

Similarly, the book would not be what it is, if it existed at all, without my tirelessly professional yet limitlessly amiable agent, Geri Thoma (of Writers House), and my extraordinarily talented and tactful editor, Denise Oswald (of Ecco and HarperCollins), as well as Emma Janaskie and her colleagues at Ecco. My amateur designs for the diagrams and maps were transformed by the skills of professionals at the press, and by my colleagues Larry Gorenflo and Janet Purdy.

The book was also made possible by the amazing professionals of the John Carter Brown Library (especially, in 2013–14, Valerie Andrews, Adelina Axelrod, Susan Danforth, Dennis Landis, John Minichiello, Susan Newbury, Maureen O'Donnell, Kim Nusco, Allison Rich, Neil Safier, and Ken Ward); by archive and library professionals such as Angelica Illueca and the staff of the Sutro Library in San Francisco, Gary Kurutz and the staff of the California State Library in Sacramento, Marcia Tucker and her colleagues at the Institute for Advanced Study, Princeton, and the dozens of professionals at the AGI, AGN, BL, BnF, and MQB (spelled out at the start of the Bibliography) who have helped me over the last decade. Likewise I am grateful to Arthur Dunkelman and the Kislak Foundation, to Chuck diGiacomantonio and the U.S. Capitol Historical Society, and to Tom Price and the Polk Home and Museum. I also thank all those audience members of talks given between 2013 and 2017 on the project at the colleges or universities of Brown, George Washington, Irvine, London, Princeton, Utah Valley, Vanderbilt, and Yale, as well as those of Bogotá: your comments and questions helped guide the book in numerous ways.

I am blessed with loving parents, parents-in-law, and daughters (Clifford, Judy, Kathy, Mariela, and Robin; Sophie, Isabel, and Lucy), whose apparent faith that what I do matters (a dubious proposition) is more uplifting than they can imagine. The girls have long been my muses, and their baby sister, Catalina, has inspired this book in ways I cannot begin to express.

It is rightfully customary to thank the spouse or partner who has endured living with the author during the writing process. In this case, Amara deserves not only gratitude for her endurance and tolerance, but also credit for the innumerable ways in which she contributed to the project's intellectual development and final fruition. As well as being the graceful author of my personal happiness, she is in effect the gracious and brilliant coauthor of this book.

STATE COLLEGE, PENNSYLVANIA

SPRING 2017

———— ⚜ ————

Language and Label, Cast and Dynasty

THE DIAGRAM BELOW REPRESENTS THE OVERLAPPING MEANINGS OF the terms *Aztec, Mexica,* and *Nahuas. Aztec* seems to have been an eighteenth-century invention. *Mexica* (pronounced "mesh-EE-ka") refers to the people of the city of Tenochtitlan or Mexico (in Nahuatl, *-co* is a locative, so that *Mexico* means "the place of the Mexica"). Note that the Mexica were not a distinct ethnicity; they were part of the larger (and very much still surviving) ethnic group of the Nahuas (pronounced "NA-wahs"), whose language was (and is) Nahuatl, and who have for many centuries lived throughout central Mexico and in some regions to the south.

Mesoamerica is the name that scholars have given to the greater civilizational area that stretched from northern Mexico into Central America, comprising the Nahuas, the Mayas, and scores of other ethnic groups. Thus I sometimes refer to Mesoamericans, avoiding the problematic term *Indian* (unless translating *indio,* as Spaniards tended to call all indigenous peoples; because the Americas were initially thought to be close to Asia, Spaniards called them *las Indias,* "the Indies," and their people *indios*—names which stuck).

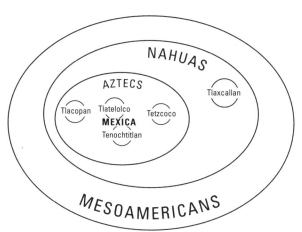

Mesoamericans did not call themselves Nahuas or Mayas or any of the other ethnic group names we use. Nor did the Aztecs have a term that translates tidily as "Aztec Empire." The Mesoamerican sense of identity was highly localized, tied to the city-state (in Nahuatl, the *altepetl*). Even the term *Mexica* was often applied specifically to those from the southern, dominant part of Tenochtitlan—people also called Tenochca, as opposed to the Tlatelolca of the smaller part, Tlatelolco. The closest that Nahuas came to using a phrase of group self-identity was *nican tlaca*, "here people" (or *i nican titlaca*, "we people here"). Outsiders—ranging from other Nahuas subject to the Aztecs to unconquered groups such as the Mayas—called the Aztecs *Culua* or *Culhúa*. This was a reference to the *altepetl* of Culhuacan, just south of Tenochtitlan (and today part of Mexico City); in Mesoamerican folk history, this seems to have been the town where the Aztecs settled before founding Tenochtitlan. But it also may have been because the people of Tetzcoco's regions of the Aztec Empire called themselves *Acolhua*.[1]

As you can see, the more one explains, the more complex the topic becomes. Bear in mind, then, that *Aztec* and other terms are familiar shorthand for a complex identity history.

The same is true of the names *Montezuma* and *Moctezuma*. As mentioned in the Preface, although they are the most common modern forms for the name, Spaniards and other Europeans used them as early as the sixteenth century. Various other renderings used in early sources, such as *Muteeçuma*, are reproduced in my translations. The emperor's real name was *Moteuctzoma*, which in his own day would never have been uttered without the *-tzin* suffix to make it reverential: *Moteuctzomatzin* ("moh-teh-ook-tsoh-mah-tseen"). After his death he began to be referenced with a second name, *Xocoyotl*, using the reverential form *Xocoyotzin* (pronounced "shock-oy-ott-seen," and meaning "the Younger," as another emperor named Moteuctzoma had ruled in the fifteenth century). It is not clear how often, if at all, the name Xocoyotzin was used in Montezuma's lifetime.

Montezuma is one of the sixteen Spanish and Nahua protagonists in the history of the Spanish-Aztec War who are mentioned most often in this book. Here are their brief biographies:[2]

Pedro de **Alvarado** was born in 1485 and settled in the Indies in the 1510s. A captain on the Grijalva and Cortés expeditions to Mexico, he remained a loyalist of the Cortesian faction, along with his four brothers (Gonzalo, Gómez, Jorge, and Juan). Together, the Alvarados were a formidable cohort, wielding more authority and making more decisions than has generally been recognized. Pedro was and is generally assumed to be responsible for the 1520 Toxcatl Massacre in Tenochtitlan. I do not dispute his reputation for cruelty; on the contrary, in that regard he was typical, not exceptional, among those conquistadors who survived the Spanish-Aztec War (1519–21). He led one of the three Spanish siege forces in 1521, and later led expeditions to highland Guatemala and northern Peru. He was granted a coat of arms. He died battling the Mixton Revolt north of central Mexico in 1541.

Cacamatzin and **Coanacochtzin** were two of the many sons of Nezahualpilli, the *tlahtoani* (king) of Tetzcoco; along with Ixtlilxochitl, they were the chief claimants to the throne when their father died in 1515 (see the Dynastic Vine). As Cacama (the *-tzin* is a reverential suffix) had the support of his uncle, Montezuma, he was confirmed in office. He met the Cortés-led conquistador company at the edge of the Valley of Mexico in November 1519 and led them to the Meeting (as it is termed in this book) in Tenochtitlan. Later caught up in the political machinations surrounding the Phoney Captivity (see Chapter 6)—Spaniards claimed he plotted against them and his uncle—he was murdered in June 1520 along with the other two Triple Alliance *tlahtoque* (Aztec imperial kings). Coanacoch succeeded him to the throne of Tetzcoco, but when his brother Ixtlilxochitl and the Spaniards marched into the city on the last day of 1520, Coanacoch fled to Tenochtitlan. Ixtlilxochitl captured him there during the siege and replaced him as ruler of Tetzcoco. In 1525, on Cortés's orders in a Maya town, Coanacoch was hanged, along with Cuauhtemoc and the captive ruler of Tlacopan—a repetition of the 1520 group murder of the triple *tlahtoque*.

Hernando **Cortés** was born in Medellín, Spain, c. 1485, and im-
migrated to Hispaniola in 1504 or 1506. He became the iconic conquistador, as much a legend and myth as a historical figure. As lead
captain of the third expedition to Mexico, he has been hailed for
five centuries as the heroic and brilliant creator of the "Conquest of
Mexico." He has also been called a slaver, assassin, uxoricide, mass
murderer, traitor, embezzler, and thief. I argue here that he was unexceptional in either regard, as leader or war criminal. He served
as the first captain-general and governor of New Spain but was removed from office in 1528 and did not again hold a senior administrative post in Mexico. Elevated to the high nobility as Marqués del
Valle in 1529, he ran his vast estates (staffed by indigenous slaves)
and fought lawsuits in Mexico from 1530 to 1540, before returning
to Spain and dying there in 1547.

Cuauhtemoc, more properly Cuauhtemoctzin, was born c. 1500
and thus was young when he became *huey tlahtoani* of Tenochtitlan, emperor of the Aztecs, in January or February 1521, following
the death (probably from smallpox) in December of Cuitlahua—his
predecessor, cousin, and a brother of Montezuma's (see the Dynastic
Vine). Because Tetzcoco, the second-ranked city-state in the empire's Triple Alliance, had switched to join the Spanish-Tlaxcalteca
alliance at the end of 1520, Cuauhtemoc was only ruler of a rump
empire. He led the Mexica for a seven-month defense of the capital city, surrendering on August 13. Cortés and Julián de Alderete
tortured the captive emperor by burning his feet, in order to discover where the *tlahtoani* had hid the imperial treasure. Taken on
the Cortés-led expedition to Honduras in 1524, he was implicated in
an alleged plot of the surviving *tlahtoque* of the old Triple Alliance;
all three captive kings were hanged in the Maya town of Acalan-
Tixchel. The fraudulent discovery of his bones in a village church in
the state of Guerrero in 1949 caused lasting controversy in Mexico,
where he has since been increasingly lauded as a national hero (to
Montezuma's expense).

Ixtlilxochitl, another of Nezahualpilli's sons, refused to accept
the Montezuma-backed appointment of his brother Cacamatzin as

tlahtoani of Tetzcoco in 1515 (see the Dynastic Vine). He became de facto ruler of Tetzcoco in 1521, baptized don Fernando Cortés Ixtlilxochitl, becoming confirmed as *tlahtoani* and *gobernador* some time in the early 1520s, ruling until his death in 1531. In accounts of the war written by his great-great-grandson, don Fernando de Alva Ixtlilxochitl, he plays a crucial leadership role both in the 1521 campaign to capture Tenochtitlan and in subsequent expeditions in Mesoamerica.

Malintzin was given to the Spanish company by the Maya rulers of Potonchan in 1519, while still a slave in her early teens. Because she was a Nahua who had been living among Mayas, she spoke both Nahuatl and Yucatec Mayan, and thus served as one of the interpreters used by the Spaniards; by the end of the war, she was the principal interpreter, given the honorific *doña* or *-tzin*. In 1522 she gave birth to a son, fathered by Cortés, named Martín (taken by his father to Spain in 1528, where he grew up as a page to Prince Philip). Little is known of her life before 1519 or after 1522. In the nineteenth and twentieth centuries she was appropriated by multiple cultural and intellectual movements—from Romanticism to the (Mexican) Revolution to second- and third-wave feminism—to create a complex "Malinche" mythology that is remote from the historical Malintzin. (Her name is explained in the Preface.)

Montezuma was born in 1468, the son of Axayacatl, and became *huey tlahtoani* of the Aztec Empire in 1502 (the ninth *tlahtoani* of Tenochtitlan). He ruled until his death at the end of June 1520, when war broke out in his capital city—he was either assassinated by his own subjects or (more likely) murdered by conquistadors. The evidence suggests that he was a strong, expansionist emperor, despite the evolution after his death of a contrary reputation whereby he was made a scapegoat for Aztec defeat. My argument that Montezuma did not surrender to the Spaniards, despite their claim, is central to this book. His surviving children and their descendants played core roles in the rule of Tenochtitlan and central Mexico after the war (see the Dynastic Vine). (His name is explained above.)

Pánfilo de **Narváez** was a tall, redheaded nobleman from a small town near Cuéllar who settled on Hispaniola around 1498. He played leading roles in the Spanish conquest campaigns on Jamaica and Cuba. In the latter, he was responsible for a massacre of Taíno villagers, condemned by the famous Dominican friar Bartolomé de Las Casas, who wrote that Narváez acted "as if made of marble" in the face of atrocity. He is best known for two failures (which, arguably, make him a typical conquistador). First, in 1520, on behalf of his longtime ally Diego de Velázquez, he led 1,100 men to Mexico to arrest Cortés and assume command of the conquistadors there; instead his men joined the Cortés-led company, and a month later most of them were killed by Aztecs. Second, in 1527 he led a company to the northern Gulf coast of Mexico, ending up accidentally in Florida; only Álvaro Cabeza de Vaca and three or four others (Narváez not among them) lived to tell the tale.

Cristóbal de **Olid**, born in Baeza in 1488, landed in Cuba in 1518 in time to join the Cortés-led company to Mexico, where he fought and survived the entire war. He was not a man of subtlety: he liked to wade, wielding his sword, into indigenous warriors and crowds ("a Hector" of hand-to-hand combat, said Bernal Díaz); his shifts between Cortesian and *Velazquista* factions were clumsy and, eventually, the death of him. One of the chief captains of the Vera Cruz plot, he was a councilman (*regidor*) for the imaginary town; then in 1521 he was caught plotting with Julián de Alderete (the man apparently behind the torture of Cuauhtemoc) to assassinate Cortés; he then fought in Michoacán, before leading a conquest expedition to Honduras—ostensibly in Cortés's name—but he stopped in Cuba en route to plot with Velázquez, resulting in two Cortés loyalists disemboweling him in Honduras in 1524.

Diego de **Ordaz**, a native of León, landed in the Indies in 1510, already thirty-two years old, tall, and brave (said Díaz), with a short black beard and a slight stammer. He joined various companies, including those to Cuba and Mexico—where he was a leading captain. A loyal *Velazquista* through the early weeks of plotting on the Gulf coast, once he saw which way the wind was blowing he permanently joined the Cortés faction (although in letters to his nephew he was candidly critical, most famously remarking that "the marquis has no more of a conscience than a dog"). He climbed Popocatepetl during the 1519 march to Tenochtitlan, claiming to come within two lances' length of the volcano's rim; his coat of arms thus featured a volcano design. He played a lead role in the Tepeaca campaign and massacre, holding official posts there through the 1520s. He missed the siege, spending a year starting October 1520 in Spain. He was there twice more (while receiving income from tens of thousands of indigenous Mexicans), until receiving in 1530 royal license to conquer the Orinoco River region—where the local environment and people gave him no less trouble than Spanish rivals, one of whom probably fatally poisoned him en route to Spain in 1532.

Gonzalo de **Sandoval** was from Cortés's hometown of Medellín. He was (according to Díaz) stocky, with chestnut hair and beard, a slight lisp, and a reputation as a fine horseman. Despite his youth, he emerged from the Vera Cruz politicking as one of the dominant captains: he was one of the four councilmen (*regidors*) of that imaginary town; he was primarily responsible for winning over the Narváez company in 1520; and he played a (arguably, the) leading role in coordinating with the Tlaxcalteca and Tetzcoca forces in the 1521 campaign to take Tenochtitlan. Although he seemed to have diplomatic rapport with Ixtlilxochitl and other Nahua leaders, he was a plunderer and enslaver like his fellow conquistadors, involved in the massacres around Tepeaca and on the 1523 Huastec campaign (which he commanded). He accompanied Cortés to Honduras in 1524–26, and then to Spain in 1528—falling ill on the voyage and dying upon arrival.

Tecuichpochtzin, aka doña Isabel Moctezuma Tecuichpo (see the Dynastic Vine), was Montezuma's most important daughter, by virtue of her royal lineage on her mother's side and her survival of the war. Supposedly "offered" to Cortés by Montezuma during the months of the Phoney Captivity (see Chapter 8) but rejected (presumably because she was still a child), she remained in Tenochtitlan after the Noche Triste; there she was betrothed to Cuitlahua and, after his death, Cuauhtemoc. Surviving the war, she married three conquistadors in succession: Alonso de Grado, Pedro Gallego, and Juan Cano. Meanwhile, Cortés impregnated her (while she was married to Gallego, according to Vásquez de Tapia); their daughter, Leonor, born in 1523, married a Spaniard. Tecuichpochtzin was given Tlacopan, of the Aztec Empire's Triple Alliance, in *encomienda* (a Spanish kind of lordship giving broad access to labor and tribute payments) and confirmed in many other privileges and properties related to her royal inheritance. She had five children by Cano, who vigorously defended her estates in the courts. She died in 1551.

Bernardino **Vásquez de Tapia** was born into a well-connected family in the Oropesa region of Castile. In his late teens he was with Pedrarias de Ávila in what is now Panama, and with Diego Velázquez in the invasion of Cuba. He held the important office of *alférez real* (royal ensign) on the Grijalva expedition, was a leading captain in the Spanish-Aztec War, and was a core pro-Cortés plotter—serving as councilman (*regidor*) of Vera Cruz in 1519. He survived the war to serve as a *regidor* of Mexico City—eventually a life appointment, until his death in 1559. He received lucrative Nahua towns in *encomienda,* including Huitzilopochco (Churubusco), and part of Tlaxcallan. In the 1520s he participated in campaigns into Pánuco and elsewhere, and twice returned to Spain; in Seville in 1527 he spent a short time in jail, due to an accusation by Cortés that he had withheld money. Thereafter he grew increasingly hostile to Cortés—and to Alvarado, whose cohort he had helped to lead in the war. Starting in 1529, he testified to excesses by both men, including cheating the Crown of its *quinto* (its 20 percent in taxes), illegally enslaving tens of thousands of indigenous women and children, and starting unprovoked massacres (by Alvarado during Toxcatl, and by Cortés at Chololan and Tepeaca). He is not to be confused with the many other Tapias (including Andrés de **Tapia**, a relative of Velázquez's who became an unswerving Cortés loyalist, giving oft-quoted hyperbolic pro-Cortés testimony and in 1539 writing his own account of the first half of the Spanish-Aztec War).

Diego **Velázquez** was born in 1465 and accompanied Columbus on his second voyage of 1493 to the New World. He rose to become the conqueror and then (de facto) governor of the island of Cuba, invaded and settled in 1511–14. He was the organizer and *adelantado* (holder of the conquest license) of increasingly large expeditions to the Mesoamerican mainland in 1517 (under Hernández de Córdoba), 1518 (under Grijalva), 1519 (under Cortés), and 1520 (under Narváez). His betrayal by the men of the 1519 and 1520 companies, and the political campaign by Cortés and his faction to secure governmental control in Mexico, fueled a bitter feud between Cortesian and *Velazquista* factions that outlasted Velázquez's death in 1524.

Xicotencatl was a young warrior captain and royal heir in Tlaxcallan in 1519 when the Spanish conquistadors first fought, and then came to terms with, his home city-state. His father, also Xicotencatl and a *tlahtoani* of Tlaxcallan, was a chief architect of the alliance with the Spaniards that allowed the Tlaxcalteca to expand their regional authority during the war of 1519–21. But Xicotencatl the son (or the Younger, or Axayacatl), despite playing an important role as a leader in the war, had doubts about the Faustian bargain with the foreigners, and in the spring of 1521 supposedly attempted to withdraw his men from the Spanish-Tetzcoco alliance; Cortés alleged a conspiracy, and Xicotencatl was hanged. More likely he was the victim of Tlaxcalteca factionalism. Viewed as a traitor in colonial sources, he is remembered today as a cultural hero in Tlaxcala and Mexico.

FOR ADDITIONAL INSIGHT INTO the kinship and marriage ties of the Aztec royal family in Tenochtitlan and Tetzcoco—and some of their ties to Spanish conquistadors and settlers—see the Dynastic Vine that follows.

This diagram presents the family trees of the royal families of Tenochtitlan (left, moving right) and Tetzcoco (right, moving left). It is designed to illustrate three phenomena central to the history of the Spanish-Aztec War and its aftermath: the extent of intermarriage between the two families, creating a single royal Aztec

dynasty; the persistence of that dynasty in the rulership of Tenochtitlan and Tetzcoco through the war and into the next century;
and the gradual insertion of Spanish men (indicated with a boxed
S) and women (a circled *S*) into the dynasty. Note that the "vine"
is not comprehensive (hundreds of spouses and children are not
included here).

THE DYNASTIC VINE

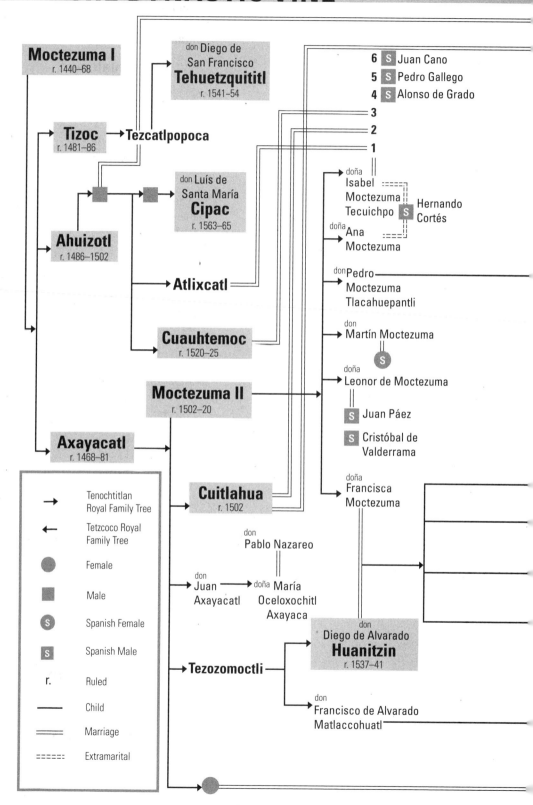

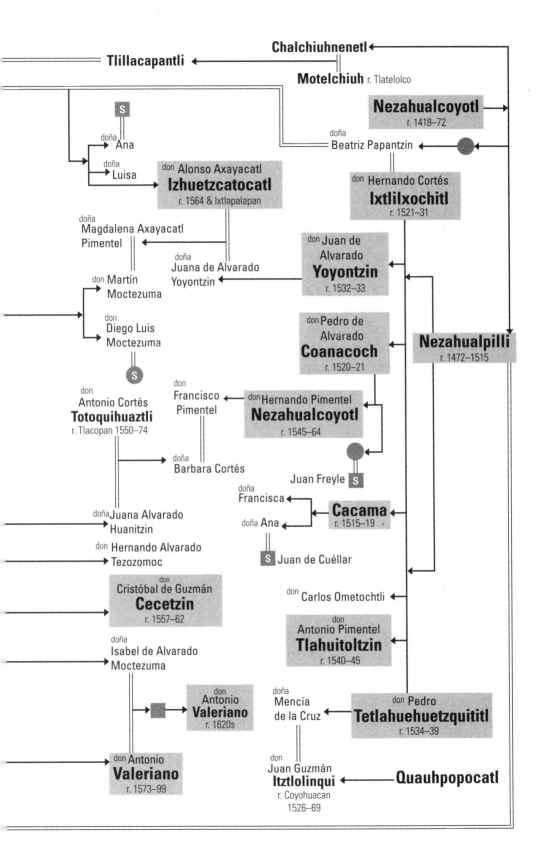

Chalchiuhnenetl

Tlillacapantli

Motelchiuh r. Tlatelolco

Nezahualcoyotl
r. 1418–72

S

doña
Ana

doña
Beatriz Papantzin

doña
Luisa

don Alonso Axayacatl
Izhuetzcatocatl
r. 1564 & Ixtlapalapan

don Hernando Cortés
Ixtlilxochitl
r. 1521–31

doña
Magdalena Axayacatl
Pimentel

doña
Juana de Alvarado
Yoyontzin

don Juan de
Alvarado
Yoyontzin
r. 1532–33

don Martín
Moctezuma

don
Diego Luis
Moctezuma

don Pedro de
Alvarado
Coanacoch
r. 1520–21

Nezahualpilli
r. 1472–1515

S

don
Antonio Cortés
Totoquihuaztli
r. Tlacopan 1550–74

don
Francisco
Pimentel

don Hernando Pimentel
Nezahualcoyotl
r. 1545–64

doña
Barbara Cortés

Juan Freyle **S**

doña
Francisca

doñaJuana Alvarado
Huanitzin

doña Ana

Cacama
r. 1515–19

don Hernando Alvarado
Tezozomoc

S Juan de Cuéllar

don
Cristóbal de Guzmán
Cecetzin
r. 1557–62

don Carlos Ometochtli

doña
Isabel de Alvarado
Moctezuma

don
Antonio Pimentel
Tlahuitoltzin
r. 1540–45

doña
Mencía
de la Cruz

don Pedro
Tetlahuehuetzquititl
r. 1534–39

don
Antonio
Valeriano
r. 1620s

don Antonio
Valeriano
r. 1573–99

don
Juan Guzmán
Itztlolinqui
r. Coyohuacan
1526–69

Quauhpopocatl

Notes

PREFACE

1. Solís (1724; preface and translation by Thomas Townsend).

PROLOGUE:
INVENTION

1. Epigraph sources, in sequence: Díaz (1632: unnumbered prefatory f. 4v); Dryden (1668 [1667]: unnumbered prefatory, p. 26); words spoken by Catherine Morland in *Northanger Abbey* (Austen 1818, but originally written 1798–99; also used as opening epigraph by Carr 1961: 6).

2. Díaz (1632: unnumbered prefatory material, p. ii) (original phrases: *el Capitan Conquistador; testigo ocular; testigo de vista*) (also 1908, I: 3; 2005, I: 3); Fuentes (1928–2012) wrote variously on Díaz, ranging from (1990: 72–77) to (2011: 25–44). Also see comments by Guillermo Serés, editor of an exhaustive 1,620-page scholarly edition of the book (Díaz 2012), who calls it "the greatest Spanish prose of the sixteenth century [*la mejor prosa castellana del siglo XVI*]" (Serés 2013).

3. "A Conqueror Captures a King" facing this Prologue's title page: The two Mercedarians were fray Alonso Remón (the editor) and fray Bartolomé de Olmedo (portrayed here). Few subsequent editions of the book reproduce or discuss this title page imagery. It is not included, for example, in Díaz (1963), (1984), or (2008); it is reproduced in Delgado-Gomez (1992: 20), Restall (2003: 138), and Díaz (2005, II: 111), for example, but not fully discussed.

4. *863-page book*: There are two surviving versions of Díaz's book: the "Guatemala Manuscript" of the 1580s comprises 863 handwritten pages (Díaz 2005); the 1632 printed edition is 508 pages (Díaz 1632; 2005; Carrasco in Díaz 2008: xxvi). *"On occasion"*: Thomas

in Díaz (2003: xi). Miralles (2008). *"Flashbacks"*: Duverger (2013: 17). While I am not persuaded that Cortés wrote the *True History*, Duverger's skepticism regarding Díaz's authorial role deserves to be taken seriously; indeed, I suspect that the original nonextant manuscript was a compilation of accounts and testimonies by multiple witnesses, lent coherence by the hand of an editor (or editors).

5. Newspaper reviews as blurbs to Díaz (2003), also quoted by Carrasco in Díaz (2008: xv). *"Historians explain"*: Menand (2015: 73). For fascinating fact/fiction accounts of the Aztec and conquistador past, written by a novelist as "history" for children and young adults, see Frías (1899–1901) (also Bonilla Reyna and Lecouvey 2015).

6. *"Every good mystery"*: Sue Grafton, speaking through her Kinsey Millhone character, in *W Is for Wasted* (New York: G. P. Putnam, 2013: 3) (not in my Bibliography); I have elided the sentence between "sleuth" and "figures." *Testigo ocular*: In Díaz's day, eyewitness reports were by definition accurate (the "Renaissance obsession . . . that eyewitness accounts were almost incontrovertibly true"; Goodwin 2015: 84), a perception that persisted into the modern era of video footage and DNA and—paradoxically—deep skepticism over the very concept of objectivity (this is a much-studied topic, but for one engaging foray into it, see Fernández-Armesto 1997: 82–102). For discussion of Díaz's own insistence that his eyewitness status trumped the learning of official historians, see Adorno (1992). For a modern example of the view that eyewitness conquistadors like Díaz and Aguilar wrote "pure truth" (*la verdad pura*) with "deep subjectivity" (*subjetividad profunda*), see Vásquez (1991: 11). For Díaz in the context of the early modern Spanish "soldierly republic of letters," see Martínez (2016).

7. *"Modern history"*: Brooks (1995: 149). *"Real discovery"*: Thomas uses the "real discovery" phrase several times (e.g., 1992).

8. Such correspondence came mostly in response to three books (Restall 1998; Restall 2003; and Restall and Solari 2011; along with non-English editions of the 2003 and 2011 books). This present book in part builds upon the 2003 volume, further exploring some of its themes and ideas, correcting arguments where the evidence has now led me to different conclusions, and with exclusive attention to the case study of central Mexico. This present book has implications for the study of the Spanish Conquest elsewhere, and I plan to follow it with another book on the Spanish-Maya wars of

invasion and conquest; but in the interests of space and focus, I leave it to others to make other connections across the Americas.

9. In sequence: Day (2008: 4); Krauze (2010: 66) (*Cómo pudo un pequeño ejército de cientos de soldados castellanos doblegar a millones de mexicas y a su ponderosa teocracia militar? Éste ha sido uno de los grandes misterios de la historia*); Wright (1993: 19; also quoted by Day); Keegan (1993: 338–39).

10. Clendinnen (1991b: 65 [2010 reprint: 49]).

11. Ballentine in Ixtlilxochitl (1969: ix).

PART I

1. Epigraph sources, in sequence: Bacon (1973 [1612]: 158); Paz quoted by Krauze (2010: 73) (*El mito nació de la ideología y solo la crítica a la ideología podrá disiparlo*).

CHAPTER 1:

MYSTERIOUS KINDNESS

1. Epigraph sources, in sequence: Cortés's Letters, hereafter cited as CCR (1522: f. 10v; 1960: 52; 1971: 86) (*no creais mas de lo que por vuestros ojos veredes*); Rowdon (1974: 122); Abbott (1904 [1856]: unnumbered p. 7; italics in original); Tuchman (1981 [1964]: 25); Fernández-Armesto (2014: xxi). Although I cite various published editions of Cortés's letters for the reader's convenience, all translations from Cortés's Second Letter are mine, made from the original texts in the 1522 Seville edition and the 1528 manuscript in Codex Vindobonensis, SN1600, ONB (also Cortés 1960 [1519–25]).

2. *"Amazed"*: Aguilar (c.1560, in J. Díaz et al. 1988: 176 and Fuentes 1963: 145) testifying as to what Ordaz told him (*otro nuevo mundo de grandes poblaciones y torres, y una mar, y dentro de ella una ciudad muy grande edificada; venia espantado de lo que habia visto; que a la verdad al parecer, ponia temor y espanto*). Note that I have varied my gloss of terms like *grande* and *espanto*, to better convey this opening point; but conquistadors like Aguilar used a limited vocabulary, and generally my translations more closely follow the original text. *"Real"*: Díaz LXXXVII (1632: f. 64v; 1910, II: 37; 2008 [1632]: 157) (*q si aquello q veian, si era entre sueños*). *"Enchantment"*: Cano in Martínez Baracs (2006: 50, 151–52) (*les parecía cosa de encantamiento y que no*

podían creer que fuese verdad sino que lo soñaban las cosas de México). Note that the "enchantment" phrase was also used by Díaz (and oft quoted as such), but he either borrowed it from Cano or, more likely, it was widely used by the conquistadors (whose imaginations were limited). *"So wondrous"*: CCR (1522: f. 12v; 1971 [1519–25]: 101–2; 1993 [1519–25]: 232) (*seran de tanta admiracion que no se podran creer . . . la grandeza, estrañas y maravillosas cosas desta grand cibdad de Temixtitan . . . los que aca con nuestros proprios ojos las veemos no las podemos con el entendimiento comprehender*).

3.   FC, XII: f. 22; Lockhart (1993: 108). This description is from Book XII of the Florentine Codex, a manuscript revisited and discussed in detail in subsequent chapters. The suggestion in this passage that the demeanors of the conquistadors and their dogs were similar is surely deliberate; it is omitted from the parallel Spanish version (op. cit.: 109).

4.   *Population*: Rojas (2012: 50–54, 88–90); Evans (2013: 549); Luna (2014). Alonso de Zuazo reported from Cuba in 1521 that Tenochtitlan had 60,000 people and Tetzcoco twice that many (CDHM, I: 366). The figure of 60,000 was commonly cited in the sixteenth century, although sometimes as houses (e.g., *sesenta mil casas*; Jeronymo Girava Tarragonez in Apiano 1575: app. p. x), encouraging exaggerated population estimates by modern scholars. The Anonymous Conquistador asserted that "most people who have seen the great city of Temistitan Mexico judge it to have sixty thousand inhabitants" (a reference to Mexico City c.1550, although often mistakenly read as referring to the pre-Conquest city); in fact, the almost fourteen square kilometers of Tenochtitlan probably did contain sixty to eighty thousand inhabitants in 1519 (and perhaps too in 1550) (CDHM, I: 391). No levels above the ground floor were residential in the Aztec city, so it could not possibly have been more densely populated than modern Manhattan; thus older claims that Tenochtitlan had half a million or even a million residents (e.g., from Abbott 1904 [1856]: 187 to Soustelle 1964: 31–32 and Vaillant 1966: 134) cannot be taken seriously, as Evans points out (2013: 549). *"Anthills"*: Mendieta (1870 [1596]: 175) (*tanto número de gente indiana, que los pueblos y caminos en lo mas de ellos no parecian sino hormigueros, cosa de admiración á quien lo veia y que debiera poner terrible terror á tan pocos españoles como los que Cortés consigo traia*).

5.   CCR (1522: f. 16v–17r; 1971 [1519–25]: 102–3, 105; 1993 [1519–
     25]: 233–34, 238) (*es tan grande la cibdad como Sevilla y Cordoba . . .
     la mas prencipal es mas alta que la torre de la iglesia mayor de Sevilla . . .
     tan grande como dos veces la plaza de la cibdad de Salamanca*) (note
     that "*la plaza de*" is missing from the 1522 and 1523 editions and
     1528 MS, but included in the Madrid MS; see 1993: 234n275).
     The comparisons of Tenochtitlan's plaza to that of Salamanca, the
     towers of its "mosques" to Granada, and its overall size to Seville
     and Córdoba, were repeated through the sixteenth century (e.g.,
     Fernández de Oviedo 1959 [1535], IV: 44–45 [Ch. X]).

6.   Included in my Bibliography as Anonymous (1522), the newsletter's
     full title was *Newe Zeitung, von dem Lande, das die Spanier funden
     haben ym 1521 Iare genant Jucatan*; the quotes above and in the cap-
     tion to the figure on p. 2 are from unnumbered pp. 5–6; translation
     mine, but indebted to Wagner (1929: 200), and to Wolfgang Gab-
     bert, personal communication, January 2014. A similar account was
     also published in Basel—but in Latin—in 1521 by Peter Martyr
     d'Anghiera (*De nuper sub D. Carolo repertis insulis*).

7.   My translation from the Spanish version by Bustamante (1986: 178)
     (*Esta ciudad es maravillosa por su tamaño, situación y artificios, puesta
     en mitad de un lago de . . .* [etc.]). Tenochtitlan was understandably a
     popular topic of fascination in Venice, featured in publications such
     as Benedetto Bordone's *Isolario*, a guide to all the world's islands,
     first published in Venice in 1528 (see Gruzinski 2014: 55 and the
     works he cites).

8.   CCR (1522: title page/frontispiece) (*haze relacio[n] de una gra[n]dis-
     sima provi[n]cia muy rica llamada Culua: e[n] la q[ua]l ay muy gra[n]
     des cuidades y de maravillosos edificios: y de gra[n]des tratos y riq[ue]zas.
     Entre las q[ua]les ay una mas maravillosa y rica q[ue] todas llamada
     Timixtita[n]*); see the image (first page of the Gallery) for the origi-
     nal text. The "urtext" quote is by Adorno (2011: 43). The title begins
     *Carta de relacio[n] e[n]biada a su S. majestad del e[m]perador n[uest]ro
     señor por el capita[n] general de la nueva [e]spaña: llamado ferna[n]do
     cortes* ("Letter of report sent to His Majesty the Emperor our Lord
     by the Captain General of New Spain, named Fernando Cortés").
     For other early Spanish descriptions of the city, see Gómara (1552:
     ff. 45v–49r; 1964: 156–67) (an author and book further discussed in
     the chapters to come). The theme of Tenochtitlan as a lost wonder

persisted through the chronicles and histories of sixteenth to eighteenth centuries, with William Robertson somewhat begrudgingly accepting the theme's legacy; he chose not to compare the Aztec city to European ones, but did note that its construction was "remarkable," that the palaces of kings and nobles "might be termed magnificent"—compared to "any other buildings which had been discovered in America"—and that the city was "the pride of the New World, and the noblest monument of the industry and art of man, while unacquainted with the use of iron, and destitute of aid from any domestic animal" (1777, II: 54–55).

9. A 1524 Antwerp edition of the Second Letter likely also included the map, but no copy of that edition has survived (Pagden in CCR 1971 [1519–25]: lx).

10. *"Azure lake"* and *"geometries"*: Mundy (1998: 11, 16). There have been about a dozen studies of the Nuremberg Map, of varying length and depth, published since the 1930s (see the historiographical summary in Boone 2011: 42n1), but three recent articles represent the map's authoritative studies to date: Mundy (1998; an abbreviated version is Mundy 2011b); Matos Moctezuma (2001); and Boone (2011). In Boone's words (op. cit.: 38), the map "presents Tenochtitlan as belonging to two temporalities"; in Mundy's (1998: 26), it is "stretched like a taut rope between Cortés's ideological programme and that of its Culhua-Mexica [Aztec] prototype." The possible connection to the *Nuremberg Chronicle* is suggested by Schreffler (2011: 257–62). For discussion of the map in the context of early European maps of "Indian" cities and understandings of indigenous barbarism, see Davies (2016: 227–30, Ch. 7).

11. CCR (1960: 57; 1971: 94) (*me trajeron figurada en un paño toda la costa*). On the coastal Nuremberg Map, see Boone (2011: 38–41). My analysis is heavily indebted to the insights in Mundy (1998: 26–28).

12. *His fame*: Hajovsky (2015: 11). *Title page*: See the Gallery; CCR (1522: frontispiece/title page (*de la q[ua]l ciudad y provi[n]cia es rey un gra[n]disimo señor llamado Muteeçuma: do[n]de le acaeciero[n] al capita[n] y los españoles espa[n]tosas cosas de oyr. Cuenta largame[n]te del gra[n]dissimo señorio del dicho Muteeçuma y de sus ritos y cerimonias. y de como se sirve*); see the Gallery figure for the original text. Also mentioned once on this page is "Your Majesty," King Carlos, pre-

sumably the monarch in the portrait (Schreffler 2016: 23–24 is clear on that fact), although I suspect the image is also meant to convey a generic monarch—taken from an old plate of a medieval Castilian king (there are similar portraits in earlier Cromberger publications) and intended to refer here both to Carlos and to Montezuma.

13. See the Gallery for an imaginative depiction of Spaniards and Aztecs before Popocatepetl and Iztaccihuatl, showing two related but separate moments, one in the background, one in the foreground. The accompanying passage in *America* parallels the background moment, recounting that all but two of the ten Spaniards who climbed one of the volcanoes had to turn back (but those two reached "the Fiery Gulph," for which "they were admir'd by the Indians for their undaunted Resolution"; Ogilby 1670: 85; Montanus 1671: 79). The foreground image of feather-dressed indigenous men begging a haughty Cortés to stop the eruption is not in this text, or supported by any account of the Spanish invasion. But the impression of "undaunted" Spaniards and credulous, superstitious "Indians" is consistent with centuries of European accounts of the early Spanish-indigenous encounters. Gómara repeats that the climb up the volcano was made by ten unnamed Spaniards; Aguilar and Díaz state that Ordaz led the group, with Díaz claiming "he took with him two of our soldiers and certain of the principal men of Guaxoçingo [the nearby Nahua town of Huexotzinco]" (LXXVII; 1632: f.54v; 2005 [1632]: 189) (*llevó consigo dos de nuestros soldados y çiertos indios principales de Guaxoçingo*). According to Díaz LXXVIII (1908, I: 288), Ordaz was granted a coat of arms depicting a smoking volcano, although I found no mention of this in the Ordaz *probanza* in AGI Patronato 150, 5, 1 (or in the 1529 Ordaz letters in AGI Justicia 712 [old citation] and Otte 1964). The events of November 1 and 2 are described by CCR (1522: f. 9v–10r; 1971 [1519–23]: 78–80; 1993 [1519–25]: 198–202) (original quotes, in order: *quisiessen perseverar en nos hazer alguna burla . . . diez de mis compañeros . . . truxeron mucha nieve y caranbalos para que los viesemos . . . algunas aldeas . . . viven muy pobremente . . . el dicho Muteeçuma los tiene cercados con su tierra . . . para todos muy complidamente de comer y en todas las posadas muy grandes fuegos y mucha leña . . . me dixeron que era hermano de Muteeçuma . . . fasta tres mill pesos de oro . . . era tierra muy pobre de comida y que para yr a ella auia muy mal camino . . . que viesse*

todo lo que queria que Muteeçuma su señor me lo mandaria dar . . . nos podrian ofender aquella noche). One of the better recent summaries of November 1–8 is Thomas (1993: 265–85).

14. CCR (1522: f. 7r; 1971 [1519–23]: 73; 1993 [1519–25]: 192–93).

15. The events of November 3–6 are described in CCR (1522: f. 10; 1971 [1519–23]: 80–81; 1993 [1519–25]: 202–3) (original quotes, in order: *unas muy buenas casas . . . hasta xl esclauas y iii mill castellanos . . . todo lo necessario pa nra comida . . . me fiziessen proueer d todas las cosas necessarias . . . y assimismo quisieran alli prouar sus fuerças con nosotros: excepto que segun parescio quisieran fazerlo muy a su salvo: i tomarnos de noche descuydados . . . espias que venian por el agua en canoas como de otras q por la tierra abarauan a ver si hauia aparejo pa efecutar su voluntad amanescieron quasi quinze o veynte q las nras las auian tomado y muerto).* A *castellano* was the same as a *peso de oro*, and was a specific weight of gold (in Cortés's day, legally equivalent to 485 *maravedís*). Obviously the Aztecs are not actually giving Cortés gold in coins (as Mesoamericans did not mint coins and did not value gold the way Europeans did), so he was probably estimating for the king the value of the gifts being given him. He was also likely exaggerating, in order to impress the king with the wealth of the land he had found; as discussed in a later chapter, this would come back to trouble Cortés for decades, as the royal inquiry into his activities repeatedly focused on the eventual location of all this alleged gold.

16. See the Gallery for the rendering of the Valley of Mexico first printed in 1869 by the Chicago atlas publisher George F. Cram, showing the route that the Spanish-Tlaxcalteca forces took November 5–8 from Chalco through Ayotzinco, Cuitlahuac, and Ixtlapalapan, into Tenochtitlan. Where Cram marked "Camp of Cortez" was not where the expedition camped, but was the gateway where Montezuma's advance entourage of a thousand men came to greet the invaders. Printed variously in color and in black and white, this example is from a 1904 edition of John Abbott's 1856 biography of Cortés (1904 [1856]: 190).

17. The events of November 7 are described in CCR (1522: f. 10; 1971 [1519–23]: 81–83; 1993 [1519–25]: 203–6) (original quotes, in order: *un gran señor mancebo fasta xxv años . . . que alla nos veriamos y*

conosceria del la voluntad que al servicio de vra alteza tenia . . . ahincaron
y purfiaron mucho . . . padesceria mucho trabajo y necessidad).

18. Today the town is called Tláhuac and is one of the sixteen districts
     (*delegaciones*) of Mexico City (the *Distrito Federal*); the lakes around
     it have long ago been almost completely drained (see Candiani
     2014) (quotes for this paragraph: *una cibdad la mas hermosa aunque*
     pequeña que fasta entonces habiamos visto assi de muy bien obradas casas
     y torres como de la buena orden que en el fundamento della habia por ser
     armada toda sobre agua . . . nos dieron bien de comer . . . me hizieron muy
     buen acogimiento . . . fasta iii mill o iiii mill castellanos y algunas esclauas
     y ropa . . . tan buenas como las mejores de España . . . bien labradas assi
     de obra de canteria como de carpinteria).

19. Díaz LXXXVII; LXXXVIII (1632: f. 64v, 65r; 1910, II: 39; 2005,
     I: 218–19, 220; 2008 [1632]: 156–57) (*ver cosas nunca oidas ni vistas,*
     ni aun soñadas, como vimos . . . y no era cosa de maravillar porque jamas
     avian visto cavallos ni hombres como nosotros).

20. CCR (1522: f. 11r; 1971 [1519–23]: 83; 1993 [1519–25]: 206–7)
     (original quotes: *que pueden ir por toda ella ocho de caballo a la par . . .*
     muy buenos edificios de casas y torres . . . estan en la costa della y muchas
     casas dellas dentro en el agua).

21. Delgado Gómez (in Cortés 1993: 210) suggests that *propuso* (from
     proponer) is intended, following the Madrid MS, not *prepuso* (from
     preponer, "to place in front, prioritize"). In fact, I think Cortés may
     have deliberately written *prepuso*, intending to convey the formality
     and legal significance of the speech.

22. Las Casas quote in LCHI, Bk. 3, Ch. 58 (1971: 196); he also de-
     nounces the Requirement in his *Very Brief Account* (2003 [1552]:
     35–36). For my earlier discussion of the Requirement, see Restall
     (2003: 87, 94–95, 98, 105); also see Seed (1995); Clayton (2012:
     66–69). Gruzinski (2014: 91) calls Montezuma's surrender speech a
     "textbook illustration" of ideal Requirement practice.

23. Faudree (2015: quote on 459); this article's important rethinking
     of the Requirement as "performative" and for a Spanish audience
     does not mention Montezuma's speech, but Faudree does rightly
     suggest that her analysis might apply to other Spanish documents
     "legitimating power" (457) in the Americas. My earlier thinking on
     the Requirement (2003: 94) did not move far beyond the Las Ca-

sas "absurd" verdict. Damian Costello, a scholar of Las Casas, has made similar arguments to Faudree in work as yet unpublished, and I thank him for sharing it and for his correspondence on the topic (October–December 2016).

24. CCR (1522: ff. 43v–44v; 1971 [1519–23]: 86–87; 1993 [1519–25]: 210–12). Potonchan was a Chontal Maya town, today in Tabasco state; Cempohuallan (Cempoala) was the Totonac capital city, near the Gulf coast, today in Veracruz state; and Tascaltecal was Tlaxcallan.

25. In other words, history is the dynamic whereby two worlds generate an encounter, which thereby alters those worlds—a self-generating dynamic built around multiple encounters. This is similar to what the structuralist anthropologist Marshall Sahlins has called "the structure of the conjuncture" (1985: xiii–xiv, 153). Also see Sewell (2005: 197–224). For a fuller treatment of my "Encounter Theory of History" and the debt it owes to Sahlins (1985 et al.), Sewell (2005), and Altman (2008), see Restall (n.d.). *"Warped"*: Fernández-Armesto (2015: 168). *"Facts"*: Carr (1961: 30).

26. Fernández-Armesto (2014: xxi); Carr (1961: 7–30); Díaz (1632); Miralles (2008); Duverger (2013); Adorno (2007; 2011: quote on 6). A brief essay that defines the New Conquest History (NCH) is Restall (2012). NCH examples that focus specifically on Mesoamerica and are illustrative of how it has evolved over the last quarter century include Lockhart (1993), Restall (1998; 2003), Wood (2003), Townsend (2006), Matthew and Oudijk (2007), Restall and Asselberg (2007), Schroeder (2010), Schwaller and Nader (2014), and Villella (2016).

27. I have borrowed the phrase *narcotic effect* from Lamana (2008: 33, writing about Spanish accounts of the Conquest of Peru).

28. *"Genes"*: Gruzinski (2014: 68). *"Configuration"*: Lamana (2008: 6).

29. Seigel (2004: 436–38) expands engagingly on the larger argument here (although neither the Spanish Conquest nor Mexico falls under her purview).

CHAPTER 2:
NO SMALL AMAZEMENT

1. Epigraph sources, in sequence: Ogilby (1670: 86); Escoiquiz (1798, III: 337) (*Cortés entró triunfante, y al Imperio / De España se agregó aquel emisferio*).

2. Although designed by Brumidi in 1859, the frieze was painted later—by him and Filippo Costaggini between 1878 and 1889. See the excellent official website on the Capitol and the frieze for its history and high-quality images: aoc.gov/history-us-capitol -building; also Hanson (2015–16: 2–10) and Restall (2016c). On the Columbus-Armstrong link, see Restall (2003: 2). I am grateful to William "Chuck" diGiacomantonio of the U.S. Capitol Historical Society for his correspondence and assistance.

3. Johannsen (1985: 150, 155, 246).

4. Cholmley (1787) is a memoir that mostly covers the exploits of Sir Hugh's father (also Sir Hugh) in the English Civil War; it includes the Tangier years but makes no mention of the Mexico paintings; on those, see Morris (1866, I: 14); Henning (1983, I: 62–63).

5. Brienen in Jackson and Brienen (2003: 57–58); Brienen and Jackson (2008: 188, 204–5). The second and third Anglo-Dutch Wars were in 1665–67 and 1672–74.

6. Solís (1684 et al.); Brienen and Jackson (2008: 189); Restall (2008: 94, 100–2); Schreffler (2008: 118–22).

7. More specifically, this sweep of sources includes the more than one hundred histories, novels, plays, poems, and paintings discussed throughout this book, including a wide variety of modern textbooks, as well as films and television shows (such as the 2015 Spanish series *Carlos, Rey Emperador*).

8. The first book-length reconstruction of the "Conquest of Mexico" was Francisco López de Gómara's 1552 biography of Cortés; since then, almost all books, be they titled as biographies or as Conquest histories, have narrated the story around Cortés. Prescott, for example, declared from the start of his *History of the Conquest of Mexico* that his "purpose" was "to exhibit the history of this Conquest, and that of the remarkable man by whom it was achieved," explaining that he chose not to end his narrative with the fall of Tenochtitlan, as Solís and others did, but to continue "to the death of Cortés, relying on the interest which the development of his character in his military career may have excited in the reader" (1994 [1843]: 9, 3). For group citations of Cortés biographies/Conquest histories, see Restall (2016a) and my notes to the chapters in Parts III–IV.

9. I am drawing here upon Brooks's insight into Cortés's Second Letter (1522) as itself a three-act drama (1995: 151–57).

10. Like the frieze in the Capitol Rotunda, the Kislak Paintings are also easily found online (in color): loc.gov/exhibits/exploring-the -early-americas/conquest-of-mexico-paintings.html.

11. For an argument against categorizing conquistadors as army soldiers, see Restall (2003: 27–37).

12. Aguilar and Malintzin are introduced in Painting #1, in a background (but well-lit) scene that brings in the important theme of religious conversion (the implied purpose and justification of the invasion). The scene is captioned as "the baptism of doña Marina and five other [women]," and the culmination of the events in the painting is "they [the people of Tabasco] make peace and are the first Christians of this New Spain" (*Entran en Tabasco las nuestros por la punta de los palmares; Bautisase D. Marina y otras cinco; Azen pazes y son los primeros cristianos desta nueva España*).

13. Kislak Paintings #2 and #3 are both included in the Gallery. The cartouche (added later) at bottom right of Painting #2 translates to: "Cortés arrives in Veracruz, anchors in Veracruz. The caciques, with the ambassadors from the emperor Montezuma, go out and bring presents of gold and textiles. Cortés receives them, after [talking] by means of the interpreters Marina and Aguilar. He eats with them and then he has the horses gallop and [cannon fire]." The key identifies: "Cortés-1, Bernal [Díaz]-2, Caciques giving presents-3, Messengers[?]-4, Those who galloped-5, The artillery-6, Marina-7, The other people-8." The original cartouche is badly faded and its corresponding numbers presumably faded too and were poorly rewritten (Díaz's "2" is on the rock off the coast, and the "1" for Cortés, himself cut off in a reframing, is in the sea). The cartouche to Painting #3 translates to "Cortés leaves for Iztapalapa, where he discovers towns and cities on the water and the straight causeway; Moctezuma comes out of Mexico to receive him and presents him with the necklace that he had around his neck. Cortés goes to put his arms around him but they restrain him, as that is not customary. Four kings carry the bier on their shoulders."

14. The cartouche in Kislak Painting #4 (also in the Gallery) translates to "Seeing themselves surrounded within the palace in Mexico, the Spaniards have Moctezuma appear on a rooftop and from there he calmed them down; but an Indian threw a stone and the other Indians shot arrows from which he died; they put the rooms to the torch."

15. The cartouche in Kislak Painting #7 (in the Gallery) reads, "The final battle for Mexico by Cortés and his men along the three causeways that go to Mexico, and across the lagoon with the brigantines, which the Indians fought savagely. Pedro de Alvarado wins the great temple of Huitzilopochtli [*alto cu de guichilobos*] and raises the flag of His Majesty." Painting #8 is not included in our Gallery.

16. Anonymous (1522 [*Newe Zeitung*]); Anonymous (1522 [*Ein Schöne Newe Zeytung*]); Wagner (1929); Martyr d'Anghiera (1521).

17. *Newe Zeitung, von dem Lande, das die Spanier funden haben ym 1521 Iare genant Jucatan* (Anonymous 1522 [*Newe Zeitung*]); because the Yucatan peninsula was the first part of Mesoamerica discovered by Spaniards on the expeditions of the late 1510s, the whole region, Mexico included, was initially called Yucatan (soon replaced by "New Spain"). Block quote: Anonymous (1522 [*Newe Zeitung*]: unnumbered p. 6), my translation, indebted to Wagner (1929: 201) and with the kind assistance of Wolfgang Gabbert (personal communication, January 2014).

18. This famous line from Gilbert and Sullivan's comic opera *The Mikado* (1885) is applied to Díaz's account (XCV; 1632: ff. 74v–75) of Montezuma's arrest in Brooks (1995: 167–68), from where I have borrowed it.

19. Anonymous (1522 [*Ein Schöne Newe Zeytung*], unnumbered p. 7); my translation, heavily indebted to Wagner (1929: 206).

20. Calvo (1522; 1985); he titled the booklet *News of the Islands and the Mainland Newly Discovered in India by the Captain of His Caesarean Majesty's Fleet*. Block quote: Calvo (1522: f. 5v; translation from the Italian is mine, but aided by 1985: 24–25). A more detailed analysis of the timing of these accounts of 1522 would need to include discussion of Carlos's own efforts to expand and retain his growing European empire.

21. I am building here upon my brief discussion of the Meeting in Restall (2003: 77–82, 87, 92, 95–98).

22. Wytfliet (1598: 57–58) is an example of the stripped-down version. The Solís version (1684: 220–27 [Bk. III, Chs. X–XI]; 1724: 59–64) was copied or paraphrased in numerous eighteenth- and nineteenth-century accounts. Also see Gómara (1552: Chs. 65–66; 1964: 140–42); Díaz LXXXIX–XC (1632: ff. 66–67v); Herrera (1601: 224–29; 1728, I: 400–4; Dec. II, Bk. VI, Chs. 5–6); Ruiz

de León (1755: Canto VI, 166); Escoiquiz (1798, I: final stanzas); Prescott (1994 [1843]: 278–86). Note that, if judged by modern standards and practices, the run of accounts from Gómara through Solís and into the eighteenth century would all be considered heavily tainted by plagiarism; they all tell the same story, misleading later historians into seeing evidence piling up, instead of Cortesian lies repeated. Perhaps the most pernicious example is Díaz, because he is still so widely read and so praised as offsetting Gómara's hagiography with the "truth" (in fact, he overwhelmingly follows Gómara, copying page after page with minor changes, sometimes adding invention to error or error to invention; Brooks 1995: 168–76), as being objective with respect to Cortés (in fact, his book is an extended defense of Cortés and an attack on Velázquez and his faction), and as being an eyewitness with an incredible memory (his invented memories and imagined presence at events have been extensively documented; Miralles 2008); no wonder Duverger (2013) concluded that Díaz was not his book's true author!

23. Properly called *General History of the Things of New Spain*, the Florentine Codex (which I have cited throughout as FC), was circulated in manuscript in sixteenth-century Mexico but not published until the nineteenth century. Sahagún quote is from his introduction in Book I (FC, I: 9); the Conquest narrative is FC, XII. *Scholar of Peru*: Lamana (2008: 8 et al.).

24. Durán LXIX, LXXIV (1967 [1581]; 1994 [1581]: especially 497–98, 530). *Ixtlilxochitl*: Ix13: 19, 21.

25. I was guided to this Nahuatl drama by Sell and Burkhart (2004: 118–45; quote on 124–25) and Burkhart (2008); my analysis of the play is slightly different from Burkhart's, but nonetheless indebted to her; in quoting from the play here and later in this book I rely on Sell and Burkhart's translations (their grasp of Nahuatl is far superior to mine). The parallel passage in the Florentine Codex where Montezuma rants against messengers and priests is in FC, XII: 100–3.

26. Aguilar (c.1560; J. Díaz et al. 1988: 179; Fuentes 1963: 147) (*gente barbada y armados*); Thomas (1857: 47 [Act III, Sc. 2]).

27. Carrasco (1992: 147) (in the original, *postconquest elaboration* is italicized). See Carrasco (1982) for a full-length study of the evidence, arguing for a somewhat different position than mine; also the citations to my Quetzalcoatl discussion in Chapter 3.

28. Escoiquiz (1798, I: 309) (*persuadido / Estoy de que el gran Rey que os ha enviado / Desciende en línea recta del temido / Quezalcoal* [sic], *autor del dilatado / Imperio Mexicano*). This epic poem on the Conquest of Mexico is in the form of ottava rima, first used by Boccaccio in the fourteenth century and used mostly by Italians as a format for heroic poetry; a full canto of 114 stanzas is devoted to the Meeting (I, 292–331). *Typical rendering*: Ranking (1827: 326–27). For a discussion of the significance of Montezuma's tears, see below (also Chapter 6 and Allen 2015).

29. "*Obviously*": Marks (1993: 129). *Dialogues*: Novo (1985: 49–59, quotes translated from p. 51) (*MALINCHE.— . . . Ellos aguardaban, por muchas generaciones atrás, el regreso de Quetzalcóatl. CARLOTA.—Y le creyeron llegado, con Cortés. MALINCHE.—Llegó en él. Para mí, al menos*). I am grateful to Megan McDonie for drawing my attention to the dialogues by Novo (1904–74).

30. Cervantes de Salazar (1914 [1560s]: 274 [Bk. 3, Ch. LXIII]) (*Dioses deben ser estos, que vienen de do nasce el sol . . . Estos deben de ser los que han de mandar y señorear nuestras personas y tierra*); Herrera (1601: 226; Dec. II, Bk. VI, Ch. 5) (*sospira[n]do dezian: Estos deuen de ser los q han de mandar, y señorear nuestras personas y tierras, pues siendo tan pocos, son tan fuertes que han vencido tantas gentes*).

31. Robertson (1777, II: 52, 53); García (1729 [1607]: 164), who used Herrera (1601: 163; Dec. II, Bk. V, Ch. 12), who drew from Gómara (1552: Chs. 66, 92; 1964: 140–42, 184–86); Marks (1993: 129).

32. FC, XII: 116–17; Monterde (lived 1894–1985) (1945: 30) (*Estaba anunciado que vendrías a tu ciudad, que regresarías a ella, y eso se ha realizado. Seas bienvenido; que descanse tu cuerpo. Nuestro señor ha llegado a su tierra. . . . Tranquilízate, señor: todos te amamos*).

33. Ogilby (1670: 86; similar passage on 258).

34. The Sepúlveda quotes have been regularly quoted in recent studies: e.g., Pagden (1982: 117); Clendinnen (1991b: 50 [2010 reprint: 65], Restall (2003: 15), and Gillespie (2008: 25). Also see Elliott (1989: 36–41); Lockhart (1993: 17); Fernández-Armesto (1992: 296). Gómara: "Montezuma must have been a cowardly little man" (1952: Ch. 89; 1964: 179; Schroeder et al. 2010: 222) (*hombre sin corazón y de poco debía ser Moteczuma*).

35. Ix13: 25; FC, XII: 80, 84; Tlatelolco account presented in a translation/summary, with some commentary, by Terraciano (2010; quote on 15).

36. Muñoz Camargo (1892 [1592]: 215 [Bk. II, Ch. VI, opening paragraph]) (*nuestros españoles y los de Tlaxcala; tan gran victoria y tomado Cholula; el capitán Cortés fué muy bien recibido de parte del gran Señor y Rey Moctheuzomatzin y de todos los Señores Mexicanos*).

37. Gemelli (1704: 558–59). Here Gemelli, like Ranking (quoted earlier) and others, is taking the story of Montezuma weeping at the second Surrender and applying it to the first; see my discussion in Chapter 6 (but also see Allen 2015).

38. Lasso (1594: ff. 232r, 223r, 231r, 232r) (*A nadie es dada tal licencia . . . donde es recebido con grande aplauso del Rey Moteçuma, y su Corte . . . inuicto y alto . . . el gran Moteçuma poderoso*).

39. *"No Greek"*: I translated this particular passage from the manuscript copy (JCB Codex Sp 63: f. 155r; Chimalpahin n.d.), but also see Gómara (1552: 83; 1964: 171) (*nunca Griego, ni Romano ni de otra nacion despuez que ai reyes hizo cosa tan igual que fernando Cortes en prender a Muteczuma rey poderosisimo en su propria casa, en lugar fortisimo, entre infinidad de gente no teniendo sino quatro cientros, y cinquenta compañeros españoles, y Amigos*). *Illustration*: "Spanish Gratitude," showing Montezuma being "Fetter'd," was used in various publications from the seventeenth and eighteenth centuries. The example in the Gallery is from *The American Traveller*, first printed in London in 1741, an account of early Spanish explorations and conquests in the Caribbean up to 1518 (thus ending before Cortés reached Mexico). Another example, almost identical but without a caption, is in a French edition of Solís (1704: facing vol. 1, p. 408). Another very similar version is the 1798 Spanish edition of Solís.

40. Thomas (1857: 51–52 [Act IV, Sc. 1]).

41. Abbott (1904 [1856]: 36, 181–88). On the "Black Legend": called such since the phrase was coined to describe it in 1914, with the phrase a battleground of debate over Spanish colonialism; see my discussion and citations in Chapter 7.

42. Dilworth (1759: 66–68; 1801: 85–88). Robertson (1777, II: 53; also quoted above) used almost identical phrasing.

43. Dilworth (1759: 68–69, 80, 88–92; 1801: 89–90, 110, 115–18).

44. *Two Nahua towns*: DC, I: 60–76 (quote on 71; *las malicias del gran Montezuma se componía de que teniéndonos allí hospedados y hacienda falso cariño*); this document is in the genre of a primordial title, but styled as a *merced* by Cortés to the two towns, created to "prove" the

immediate conversion and loyalty of these towns. *Recent retelling*: Koch (2006: 197).

45. *"Filled"* to *"allies"*: Solís (1798, II: 201–2) (*por ambos lados poblada de innumerables indios; gritos y ademanes; sus mayores fiestas; victoreaban y bendecían á los nuevos amigos*). *"Some"* to *"affection"*: Aguilar (c.1560; J. Díaz et al. 1988: 179; Fuentes 1963: 142); Díaz CXC (also cited by Thomas 1993: 251, 253) (*todos los principales le salieron a recibir con danzas y bailes y regocijos y mucho bastimento*).

46. Vargas Machuca in Lane (2010 [1612]: 94) (also see Lane 2008).

47. *"Joy"*: From the preface to a French edition of Solís (1704: unnumbered prefatory p. 7) (*Cortez revint à Mexique, où il fut reçû par les Habitans, avec les mêmes démonstrations de joie, qu'ils auroient pû témoigner pour un de leurs Empereurs*). *"Triumphant"*: Escoiquiz (1798, III: 337 [original given in Ch. 3 epigraph note]).

48. Valadés (1579: 105 [error for 205]) (my translation from Latin: *in cuius facti faelicisque victoriae memoriā ciues anniuersarium festum solemnesq; supplicationes celebrant*; also see a Spanish translation in Palomera 1988: 415). For Spaniards, the significance of a city entrance meant that the lack of an entrance was important too. In March 1530, Cortés was forbidden to enter Mexico City, by order of the queen (acting as regent while Carlos V was absent from Spain). The new colony was in the hands of a royally appointed administration, and a new president and set of judges were on their way to take office. Until they had arrived, neither "you," Cortés was told, "nor the marquesa, your wife, may enter the city of Mexico, nor may you approach it closer than ten leagues." The myth of surrender and Cortés's achievement had already become deeply rooted legend; even his denial of entry into the city was an inevitable echo and affirmation of his supposedly triumphal entry at the Meeting (CDHM, II: 30; *vos ni la marquesa, vuestra mujer, no entreis en la cibdad de Mexico, ni os llegueis a ella con diez leguas alrededor*). Failure to comply meant a fine of ten thousand castellanos. Cortés acknowledged the order, by kissing it and touching it to his head, in Tlaxcallan in August that year. Spanish history of the centuries surrounding the Spanish-Aztec War is replete with examples of triumphal entries; there are many examples just from Cortés's lifetime. For example, the same year that he reentered Tenochtitlan in triumph (1526), an elaborate, ritual meeting took place on the Portuguese-Castilian

border between a huge embassy of Spanish aristocrats and Isabella of Portugal, who was on her way to marry Carlos V; while not a triumphal entry in the sense of a war victory, the marriage was a diplomatic triumph and Isabella's entry into Castile was treated by both sides with the pomp and circumstance that imbued triumphal entries in Iberian culture. Four months later the newlyweds traveled to honeymoon in Granada, entering the city in full triumphal celebration—complete with an elaborate greeting at the gates, specially constructed arches, dancing Moriscos, and bullfights (with human, as well as bovine, fatalities) (Goodwin 2015: 54–56, 64, 68). The echoes of the 1492 triumphal entry of Carlos's grandparents were explicit and obvious to all, but the day surely also evoked other victories over heathen cities—ones hoped for (against the Ottomans, for example) and ones in recent memory (against the Aztecs, for example). Ten years later, Carlos made another elaborate and expensive triumphal entry, this time into Rome—intended to highlight his status as Holy Roman Emperor (and also, as a peaceful ceremony, to heal the wounds of the 1524 sack of the city by imperial troops) (Brandi 1980 [1939]: 370–71).

49. RC; AGI Justicia 220 through 225; DC, II.

50. AGI Patronato 184, ramo 46 (old citation 2, caja 2, legajo 5); ENE, VII, #369: 31–36; translations mine but also see Stabler and Kicza (1986); Las Casas (2003 [1552]) (*nos llama a los conquistadores tiranos y rrobadores y indinos del nonbre de xpianos . . . y en el senorio de V. Mag. Pone escrupulo y que sin liçençia pasamos a esta ptes*).

51. (*el justo titulo de V. Mag. en este nuevo mundo . . . y los murmuradores callen . . . ydolatrica . . . expurçissima y nefanda sodomia . . . no era legitimo senor . . . deshizo la compania hecha de sus pasados . . . todos los señores de la tierra fueron con nosotros . . . les hazia libres de todo cautiberio y servidumbre de los mexicanos*).

52. Suárez de Peralta (1949 [1589]: 59) (*dijo estas palabras, según las cuentan indios viejos, a quien yo las oí, y al algunos conquistadores, especialmente a mi suegro Alonso de Villanueva Tordesillas, que era secretario de la gobernación del marqués del Valle, cuando lo fue; a quien de podía dar mucho crédito, por ser como era tan principal y honrado y muy hijodalgo, natural de Villanueva de la Serena*).

53. LCHI Bk. 3, Ch. 116 (Las Casas 1951 [1561], III: 227; also quoted by Duverger 2005: 367). Note Felipe Fernández-Armesto's intrigu-

ing suggestion (personal communication, January 2017) that Cortés
may have been implying that Montezuma was a usurper because he
did not acquire his kingdom through Christ.

54. *No qualms*: For example, in LCDT: 307–9 (also partially quoted
in León-Portilla 2005 [1985]: 18–19). The judge Alonso de Zorita
echoed Las Casas's allegations in a letter to the king of 1562, but
in milder terms (AGI Patronato 182, ramo 2; see quote and discussion in my Chapter 8). *Debates*: LCHI, Bk. 3, quoted by Goodwin
(2015: 17, translation his); Gómara (1552); quote about Sepúlveda
by Goodwin (op. cit.: 102), but also see Adorno (2007; 2011: 21–26,
38–42); Lane (2010: 10, 18–29); Clayton (2012: Ch. 12); Faudree
(2015: 466–71). Fernández de Oviedo's 1535 *History of the Indies*,
reprinted in 1547 in time for the debates, was full of negative depictions of indigenous peoples as idolatrous, rebellious cannibals
(1547: e.g., Books V–VI; also see chapters throughout 1959 [1535]).

55. *Adelantado*: This formal title (literally, "invader, conqueror") gave
the license holder the right to conquer and settle, with a strong
claim to be governor of the newly acquired territories (see Restall
2003: 19–22, 38–40, 65–68). *Debate*: see Lane (2010: 10; and 41–57
for Sepúlveda's twelve "objections" to Las Casas, a dozen-pointed
argument on the justice of conquering the "Indians") (González
phrases are *escrupulo, senorio,* and *este nuevo mundo*). *Deadly baggage*:
referring to the diseases and various forms of environmental and
culture destruction that came with conquerors and colonists; phrase
borrowed from the title of Sandine (2015).

56. Prévost (1746–59, XII [1754]: 327–28) (*renferme tout-à-la-fois beaucoup d'adresse & d'ingénuité; Quoique la plûpart de ces Pieces soient
ordinairement fort suspectes, on a déja remarqué que celles ci paroissent
d'un autre ordre, parce qu'elles tirent une espece d'autenticité, de leur
resemblance dans tous les Historiens, qui doivent les avoir tirées d'une
source commune*).

57. There is no shortage of skeptical views of the Surrender and of
Montezuma's speech in more recent scholarly works. Townsend's
is one of my favorites: "In believing it [the Surrender] for so many
years, Western historians have only shown ourselves to be more
naïve than Moctezuma ever was" (2006: 86). Gruzinski's understatement also appeals: the Surrender was "rather too sudden to be
wholly credible" (2014: 114); as does Villella's characterization of

the speech as "historical ventriloquism" by Cortés (2016: 52). Over the years, the speech has been convincingly exposed as a Spanish construct by Frankl (1962), Elliott (1989 [1967]), Gillespie (1989: 180–82, 226–27; 2008), and Brooks (1995), while Clendinnen, Hassig, and León-Portilla have across various publications adopted an ambiguous position between outright rejection and acceptance. Authors more or less accepting the Cortesian account of Montezuma's speeches and his arrest are far too numerous to cite (but a recent example in a full-length scholarly study is Thomas 1993: 280–85, and a briefer, more recent one is Oudijk and Castañeda de la Paz 2017).

58. Bacon (1973 [1612]: 158, first quote; *Novum Organum* [1620] in Burtt 1939: 36, second and third quotes); Lockhart (1999: 30). The late James Lockhart was my doctoral advisor, so I had long been familiar with this essay; yet I had not considered its relevance here, so I am grateful to Pablo Ibáñez for bringing it to my attention at a 2015 conference at the University of St. Andrews. For critical insight into how history and historians rely on human memory, despite it being warped, weak, and laced with imagination, see Fernández-Armesto (2015: 167–81).

59. Widely discussed in numerous sources, but a good example is Altman (2008: 2–9), in which he primarily references work by Tzvetan Todorov and Edward Branigan.

60. Examples of this phenomenon are numerous; some examples can be found published as DC, I: 60–75; Restall, Sousa, and Terraciano (2005: 66–71); Restall and Asselbergs (2007: 18–20, 83–85).

61. *Copious*: Major recent studies include Pérez-Rocha (1998); Chipman (2005); Martínez Baracs (2006); Connell (2011); Castañeda de la Paz (2013: 329–401); and Villella (2016). Also see Pérez-Rocha and Tena (2000), cited as PRT. *"Service"*: a Cano letter of 1546; see Pérez-Rocha (1998: 50); Villella (2016: 57). *"Royal conscience"*: from Cano's so-called *Origen de los Mexicanos* (Vásquez 1991: 157) (*si V.M. manda favorecer a estos que son de linaje, parécenos que conviene a su real conciencia, especialmente a la dicha doña Isabel, pues que era subcesora de Moctezuma el que dio la obediencia e vasallaje a V.M.*).

62. Nazareo wrote two shorter letters in Latin in 1556, and a much longer one on March 17, 1566; all three are in AGI México 168 (and in facsimile in Zimmerman 1970). The quote here is from the

1566 letter (f.2r of the AGI original; also reproduced in ENE, X: 89–129; and in PRT: 333–67, quote on 342). I thank Megan Mc-Donie for help acquiring the AGI originals, and Laurent Cases for help translating the Latin (although any errors remain mine) (*nostri parentes dominus Moteucçuma nosterque pater dominus Iuanes Axayaca germanus dicti Moteucçumae facile primo omnium surrexerunt in favorem hispanorum qui primo peragrarunt has partes Indiarum, quippe qui propensissimo animo ceciderunt coronae regiae maxima reverentia, dando per manus Ducis capitanei sacrae catholicae Magestati infinita bona tantam quantitatem donorum muniliumque infinita genera ex puris auris confectorum in signum aut potius indicium quo recognoverunt verum dominium vicarium altitonantis Dei vivi, ut sit unus pastor atque unum ovile*). On Nazareo's life, see Villella (2016: 73, 81–83); on these letters also see Laird (2014: 160–62). For a Franciscan summary of the College's early decades (with don Antonio Valeriano cited as star student), see Torquemada (1614, III: 129–32; Bk. 15, Ch. 43).

63. The quotes ("superstitious," etc.) are from Hajovsky's (2015: 8) summary of Sahagún's and Durán's depictions; but see Durán LXIII, LXVII–LXIX, LXXIV–LXXV; also Hill and MacLaury (1995) and Gillespie (2007).

64. FC; the process of its gradual availability, from the earliest publications in Spanish of portions of the codex through to its full online release, stretched from the 1880s to 2010s; also see relevant discussion, with citations, in Chapter 3.

65. Myers (2015: 17).

66. See the Gallery for a one of Maurin's lithographs (discussed further in Chapter 7). On Pacini: Subirá in EC: 105–26. On Spontini: BnF, département Musique, X-309 (score and libretto of the 1817 version); Spontini (1809); Lajarte (1883: 153–83); Subirá in EC: 117–18. On the war: There is an extensive literature (not included here) on Napoleon's invasion of Spain (part of the Peninsula War of 1807–14). On Cortés's childhood house destroyed: MacNutt (1909: 2, citing Alaman's *Disertaciones*).

67. *Largely forgotten*: "It was antiwar forces that ultimately proved victorious in the battle over the memory of the 1847 war" (Greenberg 2012: 274), with Americans choosing to celebrate the "just" war of the revolution and to ignore what Ulysses Grant called a war

so "wicked" that the Civil War must have been "our punishment" for that "transgression" (ibid.). *"Emphasize a relationship"*: in Myers (2015: 266–67).

68. Here I am not just quoting but paraphrasing Myers (2015: 314, 315).

PART II

1. Sell and Burkhart (2004: 126–27); Sell and Burkhart justifiably titled the untitled play *The Three Kings*; I here use their transcription and have modified their translation (with the assistance of Christopher Valesey) for style purposes (not as a correction; their command of colonial-era Nahuatl is irreproachable).

CHAPTER 3:
SOCIAL GRACE AND MONSTROUS RITUAL

1. Epigraph sources, in sequence: Solís (1724: 206); Collis (1954: 65); Escoiquiz (1798, I: 318) (*Deseo estar en amistad unido / Con vuestro Rey, y aboliré contento / A su ruego en mi mesa la comida / De humana carne, de él aborrecida*); Prescott (1994 [1843]: 42); Clendinnen (1991a: 2).
2. Gemelli (1704: 514–15).
3. Gemelli (1704: 547); Buccini (1997: 18–20). Verne's novel was first published in French in 1873; its enormous global success since then, in every conceivable medium from musical theater to television, makes it difficult not to see earlier journeys and their accounts—such as Gemelli's—through the prism of Verne's story. Without digressing into a discussion of the modern era's shifting perceptions of reality, it is worth emphasizing that eighteenth-century readers of Gemelli, unlike Verne's modern audiences, enjoyed not only the narrated adventures of the main protagonists but also the revelations of the world's wonders by a real eyewitness traveler.
4. Gemelli (1704: 523).
5. Terry Deary's *Horrible Histories* series was started in the United Kingdom in 1993; by its twentieth anniversary, the series had sold more than 25 million copies, in thirty languages. Despite inevitably reflecting popular stereotypes on the Aztecs, as the *Angry Aztecs* cover illustrates, Deary's writing also recognizes evolving scholarly opinions ("In the 1980s clever professors reckoned that the Aztecs

had huge cannibal feasts. . . . In the 1990s even cleverer professors say this idea is potty"; Deary 1997: 54).

6. *Stories*: Ogilby (1670: 46, 62–63); Elliott (1970: 21–25); Pagden (1982: 10); Boone (1989: 55–56); Restall (2003: 103–7); Davies (2016: Chs. 1, 5–6). *Velázquez*: Instructions written in Santiago de Cuba, 23 October 1518 (DC, I: 56; CDII, XII: 245) (*diz que hay gentes de orejas grandes y anchas y otras que tienen las caras como perros, y ansi mismo donde y a que parte estan las amazonas*).

7. Whitehead (2011: 9–15, Las Casas quote on 15; original in the *Apologética*: Las Casas 1909: 380; also see a variant in LCHI Bk. 3, Ch. 117 [e.g., 1971: 231]); also see Grafton (1992: 244); Abulafia (2008: 125–30); two articles in the same issue of *Ethnohistory*, by Boruchoff (2015) and by Keegan (2015); Davies (2016: Chs. 3–4, 8); and Stone (2017). The tall tales of strange idols and human sacrifices from the Grijalva expedition, as they became repeated, were often accompanied by outlandish illustrations that bore not the slightest relation to actual Maya or Aztec architecture, culture, or religious practice (e.g., the well-known variant in Montanus 1671: 73, and its twin in Ogilby 1670: 77).

8. *"Worship"*: Anonymous (n.d. [1556]); CDHM, I: 387, 398; Bustamante (1986: 129, 157) (*adoran el miembro que tienen los hombres entre las piernas*). *"Solicitous"* to *"excessively"*: Anonymous (n.d. [1556]); CDHM, I: 371, 374, 398; Bustamante (1986: 87, 97, 157–59) (*Solían tener grandes guerras y grandes diferencias entre ellos, y todos aquellos que capturaban en la guerra o se los comían o se les hacía esclavos; Y es la gente más cruel que pueda encontrarse en guerra, porque no perdonan ni a hermano, ni a pariente, ni a amigo, les quitan la vida aunque sean mujeres y hermosas, que a todas matan y se las comen; Todos los de esta provincia de la Nueva España, e incluso los de otras provincias de su alrededor comen carne humana, y la aprecian más que todas las demás comidas del mundo, tanto que muchas veces van a la guerra y ponen en peligro su vida para matar a alguien y comérselo, son como se ha dicho, en su mayor parte sodomitas, y beben desmesuradamente*). Early modern references to "Indians of New Spain" being cannibals are numerous; e.g., Jeronymo Girava Tarragonez's *Cosmographia*, excerpted in Apiano (1575), which describes them as preoccupied with sacrificing humans, whom they then eat, but "they do not eat the flesh of friends: only that of enemies" (*no comian de la carne del enemigo:*

pero comian de la del enemigo), with the ban on eating friends a religious one that was never broken, even if it meant starvation (appendixed p. x). Also see Ruy González's 1553 Letter to Carlos V (AGI Patronato 184, ramo 46 [old citation 2, caja 2, legajo 5]; ENE, VII, #369: 31–36; Stabler and Kicza 1986; discussed in Chapter 8). Díaz's obsession with indigenous cannibalism is well known, but note that he also seems to have copied passages from (or from the same source as) this 1566 Italian *Relatione*; e.g., CCVIII (1916, V: 262–63). Also see Boruchoff (2015).

9. Cervantes de Salazar (1953 [1554]: 74).
10. *"Care and devotion"*: DC, I: 165; also in RC; AGI Justicia 220, legajo 4: ff. 342–49, with a copy (not seen by me) in AGN Hospital de Jésus cuad. 1: ff. 1–4 (*su principal motive e intencion sea apartar y desarraigar de las dichas idolatrias a todos los naturales destas partes*). *"Received reports"*: DC, I: 260; original in the archive of the ayuntamiento of Mexico City, also reproduced as CC, document 5.
11. Adorno (2011: 35–41); Sepúlveda quote from the seventh of his 1552 "Twelve Objections" to Las Casas (in Lane 2010: 50; also see 6–13); Pagden (1982: 44–47).
12. Villagrá (1610: f. 29v, f.30r; translations mine, adapted from the looser ones in 1933: 65; the original lines are *el horrible infierno / Tuvo todos los años de tributo, / De mas de cien mil almas para arriba, / Que en solos sacrificios bomitava, / La gran Ciudad de Mexico perdida*). The poem is primarily about the early history of New Mexico but seeks to tie that history to the triumph over the Aztecs and to conquistador glories in general.
13. Quoted sources, in sequence: Valadés (1579: 170); Palomera (1988: 374); Valadés (1579: 171) (Latin original: *lachrymosum profecto & flebile spectaculum*); CDII, I: 470 (Zumárraga); Padden (1967: 96, 244); Palomera (1988: 375–76).
14. Quotes from Ogilby (1670: 239, 275); also see Montanus (1671).
15. "Human Sacrifices" is included in the Gallery; it was first published in Theodore de Bry, *Peregrinationes in Americam, Germanice, Pars IX* (Frankfurt, 1601), 3rd part, Plate VIII (the image here), then again by de Bry in 1602 in his *Americae, Nona et postrema pars*, and then in numerous publications through to the present century. Boone (1989: 73) noted its "sinister and oppressive tone"; also see Klein

(2016: 275–80). *Variations*: For example, an engraving in a 1707 Dutch edition of Herrera's *Historia General*, accompanying Herrera's passage detailing the horrors of Aztec sacrifice (Aa 1706–1708, vol. 10 [1707]: 185–204). *Tell us*: Klein (2016: 293).

16. Keen (1971b: 190–92): 70; Boone (1989: 57–67); Pagden (1990: 94–97); Elliott (2006: 241); Adorno (2011: 106–9; 2014); Laird (2014; 2016). No drawings or designs of the arch have survived, but Sigüenza published a small book of explanation (Sigüenza y Góngora 1680; 1928 [1680]: 1–148). I thank Rolena Adorno for drawing my attention to Sigüenza's book. Also see Fernández (2014: 26–67).

17. León y Gama (1792); Carrasco (2012: 10–12, from whom I borrow the León y Gama quotes); Adorno (2011: 117–21).

18. Nicholson (1961: 390); Hajovsky (2012; 2015: 119).

19. Campe (1784: 176–77) (my translation from this French edition: *barbares superstitions; les portoient chez eux, & les mangeoient avec leurs amis; N'est-il pas vrai, mes enfants, que cela est horrible? Mais préparez-vous à entendre quelque chose qui l'est encore beaucoup plus*).

20. Ranking (1827: 366–67).

21. Cook (1946). Cited, for example, by Padden (1967: 73–74) as evidence that "the holocaust went on unabated for four days and nights, with tens of thousands perishing on the slabs."

22. Prescott (1994 [1843]: 42); Morgan (1876: 286, 307, 308). Carrasco (2012: 12–13) drew my attention to Morgan's views; "influential" is Carrasco's adjective, quotes also used by him. Prescott quotes also used by Clendinnen (1991a: 3).

23. Morgan (1876: 308); Abbott (1904 [1856]: 64, 182) (I used this 1904 edition, but found 1884 and 1901 editions too; Abbott lived 1805–77).

24. Spinden (1928: 201).

25. Collis (1954: 51); Gibson (1966: 26); Padden (1967: 96, 97, 99); Harris (1977: 164); Coe (1984: 146; volume first published in 1962; a seventh edition came out in 2013); Clendinnen (1991a: 2); Pennock (2008: 15); MacLachlan (2015: 9, 68, 102, 220).

26. Carrasco quote (2012: 61).

27. *"Century of genocide"*: Hobsbawn (1994: 12); Levene (2000: 305, 307). Also see Meierhenrich (2014). *Soustelle*: (1964: 112) (I have here used the published English translation of the 1955 French original). Rowdon (1974: 10–16), in one early example of how the

Aztec stereotype can be applied to those who forged it, argued that "violence became basic to Christian life in the sixteenth century" and "an essential condition of Christian survival"; "narrow-minded," incapable of respecting "the unfamiliar," quick to justify the killing "in cold blood" of those who "looked different from Christians," the Christian's "attempts to spread his civilisation were therefore rather grotesque." The literature on violence in sixteenth-century Spain, Europe, and the early modern Atlantic world is too vast to cite fully here (but recent examples that, for me, repeatedly underscored Soustelle's point include the articles in the *Journal of World History* 17:1 [March 2006]; also Barker 2005; Meierhenrich 2014; Madley 2015; 2016).

28. *Montaigne*: Quote and its translation borrowed from Elliott (1970: 46). Michel de Montaigne's essay was first published in 1580. *Ometochtzin*: AGN Inquisición tomo 2, exp. 10 (I thank Robert Schwaller for sharing copies of the original documents with me); also see Don (2010: 146–76, citing the 1910 publication of this "Proceso inquisitorial") and Benton (2017: 39–45).

29. Harris (1977: 147). Note that this book prompted "a furious controversy" in academic publications (as Carrasco put it; 1992: 126); yet Harris helped keep the debate focused on why, not if, the Aztecs were cannibals, just as Díaz (1632) did centuries ago, and arguably that focus remains (Harris lived 1927–2001).

30. Zorita and Vargas Machuca quotes in Elliott (2006: 64) (see Zorita 1994 [1566]; NCDHM, III: 71–227), but also see Vargas Machuca's *Defense and Discourse of the Western Conquests* (Lane 2010), which is effectively a polemical essay on comparative cruelty and violence (and see Lane 2008); Las Casas (2003 [1552]: 29).

31. Clendinnen (1991a: 89). A brilliant mind and gifted writer, Clendinnen (1934–2016) left us a body of work that will deservedly find readers for many generations to come.

32. Carrasco (2012: 61).

33. Carrasco (2012: 61); Graham (2011: 40–43). Also see Smith (2016: 6).

34. Ventura (2014); "The Cannibal Kingdom" is the title of the Aztecs chapter in Harris (1977: 147–66); Díaz XCII (in 1632 ed., styled LXXXXII; 1632: ff. 69v–72v; 1910, II: 81; 2005, I: 241 (*no se podrían contar porque heran muchos*); Tapia (c.1545; Fuentes 1963: 42; J. Díaz et al. 1988: 105) also claimed that another conquistador,

Gonzalo de Umbría, counted "136 thousand heads, not counting those on the towers," impaled on skull racks in the central plaza of Tenochtitlan (*hallamos haber ciento treinta y seis mill cabezas, sin las de las torres*); Gómara copied this (1552: Ch. 82; 1964: 167), and from there it became part of the traditional narrative.

35. *Skull racks*: The 2015 discovery hit the international media in August (see Martínez Torrijos 2015 but many examples are archived online). *"No evidence"*: Carrasco (2012: 62–63).

36. *"Stagger the faith"*: Prescott (1994 [1843]: 42). *Different picture*: As a sequence of fine Aztec scholars have argued, in various ways, among them Soustelle (1964 [1955]), Keen (1971b), Clendinnen (1985; 1991a), Hassig (1985; 1988; 2001a; 2016), Smith (1986; 2016: 5–7), Matos Moctezuma (1987; 2009), Boone (1989; 1992; 1994), Gillespie (1989), Carrasco (1992; 2000; 2012), López Luján (1994), Evans (1998; 2000; 2004), Burkhart (2008), Pennock (2008), Maffie (2014), and Mundy (2015) (cited works are examples drawn from larger bodies of work by these scholars), in addition to "the giants upon whose shoulders Aztec scholarship rests" (Maffie 2014: xi), Miguel León-Portilla and Alfredo López Austin.

37. *"Society"*: Carrasco (2012: 9). *"Greatness"*: Keen (1971b: 48).

38. *"Epitomize"*: Boone (1989: 55). Madariaga (1969 [1942]) rendered the god's name, with some eccentricity, as "Witchy Wolves." Our Gallery includes "Uitzilipuztli: Principal Idol of the Mexicans" (Prévost 1746–59, XII [1754]: facing p. 546), a version of an image widely reproduced for centuries (albeit a relatively restrained variant, as some included devil's horns and, above the satanic-goat legs, a monstrous face on the torso; e.g., Valadés 1579, Ogilby 1670, and Montanus 1671, Mallet 1683: 5, 311, reproduced in Boone 1989: 82, the 1707 Dutch edition of Herrera in Aa 1706–1708, vol. 10: and the 1724 Townsend edition of Solís). Such images, with the accompanying lurid descriptions of Aztec deities and their grisly sacrifical rituals, represented three centuries of European mythmaking regarding the Aztecs. Prévost was writing history at a time when the modern methodology of copious footnotes to specific sources was in its genesis; the abbot thus made it clear that his perspective was not marginal or excessively spiced with imagination, but based on his reading of the canon of early modern sources that had created the traditional narrative on the Aztecs, Montezuma, and their

imperial demise (see his preface or "Avant-Propos" and its footnotes to Benzoni, Cortés, Díaz, Gómara, Herrera, Las Casas, Ogilby, Fernández de Oviedo, Martyr d'Anghiera, Solís, and others; 1746–59, XII [1754]: v–xiii).

39. One hesitates to attribute everything to Cortés; his Letter may have been repeating what other Spaniards were saying or writing in long-lost missives (CCR 1522: f. 16v; 1960: 65; 1971: 107). The detail appears as early as June 1521 in testimony given in Cuba by conquistador Juan Álvarez, who claimed the dough contained "the blood of men, and of the hearts of the Indians who had been sacrificed" (*maíz mollido con sangre de hombre e de corazones de los indios que habían sacrificado*) (DC, I: 170–209, quote on 207). *"Virgin boys"*: Tapia (c.1545; Fuentes 1963: 41; J. Díaz et al. 1988: 103) (*con sangre de niños e niñas vírgines*); Boone (1989: 46–49). Wagner's theory (1944: 190) that Tapia wrote his brief account in Spain c.1543 specifically for Gómara remains convincing (also Nicholson 2001a: 87; Roa-de-la-Carrera 2005 has no comment; but see Martínez Martínez 2010). *Bread* to *Cortés*: García (1729 [1607]: 301). Another example of the blood-dough story is in Torquemada (1986 [1614], III: 380, 404–6; also see 1614, I: 87, 90, 620–21; Bk. 2, Chs. 1–2; Bk. 4, Ch. 100).

40. *Suggested*: Argued by Jorge Gurría Lacroix (1978: 23–34); Boone (1989: 47) is skeptical of the argument.

41. As Boone observed (1989: 49–51); Díaz XCII (in 1632 ed., styled LXXXXII; 1632: ff. 70v–72v; 1908, II: 76–77; 2005, I: 236–41). Díaz's frequent copying of Gómara—his "ill-digested plagiarism," in Brooks's words (1995: 173)—is now widely documented by scholars (e.g., Adorno 1992; Roa-de-la-Carrera 2005; Miralles 2008; Duverger 2013).

42. Acosta (2002 [1590]). Although commonly called the Codex Tovar, the manuscript (in JCB) is actually titled *Relacion del origen de los Yndios que havitan en esta Nueva Espana segun sus historias* (Tovar 1585).

43. Montanus (1671: 73, 74, 82, 220–21 inter, 223); Ogilby (1670); Boone (1989: 4).

44. *No stone statues*: This may be because Huitzilopochtli was never represented in stone, but note too that his status in the Aztec pantheon—and the precious stones that adorned his statues—would have inspired immediate looting, dismemberment, and destruction by Spaniards (Boone 1989: 2). *Codex:* image from the Telleriano-

Remensis is in the Gallery under "Divine Images"; the original codex is in BnF, image on f. 5r, this version from a 1901 reproduction (now in the public domain). The codex was created in sixteenth-century Mexico (but later acquired by Archbishop Le Tellier of Rheims, hence its name, and its location today in Paris). *Teocalli*: Found in 1926 beneath the site where Montezuma's palace once stood, the Teocalli (as it is now called; Nahuatl for "temple") is now in the National Museum of Anthropology in Mexico City. Its paired representations of Huitzilopochtli and Montezuma are on the backrest of what is a stone-carved human-scale model of an Aztec temple, probably used as a throne, created during Montezuma's reign. Huitzilopochtli is on the left of a solar disk, Montezuma on the right. Easily found in print or online.

45. *Xolotl*: Codex Xolotl is in BnF (Manuscrits, division orientale, Mexicain 1.1); see Boone (1989: 31). In another codex in BnF, the Codex Azcatitlán, Huitzilopochtli is represented simply by a man wearing a full hummingbird costume, holding a spear and shield. *Teocalli*: Boone (1989: 16–17); Hajovsky (2015: 101–2, 109–13).

46. Boone (1989: 31–37); talk and seminar discussion at Pennsylvania State University by John F. Schwaller, February 9, 2016.

47. FC, I and XII (Boone 1989: 37 cites the original MS as Med. Palat. 218, f. 10r; 220, f. 437v).

48. *"Quintessential"*: Boone (1989: 86).

49. Boone (1989: 86); Nicholson (2001a: 291); Carrasco (2000: 63–103; 2012: 29–30, 91).

50. Note that characterizing Aztec deities as having discrete areas of responsibility ("god rain," etc.) reflects European influences of how we see Aztec religion. *Ehecatl*: Nicholson (2001a: 266–91). *Cholula*: The temple to Quetzalcoatl was long ago replaced by a church dedicated to the Virgin of the Remedies, but as a result the pyramid, still mostly intact, is still a pilgrimage site (Carrasco 2012: 31–32). *St. Thomas*: Durán (1971 [1579]: 57–69); Lafaye (1976: 177–208); Nicholson (2001a: 101, 105).

51. *Cholollan*: Tapia (c.1545; Fuentes 1963: 34; J. Díaz et al. 1988: 92); Nicholson (2001a: 88). Tapia had briefly been *encomendero* of Cholula (meaning he had the right to maintain a household there and to collect tribute payments in goods and labor), so it is likely that he heard the deity's name (which he renders as "Quezalcuate")

in that town. *Sahagún*: FC, II. Beginning with Sahagún, chroniclers and historians asserted the Cortés-as-Quetzalcoatl story as if it were well-known fact; of the few who cited sources, none could claim one that predated Sahagún. For example, when Dominican friar Gregorio García remarked in the 1729 edition of his *Origin of the Indians of the New World* that "Moteçuma and his Court believed that don Hernando Cortés was Quezalcoatl," he cited Torquemada and Sahagún (García 1729 [1607]: 143). Torquemada's book was published in 1614, seven years after the original edition of García, which was in turn one of Torquemada's sources; the Torquemada citation was thus added by the editor of the 1729 edition—the circularity lending the weight of authenticity to Sahagún's fiction. Fernando Alvarado Tezozomoc, one of Montezuma's grandsons, wrote a "Mexican Chronicle" in 1598; he likewise repeats the story at the end of his book, having Montezuma conclude when the Spaniards first appear on the coast that "he is the god Quetzalcoatl for whom we have been waiting" (1878 [1598]: 687) (*es el dios que aguardamos Quetzalcoatl*). Not all contemporaries believed it worth repeating: Juan de Tovar, in his "Account of the Origins of the Indians of this New Spain," written about 1585, ignored the myth completely—including when he mentioned Quetzalcoatl (1585; 1878 [1585]: 119–20) (also see Charnay 1903).

52. *Mendoza*: Mendoza's letter was paraphrased in Fernández de Oviedo's *Historia general* (1959 [1535], IV: 245–48) (Nicholson 2001a: 88–91 cites a different edition). *Franciscans*: Carrasco (2012: 112) notes that Sahagún's claim "has resulted in endless debates" regarding its invention or its actual belief in Montezuma's court in 1519. Arguments in favor of Montezuma or Aztecs generally believing some version of it include Nicholson (2001a: 32–39; 2001b) and MacLachlan (2015: 108–9); ambivalent positions are taken by Elliott (1989 [1967]: 36–38) and Hassig (2006: 55), with Carrasco (2000: 205–40) taking a sophisticated middle position; arguments against include Frankl (1962: 10–12), Parry (1977: 319), Lockhart (1993: 235), Thomas (1993: 185), Restall (2003: 114–15), Townsend (2006: 47–50), and Villella (2016: 130–31). In a way, the issue is one of timing: Carrasco has argued that the return of Quetzalcoatl "represents not a postconquest fabrication in order to explain an incredible political collapse, but a *postconquest elaboration* of an in-

digenous tradition" (italics his; 1992: 145–47); I would argue that it is a postconquest fabrication developed to explain a political collapse. Sahagún's insistence that it was not true that Quetzalcoatl would return ("he is still expected, but it is not true; it is a falsehood"; FC, I) is ironic in view of the persistent belief "in Mexico and among some Latinos in the United States" that Quetzalcoatl still "may return one day in some powerful symbolic and political form" (Carrasco 2012: 112). *Appeal:* In the lost indigenous source that scholars call *Crónica X*, used by Durán, Tovar, Tezozomoc (1949: 90) (also see Charnay 1903), and others in the late sixteenth and early seventeenth centuries, Quetzalcoatl is "the god whom all of us await, the one who crossed the sea of heaven." Also see Chimalpahin (1997: 180–83; Nicholson 2001b: 12–13; "He is alive and will not die, and he will return to rule once again").

53. Boone (1989: 86–88); Pagden (1990: 96–102). Pagden argues that Clavigero knew that Sahagún had invented the Cortés-Quetzalcoatl connection, but that it was too useful not to use in his efforts to make Quetzalcoatl "a symbol of mestizo and *criollo* religious distinctiveness" (102); see also Lafaye (1976: 187–90).

54. Howard and Dryden (1665); Restall (2013) is linked to a performance of the semi-opera in Madrid in 2013.

55. A 1668 performance at the court of King Charles II included performances by courtiers such as the Duke and Duchess of Monmouth. One cannot but hope that the Duke played Montezuma. At the play's end, Montezuma loses his throne and commits suicide. In the real world, the Duke—who was the king's illegitimate son—rebelled when his uncle James succeeded his father Charles to the throne in 1685. For his ambitions, the Duke was beheaded. Hutner (2001: 65–88); Thompson (2008).

56. In a dedication to the published version, he reiterated that he had "neither wholly follow'd the Truth of the History, nor altogether left it: but have taken all the liberty of a Poet, to add, alter, or diminish, as I thought might best conduce to the beautifying of my Work" (also quoted at the top of my Prologue; Dryden 1668 [1667]: unnumbered prefatory pp. 26, 27).

57. Dryden (1668 [1667]: 64).

58. Quoted phrases: Dryden (1668 [1667]: 68, 65). Also see Brown (2004: 71–73).

59. *"Unstable edifice"*: Pagden (1990: 96).
60. Rueda Smithers (2009: 290–91); Collis (1954: 65–66); on Frías, see Frías (1899–1901); Bonilla Reyna and Lecouvey (2015: 61–116).
61. *"Table"*: Ranking (1827: 345).
62. Essay in Lasso (1594: ff. 295–304; quotes on ff. 295v, 296r, 300r) *(los Indios de la nueua España no eran belicosos, sino cobardes, simples, ignorantes, sin ingenio ni habilidad, ni modo de biuir . . . tan flacos de coraço[n], y ta[n] afeminados (como algunos dizen) . . . muy dieztros en las armas . . . pelear valerosamente . . . el animo y fortaleza de los Indios . . . diminuye[n] el merito q Cortes gano en ve[n]cerlos; . . . el espantoso nimbre y poder de Moteçuma Rey de Mexico . . . ni en grandeza de Reyno, ni en numero de vassallos, ni en abundancia de riquezas).*
63. Ogilby (1670: 239). See "Ruffled Feathers" (phrase inspired by a 2016 Penn State graduate seminar paper of that title by Catherine Popovici), showing the frontispiece to Ogilby's *America*. The maps scattered across this beautiful volume (and its Dutch twin, by Montanus) all feature cartouches of people surrounding the captions, with various indigenous figures wearing feathered skirts and headdresses. In an illustrated passage on the "Ancient Attire of the Mexicans," Ogilby remarked that unlike "the several barbarous Nations, that run up and down naked in *New Spain*," the Aztecs wore cotton clothing, and elaborate feathered accessories around their heads, necks, and legs (1670: 276–77). I have also included the Ogilby/Montanus portrait of Montezuma, identified in Latin as *Rex ultimus Mexicanorum* ("The Last King of the Mexicans"), and thus as a personalized portrait, yet highly generic in its details; it was reproduced for centuries in various European publications, usually varied and altered but never much—examples are a version published in Germany (Happel 1688: 101) and one in Antwerp in a Spanish edition of Herrera's *Historia General* (1728, I: facing 401).
64. Romerovargas Iturbide (1964: 21–26, quotes on 21–22, 24) *(un gran reformador y educador de su pueblo; el único gobernante de su tiempo en el mundo que exigiera la educación obligatoria de todos los miembros de la sociedad; curiosidad morbosa como pretendieron interpretar este hecho los españoles que tanto hablaban de caridad, tan mal la conocían y en nada la practicaban; de temperamento profundamente artístico; amado por su pueblo al grado de ser casi adorado).*
65. Romerovargas Iturbide (1964: 27–57; 1963–64, III: 184–85) *(figura*

excelsa . . . héroe nacional . . . fue cogido por sorpresa y tomado pri-
sionero . . . vejaciones, tormentos y martirios tanto físicos como mo-
rales . . . atormentado y reducido a la impotencia).

66. Restall (2003: 15, 100).

67. I am paraphrasing the succinct summary by Hajovsky (2015: 8, 136–38, 142); also see Gillespie (2008). Hill and MacLaury (2010) use the Sahagún/FC account of Montezuma's weaknesses to show how MacLaury's vantage theory (which uses color to categorize personality viewpoints) can be applied to sixteenth-century Aztec understandings of "person."

68. Gemelli (1704: 513–14); Vaca de Guzmán (1778: 1, 6, 16) (*el terrible Motezuma; el Rey mas arrogante; su mortal letargo*); Ranking (1827: 314, 321, 318; italics in original).

69. *White God*: This is my translation of the French title; the English edition was titled, less revealingly, *The Conquistadors*; Descola (1957 [1954]: 101–228). Valadés (1579); Palomera (1988: 31) (*leyenda pre-ñada de presagios fatalistas influía poderosamente en el ánimo religioso de los mexicanos, especialmente en el espíritu supersticioso de Moctezuma*).

70. Wolf (1959: 155–56); Todorov (1999 [1982]: 118–19); Tuchman (1984: 11–14); Le Clézio (1993: 10); MacLachlan (2015: 109, 191–92). Also see Restall (2003: 114–15, 134–35), citing some of these same sources, as well as Fernández-Armesto (1992), Gillespie (2008), and Allen (2015: 479).

71. *Essence as emperor*: Hajovsky (2009; 2015).

72. Hajovsky (2009: 338); Mundy (2011a: 175–76). Boone (2017) has recently shown that the feathered Aztecs in Weiditz's 1529 costume book, long assumed to be portraits of the Aztecs brought back to Spain by Cortés, are in fact imaginative blends of Aztec, Brazilian Tupinambá, and "Oriental" costumed featherwork. By the time of de Bry's illustrations to the 1601 volume of his *Peregrinationes in Americam*, all the prints that illustrate some aspect of Mexico feature generic Native American lords wearing feathered skirts and feathered headdresses—Montezuma's specific identification is implied on the illustrated title page of de Bry (1601; the plates are section 3 of the volume, following p. 72 of the second section). In more than one hundred images of "Indians" in Pieter vander Aa's 28-volume Dutch edition of Herrera's *Historia General*, all are shown naked or clothed only in feathers (Aa 1706–1708); the same trope runs

through editions in multiple languages of Solís and of Robertson.

73. Hajovsky (2011) is the definitive study of the Thevet portrait (quotes are from him, p. 336); also see Hajovsky (2015) for the larger context of Montezuma portraiture.

74. On the Medici portrait of Montezuma (unsigned but attributed to Rodríguez): Escalante Gonzalbo (2004: 171–77); Hajovsky (2009: 350); Schreffler (2016: 14–17). The engraving included in our Gallery as "A Noble Savage" is from *Istoria della Conquista del Messico,* an Italian edition of Solís's *History* published in Venice in 1733, although the engraving was included in Italian editions beginning in 1699; it was based on the Montezuma portrait painted by a Mexican artist that Cosimo III de' Medici had received by 1698 (and which hangs today in Florence's Medici Treasury, or Museo degli Argenti). The caption reads: "Portrait of Moctezuma, engraved from the original sent from Mexico to the Most Serene Grand Duke of Tuscany." Solís (1733: facing 243); Hajovsky (2009: 349–50); Alcalá and Brown (2014: 117).

75. Niles and Moore (1929: 128–29).

76. *Cortés wrote*: DC, I: 225, 230, et al. *Centuries*: Restall (2003: Ch. 4).

77. *Aztec Ruler*: McEwan and López Luján (2009: 23). *Revenge*: "The Aztec Two-Step" and "Montezuma's Revenge" are likely North American variants on phrases popularized by the British during World War II but surely coined generations earlier, such as "Delhi Belly," "the Rangoon Runs," "the Cairo Two-Step," "Pharaoh's Revenge," the later variant, "Ghandi's Revenge," and so on; the phrase first seems to appear in print in the United States in the 1950s (e.g., phrases.org.uk/meanings/montezumas-revenge.html). The assertion on various websites that Cortés threw up the first meal given to him by Montezuma, with every subsequent gringo regurgitation an echo of that original vengeful offering, is not supported by evidence.

CHAPTER 4:

THE EMPIRE IN HIS HANDS

1. Epigraph sources, in sequence: Durán (1967 [1581], II: 398; translation mine, but see 1994 [1581]: 389; I was led to this passage by Hajovsky 2015: 23) *(a quien todos de conformidad acudieron con sus*

votos, sin contradicción ninguna, diciendo ser de muy buena edad y muy recogido y virtuoso y muy generoso, de ánimo invencible, y adornado de todas las virtudes que en un buen príncipe se podían hallar; cuyo consejo y parecer era siempre muy acertado, especialmente en las cosas de la Guerra, en las cuales le habían visto ordenar y acometer algunas cosas que eran de ánimo invencible); Brian, Benton, and García Loaeza (2015: 19–20) (I have omitted a sentence from the middle of the quote); Dryden (1668 [1667]: unnumbered prefatory p. 25).

2. The map was published with Latin captions in Nuremberg in 1524, and with Italian ones in Venice in 1525. See Mundy (1998: 13–22) and Boone (2011: 32–38) on identifying the indigenous and European elements of the map; also Chapter 1. In addition to "Downtown," the image cluster that began this chapter, see "The Urtext" in the Gallery.

3. The original is typically called the Nuremberg Map (see Mundy 1998; 2011b). For sample variants, see differing versions, all clearly descended from the Nuremberg Map, from 1528 (in Italian, printed in Venice), 1556 (Italian, Venice; see Ramusio 1556), 1564 (French, Lyons), 1575 (Latin, Antwerp; engraved by Frans Hogenberg), 1576 (Italian, Venice; an engraving not a woodcut), 1580 (Italian, Venice), 1631 (German, Frankfurt), and 1634 (Latin, Frankfurt) (see de Bry 1634, Part 13: 125), all in JCB and all accessible through jcb.lunaimaging.com. A good example of the multiple-island variant is in Prévost (1746–59, XII [1754]: facing p. 325). Mundy (1998: 32) also lists variants published in Italy and France from 1524 to 1612; also see Kagan (2000: 89–95). The Italian rendering created by Giovanni Battista Ramusio in 1556 was reproduced widely, with minor changes, for centuries; in fact, the Ramusio Map was a more direct influence on subsequent versions than was the Nuremberg Map; a late example of the Ramusio Map, printed in Mexico City in 1858, is in CDHM, I: 390–91 inter. On the early modern "copy-cat publishing" of maps of Tenochtitlan, see Kagan (2000: 89–90).

4. *Statue*: It is eccentric enough to have prompted many theories (summarized by Boone 2011: 35); my guess is that the engraver was inspired as much by medieval images of headless savages as he was by Aztec statues with displaced heads such as those of Coatlicue and Coyolxauhqui. I am grateful to Laurent Cases for discussing the

Latin captions with me. For a list and identification of all the labels (Latin version only), see Mundy (1998: 32).

5. Anonymous, (1522 [*Ein Schöne Newe Zeytung*] unnumbered pp. 7–8); translation mine, with the kind assistance of Wolfgang Gabbert and Mitzi Kirkland-Ives; also see Wagner (1929).

6. CDHM, I: 362 (*Tenia Monteuzuma por grandeza una casa en que tenia mucha diversidad de sierpes e animalias bravas, en que habia tigres, osos, leones, puercos monteses, viboras culebras, sapos, ranas e otra mucha diversidad de serpientes y de aves, hasta gusanos; e cada cosa de estas en su lugar, e jaulas como era menester, y personas diputadas para les dar de comer y todo lo necesario, que tenian cuidado dello. Tenia otras personas monstruosas, como enanos, corcobados, con un brazo, e otros que les faltaba la una pierna, e otras naciones monstruosas que nacen ocasionadas*).

7. *Zuazo*: CDHM, I: 362–65 (*Señora de la plata*). *Ordaz*: Thomas (1993: 471); also see AGI Patronato 150, 5, 1: ff.4v–7v; Justicia 712 (old citation; Otte 1964). *Myth*: The discoveries of the Great Temple project (PTM) have been seen in Mexico as putting to bed some long-standing popular skepticism regarding the zoo (e.g., see Blanco et al. 2009; Ventura 2014); I have not found evidence of equivalent, modern skepticism outside Mexico.

8. On the lists of items sent to Spain: DC, I: 232–49; FC, XII: 58–59; Gómara (1552: Ch. 39; 1964: 84–87; Schroeder et al. 2010: 124–27); Solari (2007: 253); Russo (2011: 7–8). On buried objects, see citations to the PTM in notes to this and the previous chapter. Amara Solari's 2003 M.A. thesis and a version of it published in Mexico (2007) planted the seed for my thinking on Montezuma as a collector, thereby underpinning this chapter and providing a crucial link in the argumentative chain of the whole book.

9. *Map*: The Nuremberg Map's *casa* (Italian) and *domus* (Latin) parallel *casa* used in Spanish accounts; early modern English versions or translations of such accounts use "house," occasionally "palace" or "Pleasure-House" (e.g., Townsend version of Solís, 1724: 75). Block quote: Ogilby (1670: 88–89). On Aztec palace terminology, see Evans (2004).

10. Sahagún (1997 [c.1560]: 207); Solís (1724: 78). Such claims have appealed to later writers; Romerovargas Iturbide (1964), for example, imaginatively used them as evidence of an Aztec social welfare system.

11. Gómara (1552: Ch. 73; 1964: 151; Schroeder et al. 2010: 197); Díaz

XCI (in 1632 ed. styled as LXXXXI; 1632: f. 68; 1908, II: 67; 1984 [1632]: 169; 1963 [1632]: 229–30; 2005 [1632]: 232); Solís (1724: 76). As often, despite his claims to eyewitness reporting, Díaz simply copied Gómara, who uses the same phrases to imagine hellish zoo noise (op. cit.). (Díaz: *muchas viboras y culebras emponzoñadas, que traen en la cola uno que suena como cascabeles . . . cuando bramaban los tigres y leones, y aullaban los adives y zorros, y silbaban los sierpes, era grima oirlo y parecia infierno.*)

12. Solís (1724: 75); Gómara (1552: Ch. 73; 1964: 150–51); Schroeder et al. (2010: 196—"cranes" etc. quote is Chimalpahin's addition to Gómara's text); CCR (1524; 1960: 140; 1971: 223) (*otras que estaban junto a ellas, que aunque algo menores eran muy más frescas y gentiles, y tenía en ellas Mutezuma todos los linajes de aves que en estas partes había; y aunque a mí me pesó mucho de ello, porque a ellos les pesaba mucho más, determiné de les quemar, de que los enemigos mostraron harto pesar y también los otros sus aliados de las ciudades de la laguna*).

13. *"Lanners"*: Gómara (1552: Ch. 73; 1964: 151; Schroeder et al. 2010: 197). *Florentine Codex*: the zoo image that is "The Zookeeper" in our Gallery (FC, VIII: f. 30v in original MS) goes with Ch. 14 (41–45), Paso y Troncoso ill. #71. *"Extremely large"*: Motolinía (1951 [1541]: 269) (I have used Speck's translation here). *"Sheep"*: Solís (1724: 75–76; 1733: engraving facing p. 81): engraving included in our Gallery as one of the frames in "Picturing the War." Note that an Aztec-carrying eagle featured in an early colonial legend in which Montezuma dreamt of his empire's impeding loss, and this Solís image was also reproduced as a stone bas-relief on the atrium wall of Mexico City's St. Hippolyte church—it survives and attracts varying guidebook and online interpretations, while it slowly deteriorates (Durán LXVII; Sánchez 1886; my 2009 Mexico City field notes; also see mention of the St. Hippolyte church in Chapter 2).

14. The term I have glossed as "jackal" is *adive*; by "here they call" (*en esta tierra se llaman*) Díaz must mean Spain, or Spanish Mexico, not indigenous Mexico, as the word is Spanish of Arabic origin (Díaz XCI; 1632: f. 68r; 1984 [1632], 169; 2005 [1632]: 232; 1963 [1632]: 229, Cohen note) (*de tigres y leones de dos maneras: unos, que son de hechura de lobos, que en esta tierra se llaman adives, y zorros y otras alimañas chicas*); Gómara (1552: f.44v; Ch. 73; 1964: 150).

15. Ventura (2014); in fact, some such drawings "morphologically look more like wolves" than coyotes (in the words of Ximena Chávez Balderas, who has been doing important work on the bones found by the Great Temple project [PTM]).

16. Tapia (c.1545; Fuentes 1963: 40; J. Díaz et al. 1988: 102) (*hombres monstruos y mujeres: unos contrechos, otros enanos, otros corcovados*); Motolinía (1951 [1541]: 269) (I have used Speck's translation here); Solís (1724: 76–77). Also see CCR (1522: f. 17; 1960: 67; 1971: 111) and Gómara (1552: f.44v; Ch. 73; 1964: 150), who describe albinos as included here. *Modern Mexican historians*: e.g., Romerovargas Iturbide (1964: 21–22) (*curiosidad morbosa; para que el estado cuidase directamente de ellos por espíritu humanitario*).

17. *Status*: Aztec women's roles have been studied extensively by scholars, producing a literature that cannot be adequately covered here (but good starting points are the essays in Schroeder et al. 1997, especially one by Louise Burkhart; Evans 1998; Kellogg 2005: 18–30; and Pennock 2008). *Polygyny*: Hassig (2016; quote on p. 7); also see Townsend (2014). *Discrete compound*: e.g., Herrera (Dec. II, Bk. VII; 1728, I: 407).

18. *"Three thousand"*: Herrera (Dec. II, Bk. VII; 1728, I: 40) (*Dormían pocos hombres en esta casa Real. Avía mil mugeres: aunque otros dizen que tres mil, y esto se tiene por mas cierto, entre señoras, criadas, y esclavas*). Also see Torquemada (1614, I: 250–51; Bk. 2, Ch. 89). *Wives*: Ogilby (1670: 239) (Herrera comment is: *y assi dizen que úvo vezes que tuvo ciento y cinquenta preñadas à un tiempo: las quales à persuassion del diablo movían, tomando cosas para lançar las criaturas, para estar desembaraçadas, para dar solaz à Motezuma, ò porque sabían que sus hijos no avían de heredar*).

19. CCR (1522; 1960: 68; 1971: 112) (*todas nuevas y nunca más se les vestía otra vez*), repeated by Gómara and then misrepeated by Díaz (see Brooks 1995: 173).

20. Brussels, as a major city in the Spanish Netherlands, was part of Carlos's European empire. On the loot, the Totonacs, and their tour, see Russo (2011); van Deusen (2015a).

21. DC, I: 242–49; Fernández de Oviedo (1959 [1535], IV: 10) (*que todo era mucho de ver*).

22. Solís (1724: 77).

23. FC, VIII (Sahagún 1954, VIII: 45); CCR (1522: f. 17v; 1960: 66;

1971: 108); Tapia (c.1545; Fuentes 1963: 40–42; J. Díaz et al. 1988: 101–5); Gómara (1552: Ch. 79; 1964: 161); Gemelli (1704: 513). Examples of Aztec animal figurines are in museums such as Mexico's National Museum of Anthropology, the Peabody Museum of Archaeology and Ethnology at Harvard University, and the British Museum.

24. Las Casas (first quote), in Boone (1992: 160); Díaz XCI (1908, II: 67–68; 2005, I: 232) (*pintores y entalladores muy sublimados*). Tovar to Acosta: Boone (2000: 29); see ibid. (28–63) for an explanation of how Aztec writing was not fully hieroglyphic (as the Maya system was), but largely pictorial, with some phonetic components and abstract marks that conveyed meanings (rather than particular words), allowing the system to function in multiple languages. Cano (in Martínez Baracs 2006: 50) claimed there were five sets of books, each covering a different aspect of imperial government. On the tribute lists, see Berdan (1987: 162–74); Hassig (1985); "great house" is Díaz XCI (1632: f. 67v; 1910, II: 64; 2005, I: 230) (*y tenia destos libros una gran casa dellos*).

25. Berdan (1987: 165); Solari (2007: 254), who led me to López Luján (1994: 240–43).

26. Gómara (1552: Ch. 66; 1964: 142) (*es verdad que tengo plata, oro, plumas, armas y otras cosas y riquezas en el tesoro de mis padres y abuelos, guardado de grandes tiempos a esta parte, como es costumbre de reyes*) (Russo 2011: 12 drew my attention to this passage); Ixtlilxochitl (1985 [c.1630]: 136). Chimalpahin added to his version of Gómara: "a thousand kinds of fierce animals were kept by order of the great lord, and all because he knew his ancestors had done so" (Schroeder et. al. 2010: 196). On Nezahualcoyotl, see Martínez (1972); on Tetzcoco's palaces, Evans (2004: 24–29).

27. Solari (2007: 248–51); Durán XXIII (1967 [1581], II: 192; 1994 [1589]: 189) (*la grandeza . . . la facilidad con que los mexicanos hacían todo lo que querían . . . que os calienta con su calor y fuego, señor excelente de lo criado*).

28. FC, IX. On these first four means of acquisition, also see Berdan (1987).

29. "*Best*": Díaz XCI (1908, II: 68–69); Evans (2000). "*Trustworthy*": Motolinía (1951: 268), quoted by Solari (2007: 251). "*Bird-net*": Sahagún (1997 [c.1560]: 207).

30. Tapia (c.1545; Fuentes 1963: 40; J. Díaz et al. 1988: 101) (*asaz de oro e plata e piedras verdes*); Gómara (1552: Ch. 93; 1964: 186); Solari (2007: 241–43, 247).

31. Cortés (CCR 1522: ff. 17v–18r; 1960: 67; 1971: 110–11); Solís (1724: 75–76; 1733: 81).

32. *"thick timbers"*: Cortés (CCR 1522: f. 18r; 1960: 67; 1971: 111) (*jaulas grandes de muy gruesos maderos muy bien labrados y encajados*); FC, VIII: 44–45. *"Diseases"*: the Solís (1724: 75) version of Cortés (CCR 1522: f. 18r; 1960: 67; 1971: 110–11).

33. Zuazo in CDHM, I: 362–65; Díaz XCI–XCII (1632: ff. 66–72); CCR (1522; 1960: 51–69; 1971: 85–113); Tapia (c.1545; Fuentes 1963: 39–44; J. Díaz et al. 1988: 100–8).

34. *"Bodies"*: Gómara in Chimalpahin version (Schroeder et al. 2010: 197); Solís (1724: 76); Díaz XCI (1632: f. 68r; 1910, II: 67 and again in CCX, 1916, V: 274; 1963 [1632]: 229–30; 1983 [1632]: 169; 2005 [1632]: 232; *les davan a comer de los cuerpos de los indios que sacrificavan*). *Snakes* to *devil*: Ranking (1827: 349–50). Last line: For example, Marshall Sahlins and S. L. Washburn speculated in the *New York Review of Books* in 1979 that the zoo's function was tied to Aztec human sacrifice, with the animals fed human body parts. nybooks.com/articles/archives/1979/nov/08.

35. *"Custom"*: Solís (1724: 76).

36. Impey and MacGregor (1984); Findlen (1994); Johnson (2011: quote here is hers, 231).

37. CCR (1522: f. 17; 1971: 101; 1993: 230–32) (*otras que yo le di figuradas y el les mando hacer de oro*); Russo (2011: 10–18; 22n59) led me to Gómara (1552: Ch. 39) and Las Casas (LCHI Bk. 3, Ch. 121 [e.g., 1876, IV: 486]); Johnson (2011: Chs. 3, 6).

38. *"Died"*: Cortés writing to his father in 1527 (AGI Justicia 1005, No. 1: f. 3r; quoted more fully below). *Chorographs*: e.g., Harris (1705) reproduced in Restall (2003: xiv). *Children's book*: Herman-O'Neal (2013). Also see Solari (2007).

39. *"Darwin"*: Romerovargas Iturbide (1964: 25) (*tres siglos antes que Darwin mandó organizar parques zoológicos*). It also seems possible, and surely not mere coincidence, that the development of botanical gardens in Europe, starting in Italy in the 1540s, was influenced by descriptions of Aztec garden complexes (as suggested by Ian Mur-

sell; mexicolore.co.uk/aztecs/aztefacts/aztec-pleasure-gardens; also see López Lázaro 2007: 18–26).

40. AGI Justicia 1005, No. 1: f. 4r (letter of 23 Nov 1527 within 1531 file relating to Cortés's dealings with his cousin Francisco de Las Casas; letter also in DC, I: 480; I am grateful to Megan McDonie for acquiring copies of the original AGI documents); note that the phrase "it is booty to be gifted [*es pieça para dar*]" employs the same term—*pieza*—that Spaniards used to describe slaves (indigenous and African, acquired in war or by purchase) (*aqui en my [sic] casa se a criado un trigre [sic] desde muy pequeno y ha salido el ma[s] ermoso anymal que jamas se a visto porque demas de ser muy lindo es muy manso y andaba suelto por casa y comya a la mesa de lo que le davan y por ser tal me parescio que podria yr en el navio muy seguro y escaparía este de quantos se han muerto sup[lic]o a vra mrd se de a Su magd que de verdad es pieça para dar*).

41. Solari (2007: 240, 252).

42. *"Apex"*: Solari (2007: 260). *Great Temple*: Matos Moctezuma (1987).

43. Hajovsky (2015: 131), whose study of the portrait (2012; 2015: 118–36) underpins my discussion of it; see his work for photographs of what remains of the stone carving. He notes (personal communication, December 2016) that Bishop Zumárraga likely began the work of cultural destruction centuries before further rounds of official vandalism in the eighteenth century. The entire carving is more than six feet high, but the relief of Montezuma's body is closer to four and a half feet.

44. Quote by Hajovsky (2015: 118), who does a masterful job of exploring the richness of this iconography, devoting most of a book to it (see 2012 and 2015). I also thank him for generously sharing his drawing of the portrait.

45. *"Icon"*: Hajovsky (2012: 188).

46. Durán LII (1967 [1581], II: 398; 1994 [1581]: 389) (*por su gran valor y excelentes hechos*); Codex Tovar (Tovar c.1585); *Primeros Memoriales* (Baird 1993: Figs. 48–49); Gillespie (1989: 96–120); Solís Olguín (2009); Matos Moctezuma (2009); Hajovsky (2015: 23); Hassig (2016: 48–59).

47. In other words, that emperor was known as Ilhuicamina in his lifetime, then as Moteuczoma during the reign of his great-grandson

of the same name, and then in the post-invasion centuries gradually as Moctezuma Ilhuicamina; the designation of the second Montezuma as Montezuma Xocoyotl ("the Younger") was most likely a posthumous invention. For this argument (and contrary opinions), see Gillespie (1989: 167–70) and Hajovsky (2015: 15, 23). Also see Hassig (2016). The coronation stone is now in the Art Institute of Chicago: see photographs and comment by Elisenda Vila Llonch in McEwan and López Luján (2009: 68–69); also Hajovsky (2015: 114–15).

48.   Durán LIV (1994 [1589]: 407); Matos Moctezuma (2009); Hajovsky (2015: 23).

49.   *Tizoc*: Durán XXXIX–XL (1994 [1581]: 296–308); Gillespie 1989: 16. *Nicaragua*: Torquemada (1614, I: 193–215, 218; Bk. 2).

50.   Berdan and Anawalt (1992); reproduction of tribute listings by Lorenzana in Cortés (1770: inserted between Second and Third Letters). Codex Mendoza (Bodleian Library, Oxford University, but widely reproduced in print and online), f. 15v, shows towns and city-states (*altepeme*) conquered by Montezuma during his reign (the facing page and its reverse, f. 16, show another twenty-eight towns conquered). The towns are identified in alphabetic Nahuatl and by name-glyphs, with flames bursting from the temples to indicate defeat. The blue band on the left is a yearly calendar, with three years added post-invasion, covering the war (1519 or One Reed; 1520 or Two Flint Knife; and 1521 or Three House). *Noose*: Berdan (2009: 191).

51.   I have resisted the temptation to add physical and personality descriptions of Montezuma, because sources for such descriptions are colonial and strike me as overwhelmingly imaginary. But there is a rhetorical way to make the point regarding his character, one that I have used in lectures on this topic: the following adjectives, taken from a 1552 source, arguably apply well to Montezuma: very strong (*gran fuerça*), courageous (*mucho animo*), serene (*assentado*), devout (*devoto*), given to praying (*rezador*), well suited both to war and peace (*tuvo en la guerra buen lugar, y en paz*), much given to women (*muy dado a mugeres*), stubbornly argumentative (*rezio porfiando*), he dressed more neatly than extravagantly, being a very clean man (*vestia mas polido, que rico, y assi era ombre limpissimo*), he took delight in a large household and family (*deleitavase de tener mucha casa y familia*), he carried himself in a lordly way and with much

gravity (*tratavase muy de señor, y con tanta gravedad*), as a boy he was told that he would conquer many lands and become a very great lord (*le dixeron siendo muchacho, como avia de ganar muchas tierras, y ser grandissimo señor*). The twist here is that these all come from Gómara's description not of Montezuma but of Cortés (1552: f. 139v [Ch. 252]; translations mine, but for slightly different ones, see 1964: 409), reflecting how quickly the two men became "monstrous doubles of one another" (as Sayre 2005: 51 put it), and suggesting that inverting the stereotypes of the traditional narrative is one way to undo them.

52. On the omens, their role in the scapegoating of Montezuma, and evidence for their postwar invention, see Gillespie (1989: Ch. 6); Fernández-Armesto (1992); and Restall (2003: 114, 137, 183n36); Carrasco (2000: 236–40) takes a less skeptical position.

53. *Into the present day*: For example, a 2005 History Channel episode on "Cortés," in line with the traditional narrative, has Montezuma trying to stop the Spanish advance by bribing Cortés with gifts, "sending magicians to stop him," and ordering the Chololteca "to assassinate" him—while at the same time believing "that Cortés was a god, [that] he was immortal, that he couldn't be killed" (Bourn 2005). *"Great army"*: Aguilar (c.1560; J. Díaz et al. 1988: 166; Fuentes 1963: 143) (*Motecsuma, según pareció, tenía puesto el los caminos un gran ejército aunque no le vimos más de por la relación que nos fue hecha*).

54. Tapia (c.1545; Fuentes 1963: 33; J. Díaz et al. 1988: 90) (*los desbarataran en breve y fenecieran la guerra con ellos; e así yo que esto escribo pregunté a Muteczuma y a otros sus capitanes, qué era la cabsa porque tiniendo aquellos enemigos en medio no los acababan en un día, e me respondien: Bien lo pudiéramos hacer; pero luego no quedara donde los mancebos ejercitaran sus personas, sino lejos de aquí: y también queríamos que siempre oviese gente para sacrificar a nuestros dioses*).

55. Hassig (2006: 93).

56. *Caxtillan* or *castillan tlaca* is used in CA: 274–77 and in the Historia Tolteca-Chichimeca (Lockhart 1993: 282–87); *caxtilteca* or *castilteca* in the Annals of Cuauhtitlan (op. cit.: 280–81); also see op. cit.: 14, 21.

57. The Aztec calendar was merely one of many, similar calendars used across Mesoamerica for millennia (there were Maya equivalents of the

xihuitl, for example). The literature on the topic is extensive, but notable studies are Broda (1969), Florescano (1994), and Hassig (2001a); I also found DiCesare (2009) useful. *Panquetzaliztli:* Schwaller (see p. 401n46) argues that the dedication to Huitzilopochtli, and the central role played by merchants, were distinct to how that festival was celebrated in Tenochtitlan from the mid-fifteenth century on.

58. *"Deer":* FC, XII: 160.

59. FC, I: Ch. 18; II: Ch. 21; *Primeros Memoriales* (Baird 1993: Figs. 14, 21); Clendinnen (1985); Carrasco (1995; 2012: 75–77); Hajovsky (2015: 31–33).

PART III

1. Epigraph sources, in sequence: using the translation of Carvajal in Jáuregui (2008 [1557]: 111) (*Como! Y piensan de estorbar / que las gentes no pasasen / a las Indias a robar?*); Thevet (1676: appendix p. 78); Young (1975).

CHAPTER 5:
THE GREATEST ENTERPRISES

1. Epigraph sources, in sequence: Cervantes de Salazar (1953 [1554]: 47); Robertson (1777, II: 3); Fernández de Oviedo (1959 [1535], III: 149 [Bk. XVII, Ch. XIX]).

2. Mendieta (1870 [1596]: 174–75) (*meter debajo de la bandera del demonio á muchos de los fieles . . . el clamor de tantas almas y sangre humana derramada en injuria de su Criador . . . infinita multitud de gentes que por años sin cuento habian estado debajo del poder de Satanás*).

3. *Valiant Cortés:* Lasso de la Vega (1588; 1594: Canto XXIII, f. 259r). Forgive my unpoetic translation of *Sin dar noticia alguna a Rey Christiano, / Hasta que este varon al mundo vino, / Que fue en el año mismo que Lutero, / Monstruo contra la Iglesia horrible y fiero. Saavedra:* Saavedra (1880 [1599]: 85); Martínez (1990: 107) led me to this passage. The poem was titled *The Indiano Pilgrim* (*Indiano* did not mean "Indian," but referred to a Spaniard who went to the Indies and made his living or fortune or career there, typically returning to Spain—where he might therefore be called, respectfully, an *indiano*). *Dating problem:* Torquemada (1614, I: 374; Bk. 4, prologue). Examples are Nicolás Fernández Moratín's "Las naves

de Cortés" (Martínez 1990: 108) and Juan de Escoiquiz's *México Conquistada: Poema Heroyca* (Escoiquiz 1798). According to David Boruchoff (in a paper presented at the John Carter Brown Library, Providence, Rhode Island, in May 2015), by the middle of the seventeenth century, more than thirty Catholic writers had stated in print that Cortés and Luther were providentially born on the same day and year.

4. *"Prose"*: Adorno (2011: 46), who has keenly grasped Gómara's agenda and how much it has tainted subsequent accounts; reprinted and translated dozens of times, the book was a huge international hit, the means whereby "Cortés and Gómara bedazzled the world" (in the words of Las Casas, who denounced it as a tissue of distortions and fabrications); also see Roa-de-la-Carrera (2005). *Crony*: Las Casas (1561: f. 623v; 1951 [1561], II: 528) (from the 1561 MS: *no escrivio cosa sino lo quel mismo Cortes le dixo*). *More likely*: Martínez Martínez (2010) argues persuasively that Gómara's intimacy with Cortés has been exaggerated, and that his close relationship was with his son.

5. In the original, "*buena señal... milagro*" (Gómara 1552: f. 2v); in the early English version, "a myracle and good token . . . some sayd ye God had sente the Dove to comforte them" (1578: 4). That Christ did not begin preaching until 30 (Luke 3:23), while Cortés did not bring Christianity to indigenous Mexicans until he was about thirty-three, was probably not lost on Gómara, but making a meaningful point of such a parallel might have bordered on blasphemy.

6. Gómara (1552: f. 2r; translations mine, but see the looser translations in 1964: 7–14) (original: *harto, o arrepentido de estudiar . . . mucho peso a los padres con su ida, y se enojaron . . . era bullicioso, altivo, traviesso, amigo de armas . . . era muy buen ingenio, y habil para toda cosa . . . determino de irse por ay adelante . . . mucho oro*); Gómara (1578: 2); the anonymous "Life of Ferdinand Cortés," written in Latin in the 1550s, uses the same anecdotes and themes (probably drawn from Gómara, as Icazbalceta suggested) (Anonymous 1858 [1550s]; CDHM, I: 312–17). "French version" is Thevet, here quoted in a contemporaneous English translation (1676: 76).

7. Cervantes de Salazar (1914 [1560s]: 95–96 [Bk. 2, Ch. XV]) (*Fue Hernado [sic] Cortes, a quien Dios, con los de su compañia; tomo por instrumento para tan gran negoçio . . . muy habil*).

8. Díaz XIX–XX (1632: ff. 12v–14r); Solís (1684, et al.); Robertson (1777, II: 3).

9. Robertson (1777, II: 4).

10. Robertson (1777, II: 3, 3–6, 6–134); Thevet (1676: 76) (I have here used the 1676 English edition, not translated the French original).

11. Both the elision of Cortés's Caribbean years and their characterization as a period when he was waiting for his great moment and developing the skills he would need are part of a tradition stretching from Gómara (1552: f. 2) to the present (see, for example, Elliott 2006: 7–8).

12. The final four lines of Keats's sonnet "On First Looking into Chapman's Homer," accessed online at poetryfoundation.org/poem /173746.

13. Some pro-Cortés Spanish accounts claim that he won his *encomiendas* by helping Governor Ovando put down an indigenous rebellion, but he arrived on Hispaniola a year after the Spaniards put down Anacaona's alleged revolt by hanging her and burning other native leaders alive in the Xaragua massacre, and there is no evidence to corroborate the claim that Cortés "displayed in the field many notable feats of arms, already giving notice of his future strengths [*ejecutó en esta campaña muchos y muy notables hechos de armas, dando ya anuncios de su futuro esfuerzo*]" (Anonymous 1858 [1550s] in CDHM, I: 318).

14. *Hatuey*: LCHI Bk. 3, Ch. 25; numerous other sources. "*Obesity*": Indeed, it reflects the sniping that characterized the feud between Cortés and Velázquez (and between their allies) for decades after 1519 and even after the two men's deaths. Quote in Anonymous 1858 [1550s] in CDHM, I: 320 (*por su obesidad*). Also see Thomas (1993: 75–80).

15. *Bad leg*: Cervantes de Salazar (1914 [1560s]: 98 [Bk. 2, Ch. XVI]); Thomas (1993: 132); Duverger (2005: 98). *Explorations*: Rather than preface his *Conquest of Mexico* with coverage of conquest campaigns in which Cortés was conspicuously absent, Gómara described them in a separate book, *La Istoria de las Yndias* (1552b: ff. 18–26) (although some editions bound and sold the two works together). For eighteenth-century accounts of Spanish activities of 1504–18, when Cortés was in the Caribbean but largely absent from the story, see Prévost (1746–59, XII [1754]: 132–251) and Robertson (1777, I:

177–245), both based largely on Gómara and Herrera (the latter's coverage is in Dec. I, Libro VI through Dec. II, Libro III, e.g., Herrera 1728: 129–217). Some primary sources from the AGI are in CDII, I: 1–365, including the *repartimiento*, or allocation of groups of indigenous villagers to Spanish settlers, of the island of Hispaniola. Also see Fernández de Oviedo (1959 [1535], I: Bks. I–V; II: Bks. XVI–XVIII). For modern scholarly coverage, see Mira Caballos (1997); Livi Bacci (2008); and Stone (2014: 128–207; 2017). *American Traveller*: Anonymous (1741); this second or interior title page (p. 97), an engraving of a young, bearded Cortés, armored but sporting a soft hat and a baton of office, was used as a frontispiece to *The American Traveller*, published in London from 1741 through to the next century.

16. *"Nicaragua"*: Berry and Best (1968: 123). *Collis*: Collis (1954: 23–24).

17. *Ochoa*: DCM: #720; WWC: 99–100; Schwaller and Nader (2014: 236–37); *Alvarado brothers*: Numerous biographical details in works cited in this note, but the best starting point is DCM: #s40–44; *Bermúdez*: DCM: #130; WWC: 169; Schwaller and Nader (2014: 193); *Sopuerta*: DCM: #969; WWC: 237; Schwaller and Nader (2014: 196).

18. Mira Caballos (1997: 391–99); Livi Bacci (2008); Stone (2014; "harvest" of "Indians" plays off the title of this dissertation; 2017); Reséndez (2016: 34–45, 325). Source documentation includes AGI Contaduría 1017, which details the taking of enslaved Taínos from Hispaniola to Puerto Rico (my thanks to Scott Cave for the citation and summary); also see numerous mentions in ENE, I.

19. Gómara (1552: f. 3v; 1964: 13) (*Diego Velazquez temio por ver le armado, y a tal ora. Rogo que le cenasse, y descāsasse sin recelo; su amigo y seruidor; Tocaronse las manos por amigos, y despues de muchas platicas se acostaron juntos en una cama. Donde los hallo la mañana Diego de Orellana, que fue al ver el gouernador y al dezir le como se auia ido Cortes*).

20. Gómara (1552: f. 3v; 1964: 14) (*Por semejantes peligros y rodeos corren su camino los muy escelentes varones hasta llegandoles esta guardada su buena dicha*); Madariaga (1942: 66).

21. See "Cortés Outwits" and "Cortés Renounces" in the Gallery. Variations on "Cortés Outwits" were repeated in many versions of the Cortés story (e.g., Abbott 1904 [1856]: 47). This figure is from Dalton (1862: 61).

22. Gómara (1552: ff. 5r, 3r, 56r, 57r; 1964: 19, 12, 192, 196) (*el era demasiado mugeril; muy enojado de fernando Cortes; etaua mal anojado e indignado*). Díaz (1632; etc.) mentions Velázquez frequently, in antipathetic and critical ways, throughout his account; indeed he is consistently hostile to the Velázquez faction (as Duverger points out, arguing that Cortés was the ghost author of Díaz's book; 2013: esp. cf. 191).

23. First and second block quote: LCHI Bk. 3, Ch. 27 (1561: f. 624r-v; 1951 [1561], II: 528–29). Third block quote: LCHI Bk. 3, Ch. 21 (1951 [1561], II: 506) (*era muy gentil hombre de cuerpo y de rostro, y asi amable por ello; algo iba engordando, pero todavía perdía poco de su gentileza; era prudente, aunque tenido por grueso de entendimiento; pero engañólos con él*); Bk. 3, Ch. 27 (1561: f. 624v; 1951 [1561], II: 529).

24. Martínez in DC, I: 45n1; Thomas (1993: 75–78); Mira Caballos (1997); Stone (2014: 91–98, 135–44). Anacaona was hanged, following the massacre of her family and entourage, by an expedition led by Ovando but with Velázquez playing a leading role. Columbus's son Diego Colón was technically still governor of Cuba, and Velázquez his lieutenant governor, but Colón had returned to Spain in 1515 and exercised no power. The Velázquez-Fonseca marriage connection is stated by Gómara (1964 [1552]: 327); Elliott (1971: xiv) accepts it, but Thomas calls it a "tropical tease" (wishful thinking by Velázquez), while detailing the personal and patronage connection between the two men (1993: 78, 84, 115, 136, 337).

25. *Enslavers*: a paraphrase from Reséndez (2016: 42). *Wounds*: Gómara (1552: 3v; 1964: 14) (*iendo por indios; discubrio a Yucatan; aun que no truxo sino heridas del descubrimiento, traxo relacion como aquella tierra era rica de oro, y plata, y la gente vestida*). This summary was repeated with minor variations over the centuries (e.g., Solís 1684: 13 [Bk. I, Ch. V]). The name *Yucatan* derives from Mayas responding to Spaniards on Cozumel with phrases like *ma natic a than*, "we don't understand your language," or "we don't understand what you are saying"; or, as the Franciscan friar Diego de Landa claimed, *ci u than*, "funny talk" or "comical language" (see Restall et al., n.d., or any of the various editions of Landa's *Relación de las cosas de Yucatán*).

26. Juan Díaz's account, first published in 1520, is in CDHM, I: 282–308 (in Spanish and in Italian, the latter version being the oldest surviving one), in Díaz et al. (1988: 37–57) (in Spanish), and in

Fuentes (1963: 5–16) (in a loose English translation). Italian and Latin editions from 1520 are in JCB. Also see Martyr d'Anghiera (1521).

27. *Dismissive*: CDII, XXVII: 307 (also quoted by Thomas 1993: 114). *"Wept"*: Gómara (1552: f. 4r; 1964: 15) (*llorava por que no querian tornar con el*). *"Bobo"*: Juan de Salcedo was sent to Santo Domingo, Gonzalo de Guzmán and fray Benito Martín to Spain (Thomas 1993: 97, citing Díaz; see XVII). *Adelantado*: See introduction to the term in Chapter 2.

28. *Islands*: Vásquez de Tapia, writing years later, claimed that they "received news of the great city of Mexico [*tuvimos noticia de la gran ciudad de México*]" (in Díaz et al., 1988: 133) but he surely used hindsight to impose such details onto the general impression given to the Spaniards in 1518; more reliable is Juan Díaz, whose account refers not to a mainland but to a series of islands, the largest being Yucatan and Ulúa. The tiny island of Ulúa (as it is still called) faces today's Veracruz (the original Vera Cruz of 1519 was moved in 1521 to the site now called La Antigua de la Vera Cruz, and then in 1599 moved to its present location; see Myers 2015: 39–76 for an engaging approach to the "Three Veracruces"). *Fray Juan*: Díaz in CDHM, I: 306–7 (*habitan en casas de piedra, y tienen su leyes y ordenanzas, y lugares públicos diputados a la administración de justicia*); Díaz? [anon.] 1972 [1519]; Martyr d'Anghiera (1521: 32). *Handcrafted*: Gómara (1552: f.4; 1964: 15–17). *Nothing to do with it*: The argument that Velázquez made the Conquest of Mexico possible, but Cortés took all the credit, is of course made repeatedly in numerous Velázquez petitions and lawsuits. Fernández de Oviedo also made the point (see chapter epigraphs). Thomas (1993: 97–115) summarizes the Grijalva expedition, with clear citations to primary accounts by Bernal Díaz (see VIII), Juan Díaz, Vásquez de Tapia, etc.; also see Solís (1684: 14–26 [Bk. I, Chs. V–VIII]). For a brief imaginative summary of the Hernández and Grijalva expeditions, with fantastical illustrations of Maya sacrifices, see Ogilby (1670: 76–79).

29. *"Greedy"*: Gómara (1552: f. 5r; 1964: 19) (*Tenia poco estomago para gastar, siendo codicioso*). Baltasar and two other Bermúdez men, Agustín and Diego, joined the company; Diego died in the war, but the other two returned to Cuba in 1520 (DCM: #s129–130; Thomas 1993:

450; WWC: 169; Schwaller and Nader 2014: 193). *"Devotion"*:
Anonymous (1741: 391). *"Heart"*: Solís (1684: 27 [Bk. I, Ch. IX]) (*un
hombre de mucho corazon, y de poco espiritu*).

30. See the prosopography and indices in DCM; WWC; Schwaller
    and Nader (2014: 160–240).

31. *"Jealousy"*: Robertson (1777, II: 6–8). *"Personality"*: Palomera (1988:
    28), whose discussion is based entirely on Díaz (1632; etc.) (Palom-
    era's original: *la personalidad superior de Cortés*).

32. Ogilby (1670: 90). For modern summaries of the Garay affair, see
    Thomas (1993: 583–85); Duverger (2005: 263–65). On the Narváez
    expedition: AGI Patronato 180, ramo 2.

33. 1520 testimony in DC, I: 170–209. The four officials were Alonso
    de Estrada, Gonzalo de Salazar, Rodrigo de Albornoz, and Pedro
    Almindez Chirinos.

34. *"Evils"*: CCR (Letter of October 15, 1524; 1960: 202; 1971: 332)
    (*pienso enviar por el dicho Diego Velázquez y prenderle, y preso, enviarle
    a vuestra majestad; porque cortando la raíz de todos males, que es este
    hombre, todas las otras ramas se secarán*). *"Grave"*: Elliott (1971) in
    Cortés (1971: xxxvi). My summary of the Cortés-Velázquez feud
    owes much to Elliott (1971). Also see Duverger (2005: 227–29,
    269–70); and, on Ponce de León and Cortés, AGI Patronato 16, no.
    1, ramo 4 (first item, 1526).

35. *Cortés' parents*: Martínez Martínez (2006). Bulk of archival feud-
    related material in AGI Justicia 49 (Velázquez *residencia*) and 220–
    225 (RC, or Cortés *residencia*); México 203 (conquistador *probanzas*
    etc.); AGN Hospital de Jesús; DC, I: 91–101, 129–209; and II.

36. *"Brothers"*: The Andean *mestizo* Guaman Poma writing in 1615 of
    Andean perceptions of conquistadors (quoted in Lamana 2008: 34);
    I do not mean to suggest that Mesoamerican and Andean percep-
    tions were the same, but that Spaniards in the Americas were.

37. The paragraphs preceding and following on conquistador cohorts
    are drawn from details in numerous sources, including CCR; Díaz
    (1632); DCM; and Thomas (1993; WWC), but especially Schwaller
    and Nader (2014: 119–44 in particular).

38. DCM: #975; Díaz CXCV (1632: f. 224v; 1916, V: 142; 2005, I:
    723–24); Thomas (1993: 626–27, on the Puertocarrero-Cortés kin
    link); Gardiner (1961); Scholes (1969). Despite the robbery, and the
    Crown taking its share, Sandoval's parents received more than eight

thousand pesos in gold (sufficient to support them through old age in considerable comfort)—the spoils of Sandoval's *encomienda* income and placer mining, all acquired through unpaid indigenous labor (AGI Patronato 65, no. 1, ramo 19: ff. 1–23, is a 1562 *probanza* on Sandoval by one of his nephews; AGI Justicia 1005, no. 2, ramo 2 is a 1532 lawsuit, one of numerous documents dealing with the property of Cortés's murdered cousin, Rodrigo de Paz, this one involving the Sandoval family; also see Justicia 1017, various but esp. no. 5 [1530]; Scholes 1969: 198).

39. Andrés de Tapia, along with his relative Bernardino Vásquez de Tapia and Alonso de Ávila, was one of the conquistadors who joined Cortés in funding the Franciscan convent founded on the main site of Montezuma's zoo in 1524 (NCDHM, I: 187–93).

40. Hometown and kinship identities tied the Velázquez cohort together, as they did other cohorts: other conquistadors who did not fight in the Spanish-Aztec War but played roles in the larger story, and who were also from Cuéllar, were Juan de Grijalva, members of the Bermúdez clan (some fought in Mexico, some didn't), and Juan de Cuéllar; the red-bearded *Velazquista* Pánfilo de Narváez was from the nearby village of Navalmanzano (Thomas 1993: 151). On Ordaz: AGI Patronato 150, 5, 1; Justicia 712 (old citation; Otte 1964).

41. Elliott (1971) in Cortés (1971: xxxvii).

42. DC, IV: 267–70 (*Pensé que el haber trabajado en la juventud, me aprovechara para que en la vejez tuviera descanso, y así ha cuarenta años que me ocupado en no dormir, mal comer y a las veces ni bien ni mal, traer las armas a cuestas, poner la persona en peligros, gastar mi hacienda y edad, todo en servicio de Dios, trayendo ovejas a su corral muy remotas de nuestro hemisferio . . . sin ser ayudado de cosa alguna, antes muy estorbado por nuestros muchos émulos e envidiosos que como sanguijuelas han reventado de hartos de mi sangre . . . por defenderme del fiscal de Vuestra Majestad, que ha sido y es más dificultoso que ganar la tierra de los enemigos . . . no se me siguió reposo a la vejez, mas trabajo hasta la muerte . . . no es a culpa de V. M. . . . . magnánimo y poderoso rey*); the "prime minister" (he held various titles, which I have simplified with this Anglicism) was Francisco de los Cobos (he wrote *No hay que responder*).

43. Prescott's translation (1994 [1843]: 640–41) of excerpts from the

1544 letter gives Cortés more eloquence than he had (as is true of most translations of Cortés). Others have echoed Prescott's literal reading of the 1544 petition; e.g., Madariaga (1942: 391, 393, 473–82), who titles the final part of his biography "Self-Conquest," beginning with a chapter on "The Conqueror Conquered by his Conquest," and concludes "Poor Cortés!"

44. *"Model"*: Clendinnen (1991b: 62); in which essay she both accepts and problematizes Cortés's "passion and talent for control of self and others" (60). *"Oeuvre"*: Cortés in previously quoted petition (DC, IV: 268) (*esta obra que Dios hizo por mi medio es tan grande y maravillosa*). *"Exercise"*: I am quoting and paraphrasing (somewhat unfairly, for rhetorical purposes) Elliott (1971) in Cortés (1971: xii).

45. *Hotel*: Myers (2015: 67).

46. *Probably known*: Juan Ponce de León had accidentally stopped on the coast of Mexico or Yucatan en route from Florida back to Cuba in 1513; in 1515, a Spanish judge in Panama claimed to have a conversation, through interpreters, with a literate Mesoamerican trader or refugee (Thomas 1993: 57), so it is likely that news and knowledge were also passing in the direction, toward Tenochtitlan, in the 1510s. As early as the Hernández de Córdoba expedition of 1517, Mayas south of Campeche were already so familiar with the newcomers (who called themselves Castilians) that they called out "Castilan!" to them as they approached (according to Díaz III; 1908, I: 19).

47. *"In-waiting"*: Gruzinski (2014: 76).

48. The June 20 petition was found and published by Schwaller and Nader (2014), from which the discussion here is heavily drawn; the block quote is my translation from the facsimile and transcription (70–71), but indebted to their translation (103). The other two documents, written first week and 10th of July, 1519, respectively, are accessible in DC, I: 77–85 and in Cortés (1971: 3–46).

49. AGI Indiferente General 145, I, legajo 15: f. 1r; DC, I: 102 (*cuatrocientos hombres . . . poblaron allí . . . una villa . . . y así poblada, la dicha gente eligieron e nombraron entre sí alcaldes e regidores e otros oficiales del Consejo y nombraron al dicho Hernando Cortés por gobernador e justicia mayor de la dicha tierra*).

50. Díaz XLII (1908, I: 156) (*"Tu me lo ruegas y yo me lo quiero"* glossed by Maudslay as "You are very pressing, and I want to do it" and as

"You ask me to do what I have already made up my mind to do" by Prescott 1994 [1843]: 165).

51. LCHI Bk. 3, Ch. 115 (1876 [1561]: 453–54; 1971 [1561]: 229–30, quote); Bk. 3, Ch. 123 (1971: 243–45, on Vera Cruz).

52. Ogilby (1670: 258–59).

53. CCR (1522; 1960: 32–33; 1971: 51–52) (*tuve manera como, so color que los dichos navíos no estaban para navegar, los eché a la costa por donde todos perdieron la esperanza de salir de la tierra; se me alzarían con ellos; ver los pocos españoles que éramos; por ser criados y amigos de Diego Velázquez*) (modern English lacks a good cognate for *criado*, which I have translated here as "dependent," and which is often translated as "servant"; its early modern English equivalent was "creature"). Also see "Cortés Orders" in the Gallery.

54. *"Remarkable"*: Prescott (1994 [1843]: 186). *"Unwilling"*: Gómara (1552: Ch. 42; 1964: 90). *"Heroic"*: Díaz LIX (1908, I: 210); *Sings*: Sessions (1965: 14–16, 4). *"Hero"*: Filgueira Valverde (1960: 93–94) (*Las palabras del capitán encendieron fulgores de triunfo y de codicia sobre las pavesas de los rotos maderos. Hízose esperanza de la desesperación. Y todos se sintieron barro de historia, moldeado por las manos fortísimas de un Héroe*). *"Episode"*: Gardiner (1956: 28), who also noted the increasing exaggeration of Cortés's actions over time, citing a number of earlier chronicles and studies.

55. *Many before me*: Gardiner (1956: 29) traced this invention back to Suárez de Peralta (1949 [1589]); Elliott (1989 [1967]: 41) noted that a Spanish historian (F. Soler Jardón) was probably right that Cervantes de Salazar invented it in 1546 in order to underscore the classical analogy, later (1914 [1560s]: 180–82 [Bk. 3, Ch. XXII]) reverting to the ship-beaching version; Thomas (1993: 223) suggests Cervantes de Salazar may have misread *quebrar* ("break") for *quemar* ("burn") in conquistador testimony. Also see discussion and further references in Restall (2003: 19, 166n63–65). *Julian*: Julian burned more than a thousand river craft in A.D. 363 prior to launching a campaign to the east; the parallel with Cortés was imagined by Prescott (1994 [1843]: 186) and repeated many times since. *Centuries of chroniclers*: Gardiner (1956: 30n38) cites the run of sources from Las Casas, Motolinía, and Herrera, through Solís and Clavigero, to Bancroft and Alamán; but for some of the earlier versions stemming from Gómara, see Gómara (1964: 89–91, who virtually

admits he wrote the episode to echo the "exploits" of "great men, like Omich Barbarossa"); Aguilar (Fuentes 1963: 138–39); Tapia (1963: 25–26); Cervantes de Salazar (ibid., who helped turn Gómara's fiction into fact by insisting that Cortés's feat was superior to Barbarossa's); and Díaz LVII–LX (1908, I: 206–15).

56. *Escalante*: Gómara (1964: 91) and Díaz LVII–LVIII (1908, I: 208–9). *La Coruña*: April 29, 1520 (AGI Patronato 254, no. 3, 1, ramo 1; MacNutt 1909: 112–13). "*Unseaworthy*": Tapia (1963: 26). "*Knowledge*": Díaz LIX (1908, I: 210).

57. Bourn (2005).

58. *Machiavellian*: Mizrahi (1993: 107); Carman (2006: 49–50); both of whom cite other scholars of literature who have made Cortés Machiavellian. "*Implausible*": Clendinnen (1991b: 54) on the Meeting.

CHAPTER 6:
PRINCIPAL PLUNDERERS

1. The sources to these three epigraphs: Thevet (1676: 77); Las Casas, LCDT: 307 (León-Portilla 2005 [1985]: 18 led me to this passage) (*Tan pronto pudo entender el rey Moctezuma nuestro idioma como para comprender las estipulaciones de ese citado primer salteador, en las que se les pedía la renuncia al reino o la cesión de todo su estado real? No es verdad que sólo son válidos aquellos contratos en que las partes contratantes de entienden mutuamente?*); Krauze (2010: 69) (*una misteriosa convergencia los unió desde el primer momento: querían pensarse, descifrarse mutuamente*).

2. Works that feature Montezuma's death prominently or as the pivot to the drama or narrative are far too many to list (after the Meeting, the emperor's death and the Noche Triste are probably the most common pivot points), but an example of a book-length study built on the theme is Romero Giordano (1986) (also see n10 later in this chapter on Montezuma-themed opera).

3. CCR (1522: f. 20v; 1960: 79; 1971: 132) (*Y el dicho Mutezuma, que todavía estaba preso, y un hijo suyo, con otros muchos señores que al principio se habían tomado, dijo que le sacasen a las azoteas de la fortaleza y que él hablaría a los capitanes de aquella gente y les harían que cesase la guerra. Y yo le hice sacar, y en llegando a un pretil que salía fuera de la fortaleza, queriendo hablar a la gente que por allí combatía, le dieron una*

pedrada los suyos en la cabeza, tan grande, que de allí a tres días murió); same citations for "the fortress" (*la fortaleza*) in previous paragraph.

4. Ogilby (1670: 89). Similarly, Gemelli had "the Indians" hurling "many stones and arrows," wounding him "in the Head, Arms, and Legs, whereof he soon after dy'd" (1704: 560). There are scores of discussions of Montezuma's death, and while I have tried to present one that is based on my reading of primary sources, I have found the following useful in various ways: MacNutt (1909: 266–71); Hassig (2006: 113 has only one paragraph, but 215n21–22 lists a dozen early sources); Johansson (2010); Castañeda de la Paz (2013: 339–43); Graulich (2014: 450–59).

5. Solís (1724: 206–12; quote on 211). The claim that the Aztecs called Montezuma "effeminate [*afeminado*]" goes back through Torquemada (1614, I: 543–44; Bk. 4, Ch. 70; "*bellaco afeminado, nacido para texer, y hilar, essos perros te tienen preso porque eres una gallina*") and Ixtlilxochitl (1985 [c.1630]: 226, 229) to Cervantes de Salazar (1953 [1554]; 1914 [1560s]: 478 [Bk. 4, Ch. CXII], whom Torquemada copied, omitting the insult of "sodomite" [*cuilón*] and "you are their concubine" [*te tienen por su manceba*]; op. cit.: 481 [Bk. 4, Ch. 114]: "he was your concubine" [*fué vuestra manceba*]); see Castañeda de la Paz (2013: 339–40) and Graulich (2014: 453–54).

6. Escoiquiz (1798: II, 255) (*la funesta Piedra; le abrió sangrienta herida*). An interesting variant on this argument is by Las Casas, who in a margin note to one of his writings comments that a people cannot be forced to accept a distant lord, which is why the Aztecs stoned Montezuma (LCDT f. 69; 1958: 178–79; margin note in MS B in JCB); this, of course, contradicts his assertions elsewhere that Cortés stole Mexico instead of acquiring by legitimate conquest or donation by Montezuma. Also see "A Lamentable End" at the top of this chapter.

7. Robertson (1777, II: 90–91).

8. Dryden (1668 [1667]: 64); Cervantes de Salazar (1914 [1560s]: 478–79 [Bk. 4, Chs. CXII–CXIII]) (*ni quiso comer ni ser curado . . . el corazón se me hace pedazos . . . tú no tenías herida para morir della; mueres de pesar y descontento*); Herrera (Dec. II, Bk. X, Ch. 10; 1728: I, 476–77); Díaz LXXXVIII–CXXVII (1632: ff. 65–105; with death in CXXVI–CXXVII). *To the present*: Thomas, for example, concluded that Spanish culpability was "improbable" and that Monte-

zuma "seems either to have refused to be treated, or to have had no wish to live longer" (1993: 402, 404).

9. For a visual example of the presentation of Montezuma on the balcony as an Ecce Homo echo, see scene 32–33 in the 1698 *Conquest of Mexico* oil and mother-of-pearl paintings by the González brothers: original in the Museo Nacional del Prado, Madrid, and reproduced variously (e.g., Alcalá and Brown 2014: 41). For an art historian's suggestion that Cuauhtemoc is represented as leading the Aztec stoning of Montezuma in a seventeenth-century *biombo* (screen painting), see Mundy (2011a: 166–67).

10. Sessions (1965: 446–71, quotes on 450, 465–66, 471). Completed in 1962, with libretto by Borgese and music by Sessions, the opera debuted in Berlin in 1964. It was part of a sporadic modern return of opera to the Cortés and Montezuma theme, after the great run of such operas from Vivaldi (1733, in Italian) through works (in chronological order) by Karl Heinrich Graun (in German), Francisco di Majo (in Italian), Agustín Cordero (in Spanish), Josef Mysliveček (a Czech; libretto by an Italian), Giovanni Paisiello (in Italian), Antonio María Gasparo Sacchini (in Italian), Nicola Antonio Zingarelli (in Italian), Fermín del Rey (two operas, both in Spanish), Giuseppe Giordani (in Italian), Mariano de Bustos (in Spanish), Marcos Antonio Portugal (a Portuguese writing in Italian), Gaspare Spontini (in French; see 1809), Henry Rowley Bishop (in English), Ignaz Xavier Seyfried (in German), Giovanni Pacini (in Italian), Ignacio Ovejero (1848, in Spanish). This list is, I suspect, a small percentage of the operas written on this theme during those years. For details on some of them, see Subirá in EC: 105–26.

11. Acosta (2002 [1590]: 3); Durán LXXVI (1994 [1581]: 545); Tovar (1878 [1585]: 144–45) (*y no faltó quien dijo que porque no le viesen herida le habian metido una espada por la parte baja*); Ixtlilxochitl (1985 [c.1630]: Ch. 88); Thevet (1676: 77, "brains"); Chimalpahin (1997: 158–59). *"At night"*: quoted by Johansson (2010). *Codex Moctezuma*: the tiny image in this sixteenth-century codex, with Nahuatl text (in the Biblioteca Nacional de Antropología e Historia, Mexico City), has been interpreted as illustrating Montezuma's strangulation or—in reference to the loin-clothed Aztec dying on the ground—his death stab from a Spanish sword. While that verdict on how the emperor died may be correct, the drawing was more likely intended

to convey his status as a prisoner of the Spaniards (just as similar images in other colonial-era illustrated manuscripts—such as the *Lienzo de Tlaxcala*—showed a Spaniard holding Montezuma by a rope or chain, while the Aztec ruler spoke from the rooftop).

12. Chavero in footnote to Muñoz Camargo (1892 [1592]: 217 [Bk. II, Ch. VI]) (*no es cierto que Moteczuma muriera de la pedrada: está bien comprobado que lo mandó matar Cortés*); Romerovargas Iturbide (1964: 20) (*fue asesinado por los españoles*).

13. See the "Burned" images from FC in the Gallery; Johansson (2010).

14. The "Burned" images in the Gallery are from FC, XII: ff. 40r, 41r; Magaloni Kerpel (2003: 34–42). The Montezuma-Christ association evokes yet another twist: the question of whether the emperor "was baptized and died a Christian" or not—as Muñoz Camargo put it four centuries ago (1892 [1592]: 217 [Bk. II, Ch. VI]) (*fué bautizado y murió cristiano*). It is almost certainly apocryphal, as has been argued from Torquemada (1614, I: 544; Bk. 4, Ch. 70) to MacNutt (1909: 270) to Castañeda de la Paz (2013: 341–42), yet the question will no doubt continue to remain a topic of speculation.

15. These murders are discussed in numerous places, but, e.g., LCHI Bk. 3, Ch. 25; Lamana (2008: 92–95); Restall and Fernández-Armesto (2012: 23).

16. AGI Patronato 55, no. 3, ramo 4; PRT: 104–9. Block quote above is f. 4r (PRT: 108) (*los truxo e guyo e amparó por todos los camynos por do benyeron, hasta entrar en esta çibdad de Mexico con muchas astuçias e maneras para que no los mataron los pueblos que estaban por los camynos, los quales estaban alborotados con la venida de los dichos cristianos*). Villella (2016: 83–84) led me to this particular document in PRT (his is a book-length study of the persistence of Aztec dynastic marriage traditions through the eighteenth century); op. cit.: 84, 94, 153 on Itztlolinqui; the 1556 letter to the king is in ENE, XVI: 64–66 and PRT: 199–200 (*húmilmente suplicamos V.M. nos señale al Obispo de Chyappa don fray Bartholomé de las Casas para que tome este cargo de ser nuestro protector . . . por los muchos agravios y molestias que reçebimos de los españoles por estar entre nosotros y nosotros entre ellos*). Note that there is a portrait of Itztlolinqui in the lost, possibly fraudulent Codex Cardona (Bauer 2009: 91).

17. AGI Patronato 55, no. 3, ramo 4: f. 19v; PRT: 104 (*como a esclavos . . . muchos açotes, palos y coçes y teniendonos en cárceles, çepos y cade-*

nas como a los mayores captivos del mundo); the brief was technically a *probanza de mérito* (proof of merit) for Quauhpopocatl, with testimony (*información*) (ff. 3–18), to support Itztlolinqui's petition (ff. 1–2, 19).

18. Quauhpopocatl, called Quauhpopoca (or Quaupupuca) in colonial-era sources, has been confused with Qualpopoca (who was burned alive in Tenochtitlan during the Phoney Captivity, as we shall see); see Pagden in Cortés (1971: 469n43). On Cacama: Ix13: 21; Hassig (2006: 100). On Ixtlilxochitl's journey: Ixtlilxochitl (1985 [c.1630]: LXXX).

19. AGI Patronato 55, no. 3, ramo 4: ff. 6r, 9r, 13v–14r, 16v, 11v–12r; PRT: 110, 113, 118, 120, 115–16 (I changed Tlilançi to Tlilantzin: *los puso en salbo en esta dicha ciudad de Mexico sin peligro ni riesgo nynguno y esto que lo sabe porque lo bido*; Atenpenecatl: *ques la mytad del camino desde la Beracruz a esta çibdad . . . el dicho Quaupupuca traya a los dichos cristianos por buenos caminos y los guardón hasta metelos en salvo en esta dicha çibdad;* I changed Gucyteçoçi to Hueytecotzin: *muchas flores . . . quando el dicho Quaupupuca entró a ver el dicho Monteqsuma le echó las dichas flores delante.* I changed Guytecotle to Cuitecotle: *presente a la plática . . . sus mantas . . . le dio un collar de margaritas*).

20. My comments on Nahua perceptions of the Spaniards are indebted to Lockhart (1993: 16–21).

21. Clendinnen (1991b: 63).

22. CCR (1522; 1960: 39; 1971: 62) (*maté mucha gente; . . . en otro pueblo tan grande, que se ha hallado en él, por visitación que yo hice hacer, más de veinte mil casas, y como los tomé de sobresalto, salían desarmados, y las mujeres y niños desnudos por las calles, y comencé a hacerles algún daño*).

23. On Tlaxcalteca political factionalism, see Hassig (2001b), and on the Triple Alliance, see Hassig (1988), Carrasco (1999), and Lee (2014); for an example of the argument that "the Aztec Empire existed in name only" and was "largely a creation of Hernán Cortés and of the historiography he inspired" ("So, 'Mexica Empire'—or house of cards?. . . . there might one day have been an empire worthy of the name"), see Gruzinski (2014: 14–16).

24. My discussion of the events of September–October relies largely on Hassig (2006 [1994]: 128–40) and Ixtlilxochitl (1985 [c.1630]: 248–59 [LXXXV–LXXXVII], "invention" quote on 251) (*fue in-*

vención de los tlaxcaltecas y de algunos de los españoles). Conquistador accounts include Tapia and Aguilar (see Fuentes 1963: 33–37, 143). Early examples of the traditional narrative of the expedition through to the Meeting are Díaz VIII–LXXXVII (1632: ff. 6–65) and Torquemada (1614, Bk. 4).

25.   See Chapter 4 for full quotes and citations on the zoo as "hell."

26.   There are excellent Wikipedia pages in English and French detailing the origins of "Phoney War" (or "Phony War") and *drôle de guerre* (literally, "funny war," as a French journalist misunderstood "phoney" as "funny"). No doubt the phrase has since the 1940s been applied elsewhere, but I am not aware of it being yet applied to this interlude in the Spanish-Aztec War.

27.   Vásquez de Tapia (1546 in J. Díaz et al. 1988: 143) (*Otro día, entramos en México y estuvimos en él ocho meses, poco más o menos, hasta la venida de Pánfilo de Narváez, en el cual tiempo pasaron grandes cosas que, por no alargar, las dejo*).

28.   CCR (1522; 1960: 32; 1971: 50) (*lo habría, preso o muerto, o subdito a la corona real de vuestra majestad*). Cortés said he would capture Montezuma because it was standard practice for conquistadors to seize indigenous rulers and hold them hostage; that fact misled me in the past into accepting not only that the Spanish captains expected to do it, but that they therefore did it in Tenochtitlan (Restall 2003: 25).

29.   Abnett (2007: 6–7).

30.   CCR (1522; 1960: 60; 1971: 99) (*todos juntos y cada uno por sí prometían, y prometieron, de hacer y cumplir todo aquello que con el real nombre de vuestra majestad les fuese mandado; acudir con todos los tributos y servicios que antes al dicho Mutezuma hacían y eran obligados; lo cual todo pasó ante un escribano público y lo asentó por auto en forma*).

31.   Gómara (1578: 231). Allen (2015) argues persuasively that Montezuma's tears cannot simply be seen as evidence of the stereotype (which I have called Montezuma the Coward in Chapter 2), and that both Aztec and Spanish cultures had more complex interpretations of the significance of tears in religious, political, and ritual contexts. Note that the European (but not Mesoamerican) culture of weeping and tears has been studied extensively in the last two decades. *Engraved*: "Montezuma Surrenders Sovereignty," in the Gallery, includes the traditional narrative's detail of astonished and

tearful Aztec nobles—lending an apparent ring of truth to a scene
that was most likely invented. This image, and variants on it, accompanied many editions of Conquest accounts, from the seventeenth through twentieth centuries (this particular one is from Solís
1733: 313 facing). Visual dramatizations of this fictional moment
became increasingly popular in the eighteenth and nineteenth centuries; one of the most widely reproduced today is the oil painting
of the scene in the Museo de América.

32. CCR (1522; 1960: 65; 1971: 107) (*yo . . . sabría las cosas que debían
tener y creer mejor que no ellos; que se las dijese e hiciese entender, que ellos harían los que yo les dijese que era lo mejor*); Brooks (1995: 155); my
analysis in this section owes as much to Brooks's article as it does to
my rereading of the primary sources.

33. *Ab initio* is a Latin term meaning "from the beginning," used to lend
Cortés's imagined mass surrender a further touch of legal weight;
CCR (1522; 1960: 69; 1971: 113) (*muchos secretos de las tierras del se-
ñorío de este Mutezuma; . . . y todo con tanta voluntad y contentamiento
del dicho Mutezuma y de todos los naturales de las dichas tierras, como si de
ab initio hubieran conocido a vuestra sacra majestad por su rey y señor natural*); Cervantes de Salazar (1914 [1560s]: 479); Brooks (1995: 160).

34. *"Convergence"*: Krauze (2010: 69; see chapter-opening epigraph).
Stockholm: relevance of the syndrome suggested to me by Kris Lane
(personal communication, August 14, 2016). *Eighteenth century*: Dilworth (1759: 72–79, 122; 1801: 104–10, 158); Campe (1800: 170).
For studies suggesting that early modern Spanish understandings
of concepts like betrothal and concord influenced painted depictions of the Cortés-Montezuma relationship—beginning with the
Meeting—see Cuadriello (2001) and Hernández-Durán (2007).

35. Thevet (1676: 76).

36. Sigüenza y Góngora (1928 [1680]: 130) (I have glossed *hacer merced*
as "do favors" but it more literally means "show favor" in the sense
of kings or bishops dispensing patronage) (*Era este Rey con los Castellanos tan affable, y amoroso, que jamás pasó dia en que no hiziesse merced
á alguno*); Filgueira Valverde (1960: 108) (*Hubo días casi felices en
que el señor azteca y el capitán español, convivieron familiarmente, entre
mutuos servicios y pruebas de amistad, y horas alegradas por los azares
del juego, los lances de la caza, los finos cánticos y el grato humor del rey
preso, siempre generoso con sus guardas y servidores*).

37. *"Romance"*: Gruzinski (2014: 88). Díaz's story XCVII (1910, II: 105; 1942 [1632]: 137; 2005, I: 256–57): "Sometimes Montezuma and Cortés would play at *totoloque*, which is the name they give to a game played with some very smooth small pellets made of gold for this game"; a nephew of the emperor's kept score for him, Alvarado doing the same for Cortés, "but Alvarado always marked one point more than Cortés gained, and when Montezuma saw this he said courteously and laughingly that he did not like Tonatiuh (for so they called Pedro de Alvarado) to keep score for Cortés because he made so much *yxoxol* in what he marked down, which in their language means to say that he cheated"; at that point Cortés and all the conquistadors there laughed, as they knew Alvarado's "temperament."

38. Thomas (1993: 312, quote on 315).

39. Brooks is similarly skeptical of the Spanish spin on the Qualpopoca execution; both it and the Cacama story "are studded with absurdities" (1995: 165); see later in this chapter for a different version from the Nahuatl-language Annals of Tlatelolco.

40. *"Kings"*: from the early English edition of Gómara (1578: 230). On Cacama affair: Brooks (1995: 165–66) is as skeptical as I am; also see Hassig (2006: 106–7).

41. MacNutt (1909: 441).

42. *"Right"*: Brooks (1995: 161). *"Myth"*: Thomas (1993: 284). *"Difficult"*: Durán (1967 [1581]: 293–94; also quoted by Brooks op. cit.: 177).

43. AGI México 203, 5: ff. 1–4; AGI Patronato 73, 1, 2: ff. 46, 63; DC, II: 331–48; DCM: #s311, 549, 1009, 1060, 1102; WWC: 55–58, 123, 135–36; Schwaller and Nader (2014: 171, 177, 182, 219, 226).

44. There have survived documents written by Spaniards in the Indies during the months of the Phoney Captivity, including some in Mexico (e.g., DC, I: 105–8), but none have survived (if indeed they were written) from Tenochtitlan.

45. *"Appearances"*: MacNutt (1909: 204). *"Free"* and *"liberty"*: Brooks (1995: 176, 163); CCR (1522; 1960: 55–56; 1971: 90–92) (*vinieron muchos señores; cuando menos con él iban pasaba de tres mil hombres que los más de ellos eran señores y personas principales*); Díaz XCVI, XCVII (1910, II: 96, 108–14; 2005, I: 250–51, 259).

46. Gómara (1964: 174).

47. Abbott (1904 [1856]: 194) remarked that Montezuma "was magnificently imprisoned," but the same might more accurately be said of

the Spaniards. Conquistador descriptions of the city's palace complexes suggest that they and their slaves and servants were easily accommodated; these "beautiful and excellent houses of their lords were so large and had so many rooms, apartments, and gardens" that the so-called Anonymous Conquistador "went inside one of the houses of the great lord more than four times just to look at it, and each time I walked so far that I became tired, yet I never managed to see all of it" (Anonymous [n.d. (1556)]; CDHM, I: 395; Bustamante 1986: 151) (*muy bellas y buenas casas señoriales, tan grandes y con tantas estancias, aposentos y jardines . . . yo entré más de cuatro veces en una casa del gran señor no para otra cosa sino verla, y cada vez caminé tanto por ella que me cansé, y nunca la acabé de ver completa*). Although some sources state (and some historians assume) that the 250 or so Spaniards kept their Tlaxcalteca allies with them (e.g., Cervantes de Salazar stated that six thousand "Indian allies from the towns they had pacified" [*indios amigos de los pueblos que habia pacificado*] entered the city too; 1914 [1560s]: 272 [Bk. 3, Ch. LXIII]), it is unsupported by evidence and highly unlikely.

48. The blame assigned to Alvarado for the Toxcatl Massacre seems universal; the only split is between those arguing that he imagined an Aztec plot (gaining confirmation through torturing seized Aztecs) and those asserting it was real (e.g., Torquemada stated that the Aztecs had set up huge cauldrons in which to cook the Spaniards; MacNutt 1909: 247). A superb recent study of the Toxcatl Massacre is Scolieri (2013: 90–126).

49. From the Annals of Tlatelolco, in Lockhart (1993: 256–73; quotes on 256, 258; on its dating, 37–43; I have made only superficial adjustments to Lockhart's translation); its relatively early date, language, and authorship do not of course make the Annals intrinsically more accurate or reliable than any other source, Spanish or Nahua, but nor should it be given less weight than conquistador accounts written during the same decades.

50. Ezquerra in EC: 561–79. Either a copy or the original was in 2013 moved and placed at first-floor level on the exterior of the Royal Palace in Madrid. The Montezuma statue is one of ninety-eight statues of Spanish kings (with Montezuma and Atahuallpa viewed as such, by dint of the Spanish acquisition of their empires), created in the late eighteenth century and frequently moved around royal

gardens and palaces since then (so I cannot be entirely sure I am standing in Aranjuez, or in another garden, in that old photograph).

51. Myers (2015: 231, 260).

52. *Mass murder*: The FBI defines it as the killing of four or more people in one location in a continuous act; although these killings took place in a wartime context, the rulers were captive and probably in chains (most sources claim this), suggesting that the FBI's definition is met. See fbi.gov/stats-services/publications/serial-murder.

53. Díaz CXXVI (1632: f. 104v; 1910, II: 238) (*Y Cortés lloró por el y todos nuestros Capitanes y soldados: e hombres huuo entre nosotros, de los que le conociamos y tratavamos, que tan llorado fue, como si fuera nuestro padre*); Prescott (1994 [1843]: 399–400, 410–15, quote on 400); MacNutt (1909: 267). A common verdict is that of Vásquez (1991: 11) on the accounts by Díaz and Aguilar (1988 [c.1560]: 191), that the infirm veterans had no reason to lie, "owed nothing to Cortés or the Crown" (*debían nada a Cortés o la Corona*), and thus their versions "reflected the pure truth" (*reflejaron la verdad pura*). Also see "A Lamentable End," the image that opens this chapter.

54. Clavigero, quoted by MacNutt (1909: 268).

PART IV

1. Epigraph sources, in sequence: Jaúregui (2008 [1557]: 74–77) (whose translation I have modified slightly, to emphasize meaning, at the expense of poeticism) (*Qué campos no están regados / con la sangre, que a Dios clama, / de nuestros padres honrados, / hijos, hermanos, criados / por robar hacienda y fama? / Qué hija, mujer, ni hermana / tenemos que no haya sido / mas que pública mundana / por esta gente tirana / que todo ha corrompido?*); Keegan (1993: 3).

CHAPTER 7:
THE EPIC BOXER

1. Epigraph sources, in sequence: Solana (1938: 425) (*el caso de C y de C, difiere; fué el púgil épico, y luchó por su rey; fué el cruzado místico, y luchó por su Dios; fué el galán quijote, y adoró a su dama*); Solís (1704: unnumbered prefatory p. 2) (*Il est certain que Cortez avoit ses défauts, comme tous les autres hommes: il n'étoit peut-être pas si delicat en Politique, ni si reflexif que Solis nous le dépeint*); Duverger (2005: 27)

(*Antes que hombre, Cortés es un mito, un mito con facetas que siempre se han disputado escuelas de pensamiento concurrentes e ideologías rivales, de tal manera que cada una de ellas pudo concebir a "su" Cortés: semidiós o demonio, héroe o traidor, esclavista o protector de los indios, moderno o feudal, codicioso o gran señor . . .*); CDII, 13: 293–301; translation mine but indebted to the one by Kevin Terraciano in Restall, Sousa, and Terraciano (2005: 66–71), also adapted for Restall and Asselbergs (2007: 18–19).

2.   The bust really was shipped to Italy in 1823 (to a distant descendant of Cortés's in Palermo), where it remains today; a copy is in the Hospital de Jesús. The date of Alamán's letter to the Spanish authorities is variously cited as 1836 and 1843. My paragraphs on the history of Cortés's remains are drawn from Duverger (2005: 21–26, 368–71, App. V); Martínez Ahrens (2015) (the quote is from *El País* [*Uno de los grandes misterios históricos de América; el mayor enigma de Hernán Cortés*]; I thank Kris Lane for sending me the link to this article); notes from my visits to the Hospital de Jesús.

3.   Carvajal (2010) (*la glorificación cruel y arrogante del genocidio y un insulto al pueblo de México; falta de conocimiento; homenaje a un hijo de esta villa*).

4.   Although the theft of the Martín statue was presumably a political statement, it is historically appropriate; when he was five or six, Martín was sent to Spain to live as a page to Prince Philip, and he never saw his mother again (a point also made by Lanyon 2003: 122, who saw Martín still in situ in 2001). My field notes from visits to Mexico City, 2009 and 2016; Krauss 1997. Other statues of Cortés in Mexico are likewise in obscure locations, yet still inspire ire. One erected in the 1930s in the garden of the Hotel Casino de la Selva in Cuernavaca, for example, was denounced by Romerovargas Iturbide (1964, III: 186), who called for the removal of this "insult to the Mexican people" (*es burla para el pueblo mexicano*); the hotel was destroyed at the turn of this century to make way for a Costco and a chain supermarket, and the statue saved by the hotel's last owners but no longer on public view (Martínez Baracs 2011: 85–87; and personal communication, January 2016 and June 2016). Romerovargas Iturbide (op. cit.) likewise demanded the replacement of the equestrian statue of Carlos IV (aka *El Caballito*), which was farther down the Paseo de la Reforma from the *Glorieta*

de Cuauhtémoc mentioned earlier, with a new statue of Montezuma; Carlos IV is now in a far smaller square in the city; no *glorieta* to Montezuma has been placed on the Paseo de la Reforma.

5. Written in his *History of the Indians of New Spain*, first published in 1541, six years before Cortés's death; Motolinía (1951 [1541]: 273) (I have used Steck's translation here). Different versions of a section of this chapter were published as Restall (2016a; 2016b).

6. For a page-long footnote listing a significant sampling of Cortés biographies and books that are effectively such, stretching from Gómara (1552) to Sandine (2015), see Restall (2016a: 33–34). "*Myth*": Duverger (2005: 27), quoted in this chapter's epigraphs. There is much fine work by literary scholars on Gómara (e.g., Roa-de-la-Carrera 2005; Carman 2006; Adorno 2007).

7. My thanks to Michael Kulikowski (personal communication, May 5, 2014), for help in translating the motto. Josephus's account of *The Jewish War*, which culminated in the fall and destruction of Jerusalem in the First Jewish-Roman War, in A.D. 70, would have been available in Latin to Gómara, who provided the full motto at the very end of his *Conquest of Mexico* (1552: f. 139v; 1964 [1552]: 410). On Spaniards and the ancients: for example, Francisco de ·Jerez (who fought in South America) wrote in 1534 that Spaniards achieved more, against greater odds, than the armies of ancient Rome; Bernardo de Vargas Machuca, a veteran conquistador writing at century's end, likewise argued that Spanish success was even more astonishing than the most famous feats of the Greeks and Romans (Vargas Machuca 1599: ff. 25v–26v; 2010 [1612]: 92–96; Restall 2003: 1, 27–28). Such comparisons were commonplace by the seventeenth century (e.g., Juan de Solórzano's 1631 *Discurso y alegación en derecho* in JCB, Codex Sp 26: ff. 7r, 76).

8. Lupher (2003: 8–42).

9. Gómara (1552b: 26v) (*por quanto el hizo muchas, y grandes hazañas en las guerras que, alli tuuo, que sin perjuycio de ningun español de Yndias, fueron las mejores de quantas se han hecho en aquellas partes del nuevo mundo, las escrivire por su parte: a imitacion de Polivio, y de Salustio que sacaron de las istorias Romanas q[ue] juntas, y enteras, hazian, este la de Mario y aquel lo de Scipion*).

10. Gómara (1552b: 2, 58). "*Official history*": Kagan (2009: 160). As Kagan deftly observes, Gómara started his book while working for

Cortés (although perhaps not as his secretary-chaplain, a common assumption that Martínez Martínez 2010 disputes), finishing it just a few years after the old conquistador's death; but it was Cortés's son, (the legitimate) don Martín, who commissioned the *Historia*. Martín hoped that the book would inspire the king to restore some of the privileges that his father had once held. Gómara, for his part, saw the *Historia* as an elaborate job application, which he hoped would lead to his appointment by the king as official chronicler of the empire (*coronista de las Indias*). Martín Cortés also wrote letters in support of Gómara's ambitions, as the writer's advancement could only help his own plans advance. As it turned out, neither achieved his goals; but Gómara's laudatory treatment of Cortés and his critical account of the conquest wars in Peru has resonated across centuries of literature, both scholarly and popular.

11. Cervantes de Salazar (1546: f. 4r) (also see Elliott 1989: 41; Restall 2003: 15; Lyons 2015: 133–230). My translations from Villagrá (1610: f. 16v; 1933: 54; block quote from 1610: ff. 30v–31r; but also see 1933: 65).

12. Díaz CCXII (1916, V: 291; also quoted by Lupher 2003: 14). "*Antiquity*": Quoting an early English edition: Solís (1724: unnumbered first page of Preface). Solís was widely read until replaced partly by Robertson's account of the 1770s and then firmly by Prescott's of the 1840s (Kagan 2009: 268–73). "*BRITISH*": Dilworth (1759: title page; 1801: British youth comment not on title page).

13. E.g., Vasconcelos (1941); Alcala (1950); Lyons (2015); to some extent Benito (1944). "*Boxer*": Solana (1938: 425) (*el púgil épico; el cruzado místico*).

14. "Caesar Borgia" quote by the Argentine novelist and literary critic Enrique Anderson Imbert (1962: 33); other quotes by the Mexican scholar José Valero Silva (1965: 40); both quoted in Mizrahi (1993). Also see Carman (2006: 49–50). An earlier version of *The Prince* was circulated in 1512, but it was in Latin in manuscript form, and Cortés had already been in the Caribbean for eight years. It is possible, perhaps probable, that the ideas on political action that ended up being most closely associated with *The Prince* were circulating sufficiently in the 1510s that they reached Cortés in Cuba (as Mizrahi 1993 suggests); but by framing such a possibility not in terms of the larger context of the intellectual world of the pre-1520 Span-

ish Caribbean, but in terms of a specific Cortés-Machiavelli link, the tradition of Cortés as exceptional and foundational—as legendary—is merely reinforced.

15. Alcalá (1950: 168); Mizrahi (1993: 109–11) (I thank Russell Lohse for sending me this article).

16. Valadés (1579: 204–105 [*sic*]); my translation from the Latin original (*Nolim deprimere magnanimitatem Romanorum . . . Sed maioribus praeconiis nouaque maiestate verborum efferenda est inaudita fortitudo Ferdinandi Cortesii & religiosorum qui nouos illos orbes adierunt . . . cum ea parte Indiarum, quae in nostras manus venit: haec infinitis partibus amplior est . . . Hic itaq suā virtutem exercuit bonus ille Cortesius . . . sacrificiisq illorum diabolicis . . . maxime heroicum*) (also see a Spanish version in Palomera 1988: 413–14).

17. Valadés was born in Tlaxcallan in 1533; his *Rhetorica Christiana* (1579), written entirely in Latin, was the first book by someone of Native American ancestry to be published in Europe. His father was the conquistador Diego Valadés, who arrived with Narváez in 1520, survived the war, fathered a son in Tlaxcallan, and was awarded a coat of arms for the heroic action he claimed he had performed in the war. Of the friar's Tlaxcalteca mother, her willingness and treatment, we know nothing; neither Diego Valadés, father or son, wrote about her. DCM: #1070; AGN and AGI testimony by Diego Valadés, the father, in Palomera (1988: 153–59). *Long-lasting tradition*: see Torquemada (1614, III: 191–97; 1986 [1614]: 3, 166–69; Bk. 16, Ch. 13); the narrative promoted by Mexican Bishop Lorenzana; Wood (2003: 85–94); Pardo (2004: 20–24).

18. Muñoz Camargo (1892 [1592]: 189–205; 1998 [1592]: 195–205) (*nos llamamos* cristianos, *porque lo somos por ser hijos del verdadero Dios; no hay más de un solo Dios verdadero*); also see Gibson (1952: 28–31); Pardo (2004: 23, who noted that mythistories like that of the 1520 Tlaxcallan meeting have "the odd quality of giving historical turning points an air of inevitability"); Martínez Baracs (2008); Cuadriello (2011).

19. Mendieta (1870 [1596]: 210–11 on Cortés's support for the Twelve); Phelan (1970: 92–102); Pardo (2004: 2–4); Restall and Solari (2011: 67–89).

20. Mendieta (1870 [1596]: 174–75) (*meter debajo de la bandera del demonio á muchos de los fieles . . . infinita multitud de gentes que por años*

*sin cuento habian estado debajo del poder de Satanás . . . el clamor de
tantas almas y sangre humana derramada en injuria de su Criador . . .
como á otro Moisen á Egipto).* For further discussion and citations,
see Chapter 5.

21. Mendieta (1870 [1596]: 174–75). Further proof was the fact that, just
as God had given Moses an interpreter to speak with the pharaoh
of Egypt, so did God "miraculously provide" Cortés with interpreters (Malintzin, or Malinche, and Gerónimo de Aguilar). The conquistador captain showed "great zeal" and "diligence" everywhere he
went, "in the honor and service of God and the saving of souls"; he
"toppled idols, raised up crosses, and preached the faith and belief
in the one true God" (op. cit.: 175–77, 182–84, 211–12, 228) (*Cortés
elegido como otro Moisen para librar el pueblo indiano . . . sin alguna
dubda eligió Dios señaladamente y tomó por instrumento á este valeroso
capitan D. Fernando Cortés, para por medio suyo abrir la puerta y hacer
camino á los predicadores de su Evangelio es este nuevo mundo . . . co-
menzó Lutero á corromper el Evangelio . . . á publicarlo fiel y sinceramente
á las gentes que nunca de él habian tenido noticia . . . proveido miracu-
losamente . . . se confirma esta divina eleccion de Cortés para obra tan alta
en el ánimo, y extraña determinacion que Dios puso en su corazon . . . este
su negocio . . . tan buen celo como tuvo de la honra y servicio de ese mismo
Dios y salvacion de las almas . . . derrocase los ídolos . . . levantase cruces y
predicase la fe y creencia de un solo Dios verdadero).*

22. Saavedra (1880 [1599]); Vecchietti (n.d.); García (1729 [1607]: 94)
(*Y aunque la reverencia, i postracion de rodillas que aora hacen los In-
dios de Nueva-España à los Sacerdotes, se la enseñò D. Fernando Cortès,
Marquès del Valle, de felice memoria).*

23. *"Fanaticism"* to *"Christ"*: Abbott (1904 [1856]: 44), although the argument is made to various degrees of subtlety from Robertson in the
1770s through the twentieth century. *"Sincerity"* to *"waver"*: MacNutt
in Cortés (1908: I, 207). *"So far as"* to *"Faith"*: Braden (1930: 80).

24. Valadés (1579: 205 but "105" erroneously printed as the page number). Villagrá (1610: f. 18r, f. 16; using the translations in 1933: 55,
54). Note that in 2009–14 Manuel Martín-Rodríguez published a
three-volume study of Villagrá and his writings that I did not use
here.

25. *Archival*: Obvious examples are in conquistador *probanzas* in AGI
Justicia and in AGI México 203, but less obvious ones include a

little-known document in JCB, Codex Sp 138, f. 6. Engaging for
its rare use of sarcasm in an official report, it was written by don José
Ignacio Flores de Vergara y Ximénez de Cárdenas, who served as
the senior Spanish official in Bolivia in the early 1780s (his title was
president of the Audiencia of Charcas). For his role in the suppression of the Tupac Amaru rebellion in 1781, he earned the nickname
"Pacifier of Peru" (*el Pacificador del Perú*), but he also came under attack from a royal judge (an *oidor*) sent to report on the president's actions. In his defense, Flores de Vergara scoffed that the *oidor* would
have tried to discredit even Cortés himself. In doing so, wrote the
president, the *oidor* would have dismissed Cortés's burning of his
ships as a "meagre feat," likewise his entry into Mexico "without
losing more than a very few men." No doubt he also would have
called Cortés "crazy" for leaving Pedro de Alvarado in charge when
he left Tenochtitlan to meet the Narváez expedition, and "stupid
and lazy" for taking so long to besiege the city. Not that Flores
de Vergara was comparing himself to Cortés, he insisted—adding,
"I'm not that vain" (*poca Asaña; sin haver perdido mas que mui pocos
hombres; loco; tonto y floxo*). *Epic*: Lasso de la Vega (1588; 1594); Saavedra (1599; 1880 [1599]).
26. Lasso de la Vega (1601); Weiner (2006: 93–120).
27. Lasso de la Vega (1588: f. 4v) (*Con Dulce son, de nuevo se derrama /
De mi invencible Abuelo la grandeza / Los trabajos, peligros, y braveza
/ Con que tiene ganada eterna fama*). Gerónimo was a son of don
Martín, who had inherited the title of Marqués del Valle from his
father.
28. *Invincible*: Saavedra (1880 [1599]: 20, 33) (*Con animo invencible y
fortaleza / del gran Cortés*). *Lasso*: See "Portrait of the Conqueror
as an Old Man" in the Gallery. Among the many imaginary portraits of Cortés a fair number derive from two images created in
his lifetime. One, the Weiditz Medallion, has survived (and is
frequently reproduced). The other is long lost but must have been
commissioned to hang in the church of one of the hospitals Cortés
helped endow; it would have featured the Marquis gazing piously
upward, no doubt on his knees praying. Numerous images of Cortés descended from that lost painting. A few show him in blatant
religious pose, but most of them show his head in a slightly pious
gaze, either grafted onto a body (as in the full-length portrait still

hanging in the Hospital de Jesús) or a bust—as in the engraving
used in all three of Gabriel Lasso de la Vega's works praising Cortés, with the Latin caption glossed as: "Fernando Cortés, Invincible
Leader, Aged 63" (Lasso de la Vega 1588: f. 2r). The other image
in "Portrait of the Conqueror as an Old Man" is a frontispiece to
the 1778 Italian edition of Robertson's *Storia di America* [The History of America], with captioning translating to "Engraved from an
original first made when he had achieved the conquest of Mexico"
(Robertson 1778, III: frontispiece). This image is probably one of
many that evolved from the rendering used with Lasso's poems. On
Cortés portraits: Romero de Terreros (1944: 19, and figures following 36); Duverger (2005: "Álbum de Fotos" following 440). *Valiant*:
Vargas Machuca (2010 [1612]: 92, 96); Díaz (1632: unnumbered
prefatory material, p. ii, by fray Diego Serrano, head of the Mercedarians; *el ilustre y esforçado Cauallero*); Mendieta (1870 [1596]:
173). Torquemada, whose *Monarquia Indiana* drew heavily upon
(by modern standards, plagiarized) Mendieta, has the same phrase
in the Prologue to his Book 4 (1614: I, 373; *el famosísimo y ven-*
turosísimo capitan D. Fernando Cortés [que despues fué meritísimo mar-
qués del Valle]). Another term that some poets could not resist was
"courteous," because it played on the conquistador's surname (e.g.,
Thevet 1676: 75), although it was not an obviously martial quality,
as noted by Luis de Vargas Manrique in the final lines of a sonnet
that preceded the prologue to Lasso de la Vega (1594): "He is the
son of courtesy, and of courage, and although the son of both, he
chose his mother's surname [*Este es el hijo de la cortesia, / Y del valor, y*
aunque de entrãbos hijo, / Escogio de la madre el apellido]." Presumably
Lasso was amused by the joke, which rather damned Cortés with
faint praise, but it was too subtle to trouble don Gerónimo Cortés.
(I am grateful to Miguel Martínez for helpfully discussing these
lines with me.)

29. From the late sixteenth to mid-eighteenth centuries, Cortés's Let-
     ters saw no new edition, but Lorenzana's volume inspired new edi-
     tions in French, German, and Dutch within a few years (Cortés
     1770; 1778; 1779; 1780). Some credit may also lie with the ear-
     lier inclusion of Cortés's four Letters in the sources compiled by
     González Barcía (1749). After the flurry of editions in the 1770s,
     there were regular reprints or new editions in European languages

through the twentieth century (see the discussions in Cortés 1843: iii–iv and Pagden in Cortés 1971: xxxixlx). Escoiquiz (1798): see the illustration facing this chapter's title page: the "Fat Cortés" portrait is best known (and perhaps originated with) Paul Methuen's engraving for the 1724 English edition of Solís; it appeared variously during the eighteenth century, including in this cropped form in Escoiquiz's book and in an edition of Solís likewise (and presumably not coincidentally) published in Madrid in 1798. Cortés as a soft-hatted, portly gentleman is a far cry from the robust warrior of most portraits of the conquistador; arguably, it better represents how he lived for most of his life.

30. Ruiz de León (1755). The poem's subtitle was *Triumphos de la Fe, y Gloria de las Armas Españolas. Poema Heroyco. Conquista de Mexico, Cabeza del Imperio Septentrional de la Nueva-España. Proezas de Hernan-Cortes, Catholicos Blasones Militares, y Grandezas del Nuevo Mundo.*

31. Nicolás Fernández de Moratín and Joseph María Vaca de Guzmán, in 1765 and 1778, respectively (*Las Naves de Cortés Destruidas*); Vaca de Guzmán (1778: 1, 9, 8) (*El Héroe grande; Del nuevo Cid, del Español Aquíles; Ese el teatro, donde el mar de Atlante / Al Castellano veneró triunfante*); Escoiquiz (1798).

32. "Black Legend" was coined in 1914 by Julián Juderías y Loyot; for the mid-twentieth century debate among U.S. historians Charles Gibson, Lewis Hanke, Benjamin Keen, and William Maltby, see Keen (1969; 1971a); for more recent studies that summarize, cite, and update earlier ones, see Cárcel (1992), Hillgarth (2000), and Villaverde Rico and Castilla Urbano (2016).

33. Thomas Nicholas in Gómara (1578 [1552], Nicholas trans.: i–ii); italics in original.

34. Nicholas briefly recounts falling in with a seventy-year-old conquistador on the road leaving Toledo. Named Zárate, this veteran of the conquests and "the civil warres of *Pirru*," rather than resting on his laurels and the wealth of his "good lands and possessions" in Peru, was on his way to petition the king for a license "to discover and conquere a certayne parte of India, whyche adioyneth *Brazile* and is part of the Empire of *Pirru*." "You are not wel in your wit," responds Nicholas bluntly; "for what would you have? Wil not reason suffice you? Or else would you now in your old days be an Emper-

our?" The old *indiano* responds with a noble speech showing that he is neither crazy nor power-hungry, but an altruistic gentleman, devoted to "God and my Prince." A true Christian is born to help others, says Zárate, "not for his owne private wealth and pleasure." He intends to spend the rest of his days enlarging "the royall estate of my Prince" and showing "valiante yong Gentlemen" the virtues of hard work and service. Nicholas in Gómara (1578 [1552], Nicholas trans.: ii–v); italics in original. Nicholas's Zárate, if apocryphal, may have been inspired by Agustín de Zaráte, who served briefly as a royal official in Peru in the 1540s and is known primarily for his account of the conquest of Peru, first published in 1555.

35. Solís (1724: unnumbered first page of Dedication).

36. Vasconcelos (1941: 172).

37. Spontini and Maurin are both discussed in Chapter 2. On Spontini: BnF, département Musique, X-309 (score and libretto of the 1817 version); Spontini (1809); Lajarte (1883: 153–83); Subirá in EC: 117–18G. Spontini's opera was performed repeatedly in Paris, where Maurin lived, through the decades of both men's adult lives (they died within months of each other in 1850–51) (also see the anonymous curator's commentary to the copies of Maurin's lithographs in the Museo de América, Madrid, accessible at mecd.gob.es/museodeamerica). I first accessed prints of two of the Maurin lithographs in the California State Library, Sacramento (CSL-Sac, Rare Prints #2001–0019) (*Se place fièrement sur le trône; ton empire est détruit, je suis seul maître ici, et tu vas subir le sort qui t'est réservé; il en coute la vie pour résister à Cortès; ton coeur est noble, Cortés, il sera généreux aussi, et ce moment va décider si c'est un héros magnanime où un soldat barbare à qui j'ai donné mon amour*).

38. The quoted sources are, in sequence: MacNutt (1909: xii, v) (earned by his "preeminent qualities both as a statesman and general"); Descola (1957 [1954]: 227); Madariaga (1969 [1942]: 108 et al.); Schurz (1964: 112); Elizondo Alcaraz (1996: 11) (*luces y sombras; en verdad extraordinaria; un personaje apasionante*); Berry and Best (1968: 134).

39. The Darryl F. Zanuck/Twentieth Century Fox movie, directed by Henry King and starring Tyrone Power, was based on the first half of the 1945 novel by Samuel Shellabarger (Zanuck and King 1947) (note that after making the film, Power bought one of Cortés's old

estates; Bauer 2009: 99). *Carlos*: Cortés is depicted as strangling his first wife, Catalina Suárez, in episode 7 of the series, directed by Oriol Ferrer and produced by Diagonal TV for RTVE, Spain (Ferrer 2015); the scene is revisited at the start of Chapter 8. It is a curiosity of modern creative representations and usages of the "Conquest of Mexico" that it has inspired numerous operas (see relevant discussions and notes in Chapter 6 and the Epilogue), plays, and novels (e.g., Dryden 1668, Planché 1823, Bird 1835, Thomas 1857, García Iglesias 1946, Thomas 1998, Spinrad 2005, Aguirre 2008), but very few feature films. I suspect (based anecdotally on half a dozen conversations with filmmakers in Los Angeles and Mexico spread over the last thirty years, as well as recent conversations and communications with Stuart Schwartz) that many movies on the topic have been planned but never made due to the costs and logistical challenges of re-creating and then destroying the Tenochtitlan of 1519–21; but I like to think that another deterrent has been the realization that historical accuracy cannot easily be reconciled with the racist romanticism of the traditional narrative.

40. RC (AGI Justicia 220–225), with scores of additional documents in Justicia (e.g., in 1004, in 1005, and in 1018), Patronato, and México; relevant documents also in all four volumes of DC. Cortés was involved in more than fifty lawsuits just in the 1530s alone.

41. *Manuscripts*: LCDT; LCHI. *"False"*: Krauze (2010: 59). Also see Fernández (2014: 103–72).

42. *"Bandit"*: Romerovargas Iturbide (1964: quotes in sequence on 186, 184).

43. *Muralists*: Rivera's version is in one of the scenes in the Palacio Nacional (completed in 1945); Orozco's 1926 fresco painting is in the Colegio de San Idelfonso, both in Mexico City. As Krauze notes (2010: 72), the oldest public monument in Mexico City that shows Cortés is the 1887 *glorieta* mentioned earlier. *Paz*: Paz (1987); Paz interpreted the Orozco fresco of Cortés and "la Malinche" not as a peaceful genesis but as evoking the sexual violence of the Conquest; see also Hernández (2006: 87). *Guzmán*: on her battle in the 1940s and 1950s to publish an edition of Cortés's Letters (CCR; Guzmán 1958) that included a damning critique of Cortesian claims—certainly "ahead of its time" and in many ways in the spirit of this book—and the impact of the controversy surrounding Cuauhtemoc's faked tomb, revealed in 1949 and endorsed by Guzmán, see

Gillingham (2011: 51–69, above quotation on 52). *"Controversial"*: Felipe Solís interviewed in the History Channel's "Cortés" documentary (Bourn 2005); Benjamin Keen in Zorita (1994 [1566]: 19). *"Gentleman-adventurer"*: Keen in Zorita (1994 [1566]: 19).

44. Young (1975); also see the liner notes to *Decade* (Warner Bros. 1977), on which "Cortez the Killer" was included; Manrique (2012).

45. Candelaria (2011: 6).

46. *"Rebellion"*: Fray Francisco Cárdenas y Valencia on Maya resistance to invasion in northeast Yucatan (in his *Relación historial*: BL, Egerton MS 1791: f. 14v). My explanation of the "myth of completion" is Chapter 4 of Restall (2003).

47. Prescott (1994 [1843]); Gómara (1552; 1964); Carrasco in Díaz (2008 [1632]: xiv, xxviinn3–4). Díaz (1632) has 214 chapters, with Tenochtitlan's capture in Chapter 156, which is where the widely read Penguin edition ends (1963 [1632]); Maudslay's original five-volume edition included the whole text (1908–16 [1632]), but the abridged edition (printed many times by various publishers; e.g., 1942 [1632]), likewise ends in 1521.

48. The 1550 end date is a soft one, as wars came to an end variously in different regions to the west, north, and south in the 1540s (an argument can be made for 1547 as an end date, allowing us to dub this another Thirty Years' War, or the Mesoamerican Thirty Years' War, although the year unfortunately happens to be that of Cortés's death). On the New Galicia wars, which Ida Altman dates 1524–50, see Altman (2010); on ex-Aztecs fighting after 1521, see Matthew and Oudijk (2007) and Oudijk and Restall (2014); on the Maya wars, see Restall (1998; 2014); Restall and Asselbergs (2007); Graham (2011).

49. Ix13; CA: ff. 42r–45v; the two different Tlatelolco accounts called the Annals (in Lockhart 1993: 256–73) and the List of Rulers (see Terraciano 2010: 15–18); FC, XII (note that the exception to the pattern is the attention given here to pre-1520 events, a third of the whole account, a section that Lockhart 1993: 16–17 argues "is quite anomalous").

50. *Unread reports*: these are the *probanzas de mérito*, mentioned above, that have survived by the hundreds, mostly in the AGI; point suggested to me by Richard Conway (personal communication, December 7, 2016).

51. *"Brilliant"*: Palomera (1988: 34; *brillante victoria*). Narváez expedition: AGI Patronato 180, ramo 2. Usagres: DCM: #s1067–68; Díaz CXVII, CXXII, CLXIV (1910, II: 181, 206; 1912, IV: 272).

52. This paragraph is drawn from reading between the lines of Díaz CXXXVII–CLVII (1912, IV: 1–203); Ix13: 27–59; Townsend (2006: 109–25); and Hassig (2006: 131–75); also see the admittedly partisan Gardiner (1961); AGI sources on the brigantines include Escribanía 178A, no. 4. *Plaza-Toro*: a line of Fernández-Armesto's in Restall and Fernández-Armesto (2012: 82). *"Cowards"*: Ix13: 22. (This was hardly the first time Cortés had been called a coward in print: Velázquez accused him of it as early as November 1519; DC, I: 99). I found a possible variation on this theme in an unlikely place: the sonnet dedicated to the portrait of Cortés in Lasso de la Vega's 1594 epic poem, *Mexicana* (quoted in the notes to this chapter), suggesting that Cortés chose to be the feminized courtier rather than the valiant warrior of legend.

53. *"Veritable"*: Benton (2017: 4); my discussion of Tetzcoco draws heavily upon the work of Bradley Benton, who generously allowed me to access his book while still in manuscript form; also useful were Ix13; Ixtlilxochitl (1985 [1620s–30s]); Offner (1983); and Lee and Brokaw (2014).

54. Benton (2017: 25–28); Hassig (2016: 107–9, 132–33); Ixtlilxochitl (1985 [1620s–30s]: 220–23); as the latter noted, Tetzcoco's divided rule did not prevent it from participating in successful Aztec conquest campaigns in the late 1510s.

55. Sources vary as to whether this brother (named Nezahualquentli) was beaten by a Spanish captain, then hanged by Cortés, or hanged by Cacama. Ix13: 21–24; Ixtlilxochitl (1985 [1620s-30s]: 248–56). Also see Díaz C–CVI (1910, II: 115–46; 2005, I: 264–82); Benton (2017: 29–33).

56. CDII, XXVII: 243–47, 385, 519; Díaz CXXXVII (1912, IV: 6–7).

57. Ix13: 28.

58. On Tlaxcala, see Martínez Baracs (2008: 37–69) and Cuadriello (2011). On Ixtlilxochitl's accounts, see 1985 [1620s–30s]; Ix13; the fine new work being done by Bradley Benton (e.g., 2014; 2017) and Amber Brian (e.g., 2010; 2014, especially 206–7 on the link to Wallace's novel, *The Fair God* [Wallace 1873]); as well as García Loaeza (2014) and Kauffmann (2014).

59. On the hanging of the three deposed *tlatoque* of the old Triple Alliance, see Ix13: 89–94; Restall (2003: 147–57); Terraciano (2010); all of which lead to numerous primary and secondary sources on the incident.

60. Ix13: 31–32.

61. For a smart summary of these months of warfare, dependent upon the traditional narrative but not uncritical of it, see Hassig (2006: 131–175; also 2001b). For a summary in which Ixtlilxochitl leads the entire campaign and siege, with warriors from an expanding Tetzcoca territory at times outnumbering Spanish allies 1,000:1, and Ixtlilxochitl helping a hapless Cortés at every turn (even personally saving his life in combat), see Ix13: 31–59.

62. *Radical suspension*: paraphrases Benton (2017: 20; also see 36–39). *Cohorts*: Hassig (2016: 48–59).

63. Benton (2014; 2017: 48–105). Don Antonio Pimentel Tlahuitoltzin was the eighth son of Nezahualpilli to rule as *tlahtoani*, or the tenth if we count Tecolol and another brother that some Spanish sources claim ruled very briefly between Tecolol and Ixtlilxochitl (see the Dynastic Vine). There was only one other succession dispute of note: Yet another of the sons of Nezahualpilli, don Carlos Ometochtzin (aka Chichimecatecuhtli), agitated in the 1530s to succeed his brother don Pedro. When don Pedro died, don Carlos tried to take his sister-in-law as a second wife, in accordance with Aztec custom; she and don Carlos's wife, both Christians, denounced him to the Inquisition, whose investigation made him vulnerable to various other accusations by his enemies. Bishop Zumárraga jumped on one accusation—that of "idolatry"—and just two months after don Pedro's death, don Carlos was burned alive at the stake in Tenochtitlan/Mexico City. While the theme of the spiritual conquest is obviously important (see Don 2010: 146–76), as is that of political subversion (see Ruiz 2014), Benton (2014; 2017: 39–45) argues persuasively that this was the old succession dispute among Nezahualpilli's sons rearing its head for the last time (also see AGN Inquisición, tomo 2, exp. 10; thanks again to Robert Schwaller for sharing copies of the original documents with me). For an argument on how the imposition of monogamy helped undo the Aztec Empire, in whose rise polygyny had "played a crucial role," see Hassig (2016: 123–47, quote on 142).

64. Las Casas (1697: unnumbered prefatory p. v) (*un grand Empire, dont Montezume fut le dernier Roi. Fernand Cortez y entra l'an 1519, prit ce Prince, & conquit tout son Païs*). Solís in Townsend translation (1724, V: 151–52). Solís's book is 567 oversize pages in the 1724 English edition.

65. Vargas Machuca (2010 [1612]: 96) (I have slightly altered Johnson's translation).

66. Solís in Townsend translation (1724, V: 152); Abnett (2007: 21); an earlier page of the same book (2007: 6–7), included in our Gallery, similarly captures elements of the traditional narrative: a clever Cortés controlling a passive Montezuma, happily complicit in his own manipulation; and a hotheaded Pedro de Alvarado destined to wreck the peace.

67. *Swords:* Johnson (1975: 160). *Warriors:* Matthew and Oudijk (2007); Oudijk and Restall (2014). *Pair of ships:* van Deusen (2015b: 285). For an early account from Tlatelolco of two of the royal passengers headed for Spain, both informed by Malintzin that they will die in Castile, prompting one to jump overboard, see the translated summary in Terraciano (2010: 15–18).

68. *Myth:* Mundy (2015: 72; quotes Motolinía on 73); in referring to the city's "life" and "death" I am also alluding to the title of Mundy's book. *Stumbled:* Díaz CLVI (1912, IV: 187; 2005, I: 510) (*algunos pobres mexicanos que no podian salir; tan flacos y amarillos y suzios y hidiondos que era lastima de los ver*); FC, XII: 248–49; *Annals of Tlatelolco* in Lockhart (1993: 268–69).

69. This and my discussion of Tenochtitlan in the 1520s–30s rely heavily on Mundy (2014; 2015: 72–113); also see López (2014).

70. *Aubin:* Gallery image titled "Once and for All": The entry, bottom left, beside the pictographic representation of Two Flint Knife (1520), translates from Nahuatl as "The tenth king, Cuitlahuatzin, was installed in [the month of] Ochpaniztli. He ruled for only eighty days, dying at the end of Quecholli of pustules [smallpox], when the Castilians had gone to Tlaxcallan." The next entry, top right, following a pictogram of Three House (1521), translates as "The eleventh king, Cuauhtemoc, was installed during Nemontemi and Quahuitl-ehua. And this was the moment when Mexico Tenochtitlan as an entity collapsed. This was when the Spaniards came in once and for all." Halfway down the page the 1523 entry

depicts "*Cihuacoatl* Tlacotzin, here seated as ruler" (CA: ff. 44v–45r; I have worked from this original in BM, but am indebted greatly to Lockhart 1993: 278–79).

71. CA: f. 76; Chimalpahin (1997: 166–73); Mundy (2015: 77–84). Much has been made of the administrative paperwork generated by Cortés during his term as governor and captain-general. Indeed, viewed in isolation, the many edicts and orders that flew off his desk in the 1520s would seem to support the interpretation that he had some sort of governmental vision—seen by his biographers as pious or putatively patriotic or even "mestizo" (Vasconcelos 1941; Duverger 2005). In fact, much of it was smoke and mirrors, designed to impress the court in Spain of his administrative acumen and accomplishments—as much a performance of due process as was the Requirement. His objection to Aztec "idols" was entirely expected and his support for the Franciscans politically expedient; his requests to the king in 1524 that "*personas religiosas*" be sent to Mexico did not show exceptional piety, but normal understandings of the need to create an alliance with the church and show to the king the appropriate forms of commitment to settlement (CDII, V: 556–59; letter written in Tenochtitlan, October 15, 1524). Ogilby (1670: 92) summarized the Spanish and Cortesian 1520s with wry brevity: "the *Spanish* Officers has these Civil Broyls one against another" until royal officials arrived, and "at last, after all these Services, *Cortez* disagreeing with the Vice-Roy *Don Antonio Mendoza*, being about that time sent over, went male-contented [*sic*] into *Spain*."

72. CA: ff. 76v77r; the *Primeros Memoriales* (Sahagún 1997 [c.1560]: 193); Castañeda de la Paz (2013: 251–57); Mundy (2015: 99–117). On continuities in Mexica rule and status through and beyond Huanitzin's day, see various articles by Castañeda de la Paz (e.g., 2009).

73. AGI Patronato 21, no. 2, ramo 4 (old citation 16, ramo 4): quotes all f. 1; also published in Mathes (1973: 101–5), whose translations I followed. I thank Megan McDonie for helping me locate the original documents.

74. AGI Mapas y Planos, México 6 (and referenced in AGI Patronato 21, no. 2, ramo 4: f. 7); also reproduced in Mathes (1973: 102).

75. Edict of 1529: AGI Patronato 16, no. 2, ramo 19, quote on f.1r; also published in Mathes (1973: 107–14).

76. Cortés to Oñate: AGI Patronato 16, no. 1, ramo 15, quote on f.1r; also published (including facsimile of the letter) in Mathes (1973: 115–18). *Paltry Spanish colony*: Founded by Sebastián Vizcaíno (AGI Patronato 20; Mathes 1968) as La Paz, which name it retains. Also see León-Portilla (2005 [1985]: 117–22).

77. *Biographers*: Madariaga (1969 [1942]); Martínez (1990; DC).

78. CCR (Letter of May 15, 1522; 1960: 170; 1971: 277); Mathes (1973: 17).

79. Mathes (1973: 18–19).

80. DC, I: 439–75 (quotes, in sequence, on 459, 467, 445) (*quiso preferir . . . que por su bondad quiso le fuse emperador del universe . . . ocho o diez cartas en latín, los nombres en blanco . . . porque como lengua mas general en el universo . . . que halleis judios o otras personas que las sepan leer*); Mathes (1973: 18–19); Gruzinski (2014: 202); León-Portilla (2005 [1985]: 68–84).

81. Decrees in DC, III: 49–58 (four of July 6), 59–62 (two of July 27) (also see AGN Hospital de Jesús legajos 123 and 124; CC: 125–39; González-Gerth 1983: 85).

82. Previous two paragraphs based on DC, I: 439–75, 491–503 (documents of 1527–28, mostly transcribed from AGI and AGN); also see Mathes (1973: 20); Gruzinski (2014: 203–7); León-Portilla (2005 [1985]: 123–65). Hernando de Grijalva, a relative of Juan, joined the war in Mexico in 1520, thereafter remaining a Cortesian loyalist.

83. Gruzinski (2014: 207).

84. *Conversations*: Martínez Martínez (2010). *Mediterranean*: Goodwin (2015: 108).

85. I have obviously made no attempt to poetically translate Vaca de Guzmán (1778: 7) (*Si quieres ver el ánimo valiente, / Que tanta gloria á tu Nacion ha dado, Prevenido en los riesgos, y prudente, / Resuelto en las empresas, y arrestado, / Un General de la Española gente, / Cuyo valor el mundo ha respetado, / En el grande Cortés lo verás todo, / En el grande Cortés, mas de este modo: . . .*).

86. *"Bed"*: Duverger (2013: 25) (*Es el único de los conquistadores en morir en su cama*). *Medal*: Yoeli and Rand (2015: "Sunday Review," 10).

CHAPTER 8:
WITHOUT MERCY OR PURPOSE

1. Epigraph sources, in sequence: CA: f. 42v (using translation in Lockhart 1993: 274–75); ENE, XVI: 64; PRT: 199 (*por los muchos agravios y molestias que reçebimos de los españoles por estar entre nosotros y nosotros entre ellos*); Gopnik (2015: 104) (I have omitted five sentences between "things" and "Frightened"); Candelaria (2011: 6).

2. The scene is in episode 7 of the TVE series, originally broadcast in 2015 (I thank Jorge Gamboa in Colombia and Enrique Gomáriz in Costa Rica for bringing the series to my attention). (*Soy vos tu esposo, soy el gobernador de la Nueva España; tengo un mundo entero a mis pies, yo aqui soy un dios, un dios; un demonio, un demonio loquecido.*)

3. As Fernández del Castillo (1980 [1929]: 37) pointed out, the prominent signatures of Cortesian enemies Nuño de Guzmán and Ortiz Matienzo, the connections back to Cobos (royal minister and supporter of the late Velázquez) in Spain, and the precise timing of the accusation by doña Catalina's mother with the start of the *residencia* inquiry suggest strongly an orchestration of the allegation (which does not make it untrue).

4. Juan de Salcedo also testified that she had been "very ill with [*muy enferma del*] mal de madre"; WWC: 386–88; *residencia* testimony on Catalina's death in RC; AGI Justicia 220, no. 5; 221, part 4; 222, parts 3 and 5; DC, II: 53–54, 59, 75–101.

5. "*Not proven*": Abbott (1904 [1856]: 304; italics his). "*Bad behavior*": Townsend (2006: 138). The claim by one of doña Catalina's maids that, when told that the whole city "is saying you killed your wife," Cortés responded, "She lay down fine and woke up dead," if true, would seem to support the notion of a man so callous he was capable of uxoricide (1529 testimony by Ana Rodríguez; DC, II: 83) (*dicen que mataste a vuestra mujer; ella se echo buena e amaneció muerta*). Among numerous verdicts by writers and historians, two competing books published in Mexico in the 1920s offered rival verdicts (innocent: Fernández del Castillo 1980 [1929]; guilty: Toro 1922); also see Solana (1938: 22, 161–74); Martínez (1990: 382–94); Thomas (1993: 579–82, 635–36; WWC: 385–89); Miralles (2008: 144, 189, 203). The inclusion in the Codex Cardona of an image of Cortés placing a hand on doña Catalina's coffin intriguingly sug-

gests that—should this now-lost and possibly fraudulent document resurface—there will always be something to prod interest in such mysteries (Bauer 2009: 3).

6. The conversation was reported by Isidro Moreno, Cortés's majordomo; see AGI Justicia 220, no. 5: ff.336–43; CDII, XXVI: 338–40; DC, II: 87–89 (quotes 88–89) (*Vos, Solís, no queries sino ocupar a mis indios en otras cosas de lo que yo les mando e no se face lo que yo quiero; Yo, señora, no los ocupo, ahí está su merced que los manda e ocupa; Yo vos prometo que antes de muchos días haré yo de manera que no tenga nadie que entender con lo mío; Con lo vuestro, señora? Yo no quiero nada de lo vuestro*); also quoted by Martínez (1990: 383–84) and Thomas (1993: 580; WWC: 386); Cortés's cruel double entendre is not spotted as often as one might think: Pérez Martínez noticed, and called it "malevolent [*malévola*]" (2014 [1944]: 204); it is fully articulated by Townsend (2006: 138).

7. Catalina Suárez (or Xuárez) arrived in Hispaniola with her mother, brother, and sisters in 1509 or 1510, settling in Cuba after its conquest by Velázquez (who allegedly fell in love with one of the sisters). According to Gómara, "*las Xuarez*" were "*bonicas* [pretty]" (1552: f. 3r), the local Spaniards competed for their favors, and "Cortés courted Catalina and eventually married her, although at first there was some quarrelling over it and he was imprisoned, because he did not want her as his wife and she sued him to keep his word" (1552: f. 3r; 1964: 11) (*las festajavan muchos, y Cortes a la Catalina. Y en fin se caso con ella. Aun que primero tuuo algunos pendencias, y estuuo preso. La no la queria por muger. Y ella le demandaba la palabra*); also see Fernández del Castillo (1980 [1929]: 10–43); Duverger (2005: 104–8). On Díaz being wrong about the surprise trip, and claims that Cortés sent doña Catalina's brother to Cuba to fetch her, see WWC: 385–86. On daughter Catalina's fate and her father's will: DC, IV: 313–41; Conway (1940); Johnson (1975: 220). On her mother Leonor and Salcedo: DCM: #940; Thomas (1993: 635).

8. *Rodríguez*: CDII, XII: 255; DC, II: 81–83; hers and Tapia's quotes also in Thomas (translated slightly differently; respectively WWC: 387; and 1993: 765n50) (*don Fernando festejaba damas e mujeres que estaban en estas partes; era celosa de su marido*). *Another conquistador*: Antonio de Carvajal in DC, II: 58 (*vido en casa del dicho don FC a muchas fijas de señores desta tierra*).

9. *"Family Matters"*: The caption from this Codex Cozcatzin image reads, "Don Alonço de Alvarado married the daughter of the prince of Muntesçuma: Doña Yssabel de Muntesçuma, sister of don Pedro Tlacaquepan, who went to Spain. They are son and daughter of the Emperor Muntesçuma of Mexico." Image discussed by Hajovsky (2015: 52) and Mundy (2015: 192–93), who also reproduces it; the original codex is in BnF, Ms. Mexicain 41–45. *Gemelli visited*: Gemelli (1704: 544).

10. DC, II: 44. Leonor had a daughter, named doña Isabel de Tolosa Cortés Moctezuma, who married Juan de Oñate, the first governor of New Mexico. Spaniards laid claim for generations to the status of royal Aztec lineage, surely aware of the "conquest" circumstances of its genesis (one can read between such lines as Villagrá's trumpeting how a fellow conquistador in New Mexico, Cristóbal de Oñate, was descended from both Cortés and Montezuma: "The Great Marquis of the Valley begat a daughter / By a princess, one of three girls to Montezuma born"; Villagrá 1610; also quoted by Goodwin 2015: 255). On doña Isabel Moctezuma Tecuichpo, see Chipman (2005), Martínez Baracs (2006), Castañeda de la Paz (2013), and Villella (2016); her story has inspired several novels (e.g., Haggard 1893; García Iglesias 1946; Aguirre 2008).

11. *"Very publicly"*: Vásquez de Tapia in DC, II: 41–42 (*muy publico en este pueblo e fuera dél que se echó con dos o tres hermanas hijas de Motunzuma [sic] . . . por amiga, e que teniendola*); also DC, II: 44, 45 (Vásquez de Tapia again, and Gonzalo Mejía, both in 1529). *Modern historian*: Townsend (2006: 106). *Cuéllar*: DCM: #249.

12. Thomas (1993: 765n52; WWC: 386). I previously argued (2003: 83) that the timing of Malintzin's pregnancy suggested that Cortés refrained from making sexual demands on her until the campaign was over, as she was too valuable as an interpreter to be lost to pregnancy or childbirth complications (an idea that I believe originated with Frances Karttunen, personal communication, although I did not cite it as such); Townsend (2006: 139) argued that this gives Cortés too much credit, and that more likely her "poor diet, sleep deprivation, and psychological strain" during the war prevented conception—a disturbing point that is well taken.

13. *"In Cuba"*: That accusation is common in the *residencia* documents; e.g., Vásquez de Tapia in DC, II: 41 (*con primas e con hermanas; "ha-*

biendo tenido a mi hija públicamente en Cuba"; etc.); Juan de Burgos in DC, II: 53–54; Antonio de Carvajal in DC, II: 58; and Gonzalo Mejía in DC, II: 45. *"Niece"*: Ibid. (*se echaba el dicho don Fernando con Marina, en quienes hubo ciertos hijos, que era mujer de la tierra, e con otra sobrina suya*). *"Daughter of hers"*: Alonso Pérez in DC, II: 62 (*don Fernando Cortés se ha echado carnalmente con dos hermanas fijas de Motezuma [sic] e con Marina, la lengua, e con una fija suya e demas deste vido este testigo dos o tres indios ahorcados en Cuyoacan [sic] en un árbol dentro de las casa del dicho don Fernando Cortés . . . los habia mandando ahorcado porque se habian echado con la dicha Marina*).

14. Townsend (2006: 200), who also (op. cit.: 153) translates and quotes Herren (1992: 141): "If anyone ever really loved Marina, it was not don Hernán Cortés." One might add, if Cortés ever loved anyone, it was his Taíno family of Leonor and Catalina.

15. Thomas (1857: 39–40 [Act III, Sc. 1]).

16. *"Of noble"* to *"Christianity"*: Ranking (1827: 320), who elaborated upon Clavigero's elaboration upon a few comments by Díaz. *"Extraordinary"* to *"union"*: Abbott (1904 [1856]: 80).

17. Abbott (1904 [1856]: 81); Novo (1985: 52) (*Yo lo sentía soñar sus sueños de oro; sus sueños pueriles e inagotables de riqueza y poder. Pero yo acariciaba el oro vivo de sus cabellos. Era mío el tesoro de su cuerpo que respiraba, que vivía. Por conservarlo junto a mí, le habría abierto las puertas de cien ciudades*).

18. "A Clement Cortés" in the Gallery is another lithograph in the same series (CSL-Sac, Rare Prints #2001–0008); Maurin lived in Paris in the first half of the nineteenth century (see discussions in Chapters 2 and 7) (*Cortès accepta l'inappréciable cadeau du chef Cacique, et ce jour fut le premier d'une passion qui jeta quelque douceur sur les sanglans triomphes du vainqueur du Mexique*).

19. *"Traitor"*: phrase is Townsend's (2006: 2), who points out that one of the earliest examples in literature of this interpretation is Anonymous (1999 [1826]).

20. *"Symbol"*: a 1999 phrase by Jean Franco, as quoted by Townsend (2006: 3); also see Hassig (1998).

21. Richmond (1885: 158); Abbott (1904 [1856]: 81).

22. Díaz CCIII (1632: f. 238r); Thomas (1993: 622); Abbott (1904 [1856]: 31, 38, 80–81). *"Temperament"*: MacNutt (1909: 448). *"New type"* to *"species"*: Solana (1938: 19, 21) (*un tipo nuevo en el ser hu-*

mano . . . El pasaje del amor carnal de Don Hernando Cortés, Marqués del Valle de Oajaca, tiene toda la magnitud de un versílico bíblico donde Jehová bendecía la fecundidad, tantas veces incestuosa, de los patriarcas porque ella continuaba la especie).

23. *"Amorous"*: Benito (1944: 127) (*los lances amorosos de aquel conquistador de reinos y de damas*). See "A Clement Cortés" in the Gallery, and "Conquest as Crucible," the painting that faces the Epilogue's title page.

24. *"Heathen"*: *residencia* testimony in DC, II: 41 (*pero que otras cosas tenía más de gentílico que de buen cristiano especialmente que tenía infinitas mujeres dentro de su casa*).

25. My verdict on doña Catalina's death is essentially the same as Hugh Thomas's; he likewise read all the testimony in the *residencia* inquiry, and speculated that while "Cortés was capable of murder," she probably "had a heart attack and died" after he shook her when they were arguing (1993: 582).

26. Prévost (1746–59, XII [1754]: 265) (*le prétexte qi les fit recevoir; main il est certain que Cortez prit de l'inclination pur une de ces Femmes, qu'il fit batiser sous le nom de Marina, & dont il fit la Maîtresse. Elle étoit, suivant Diaz, d'une beauté rare & d'une condition relevée*). See the images "Gifts of Women" atop this chapter (Anonymous 1760–61, 2 [of 20 volumes]: facing p. 19) and "To Make Corn Bread" in the Gallery (Prévost 1746–59, XII [1754]: 265) (*le Cacique de Tabasco fit accepter à Cortez vingt Femmes indiennes, pour faire du pain de Maïs à ses Trouppes*). Other examples of the Prévost image printed in the eighteenth century reversed the right–left orientation.

27. On Las Casas's whereabouts: Orique (2017); Clayton (2012: 342–47). Edict: CI, IV: 369–70; CC #88: 312–14; DC, IV: 342–43 (*entre otros cargos que fueron hechos . . . nadie con buena conciencia y título pueda tener los dichos indios por esclavos . . . los pongais en libertad y ansi mismo a todos los hijos y descendientes de las mujeres que quedaron pos esclavos de la dicha razón . . . que habia tomado de paz . . . don Hernando habia hecho apartar de los dichos indios cuatrocientos hombres que eran para pelear, y los habia hecho matar todos y los otros que habian quedado, que eran mujeres y niños en cantidad de hasta tres mil, los habia hecho herrar por esclavos . . . estando los indios del dicho pueblo y pueblos a él sujetos de paz, dio en los dichos indios y mató a muchos dellos y prendió a otros y a mujeres y los trajo al dicho pueblo de Tezcuco . . . y los habia hecho*

herrar por esclavos y vendídolos . . . habían hecho herrar más de quinien-
tos ánimas por esclavos . . . quando el dicho don Hernando fue de Guerra
sobre la ciudad de Chulula . . . cuatro mil indios, poco más o menos . . . sin
causa alguna habia mandado a los dichos españoles que les matasen y que
así habia muerto muchos dellos y hechos esclavos otros).

28. RC; AGI Justicia 224, 1: f. 294; Justicia 223, 2: f. 227; CDII,
     XXVII: 28, 231–32; DC, I: 208; Thomas (1993: 435–38); also CCR;
     Díaz CXLIII, CCXIII (1912, IV: 54; 1916, V: 306–7) ("wrecked"
     quote from Díaz); and Cervantes de Salazar (1914 [1560s]: 523–33
     [Bk. 5, Chs. IX–XVI]), on Tepeaca massacre and enslavement.

29. *Proceedings*: Cortés's will has been frequently published (e.g., Conway
     1940; DC, IV: 313–41); for the record of the 1548 auction of Cortés's
     household goods on the steps of Seville's cathedral, see DC, IV: 352–
     57; for a 1549 debt settlement using 93 kilos' worth of gold and silver
     jewelry from Cortés's estate, see DC, IV: 358–61. *"Poverty"*: quote by
     a Mexican-American filmmaker and university student, expressing a
     common view, in Myers (2015: 309); this myth of Cortés's final years
     goes at least back to the eighteenth century, with the dovetailing of
     him and Columbus often made explicit (e.g., "this great, this merito-
     rious man, now found himself at the close of his life in circumstances
     similar to those of Columbus, compelled to supplicate justice at the
     hands of an ungrateful King and malicious ministers"; Campe 1800:
     269, who even shaves off Cortés's last seventeen years to have him
     die in Spain in 1530). *Inventory*: AGN Hospital de Jesús 28; DC, IV:
     364–432 (quote on 393) (*una prisión de esclavo, con cuatro eslabones de*
     hierro); also see AGN Hospital de Jesús 398; Riley (1973).

30. DC, IV: 370–415. I have taken Xitl's occupation (*formero*) to be
     hornero, meaning he worked the sugar-boiling furnaces and ovens,
     but I might be wrong (*Juan Ucelote, indio, natural de Ecatepeque, de*
     edad de cincuenta años, e así lo parecía . . . Isabel Siguaquesuchil, india,
     natural de Tlaxcala, de edad de cuarenta y tres años . . . Juan Xitl, indio,
     natural de Guaxaca, de edad de cuarenta e un años, e dijo ser formero . . .
     Cecilia, esclava india, condenada por veinte años, natural de Tepexi, de
     edad de cuarenta años . . . Cristóbal, indio natural desta Nueva España,
     e dijo que no sabe de dónde es natural, porque vino pequeño a poder de
     españoles, de edad de treinta e cinco años poco más o menos).

31. *"Toleration"*: MacNutt (1909: xi). *"Abhorrent"*: Johnson (1975: 176).
     "Richest": Reséndez (2016: 66).

32. The literature on these topics is vast, but the broad number of Africans enslaved and transported to the Americas, in the late fifteenth through nineteenth centuries, is 10–15 million; recent work on indigenous enslavement in the Americas, for the same centuries, has produced a range of 2.5–5 million (see the massively documented table in Reséndez 2016: 324). Vásquez de Tapia's number of 20,000 is suspicious (it is a nice round sum and he was not a friendly witness in the Cortés *residencia*), but it is also plausible that such a number passed through the markets on Cortés's behalf.

33. Díaz CCXIII (1908–16, V: 306; 2005, I: 833) (*diesen liçençia para que de los indios mexicanos y naturales de los pueblos que se avian alçado y muerto españoles, que si los tornásemos a requerir tres vezes que vengan de paz, y que si no quisieren venir y diesen guerra, que le pudiésemos hazer esclavos, y echar un hierro en la cara que fue una 'g' como esta*).

34. On Garrido, see Restall (2003: 44, 55–63) (on his illicit sale of a Nahua slave in Spain, see van Deusen 2015b: 289–92).

35. "*Bondage*": Reséndez's phrase, used variously (e.g., 2016); also see Seijas (2014: 215–21); Stone (2014); van Deusen (2015b: 296).

36. "*Complexion*" and "*climate*": quoted in Earle (2014: 143–44). When Sandoval died of a sudden illness shortly after landing in Spain in 1528, among his property were two "Indians," two enslaved indigenous men who were freed in Sandoval's will. No mention is made of providing for them, so presumably they were set loose, penniless, in southern Spain—the ultimate displacement (AGI Justicia 1005, no. 2, ramo 2; Scholes 1969: 189).

37. *Francisco Manuel*: case in AGI Justicia 1007, no. 1, ramo 1; and Justicia 1022, no. 1, ramo 2; but expertly summarized by van Deusen (2015b: 298–300).

38. *Melgarejo*: ENE, VIII, #s447, 454, 461, 478: 128–30, 145–46, 182–84, 245–46; also see VI: 120–23, 208–9; VII: 270–72; IX: 102–6; Reséndez (2016: 72–74) (*ni he podido abogar por los que tienen indios por esclavos y bastaría aunque esto cesara para no venir a mí la gran enemistad común que me han tenido . . . mi odioso trabajo . . . de peor condición que los dichos indios esclavos que se han libertado*).

39. AGI Santo Domingo 99, ramo 1, no. 17 (I thank Scott Cave for sharing and transcribing this document with me) (*de la mucha cantidad de yndios que se sacaron en las armadas que para ello se hizieron que quando esta ysla muy despoblada y ansi mismo rrescivio mucho daño . . . a*

otras algunas personas eçesivos repartimientos . . . todos los demas vecinos de la ysla y se fueron muchos della de la nueva españa llevando consigo muchas de las naburias y yndios que les fueron encomendados e los demas vendian e barataban).

40. *Maltreatment*: CCR (1971: 57–58). *Ávila*: DC, I: 170–209 (quote on 201) (*los españoles truequen con los indios caribes los indios que traen de las entradas pos gallinas e por otras cosas, e este testigo ha visto trocar muchos de los dichos indios publicamente a los españoles*).

41. AGI Patronato 2, caja 1, legajo 1, no. 1, ramo 13; ENE, II, #107: 127–31; WWC: 170–71. On accusations of Velázquez abusing the rules on indigenous slaves, Justicia 49, e.g., 1, 1: ff.98–127. On slave markets in Mexico, e.g., RC; AGI Justicia 222, no. 3: ff. 61–68 (indigenous slaves sold at twenty to thirty pesos each); also see various items in ENE, I–III; there are also fleeting textual and visual references to indigenous slaves in early colonial Mexico in codices such as the Azcatitlan and Vaticano A (see Castañeda de la Paz and Oudijk 2012: 74–76).

42. ENE, VII, #391: 183–84 (letter of 1554, original in Simancas, not accessed by me) (*en tiempos pasados se llevaron muchos de los naturales de aquella provincial a las islas y otras partes y con lo que le dan en tributo no se puede sustentar por ser de poco provecho*). Also see ENE, I, #78: 153–66, a 1529 request to ship indigenous slaves from Mexico to the islands in order to exchange them for horses and other livestock.

43. From the king himself down to the humblest conquistador-settler, Spaniards believed that "the king's gold and treasure" (*el oro del rey; todo el oro e joyas de Su Majestad*; etc.), worth tens of thousands of pesos (equivalent to millions of dollars), had been lost during the Noche Triste. The rumors were fueled for decades by claims by conquistadors like Vásquez de Tapia that specific sums were secreted out of Tenochtitlan by certain Cortés cronies; in turn, Cortés loyalists insisted that Montezuma had revealed in 1520 "the secrets of the land," and its "many riches of diverse kinds, especially the silver mines" (*los secretos de la tierra . . . muchas riquezas de diversas maneras, especialmente las minas de plata*): DC, I: 114–28, 156–63 (quote on 156); Conway (1943); hundreds of testimonies in RC (Cortés *residencia*: RC; AGI Justicia 220–225; DC, II: 29, 43, 46, 48, 51, 56, numerous in 145–362) (e.g., in response to question #47 of the *residencia*: Vásquez de Tapia claimed Alvarado had buried in three or

four places near the city "a million and more of the treasure that was Montezuma's [*un millón e más el thesoro que huvo de Motezuma*]").

44. Mira Caballos (1997: 288–89); van Deusen (2015a; 2015b); Reséndez (2016: 50–51).

45. Hoig (2013: 4, 21). Also see Goldwert (1983); Alves (1996: 213–31).

46. *González*: Schwaller and Nader (2014: 179). *Vásquez*: DCM: #1102; Schwaller and Nader (2014: 176–77). *Suárez*: DCM: #1025; Schwaller and Nader (2014: 210–11); AGN Inquisición 37: f. 1; Díaz CCV (1916, V: 233–34).

47. *Sopuerta*: DCM: #969; WWC: 237; Schwaller and Nader (2014: 196). *Granada*: DCM: #414; WWC: 64; Schwaller and Nader (2014: 188–89). *Sedeño*: DCM: #991; Schwaller and Nader (2014: 213).

48. *Gutiérrez*: DCM: #434; Schwaller and Nader (2014: 214). *Galingo*: DCM: #972; Schwaller and Nader (2014: 215). *Sánchez*: ENE, XV, #842; DCM: #959; Schwaller and Nader (2014: 216–17). *Pérez*: DCM: #793; Schwaller and Nader (2014: 235–36).

49. *"Infect"*: Cervantes de Salazar (1914 [1560s]: 98 [Bk. 2, Ch. XVI]) (*Decían sus amigos que eran las bubas, porque siempre fué amigo de mujeres, y las indias mucho más que las españolas inficionan a los que las tratan*). *"Pain"*: DC, I: 439–49 (quote on 449; letter of 1527 written in Tenochtitlan to Saavedra Cerón) (*los naturales de aquellas partes son muy celosos e de ninguna cosa reciben mayor pena que de tratarles con sus mujeres*).

50. Díaz CXL, CXLII, CXLIV, CXLVI, CLXII, CLXXV, CLXXVIII, CLXXXIV (1912, IV: 25, 50, 51, 67, 69, 90, 265; 1916, V: 12, 38, 41, 42, 66–67; 2005, I: 407, 422, 433, 434, 448, 561, 639, 655, 657, 658, 675) (*en buscar una buena india o aver algún despojo; muy buenas pieças de indias; aqui se ovieron muy buenas indias e despojo; dimos muy de presto en la casa y prendimos tres indios y dos mugeres moças y hermosas para ser indias y una vieja; treinta gallinas y melones de la tierra . . . y apañamos . . . tres mugeres, y tuvimos buena Pasqua; le enbiaron muchas indias y gente menuda*). Note that the Díaz citations in this and adjacent notes are by no means a comprehensive list of such references.

51. Díaz CXLIII, CXLVI (1912, IV: 54–55, 90; 2005, I: 424–25, 448) (*para capitanes, y si heran hermosas y buenas indias las que metiamos a herrar las hurtavan de noche del montón; qual tratavan bien a las indias y naborias que tenian, o qual as tratava mal; de presto les desaparesçian y no las vian mas*).

52. CA: f.42v (using translation in Lockhart 1993: 274–75).

53. FC, XII: 248–49; *Annals of Tlatelolco* in Lockhart (1993: 268–69) (*ninguna cosa otra tomauan sino el oro y las mugeres moças hermosas*).

54. Díaz CLXXX (1916, V: 51–52; 2005, I: 664) (*las mugeres tomadas; a rogar a Cortés; çiertas joyezuelas de oro; todos los indios de aquel pueblo; dan una buen mano de vara y piedra y flecha a Cortés y a sus soldados, de manera que hirieron al mismo Cortés en la cara y a otros doze de sus soldados*).

55. Díaz LI, LII (1908–16, I: 185, 191; 2005, I: 124, 127).

56. DC, IV: 401. To place the fate of indigenous women slaves in a larger context, see van Deusen (2012).

57. Motolinía quote by Reséndez (2016: 62); *residencia* charge in DC, II: 114 (*don Hernando Cortés, con la gente que con él iba, mató muchos indios e fizo herrar a más de quinientas animas por esclavos*).

58. *"Handful"* quotes: Maudslay, in Díaz (1942: xv); the great J. H. Plumb in Johnson (1975: xii); Ballentine in Ixtlilxochitl (1969: ix). Also see the quotes and citations in the Prologue; and Restall (2003: Ch. 1).

59. My discussion of conquistador totals is drawn from the numbers in Hassig (2006: 58, 62, 71, 74, 76–77, 84, 86, 93, 100, 104, 107, 111–12, 119–20, 122, 124, 135, 165, 175, 176), checked against comments made by Aguilar, Cortés, Díaz (e.g., CCX; 1916, V: 274–75 gives numbers totaling over three thousand), Durán, Gómara, and Sahagún. Of the original 450 men, 35 were killed by Mayas at Potonchan (dying later of wounds and infections). The surviving 415 were supplemented by a dozen or so new arrivals in the summer (1519), but a comparable number left on the ship sent to Spain. In August, 300 marched to Tlaxcallan, leaving very approximately 100 in Vera Cruz. The Tlaxcalteca killed 50 or more, so only 250 reached Tenochtitlan in November (with numbers in Vera Cruz also falling due to battle, illness, and perhaps flight). The end of 1519 was thus the first numerical low point. A trickle of new arrivals in the early months of 1520 brought Spanish numbers in Tenochtitlan to about 350 by the time Narváez landed on the coast in April with 1,100. By June there were thus some 1,500 Spaniards in the capital city (the war's numerical high point), but perhaps 900 were soon killed in the city and another hundred or so died in the march back to Tlaxcallan; the second low point was thus late summer 1520, when numbers dropped below 500, perhaps as low as the

original number of 450. Hundreds more arrived in 1521, perhaps 500 or 600, so that even with Spanish mortality during the siege at over a hundred men, there were close to a thousand in the valley when Tenochtitlan fell in August.

60. *"Secret"*: Bourn (2005). *Formula*: Hassig comments in ibid. (also 2006 [1994]).

61. Brooks (1993: 1–12); Hassig (2006: 123–25, 187–89); Sandine (2015: 153–59).

62. Motolinía (1950: 38); point made by Brooks (1993: 8–10, 22–23) and Sandine (2015: 156). *"In large part"*: McNeill (1979: 192), quoted by Brooks (op. cit.: 8).

63. Brooks (1993: 15–29); Hassig (2006 [1994]: 125); Sandine (2015: 153–59).

64. Both numbers from Luis de Cárdenas, in a denunciation of Cortés made in Madrid in 1528 (hence my assumption of exaggeration), in AGI Patronato 1, 1, 2; CDII, XL: 370; and DC, III: 19 (*así hizo capitán a Pedro de Alvarado de los cincuenta mil indios, cuando fue sobre Francisco de Garay y le mató los trescientos cristianos en una noche, por mandado de Hernando Cortés*).

65. Between 1512 and 1519, the power balance between the two Triple Alliances had shifted in favor of the Aztecs, with the Tlaxcalteca losing one of its three partners, Huexotzinco, for much of 1512–16, and then briefly Cholollan too. This magnified the impact of the pendulum swing toward the Tlaxcalteca in 1519–21. On this, and the Flower Wars, see the various treatments in Carrasco (1999) and Hassig (1988; 2006 [1994]). I use "total warfare"—a highly debated concept applicable primarily to the twentieth century—loosely and somewhat rhetorically.

66. *"Ordinary men"*: The phrase is a reference to the title of Browning (1998), whose "ordinary men" are German policemen drawn into committing mass murder in Poland in the early 1940s. I am grateful to Garrett Fagan for introducing me to Browning's work.

67. Archival references to González: RC; AGI Justicia 223: f. 22ff; Justicia 237; Patronato 2, caja 1, legajo 1; DC, II: 195, 285; ENE, II, #81: 6–8; VII, #369: 31–36. Translations of his 1530 commendation in ENE, II, #81 are mine (*la provincia de Tepeaca donde pasastes muchos peligros y trabajos peleando muchas veces con los indios*), as is the quote from the letter in ENE, VII, #369 but also see Stabler and

Kicza (1986); the final word in the quote ("elsewhere") is actually a missing word due to document damage (Paso y Troncoso imagines "Italia"; ENE op. cit.). Also Grunberg (2001: 208–10) (*la guerra y conquista deste rreynos no parezca ta Reuirosa y sin razon, como algunos con sus pocas letras lo afirmaban y prueban que esta gente era barbara ydolatrica sacrificadora, matadora de ynoçentes, comedora de carne humana, expurçissima y nefanda sodomia, y si me quiere dezir que tales y tantos pecados diños son de guerra y de perdamjo de rreyno, mas que en la guerra se tuvo modo eçesivo y grandes ynadvertençias y notables desordenes y pecados y ansi lo creo, paguenlo los que los cometieron, y no todos; castiguen a aquellos, y no perdamos nosotros o que tan bien y con tanto trabajo y en sevicio de dios y de V. Mag. Ganamos y a la verdad despues que la Guerra se comiença aunque sea muy justa y en gente muy xriana no creo que podra ser menos que desordenes, como consta de la guerras de francia y rroma e . . .*).

68. Todorov (1999 [1982]: 145).

69. Las Casas (2003 [1552]); Gardiner (1961) (on Sandoval); Butterfield (1955) (on Aguilar); Anonymous (1999 [1826]: 119) (I consulted only this fine English edition of the novel, first published in Philadelphia but in Spanish and almost certainly by a Mexican; op. cit.: 1–2).

70. Martínez's comments in Bourn (2005).

71. Mendieta (1870 [1596]: 177) (*tanta multitud de enemigos, unos claros y otros ocultos . . . tan pocos compañeros . . . tan cobdiciosos del oro . . . Y aunque él mismo pronunciase la sentencia de muerte en causa no justificada, diciendo: ahorquen á tal indio, quemen á este otro, den tormento á fulano, porque en dos palabras le traian hecha la informacion, que era un tal por cual, que hizo matar españoles, que conspiró, que amotinó, que intentó, y otras cosas semejantes, que aunque él muchas veces sintiese que no iban muy justificadas, habia de condescender con la compañia y con los amigos, porque no se le hiciesen enemigos y lo dejasen solo*).

72. Robertson (1777, II: 48).

73. Ibid.; Prescott (1994 [1843]); MacNutt (1909: 168). Also Thomas (1993: 434–39) is a good summary of the 1520 massacres. Grotius quoted by Carr (2003: 78–79).

74. *"Minds"*: Myers (2015: 124). *"Traitors"*: Isabel Sánchez de García speaking c.2006 to Myers (op. cit.). *"Forgive"* and *"things happen"*: Hersh (2015: quotes on 56, 59).

75. DCM: #41; #44; WWC: 5–12; Schwaller and Nader (2014: 160–62).

76. DCM: #141; WWC: 170–71; Díaz CLX (1912, IV: 240–41); Thomas (1993: 99, 358, 360, 377–78, 437, 450, 554); Schwaller and Nader (2014: 169–70).

77. DCM: #820; RC; AGI Justicia, 223: f. 18; NCDHM, II: 217–19. Schwaller and Nader (2014: 196) speculate that Portillo may have been the "Diego Enos" who signed the 1519 First Letter in Vera Cruz. Díaz (CCV; 1916, V: 243) claimed "he performed miracles, and he was almost a saint"—that is, in Maudslay's translation; the original reads *fue de santa bida* ("he lived a holy life") (2005, I: 788).

78. *Scholar of the Holocaust*: Browning (1998: 160).

79. *Paz*: AGI Justicia 1018, no. 1, ramos 1 and 2 (lawsuits by Paz's family members, including details of Paz being racked, waterboarded, and foot-burned; e.g., "many kinds of torture by cords, garrotte, water, and hot bricks [*muchos generos de tormentos de cordeles, garrotes, de agua, fuego de ladrillos*]" in Justicia 1018, no. 1, ramo 1: f.2); the account in Díaz CLXXXV (1916, V: 77–78) barely begins to convey the horror of Paz's slow death. *García de Llerena*: A veteran of the Spanish-Aztec War and Cortesian loyalist, he acted as one of Cortés's legal representatives in the late 1520s and in 1529 mounted the first defense in Tenochtitlan against the accusations of the *residencia* inquiry. In retaliation, the royal judges arrested him and a priest who had helped him hide; the latter was hanged and quartered, while García de Llerena was given a hundred lashes and condemned to have a foot severed (Martínez in DC, I: 80–81). Foot severing was actually the removal of some toes—so the victim could still walk, but with a humiliating limp—and was a standard "punishment" among Spaniards; Cortés allegedly had Gonzalo de Umbría likewise maimed for *Velazquista* plotting (DC, II: 42; Díaz LVI).

80. *"Numbed"*: Browning (1998: 160).

81. *Recent studies*: e.g., Woolford, Benvenuto, and Laban Hinton (2014); Madley (2015; 2016). *"Government policy"*: Browning (1998: 161). For discussion of definitions of genocide that underpin my suggestion that we can usefully see genocide in effect and micro-genocidal moments in the Spanish-Aztec War and its aftermath, see Woolford, Benvenuto, and Laban Hinton (2014: 2), and Madley (2016: 4–5). The 150 readings in Meierhenrich (2014) show that debates over the definition and applicability of concepts of genocide

have only served to fuel the dynamism of the field of genocide studies since the 1990s; it will be to the benefit of "Conquest" studies if
the arguments made by Todorov (1999 [1982]: 127–45), Stannard
(1993), Madley, and others remain debated, and if the relevance of
the term to European colonization in the Americas continues to be
"an empirically contested question" (Meierhenrich 2014: 30).

EPILOGUE:
HALLS OF THE MONTEZUMAS

1. Epigraph sources, in sequence: Thomas (1857: 47–48 [Act III, Sc. 3]); Navarra, aka Pedro de Albret, a humanist bishop from Navarre, in Martínez (2016: 84), whose translation I adjusted very slightly, using his transcription; Matos Moctezuma (1987: 199), writing about how Aztecs understood their Great Temple; MacNutt (1909: 173); Grafton, *V Is for Vengeance* (New York: G. P. Putnam, 2011: 432) (not included in Bibliography).

2. On the life of Malintzin's son, Martín, see the excellent Lanyon (2003); also Townsend (2006: 151–52, 188–213). On Prince Philip's youth and education, see Parker (2014: 8–31).

3. Letter of April 1, 1562 (AGI Patronato 182, ramo 2; partially transcribed in Romerovargas Iturbide 1964, II: 229–30).

4. Trueba y Cosío (1829: 342).

5. *Modern historian*: Butterfield (1955: 1). The claim by historians that the "Conquest of Mexico" seems more like "an epic poem or chivalric romance" goes back to the early nineteenth century (here I'm quoting Chevalier 1846: 83), repeated scores of time since then, and is often found beside expressions of wonder over the "miraculous" and "stupendous" achievement of "a handful of adventurers" (see Restall 2003: Ch. 1; and discussion in the Prologue and Chapter 8).

6. *"Misrepresented"*: Lane (2010: ix).

7. Brooks (1995: 149) calculated the twenty-seven years and twenty-seven days.

8. Díaz CCXIII (1919, V: 301–11; 2005, I: 830–36).

9. Op. cit.: block quote: 308; 834; *"pride"*: 310; 836 (*nos preçiamos de aver hecho tan buena obra*).

10. On Aztec victory tradition: Mundy (2015: 95).

11. Nahuatl original and English translation in Sell and Burkhart (2004: quote on 124–25) (also discussed in Chapter 2).

12. *"Latin as elegant"*: CDII, II: 149–50 (also quoted in Gruzinski 2002: 94). *San Francisco*: In the Sutro Library: Mathes (1985) details the fascinating story of how the Tlatelolco library prospered and suffered, by turns, with volumes lost with every move and disaster, yet surviving to a miraculous degree (including escaping the 1906 San Francisco earthquake). I am most grateful to Sutro librarian Angelica Illueca for generously sharing the collection with me in July 2014.

13. Carochi (2001 [1645]: 253).

14. "Mexico City Idealized," in the Gallery, is the front of the *biombo*, showing the city Spaniards made on that site, albeit in a somewhat idealized and sanitized form. Although many of these buildings can still be seen in downtown Mexico City today, this midcolonial metropolis is closer to the Tenochtitlan with which it merged and which it submerged—with its midlake location, dominant central plaza, canals, aqueduct, and the Franciscan complex in the foreground on one of the main sites of Montezuma's zoo. The screen's reverse side portrays the "Conquest of Mexico," in the form of a stylized view of Tenochtitlan highlighting where nine events took place during the war. The full map is reproduced to varying degrees of utility, with brief discussion, in Kagan (2000: 153–59); Rivero Borrell M. et al. (2002: 83–87); Schreffler (2007: 22–24); Terraciano (2011: 76–77); Alcalá and Brown (2014: 113–15). I am grateful to Janet Purdy for helping create the map and its graphic.

15. Reprinted in his *Obras*: Sigüenza y Góngora (1928: 271–346).

16. *"Cursed name"*: Krauze (2010: 72–73) (*Ninguna calle, ninguna estatua, ninguna ciudad, apenas algunos sitios que marcan su itinerario [el Mar de Cortés en California, el Paso de Cortés entre los volcanes, el Palacio de Cortés en Cuernavaca] se atreven a mencionar el nombre maldito*).

17. Nelson and Nelson (1892: 142–43, 198–99); Tom Price, curator of the President James K. Polk Home and Museum, personal communication, July 19, 2016 (to whom I am grateful for his help, and for sending me an 1891 photograph of Polk Place's entrance hall, with the Cortés painting visible on the wall); also see the White House Historical Association's page, whitehousehistory.org/a-portrait-of

-spanish-conquistador-hernan-cortes (written by the museum's director, John Holtzapple); and Greenberg (2012: 268, 275, et al.) (I have enjoyed and benefited greatly from conversations with Amy Greenberg on Polk-related matters).

18. On the shifts in Tenochtitlan's nomenclature of the 1520s–40s, see Mundy (2015: 132–33). The colored-tile replacement to the concrete plaque (shown in the Gallery) is a reproduction of the seventeenth-century *biombo* depictions of the Meeting and "Conquest"; at the time of writing, its artwork had proved less inviting to vandals or political protestors.

19. For a captivating visual record of the half-destroyed palace, see the 1695 painting by Cristóbal de Vallalpando, frequently reproduced (e.g., Kagan 2000: 163 and dust jacket; and with important discussion in Schreffler 2007: 32–35).

20. *"Flag"* to *"cowardly"*: Kendall (1851: 45–46; lithograph facing p. 45). The earlier lithograph of the *zócalo* was published variously in the 1830s and '40s; both versions are easily found in modern publications and online. Also see Johannsen (1985: 228–29, 259).

21. Thomas (1857: 4 [unnumbered], 47–48 [Act III, Sc. 3], 74).

22. *Prescott*: Prescott (1994 [1843]); Gardiner (1959: 10–12, 213, 243). *Occupation*: Myers (2015: 51–53). *Hymn*: The rest of the opening verse is "First to fight for right and freedom, / And to keep our honor clean. / We are proud to claim the title of United States Marine" (published widely online and in print, but the earliest version that I found, complete with musical score, is Niles and Moore 1929: 72–74).

23. *"Forgotten"*: title to Kurutz and Mathes (2003); also see Johannsen (1985); Greenberg (2012).

24. Vivaldi (1733); Lajarte (1883); Subirá (1948); Riding (2005); interview with Máynez in the Mexican magazine *Proceso*, November 10, 2006, accessed at proceso.com.mx/223158/maynez-reescribe -en-nahuatl-moctezuma-de-vivaldi (not included in Bibliography) (*inventó un romance amoroso bastante trivial; una bazofia, absurdo, una farsa tragicómica*); Ng (2009).

25. By 1529, the Franciscans were established enough on the site of the old zoo to acquire another lot across the canal, westward toward the lake edge (and due south of where the Palacio de Bellas Artes now sits), where a hospital was built "for the sick indigenous boys

(*muchachos naturales de esta tierra . . . enfermos*); part of that building complex still stands (copy of the city's Actas de Cabildo in Newberry Library, Chicago; Ayer MS 1143, v.2: f. 11r; my thanks to Scott Cave for finding and sharing this document).

APPENDIX:

LANGUAGE AND LABEL, CAST AND DYNASTY

1. Lockhart (1993: 13).
2. For prosopographies of the conquistadors who fought in Mexico, presented in variants on the encyclopedia and dictionary formats, see DCM; WWC; Díaz CCVI (1916, V: 252–59); and Schwaller and Nader (2014). My biographies here are based on a combination of those four sources with various archival and other items cited throughout the book.

Bibliography of References and Sources

—— ⚘ ——

BIBLIOGRAPHICAL NOTE

THE TWO BIBLIOGRAPHIES BELOW constitute a comprehensive list of the sources I consulted in writing this book; all of them can also be found cited in the notes. Because many of the early printed sources are very rare, hard-to-find books, I have indicated in which library I found copies of all rare books listed below under "Primary Sources." I have treated most books published before the somewhat arbitrary date of 1940 as "Primary," and most items published before 1920 as rare. As this book's arguments reflect, the historian's dividing line between primary and secondary sources, normally solid, is here very blurred—because the topic's history and its protagonists have had complex posthumous lives for five centuries.

Note that I only cite the libraries where I consulted such copies (and in the order I did so); I do not cite all libraries holding copies of such books. Most of the research (and much of the writing) for the project was done in the AGI, BL, MQB, and above all in the JCB (all abbreviations listed below). The archives and libraries listed below were visited on-site unless otherwise indicated.

There are inevitably sources I did not consult, either because they could not be found or did not come to my attention; there is, after all, half a millennium of written and visual material on this subject. In other words, this is not a bibliography of everything written on all topics relevant to the book. But I consulted whatever I could get my hands on, and I hope it is a representative body of work.

BIBLIOGRAPHY OF REFERENCES:
PRIMARY SOURCES AND ABBREVIATIONS

AGI   Archivo General de Indias, Seville, Spain

AGN   Archivo General de la Nación, Mexico City, Mexico

BL   British Library, London, England

BLY   Beinecke Rare Book & Manuscript Library, Yale University, New Haven, USA

BM   British Museum, London, England

BnF   Bibliothèque national de France, Paris, France

CA   Codex Aubin in BM (item # Am2006, Drg.31219; available online; also see Lockhart 1993: 274–79)

CC   *Cedulario cortesiano* (see Arteaga Garza and Pérez San Vicente 1949)

CCR   Cortés's *Cartas de relación,* or Letters to the King; translations mine from first editions (Cortés 1522, etc.) and the 1528 manuscript in Codex Vindobonensis, SN1600, ONB (also Cortés 1960 [1519–25])

CDHM   *Colección de Documentos para la Historia de México* (see García Icazbalceta 1858–66)

CDII   *Colección de documentos inéditos de Indias* (see Torres de Mendoza et al. 1864–84)

CI   *Cedulario Indiano* (see Anonymous 1596)

CSL-Sac   California History Room, California State Library, Sacramento, USA

CSL-SL   Sutro Library, California State Library, San Francisco, USA

DC   *Documentos Cortesianos* (see Martínez 1991)

DCM   *Dictionnaire des Conquistadores de Mexico* (see Grunberg 2001)

DHM   *Documentos para la Historia de México* (see López Rayon 1852–53)

EC   *Estudios Cortesianos: Recopilados con motivo del IV centenario de la muerte de Hernán Cortés* (Madrid: Consejo Superior de Investigaciones Científicas, 1948)

ENE   *Epistolario de Nueva España* (see Paso y Troncoso 1939–42)

FC   Florentine Codex (see Sahagún 1950–82 for all references to Books I through XI [FC, I–XI]; Lockhart 1993 for all references to Book XII [FC, XII]; and Sahagún 1989 [1585] for references to the revised Book XII)

HAHR   *Hispanic American Historical Review*

JCB   John Carter Brown Library, Brown University, Providence, USA

Ix13   Ixtlilxochitl's *Thirteenth Relation* (see Ixtlilxochitl 1969; 2015; but all references are to the English translation in Brian, Benton, and García Loaeza 2015)

LCDT   Las Casas's *De Thesauris* (cited by folio number; see Las Casas 1561b)

LCHI   Las Casas's *History of the Indies* (cited by original book and chapter, but also see below under Las Casas the manuscript and various editions consulted and variously cited)

LML-H   Loeb Music Library, Harvard University (accessible through harvard.edu/libraries/loebmusic)

LOC   Library of Congress, Washington, DC, USA

MQB   Musée du quai Branly (médiathèque), Paris, France

NCDHM *Nueva Colección de Documentos para la Historia de México* (see García Icazbalceta 1886–92)

ONB   Österreichische Nationalbibliothek, Vienna, Austria

PRT   Documents collected by Pérez-Rocha and Tena (2000)

PSU-SC   Pennsylvania State University, Special Collections Library, University Park, PA, USA

PTM   Proyecto Templo Mayor, or Great Temple archaeological project in central Mexico City, 1978–present

RC   *Residencia* and *Pesquisa Secreta* investigation (1526–45) into Cortés by Crown officials; original documents in the AGI; excerpts published in DC and DHM

WWC   *Who's Who of the Conquistadors* (see Thomas 2000)

BIBLIOGRAPHY OF REFERENCES:
PRINTED PRIMARY SOURCES (HISTORICAL AND LITERARY)

Aa, Pieter vander. 1706–1708. *Naaukeurige versameling der gedenk-waardigste zee en land-reysen na Oost en West-Indiën.* 28 vols. Leiden: Pieter vander Aa. [1st ed.; Dutch version of Herrera's *Historia General*; see Herrera 1728; in JCB.]

Abbott, John S. C. 1904 [1856]. *Makers of History: Hernando Cortez.* New York: Harper and Brothers. [In CSL-SL.]

Acosta, José de. 2002 [1590]. *Natural and Moral History of the Indies.* Jane E. Mangan, ed. Frances López-Morillas, trans. Durham: Duke University Press.

Aguilar, fray Francisco de. 1938 [c.1560]. *Historia de la Nueva España.* Alfonso Teja Zabre, ed. Mexico City: Ediciones Botas.

———. 1977 [c.1560]. *Relación breve de la conquista de la Nueva España.* Jorge Gurría Lacroix, ed. Mexico City: UNAM.

———. 1988 [c.1560]. *Relación breve de la conquista de la Nueva España.* In J. Díaz, A. Tapia, B. Vásquez, and F. Aguilar, *La conquista de Tenochtitlán.* Germán Vásquez, ed. Madrid: historia 16, pp. 155–206.

Anonymous. 1522. *Newe Zeitung, von dem Lande, das die Spanier funden haben ym 1521 Iare genant Jucatan.* Augsburg. [1st ed.; in JCB.]

———. 1522. *Ein Schöne Newe Zeytung so Kayserlich Mayestet aus India yetz nemlich zukommen seind.* Augsburg: Sigmund Grimm. [1st ed.; in JCB.]

Anonymous [uno gentil'homo del Signor Fernando Cortese; el Conquistador Anónimo]. n.d. [1556]. "Relatione di Alcune Cose della Nuova Spagna [Relación de Algunas Cosas de la Nueva España]." In Giovanni Battista Ramusio, *Navigationi et Viaggi.* Venice: Giunti. [1st ed.; in JCB. Spanish editions cited are CDHM, vol. I, pp. 368–98; and Bustamante 1986.]

Anonymous. 1596. *Libro Quarto de Provisiones, Cedulas, Capitulos, de ordenanças, instruciones, y cartas* [etc.; aka *Cedulario Indiano,* vol. IV]. Madrid: Imprenta Real. [In LOC.]

Anonymous. 1741. *The American Traveller; Being a New Historical Collection Carefully compiled from Original Memoirs in several Languages, And the most authentic Voyages and Travels [etc.].* London: J. Fuller. [In BL and JCB.]

Anonymous. 1760–61. *The World displayed; or, a Curious Collection of Voyages and Travels, Selected from the Writers of all Nations.* 20 vols. London: J. Newberry. [In JCB.]

Anonymous. 1858 [1550s]. *Vida de Hernan Cortés [De Rebus Gestis Ferdinandi Cortesii].* Latin transcription and Spanish translation in CDHM, vol. I, pp. 309–57.

Anonymous. 1999 [1826]. *Xicoténcatl: An anonymous historical novel about the events leading up to the conquest of the Aztec Empire.* Guillermo I. Castillo-Feliú, trans. Austin: University of Texas Press.

Apiano, Pedro. 1575. *La Cosmographia de Pedro Apiano, corregida y añadida por Gemma Frisio, Medico y Mathematico.* Antwerp: Juan Bellero al Aguila de Oro. [In JCB.]

Argensola, Bartolomé Leonardo de. 1940 [1620s?]. *La Conquista de México.* Joaquín Ramírez Cabañas, ed. Mexico City: Pedro Robredo.

Arteaga Garza, Beatriz, and Guadalupe Pérez San Vicente, eds. 1949. *Cedulario cortesiano.* Mexico City: Editorial Jus.

Austen, Jane. 1818. *Northanger Abbey.* London: Murray.

Bacon, Francis. 1973 [1612]. *Essays.* London: Dent.

Baird, Ellen T. 1993. *The Drawings of the Sahagún's Primeros Memoriales: Structure and Style.* Norman: University of Oklahoma Press.

Barker, George. n.d. [1960s?] *The Degradations of Guatemozin*. Play, in original typescript with handwritten corrections by the playwright. [In BL.]

Beauvois, E. 1885. *Les Deux Quetzalcoatl Espagnols: J. de Grijalva et F. Cortés*. Louvain: Ch. Peeters. [In MQB.]

Berdan, Frances and Patricia Reiff Anawalt, eds. 1992. *The Codex Mendoza*. 4 vols. Berkeley: University of California Press.

Bird, Robert Montgomery. 1835. *The Infidel; or, The Fall of Mexico. A Romance*. Philadelphia: Carey, Lea & Blanchard. [In BLY.]

Braden, Charles S. 1930. *Religious Aspects of the Conquest of Mexico*. Durham: Duke University Press.

Brian, Amber, Bradley Benton, and Pablo García Loaeza. 2015. *The Native Conquistador: Alva Ixtlilxochitl's Account of the Conquest of New Spain*. Latin American Originals #10. University Park, PA: Penn State University Press.

Bry, Theodore de. 1601. *Peregrinationes in Americam*. Part 9. German printing. Frankfurt: Wolffgang Richter. [In JCB.]

———. 1634. *Peregrinationes in Americam*. Part 13. Latin printing. Frankfurt: Matthaei Meriani. [In JCB.]

Burtt, Edwin A. 1939. *The English Philosophers from Bacon to Mill*. New York: Random House.

Bustamante, Jesús, ed. and trans. 1986. *Conquistador Anónimo: Relación de la Nueva España*. Madrid: Polifemo.

Calvo, Andrea. 1522. *Noue de le Isole & Terra ferma Nouamente trouate In India per el Capitaneo de larmata de la Cesarea Maiestate*. Milan: Andrea Calvo. [1st ed.; in BL.]

———. 1985. *News of the Islands and the Mainland newly discovered in India by the Captain of his Imperial Majesty's Fleet*. Edward F. Tuttle, trans. and ed. Culver City, CA: Labyrinthos.

Campe, J. H. 1784. *La Découverte de L'Amerique, pour l'instruction et l'amusement des jeunes gens*. Vol. 2. Switzerland ["En Suisse"]: Les Libraires Associés. [In CSL-SL and MQB.]

———. 1800. *Cortes: or, the Discovery of Mexico; Being a Continuation of the Discovery of America. For the Use of Children and Young Persons*. Translated from the German original. Birmingham, England: J. Belcher. [In BLY.]

Carochi, Horacio. 2001 [1645]. *Grammar of the Mexican Language, with an explanation of its adverbs (1645)*. James Lockhart, trans. and ed. Stanford and Los Angeles: Stanford University Press and UCLA Latin American Center Publications.

Cervantes de Salazar, Francisco. 1546. *Obras, que Francisco Cervantes de Salazar, ha hecho, glosado, y traduzido.* Alcalá. [In JCB.]

———. 1953 [1554]. *Life in the Imperial and Loyal City of Mexico in New Spain and the Royal and Pontifical University of Mexico as Described in the Dialogues for the Study of the Latin Language.* Austin: University of Texas Press.

———. 1914 [1560s]. *Crónica de la Nueva España.* Madrid: Hispanic Society of America. [Lingkua.com has transcription (Barcelona: Red Ediciones, 2012) of Madrid: Hauser y Menet, 1914 edition.]

Charnay, D. 1903. *Manuscrit Ramirez: Histoire de l'origine des Indiens qui habitant la Nouvelle Espagne, selons leurs traditions.* Paris: Leroux. [In MQB.]

Chevalier, Michel. 1846. *Mexico: Before and After the Conquest.* Fay Robinson, trans. Philadelphia: Carey and Hart. [In MQB.]

Chimalpahin, Domingo de San Antón Muñoz Quauhtleuanitzin. 1997. *Codex Chimalpahin, Volume 1: Society and Politics in Mexico Tenochtitlan, Tlatelolco, Texcoco, Culhuacan, and Other Nahua Altepetl in Central Mexico.* Arthur J. O. Anderson and Susan Schroeder, trans. and eds. Norman: University of Oklahoma Press.

———. n.d. *Historia de la Conquista de Mexico.* Manuscript. [In JCB as Codex Sp 63; also see Roa-de-la-Carrera; Gómara 1552.]

Cholmley, Hugh. 1787. *The Memoirs of Sir Hugh Cholmley; and an Account of Tangier.* London. [In BL.]

Conway, G. R. G. 1940. *Postrera Voluntad y Testamento de Hernando Cortés, Marqués del Valle.* Mexico City: Pedro Robredo.

———. 1943. *La Noche Triste. Documentos: Segura de la Frontera en Nueva España, Año de MDXX.* Mexico City: Gante.

Cortés, Hernando. 1522. *Carta de relacio[n] e[m]biada a Su S. Majestad [etc.].* Seville: Jacobo Cromberger. [In JCB.]

———. 1523. *Carta de relacio[n] e[m]biada a Su S. Majestad [etc.].* Zaragoza: George Zoci. [In JCB.]

———. 1770. *Historia de Nueva-España, Escrita Por Su Esclarecido Conquistador Hernan Cortés, [etc.].* Archbishop Francisco Antonio Lorenzana, ed. Mexico City: J. H. de Hogal. [In JCB.]

———. 1778. *Correspondence de Fernand Cortès avec l'empereur Charles-Quint, sur la conquête du Mexique.* French edition of Lorenzana's edition of Cortés 1770. Paris: Cellot & Jombert Fils jeune (A 2nd ed. is: En Suisse, chez les Libraires Associés, 1779). [Both in JCB.]

———. 1779. *Briefe des Ferdinand Cortes an Kayser Carl [etc.].* Heidelberg: Gebrüden Pfähler. [In JCB.]

———. 1780. *Brieven van Ferdinand Cortes, aan Keiser Karel V. [etc.].* Amsterdam: Yntema en Tieboel. [In JCB.]

———. 1843. *The Despatches of Hernando Cortes, the Conqueror of Mexico, addressed to the Emperor Charles V.* George Folsom, ed. New York: Wiley and Putnam. [In JCB.]

———. 1908. *Letters of Hernando Cortés to Charles V.* Francis A. MacNutt, ed. and trans. 2 vols. New York: G. P. Putnam's Sons.

———. 1960. *Cartas de Relacíon.* Manuel Alcalá, ed. Mexico City: Porrúa.

———. 1962. *Conquest: Dispatches of Cortes from the New World.* Irwin R. Blacker and Harry M. Rosen, eds. New York: Grosset and Dunlap.

———. 1971. *Hernán Cortés: Letters from Mexico.* A. R. Pagden, trans. and ed. New York: Grossman.

———. 1993. *Cartas de Relación.* Ángel Delgado Gómez, ed. Madrid: Clásicos Castalia.

Dalton, William. 1862. *Cortes and Pizarro. The Stories of the Conquests of Mexico and Peru, with a Sketch of the Early Adventures of the Spaniards in the New World. Re-Told for Youth.* London: Griffin, Bohn, and Company. [In BLY.]

De Laet, Ioannes. 1629. *Hispania.* Leiden: Ex officina Elzeviriana. [In JCB.]

Díaz del Castillo, Bernal. 1632. *Historia Verdadera de la Conquista de la Nueva España.* Fray Alonso Remón, ed. Madrid: Emprenta del Reyno. [In JCB.]

———. 1908–16. *The True History of the Conquest of New Spain.* A. P. Maudslay, trans. and ed. 5 vols. London: Hakluyt Society.

———. 1942. *The Discovery and Conquest of Mexico, 1517–1521.* A. P. Maudslay, trans. and ed. Miguel Covarrubias, ill. Mexico City: Limited Editions Club. [Author's collection; also in CSL-SL.]

———. 1963 [1632]. *The Conquest of New Spain.* J. M. Cohen, ed. London: Penguin.

———. 1984 [1632]. *Historia Verdadera de la Conquista de la Nueva España.* Miguel León-Portilla, ed. Madrid: historia 16.

———. 2003 [1632]. *The Discovery and Conquest of Mexico, 1517–1521.* Hugh Thomas, intro. Cambridge, MA: Da Capo Press.

————. 2005. *Historia verdadera de la conquista de la Nueva España (Manuscrito "Guatemala").* 2 paginated parts. José Antonio Barbón Rodríguez, ed. Mexico City: El Colegio de México.

————. 2008 [1632]. *The History of the Conquest of New Spain.* Davíd Carrasco, ed. Albuquerque: University of New Mexico Press.

————. 2012 [1632]. *Historia verdadera de la conquista de la Nueva España.* Guillermo Serés, ed. Barcelona: Real Academia Española.

Díaz, J., A. Tapia, B. Vásquez, and F. Aguilar. 1988. *La conquista de Tenochtitlán.* Germán Vásquez, ed. Madrid: historia 16.

Díaz, Juan (author given as anon.)? 1972 [1519]. *Littera mandata della Insula de Cuba d ndia* [sic]. Mexico City: Editorial Juan Pablos.

Dillinger, Georg Adam. 1770. *Nach dem jezigen Staat eingerichtete Bilder-Geographie.* Nuremberg: Christoph Riegels. [In JCB.]

Dilworth, W. H. 1759. *The History of the Conquest of Mexico, By the Celebrated Hernan Cortes.* 2 vols. [published as one]. London: William Anderson. [In JCB; also Philadelphia: H. Sweitzer, 1801, in BLY, 1st vol. only.]

Dryden, John. 1665. See Howard, Sir Robert.

————. 1668 [1667]. *The Indian Emperour, or, the Conquest of Mexico by the Spaniards. Being the Sequel of the Indian Queen.* 2nd ed. London: H. Herringman. [In JCB.]

Durán, fray Diego. 1867 [1581]. *Historia de las Indias de Nueva-España y Islas de Tierra Firme.* José F. Ramirez, ed. Mexico City: J. M. Andrade & F. Escalante. [In BLY.]

————. 1967 [1581]. *Historia de las Indias de Nueva España e Islas de Tierra Firme.* 2 vols. Mexico City: Editorial Porrúa.

————. 1971 [1579]. *Book of the Gods and Rites and the Ancient Calendar by Fray Diego Durán.* Fernando Horcasitas and Doris Heyden, trans. and eds. Norman: University of Oklahoma Press.

————. 1994 [1581]. *The History of the Indies of New Spain.* Doris Heyden, trans. Norman: University of Oklahoma.

Escoiquiz, Juan de. 1798. *México Conquistada. Poema Heroyco.* Madrid: Imprenta Real. [In JCB.]

Fernández del Castillo, Francisco. 1927. *Tres Conquistadores y Pobladores de la Nueva España: Cristóbal Martín Millán de Gamboa, Andrés de Tapia, Jerónimo López.* Mexico City: Publicaciones del Archivo General de la Nación, Talleres Gráficos de la Nación.

————. 1980 [1929]. *Doña Catalina Xuárez Marcaida, primera esposa de Hernán Cortés, y su familia.* Mexico City: Editorial Cosmos.

Fernández de Oviedo y Valdés, Gonzalo. 1547. *Coronica de la Indias. La hystoria general de las Indias agorà nuevamente impressa corregida y emendada.* Salamanca: n.p. [In JCB.]

————. 1959 [1535]. *Historia general y natural de las Indias.* Juan Pérez de Tudela Bueso, ed. 5 vols. Madrid: Ediciones Atlas.

Frías, Heriberto. 1899–1901. *Biblioteca del Niño Mexicano.* 110 parts. Mexico City: Maucci Hermanos de México. [In BL.]

Fuentes, Patricia de, ed. and trans. 1963. *The Conquistadors: First-Person Accounts of the Conquest of Mexico.* New York: Orion Press.

García, fray Gregorio. 1729 [1607]. *Origen de los Indios de el Nuevo Mundo, e Indias Occidentales.* Rev. ed. Madrid: Francisco Martínez Abad. [In CSL-Sac.]

García Icazbalceta, Joaquín, ed. 1858–66. *Colección de Documentos para la Historia de México* 2 vols. Mexico City: Andrade. [Cited as CDHM.]

————. 1886–92. *Nueva Colección de Documentos para la Historia de México.* 5 vols. Mexico City: Antigua Librería de Andrade y Morales. [Cited as NCDHM.]

Gemelli Careri, John Francis [Giovanni Francesco]. 1704. *A Voyage Around the World.* English edition of *Giro del Mondo* (Naples, 1699). Published as vol. 4, pp. 1–606 of *A Collection of Voyages and Travels.* London: H. C. for Awnsham and John Churchill. [Copy in JCB.]

Gómara, Francisco López de. 1552. *La Conquista de México.* Zaragoza. [In JCB.]

————. 1552b. *La Istoria de las Yndias.* Zaragoza. [In JCB.]

————. 1578. *The Pleasant Historie of the Conquest of the Weast India, now called new Spayne.* Thomas Nicholas, trans. London: Henry Bynneman. [Translation of Gómara 1552, although original author and book not mentioned; in JCB.]

————. 1964. *Cortés: The Life of the Conqueror by His Secretary.* Lesley Byrd Simpson, trans. and ed. Berkeley: University of California Press. [Translation of Gómara 1552.]

González Barcía, Andrés. 1749. *Historiadores Primitivos de las Indias Occidentales.* Madrid. [In JCB.]

Guzmán, Eulalia. 1958. *Relaciones de Hernán Cortés a Carlos V sobre la invasión de Anáhuac.* Mexico City: Libros Anáhuac.

Haggard, Henry Rider. 1893. *Montezuma's Daughter.* London: Longman's. [In BL.]

Happel, Eberhard Werner. 1688. *Thesaurus exoticorum: [etc.].* Hamburg: Thomas von Wiering. [In JCB.]

Harris, John. 1975. *Navigantium atque itinerantium bibliotheca, or, a compleat collection of voyages and travels.* London: Thomas Bennet, et al. [In JCB.]

Helps, Arthur. 1894. *The Life of Hernando Cortes.* 2 vols. London: George Bell & Sons.

Herrera y Tordesillas, Antonio de. 1728 [1601–15]. *Historia General de los hechos de los castellanos.* 4 vols. Antwerp: Juan Bautista Verdussen. Also known as *Décadas.* [In JCB.]

Howard, Sir Robert, and John Dryden. 1665. *The Indian-Queen, A Tragedy.* London: H. Herringman. [Attributed in this edition to Howard alone; in JCB.]

Ixtlilxochitl, Fernando de Alva. 1969. *Ally of Cortés. Account 13: Of the coming of the Spaniards and the beginning of the evangelical law.* Douglass K. Ballentine, ed. and trans. El Paso: Texas Western Press.

———. 1985 [1620s–30s]. *Historia de la nación chichimeca.* Germán Vásquez, ed. Madrid: historia 16.

———. 2015. *Thirteenth Relation.* [See Brian, Benton, and García Loaeza 2015].

Jáuregui, Carlos A. 2008. *The Conquest on Trial: Carvajal's Complaint of the Indians in the Court of Death.* Latin American Originals #3. University Park: Penn State University Press. [Text of Carvajal's play cited as Jáuregui 2008 (1557).]

Kendall, George Wilkins. 1851. *The War Between the United States and Mexico Illustrated, embracing pictorial drawings of all the principal conflicts, by Carl Nebel.* New York: Appleton. [In CSL-Sac.]

Lafaye, Jacques, ed. 1972. *Manuscrit Tovar: Origines et Croyances des Indiens du Mexique.* "Edition établie d'après le manuscrit de la John Carter Brown Library." Graz: Akademische Druck-u. Verlagsanstalt.

Lajarte, Théodore de. 1883. *Curiosités de l'Opéra.* Paris: Calmann Lévy.

Lane, Kris, ed. 2008. *The Indian Militia and Description of the Indies, by Captain Bernardo de Vargas Machuca.* Durham: Duke University Press.

———. 2010. [See Vargas Machuca 2010 (1612).]

Las Casas, fray Bartolomé de. 1561a. *Historia de las Indias.* Manuscript. [Handwritten 962-folio manuscript, possibly made in 1597, in JCB.]

———. 1561b. *De Thesauris in Peru.* [Manuscript in Latin in Las Casas's hand, in Biblioteca de Palacio, Madrid, published as *Los Tesoros del Peru*, Angél Losada, ed., Madrid: Consejo Superior de Investigaciones Cientificas, 1958; 1565 version by Las Casas, titled *De Thesauris in sepulchris Indorum latentibus*, called Manuscrito B by Losada, in JCB; copy signed by Las Casas, called Manuscrito C by Losada, in Biblioteca Nacional, Madrid; I only consulted Losada 1958 and MS B in JCB.]

————. 1697 [1552]. *La Découverte des Indes Occidentales par Les Espagnols*. [French version of the *Brevísima relación de la destruición de las Indias*.] Paris: André Pralard. [In JCB.]

————. 1876 [1561]. *Historia de las Indias*. Vol. 4. José Sancho Rayon, ed. Madrid: Miguel Ginesta.

————. 1909. *Apologética historia de las Indias*. Madrid: Bailly-Baillere é Hijos.

————. 1951 [1561]. *Historia de las Indias*. Agustín Millares Carlo, ed. Mexico City: Fondo de Cultura Económica.

————. 1971 [1561]. *History of the Indies*. Andrée Collard, ed. and trans. New York: Harper Torchbooks.

————. 1993. *The Only Way*. Helen Rand Parish, ed. Francis Patrick Sullivan, trans. New York: Paulist Press.

————. 2003 [1552]. *An Account, Much Abbreviated, of the Destruction of the Indies*. Franklin Knight, ed. Andrew Hurley, trans. [English version of the *Brevísima relación de la destruición de las Indias*.] Indianapolis: Hackett.

Lasso de la Vega, Gabriel. 1588. *Primera Parte de Cortés valeroso, y Mexicana*. Madrid: Pedro Madrigal. [In JCB.]

————. 1594. *Mexicana, emendad y añadida*. Madrid: Luis Sanchez. [In JCB.]

————. 1601. *Elogios en Loor de los Tres Famosos Varones*. Zaragoza: Alonso Rodriguez. [In JCB.]

León y Gama, Antonio de. 1792. *Descripción Histórica y Cronológica de las Dos Piedras Que Con Occasion del Nuevo Empredado Que Se Está Formando el la Plaza Principal de México*. Mexico City: Don Felipe de Zúñiga y Ontiveros. [In LOC.]

Lockhart, James. 1993. *We People Here: Nahuatl Accounts of the Conquest of Mexico*. Berkeley: University of California Press.

López Rayon, Ignacio, ed. 1852–53. *Documentos para la Historia de México*. 2 vols. Mexico City: Vicente García Torres. [Cited as DHM.]

MacNutt, Francis A. 1909. *Fernando Cortes and the Conquest of Mexico, 1485–1547*. New York: G. P. Putnam's Sons.

Mallet, Alain Manesson. 1683. *Description de L'Univers*. Paris. [In BL.]

Martínez Martínez, María del Carmen, ed. 2006. *En el nombre del hijo: Cartas de Martín Cortés y Catalina Pizarro*. Mexico City: Universidad Nacional Autónoma de México.

Martyr (Pietro Martire) d'Anghiera, Peter. 1521. *De nuper sub D. Carolo repertis insulis, simulatque incolarum moribus*. Basle. [In BLY.]

Mathes, W. Michael, trans. and ed. 1973. *The Conquistador in California: 1535. The Voyage of Fernando Cortés to Baja California in Chronicles and Documents*. Los Angeles: Dawson's Book Shop.

Mendieta, Gerónimo de. 1870 [1596]. *Historia Eclesiástica Indiana*. Joaquín García Icazbalceta, ed. Mexico City: Antigua Librería. [In JCB.]

Montanus, Arnoldus. 1671. *De Nieuwe en Onbekende Weereld: of Beschryving van America*. Amsterdam: Jacob Meurs. [In CSL-Sac.]

Monterde, Francisco. 1945. *Moctezuma: El de la Silla de Oro*. Mexico City: Imprenta Universitaria.

Morris, Francis Orpen. 1866. *The County Seats of the Noblemen and Gentlemen of Great Britain and Ireland*. 6 vols. London: Longmans, Green. [In BL.]

Motolinía, [Toribio de Benavente]. 1950. *Motolinia's History of the Indians of New Spain*. Elizabeth Andros Foster, trans. and ed. Berkeley: Cortés Society.

———. 1951 [1941]. *Motolinia's History of the Indians of New Spain*. Francis Borgia Steck, ed. Washington, DC: Academy of American Franciscan History.

Muñoz Camargo, Diego. 1892 [1592]. *Historia de Tlaxcala*. Alfredo Chavero, ed. Mexico City: Secretaria de Fomento. [In JCB.]

———. 1998 [1592]. *Historia de Tlaxcala*. Luis Reyes Garcia, ed. Tlaxcala: Gobierno del Estado de Tlaxcala and Universidad Autónoma de Tlaxcala.

Niles, John J., and Douglas S. Moore. 1929. *The Songs My Mother Never Taught Me*. New York: Macaulay.

Ogilby, John. 1670. *America: Being an Accurate Description of the New World [etc.]*. London: Tho. Johnson. [In JCB, which also has three 1671 editions, reprinted from the 1670 original, with subtitle *Being the Latest, and Most Accurate Description of the New World (etc.)*. London: "Printed by the Author." Same edition in CSL-Sac.]

Otte, Enrique. 1964. "Nueve Cartas de Diego de Ordás," in *Historia Mexicana* 14:1, 102–30.

Paso y Troncoso, Francisco del. 1939–42. *Epistolario de Nueva España, 1505–1818.* 16 vols. Mexico City: Antigua Librería Robredo (Porrúa). [Cited as ENE.]

Peón Contreras, José. 1872. *Moteuczoma Xocoyotzin. Leyenda Histórica.* Mexico City: Imprenta del "Federalista" Escalerillas. [In CSL-SL.]

Pérez-Rocha, Emma. 1998. *Privilegios en lucha: La información de doña Isabel Moctezuma.* Mexico City: INAH.

Pérez-Rocha, Emma, and Rafael Tena, eds. 2000. *La Nobleza Indígena del Centro de México, Después de la Conquista.* Mexico City: CONACULTA and INAH. [Cited as PRT.]

Planché, J. R. 1823. *Cortez; or, The Conquest of Mexico. An Historical Drama, in Three Acts.* London: John Lowndes. [In BLY.]

Pomar, Juan Baptista de. 1582. "Relación de Tezcoco." In NCDHM, III: 1–69.

Prescott, William. 1994 [1843]. *History of the Conquest of Mexico, with a preliminary view of the Ancient Mexican Civilization and the life of the conqueror Hernando Cortés.* Felipe Fernández-Armesto, intro. London: Folio.

Prévost, Antoine François. 1746–59. *Histoire Générale des Voyages, ou Nouvelle Collection de Toutes les Relations de Voyages par Mer et par Terre [etc.].* 15 vols. Paris: Didot. [In JCB.]

Ramusio, Giovanni Battista. 1556. *Navigationi et Viaggi.* Venice: Giunti. [In JCB.]

Ranking, John. 1827. *Historical Researches on the Conquest of Peru, Mexico, Bogota, Natchez, and Talomeco, in the Thirteenth Century, by the Mongols.* London: Longman, Rees, Orme, Brown, and Green. [In JCB.]

Richmond, Hiram Hoyt. 1885. *Montezuma. An Epic on the Origin and Fate of the Aztec Nation.* San Francisco: Golden Era. [In CSL-Sac.]

Robertson, William. 1777. *The History of America.* 2 vols. London: W. Strahan, T. Cadell, and J. Balfour. [1st ed.; 2nd ed., 1778; both in JCB.]

———. 1778. *Storia di America.* 4 vols. Venice: Presso Giovanni Gatti. [First Italian edition of Robertson 1777; in JCB.]

Robinson, Henry Morton. 1931. *Stout Cortez: A Biography of the Spanish Conquest.* New York: Century. [In CSL-Sac.]

Ruiz de León, Francisco. 1755. *Hernandia. Triumphos de la Fe, y Gloria de las Armas Españolas. Poema Heroyco. [Etc.].* Madrid: Viuda de Manuel Fernández. [In JCB, CSL-SL, and CSL-Sac.]

Saavedra y Guzmán, Antonio de. 1599. *El Peregrino Indiano*. Madrid: Pedro Madrigal. [In JCB.]

———. 1880 [1599]. *El Peregrino Indiano*. Joaquín García Icazbalceta, ed. Mexico City: José María Sandoval. [Also: 2007. María José Rodilla León, ed. Madrid: Iberoamericana.]

Sahagún, fray Bernardino de. 1950–82 [1555–80]. *Florentine Codex: General History of the Things of New Spain*. Arthur J. O. Anderson and Charles E. Dibble, trans. 13 vols. Salt Lake City and Santa Fe: University of Utah Press and School of American Research.

———. 1997 [c.1560]. *Primeros Memoriales*. Thelma Sullivan et al., trans. and ed. Norman: University of Oklahoma Press.

Sánchez, Jesús. 1886. "El sueño de Motecuhzoma." In *Anales del Museo Nacional de México* 1, 1: 301–4.

Sell, Barry D. and Louise M. Burkhart, eds. 2004. *Nahuatl Theatre, Volume 1: Death and Life in Colonial Nahua Mexico*. Norman: University of Oklahoma Press.

Sigüenza y Góngora, Carlos. 1680. *Teatro de virtudes políticas que constituyen a un príncipe, advertidas en los monarchos antiguos del México imperial*. Mexico City: Viuda de Bernardo Calderon.

———. 1928 [1680]. *Teatro de virtudes políticas que constituyen a un príncipe, advertidas en los monarchos antiguos del México imperial*. In *Obras*. Mexico City: Sociedad de Bibliofilos Mexicanos, 1–148.

Solana y Gutierrez, Mateo. 1938. *Don Hernando Cortés, Marqués del Valle de Oajaca*. Mexico City: Ediciones Botas.

Solís, Antonio de. 1684. *Historia de la Conquista de Mexico*. Madrid: Bernardo de Villa-Diego. [In JCB and CSL-SL.]

———. 1704. *Histoire de la Conqueste du Mexique ou de la Nouvelle Espagne, par Fernand Cortez*. "L'Auteur du Triumvirat," trans. and ed. 2 vols. Paris: Jean and Michel Guignard. [In JCB.]

———. 1724. *The History of the Conquest of Mexico by the Spaniards*. Thomas Townsend, trans. and ed. London: Woodward, Hooke, and Peele. [In JCB.]

———. 1733. *Istoria della Conquista del Messico*. Venice: Andrea Poletti. [In JCB.]

———. 1776. *Historia de la Conquista de México, poblacion y progresos de la América Septentrional, conocida por el nombre de Nueva España*. Madrid: Blas Román. [In PSU-SC (catalogued as 1790).]

———. 1798. *Historia de la Conquista de México, poblacion y progresos de la*

América Septentrional, conocida por el nombre de Nueva España. Madrid: Cano. [In JCB.]

Solórzano Pereyra, Juan de. 1736. *Política Indiana.* Madrid: Matheo Sacristan. [In CSL-SL.]

Stabler, Arthur P., and John E. Kicza. 1986. "Ruy González's 1553 Letter to Emperor Charles V: An Annotated Translation," in *The Americas* 42:4 (April): 473–87.

Suárez de Peralta, Juan. 1949 [1589]. *Tratado del Descubrimiento de las Indias.* Mexico City: Secretaria de Educación Pública.

Tapia, Andrés de. c.1545. *Relación de algunas cosas de las que acaecieron al Muy Ilustre Señor don Hernando Cortés [etc.].* In CDHM, II: 554–94; Fuentes (1963: 19–48); J. Díaz et al. (1988).

Tezozomoc, Fernando Alvarado. 1878 [1598]. *Cronica Mexicana.* Manuel Orozco y Berra, ed. Also known as *Cronica Mexicayotl.* Mexico City: Ireneo Paz. [In JCB.]

———. 1949 [1598]. *Cronica Mexicayotl.* Adrián León, trans. and ed. Mexico City: Imprenta Universitaria.

Thevet, André. 1676. *Select Lives Collected out of A. Thevet, the French Historiographer. Englished by I.S.A.M.* [Appended to Plutarch's *Lives.*] Cambridge: John Hayes. [In JCB.]

Thomas, Lewis Foulk. 1857. *Cortez, the Conqueror. A Tragedy in Five Acts. [Founded on the Conquest of Mexico.]* Washington, DC: B. W. Ferguson. [In BLY.]

Toro, Alfonso. 1922. *Un Crimen de Hernán Cortés: La Muerte de Doña Catalina Xuárez, estudio histórico y medico legal.* Mexico City: Ediciones M. Mañon.

Torquemada, fray Juan de. 1614. *Los Veynte y Un Libros Rituales y Monarquía Indiana, con el origen y guerras de los Yndios Occidentales.* 3 vols. Seville: Matthias Clavijo. [In JCB.]

———. 1986 [1614]. *Monarquía Indiana.* Miguel León-Portilla, ed. Mexico City: Porrúa.

Torres de Mendoza, Luis, Joaquín Francisco Pacheco, and Francisco de Cárdenas, eds. 1864–84. *Colección de documentos inéditos de Indias,* also titled *Colección de documentos inéditos relativos al descubrimiento, conquista y organización de las antiguas posesiones españoles de América y Oceanía.* 42 vols. Madrid: variously, Manuel Hernández, and Frias y compañia. [Cited as CDII; in CSL-SL and PSU-SC.]

Tovar, Juan de. c.1585. *Relacion del origen de los Yndios que havitan en esta*

Nueva Espana segun sus historias. Manuscript. Also known as Codex Tovar (a contemporary copy is known as the Codex Ramírez). Also see Charnay 1903; Lafaye 1972. [In JCB.]

———. 1878 [c.1585]. *Relacion del origen de los Indios que habitan en esta Nueva España segun sus historias.* Manuel Orozco y Berra, ed. Included with the *Cronica Mexicana* (Tezozomoc 1878 [1598]). Mexico City: Ireneo Paz. [In JCB.]

Trueba y Cosio, Joaquín Telesforo de. 1829. *Life of Hernan Cortes.* Edinburgh: Constable. [In BL.]

Vaca de Guzmán, Joseph María. 1778. *Las Naves de Cortés Destruidas.* Madrid: Joachin Ibarra. [In JCB.]

Valadés, Diego. 1579. *Rhetorica Christiana.* Perusia (Perugia, Italy): Petrumiacobum Petrutium. [In JCB.]

Vargas Machuca, Bernardo de. 1599. *Milicia y Descripción de las Indias.* Madrid: Pedro Madrigal. [In JCB.]

———. 2010 [1612]. *Defending the Conquest: Bernardo de Vargas Machuca's Defense and Discourse of the Western Conquests.* Kris Lane, ed. Timothy F. Johnson, trans. Latin American Originals #4. University Park, PA: Penn State University Press. [Translated text cited as Vargas Machuca in Lane (2010 [1612]).]

Vásquez, Germán, ed. 1991. *Varios Relaciones de la Nueva España.* Madrid: historia 16.

Vásquez de Tapia, Bernardino. 1546. In: 1972. *Relación de méritos y servicios del conquistador Bernardino Vásquez de Tapia, vecino y regidor de esta gran ciudad de Tenustitlan, Mexico.* Jorge Gurría Lacroix, ed. Mexico City: Universidad Autónoma de México. [Also in J. Díaz et al. 1988.]

Vecchietti, Girolamo. n.d. [17th century?] *Ferrante Cortese.* Epic poem in manuscript. [In BL.]

Villagrá, Gaspar de. 1610. *Historia de la Nueva Mexico.* Alcala: Luys Martinez Grande. [In JCB.]

———. 1933 [1610]. *History of New Mexico.* Gilberto Espinosa, trans. Los Angeles: Quivira Society.

Wagner, Henry R. 1929. "Three Accounts of the Expedition of Fernando Cortés, Printed in Germany Between 1520 and 1522." *HAHR* 9:2, 176–212, 361–63.

———. 1942. *The Discovery of New Spain in 1518 by Juan de Grijalva: A Translation of the Original Texts.* Berkeley: Cortés Society.

Wallace, Lew. 1873. *The Fair God or, the Last of the 'Tzins: A Tale of the Conquest of Mexico*. Boston: James R. Osgood.

Wytfliet, Cornelius. 1598. *Descriptionis Ptolemaicae Augmentum*. Louvain: Gerardi Riuij. [In CSL-Sac.]

Zimmerman, Günter. 1970. *Briefe der indianischen Nobilität aus Nesupanien an Karl V und Philipp II um die Mitte des 16. Jahrhunderts*. Hamburg: Klaus Renner.

Zorita, Alonso de. 1994 [1566]. *Life and Labor in Ancient Mexico: The Brief and Summary Relation of the Lords of New Spain*. Benjamin Keen, trans. and ed. 2nd ed. [1st ed., 1963]. Norman: University of Oklahoma Press. [Also see transcription of original in NCDHM, III: 71–227.]

BIBLIOGRAPHY OF REFERENCES:
PRINTED SECONDARY SOURCES

Abulafia, David. 2008. *The Discovery of Mankind: Atlantic Encounters in the Age of Columbus*. New Haven: Yale University Press.

Adorno, Rolena. 1992. "The Discursive Encounter of Spain and America: The Authority of Eyewitness Testimony in the Writing of History." *William and Mary Quarterly* 49:2 (April): 210–28.

———. 2007. *The Polemics of Possession in Spanish American Narrative*. New Haven: Yale University Press.

———. 2011. *Colonial Latin American Literature: A Very Short Introduction*. Oxford: Oxford University Press.

———. 2014. "Carlos de Sigüenza y Góngora (1645–1700): 'El Amante Más Fino de Nuestra Patria.'" *Hispanófila* 117: 10–125.

Aguirre, Eugenio. 2008. *Isabel Moctezuma*. Mexico City: Editorial Planeta.

Alcalá, Luisa Elena, and Jonathan Brown, eds. 2014. *Painting in Latin America, 1550–1820*. New Haven: Yale University Press.

Alcalá, Manuel. 1950. *César y Cortés*. Mexico City: Editorial Jus.

Allen, Heather. 2015. "'Llorar amargamente': Economies of Weeping in the Spanish Empire." *Colonial Latin American Review* 24:4 (May): 479–504.

Altman, Ida. 2010. *The War for Mexico's West: Indians and Spaniards in New Galicia, 1524–1550*. Albuquerque: University of New Mexico Press.

Altman, Rick. 2008. *A Theory of Narrative*. New York: Columbia University Press.

Alves, Abel A. 1996. *Brutality and Benevolence: Human Ethnology, Culture, and Birth of Mexico*. Westport, CT: Greenwood Press.

Anderson Imbert, Enrique. 1962. *Historia de la literatura hispanoamericana*. Mexico City: Fondo de Cultura Económica.

Barjau, Luis. 2009. *La Conquista de la Malinche*. Mexico City: Instituto Nacional de Antropología e Historia.

Barker, Juliet. 2005. *Agincourt: The King, the Campaign, the Battle*. London: Little, Brown.

Bauer, Arnold J. 2009. *The Search for the Codex Cardona: On The Trail of a Sixteenth-Century Mexican Treasure*. Durham: Duke University Press.

Benítez, Fernando. 1965. *The Century after Cortés*. Joan MacLean, trans. (of *Los primeros Mexicanos: La vida criolla en el siglo XVI*, 1962). Chicago: University of Chicago Press.

Benito, José de. 1944. *Hernán Cortés: Boceto Biográfico*. Mexico City: Ediciones Nuevas.

Benton, Bradley. 2014. "Beyond the Burned Stake: The Rule of Don Antonio Pimentel Tlahuitoltzin in Tetzcoco." In Jongsoo Lee and Galen Brokaw, eds., *Texcoco: Prehispanic and Colonial Perspectives*. Boulder: University Press of Colorado, 183–200.

———. 2017. *The Lords of Tetzcoco: The Transformation of Indigenous Rule in Postconquest Central Mexico*. Cambridge: Cambridge University Press.

Berdan, Frances F. 1987. "The Economics of Aztec Luxury Trade and Tribute." In Elizabeth Hill Boone, ed., *The Aztec Templo Mayor*. Washington, DC: Dumbarton Oaks, 161–83.

———. 2009. "Moctezuma's Military and Economic Rule." In Colin McEwan and Leonardo López Luján, eds., *Moctezuma: Aztec Ruler*. London: British Museum, 182–95.

Berry, Erick, and Herbert Best. 1968. *Men Who Changed the Map: AD 400 to 1914*. New York: Funk and Wagnalls.

Blanco, Alicia, Gilberto Pérez, Bernardo Rodríguez, Nawa Sugiyama, Fabiola Torres, and Raúl Valadez. 2009. "El zoológico de Moctezuma. Mito o realidad?" in *AMMVEPE* 20:2: 28–39.

Bonilla Reyna, Helia Emma, and Marie Lecouvey. 2015. *La modernidad en la* Biblioteca del Niño Mexicano*: Posada, Frías y Maucci*. Mexico City: Instituto de Investigaciones Estéticas, UNAM.

Boone, Elizabeth Hill. 1989. "Incarnations of the Aztec Supernatural:

The Image of Huitzilopochtli in Mexico and Europe." *Transactions of the American Philosophical Society* 79:2: 1–107.

———. 1992. "Glorious Imperium: Understanding Land and Community in Moctezuma's Mexico." In Davíd Carrasco and Eduardo Matos Moctezuma, eds., *Moctezuma's Mexico: Visions of the Aztec World*. Boulder: University Press of Colorado, 159–73.

———. 1994. *The Aztec World*. Montreal and Washington, DC: St. Remy Press and Smithsonian Books.

———. 2000. *Stories in Red and Black: Pictorial Histories of the Aztecs and Mixtecs*. Austin: University of Texas Press.

———. 2011. "This New World Now Revealed: Hernán Cortés and the Presentation of Mexico to Europe." *Word & Image* 27:1 (January–March): 31–46.

———. 2017. "Seeking Indianness: Christoph Weiditz, the Aztecs, and feathered Amerindians." *Colonial Latin American Review* 26:1 (April): 39–61.

Boruchoff, David A. 2015. "Indians, Cannibals, and Barbarians: Hernán Cortés and Early Modern Cultural Relativism." *Ethnohistory* 62:1 (January): 17–38.

Brandi, Karl. 1980 [1939]. *The Emperor Charles V*. London: Harvester Press.

Brian, Amber. 2010. "Don Fernando de Alva Ixtlilxochitl's Narratives of the Conquest of Mexico: Colonial Subjectivity and Circulation of Native Knowledge." In Susan Schroeder, ed., *The Conquest All Over Again: Nahuas and Zapotecs Thinking, Writing, and Painting Spanish Colonialism*. Brighton, UK: Sussex Academic Press, 124–43.

———. 2014. "The Alva Ixtlilxochitl Brothers and the Nahua Intellectual Community." In Jongsoo Lee and Galen Brokaw, eds., *Texcoco: Prehispanic and Colonial Perspectives*. Boulder: University Press of Colorado, 201–18.

Brienen, Rebecca P., and Margaret A. Jackson, eds. 2008. *Invasion and Transformation: Interdisciplinary Perspectives on the Conquest of Mexico*. Boulder: University Press of Colorado.

Broda, Johanna. 1969. *The Mexican Calendar as Compared to Other Mesoamerican Calendar Systems*. Vienna: Englebert Stiglmayr.

Brooks, Francis J. 1993. "Revising the Conquest of Mexico: Smallpox, Sources, and Populations." *Journal of Interdisciplinary History* 24:1 (Summer): 1–29.

———. 1995. "Motecuzoma Xocoyotl, Hernán Cortés, and Bernal Díaz del Castillo: The Construction of an Arrest." *HAHR* 75:2 (May): 149–83.

Brotherston, Gordon. 1995. *Painted Books from Mexico: Codices in the UK Collections and the World They Represent.* London: British Museum Press.

Brown, Laura. 2004. "Dryden and the Imperial Imagination." In Steven N. Zwicker, ed., *The Cambridge Companion to John Dryden.* Cambridge: Cambridge University Press, 59–74.

Browning, Christopher R. 1998. *Ordinary Men: Reserve Police Batallion 101 and the Final Solution in Poland.* Reissued ed. New York: Harper Perennial.

Buccini, Stefania. 1997. *The Americas in Italian Literature and Culture, 1700–1825.* University Park, PA: Penn State University Press.

Burkhart, Louise M. 2008. "Meeting the Enemy: Moteuczoma and Cortés, Herod and the Magi." In Rebecca P. Brienen and Margaret A. Jackson, eds., *Invasion and Transformation: Interdisciplinary Perspectives on the Conquest of Mexico.* Boulder: University Press of Colorado, 11–23.

Butterfield, Marvin E. 1955. *Jerónimo de Aguilar, Conquistador.* Pamphlet. University of Alabama Latin American Studies Program.

Candelaria, Xochiquetzal. 2011. *Empire.* Tucson: University of Arizona Press.

Candiani, Vera S. 2014. *Dreaming of Dry Land: Environmental Transformation in Colonial Mexico City.* Stanford: Stanford University Press.

Carman, Glen. 2006. *Rhetorical Conquests: Cortés, Gómara, and Renaissance Imperialism.* West Lafayette, IN: Purdue University Press.

Carr, Caleb. 2003. *The Lessons of Terror: A History of Warfare against Civilians.* Rev. ed. New York: Random House.

Carr, E. H. 1961. *What Is History?* London: Macmillan.

Carrasco, Davíd. 2000 [1982]. *Quetzalcoatl and the Irony of Empire: Myths and Prophecies in the Aztec Tradition.* Rev. ed. Boulder: University Press of Colorado.

———. 1992. "Toward the Splendid City: Knowing the Worlds of Moctezuma." In Davíd Carrasco and Eduardo Matos Moctezuma, eds., *Moctezuma's Mexico: Visions of the Aztec World.* Boulder: University Press of Colorado, 99–148.

———. 1995. "Give Me Some Skin: The Charisma of the Aztec Warrior." *History of Religions* 35:1 (August): 1–26.

———. 2012. *The Aztecs: A Very Short Introduction.* Oxford: Oxford University Press.

Carrasco, Pedro. 1999. *The Tenochca Empire of Ancient Mexico: The Triple Alliance of Tenochtitlan, Tetzcoco, and Tlacopan.* Norman: University of Oklahoma Press.

Carvajal, Álvaro. 2010. "Manchan con pintura roja una estatua de Hernán Cortés por ser un 'insulto a México.'" *El Mundo* (August 12) "España" section, accessed online November 18, 2015.

Castañeda de la Paz, María. 2009. "Central Mexican Indigenous Coats of Arms and the Conquest of Mesoamerica." *Ethnohistory* 56:1 (January): 125–61.

———. 2013. *Conflictos y alianzas en tiempos de cambio: Azcapotzalco, Tlacopan, Tenochtitlan y Tlatelolco (siglos XII–XVI).* Mexico City: Universidad Nacional Autónoma de México.

Castañeda de la Paz, María, and Michel R. Oudijk. 2012. "La conquista y la colonia en el *Códice Azcatitlan.*" *Journal de la Société des Américanistes* 98:2: 59–95.

Chipman, Donald E. 2005. *Moctezuma's Children: Aztec Royalty Under Spanish Rule, 1520–1700.* Austin: University of Texas Press.

Clayton, Lawrence A. 2012. *Bartolomé de las Casas: A Biography.* Cambridge: Cambridge University Press.

Clendinnen, Inga. 1985. "The Cost of Courage in Aztec Society." *Past and Present* 107 (May): 44–89. Reprinted in *The Cost of Courage in Aztec Society: Essays on Mesoamerican Society and Culture.* Cambridge: Cambridge University Press, 2010, 6–48.

———. 1991a. *Aztecs: an interpretation.* Cambridge: Cambridge University Press.

———. 1991b. "'Fierce and Unnatural Cruelty': Cortés and the Conquest of Mexico." *Representations* 33 (Winter): 65–100. Reprinted in *The Cost of Courage in Aztec Society: Essays on Mesoamerican Society and Culture.* Cambridge: Cambridge University Press, 2010, 49–90.

Coe, Michael D. 1984. *Mexico.* 3rd ed. London and New York: Thames and Hudson.

Collis, Maurice. 1954. *Cortés and Montezuma.* London: Clark. Reprinted New York: New Directions, 1994.

Connell, William F. 2011. *After Moctezuma: Indigenous Politics and Self-Government in Mexico City, 1524–1730.* Norman: University of Oklahoma Press.

Cook, Sherburne F. 1946. "Human Sacrifice and Warfare as Factors in the Demography of Pre-Colonial Mexico." *Human Biology* 18:2 (May): 81–102.

Cuadriello, Jaime. 2001. "El encuentro de Cortés y Moctezuma como escena de Concordia." In Arnulfo Herrera Curiel, ed., *El amor y desamor en las artes*. Mexico City: Universidad Nacional Autónoma de México, 263–92.

———. 2011. *The Glories of the Republic of Tlaxcala: Art and Life in Viceregal Mexico*. Austin: University of Texas Press.

Davies, Surekha. 2016. *Renaissance Ethnography and the Invention of the Human: New World, Maps and Monsters*. Cambridge: Cambridge University Press.

Day, David. 2008. *Conquest: How Societies Overwhelm Others*. Oxford: Oxford University Press.

Deary, Terry. 1997. *Angry Aztecs*. Illustrated by Martin Brown. London: Scholastic.

Delgado-Gomez, Angel. 1992. *Spanish Historical Writing About the New World, 1493–1700*. Providence: John Carter Brown Library.

Descola, Jean. 1957 [1954]. *The Conquistadors*. Malcolm Barnes, trans. New York: Viking.

DiCesare, Catherine R. 2009. *Sweeping the Way: Divine Transformation in the Aztec Festival of Ochpaniztli*. Boulder: University Press of Colorado.

Don, Patricia Lopes. 2010. *Bonfires of Culture: Franciscans, Indigenous Leaders, and Inquisition in Early Mexico, 1524–1540*. Norman: University of Oklahoma Press.

Duverger, Christian. 2005. *Hernán Cortés: Más allá de la leyenda*. Madrid: Taurus.

———. 2013. *Crónica de la Eternidad: ¿Quién escribió la Historia veradera de la conquista de la Nueva España?* Madrid: Taurus. [Also published the same year as *Cortés et son double: Enquête sur une mystification*. Paris: Seuil.]

Earle, Rebecca. 2014. "Diet, Travel, and Colonialism in the Early Modern World." In Bethany Aram and Bartolomé Yun-Casalilla, eds., *Global Goods and the Spanish Empire, 1492–1824: Circulation, Resistance and Diversity*. Basingstoke, UK: Palgrave Macmillan, 137–52.

Elizondo Alcaraz, Carlos. 1996. *El Escorpión de Oro: Luces y sombras en la extraordinaria vida de Hernán Cortés*. Mexico City: Edamex.

Elliott, J. H. 1970. *The Old World and the New, 1492–1650.* Cambridge: Cambridge University Press.

———. 1971. "Cortés, Velásquez and Charles V." In Cortés (1971: xi–xxxvii).

———. 1989 [1967]. "The Mental World of Hernán Cortés." In *Spain and Its World, 1500–1700.* New Haven: Yale University Press, 27–41.

———. 2006. *Empires of the Atlantic World: Britain and Spain in America, 1492–1830.* New Haven: Yale University Press.

Escalante Gonzalbo, Pablo. 2004. "Portrait of Moctezuma." In Donna Pierce et al., *Painting a New World: Mexican Art and Life, 1521–1821.* Denver: Denver Art Museum, 171–77.

Evans, Susan Toby. 1998. "Sexual Politics in the Aztec Palace: Public, Private, and Profane." *RES: Journal of Anthropology and Aesthetics* 33: 165–83.

———. 2000. "Aztec Royal Pleasure Parks: Conspicuous Consumption and Elite Status Rivalry." *Studies in the History of Gardens and Designed Landscapes* 20:3 (July–September): 206–28.

———. 2004. "Aztec Palaces and Other Elite Residential Architecture." In Susan Toby Evans and Joanne Pillsbury, eds., *Palaces of the Ancient New World.* Washington, DC: Dumbarton Oaks, 7–58.

———. 2013. *Ancient Mexico and Central America.* London and New York City: Thames and Hudson.

Ezquerra, Ramón. 1948. "Rincones Americanistas: Motezuma [*sic*] y Atahualpa en los Jardines de Aranjuez," in EC: 573–79.

Faudree, Paja. 2015. "Reading the *Requerimiento* Performatively: Speech Acts and the Conquest of the New World." *Colonial Latin American Review* 24:4: 456–78.

Fernández, María. 2014. *Cosmopolitanism in Mexican Visual Culture.* Austin: University of Texas Press.

Fernández-Armesto, Felipe. 1992. "Aztec Auguries and Memories of the Conquest of Mexico." *Renaissance Studies* 6:3–4, 287–305.

———. 1997. *Truth: A History and a Guide for the Perplexed.* London: St. Martin's Press.

———. 2014. *Our America: A Hispanic History of the United States.* New York: Norton.

———. 2015. *A Foot in the River: Why Our Lives Change—and the Limits of Evolution.* Oxford: Oxford University Press.

Filgueira Valverde, José. 1960. *Hernán Cortés: su vida contada a los mucha-chos de las dos Españas*. Madrid: Ediciones Cultura Hispanica.

Findlen, Paula. 1994. *Possessing Nature: Museums, Collecting, and Scientific Culture in Early Modern Europe*. Berkeley: University of California Press.

Florescano, Enrique. 1994. *Memory, Myth, and Time in Mexico: From the Aztecs to Independence*. Austin: University of Texas Press.

Frankl, Victor. 1962. "Hernán Cortés y la tradición de las Siete Partidas." *Revista de Historia de América* 53–54, 9–74.

Fuentes, Carlos. 1990. *Valiente mundo nuevo: Épica, utopía y mito en la novela hispanoamericana*. Mexico City: Fondo de Cultura Económica.

————. 2011. *La gran novela latinoamericana*. Mexico City: Alfaguara.

García Cárcel, Ricardo. 1992. *La Leyenda Negra: Historia y Opinión*. Madrid, Alianza.

García Iglesias, Sara. 1946. *Isabel Moctezuma, la Ultima Princesa Azteca*. Mexico City: Ediciones Xochitl.

García Loaeza, Pablo. 2014. "Fernando de Alva Ixtlilxochitl's Texcocan Dynasty: Nobility, Genealogy, and Historiography." In Jongsoo Lee and Galen Brokaw, eds., *Texcoco: Prehispanic and Colonial Perspectives*. Boulder: University Press of Colorado, 219–42.

Gardiner, C. Harvey. 1956. *Naval Power in the Conquest of Mexico*. Austin: University of Texas Press.

————. 1959. *Prescott and His Publishers*. Carbondale: Southern Illinois University Press.

————. 1961. *The Constant Captain: Gonzalo de Sandoval*. Carbondale: Southern Illinois University Press.

Gerbi, Antonello. 1985. *Nature in the New World: From Christopher Columbus to Gonzalo Fernández de Oviedo*. Jeremy Moyle, trans. Pittsburgh: University of Pittsburgh Press.

Gibson, Charles. 1952. *Tlaxcala in the Sixteenth Century*. Stanford: Stanford University Press.

————. 1966. *Spain in America*. New York: Harper Colophon.

Gillespie, Susan D. 1989. *The Aztec Kings: The Construction of Rulership in Mexica History*. Tucson: University of Arizona Press.

————. 2008. "Blaming Moteuczoma: Anthropomorphizing the Aztec Conquest." In Rebecca P. Brienen and Margaret A. Jackson, eds., *Invasion and Transformation: Interdisciplinary Perspectives on the Conquest of Mexico*. Boulder: University Press of Colorado, 25–55.

Gillingham, Paul. 2011. *Cuauhtémoc's Bones: Forging National Identity in Modern Mexico*. Albuquerque: University of New Mexico Press.

Goldwert, Marvin. 1983. *Machismo and Conquest: The Case of Mexico*. Lanham, MD: University Press of America.

Gómez de Orozco, Federico. 1953. "El Conquistador Anónimo." *Historia Mexicana* 2:3: 401–11.

González-Gerth, Miguel. 1983. "Hernando Cortés, Captain-General of New Spain." Institute of Latin American Studies, offprint no. 236. Austin: University of Texas.

Goodwin, Robert. 2015. *Spain: The Centre of the World, 1519–1682*. London: Bloomsbury.

Gopnik, Adam. 2015. "Blood and Soil: A Historian Returns to the Holocaust." *New Yorker* (September 21): 100–104.

Gordon, Helen Heightsman. 1995. *Voice of the Vanquished: The Story of the Slave Marina and Hernán Cortés*. Huntington, WV: University Editions.

Grafton, Anthony. 1992. *New Worlds, Ancient Texts: The Power of Tradition and the Shock of Discovery*. Cambridge, MA: Belknap Press of Harvard University Press.

Graham, Elizabeth. 2011. *Maya Christians and Their Churches in Sixteenth-Century Belize*. Gainesville: University Press of Florida.

Graulich, Michel. 2014. *Moctezuma: Apogeo y caida del imperio azteca*. Mexico City: Ediciones Era.

Greenberg, Amy S. 2012. *A Wicked War: Polk, Clay, Lincoln, and the 1846 U.S. Invasion of Mexico*. New York: Knopf.

Grunberg, Bernard. 2001. *Dictionnaire des Conquistadores de Mexico*. Paris: L'Harmattan.

Gruzinski, Serge. 2002. *The Mestizo Mind: The Intellectual Dynamics of Colonization and Globalization*. Trans. of *La Pensée Métisse* (1999). New York: Routledge.

———. 2014. *The Eagle and the Dragon: Globalization and European Dreams of Conquest in China and America in the Sixteenth Century*. Cambridge, UK: Polity Press.

Gurría Lacroix, Jorge. 1978. "Andrés de Tapia y la Coatlicue." *Estudios de Cultura Náhuatl* 13: 23-34.

Hajovsky, Patrick Thomas. 2009. "André Thevet's 'True' Portrait of Moctezuma and Its European Legacy." *Word & Image* 25:4: 335–52.

———. 2012. "Without a Face: Voicing Moctezuma II's Image at

Chapultepec Park, Mexico City." In Dana Leibsohn and Jeanette Favrot Peterson, eds., *Seeing Across Cultures in the Early Modern World*. Farnham, UK: Ashgate, 171–92.

————. 2015. *On the Lips of Others: Moteuczoma's Fame in Aztec Monuments and Rituals*. Austin: University of Texas Press.

Hanson, Debra. 2015–16. "Modern Muralists of the Capitol: Allyn Cox and Jeffrey Greene." *Capitol Dome* 52:3 (Winter): 2–10.

Harris, Marvin. 1977. *Cannibals and Kings*. New York: Vintage.

Hassig, Ross. 1985. *Trade, Tribute, and Transportation: The Sixteenth-Century Political Economy of the Valley of Mexico*. Norman: University of Oklahoma Press.

————. 1988. *Aztec Warfare: Imperial Expansion and Political Control*. Norman: University of Oklahoma Press.

————. 1998. "The Maid of the Myth: La Malinche and the History of Mexico." *Indiana Journal of Hispanic Literatures* 12: 101–33.

————. 2001a. *Time, History, and Belief in Aztec and Colonial Mexico*. Austin: University of Texas Press.

————. 2001b. "Xicotencatl: Rethinking an Indigenous Mexican Hero." *Estudios de Cultura Náhuatl* 32: 29–49.

————. 2006 [1994]. *Mexico and the Spanish Conquest*. 2nd ed. Norman: University of Oklahoma Press.

————. 2016. *Polygamy and the Rise and Demise of the Aztec Empire*. Albuquerque: University of New Mexico Press.

Henning, Basil Duke. 1983. *The House of Commons, 1660–1690*. Vol. 1. London: Secker and Warburg.

Herman-O'Neal, Jackie. 2013. *Moctezuma's Zoo: A Tale from an Enchanted City*. Frederick, MD: America Star Books.

Hernández-Durán, Ray. 2007. *"El Encuentro de Cortés y Moctezuma*: The Betrothal of Two Worlds in Eighteenth-Century New Spain." In *Women and Art in Early Modern Latin America*. Leiden: Brill, 181–206.

Hernández, Mark A. 2006. *Figural Conquistadors: Rewriting the New World's Discovery and Conquest in Mexican and River Plate Novels of the 1980s and 1990s*. Lewisburg, PA: Bucknell University Press.

Herren, Ricardo. 1992. *Doña Marina, La Malinche*. Mexico City: Planeta.

Hersh, Seymour M. 2015. "The Scene of the Crime: A Reporter's Journey to My Lai and the Secrets of the Past." *New Yorker* (March 30): 53–61.

Hill, Jane H., and Robert MacLaury. 2010 [1995]. "The Terror of Moctezuma: Aztec History, Vantage Theory, and the Category of 'Person.'" In John R. Taylor and Robert E. MacLaury, eds., *Language and the Cognitive Construal of the World*. Munich: De Gruyter Mouton, 277–329.

Hillgarth, J. N. 2000. *The Mirror of Spain, 1500–1700: The Formation of a Myth*. Ann Arbor: University of Michigan Press.

Hobsbawn, Eric. 1994. *Age of Extremes: The Short Twentieth Century, 1914–1991*. London: Abacus.

Hoig, Stan. 2013. *Came Men on Horses: The Conquistador Expeditions of Francisco Vásquez de Coronado and Don Juan de Oñate*. Boulder: University Press of Colorado.

Hutner, Heidi. 2001. *Colonial Women: Race and Culture in Stuart Drama*. New York: Oxford University Press.

Impey, Oliver, and Arthur MacGregor, eds. 1985. *The Origins of Museums: The Cabinet of Curiosities in Sixteenth- and Seventeenth-Century Europe*. Oxford: Clarendon Press.

Jackson, Margaret A., and Rebecca P. Brienen, eds. 2003. *Visions of Empire: Painting the Conquest in Colonial Mexico*. Coral Gables, FL: University of Miami and Kislak Foundation.

Johannsen, Robert W. 1985. *To the Halls of the Montezumas: The Mexican War in the American Imagination*. New York: Oxford University Press.

Johansson, Patrick. 2010. "The Death of Moctezuma." *Mexicolore*. mexico lore.co.uk/aztecs/moctezuma/death-of-moctezuma-1.

Johnson, Carina L. 2011. *Cultural Hierarchy in Sixteenth-Century Europe: The Ottomans and Mexicans*. Cambridge: Cambridge University Press.

Johnson, William Weber. 1975. *Cortés*. Boston: Little, Brown.

Kagan, Richard L. 2000. *Urban Images of the Hispanic World, 1493–1793*. New Haven: Yale University Press.

———. 2009. *Clio and the Crown: The Politics of History in Medieval and Early Modern Spain*. Baltimore: Johns Hopkins University Press.

Kauffmann, Leisa. 2014. "The Reinvented Man-God of Colonial Texcoco: Alva Ixtlilxochitl's Nezahualcoyotl." In Jongsoo Lee and Galen Brokaw, eds., *Texcoco: Prehispanic and Colonial Perspectives*. Boulder: University Press of Colorado, 243–59.

Keegan, John. 1993. *A History of Warfare*. New York: Vintage.

Keegan, William F. 2015. "Mobility and Disdain: Columbus and Cannibals in the Land of Cotton." *Ethnohistory* 62:1 (January): 1–15.

Keen, Benjamin. 1969. "The Black Legend Revisited: Assumptions and Realities." *HAHR* 49:4 (November): 703–19.

———. 1971a. "The White Legend Revisited: A Reply to Professor Hanke's 'Modest Proposal.'" *HAHR* 51:2 (May): 336–55.

———. 1971b. *The Aztec Image in Western Thought*. New Brunswick, NJ: Rutgers University Press.

Kellogg, Susan. 2005. *Weaving the Past: A History of Latin America's Indigenous Women from the Prehispanic Period to the Present*. New York: Oxford University Press.

Klein, Cecelia F. 2016. "Death in the Hands of Strangers: Aztec Human Sacrifice in the Western Imagination." In John M. D. Pohl and Claire L. Lyons, eds., *Altera Roma: Art and Empire from Mérida to Mexico*. Los Angeles: Cotsen Institute of Archaeology at UCLA, 257–311.

Koch, Peter O. 2006. *The Aztecs, the Conquistadors, and the Making of Mexican Culture*. Jefferson, NC: McFarland.

Krauss, Clifford. 1997. "After 500 Years, Cortés' Girlfriend Is Not Forgiven." *New York Times*, Mexico City Journal (March 26).

Krauze, Enrique. 2010. *De héroes y mitos*. Mexico City: Tusquets Editores.

Kubler, George, and Charles Gibson. 1951. "The Tovar Calendar: An Illustrated Mexican Manuscript ca. 1585." *Memoirs of the Connecticut Academy of Arts & Sciences*, vol. 11. New Haven: CAAS and Yale University Press.

Kurutz, Gary F., and W. Michael Mathes. 2003. *The Forgotten War: The Conflict Between Mexico and the United States, 1846–1849*. Sacramento: California State Library Foundation.

Lafaye, Jacques. 1976. *Quetzalcoatl and Guadalupe: The Formation of Mexican National Consciousness*. Benjamin Keen, trans. Chicago: University of Chicago Press.

Laird, Andrew. 2014. "Nahuas and Caesars: Classical Learning and Bilingualism in Post-Conquest Mexico; An Inventory of Latin Writings by Authors of the Native Nobility." *Classical Philology* 109, no. 2 (April): 150–69.

———. 2016. "Aztec and Roman Gods in Sixteenth-Century Mexico: Strategic Uses of Classical Learning in Sahagún's *Historia General*." In John M. D. Pohl and Claire L. Lyons, eds., *Altera Roma: Art and Empire from Mérida to Mexico*. Los Angeles: Cotsen Institute of Archaeology at UCLA, 167–87.

Lamana, Gonzalo. 2008. *Domination Without Dominance: Inca-Spanish Encounters in Early Colonial Peru*. Durham: Duke University Press.

Lanyon, Anna. 2003. *The New World of Martín Cortés*. Crows Nest, Australia: Allen and Unwin.

Le Clézio, J. M. G. 1993. *The Mexican Dream: Or, The Interrupted Thought of Amerindian Civilizations*. Teresa Lavender Fagan, trans. Chicago: University of Chicago Press.

Lee, Jongsoo. 2014. "The Aztec Triple Alliance: A Colonial Transformation of the Prehispanic Political Tributary System." In Jongsoo Lee and Galen Brokaw, eds., *Texcoco: Prehispanic and Colonial Perspectives*. Boulder: University Press of Colorado, 63–92.

Lee, Jongsoo, and Galen Brokaw, eds. 2014. *Texcoco: Prehispanic and Colonial Perspectives*. Boulder: University Press of Colorado.

León-Portilla, Miguel. 2005 [1985]. *Hernán Cortés y la Mar del Sur*. Madrid: Algaba Ediciones.

Levene, Mark. 2000. "Why Is the Twentieth Century the Century of Genocide?" *Journal of World History* 11:2 (Fall): 305–36.

Livi Bacci, Massimo. 2008. *Conquest: The Destruction of the American Indios*. Cambridge, UK: Polity.

Lockhart, James. 1999. *Of Things of the Indies: Essays Old and New in Early Latin American History*. Stanford: Stanford University Press.

López, John F. 2014. "Indigenous Commentary on Sixteenth-Century Mexico City." *Ethnohistory* 61, no. 2 (special issue on *The Ethnohistorical Map in New Spain*): 253–75.

López Lázaro, Fabio. 2007. "Sweet Food of Knowledge: Botany, Food, and Empire in the Early Modern Spanish Kingdoms." In Timothy J. Tomasik and Juliann M. Vitullo, eds. *At the Table: Metaphorical and Material Cultures of Food in Medieval and Early Modern Europe*. Turnhout, Belgium: Brepols, 3–28.

López Luján, Leonardo. 1994. *The Offerings of the Templo Mayor of Tenochtitlán*. Boulder: University Press of Colorado.

Luna, Greg. 2014. "Modeling the Aztec Agricultural Waterscape of Lake Xochimilco: A GIS Analysis of Lakebed Chinampas and Settlement." Ph.D. diss., Pennsylvania State University.

Lupher, David A. 2003. *Romans in a New World: Classical Models in Sixteenth-Century Spanish America*. Ann Arbor: University of Michigan Press.

Lyons, Justin D. 2015. *Alexander the Great and Hernán Cortés: Ambiguous Legacies of Leadership*. Lanham, MD: Lexington Books.

MacLachlan, Colin M. 2015. *Imperialism and the Origins of Mexican Culture*. Cambridge, MA: Harvard University Press.

Madariaga, Salvador. 1969 [1942]. *Hernán Cortés: Conqueror of Mexico*. New York: Doubleday.

Madley, Benjamin. 2015. "Reexamining the American Genocide Debate: Meaning, Historiography, and New Methods." *American Historical Review* (February): 98–139.

———. 2016. *An American Genocide: The United States and the California Indian Catastrophe, 1846–1873*. New Haven: Yale University Press.

Maffie, James. 2014. *Aztec Philosophy: Understanding a World in Motion*. Boulder: University Press of Colorado.

Magaloni Kerpel, Diana. 2003. "Imágenes de la conquista de México en los codices del siglo XVI." *Anales del Instituto de Investigaciones Estéticas* 82: 5–45.

Manrique, Diego A. 2012. "Los discos prohibidos del franquismo." *El País* (January 20), "Cultura" section, accessed online November 23, 2015.

Marks, Richard Lee. 1993. *Cortés: The Great Adventurer and the Fate of Aztec Mexico*. New York: Knopf.

Martínez, José Luis. 1972. *Nezahualcóyotl, vida y obra*. Mexico City: Fondo de Cultura Economica.

———. 1990. *Hernán Cortés*. Mexico City: UNAM and Fondo de Cultura Economica. ("Versión abreviada," 1992.)

———. 1991. *Documentos Cortesianos*. 4 vols. Mexico City: Fondo de Cultura Economica.

Martínez, Miguel. 2016. *Front Lines: Soldiers' Writing in the Early Modern Hispanic World*. Philadelphia: University of Pennsylvania Press.

Martínez Ahrens, Jan. 2015. "La tumba secreta de Hernán Cortés." *El País* (June 3), "Opinión" section, accessed online June 4, 2015.

Martínez Baracs, Andrea. 2008. *Un gobierno de indios: Tlaxcala, 1519–1750*. Mexico City: Fondo de Cultura Económica.

———. 2011. *Repertorio de Cuernavaca*. Mexico City: Editorial Clío.

Martínez Baracs, Rodrigo. 2006. *La perdida Relación de la Nueva España y su conquista de Juan Cano*. Mexico City: Instituto Nacional de Antropología e Historia.

Martínez Martínez, María del Carmen. 2010. "Francisco López de Gómara y Hernán Cortés: nuevos testimonios de la relación del cronista con los marqueses del Valle de Oaxaca." *Anuario de Estudios Americanos* 67:1 (January-June), 267–302.

Martínez Torrijos, Reyes. 2015. "Hallan el Huey Tzompantli de Tenoch-titlán." *La Jornada* (August 21), "Cultura" section, p. a40, accessed on-line August 31, 2015.

Mathes, W. Michael. 1968. *Vizcaíno and Spanish Expansion in the Pacific Ocean: 1580–1630.* San Francisco: California Historical Society.

———. 1985. *The Americas' First Academic Library: Santa Cruz de Tlate-lolco.* Sacramento: California State Library Foundation.

Matos Moctezuma, Eduardo. 1987. "Symbolism of the Templo Mayor." In Elizabeth Hill Boone, ed., *The Aztec Templo Mayor.* Washington, DC: Dumbarton Oaks, 185–209.

———. 2001. "Reflexiones acerca del plano de Tenochtitlan publicado en Nuremberg en 1524." In *Caravelle: Cahiers du monde hispanique et luso-brésilien,* 76–77, 183–95.

———. 2009. "The Coronation of Moctezuma II." In Colin McEwan and Leonardo López Luján, eds., *Moctezuma: Aztec Ruler.* London: British Museum Press, 56–67.

Matos Moctezuma, Eduardo, and Felipe Solís Olguín, eds. and curators. 2002. *Aztecs.* Exhibition catalog. London: Royal Academy of Arts.

Matthew, Laura, and Michel Oudijk, eds. 2007. *Indian Conquistadors: Indigneous Allies in the Conquest of Mesoamerica.* Norman: University of Oklahoma Press.

McEwan, Colin, and Leonardo López Luján, eds. 2009. *Moctezuma: Aztec Ruler.* London: British Museum Press.

McNeill, William H. 1979. *Plagues and Peoples.* London: Anchor.

Meierhenrich, Jens. 2014. *Genocide: A Reader.* New York: Oxford University Press.

Menand, Louis. 2015. "Thinking Sideways: The One-Dot Theory of History." *New Yorker* (March 30): 73–76.

Mira Caballos, Esteban. 1997. *El indio antillano: Repartimiento, enco-mienda y esclavitud, 1492–1542.* Seville: Muñoz Moya Editor.

———. 2010. *Hernán Cortés: El fin de una leyenda.* Trujillo, Spain: Pala-cio de los Barrantes Cervantes.

Miralles, Juan. 2008. *Y Bernal Mintió: El lado oscuro de su Historia ver-dadera de la conquista de la Nueva España.* Mexico City: Taurus.

Mizrahi, Irene. 1993. "El maquiavelismo renacentista en las cartas de relación de Hernán Cortés." *Dactylus* 12: 98–115.

Morgan, Lewis H. 1876. "Montezuma's Dinner." *North American Re-view,* 122. Boston: Osgood, 265–308.

Mundy, Barbara E. 1998. "Mapping the Aztec Capital: The 1524 Nuremberg Map of Tenochtitlan, Its Sources and Meanings." *Imago Mundi* 50: 11–33.

———. 2011a. "Moteuczoma Reborn: Biombo Paintings and Collective Memory in Colonial Mexico City." *Winterthur Portfolio* 45:2–3, 161–76.

———. 2011b. "Indigenous Civilization: Map of Tenochtitlán (Mexico), 1524." In Jordana Dym and Karl Offen, eds., *Mapping Latin America: A Cartographic Reader*. Chicago: University of Chicago Press, 42–45.

———. 2014. "Place-Names in Mexico-Tenochtitlan." *Ethnohistory* 61:2 (special issue on *The Ethnohistorical Map in New Spain*): 329–55.

———. 2015. *The Death of Aztec Tenochtitlan, the Life of Mexico City*. Austin: University of Texas Press.

Myers, Kathleen Ann. 2015. *In the Shadow of Cortés: Conversations Along the Route of Conquest*. Tucson: University of Arizona Press.

Nelson, Anson, and Fanny Nelson. 1892. *Memorials of Sarah Childress Polk*. New York: Anson D. F. Randolph.

Ng, David. 2009. "Vivaldi's 'Motezuma' Lost, Found, Restored, Reimagined." *Los Angeles Times* (March 22).

Nicholson, H. B. 1961. "The Chapultepec Cliff Sculpture of Motecuhzoma Xocoyotzin." *El México Antiguo* 9: 379–444.

———. 2001a. *Topiltzin Quetzalcoatl, the Once and Future Lord of the Toltecs*. Boulder: University Press of Colorado.

———. 2001b. *The 'Return of Quetzalcoatl': Did It Play a Role in the Conquest of Mexico?* Pamphlet. Lancaster, PA: Labyrinthos.

Novo, Salvador. 1985. *Diálogos Teatro Breve*. Mexico City: Editores Mexicanos Unidos.

Offner, Jerome A. 1983. *Law and Politics in Aztec Tetzcoco*. New York: Cambridge University Press.

Orique, David T. 2009. "Journey to the Headwaters: Bartolomé de Las Casas in a Comparative Context." *Catholic Historical Review* 95:1 (January). doi:10.1353/cat.0.0312.

———. 2017. *To Heaven or to Hell: Bartolomé de Las Casas's Confessionary Road Map to Temporal Justice and Eternal Life*. Latin American Originals #13. University Park, PA: Penn State University Press.

Oudijk, Michel R., and María Castañeda de la Paz. 2017. "Nahua Thought and the Conquest." In Deborah L. Nichols and Enrique

Rodríguez-Alegría, eds., *The Oxford Handbook of the Aztecs*. Oxford: Oxford University Press, 161–71.

Oudijk, Michel R., and Matthew Restall. 2014. *Conquista de Buenas Palabras y de Guerra: una visión indígena de la conquista*. Mexico City: UNAM [transcription of AGI Patronato 245, R. 10 also available at iifl. unam.mx/publicaciones-digitales/conquista-buenas-palabras-y-guerra].

Padden, R. C. 1967. *The Hummingbird and the Hawk*. Columbus: Ohio State University Press.

Pagden, Anthony. 1982. *The Fall of Natural Man: The American Indian and the Origins of Comparative Ethnology*. Cambridge: Cambridge University Press.

———. 1990. *Spanish Imperialism and the Political Imagination*. New Haven: Yale University Press.

Palomera, Esteban J. 1988. *Fray Diego Valadés, O.F.M., evangelizador humanista de la Nueva España: el hombre, su época y su obra*. Mexico City: Universidad Iberoamericana.

Pardo, Osvaldo F. 2004. *The Origins of Mexican Catholicism: Nahua Rituals and Christian Sacraments in Sixteenth-Century Mexico*. Ann Arbor: University of Michigan Press.

Parker, Geoffrey. 2014. *Imprudent King: The New Life of Philip II*. New Haven: Yale University Press.

Parry, J. H. 1977. "Juan de Tovar and the History of the Indians." *Proceedings of the American Philosophical Society* 121:4: 316–19.

Paz, Octavio. 1987 [1985]. "Hernán Cortés: Exorcismo y liberación." In Octavio Paz and L. M. Schneider, eds., *México en la obra de Octavio Paz: El peregrino en su patria*. Mexico City, I, 101–6.

Pennock, Caroline Dodds. 2008. *Bonds of Blood: Gender, Lifecycle, and Sacrifice in Aztec Culture*. Basingstoke, UK: Palgrave Macmillan.

Pérez Martínez, Héctor. 2014 [1944]. *Cuauhtémoc, vida y muerte de una cultura*. Mexico City: CONACULTA.

Phelan, John Leddy. 1970. *The Millennial Kingdom of the Franciscans of the New World*. 2nd ed. Berkeley: University of California Press.

Reséndez, Andrés. 2016. *The Other Slavery: The Uncovered Story of Indian Enslavement in America*. Boston: Houghton Mifflin Harcourt.

Restall, Matthew. 1998. *Maya Conquistador*. Boston: Beacon Press.

———. 2003. *Seven Myths of the Spanish Conquest*. New York: Oxford University Press.

————. 2008. "Spanish Creation of the Conquest of Mexico." In Rebecca P. Brienen and Margaret A. Jackson, eds., *Invasion and Transformation: Interdisciplinary Perspectives on the Conquest of Mexico*. Boulder: University Press of Colorado, 93–102.

————. 2012. "The New Conquest History." *History Compass* 10. historycompass.com/caribbean-latin-america.

————. 2013. "Mirarse en el espejo del otro: *La Conquista de México* y *The Indian Queen*." *La Revista del Real* 17 (September–November): 6. teatro-real.com/assets.

————. 2014. "Invasion: The Maya at War, 1520s–1540s." In Andrew Scherer and John Verano, eds., *Embattled Bodies, Embattled Places: Conflict, Conquest, and the Performance of War in Pre-Columbian America*. Washington, DC: Dumbarton Oaks, 93–117.

————. 2016a. "Moses, Caesar, Hero, Anti-hero: The Posthumous Faces of Hernando Cortés." *Leidschrift* 31:2 (May): 33–58.

————. 2016b. "La Contradictoria Inmortalidad de Hernán Cortés." *Letras Libres* (December): 16–22.

————. 2016c. "Montezuma Surrenders in the Capitol." *The Capitol Dome* 53:2 (Fall), 2–10.

————. n.d. "Encounter: Spaniards, Britons, Aztecs, and a Theory of History." Unpublished article manuscript.

Restall, Matthew, and Florine Asselbergs. 2007. *Invading Guatemala: Spanish, Nahua, and Maya Accounts of the Conquest Wars*. Latin American Originals #2. University Park, PA: Penn State University Press.

Restall, Matthew, and Felipe Fernández-Armesto. 2012. *The Conquistadors: A Very Short Introduction*. Oxford: Oxford University Press.

Restall, Matthew, and Amara Solari. 2011. *2012 and the End of the World: The Western Roots of the Maya Apocalypse*. Lanham, MD: Rowman & Littlefield.

Restall, Matthew, Amara Solari, John F. Chuchiak, and Traci Ardren. n.d. *The Friar and the Maya: Diego de Landa's Account of the Things of Yucatan*. Boulder: University Press of Colorado, forthcoming.

Restall, Matthew, Lisa Sousa, and Kevin Terraciano, eds. 2005. *Mesoamerican Voices: Native Writings from Colonial Mexico, Oaxaca, and Yucatan*. Cambridge: Cambridge University Press.

Riding, Alan. 2005. "Lost Vivaldi Opera Finally Gets Its Music and Words Together." *New York Times* (June 13).

Riley, G. Micheal. 1973. *Fernando Cortes and the Marquesado in Morelos,*

1522–1547. A Case Study in the Socioeconomic Development of Sixteenth-Century Mexico. Albuquerque: University of New Mexico Press.

Rivero Borrell M., Héctor, et al. 2002. *The Grandeur of Viceregal Mexico: Treasures from the Museo Franz Mayer / La grandeza del México virreinal: tesoros del Museo Franz Mayer.* Mexico City and Houston: Museo Franz Mayer and Museum of Fine Arts.

Roa-de-la-Carrera, Cristián. 2005. *Histories of Infamy: Francisco López de Gómara and the Ethics of Spanish Imperialism.* Boulder: University Press of Colorado.

———. 2012. *Chimalpáhin y La Conquista de México: La crónica de Francisco López de Gómara comentada por el historiador Nahua.* Mexico City: Universidad Nacional Autónoma de México.

Rojas, José Luis de. 2012. *Tenochtitlan: Capital of the Aztec Empire.* Gainesville: University Press of Florida.

Romero de Terreros, Manuel. 1944. *Los Retratos de Hernán Cortés: Estudio Iconográfico.* Mexico City: Porrúa.

Romero Giordano, Carlos. 1986. *Moctezuma II: El Misterio de Su Muerte.* Mexico City: Editorial Panorama.

Romerovargas Iturbide, Ignacio. 1964. *Moctezuma el Magnífico y la Invasión de Anáhuac.* Selección de Estudios y Conferencias #5. Mexico City: Sociedad Mexicana de Geografía y Estadística. (Single volume edition of self-published first edition, *Motecuhzoma Xocoyotzin o Moctezuma el Magnífico y la Invasión de Anáhuac*, 3 vols., 1963–64.)

Rowdon, Maurice. 1974. *The Spanish Terror: Spanish Imperialism in the Sixteenth Century.* New York: St. Martin's Press.

Rueda Smithers, Salvador. 2009. "Rethinking Moctezuma." In Colin McEwan and Leonardo López Luján, eds., *Moctezuma: Aztec Ruler.* Exhibition catalog. London: British Museum Press, 288–93.

Ruiz Medrano, Ethelia. 2014. "Don Carlos de Tezcoco and the Universal Rights of Emperor Carlos V." In Jongsoo Lee and Galen Brokaw, eds., *Texcoco: Prehispanic and Colonial Perspectives.* Boulder: University Press of Colorado, 165–82.

Russo, Alexandra. 2011. "Cortés's Objects and the Idea of New Spain." *Journal of the History of Collections* 23:2: 229–52.

Sahlins, Marshall. 1985. *Islands of History.* Chicago: University of Chicago Press.

Sandine, Al. 2015. *Deadly Baggage: What Cortés Brought to Mexico and How It Destroyed the Aztec Civilization.* Jefferson, NC: McFarland.

Sayre, Gordon M. 2005. *The Indian Chief as Tragic Hero: Indian Resistance and the Literatures of America, from Moctezuma to Tecumseh.* Chapen Hill: University of North Carolina Press.

Scholes, France V. 1969. *The Last Days of Gonzalo de Sandoval, Conquistador of New Spain.* Pamphlet. Madrid: Ediciones José Porrúa Turanzas.

Schreffler, Michael J. 2007. *The Art of Allegiance: Visual Culture and Imperial Power in Baroque New Spain.* University Park, PA: Penn State University Press.

———. 2008. "The Conquest of Mexico and the Representation of Imperial Power in Baroque New Spain." In Rebecca P. Brienen and Margaret A. Jackson, eds., *Invasion and Transformation: Interdisciplinary Perspectives on the Conquest of Mexico.* Boulder: University Press of Colorado, 103–24.

———. 2011. "'Threads of Every Color': On *Mudéjar* and Cultural Comparison in Colonial Latin America." In Jonathan Bloom and Sheila Blair, eds., *And Diverse Are Their Hues: Color in Islamic Art and Culture.* New Haven: Yale University Press, 245–69.

———. 2016. "Cortés and Moctezuma: Words, Pictures, and Likeness in Sixteenth-Century New Spain." In Donna Pierce, ed., *New England / New Spain: Portraiture in the Colonial Americas, 1492–1850.* Norman and Denver: University of Oklahoma Press and Denver Art Museum, 11–25.

Schroeder, Susan, ed. 2010. *The Conquest All Over Again: Nahuas and Zapotecs Thinking, Writing, and Painting Spanish Colonialism.* Brighton, UK: Sussex Academic Press.

Schroeder, Susan. 2011. "The Truth about the *Crónica Mexicayotl.*" *Colonial Latin American Review* 20:2: 233–47.

Schroeder, Susan, David Tavárez, and Cristián Roa-de-la-Carrera. 2010. *Chimalpahin's Conquest: A Nahua Historian's Rewriting of Francisco López de Gómara's La conquista de México.* Stanford: Stanford University Press. [Also see all entries under Gómara; and Roa-de-la-Carrera 2012.]

Schroeder, Susan, Stephanie Wood, and Robert Haskett, eds. 1997. *Indian Women of Early Mexico.* Norman: University of Oklahoma Press.

Schurz, William L. 1964. *This New World: The Civilization of Latin America.* New York: Dutton.

Schwaller, John F., with Helen Nader. 2014. *The First Letter from New Spain: The Lost Petition of Cortés and His Company, June 20, 1519.* Austin: University of Texas Press.

Scolieri, Paul A. 2013. *Dancing the New World: Aztecs, Spaniards, and the Choreography of Conquest.* Austin: University of Texas Press.

Sedgwick, Henry Dwight. 1926. *Cortés the Conqueror.* Indianapolis: Bobbs-Merrill.

Seed, Patricia. 1995. *Ceremonies of Possession in Europe's Conquest of the New World, 1492–1640.* Cambridge: Cambridge University Press.

Seigel, Micol. 2004. "World History's Narrative Problem." *HAHR* 84:3 (August): 431–46.

Seijas, Tatiana. 2014. *Asian Slaves in Colonial Mexico: From Chinos to Indians.* Cambridge: Cambridge University Press.

Serés, Guillermo. 2013. "El verdadero autor de 'La historia verdadera.'" *El País* (February 21), "Cultura" section, accessed online January 27, 2014.

Sewell, William H., Jr. 2005. *Logics of History: Social Theory and Social Transformation.* Chicago: University of Chicago Press.

Smith, Michael E. 1986. "The Role of Social Stratification in the Aztec Empire: A View from the Provinces." *American Anthropologist* 88:1: 70–91.

———. 2016. *At Home With the Aztecs: An Archaeologist Uncovers Their Daily Life.* New York: Routledge.

Solari, Amara. 2007. "'The Lords of All Created Things': Aztec Political Ideology in the Collections of Motecuhzoma II." In Guztavo Curiel, ed., *Orientes–Occidentes: El arte y la mirada del otro.* Mexico City: Instituto de Investigaciones Estéticas, UNAM., 239–60.

Solís Olguín, Felipe. 2009. "Family Histories: The Ancestors of Moctezuma II." In Colin McEwan and Leonardo López Luján, eds., *Moctezuma: Aztec Ruler.* London: British Museum Press, 25–39.

Somonte, Mariano G. 1969. *Doña Marina, "La Malinche."* [2nd ed., 1971.] Mexico City: Author.

Soustelle, Jacques. 1964 [1955]. *The Daily Life of the Aztecs.* (Translation of *La Vie quotidienne des Aztèques à la vielle de la conquête espagnole.* Paris: Hachette). Harmondsworth, UK: Penguin.

Spinden, Herbert J. 1928. *Ancient Civilizations of Mexico and Central America.* New York: American Museum of Natural History.

Spinrad, Norman. 2005. *Mexica: A Novel.* London: Little, Brown.

Stannard, David E. 1993. *American Holocaust: The Conquest of the New World.* New York: Oxford University Press.

Stone, Erin Woodruff. 2014. "Indian Harvest: The Rise of the Indigenous Slave Trade and Diaspora from Española to the Circum-Caribbean, 1492–1542." Ph.D. diss., Vanderbilt University.

————. 2017. "Slave Raiders vs. Friars: Tierra Firme, 1513–1522." *The Americas* 17:2 (April), 139–70.

Streeby, Shelley. 2002. *American Sensations: Class, Empire, and the Production of Popular Culture*. Berkeley: University of California Press.

Subirá, José. 1948. "Hernán Cortés en la Música Teatral." *EC:* 105–26.

Terraciano, Kevin. 2010. "Three Views of the Conquest of Mexico from the *Other* Mexica." In Susan Schroeder, ed., *The Conquest All Over Again: Nahuas and Zapotecs Thinking, Writing, and Painting Spanish Colonialism*. Brighton, UK: Sussex Academic Press, 15–40.

————. 2011. "Competing Memories of the Conquest of Mexico." In Ilona Katzew, ed., *Contested Visions in the Spanish Colonial World*. Los Angeles and New Haven: LACMA and Yale University Press, 54–77.

Thomas, Hugh. 1992. *The Real Discovery of America: Mexico, November 8, 1519*. Pamphlet. Mount Kisco, NY: Moyer Bell.

————. 1993. *Conquest: Montezuma, Cortés, and the Fall of Old Mexico*. New York: Simon and Schuster.

————. 1998. *Yo, Moctezuma, emperador de los Aztecas*. Barcelona: Editorial Planeta.

————. 2000. *Who's Who of the Conquistadors*. London: Cassell.

Thompson, Ayanna. 2008. *Performing Race and Torture on the Early Modern Stage*. London: Routledge.

Todorov, Tzvetan. 1999 [1982]. *The Conquest of America: The Question of the Other*. Richard Howard, trans. Norman: University of Oklahoma Press.

Townsend, Camilla. 2006. *Malintzin's Choices: An Indian Woman in the Conquest of Mexico*. Albuquerque: University of New Mexico Press.

————. 2014. "Polygyny and the Divided Altepetl: The Tetzcocan Key to Pre-conquest Nahua Politics." In Jongsoo Lee and Galen Brokaw, eds., *Texcoco: Prehispanic and Colonial Perspectives*. Boulder: University Press of Colorado, 93–116.

Trueba y Cosio, Telesforo de. 1829. *Life of Hernan Cortes*. Edinburgh: Constable. [In BL.]

Tuchman, Barbara. 1981 [1964]. "When Does History Happen?" In *Practicing History*. New York: Knopf.

————. 1984. *The March of Folly: From Troy to Vietnam*. New York: Ballantine.

Valero Silva, José. 1965. *El legalismo de Cortés como instrumento de su conquista*. Mexico City: Universidad Nacional Autónoma de México.

Vaillant, George C. 1966. *Aztecs of Mexico: Origin, Rise, and Fall of the Aztec Nation.* Baltimore: Penguin.

van Deusen, Nancy E. 2012. "The Intimacies of Bondage: Female Indigenous Servants and Slaves and Their Spanish Masters, 1492–1555." In *Journal of Women's History* 24:1 (Spring), 13–43.

———. 2015a. *Global Indios: The Indigenous Struggle for Justice in the Sixteenth Century.* Durham: Duke University Press.

———. 2015b. "Coming to Castile with Cortés: Indigenous 'Servitude' on the Sixteenth Century." *Ethnohistory* 62:2 (April): 285–308.

Vasconcelos, José. 1941. *Hernán Cortés: Creador de la Nacionalidad.* Mexico City: Ediciones Xochitl.

Ventura, Abida. 2014. "El zoológico de Moctezuma no es un mito." *El Universal* (December 6), "Cultura" section, accessed online December 17, 2014.

Villaverde Rico, María José, and Francisco Castilla Urbano, eds. 2016. *La sombra de la leyenda negra.* Madrid: Editorial Tecnos.

Villella, Peter B. 2016. *Indigenous Elites and Creole Identity in Colonial Mexico, 1500–1800.* Cambridge: Cambridge University Press.

Wagner, Henry R. 1944. *The Rise of Fernando Cortés.* Berkeley: Cortés Society.

Weiner, Jack. 2006. *Cuatro Ensayos Sobre Gabriel Lobo Laso de la Vega (1555–1615).* Valencia: Publicacions Universitat de València.

White, Jon Manchip. 1971. *Cortés and the Downfall of the Aztec Empire: A Study in a Conflict of Cultures.* New York: St. Martin's Press.

Whitehead, Neil L. 2011. *Of Cannibals and Kings: Primal Anthropology in the Americas.* University Park, PA: Penn State University Press.

Wolf, Eric R. 1959. *Sons of the Shaking Earth: The People of Mexico and Guatemala, Their Land, History, and Culture.* Chicago: University of Chicago Press.

Wood, Stephanie. 2003. *Transcending Conquest: Nahua Views of Spanish Colonial Mexico.* Norman: University of Oklahoma Press.

Woolford, Andrew, Jeff Benvenuto, and Alexander Laban Hinton, eds. 2014. *Colonial Genocide in Indigenous North America.* Durham: Duke University Press.

Wright, Ronald. 1993. *Stolen Continents: The 'New World' Through Indian Eyes.* New York: Mariner Books.

Yoeli, Erez and David Rand. 2015. "The Trick to Acting Heroically." *New York Times* (August 30).

BIBLIOGRAPHY OF REFERENCES:
SECONDARY SOURCES IN ALTERNATIVE MEDIA
(FILM, ANIMATION, LYRICS, OR LIBRETTO TO MUSIC, GRAPHIC BOOK)

Abnett, Dan. 2007. *Hernán Cortés and the Fall of the Aztec Empire*. Jr. Graphic Biographies. New York: PowerKids Press.

Bourn, Sonya Gay (writer and producer). 2005. "Cortés: Conqueror of Mexico." Television documentary series *The Conquerors* (The History Channel/A&E Television Networks).

Ferrer, Oriol (director). 2015. *Carlos, Rey Emperador*. Television drama series (produced by Diagonal TV for RTVE, Spain).

Sessions, Roger (music) and G. Antonio Borgese (libretto). 1965. *Montezuma: Opera in Three Acts*. (First performance 1964, Berlin.) New York: Marks Music Corporation.

Spontini, Gaspare. 1809. *Fernand Cortez. Opéra (Arrangé pour le Piano)*. Paris: Imbault. [In LML-H.]

Vivaldi, Antonio. 1733. *Motezuma: Drama Per Musica*. Venice: Marino Rossetti. [Libretto by Girolamo Alvise Giusti, transcription available online at librettidopera.it/zpdf/motezuma.]

Young, Neil (writer and recording artist). 1975. "Cortez the Killer." Song first released on the LP, Neil Young and Crazy Horse, *Zuma* (Reprise Records).

Zanuck, Darryl F. (producer) and Henry King (director). 1947. *Captain from Castile*. Twentieth Century Fox feature film (based on the first half of the 1945 novel by Samuel Shellabarger).

Index